AFRICA DEVELOPMENT INDICATORS 2011

THE WORLD BANK

ISBN: 978-0-8213-8731-3
e-ISBN: 978-0-8213-8732-0
DOI: 10.1596/978-0-8213-8731-3
SKU: 18731

Library of Congress Cataloging-in-Publication data have been requested.

Cover design: Communications Development Incorporated.

Photo credits: front cover, Arne Hoel/World Bank; back cover, Arne Hoel/World Bank and Jonathan Ernst/World Bank.

The map of Africa is provided by the Map Design Unit/World Bank.

To order *Africa Development Indicators 2011, The Little Data Book on Africa 2011* (available online only), or Africa Development Indicators 2011–Multiple User CD-ROM, please visit www.worldbank.org/publications. To subscribe to Africa Development Indicators Online please visit http://publications.worldbank.org/ADI.

For more information about Africa Development Indicators and its companion products, please visit www.worldbank.org/africa or email ADI@worldbank.org.

Contents

Foreword

This year's *Africa Development Indicators*, which covers some 1,700 macroeconomic, sectoral, and human development indicators dating to the 1960s, comes at a critical time for Sub-Saharan Africa's 48 countries and 841 million people. After a decade of economic growth at nearly 5 percent a year, Africa—along with the rest of the world—was hit hard by the global economic crisis, but it rebounded within a year. In 2011 the continent's growth is expected to return to precrisis levels. The poverty rate has been declining at about 1 percentage point a year, and progress on the Millennium Development Goals, while insufficient to reach the 2015 targets in many countries, has been substantial.

Yet, Africa faces some of the most formidable development challenges in the world. First, growth has been uneven, with about 20 fragile and conflict-affected states seemingly trapped in persistent poverty. Second, economic growth has not translated to productive jobs and more earning opportunities for Africa's labor force—most of which is engaged in agriculture and informal enterprises—and especially for the 7–10 million young people entering the labor force each year. And third, Africa's growth could be faster and more widespread (and abject poverty eliminated) if it could address its most fundamental challenges—improving governance and increasing public sector capacity.

Just as the World Bank's Africa strategy, *Africa's Future and World Bank Support to It,* seeks to harness the continent's recent dynamic growth to address these development challenges, so too do statistics in general, and *Africa Development Indicators* in particular, reflect both the progress and the potential of the continent. *Africa Development Indicators* permits policymakers, private actors, civil society, development partners, and citizens to monitor, study, and document Africa's economic and social development. It also shows where we need to improve. Just 18 of 48 countries have poverty data for 2007–10. And in the 2000s Africa averaged 1.5 poverty figures per country, less than half the world's average of 3.8. One reason for the shortcomings is lack of statistical capacity—as of 2010 only six countries have statistical capacity building indicators of 70–84 percent. But here too there has been progress: all but four countries now have an official national statistics website, compared with 50 percent a few years ago. More than 20 countries have made their household survey datasets available on their national data archive website, and more than 75 percent of Africa's people are covered by a population census less than 10 years old.

Since 2005 countries have developed their national statistical systems by designing and implementing a National Strategy for the Development of Statistics, which links data with poverty reduction strategies. The World Bank, in collaboration with other partners, is providing financial support and technical advice through lending operations such as STATCAP, through trust funds (in particular the Trust Fund for Statistical Capacity Building and the Statistics for Results Catalytic Fund), and through international initiatives. Moving forward, the Bank will scale up its statistical capacity development activities, not least because it is only with credible statistics that progress on the Africa strategy can be monitored. In addition, technology is being used to accelerate data collection, especially in underserved areas. For instance, in Africa's newest country, the Republic of South Sudan, the Bank is collaborating with the local statistics office to collect information on people's economic situation, security, and outlook using cell phones distributed to 1,000 households in 10 state capitals.

Africa Development Indicators has another, more fundamental role in Africa's development. Statistics—and the information contained in them—can empower citizens to hold their governments accountable. From the first public expenditure tracking survey of education in Uganda to the Ushahidi platform for tracking political violence and natural disasters, Africans have demonstrated how systematic data can mobilize citizens to spur their governments to action. Inasmuch as governance was identified as the fundamental constraint to African development, *Africa Development Indicators* is a major instrument in relaxing that constraint.

To that end, since April 2010 the World Bank has made all its data freely available, resulting in continually growing use of its online resources. This volume is part of the Africa Development Indicators suite of products, which also includes *The Little Data Book on Africa 2011* (available online only), the Africa Development Indicators 2011–Multiple User CD-ROM, and a data query and charting application for mobile services.

A tool for learning, capacity strengthening, and accountability, *Africa Development Indicators 2011* will continue to play a critical role in Africa's economic transformation.

Obiageli K. Ezekwesili
Vice President
The World Bank Group
Africa Region

Acknowledgments

Africa Development Indicators is a product of the Africa Region of the World Bank.

This report has been prepared by a core team led by Rose Mungai comprising Francoise Genouille and Jane Njuguna in the production of this book and its companions—Africa Development Indicators Online 2011, Africa Development Indicators 2011—Multiple User CD-ROM, and *The Little Data Book on Africa 2011* (online only). Yohannes Kebede coordinated the *Africa Development Indicators* Online apps platform while Mapi Buitano coordinated the dissemination of the book and its companions, and Jane Njuguna coordinated production. The overall work was carried out under the guidance of Shantayanan Devarajan, Chief Economist of the Africa Region.

The technical box contributors were:

- Ghislaine Delaine and Antoine Simonpietri (African statistical systems).
- Shantayanan Devarajan (Africa's future and the World Bank's support to it).
- Quy-Toan Do (Multidimensional indices of poverty).
- Punam Chuhan-Pole and Manka S. Angwafo (Transformation of Rwanda's coffee sector: an African success story).
- Sailesh Tiwari and Hassan Zaman (Food prices in Africa).
- Dilip Ratha, Sanket Mohapatra, Caglar Ozden, Sonia Plaza, and Abebe Shimeles (Migration and remittances in Africa).
- Bernard Harborne, Noro Aina Andriamihaja, and Viola Erdmannsdoerfer (Conflict-affected and fragile states in Africa).
- Stuti Khemani (The political economy of public policies and government failures).

Azita Amjadi, Abdolreza Farivari, Shelley Lai Fu, Ugendran Machakkalai, Shanmugam Natarajan, Lakshmikanthan Subramanian, and Malarvizhi Veerappan collaborated in the online data production. Maja Bresslauer, Mahyar Eshragh-Tabary, Masako Hiraga, and Soong Sup Lee collaborated in the update of the live database. Software preparation and testing for the CD-ROM and mobile applications was managed by Vilas Mandelkar, with the assistance of Ramgopal Erabelly, Parastoo Oloumi, William Prince, and Jomo Tariku. William Prince also collaborated in the production of *The Little Data Book on Africa 2011*.

Jeffrey Lecksell and Bruno Bonansea of the World Bank's Map Design Unit coordinated preparation of the maps.

Ann Karasanyi and Kenneth Omondi provided administrative and logistical support. The core team would like to thank the many people who provided useful comments on the publication. Their feedback and suggestions helped improve this year's edition.

Staff from External Affairs oversaw printing and dissemination of the book and its companions.

Several institutions provided data to *Africa Development Indicators*. Their contribution is very much appreciated.

Communications Development Incorporated provided design direction, editing, and layout.

Indicator tables

Users guide

Tables

The tables are numbered by section. Countries are listed alphabetically by subregion (Sub-Saharan Africa and North Africa). Indicators are shown for the most recent year or period for which data are available and, in most tables, for an earlier year or period (usually 1980, 1990, or 1995). Time-series data are available on the Africa Development Indicators—Multiple User CD-ROM and Africa Development Indicators Online. The term *country,* used interchangeably with *economy,* does not imply political independence but refers to any territory for which authorities report separate social or economic statistics. Known deviations from standard definitions or breaks in comparability over time or across countries are noted in the tables. When available data are deemed too weak to provide reliable measures of levels and trends or do not adequately adhere to international standards, the data are not shown.

Aggregate measure for region and subclassifications

The aggregates are based on the World Bank's regional classification for Sub-Saharan Africa and North Africa, which may differ from common geographic usage. Former Spanish Sahara is not included in any aggregates.

Statistics

Data are shown for economies as they were constituted in 2008, and historical data are revised to reflect current political arrangements. Exceptions are noted in the tables. Consistent time-series data for 1961–2009 are available on the Africa Development Indicators—Multiple User CD-ROM and Africa Development Indicators Online. Data for some indicators, including macroeconomic statistics, Doing Business indicators, investment climate indicators, governance and anticorruption indicators, and Country Policy and Institutional Assessment ratings are provided for 2010.

Data consistency, reliability, and comparability

Considerable effort has been made to harmonize the data, but full comparability cannot be assured, and care must be taken in interpreting indicators. Many factors affect data availability, comparability, and reliability. Data coverage may be incomplete because of circumstances affecting the collection and reporting of data, such as conflicts. Although drawn from sources thought to be the most authoritative, data should be construed as indicating trends and characterizing differences across economies. Discrepancies in data presented in earlier editions of *Africa Development Indicators* reflect updates from countries as well as revisions to historical series and changes in methodology. Readers are therefore advised not to compare data series between editions or across World Bank publications.

Classification of economies

For operational and analytical purposes the World Bank's main criterion for classifying economies is gross national income (GNI) per capita (calculated by the *World Bank Atlas* method; box 1). Every economy is classified as low income, middle income (subdivided into lower middle and upper middle), or high income (table 1). Low- and middle-income economies are sometimes referred to as developing economies. The term is used for convenience; it is not intended to imply that all economies in the group are experiencing similar development or that other economies have reached a preferred or final stage of development. Classification by income does not necessarily reflect development status. Because GNI per capita changes over time, the

Box 1 The *World Bank Atlas* method for converting gross national income to a common denominator

In calculating GNI and GNI per capita in U.S. dollars for certain operational purposes, the *World Bank Atlas* conversion factor is used to reduce the impact of exchange rate fluctuations in cross-country comparison of national incomes. The *World Bank Atlas* conversion factor for any year is the average of the official exchange rate or alternative conversion factor for that year and the two preceding, adjusted for the difference between the rate of inflation in the country and that in Japan, the United Kingdom, the United States, and the euro area. A country's inflation rate is measured by the change in its GDP deflator.

The inflation rate for Japan, the United Kingdom, the United States, and the euro area, representing international inflation, is measured by the change in the "special drawing rights (SDR) deflator." The SDR is the International Monetary Fund's unit of account and is calculated as a weighted average of these countries' GDP deflators in SDR terms, the weights being the amount of each country's currency in one SDR unit. Weights vary over time because both the composition of the SDR and the relative exchange rates for each currency change. The SDR deflator is calculated in SDR terms first and then converted to U.S. dollars using the SDR-to-dollar *World Bank Atlas* conversion factor. The conversion factor is then applied to a country's GNI. The resulting GNI in U.S. dollars is divided by the midyear population for the latest of the three years to derive GNI per capita.

When official exchange rates are deemed unreliable or unrepresentative of the effective exchange rate during a period, an alternative estimate of the exchange rate is used in the *World Bank Atlas* formula below.

The following formulas describe the procedures for computing the conversion factor for year *t:*

$$e_t^* = \frac{1}{3}\left[e_{t-2}\left(\frac{p_t}{p_{t-2}} \Big/ \frac{p_t^{S\$}}{p_{t-2}^{S\$}}\right) + e_{t-1}\left(\frac{p_t}{p_{t-1}} \Big/ \frac{p_t^{S\$}}{p_{t-1}^{S\$}}\right) + e_t\right]$$

and for calculating per capita GNI in U.S. dollars for year *t:*

$$Y_t^{\$} = \left(\frac{Y_t}{N_t}\right) / e_t^*$$

where e_t^* is the *World Bank Atlas* conversion factor (national currency to the U.S. dollar) for year *t*, e_t is the average annual exchange rate (national currency to the U.S. dollar) for year *t*, p_t is the GDP deflator for year *t*, $p_t^{S\$}$ is the SDR deflator in U.S. dollar terms for year *t*, $Y_t^{\$}$ is current GNI per capita in U.S. dollars in year *t*, Y_t is current GNI (local currency) for year *t*, and N_t is midyear population for year *t*.

country composition of income groups may change from one edition of *Africa Development Indicators* to the next. Once the classification is fixed for an edition, based on GNI per capita in the most recent year for which data are available (2008 in this edition), all historical data are based on the same country grouping. Low-income economies are those with a GNI per capita of $995 or less in 2008. Middle-income economies are those with a GNI per capita of more than $995 but less than $12,126. Lower middle-income and upper middle-income economies are separated at a GNI per capita of $3,945. High-income economies are those with a GNI per capita of $12,126 or more.

Alternative conversion factors

The World Bank systematically assesses the appropriateness of official exchange rates as conversion factors. An alternative conversion factor is used when the official exchange rate is judged to diverge by an exceptionally large margin from the rate effectively applied to domestic transactions of foreign currencies and traded products. This applies to only a small number of countries. Alternative conversion factors are used in the *Atlas* methodology and elsewhere in *Africa Development Indicators* as single-year conversion factors.

Symbols

..	means that data are not available or that aggregates cannot be calculated because of missing data in the years shown.
$	means current U.S. dollars unless otherwise noted.
<	means less than
>	means greater than
0 or 0.0	means zero or small enough that the number would round to zero at the displayed number of decimal places.

Data presentation conventions

A blank means not applicable or, for an aggregate, not analytically meaningful.

A billion is 1,000 million.

Growth rates are in real terms, unless otherwise specified.

The cutoff date for data is May 2011. However, the database may have more recent data by the time of publication.

Table 1 World Bank classification of economies, 2009 (GNI per capita)

Low income	Lower middle income	Upper middle income	High income
$995 or less	**$996–$3,945**	**$3,946–$12,195**	**$12,196 or more**
Benin	Algeria	Botswana	Equatorial Guinea
Burkina Faso	Angola	Gabon	
Burundi	Cameroon	Libya	
Central African Republic	Cape Verde	Mauritius	
Chad	Congo, Rep.	Seychelles	
Comoros	Djibouti	South Africa	
Congo, Dem. Rep.	Egypt, Arab Rep.		
Côte d'Ivoire	Lesotho		
Eritrea	Morocco		
Ethiopia	Namibia		
Gambia, The	Sudan		
Ghana	Swaziland		
Guinea	Tunisia		
Guinea-Bissau			
Kenya			
Liberia			
Madagascar			
Malawi			
Mali			
Mauritania			
Mozambique			
Niger			
Nigeria			
Rwanda			
São Tomé and Príncipe			
Senegal			
Sierra Leone			
Somalia			
Tanzania			
Togo			
Uganda			
Zambia			
Zimbabwe			

Source: World Bank.

Table 1.1 Basic indicators

	Population		Land area (thousands of sq km)	Population density (people per sq km)	GNI per capita, *World Bank Atlas* method (current $)	GDP per capita Constant 2000 prices		Life expectancy at birth (years)	Under-five mortality rate (per 1,000)	Gini index	Adult literacy rate (% ages 15 and older)		Net official development assistance per capita (current $)
	Total (millions)	Growth (annual %)				$	Average annual growth (%)				Male	Female	
	2009	2009	2009	2009	2009	2009[a]	2000–09	2009	2009	2000–09[b]	2009	2009	2009
SUB-SAHARAN AFRICA	**841.0**	**2.5**	**23,636**	**35.6**	**1,130**	**618**	**2.6**	**52.5**	**130**		**74.8**	**56.3**	**53.2**
Excluding South Africa	791.6	2.6	22,422	35.3	844	428	3.1	52.6	132		74.8	56.3	55.1
Excl. S. Africa & Nigeria	636.9	2.6	21,511	29.6	757	408	2.8	53.6	131		..	..	65.9
Angola	18.5	2.6	1,247	14.8	3,750	1,313	9.9	47.6	161	58.6	82.9	57.6	12.9
Benin	8.9	3.1	111	80.8	750	363	0.6	61.8	118	38.6	54.2	29.1	76.4
Botswana	1.9	1.5	567	3.4	6,260	4,082	3.0	55.0	57	..	83.8	84.4	143.4
Burkina Faso	15.8	3.4	274	57.6	510	264	1.9	53.3	166	39.6	..	..	68.8
Burundi	8.3	2.8	26	323.3	150	112	0.2	50.9	166	33.3	72.6	60.9	66.1
Cameroon	19.5	2.2	473	41.3	1,190	694	1.0	51.4	154	44.6	..	..	33.3
Cape Verde	0.5	1.4	4	125.5	3,010	1,763	4.8	71.3	28	50.4	90.1	80.2	387.5
Central African Republic	4.4	1.9	623	7.1	450	233	−1.0	47.3	171	43.6	69.1	42.1	53.6
Chad	11.2	2.6	1,259	8.9	600	265	6.7	48.9	209	39.8	44.5	23.1	50.1
Comoros	0.7	2.4	2	354.2	810	367	−0.3	65.8	104	64.3	79.7	68.7	76.8
Congo, Dem. Rep.	66.0	2.7	2,267	29.1	160	97	2.1	47.8	199	44.4	79.5	54.9	35.6
Congo, Rep.	3.7	1.9	342	10.8	2,080	1,267	1.8	53.7	128	47.3	..	..	76.8
Côte d'Ivoire	21.1	2.3	318	66.3	1,070	536	−1.3	58.0	119	41.5	64.7	45.3	112.3
Djibouti	0.9	1.7	23	37.3	1,280	904	2.1	55.7	94	39.9	..	..	187.7
Equatorial Guinea	0.7	2.6	28	24.1	12,420	8,011	13.6	50.6	145	..	97.0	89.8	46.7
Eritrea	5.1	2.9	101	50.2	320	133	−3.4	59.9	55	..	77.9	56.0	28.5
Ethiopia	82.8	2.6	1,000	82.8	330	201	5.7	55.7	104	29.8	..	..	46.1
Gabon	1.5	1.8	258	5.7	7,370	4,054	0.1	60.9	69	41.5	91.4	84.1	52.6
Gambia, The	1.7	2.7	10	170.5	440	382	2.1	56.2	103	47.3	57.6	35.8	75.1
Ghana	23.8	2.1	228	104.8	1,190	343	3.5	56.8	69	42.8	72.8	60.4	66.4
Guinea	10.1	2.4	246	41.0	370	400	1.0	58.3	142	39.4	50.8	28.1	21.3
Guinea-Bissau	1.6	2.2	28	57.3	510	143	−1.4	48.2	193	35.5	66.9	38.0	90.3
Kenya	39.8	2.6	569	69.9	760	452	1.7	54.9	84	47.7	90.5	83.5	44.7
Lesotho	2.1	0.8	30	68.1	980	471	2.1	45.4	84	52.5	82.9	95.3	59.5
Liberia	4.0	4.2	96	41.1	160	148	−3.5	58.7	112	38.2	63.7	54.5	127.7
Madagascar	19.6	2.7	582	33.7	430	255	0.8	60.8	58	47.2	..	..	22.7
Malawi	15.3	2.8	94	162.2	290	168	1.9	53.8	110	39.0	80.6	67.0	50.6
Mali	13.0	2.4	1,220	10.7	680	304	2.8	48.8	191	39.0	..	..	75.7
Mauritania	3.3	2.3	1,031	3.2	990	462	2.0	57.0	117	39.0	64.5	50.3	87.1
Mauritius	1.3	0.5	2	628.2	7,250	4,917	2.9	72.6	17	..	90.6	85.3	122.0
Mozambique	22.9	2.3	786	29.1	440	371	5.2	48.1	142	45.6	70.1	41.5	87.9
Namibia	2.2	1.9	823	2.6	4,270	2,673	3.3	61.6	48	..	88.9	88.1	150.2
Niger	15.3	3.9	1,267	12.1	340	173	0.5	52.0	160	34.0	..	..	30.7
Nigeria	154.7	2.3	911	169.0	1,190	506	4.0	48.1	138	42.9	72.0	49.8	10.7
Rwanda	10.0	2.8	25	405.3	490	334	5.1	50.6	111	53.1	75.0	66.8	93.5
São Tomé and Príncipe	0.2	1.6	1	169.5	1,130	..	..	65.8	78	50.6	93.7	84.0	188.7
Senegal	12.5	2.6	193	65.1	1,040	534	1.6	55.9	93	39.2	61.8	38.7	81.2
Seychelles	0.1	1.2	0	191.2	8,480	7,389	0.9	73.7	12	65.8	..	..	263.7
Sierra Leone	5.7	2.4	72	79.5	340	265	5.8	47.9	192	42.5	52.7	30.1	76.8
Somalia	9.1	2.3	627	14.6	..	..	..	50.1	180	..	..	..	72.4
South Africa	49.3	1.1	1,214	40.6	5,760	3,689	2.8	51.6	62	57.8	..	..	21.8
Sudan	42.3	2.2	2,376	17.8	1,220	537	5.0	58.5	108	..	79.6	60.8	54.1
Swaziland	1.2	1.5	17	68.9	2,470	1,553	1.6	46.3	73	50.7	87.8	86.2	48.9
Tanzania	43.7	2.9	886	49.4	490	426	4.2	56.3	108	37.6	79.0	66.9	67.1
Togo	6.6	2.4	54	121.7	440	247	−0.1	62.9	98	34.4	..	..	75.4
Uganda	32.7	3.3	197	166.0	460	366	4.3	53.4	128	44.3	..	..	54.6
Zambia	12.9	2.5	743	17.4	960	401	3.0	46.3	141	50.7	80.6	61.3	98.1
Zimbabwe	12.5	0.5	387	32.4	360	288	−7.4	45.4	90	..	94.7	89.4	58.8
NORTH AFRICA	**166.7**	**1.6**	**5,738**	**29.1**	**3,280**	**2,191**	**3.1**	**71.5**	**26**		**..**	**..**	**17.2**
Algeria	34.9	1.5	2,382	14.7	4,420	2,190	2.5	72.6	32	..	..	..	9.1
Egypt, Arab Rep.	83.0	1.8	995	83.4	2,070	1,836	3.0	70.3	21	32.1	..	..	11.1
Libya	6.4	2.0	1,760	3.6	12,020	7,692	3.3	74.5	19	..	95.2	82.0	6.1
Morocco	32.0	1.2	446	71.7	2,810	1,809	3.8	71.6	38	40.9	68.9	43.9	28.5
Tunisia	10.4	1.0	155	67.2	3,720	2,805	3.9	74.5	21	40.8	..	..	45.4
ALL AFRICA	**1,007.7**	**2.3**	**29,375**	**34.3**	**1,487**	**879**	**2.6**	**55.6**	**119**		**..**	**..**	**47.2**

a. Provisional.
b. Data are for the most recent year available during the period specified.

Table

2.1 Gross domestic product, nominal

	Current prices ($ millions)									Annual average growth (%)		
	1980	1990	2003	2004	2005	2006	2007	2008	2009[a]	1980–89	1990–99	2000–09
SUB-SAHARAN AFRICA	**272,131**	**300,900**	**448,082**	**559,094**	**653,676**	**763,395**	**879,541**	**1,009,865**	**954,357**	**1.0**	**1.5**	**15.2**
Excluding South Africa	193,303	189,013	279,985	340,092	406,780	502,768	593,774	734,377	669,740	–0.7	1.2	16.7
Excl. S. Africa & Nigeria	124,769	160,605	212,189	252,030	294,213	355,441	427,372	526,649	496,310	3.0	0.8	15.7
Angola	..	10,260	13,956	19,775	30,632	45,163	59,263	84,179	75,493	..	–3.8	32.9
Benin	1,405	1,845	3,558	4,047	4,287	4,735	5,546	6,683	6,656	2.3	3.5	13.8
Botswana	1,061	3,792	8,087	10,049	10,255	11,255	12,386	13,545	11,823	12.6	4.6	10.8
Burkina Faso	1,929	3,101	4,270	5,109	5,427	5,771	6,767	8,046	8,141	4.8	0.0	14.4
Burundi	920	1,132	595	664	796	919	980	1,169	1,325	2.2	–3.3	8.4
Cameroon	6,741	11,152	13,622	15,775	16,588	17,957	20,686	23,736	22,186	7.3	–2.5	11.2
Cape Verde	..	339	797	925	999	1,108	1,331	1,531	1,549	..	6.4	14.1
Central African Republic	797	1,488	1,139	1,270	1,350	1,477	1,712	1,988	2,006	8.1	–4.3	9.5
Chad	1,033	1,739	2,737	4,415	5,302	6,099	7,016	8,357	6,839	5.7	–1.3	23.2
Comoros	124	250	324	362	387	403	465	530	535	8.0	–2.0	12.0
Congo, Dem. Rep.	14,395	9,350	5,673	6,570	7,104	8,543	9,977	11,588	10,575	–6.2	–7.1	12.0
Congo, Rep.	1,706	2,799	3,496	4,649	6,087	7,731	8,344	11,789	9,580	2.3	–2.4	18.2
Côte d'Ivoire	10,175	10,796	13,737	15,481	16,363	17,367	19,796	23,414	23,304	2.0	2.2	10.4
Djibouti	..	452	622	666	709	769	848	983	1,049	..	1.7	7.6
Equatorial Guinea	..	132	2,952	5,241	8,217	9,603	12,576	18,525	10,413	..	22.5	34.1
Eritrea	..	..	771	939	1,171	1,281	1,374	1,654	1,873	..	7.2	13.7
Ethiopia	..	12,083	8,539	10,034	12,286	15,134	19,182	25,899	28,526	5.9	–5.7	16.9
Gabon	4,279	5,952	6,055	7,178	8,666	9,546	11,571	14,535	11,062	–0.5	–1.7	13.4
Gambia, The	241	317	367	401	461	508	651	822	733	1.7	3.6	8.6
Ghana	4,445	5,886	7,624	8,872	10,720	20,388	24,632	28,527	26,169	3.2	2.6	25.0
Guinea	..	2,667	3,446	3,666	2,937	2,821	4,209	3,778	4,103	..	3.0	3.2
Guinea-Bissau	111	244	475	535	590	597	692	847	837	3.7	–0.6	19.4
Kenya	7,265	8,591	14,904	16,096	18,738	22,502	27,166	30,031	29,376	2.6	7.7	11.8
Lesotho	431	541	947	1,206	1,315	1,417	1,577	1,594	1,579	–0.8	4.1	11.8
Liberia	954	384	410	460	530	612	735	843	876	–0.5	1.8	6.1
Madagascar	4,042	3,081	5,474	4,364	5,039	5,515	7,343	9,424	8,590	–5.2	3.4	9.5
Malawi	1,238	1,881	2,425	2,625	2,755	3,117	3,458	4,074	4,727	1.8	0.2	10.9
Mali	1,787	2,421	4,362	4,874	5,305	5,866	7,146	8,722	8,996	3.4	0.4	16.3
Mauritania	709	1,020	1,285	1,548	1,858	2,699	2,838	3,589	3,024	3.5	1.4	15.9
Mauritius	1,137	2,653	5,610	6,386	6,284	6,507	7,521	9,310	8,589	8.8	5.8	8.5
Mozambique	3,526	2,463	4,666	5,698	6,579	7,096	8,030	9,867	9,790	–4.7	8.3	11.8
Namibia	2,169	2,350	4,934	6,606	7,262	7,981	8,806	8,970	9,265	0.1	4.6	13.3
Niger	2,509	2,481	2,731	3,053	3,405	3,645	4,246	5,357	5,383	–0.2	–1.8	13.8
Nigeria	64,202	28,472	67,656	87,845	112,249	146,867	165,921	207,118	173,004	–12.0	3.2	19.9
Rwanda	1,163	2,584	1,846	2,089	2,581	3,111	3,741	4,691	5,216	8.6	–2.0	15.0
São Tomé and Príncipe	..	..	98	107	114	125	145	174	191	..	..	11.5
Senegal	3,503	5,717	6,871	8,041	8,703	9,378	11,334	13,175	12,822	6.2	–1.8	13.4
Seychelles	147	369	706	700	884	968	1,026	926	764	9.3	6.0	4.9
Sierra Leone	1,101	650	991	1,096	1,239	1,422	1,664	1,955	1,942	–4.3	0.6	13.1
Somalia	604	917	..	..	..	..	..	..	..	6.4	..	..
South Africa	80,710	112,014	168,219	219,093	247,064	261,007	286,302	276,451	285,366	4.1	2.1	12.2
Sudan	7,617	12,409	17,780	21,684	27,386	36,401	46,531	58,032	54,681	10.1	0.8	21.2
Swaziland	543	1,115	1,796	2,282	2,524	2,670	2,950	2,840	3,001	1.9	4.4	11.3
Tanzania	..	4,259	11,659	12,826	14,142	14,331	16,826	20,715	21,368	..	10.1	9.1
Togo	1,136	1,628	1,759	2,061	2,108	2,218	2,499	2,899	2,855	4.5	–0.1	10.0
Uganda	1,245	4,304	6,337	8,469	9,000	9,922	11,892	14,441	16,043	20.7	8.8	12.6
Zambia	3,884	3,288	4,374	5,423	7,157	10,675	11,410	14,382	12,805	–3.1	0.2	20.3
Zimbabwe	6,679	8,784	5,658	5,671	5,583	5,203	5,018	4,247	5,625	–0.1	–1.5	–3.6
NORTH AFRICA	**111,546**	**172,192**	**249,820**	**282,321**	**324,517**	**377,737**	**448,926**	**556,721**	**522,285**	**4.8**	**4.2**	**11.2**
Algeria	42,345	62,045	68,019	85,014	102,339	117,169	135,804	170,989	140,577	4.5	–1.2	14.6
Egypt, Arab Rep.	22,912	43,130	82,924	78,845	89,686	107,484	130,473	162,836	188,413	6.8	10.8	7.7
Libya	..	28,905	24,063	33,385	44,000	56,484	71,803	93,168	62,360	..	–0.9	15.0
Morocco	18,821	25,821	49,823	56,948	59,524	65,637	75,226	88,883	91,375	3.7	5.1	11.6
Tunisia	8,743	12,291	24,992	28,129	28,968	30,962	35,620	40,845	39,561	2.3	6.0	9.3
ALL AFRICA	**386,556**	**472,997**	**697,735**	**841,140**	**977,859**	**1,140,739**	**1,328,046**	**1,566,195**	**1,476,265**	**2.2**	**2.5**	**13.7**

a. Provisional.

Table 2.2 Gross domestic product, real

	Constant prices (2000 $ millions)									Annual average growth (%)		
	1980	1990	2003	2004	2005	2006	2007	2008	2009[a]	1980–89	1990–99	2000–09
SUB-SAHARAN AFRICA	**227,433**	**273,288**	**383,153**	**407,008**	**430,323**	**457,294**	**486,811**	**511,548**	**520,086**	**1.8**	**2.4**	**5.1**
Excluding South Africa	132,121	162,355	237,556	254,798	270,086	288,086	308,333	326,524	338,402	2.1	2.7	5.8
Excl. S. Africa & Nigeria	99,187	127,336	184,367	195,958	208,072	222,229	238,231	252,216	259,922	2.6	2.8	5.5
Angola	..	8,464	11,137	12,383	14,935	17,707	21,298	24,136	24,295	..	1.0	13.1
Benin	1,084	1,412	2,571	2,650	2,727	2,839	2,970	3,121	3,240	2.7	4.7	4.0
Botswana	1,209	3,395	6,751	7,154	7,271	7,643	8,010	8,260	7,959	10.9	4.8	4.4
Burkina Faso	1,101	1,556	3,150	3,296	3,505	3,698	3,831	4,023	4,164	4.0	5.5	5.4
Burundi	559	865	747	783	790	830	860	899	930	4.5	–3.2	3.0
Cameroon	6,339	8,793	11,393	11,815	12,087	12,476	12,913	13,287	13,553	4.5	1.3	3.3
Cape Verde	..	303	613	608	681	750	815	867	891	6.3	5.9	6.4
Central African Republic	735	815	884	892	914	949	984	1,005	1,029	1.6	1.8	0.8
Chad	665	1,106	1,925	2,572	3,018	3,024	3,030	3,018	2,970	6.7	2.3	10.2
Comoros	136	181	223	222	232	234	236	238	242	2.9	1.2	1.9
Congo, Dem. Rep.	7,016	7,659	4,614	4,921	5,239	5,505	5,849	6,212	6,379	2.1	–5.0	5.2
Congo, Rep.	1,746	2,796	3,524	3,647	3,932	4,173	4,107	4,335	4,665	3.8	0.8	4.0
Côte d'Ivoire	7,727	8,298	10,106	10,287	10,417	10,488	10,668	10,904	11,296	0.7	3.5	0.8
Djibouti	..	660	596	619	638	669	703	744	781	..	–2.3	4.0
Equatorial Guinea	..	207	2,764	3,815	4,187	4,239	5,148	5,730	5,418	..	20.7	16.8
Eritrea	..	..	692	702	720	713	722	652	675	..	7.9	0.2
Ethiopia	..	6,234	8,798	9,993	11,174	12,384	13,803	15,291	16,623	2.1	3.7	8.5
Gabon	3,594	4,298	5,290	5,361	5,523	5,588	5,899	6,035	5,978	0.5	2.9	2.1
Gambia, The	213	305	460	493	518	552	587	623	651	3.5	2.7	5.2
Ghana	2,640	3,267	5,691	6,010	6,364	6,771	7,209	7,817	8,181	2.6	4.3	5.8
Guinea	..	2,088	3,503	3,585	3,692	3,784	3,851	4,041	4,030	..	4.4	3.0
Guinea-Bissau	115	186	195	201	211	215	216	224	230	3.8	1.4	1.0
Kenya	7,078	10,544	13,631	14,327	15,173	16,132	17,263	17,531	17,985	4.1	2.2	4.4
Lesotho	380	504	819	838	847	902	924	965	973	2.3	4.0	3.1
Liberia	1,391	433	411	422	444	479	524	561	587	–3.3	0.2	0.0
Madagascar	3,099	3,266	3,941	4,148	4,339	4,557	4,842	5,187	4,997	0.8	1.7	3.6
Malawi	1,000	1,243	1,778	1,875	1,924	2,072	2,192	2,381	2,562	2.4	3.8	4.8
Mali	1,536	1,630	3,039	3,105	3,294	3,469	3,618	3,795	3,958	0.5	3.9	5.3
Mauritania	693	816	1,188	1,249	1,317	1,573	1,483	1,537	1,521	1.9	2.9	4.7
Mauritius	1,519	2,726	4,975	5,261	5,327	5,537	5,842	6,140	6,271	6.1	5.0	3.7
Mozambique	2,462	2,199	5,485	5,918	6,414	6,971	7,478	7,982	8,488	–0.9	6.0	7.9
Namibia	2,292	2,591	4,320	4,850	4,972	5,324	5,610	5,851	5,804	1.1	4.0	5.3
Niger	1,523	1,507	2,089	2,091	2,185	2,312	2,380	2,615	2,641	–0.4	2.4	4.3
Nigeria	31,452	34,978	53,102	58,731	61,903	65,740	69,981	74,179	78,333	0.0	2.4	6.6
Rwanda	1,368	1,673	2,135	2,293	2,507	2,737	2,888	3,211	3,343	2.5	–1.6	7.6
São Tomé and Príncipe	..	..	..	..	..	..	..	..	..	..	..	..
Senegal	2,683	3,463	5,268	5,579	5,893	6,042	6,335	6,546	6,691	2.7	2.8	4.3
Seychelles	292	395	572	556	598	647	710	704	650	3.1	4.5	1.7
Sierra Leone	929	1,014	1,047	1,125	1,206	1,294	1,377	1,454	1,512	0.5	–5.3	9.5
Somalia	..	..	..	..	..	..	..	..	..	..	..	..
South Africa	95,503	110,945	145,693	152,329	160,367	169,354	178,644	185,216	181,923	1.4	2.0	4.1
Sudan	5,525	7,062	14,821	15,579	16,564	18,434	20,308	21,697	22,678	2.4	5.4	7.3
Swaziland	470	1,033	1,592	1,632	1,668	1,715	1,776	1,818	1,840	7.4	3.1	2.6
Tanzania	..	7,547	12,367	13,335	14,318	15,282	16,375	17,593	18,652	..	2.8	7.1
Togo	964	1,071	1,419	1,461	1,479	1,537	1,566	1,594	1,634	1.5	3.6	2.5
Uganda	..	3,215	7,542	8,055	8,565	9,489	10,287	11,183	11,973	2.3	7.4	7.8
Zambia	2,730	3,028	3,687	3,886	4,089	4,342	4,611	4,880	5,192	1.0	0.2	5.4
Zimbabwe	3,699	5,691	5,069	4,720	4,431	4,284	4,127	3,415	3,609	3.3	2.7	–7.5
NORTH AFRICA	**118,981**	**178,165**	**273,922**	**286,676**	**301,162**	**318,159**	**334,909**	**352,333**	**365,307**	**4.2**	**3.2**	**4.8**
Algeria	35,291	46,367	62,918	66,190	69,565	70,956	73,085	74,839	76,411	2.9	1.7	4.0
Egypt, Arab Rep.	38,506	65,579	109,198	113,666	118,749	126,876	135,869	145,592	152,360	5.5	4.3	4.9
Libya	..	..	36,180	37,771	41,511	43,960	46,598	48,368	49,384	..	..	5.4
Morocco	20,086	29,312	43,735	45,835	47,201	50,863	52,240	55,158	57,888	4.2	2.4	5.0
Tunisia	8,622	12,237	21,891	23,213	24,136	25,503	27,118	28,376	29,265	3.2	4.6	4.9
ALL AFRICA	**348,882**	**452,854**	**657,068**	**693,666**	**731,462**	**775,424**	**821,680**	**863,841**	**885,368**	**2.6**	**2.7**	**5.0**

a. Provisional.

Table 2.3 Gross domestic product growth

	Annual growth (%)											
										Annual average		
	1980	1990	2003	2004	2005	2006	2007	2008	2009[a]	1980–89	1990–99	2000–09
SUB-SAHARAN AFRICA	**4.0**	**1.1**	**4.2**	**6.2**	**5.7**	**6.3**	**6.5**	**5.1**	**1.7**	**2.2**	**2.1**	**4.6**
Excluding South Africa	1.7	2.1	5.0	7.3	6.0	6.7	7.0	5.9	3.6	2.1	2.5	5.2
Excl. S. Africa & Nigeria	0.7	0.6	3.5	6.3	6.2	6.8	7.2	5.9	3.1	2.5	2.4	5.0
Angola	..	–0.3	3.3	11.2	20.6	18.6	20.3	13.3	0.7	4.2	1.0	10.9
Benin	6.8	3.2	3.9	3.1	2.9	4.1	4.6	5.1	3.8	3.1	4.5	4.3
Botswana	12.0	6.8	6.3	6.0	1.6	5.1	4.8	3.1	–3.7	11.5	5.3	4.2
Burkina Faso	0.8	–0.6	8.0	4.6	6.4	5.5	3.6	5.0	3.5	3.7	5.1	5.0
Burundi	1.0	3.5	–1.2	4.8	0.9	5.1	3.6	4.5	3.5	4.3	–1.4	2.7
Cameroon	–2.0	–6.1	4.0	3.7	2.3	3.2	3.5	2.9	2.0	4.0	0.4	3.4
Cape Verde	..	0.7	6.2	–0.7	11.9	10.1	8.6	6.5	2.8	6.4	5.2	6.0
Central African Republic	–4.5	–2.1	–7.6	1.0	2.4	3.8	3.7	2.2	2.4	0.9	1.3	1.0
Chad	–6.0	–4.2	14.7	33.6	17.3	0.2	0.2	–0.4	–1.6	5.4	2.2	8.3
Comoros	..	5.1	2.5	–0.2	4.2	1.2	0.5	1.0	1.8	2.7	1.6	2.0
Congo, Dem. Rep.	2.2	–6.6	5.8	6.6	6.5	5.1	6.3	6.2	2.7	1.8	–5.5	3.4
Congo, Rep.	17.6	1.0	0.8	3.5	7.8	6.1	–1.6	5.6	7.6	6.8	0.8	4.6
Côte d'Ivoire	–11.0	–1.1	–1.6	1.8	1.3	0.7	1.7	2.2	3.6	–0.2	2.6	0.5
Djibouti	..	..	3.2	3.8	3.2	4.8	5.1	5.8	5.0	..	–2.0	3.6
Equatorial Guinea	..	3.3	14.0	38.0	9.7	1.3	21.4	11.3	–5.4	0.9	20.2	18.5
Eritrea	..	..	–2.7	1.5	2.6	–1.0	1.3	–9.8	3.6	..	8.1	–0.6
Ethiopia	..	2.7	–2.2	13.6	11.8	10.8	11.5	10.8	8.7	2.4	2.7	8.1
Gabon	2.6	5.2	2.5	1.3	3.0	1.2	5.6	2.3	–1.0	1.9	2.5	1.5
Gambia, The	6.3	3.6	6.9	7.1	5.1	6.6	6.3	6.1	4.6	3.9	3.1	5.1
Ghana	0.5	3.3	5.2	5.6	5.9	6.4	6.5	8.4	4.7	2.0	4.3	5.5
Guinea	..	4.3	5.4	2.3	3.0	2.5	1.8	4.9	–0.3	4.5	4.3	2.8
Guinea-Bissau	–16.0	6.1	–2.9	3.1	5.0	2.2	0.3	3.5	3.0	2.9	2.0	1.5
Kenya	5.6	4.2	2.9	5.1	5.9	6.3	7.0	1.6	2.6	4.2	2.2	3.6
Lesotho	–2.7	6.5	4.3	2.3	1.1	6.5	2.4	4.5	0.9	2.1	4.1	3.3
Liberia	–4.1	–51.0	–31.3	2.6	5.3	7.8	9.4	7.1	4.6	–4.5	1.2	3.8
Madagascar	0.8	3.1	9.8	5.3	4.6	5.0	6.2	7.1	–3.7	0.4	1.6	3.2
Malawi	0.4	5.7	5.5	5.5	2.6	7.7	5.8	8.6	7.6	1.7	4.1	4.2
Mali	–4.3	–1.9	7.4	2.2	6.1	5.3	4.3	4.9	4.3	0.6	3.6	5.4
Mauritania	3.4	–1.8	5.6	5.2	5.4	19.4	–5.7	3.7	–1.1	2.2	2.6	3.8
Mauritius	–10.1	7.2	3.7	5.7	1.2	3.9	5.5	5.1	2.1	4.3	5.2	4.1
Mozambique	..	1.0	6.0	7.9	8.4	8.7	7.3	6.7	6.3	0.4	5.5	7.3
Namibia	..	2.5	4.2	12.3	2.5	7.1	5.4	4.3	–0.8	1.1	4.1	4.4
Niger	–2.2	–1.3	5.3	0.1	4.5	5.8	3.3	9.5	1.0	0.0	1.9	3.8
Nigeria	4.2	8.2	10.3	10.6	5.4	6.2	6.4	6.0	5.6	0.9	3.1	6.1
Rwanda	9.0	–2.4	2.2	7.4	9.3	9.2	5.5	11.2	4.1	3.2	2.1	7.7
São Tomé and Príncipe	..	..	..	..	..	..	..	..	..	..	..	..
Senegal	–3.3	–0.7	6.7	5.9	5.6	2.5	4.9	3.3	2.2	2.4	2.7	4.0
Seychelles	–4.2	7.0	–5.9	–2.9	7.5	8.3	9.7	–0.9	–7.6	2.1	4.9	1.1
Sierra Leone	4.8	3.4	9.3	7.5	7.2	7.3	6.4	5.5	4.0	1.1	–4.3	9.7
Somalia	..	..	..	..	..	..	..	..	..	..	..	..
South Africa	6.6	–0.3	2.9	4.6	5.3	5.6	5.5	3.7	–1.8	2.2	1.4	3.6
Sudan	1.5	–5.5	7.1	5.1	6.3	11.3	10.2	6.8	4.5	3.4	4.4	7.1
Swaziland	12.4	9.8	3.9	2.5	2.2	2.9	3.5	2.4	1.2	8.6	3.7	3.1
Tanzania	..	7.0	6.9	7.8	7.4	6.7	7.1	7.4	6.0	3.8	3.3	6.8
Togo	14.6	–0.2	2.7	3.0	1.2	3.9	1.9	1.8	2.5	2.6	2.6	2.0
Uganda	..	6.5	6.5	6.8	6.3	10.8	8.4	8.7	7.1	3.0	7.1	7.2
Zambia	3.0	–0.5	5.1	5.4	5.2	6.2	6.2	5.8	6.4	1.4	0.4	5.2
Zimbabwe	14.4	7.0	–17.2	–6.9	–6.1	–3.3	–3.7	–17.3	5.7	5.2	2.6	–5.9
NORTH AFRICA	**5.2**	**4.0**	**5.9**	**4.7**	**5.1**	**5.6**	**5.3**	**5.2**	**3.7**	**4.3**	**3.3**	**4.5**
Algeria	0.8	0.8	6.9	5.2	5.1	2.0	3.0	2.4	2.1	2.8	1.6	3.6
Egypt, Arab Rep.	10.0	5.7	3.2	4.1	4.5	6.8	7.1	7.2	4.6	5.9	4.3	4.9
Libya	..	..	13.0	4.4	9.9	5.9	6.0	3.8	2.1	..	..	4.3
Morocco	3.6	4.0	6.3	4.8	3.0	7.8	2.7	5.6	4.9	3.9	2.8	4.8
Tunisia	7.4	7.9	5.6	6.0	4.0	5.7	6.3	4.6	3.1	3.6	5.1	4.7
ALL AFRICA	**4.4**	**2.2**	**4.9**	**5.6**	**5.4**	**6.0**	**6.0**	**5.1**	**2.5**	**2.9**	**2.5**	**4.6**

a. Provisional.

Table 2.4 Gross domestic product per capita, real

	Constant prices (2000 $)									Annual average growth (%)		
	1980	1990	2003	2004	2005	2006	2007	2008	2009[a]	1980–89	1990–99	2000–09
SUB-SAHARAN AFRICA	**587**	**530**	**528**	**547**	**564**	**585**	**608**	**623**	**618**	**–0.9**	**–0.6**	**2.6**
Excluding South Africa	367	338	350	365	378	393	410	423	428	–0.8	–0.2	3.1
Excl. S. Africa & Nigeria	347	332	338	350	362	377	394	406	408	–0.2	–0.3	2.8
Angola	..	794	712	767	899	1,036	1,213	1,339	1,313	..	–2.4	9.9
Benin	305	294	349	348	347	349	354	360	363	–0.4	1.3	0.6
Botswana	1,227	2,512	3,764	3,941	3,954	4,099	4,233	4,300	4,082	7.6	2.5	3.0
Burkina Faso	160	177	245	248	255	260	260	264	264	1.4	2.8	1.9
Burundi	135	152	107	109	107	109	110	111	112	1.2	–3.4	0.2
Cameroon	698	719	670	678	678	684	692	696	694	1.4	–1.6	1.0
Cape Verde	..	854	1,325	1,294	1,426	1,547	1,657	1,739	1,763	..	3.4	4.8
Central African Republic	324	278	223	222	223	227	231	232	233	–1.2	–0.9	–1.0
Chad	144	181	206	265	301	293	285	277	265	3.4	–0.6	6.7
Comoros	405	416	387	378	386	382	375	370	367	0.0	–1.1	–0.3
Congo, Dem. Rep.	258	207	83	86	89	91	94	97	97	–1.3	–8.8	2.1
Congo, Rep.	962	1,143	1,081	1,092	1,151	1,197	1,157	1,199	1,267	2.1	–1.4	1.8
Côte d'Ivoire	918	658	548	546	541	533	530	530	536	–3.2	–0.3	–1.3
Djibouti	..	1,178	767	782	793	816	843	876	904	..	–4.7	2.1
Equatorial Guinea	..	547	4,796	6,439	6,877	6,779	8,017	8,692	8,011	..	15.2	13.6
Eritrea	..	..	167	163	161	154	151	132	133	..	..	–3.4
Ethiopia	..	129	124	137	150	162	176	189	201	..	–0.7	5.7
Gabon	5,274	4,640	4,020	3,993	4,034	4,004	4,148	4,168	4,054	–1.6	–0.9	0.1
Gambia, The	346	340	321	333	340	351	363	375	382	–0.2	–0.8	2.1
Ghana	239	218	272	280	290	302	315	335	343	–1.1	1.6	3.5
Guinea	..	340	395	397	400	402	401	411	400	..	1.0	1.0
Guinea-Bissau	137	182	139	140	143	143	140	142	143	2.8	–1.6	–1.4
Kenya	435	450	401	411	424	439	457	452	452	0.3	–1.0	1.7
Lesotho	293	315	419	424	424	448	455	471	471	0.3	2.1	2.1
Liberia	728	200	131	131	133	138	144	148	148	–6.7	–1.9	–3.5
Madagascar	360	290	237	242	246	252	260	271	255	–2.4	–1.7	0.8
Malawi	161	132	138	141	141	148	152	160	168	–2.4	1.4	1.9
Mali	214	188	270	269	278	286	292	299	304	–1.0	2.1	2.8
Mauritania	454	410	420	430	441	514	472	478	462	–0.6	0.2	2.0
Mauritius	1,573	2,579	4,069	4,266	4,284	4,419	4,634	4,839	4,917	4.8	3.6	2.9
Mozambique	203	185	277	291	308	326	342	357	371	–1.0	2.8	5.2
Namibia	2,262	1,828	2,233	2,460	2,475	2,599	2,686	2,747	2,673	–2.2	1.6	3.3
Niger	257	191	171	166	167	170	169	178	173	–2.8	–1.2	0.5
Nigeria	422	359	396	427	439	456	474	491	506	–2.4	0.0	4.0
Rwanda	263	234	246	260	279	297	306	330	334	–1.1	–0.9	5.1
São Tomé and Príncipe	..	..	..	..	..	..	..	..	..	..	..	..
Senegal	476	460	492	508	522	522	533	536	534	0.0	0.3	1.6
Seychelles	4,532	5,645	6,913	6,740	7,209	7,651	8,350	8,092	7,389	1.8	2.9	0.9
Sierra Leone	285	248	221	229	236	246	254	261	265	–1.7	–5.7	5.8
Somalia	..	..	..	..	..	..	..	..	..	..	..	..
South Africa	3,463	3,152	3,159	3,264	3,398	3,548	3,702	3,796	3,689	–0.8	–0.7	2.8
Sudan	269	261	399	411	428	466	502	525	537	0.5	2.8	5.0
Swaziland	780	1,196	1,437	1,463	1,483	1,509	1,542	1,557	1,553	4.1	0.7	1.6
Tanzania	..	297	335	351	367	381	397	414	426	..	–0.2	4.2
Togo	346	273	249	250	247	250	249	247	247	–2.3	–0.4	–0.1
Uganda	..	181	281	290	298	320	336	353	366	..	3.7	4.3
Zambia	473	383	329	339	348	361	375	387	401	–2.0	–2.5	3.0
Zimbabwe	508	544	405	378	355	344	332	274	288	0.3	0.1	–7.4
NORTH AFRICA	**1,290**	**1,480**	**1,808**	**1,862**	**1,925**	**2,001**	**2,073**	**2,147**	**2,191**	**1.3**	**1.3**	**3.1**
Algeria	1,876	1,834	1,973	2,045	2,117	2,128	2,159	2,177	2,190	–0.1	–0.3	2.5
Egypt, Arab Rep.	867	1,135	1,470	1,501	1,539	1,614	1,697	1,786	1,836	2.6	2.1	3.0
Libya	..	..	6,364	6,509	7,009	7,272	7,554	7,685	7,692	..	..	3.3
Morocco	1,027	1,182	1,467	1,520	1,548	1,649	1,673	1,745	1,809	1.3	0.9	3.8
Tunisia	1,351	1,501	2,225	2,337	2,407	2,518	2,652	2,748	2,805	0.6	3.0	3.9
ALL AFRICA	**727**	**712**	**749**	**773**	**796**	**825**	**854**	**877**	**879**	**–0.2**	**0.0**	**2.6**

a. Provisional.

Table

2.5 Gross domestic product per capita growth

	Annual growth (%)											
										Annual average		
	1980	1990	2003	2004	2005	2006	2007	2008	2009[a]	1980–89	1990–99	2000–09
SUB-SAHARAN AFRICA	**1.0**	**–1.6**	**1.6**	**3.6**	**3.2**	**3.7**	**3.9**	**2.5**	**–0.8**	**–0.7**	**–0.6**	**2.1**
Excluding South Africa	–1.3	–0.7	2.3	4.6	3.3	4.0	4.3	3.3	1.1	–0.9	–0.2	2.6
Excl. S. Africa & Nigeria	–2.3	–2.3	0.9	3.6	3.5	4.1	4.5	3.2	0.4	–0.4	–0.4	2.3
Angola	..	–3.1	0.1	7.8	17.1	15.3	17.1	10.4	–1.9	1.5	–1.9	7.7
Benin	3.8	–0.1	0.4	–0.3	–0.5	0.8	1.3	1.8	0.6	0.2	1.1	0.9
Botswana	8.0	3.7	5.0	4.7	0.3	3.7	3.3	1.6	–5.1	7.9	3.2	2.7
Burkina Faso	–1.4	–3.3	4.6	1.2	2.8	2.0	0.1	1.5	0.1	1.2	2.2	1.6
Burundi	–1.9	0.9	–3.9	1.8	–2.1	2.0	0.5	1.4	0.6	1.0	–2.8	0.0
Cameroon	–4.8	–8.9	1.6	1.3	0.0	0.9	1.2	0.6	–0.3	1.0	–2.2	1.1
Cape Verde	..	–1.5	4.4	–2.3	10.2	8.5	7.1	5.0	1.4	4.2	3.0	4.4
Central African Republic	–7.0	–4.4	–9.2	–0.8	0.6	1.9	1.8	0.3	0.5	–1.6	–1.2	–0.9
Chad	–8.0	–7.2	10.6	29.1	13.6	–2.8	–2.6	–3.1	–4.2	2.6	–1.0	4.9
Comoros	..	2.4	0.3	–2.3	2.1	–0.9	–1.9	–1.4	–0.6	0.1	–0.7	–0.2
Congo, Dem. Rep.	–0.7	–9.9	2.5	3.4	3.3	2.1	3.3	3.3	0.0	–1.2	–8.5	0.4
Congo, Rep.	14.0	–1.8	–1.7	1.0	5.4	4.0	–3.4	3.7	5.6	3.6	–1.4	2.4
Côte d'Ivoire	–15.0	–4.6	–3.6	–0.3	–0.9	–1.5	–0.6	–0.1	1.2	–4.3	–0.7	–1.8
Djibouti	..	..	1.3	2.0	1.4	2.9	3.2	3.9	3.2	..	–4.5	1.6
Equatorial Guinea	..	–0.1	10.8	34.2	6.8	–1.4	18.3	8.4	–7.8	–2.9	16.3	15.3
Eritrea	..	..	–6.7	–2.6	–1.2	–4.3	–1.9	–12.5	0.6	..	6.5	–4.1
Ethiopia	..	–0.6	–4.7	10.7	9.0	8.0	8.6	7.9	5.9	–0.8	–0.5	5.3
Gabon	–0.3	1.9	0.4	–0.7	1.0	–0.7	3.6	0.5	–2.7	–1.2	–0.5	–0.5
Gambia, The	2.7	–0.5	3.5	3.8	2.0	3.5	3.4	3.2	1.8	0.2	–0.7	1.9
Ghana	–1.9	0.5	2.8	3.2	3.6	4.1	4.2	6.2	2.5	–1.0	1.5	3.2
Guinea	..	0.6	3.5	0.4	1.0	0.4	–0.4	2.6	–2.6	1.4	1.0	0.8
Guinea-Bissau	–18.5	3.6	–5.3	0.6	2.6	–0.1	–1.9	1.2	0.7	0.8	–0.5	–0.9
Kenya	1.7	0.7	0.3	2.4	3.2	3.6	4.2	–1.1	–0.1	0.4	–0.8	1.0
Lesotho	–5.2	4.9	3.3	1.3	0.1	5.5	1.5	3.6	0.0	–0.1	2.4	2.2
Liberia	–7.3	–50.0	–33.1	–0.2	1.8	3.6	4.7	2.4	0.3	–6.2	–2.3	–0.4
Madagascar	–1.8	0.1	6.7	2.3	1.7	2.2	3.4	4.3	–6.2	–2.3	–1.4	0.4
Malawi	–2.6	1.8	2.6	2.6	–0.2	4.7	2.9	5.6	4.7	–2.4	1.8	1.2
Mali	–6.0	–3.8	4.9	–0.2	3.6	2.8	1.9	2.4	1.9	–1.3	1.6	3.0
Mauritania	0.5	–4.3	2.7	2.4	2.7	16.4	–8.0	1.2	–3.3	–0.5	–0.1	1.1
Mauritius	–11.4	6.4	2.6	4.8	0.4	3.1	4.9	4.4	1.6	3.3	4.0	3.3
Mozambique	..	–0.3	3.2	5.1	5.7	6.0	4.8	4.3	4.0	–0.6	2.6	4.6
Namibia	..	–1.3	2.3	10.2	0.6	5.0	3.3	2.3	–2.7	–2.2	1.4	2.4
Niger	–5.1	–4.3	1.8	–3.3	0.8	1.9	–0.6	5.3	–2.9	–2.8	–1.4	0.1
Nigeria	1.2	5.4	7.7	8.0	2.9	3.7	4.0	3.6	3.2	–1.8	0.5	3.6
Rwanda	5.4	–2.0	0.5	5.8	7.2	6.6	2.8	8.2	1.2	–0.4	1.3	4.5
São Tomé and Príncipe	..	..	3.6	4.8	3.9	5.0	4.3	4.1	2.4	..	..	4.7
Senegal	–6.0	–3.5	3.9	3.2	2.9	–0.1	2.1	0.6	–0.4	–0.5	–0.1	1.3
Seychelles	–5.4	6.1	–4.9	–2.5	7.0	6.1	9.1	–3.1	–8.7	1.2	3.3	0.2
Sierra Leone	2.6	2.1	4.8	3.3	3.4	3.9	3.5	2.9	1.5	–1.2	–4.5	6.2
Somalia	–9.0	–1.9	..	..	..	..	..	..	..	0.9	–1.9	..
South Africa	4.2	–2.3	1.6	3.3	4.1	4.4	4.3	2.5	–2.8	–0.3	–0.8	2.2
Sudan	–1.7	–7.7	5.0	3.0	4.1	8.9	7.7	4.5	2.2	0.5	1.8	4.9
Swaziland	9.1	6.0	3.3	1.9	1.4	1.8	2.2	1.0	–0.3	4.8	1.2	2.0
Tanzania	..	3.7	4.1	4.9	4.4	3.8	4.1	4.4	3.0	0.6	0.2	3.9
Togo	11.1	–3.0	0.1	0.4	–1.3	1.3	–0.6	–0.7	0.0	–0.9	–0.3	–0.6
Uganda	..	2.7	3.1	3.4	2.9	7.2	4.9	5.2	3.6	–0.5	4.1	3.8
Zambia	–0.3	–3.4	2.8	3.1	2.8	3.7	3.7	3.3	3.8	–1.7	–2.4	2.7
Zimbabwe	10.4	3.9	–17.1	–6.7	–6.0	–3.2	–3.6	–17.3	5.2	1.4	0.6	–6.0
NORTH AFRICA	**2.4**	**1.6**	**4.3**	**3.0**	**3.4**	**4.0**	**3.6**	**3.5**	**2.1**	**1.5**	**1.3**	**2.8**
Algeria	–2.5	–1.7	5.3	3.6	3.5	0.5	1.5	0.9	0.6	–0.3	–0.4	2.1
Egypt, Arab Rep.	7.4	3.2	1.2	2.1	2.5	4.9	5.1	5.2	2.8	3.2	2.3	2.9
Libya	..	..	10.7	2.3	7.7	3.8	3.9	1.7	0.1	..	..	2.2
Morocco	1.0	2.1	5.2	3.7	1.8	6.5	1.5	4.3	3.7	1.4	1.2	3.5
Tunisia	4.6	5.4	4.9	5.1	3.0	4.6	5.3	3.6	2.1	1.0	3.3	3.6
ALL AFRICA	**1.4**	**–0.6**	**2.5**	**3.1**	**3.0**	**3.6**	**3.5**	**2.7**	**0.2**	**0.0**	**–0.1**	**2.2**

a. Provisional.

Table 2.6 Gross national income, nominal

	Current prices ($ millions)									Annual average growth (%)		
	1980	1990	2003	2004	2005	2006	2007	2008	2009[a]	1980–89	1990–99	2000–09
SUB-SAHARAN AFRICA	**261,499**	**284,576**	**425,226**	**529,902**	**616,553**	**728,169**	**827,908**	**947,512**	**909,888**	**0.9**	**1.8**	**15.1**
Excluding South Africa	186,001	176,977	261,709	315,160	374,531	472,616	551,831	680,851	631,533	–1.0	1.5	16.7
Excl. S. Africa & Nigeria	120,669	151,469	201,604	236,870	275,384	330,873	397,306	485,559	468,215	2.8	1.1	15.4
Angola	..	8,214	12,230	17,295	26,601	39,679	50,485	69,675	67,478	..	–2.4	33.5
Benin	1,402	1,806	3,515	4,006	4,259	4,623	5,428	6,672	6,646	2.1	3.7	13.8
Botswana	1,028	3,686	7,368	9,089	9,420	10,482	11,647	12,843	11,341	10.8	4.2	11.0
Burkina Faso	1,924	3,094	4,269	5,102	5,411	5,756	6,752	7,932	8,019	4.8	0.0	14.2
Burundi	922	1,117	577	646	776	910	974	1,165	1,331	1.9	–3.3	8.5
Cameroon	5,618	10,674	13,097	15,374	16,126	17,706	20,608	23,407	22,059	9.0	–2.4	12.0
Cape Verde	..	340	781	907	966	1,063	1,305	1,484	1,499	..	6.2	13.8
Central African Republic	800	1,465	1,137	1,268	1,348	1,473	1,702	1,966	1,983	7.8	–4.3	9.5
Chad	1,038	1,721	2,279	3,720	4,277	4,888	5,817	6,687	6,124	5.5	–1.2	20.7
Comoros	124	249	322	360	386	404	467	530	535	7.9	–2.0	12.0
Congo, Dem. Rep.	14,102	8,579	5,485	6,276	6,760	8,143	9,621	10,266	9,831	–6.8	–7.0	12.0
Congo, Rep.	1,544	2,324	2,580	3,159	4,039	5,105	5,747	8,728	6,869	1.9	–5.2	18.1
Côte d'Ivoire	9,680	9,209	13,018	14,763	15,643	16,589	18,911	22,438	22,406	1.3	3.3	10.7
Djibouti	..	..	673	731	776	854	936	1,073	1,120	..	1.3	8.4
Equatorial Guinea	..	124	1,392	2,312	4,173	5,163	6,674	11,868	6,715	..	16.9	35.3
Eritrea	..	..	761	923	1,162	1,272	1,365	1,642	1,856	..	7.3	13.7
Ethiopia	..	12,016	8,473	9,971	12,250	15,095	19,196	25,931	28,489	5.8	–5.8	17.0
Gabon	3,856	5,336	5,342	5,987	7,708	7,902	10,044	12,364	9,549	–0.1	–1.9	13.2
Gambia, The	237	291	336	366	418	460	597	776	690	1.6	3.7	8.5
Ghana	4,426	5,774	7,459	8,674	10,590	20,261	24,494	28,268	25,871	2.9	2.6	25.3
Guinea	..	2,518	3,201	3,391	2,658	2,496	3,819	3,321	3,692	..	3.3	1.9
Guinea-Bissau	105	233	463	524	579	588	681	834	826	3.4	–0.7	20.2
Kenya	7,043	8,224	14,738	15,955	18,732	22,540	27,208	30,134	29,311	2.6	8.3	12.0
Lesotho	695	902	1,202	1,515	1,619	1,797	1,995	2,014	1,934	–0.2	1.5	11.5
Liberia	930	..	350	373	417	444	560	673	645	–3.2	..	6.3
Madagascar	4,024	2,958	5,394	4,285	4,960	5,435	7,288	9,372	8,498	–6.0	3.8	9.6
Malawi	1,138	1,837	2,385	2,582	2,714	3,078	3,437	4,051	4,656	2.2	0.2	11.1
Mali	1,768	2,405	4,203	4,679	5,099	5,524	7,146	8,722	8,996	2.8	0.1	17.0
Mauritania	672	1,076	1,343	1,613	1,922	2,334	2,828	3,619	3,041	4.8	1.8	15.3
Mauritius	1,113	2,631	5,580	6,371	6,276	6,559	7,746	9,482	8,874	9.1	5.7	8.9
Mozambique	3,550	2,320	4,469	5,398	6,219	6,472	7,445	9,239	9,696	–5.6	8.6	11.9
Namibia	1,818	2,388	5,163	6,000	7,149	7,928	8,629	8,752	9,174	0.2	4.5	12.8
Niger	2,476	2,423	2,718	3,039	3,397	3,645	4,246	5,338	5,281	0.1	–1.7	13.8
Nigeria	61,079	25,585	59,996	78,110	98,881	141,275	154,068	194,690	162,901	–12.5	3.7	20.8
Rwanda	1,165	2,572	1,816	2,055	2,554	3,083	3,724	4,656	5,179	8.5	–2.0	15.1
São Tomé and Príncipe	..	..	..	..	111	127	151	170	194	..	..	..
Senegal	3,403	5,520	6,766	7,949	8,546	9,290	11,238	13,127	12,778	6.1	–1.8	13.6
Seychelles	142	355	663	666	844	924	954	823	655	8.9	5.9	4.0
Sierra Leone	1,071	580	958	1,034	1,176	1,364	1,629	1,916	1,901	–4.8	1.5	13.3
Somalia	603	835	..	..	..	..	..	..	..	5.5	..	..
South Africa	77,378	107,746	163,610	214,782	242,122	255,872	276,534	267,509	279,023	4.2	2.2	12.2
Sudan	7,570	11,409	16,428	19,990	25,397	33,503	41,985	52,236	49,255	9.7	1.9	20.9
Swaziland	..	1,174	1,754	2,284	2,702	2,684	2,991	2,833	2,874	..	4.5	10.7
Tanzania	..	4,072	11,601	12,775	14,114	14,331	16,839	20,731	21,385	..	10.6	9.3
Togo	1,096	1,598	1,736	2,033	2,073	2,180	2,478	2,892	2,850	4.6	–0.1	10.2
Uganda	1,237	4,227	6,219	8,338	8,771	9,679	11,664	14,161	15,711	20.7	9.1	12.5
Zambia	3,594	3,008	4,231	5,026	6,761	9,506	10,026	12,982	11,444	–4.1	0.7	19.2
Zimbabwe	6,530	8,512	5,439	5,388	5,308	4,890	4,654	3,879	5,213	–0.2	–1.7	–4.0
NORTH AFRICA	**103,183**	**159,989**	**257,561**	**289,635**	**332,058**	**390,836**	**469,628**	**580,537**	**542,401**	**4.9**	**5.4**	**11.8**
Algeria	41,147	59,955	65,319	81,414	97,259	112,669	134,004	169,689	139,577	4.5	–1.3	15.1
Egypt, Arab Rep.	21,453	42,025	82,816	78,638	89,432	108,015	131,650	164,196	188,575	7.5	11.2	7.6
Libya	..	..	24,603	33,139	43,719	57,559	74,070	93,533	61,985	..	..	22.8
Morocco	18,402	24,835	48,783	55,961	58,760	64,703	74,246	87,411	89,489	3.3	5.3	11.7
Tunisia	8,450	11,882	23,957	26,895	27,309	29,553	33,625	38,471	37,328	2.0	6.0	9.1
ALL AFRICA	**369,585**	**448,242**	**684,475**	**822,420**	**952,088**	**1,123,145**	**1,301,612**	**1,531,638**	**1,456,113**	**2.1**	**3.0**	**13.9**

a. Provisional.

Table 2.7 Gross national income, *World Bank Atlas* method

	Current prices ($ millions)									Annual average growth (%)		
	1980	1990	2003	2004	2005	2006	2007	2008	2009[a]	1980–89	1990–99	2000–09
SUB-SAHARAN AFRICA	**248,179**	**296,836**	**372,146**	**464,775**	**582,430**	**688,914**	**784,038**	**902,495**	**950,647**	**0.8**	**1.6**	**15.0**
Excluding South Africa	183,411	177,652	240,847	296,269	354,076	428,060	506,838	617,236	667,916	–1.2	1.1	16.5
Excl. S. Africa & Nigeria	122,461	152,211	184,869	222,371	265,832	307,548	363,836	439,072	482,054	2.1	0.8	14.6
Angola	..	7,700	10,678	14,638	21,938	32,662	45,510	60,022	69,373	..	–2.3	34.9
Benin	1,433	1,723	2,985	3,708	4,316	4,606	5,091	6,062	6,715	1.1	3.2	13.3
Botswana	860	3,311	6,616	7,991	9,506	10,640	11,477	12,592	12,211	9.4	5.1	11.3
Burkina Faso	2,016	2,923	3,684	4,634	5,527	5,990	6,399	7,242	8,036	3.4	–1.1	13.6
Burundi	897	1,187	623	666	723	843	956	1,093	1,232	3.6	–4.1	6.0
Cameroon	4,613	10,553	11,393	14,184	16,293	17,783	19,489	21,731	23,189	8.7	–1.5	11.6
Cape Verde	..	334	678	807	1,001	1,119	1,257	1,411	1,520	..	6.3	13.4
Central African Republic	785	1,384	1,003	1,187	1,358	1,470	1,602	1,799	1,975	6.9	–4.1	8.8
Chad	929	1,504	1,999	3,254	4,218	4,625	5,213	5,845	6,692	4.5	–0.6	20.4
Comoros	..	234	270	326	390	411	435	483	531	10.5	–1.7	11.7
Congo, Dem. Rep.	14,859	7,912	5,455	6,365	6,950	7,741	8,899	9,702	10,609	–8.4	–5.7	12.2
Congo, Rep.	1,471	2,185	2,365	2,687	3,456	4,414	5,238	7,158	7,671	2.2	–5.8	18.8
Côte d'Ivoire	9,319	9,253	11,191	13,655	15,689	16,521	17,770	20,252	22,545	0.8	2.9	9.9
Djibouti	..	..	675	754	803	864	925	1,029	1,106	..	0.6	8.5
Equatorial Guinea	..	124	1,232	1,928	3,170	4,296	6,236	9,874	8,398	..	15.5	37.4
Eritrea	..	..	707	818	1,019	1,163	1,312	1,368	1,620	..	4.2	11.9
Ethiopia	..	11,542	8,162	9,942	12,172	14,272	17,525	22,441	27,149	6.4	–4.9	14.9
Gabon	3,337	4,577	4,727	5,357	7,009	7,398	9,175	10,606	10,869	0.3	–1.4	13.8
Gambia, The	243	292	369	392	417	456	537	668	743	0.7	3.5	6.8
Ghana	4,643	5,847	6,549	8,144	10,018	13,302	18,374	26,845	28,383	4.0	1.9	21.7
Guinea	..	2,588	3,096	3,424	3,272	2,921	3,090	3,328	3,771	..	4.1	0.8
Guinea-Bissau	115	219	235	358	580	609	641	732	826	3.4	–1.1	20.4
Kenya	7,446	8,848	14,032	16,078	18,607	21,046	24,831	28,305	30,269	2.4	5.7	11.2
Lesotho	502	879	987	1,211	1,523	1,819	1,941	2,075	2,036	2.5	2.4	11.1
Liberia	849	..	342	365	407	431	531	645	651	–3.2	..	5.8
Madagascar	4,018	2,785	4,858	5,184	5,377	5,353	6,359	7,911	8,533	–4.3	4.1	9.1
Malawi	1,169	1,723	2,290	2,813	2,828	3,094	3,382	3,913	4,433	2.0	0.7	11.7
Mali	1,752	2,270	3,477	4,366	5,194	5,546	6,534	7,723	8,862	1.2	0.6	16.2
Mauritania	719	1,102	1,310	1,532	1,797	2,043	2,532	3,153	3,250	4.8	3.1	13.7
Mauritius	1,203	2,579	5,164	6,158	6,658	6,935	7,535	8,523	9,243	7.6	6.3	8.7
Mozambique	..	2,338	4,491	5,186	6,107	6,663	7,437	8,552	9,964	–2.2	6.6	10.7
Namibia	..	2,300	4,292	5,537	6,863	7,966	8,567	9,071	9,264	0.2	5.4	13.5
Niger	2,442	2,368	2,382	2,812	3,347	3,703	4,029	4,821	5,199	–0.3	–2.4	13.1
Nigeria	55,754	25,520	55,622	73,423	87,677	119,729	142,074	177,005	184,656	–10.9	2.7	22.8
Rwanda	1,298	2,546	1,806	2,037	2,469	2,896	3,403	4,252	4,896	8.2	–3.5	11.9
São Tomé and Príncipe	..	..	..	..	117	130	145	164	185	..	..	..
Senegal	2,977	5,046	5,878	7,378	8,684	9,327	10,368	11,960	13,062	5.0	–1.0	12.3
Seychelles	134	351	620	680	803	909	1,004	915	746	9.5	5.9	5.6
Sierra Leone	1,074	768	1,026	1,086	1,200	1,341	1,543	1,788	1,938	–6.6	0.6	12.5
Somalia	656	959	..	..	..	..	..	..	..	5.9	..	..
South Africa	69,282	119,309	131,765	169,056	228,919	261,586	278,167	286,605	284,270	4.5	2.3	12.2
Sudan	7,909	12,988	15,277	18,512	22,943	29,254	36,800	46,260	51,524	10.0	0.4	20.5
Swaziland	..	940	1,418	1,804	2,542	2,685	2,930	2,991	2,932	..	7.3	10.0
Tanzania	..	4,836	11,853	13,314	14,699	15,366	16,636	18,992	21,411	..	7.2	8.8
Togo	1,137	1,516	1,561	1,877	2,104	2,253	2,382	2,652	2,883	3.2	–0.3	9.4
Uganda	..	5,396	6,548	7,692	8,678	10,153	11,280	13,163	15,200	21.2	6.3	11.1
Zambia	3,610	3,491	4,007	4,593	5,847	7,222	9,117	11,929	12,473	–6.1	–0.2	18.7
Zimbabwe	6,692	9,014	5,186	5,289	5,357	5,157	4,858	3,958	4,564	0.1	–2.3	–4.0
NORTH AFRICA	**101,468**	**161,543**	**255,081**	**279,856**	**316,979**	**362,189**	**420,732**	**502,217**	**546,929**	**5.8**	**4.2**	**10.6**
Algeria	38,814	61,138	62,070	73,991	89,341	104,132	122,798	146,510	154,202	6.3	–2.5	15.2
Egypt, Arab Rep.	21,726	42,481	92,987	90,595	92,761	101,678	120,059	146,909	172,048	8.6	9.5	5.7
Libya	..	..	26,540	28,216	37,258	49,554	63,057	77,898	77,185	..	..	20.7
Morocco	18,734	24,777	44,364	53,199	60,341	66,321	70,682	80,878	89,933	1.9	4.7	11.0
Tunisia	8,689	11,649	22,258	26,325	28,750	30,761	32,816	36,510	38,845	2.0	6.2	8.8
ALL AFRICA	**353,620**	**462,592**	**627,017**	**744,930**	**900,271**	**1,052,308**	**1,206,017**	**1,405,886**	**1,498,551**	**2.4**	**2.5**	**13.3**

a. Provisional.

Table

2.8 Gross national income per capita, *World Bank Atlas* method

	Current prices ($)									Annual average growth (%)		
	1980	1990	2003	2004	2005	2006	2007	2008	2009[a]	1980–89	1990–99	2000–09
SUB-SAHARAN AFRICA	**640**	**576**	**513**	**625**	**764**	**882**	**979**	**1,100**	**1,130**	**-2.0**	**-1.1**	**12.2**
Excluding South Africa	509	370	354	425	495	583	673	800	844	-4.0	-1.6	13.6
Excl. S. Africa & Nigeria	429	397	339	397	463	522	602	707	757	-0.8	-1.9	11.7
Angola	..	720	680	910	1,320	1,910	2,590	3,330	3,750	..	-5.0	31.1
Benin	400	360	410	490	550	570	610	700	750	-1.9	-0.2	9.7
Botswana	870	2,450	3,690	4,400	5,170	5,710	6,060	6,550	6,260	6.0	2.5	9.8
Burkina Faso	290	330	290	350	400	420	430	480	510	1.0	-3.9	9.8
Burundi	220	210	90	90	100	110	120	140	150	0.3	-5.3	3.3
Cameroon	510	860	670	810	910	980	1,040	1,140	1,190	5.4	-4.1	9.1
Cape Verde	..	940	1,470	1,720	2,100	2,310	2,560	2,830	3,010	..	4.0	11.6
Central African Republic	350	470	250	290	330	350	380	410	450	4.2	-6.4	6.9
Chad	200	250	210	340	420	450	490	540	600	1.7	-3.6	16.6
Comoros	..	540	470	550	650	670	690	750	810	7.4	-3.9	9.3
Congo, Dem. Rep.	550	210	100	110	120	130	140	150	160	-11.1	-8.5	9.1
Congo, Rep.	810	890	730	800	1,010	1,270	1,470	1,980	2,080	-0.8	-7.8	16.2
Côte d'Ivoire	1,110	730	610	720	820	840	880	980	1,070	-3.3	-0.3	7.6
Djibouti	..	..	870	950	1,000	1,050	1,110	1,210	1,280	..	-2.1	6.5
Equatorial Guinea	..	330	2,140	3,250	5,210	6,870	9,710	14,980	12,420	..	11.5	33.7
Eritrea	..	..	170	190	230	250	270	280	320	..	1.7	7.8
Ethiopia	..	240	120	140	160	190	220	280	330	3.3	-7.6	11.7
Gabon	4,900	4,940	3,590	3,990	5,120	5,300	6,450	7,320	7,370	-2.7	-4.2	11.5
Gambia, The	390	330	260	260	270	290	330	400	440	-3.1	-0.4	3.5
Ghana	420	390	310	380	460	590	800	1,150	1,190	0.9	-0.9	19.0
Guinea	..	420	350	380	350	310	320	340	370	..	0.8	-1.2
Guinea-Bissau	140	210	170	250	390	400	420	460	510	1.3	-3.3	17.2
Kenya	460	380	410	460	520	570	660	730	760	-1.3	2.5	8.4
Lesotho	390	550	500	610	760	900	960	1,010	980	0.3	0.7	10.1
Liberia	440	..	110	110	120	120	150	170	160	-4.8	..	1.8
Madagascar	470	250	290	300	310	300	340	410	430	-6.8	1.0	6.0
Malawi	190	180	180	210	210	220	230	260	290	-2.5	-1.3	8.2
Mali	240	260	310	380	440	460	530	610	680	-0.6	-1.4	13.3
Mauritania	470	550	460	530	600	670	810	980	990	2.1	0.4	10.9
Mauritius	1,250	2,440	4,220	4,990	5,350	5,540	5,980	6,720	7,250	6.7	5.0	7.9
Mozambique	..	170	230	260	290	310	340	380	440	-2.7	3.5	7.9
Namibia	..	1,620	2,220	2,810	3,120	3,890	4,100	4,260	4,270	-3.5	2.8	11.3
Niger	410	300	200	220	260	270	280	330	340	-3.0	-5.5	9.1
Nigeria	750	260	410	530	620	830	960	1,170	1,190	-13.2	0.1	19.9
Rwanda	250	360	210	230	270	310	360	440	490	4.3	-3.6	9.3
São Tomé and Príncipe	..	..	..	..	760	840	920	1,020	1,130	..	..	..
Senegal	530	670	550	670	770	810	870	980	1,040	1.9	-3.6	9.1
Seychelles	2,080	5,020	7,490	8,240	9,680	10,740	11,800	10,530	8,480	8.6	4.3	4.7
Sierra Leone	330	190	220	220	240	250	280	320	340	-8.8	0.8	8.8
Somalia	100	150	..	..	..	..	..	..	..	6.0	..	..
South Africa	2,510	3,390	2,860	3,620	4,850	5,480	5,760	5,870	5,760	1.9	0.0	10.9
Sudan	390	480	410	490	590	740	910	1,120	1,220	6.8	-2.2	18.0
Swaziland	..	1,090	1,280	1,620	2,260	2,360	2,540	2,560	2,470	..	4.9	8.9
Tanzania	..	190	320	350	380	380	400	450	490	..	4.1	5.9
Togo	410	390	270	320	350	370	380	410	440	-0.5	-3.0	6.7
Uganda	..	300	240	280	300	340	370	420	460	17.0	3.1	7.5
Zambia	630	440	360	400	500	600	740	950	960	-9.0	-3.0	15.8
Zimbabwe	920	860	410	420	430	410	390	320	360	-3.6	-4.1	-4.0
NORTH AFRICA	**1,100**	**1,342**	**1,683**	**1,818**	**2,026**	**2,278**	**2,605**	**3,060**	**3,280**	**3.0**	**2.3**	**8.8**
Algeria	2,060	2,420	1,950	2,290	2,720	3,120	3,630	4,260	4,420	3.2	-4.4	13.5
Egypt, Arab Rep.	490	740	1,250	1,200	1,200	1,290	1,500	1,800	2,070	5.7	7.4	3.7
Libya	..	..	4,670	4,860	6,290	8,200	10,220	12,380	12,020	..	..	18.2
Morocco	960	1,000	1,490	1,760	1,980	2,150	2,260	2,560	2,810	-0.6	3.1	9.7
Tunisia	1,360	1,430	2,260	2,650	2,870	3,040	3,210	3,540	3,720	-0.5	4.5	7.7
ALL AFRICA	**737**	**727**	**715**	**830**	**980**	**1,119**	**1,253**	**1,428**	**1,487**	**-0.5**	**-0.1**	**10.7**

a. Provisional.

Table 2.9 Gross domestic product deflator (local currency series)

Index (2000 = 100)

	1980	1990	2003	2004	2005	2006	2007	2008	2009[a]	Annual average 1980–89	1990–99	2000–09
SUB-SAHARAN AFRICA	**20**	**40**	**118**	**127**	**140**	**149**	**164**	**189**	**195**	**26**	**67**	**140**
Excluding South Africa	20	41	117	127	139	148	164	192	196	27	68	140
Excl. S. Africa & Nigeria	20	42	117	127	139	147	162	189	195	27	69	139
Angola	..	0	931	1,329	1,780	2,041	2,126	2,606	2,455	0	3	1,404
Benin	38	50	113	113	116	122	126	135	136	47	73	118
Botswana	14	43	116	129	141	168	186	217	205	23	66	150
Burkina Faso	52	76	111	115	115	115	119	126	130	67	84	114
Burundi	21	31	120	130	151	158	171	214	243	24	51	150
Cameroon	34	58	106	107	110	115	117	122	118	50	79	110
Cape Verde	..	66	106	113	109	109	110	111	115	60	81	108
Central African Republic	32	70	105	106	109	114	117	124	129	54	83	112
Chad	46	60	116	127	130	148	156	174	153	55	78	133
Comoros	36	70	119	121	124	126	133	140	147	54	82	123
Congo, Dem. Rep.	0	0	722	766	931	1,053	1,276	1,523	1,983	0	2	948
Congo, Rep.	29	38	81	95	115	136	137	171	136	39	50	114
Côte d'Ivoire	39	50	111	112	116	122	125	135	137	50	75	117
Djibouti	..	69	104	108	111	115	121	132	134	..	85	113
Equatorial Guinea	..	24	87	102	145	166	164	203	135	26	41	128
Eritrea	..	..	161	192	260	287	304	406	443	..	66	241
Ethiopia	..	49	102	106	117	130	153	200	248	42	79	134
Gabon	35	53	93	99	116	125	132	151	123	44	63	113
Gambia, The	15	64	170	191	199	202	216	229	234	31	82	179
Ghana	0	11	213	244	280	506	589	708	826	3	37	377
Guinea	..	48	112	130	166	228	258	294	310	31	77	180
Guinea-Bissau	0	6	199	198	208	203	215	238	241	1	47	180
Kenya	10	24	109	117	122	132	139	155	166	16	57	124
Lesotho	13	40	126	134	142	153	174	197	204	22	68	146
Liberia	2	2	145	146	166	181	210	232	249	2	22	168
Madagascar	4	21	127	145	172	192	210	229	248	10	54	165
Malawi	2	7	223	256	285	344	371	404	437	3	29	275
Mali	35	57	117	116	119	124	133	145	151	50	79	122
Mauritania	20	42	119	133	157	193	207	233	218	29	75	158
Mauritius	22	55	120	127	133	142	154	164	167	34	76	133
Mozambique	0	6	131	141	153	167	180	194	201	1	45	151
Namibia	11	34	124	127	134	146	159	182	194	19	55	140
Niger	49	63	107	108	115	116	120	129	135	63	78	114
Nigeria	2	7	162	195	234	280	293	325	323	3	41	217
Rwanda	20	33	119	135	147	161	182	205	228	25	70	147
São Tomé and Príncipe	..	..	..	..	..	..	..	..	..	..	..	..
Senegal	39	63	107	107	110	114	121	128	127	55	81	112
Seychelles	56	87	117	121	142	144	170	218	280	70	92	151
Sierra Leone	0	5	106	126	142	156	172	192	204	1	41	140
Somalia	..	..	..	..	..	..	..	..	..	..	..	..
South Africa	9	38	126	134	141	150	163	178	191	18	65	141
Sudan	0	1	122	140	157	167	180	217	216	0	35	151
Swaziland	13	40	123	130	139	152	169	186	196	19	69	142
Tanzania	..	14	122	131	139	147	160	176	189	10	46	138
Togo	35	58	101	105	106	106	107	114	116	49	78	106
Uganda	..	29	109	126	124	127	136	145	169	4	70	124
Zambia	0	1	180	214	251	285	318	355	400	0	32	238
Zimbabwe	181	154	112	120	126	121	122	124	156	161	122	118
NORTH AFRICA	**21**	**54**	**111**	**123**	**133**	**143**	**161**	**181**	**178**	**33**	**77**	**134**
Algeria	6	16	111	123	143	159	171	196	178	9	50	138
Egypt, Arab Rep.	13	43	112	125	133	143	161	181	200	20	73	136
Libya	..	..	166	224	279	321	367	460	309	..	84	248
Morocco	35	68	103	104	105	107	111	118	120	50	84	107
Tunisia	30	64	107	110	114	118	123	129	133	46	82	114
ALL AFRICA	**20**	**42**	**117**	**127**	**139**	**148**	**163**	**186**	**194**	**26**	**69**	**139**

a. Provisional.

Table 2.10 Gross domestic product deflator

(U.S. dollar series)

	Index (2000 = 100)									Annual average		
	1980	1990	2003	2004	2005	2006	2007	2008	2009[a]	1980–89	1990–99	2000–09
SUB-SAHARAN AFRICA	**120**	**110**	**117**	**137**	**152**	**167**	**181**	**197**	**184**	**106**	**109**	**142**
Excluding South Africa	146	116	118	133	151	175	193	225	198	119	105	150
Excl. S. Africa & Nigeria	126	126	115	129	141	160	179	209	191	116	113	142
Angola	..	121	125	160	205	255	278	349	311	95	91	198
Benin	130	131	138	153	157	167	187	214	205	103	116	154
Botswana	88	112	120	140	141	147	155	164	149	77	110	132
Burkina Faso	175	199	136	155	155	156	177	200	196	147	135	149
Burundi	164	131	80	85	101	111	114	130	142	153	123	104
Cameroon	106	127	120	134	137	144	160	179	164	102	125	133
Cape Verde	..	112	130	152	147	148	163	177	174	95	117	140
Central African Republic	108	183	129	142	148	156	174	198	195	117	143	145
Chad	155	157	142	172	176	202	232	277	230	121	129	176
Comoros	91	138	146	163	167	172	197	223	221	89	125	161
Congo, Dem. Rep.	205	122	123	134	136	155	171	187	166	133	126	141
Congo, Rep.	98	100	99	127	155	185	203	272	205	84	81	152
Côte d'Ivoire	132	130	136	150	157	166	186	215	206	108	123	153
Djibouti	..	69	104	108	111	115	121	132	134	..	85	113
Equatorial Guinea	..	64	107	137	196	227	244	323	192	54	65	170
Eritrea	..	..	111	134	163	180	190	254	278	..	99	160
Ethiopia	..	194	97	100	110	122	139	169	172	167	151	119
Gabon	119	138	114	134	157	171	196	241	185	96	104	148
Gambia, The	113	104	80	81	89	92	111	132	113	91	109	98
Ghana	168	180	134	148	168	301	342	365	320	177	166	209
Guinea	..	128	98	102	80	75	109	93	102	117	136	94
Guinea-Bissau	97	131	244	267	280	277	320	379	363	105	116	242
Kenya	103	81	109	112	123	139	157	171	163	86	86	127
Lesotho	114	107	116	144	155	157	171	165	162	95	120	134
Liberia	69	89	100	109	119	128	140	150	149	76	101	118
Madagascar	130	94	139	105	116	121	152	182	172	108	101	132
Malawi	124	151	136	140	143	150	158	171	185	118	132	145
Mali	116	149	144	157	161	169	198	230	227	108	132	160
Mauritania	102	125	108	124	141	172	191	233	199	108	140	147
Mauritius	75	97	113	121	118	118	129	152	137	72	106	118
Mozambique	143	99	85	96	103	102	107	124	115	157	93	100
Namibia	95	91	114	136	146	150	157	153	160	79	97	129
Niger	165	165	131	146	156	158	170	205	204	137	127	149
Nigeria	204	81	127	150	181	223	237	279	221	127	70	174
Rwanda	85	154	86	91	103	114	130	146	156	112	123	109
São Tomé and Príncipe	..	..	..	..	..	..	..	..	..	..	..	..
Senegal	131	165	130	144	148	155	179	201	192	120	136	146
Seychelles	50	93	123	126	148	150	145	132	118	65	103	126
Sierra Leone	119	64	95	97	103	110	121	134	128	98	99	109
Somalia	..	..	..	..	..	..	..	..	..	..	..	..
South Africa	85	101	115	144	154	154	160	149	157	88	115	130
Sudan	138	176	120	139	165	197	229	267	241	196	122	167
Swaziland	115	108	113	140	151	156	166	156	163	87	123	131
Tanzania	..	56	94	96	99	94	103	118	115	69	72	101
Togo	118	152	124	141	143	144	160	182	175	106	131	137
Uganda	..	134	84	105	105	105	116	129	134	157	109	105
Zambia	142	109	119	140	175	246	247	295	247	111	111	178
Zimbabwe	181	154	112	120	126	121	122	124	156	161	122	118
NORTH AFRICA	**94**	**97**	**91**	**98**	**108**	**119**	**134**	**158**	**143**	**91**	**93**	**113**
Algeria	120	134	108	128	147	165	186	228	184	128	101	144
Egypt, Arab Rep.	60	66	76	69	76	85	96	112	124	62	76	91
Libya	..	..	67	88	106	128	154	193	126	..	93	111
Morocco	94	88	114	124	126	129	144	161	158	72	99	125
Tunisia	101	100	114	121	120	121	131	144	135	89	111	119
ALL AFRICA	**111**	**104**	**106**	**121**	**134**	**147**	**162**	**181**	**167**	**100**	**102**	**130**

a. Provisional.

Table 2.11 Consumer price index

	Annual growth (%)											
										Annual average		
	1980	1990	2003	2004	2005	2006	2007	2008	2009[a]	1980–89	1990–99	2000–09
SUB-SAHARAN AFRICA	..	..	..	..	..	..	..	..	..	..	..	..
Angola	..	..	98.2	43.5	23.0	13.3	12.2	12.5	13.7	..	1,122.5	80.3
Benin	..	..	1.5	0.9	5.4	3.8	1.3	7.9	2.2	..	9.7	3.4
Botswana	13.6	11.4	9.2	6.9	8.6	11.6	7.1	12.7	8.0	10.8	10.8	8.7
Burkina Faso	12.2	−0.5	2.0	−0.4	6.4	2.3	−0.2	10.7	2.6	5.0	4.5	3.0
Burundi	2.5	7.0	10.8	7.9	13.5	2.8	8.3	24.1	11.0	7.2	13.5	11.1
Cameroon	9.6	1.1	0.6	0.2	2.0	5.1	0.9	5.3	3.0	9.1	5.6	2.6
Cape Verde	..	10.7	1.2	−1.9	0.4	5.4	4.4	6.8	1.0	6.7	6.4	2.0
Central African Republic	..	0.0	4.1	−2.1	2.9	6.7	0.9	9.3	3.5	3.6	3.9	3.5
Chad	..	−0.7	−1.8	−5.4	7.9	8.0	−9.0	10.3	10.0	3.0	5.5	4.2
Comoros	..	..	..	..	..	..	..	..	..	..	..	..
Congo, Dem. Rep.	46.6	81.3	12.9	4.0	21.3	13.1	16.9	17.3	..	57.0	3,367.2	110.1
Congo, Rep.	..	2.9	−0.6	2.4	3.1	6.5	2.7	7.3	5.0	1.0	−3.5	3.0
Côte d'Ivoire	14.7	−0.8	3.3	1.4	3.9	2.5	1.9	6.3	1.0	6.7	6.0	3.0
Djibouti	12.1	..	2.0	3.1	3.1	3.5	5.0	12.0	1.7	5.3	..	3.6
Equatorial Guinea	..	0.9	7.3	4.2	5.6	4.4	2.8	6.6	..	−5.5	6.6	5.8
Eritrea	..	..	..	..	..	..	..	..	..	..	..	..
Ethiopia	4.5	5.2	17.8	3.3	11.6	12.3	17.2	44.4	8.5	4.6	8.0	10.9
Gabon	12.3	7.7	2.2	0.4	3.7	−1.4	5.0	5.3	1.9	6.5	3.7	2.0
Gambia, The	6.8	12.2	17.0	14.2	4.8	2.1	5.4	4.5	4.6	17.5	5.4	6.6
Ghana	50.1	37.3	26.7	12.6	15.1	10.9	10.7	16.5	19.3	48.3	27.6	18.5
Guinea	..	..	..	..	..	..	..	18.4	4.7	..	..	11.5
Guinea-Bissau	..	33.0	−3.5	0.9	3.3	2.0	4.6	10.5	−1.7	70.5	37.5	3.1
Kenya	13.9	17.8	9.8	11.6	10.3	14.5	9.8	26.2	9.2	11.8	17.4	10.9
Lesotho	16.3	11.6	6.7	5.0	3.4	6.0	8.0	10.7	7.2	13.9	−1.7	7.7
Liberia	14.7	..	..	..	..	..	..	..	..	5.6	..	..
Madagascar	18.2	11.8	−1.2	13.8	18.5	10.8	10.3	9.2	9.0	18.6	17.3	10.5
Malawi	..	11.8	9.6	11.4	15.4	14.0	8.0	8.7	8.4	16.8	31.0	14.3
Mali	..	0.6	−1.3	−3.1	6.4	1.5	1.4	9.2	2.2	−0.1	4.2	2.6
Mauritania	..	6.6	5.2	10.4	12.1	6.2	7.3	7.3	2.2	7.5	6.4	6.3
Mauritius	42.0	13.5	3.9	4.7	4.9	8.9	8.8	9.7	2.5	11.2	7.6	6.0
Mozambique	..	47.0	13.4	12.7	7.2	13.2	8.2	10.3	3.3	−3.2	34.5	10.7
Namibia	..	..	7.2	4.1	2.3	5.1	6.7	10.4	8.8	..	..	6.4
Niger	10.3	−0.8	−1.6	0.3	7.8	0.0	0.1	11.3	4.3	3.6	4.3	3.2
Nigeria	10.0	7.4	14.0	15.0	17.9	8.2	5.4	11.6	11.5	20.9	30.6	12.2
Rwanda	7.2	4.2	7.4	12.3	9.0	8.9	9.1	15.4	10.4	4.7	−3.4	8.2
São Tomé and Príncipe	..	..	..	..	..	..	..	..	..	..	..	..
Senegal	8.7	0.3	0.0	0.5	1.7	2.1	5.9	5.8	−1.1	6.9	4.5	2.1
Seychelles	13.6	3.9	3.3	3.9	0.9	−0.4	5.3	37.0	31.8	4.0	2.0	9.4
Sierra Leone	..	..	..	..	..	..	11.6	14.8	9.3	..	..	11.9
Somalia	..	..	..	..	..	..	..	..	..	..	..	..
South Africa	13.7	14.3	5.9	1.4	3.4	4.6	7.1	11.5	7.1	14.6	9.9	6.1
Sudan	25.4	65.2	7.7	8.4	8.5	7.2	8.0	14.3	11.2	36.2	80.4	8.7
Swaziland	18.7	13.1	7.3	3.4	4.8	5.3	9.5	13.4	7.3	15.0	9.5	8.1
Tanzania	30.2	35.8	5.3	4.7	5.0	7.3	7.0	10.3	12.1	30.1	23.1	6.8
Togo	12.3	1.0	−1.0	0.4	6.8	2.2	1.0	8.7	2.0	5.0	7.1	2.9
Uganda	..	33.1	8.7	3.7	8.4	7.3	6.1	11.6	13.4	111.2	13.0	6.4
Zambia	..	107.0	21.4	18.0	18.3	9.0	10.7	12.4	13.4	69.3	76.2	17.3
Zimbabwe	5.4	17.4	431.7	282.4	302.1	1,096.7	24,411.0	..	..	12.8	28.6	3,349.6
NORTH AFRICA	..	..	..	..	..	..	..	..	..	..	..	..
Algeria	9.5	16.7	2.6	3.6	1.6	2.5	3.5	4.4	5.7	9.0	18.6	3.0
Egypt, Arab Rep.	20.8	16.8	4.5	11.3	4.9	7.6	9.3	18.3	11.8	17.4	10.5	7.5
Libya	9.7	8.5	−2.2	−2.2	2.7	1.5	6.3	10.4	2.5	7.9	6.7	−0.3
Morocco	9.4	6.8	1.2	1.5	1.0	3.3	2.0	3.7	1.0	7.6	4.4	1.9
Tunisia	..	6.5	2.7	3.6	2.0	4.5	3.1	4.9	3.8	7.6	4.9	3.2
ALL AFRICA	..	..	..	..	..	..	..	..	..	..	..	..

a. Provisional.

Table 2.12 Price indexes

	Inflation, GDP deflator (annual %)		Consumer price index (2000 = 100)		Exports of goods and services price index (2000 = 100)		Imports of goods and services price index (2000 = 100)	
	2008	2009[a]	2008	2009[a]	2008	2009[a]	2008	2009[a]
SUB-SAHARAN AFRICA	**10.6**	**4.3**	**126.6**	**134.2**	..	..	**173.0**	**153.9**
Excluding South Africa	10.8	4.1	126.7	134.6	..	..	..	..
Excl. S. Africa & Nigeria	10.6	4.3	126.6	134.0	..	..	178.1	..
Angola	22.6	–5.8	143.0	162.7	..	..	..	..
Benin	7.1	1.2	113.5	115.9	..	..	..	..
Botswana	17.0	–5.7	134.6	145.4	138.8	135.2	159.8	163.5
Burkina Faso	5.8	3.1	113.0	115.9	..	..	..	..
Burundi	25.1	13.6	138.2	153.4	..	..	..	..
Cameroon	4.2	–3.4	111.7	115.2	338.8	271.8	296.7	254.4
Cape Verde	1.0	3.8	117.5	118.6	74.2	70.4	126.5	120.0
Central African Republic	6.2	3.9	117.7	121.8	..	..	..	..
Chad	11.9	–12.4	108.5	119.3	..	..	..	..
Comoros	5.5	4.6	..	..	..	..	..	..
Congo, Dem. Rep.	19.4	30.2	155.1	..	179.4	64.1	127.8	74.6
Congo, Rep.	25.1	–20.4	117.4	123.3	..	..	..	..
Côte d'Ivoire	8.1	1.3	111.0	112.1	194.2	158.6	211.5	165.0
Djibouti	9.5	1.7	121.6	123.6	..	..	..	..
Equatorial Guinea	23.7	–33.5	114.4	..	..	..	..	..
Eritrea	33.4	9.3	..	..	..	..	..	..
Ethiopia	30.5	24.4	190.1	206.2	145.0	138.4	135.4	120.1
Gabon	14.7	–19.0	109.0	111.1	330.3	207.2	204.3	166.6
Gambia, The	6.2	2.4	112.3	117.4	121.3	108.5	170.5	152.1
Ghana	20.2	16.7	143.1	170.7	..	..	..	..
Guinea	14.1	5.2	118.4	123.9	139.1	179.2	165.7	181.3
Guinea-Bissau	10.6	1.1	117.8	115.9	..	..	..	..
Kenya	11.9	6.7	158.6	173.2	174.8	168.1	163.6	146.8
Lesotho	13.4	3.4	126.8	135.9	130.4	136.0	87.1	86.5
Liberia	10.4	7.4	..	..	..	..	..	..
Madagascar	9.2	8.3	133.5	145.4	151.0	135.3	164.0	153.3
Malawi	8.9	8.4	133.8	145.0	..	..	..	..
Mali	8.7	4.3	112.4	114.9	..	..	..	..
Mauritania	12.4	–6.2	122.3	125.0	..	..	..	..
Mauritius	7.0	1.5	130.1	133.4	142.7	126.6	185.1	156.4
Mozambique	8.2	3.3	135.1	139.5	113.8	85.5	211.2	173.3
Namibia	14.3	6.5	123.7	134.6	175.5	184.1	136.1	133.2
Niger	7.7	4.9	111.4	116.2	..	..	..	..
Nigeria	11.0	–0.6	127.3	142.0	..	..	..	..
Rwanda	12.7	11.0	137.1	151.3	..	..	..	..
São Tomé and Príncipe	23.1	15.6	1,171.2	..	..	..	..	..
Senegal	5.9	–0.5	114.3	113.1	183.3	178.1	198.8	193.0
Seychelles	28.5	28.6	143.8	189.4	96.9	73.1	96.9	73.1
Sierra Leone	11.2	6.3	128.2	140.1	..	..	..	..
Somalia	..	..	..	..	..	..	..	..
South Africa	9.2	7.3	125.0	133.9	196.5	194.1	168.0	153.7
Sudan	21.0	–0.8	132.3	147.2	255.0	..	254.3	..
Swaziland	10.1	5.5	130.7	140.3	97.2	103.4	97.2	103.4
Tanzania	10.1	7.4	126.6	142.0	137.4	125.9	129.7	105.5
Togo	6.5	1.3	112.2	114.4	..	..	..	..
Uganda	6.5	16.5	127.2	144.3	108.0	99.5	153.9	148.0
Zambia	11.5	12.7	135.7	153.8	..	..	..	..
Zimbabwe	2.3	25.3	..	..	187.3	201.5	217.9	196.2
NORTH AFRICA	**12.2**	**1.8**	**113.1**	**117.4**	..	..	**160.1**	**152.8**
Algeria	14.6	–9.4	110.9	117.2	292.8	216.7	188.8	209.7
Egypt, Arab Rep.	12.2	10.8	139.2	155.6	92.2	94.6	90.9	105.6
Libya	25.4	–32.8	119.0	121.9	..	..	..	..
Morocco	5.9	1.8	109.3	110.4	176.3	159.2	188.5	160.0
Tunisia	5.4	2.9	113.1	117.4	198.7	168.9	204.5	159.4
ALL AFRICA	**10.8**	**3.8**	**124.4**	**133.4**	..	..	**167.6**	**153.4**

a. Provisional.

Table 2.13 Gross domestic savings

	Share of GDP (%)											
										Annual average		
	1980	1990	2003	2004	2005	2006	2007	2008	2009[a]	1980–89	1990–99	2000–09
SUB-SAHARAN AFRICA	**25.3**	**17.1**	**16.0**	**15.9**	**15.7**	**15.9**	**16.7**	**16.1**	**15.5**	**20.1**	**15.4**	**16.0**
Excluding South Africa	..	11.7	13.4	14.2	14.2	14.6	15.2	13.3	12.5	11.9	11.7	13.7
Excl. S. Africa & Nigeria	11.7	11.7	13.4	14.2	14.2	14.6	15.2	13.3	12.5	11.8	11.7	13.7
Angola	..	29.7	19.2	25.1	37.9	49.1	45.0	41.1	20.8	24.0	22.0	31.9
Benin	–6.3	2.2	6.0	5.5	6.9	6.9	6.1	7.1	10.7	–2.4	3.8	6.5
Botswana	26.7	42.6	41.0	40.5	43.1	40.4	37.8	32.3	13.0	35.3	38.8	36.5
Burkina Faso	–7.2	5.4	4.5	1.8	4.8	2.8	..	..	..	–1.6	9.0	2.6
Burundi	–0.6	–5.4	–8.7	–11.0	–23.1	–19.9	..	..	..	3.1	–5.2	–12.3
Cameroon	21.7	20.7	17.8	18.5	18.1	18.9	18.5	..	..	24.2	18.5	18.8
Cape Verde	..	–8.1	–15.8	–1.5	4.4	5.0	5.8	9.2	12.0	–2.2	–5.6	–2.6
Central African Republic	–8.9	–0.6	1.6	0.0	0.1	1.4	1.5	–1.0	2.7	–1.1	3.7	2.0
Chad	..	–7.7	18.0	24.5	35.1	36.4	20.5	27.4	5.9	–8.1	–0.5	13.8
Comoros	–10.1	–3.2	–3.4	–8.5	–12.3	–14.8	–15.4	–20.1	–21.1	–4.5	–4.9	–11.1
Congo, Dem. Rep.	10.1	9.3	5.0	4.0	5.9	–0.6	8.8	8.6	17.7	10.9	8.8	6.1
Congo, Rep.	35.7	23.8	30.9	52.2	52.0	43.3	49.6	48.4	45.5	31.9	28.8	48.3
Côte d'Ivoire	20.4	11.3	21.0	20.0	17.2	19.6	14.6	17.9	19.2	19.6	17.8	19.4
Djibouti	..	–10.4	5.3	4.3	8.6	12.1	17.4	..	..	..	–6.4	5.7
Equatorial Guinea	..	–20.1	80.1	78.9	83.7	86.1	86.9	72.8	72.2	..	13.7	79.5
Eritrea	..	..	–40.9	–41.5	–27.2	–17.2	–17.7	..	..	..	–29.7	–29.2
Ethiopia	..	9.6	7.7	8.8	2.6	1.5	4.2	0.4	4.1	10.5	9.7	5.7
Gabon	60.6	36.9	48.2	54.6	58.3	56.0	55.3	58.9	47.3	44.3	43.6	53.2
Gambia, The	5.8	10.7	11.1	8.9	4.0	11.2	6.6	6.1	6.3	6.5	7.4	8.8
Ghana	4.9	5.5	7.0	7.3	3.7	6.1	3.8	2.0	8.7	4.8	7.5	5.9
Guinea	..	22.2	21.5	18.4	18.3	13.9	9.7	10.3	16.9	16.6	18.3	15.1
Guinea-Bissau	–1.0	2.8	..	..	..	..	..	..	..	–0.9	1.5	–13.2
Kenya	18.1	18.5	10.5	10.8	9.5	8.1	8.0	6.1	7.8	18.3	14.6	8.7
Lesotho	–52.0	–49.1	–25.9	–25.7	–27.9	–23.6	–27.1	–25.3	–29.1	–69.5	–37.6	–26.4
Liberia	14.8	..	–3.2	–0.7	2.4	–34.6	–142.5	–121.5	..	2.2	..	–38.4
Madagascar	–1.4	5.5	8.9	8.5	4.9	9.3	10.6	9.9	8.9	2.9	4.2	9.2
Malawi	10.8	13.4	3.2	0.0	–5.5	1.2	18.9	8.9	17.2	12.7	3.4	5.4
Mali	1.1	6.4	13.3	8.6	11.0	14.8	13.0	..	..	–0.4	7.6	12.2
Mauritania	–3.5	4.9	–5.0	–3.1	–15.0	18.6	8.0	5.6	7.4	3.1	2.4	0.9
Mauritius	10.4	23.0	24.9	22.0	16.5	15.3	16.6	12.5	10.8	20.3	24.1	19.6
Mozambique	–8.9	–5.8	3.5	7.7	6.5	8.8	6.3	1.6	2.2	–6.2	–2.9	6.0
Namibia	38.4	18.2	10.3	16.8	19.8	20.6	22.4	21.4	13.9	10.8	12.7	17.1
Niger	14.6	1.2	5.0	3.9	13.4	..	..	..	..	7.3	2.7	5.9
Nigeria[b]	..	..	..	..	..	..	..	..	..	..	..	..
Rwanda	4.2	6.2	0.4	1.4	2.0	1.8	3.5	7.0	4.2	5.0	–5.5	2.4
São Tomé and Príncipe	..	..	..	..	..	..	..	..	..	..	..	..
Senegal	2.1	2.4	8.8	7.9	14.1	10.7	8.6	3.6	8.0	4.3	5.4	8.9
Seychelles	27.1	20.3	21.5	14.7	3.1	8.1	–1.7	6.0	15.9	24.1	21.7	13.3
Sierra Leone	0.9	8.7	–3.7	–0.4	4.1	7.6	6.1	1.7	2.3	9.1	2.8	–1.6
Somalia	–12.9	–12.5	..	..	..	..	..	..	..	–6.3	–12.5	..
South Africa	37.9	23.2	19.0	17.8	17.5	17.2	18.3	18.9	18.6	28.5	19.4	18.5
Sudan	2.1	8.2	15.7	18.7	19.0	18.6	26.7	26.8	19.4	4.2	9.6	18.4
Swaziland	1.2	5.3	18.1	13.5	11.2	11.5	12.7	–0.2	0.2	3.7	2.0	9.4
Tanzania	..	1.3	16.1	15.2	14.0	11.0	12.6	10.3	17.9	..	2.9	13.7
Togo	23.2	14.7	5.3	4.5	1.5	..	..	..	..	12.3	6.7	1.8
Uganda	–0.4	0.6	7.2	10.1	11.7	8.1	8.8	15.3	12.5	2.3	4.3	9.5
Zambia	19.3	16.6	13.0	19.9	21.8	31.5	30.5	25.1	25.6	14.0	9.0	18.1
Zimbabwe	13.8	17.5	2.3	–2.8	–7.6	–9.8	–1.6	–22.6	–26.9	16.5	17.1	–3.9
NORTH AFRICA	**22.8**	**20.8**	**27.2**	**27.7**	**29.9**	**33.5**	**32.8**	**33.7**	**23.8**	**20.3**	**19.2**	**27.9**
Algeria	43.1	27.1	44.9	47.7	54.9	56.6	57.5	56.7	45.5	31.5	30.1	49.1
Egypt, Arab Rep.	15.2	16.1	14.3	15.6	15.7	17.1	16.3	16.8	12.4	15.5	14.2	14.8
Libya	..	27.2	46.8	42.7	48.1	66.8	63.6	67.8	..	..	17.6	46.6
Morocco	14.9	19.9	24.5	24.2	23.2	24.0	23.4	24.7	25.1	16.7	17.8	23.7
Tunisia	24.0	20.0	21.2	21.2	21.4	21.5	22.0	22.4	23.5	22.7	22.3	22.2
ALL AFRICA	**24.2**	**18.8**	**21.0**	**21.2**	**22.1**	**23.8**	**24.0**	**24.3**	**19.1**	**20.2**	**17.1**	**21.4**

a. Provisional.

b. For 1994–2000 Nigeria's values were distorted because the official exchange rate used by the government for oil exports and oil value added was significantly overvalued.

Table 2.14 Gross national savings

	Share of GDP (%)											
										Annual average		
	1980	1990	2003	2004	2005	2006	2007	2008	2009[a]	1980–89	1990–99	2000–09
SUB-SAHARAN AFRICA	**23.4**	**15.8**	**16.0**	**16.4**	**16.4**	**16.1**	**15.9**	**15.5**	**15.4**	**18.6**	**15.2**	**15.8**
Excluding South Africa	..	12.8	16.3	17.8	18.3	..	..	..	..	13.0	13.9	16.3
Excl. S. Africa & Nigeria	10.9	12.8	16.3	17.8	18.3	18.0	18.0	16.2	..	12.4	13.9	16.7
Angola	..	9.0	7.6	12.6	24.8	36.5	29.9	23.6	9.7	13.8	1.6	17.7
Benin	4.2	5.3	6.7	6.8	10.1	10.0	8.8	10.6	..	4.6	7.8	9.3
Botswana	28.7	41.6	35.7	36.2	41.5	41.2	40.8	34.8	16.4	33.8	40.5	35.4
Burkina Faso	9.3	15.9	9.4	5.4	8.8	7.0	..	..	..	14.6	21.5	6.8
Burundi	..	8.7	9.1	9.5	4.5	4.1	..	..	..	11.2	6.2	5.8
Cameroon	5.2	16.2	14.9	17.0	16.7	19.2	20.3	..	..	18.8	13.4	16.5
Cape Verde	..	17.8	9.3	22.0	29.1	27.1	26.5	26.7	31.3	24.3	21.8	19.8
Central African Republic	1.6	6.2	..	..	..	..	..	..	..	6.1	8.1	..
Chad	..	2.3	..	..	..	..	..	..	..	6.2	4.6	..
Comoros	−0.4	14.4	..	..	..	..	..	..	..	15.0	15.4	..
Congo, Dem. Rep.	..	..	..	..	..	..	..	..	..	..	..	..
Congo, Rep.	26.1	6.9	4.2	19.7	18.9	9.0	18.0	..	..	25.5	5.3	18.0
Côte d'Ivoire	8.6	−5.1	12.3	12.4	10.0	12.1	8.4	12.3	14.8	6.8	6.0	11.7
Djibouti	..	..	24.6	24.4	28.3	33.4	37.1	..	..	..	11.4	22.3
Equatorial Guinea	..	2.1	..	..	..	..	..	..	..	..	14.7	..
Eritrea	..	..	..	..	..	..	..	..	..	..	32.8	4.4
Ethiopia	..	12.8	21.4	22.1	13.7	9.7	21.9	17.1	16.1	13.4	15.5	17.8
Gabon	47.8	24.3	33.4	35.4	44.2	..	..	..	..	33.7	29.3	37.1
Gambia, The	16.4	21.9	17.1	16.7	10.2	18.9	17.3	10.4	18.8	16.9	16.9	15.6
Ghana	6.3	10.5	21.1	22.9	19.2	16.5	11.5	8.8	15.5	7.3	13.5	17.4
Guinea	..	19.2	18.3	11.4	..	..	−1.6	1.4	7.7	12.4	18.7	9.9
Guinea-Bissau	..	14.5	..	..	..	..	..	..	..	1.8	9.0	−7.3
Kenya	17.2	18.5	15.2	16.2	16.1	16.2	16.0	14.2	15.4	18.0	21.8	15.1
Lesotho	49.6	70.5	18.9	20.6	18.0	30.7	39.0	33.5	28.1	42.0	49.5	24.9
Liberia	13.1	..	..	142.2	128.1	134.1	−11.4	−2.1	..	−3.5	..	78.2
Madagascar	−0.7	9.1	13.0	14.1	8.0	..	..	..	..	3.0	5.1	11.8
Malawi	7.8	16.4	..	..	..	..	..	..	..	12.5	8.1	8.9
Mali	8.4	15.0	14.4	8.6	11.4	14.5	18.6	..	..	6.1	14.7	13.1
Mauritania	3.9	18.8	..	..	..	..	..	..	..	12.2	10.5	..
Mauritius	10.4	25.8	25.3	22.6	17.4	17.1	21.3	16.7	16.7	20.2	26.5	21.9
Mozambique	−6.6	6.6	4.1	8.0	7.1	7.1	6.6	3.8	9.1	−2.2	6.0	7.8
Namibia	..	34.8	24.3	28.2	27.5	31.7	31.8	31.6	26.5	..	27.5	27.8
Niger	17.1	−0.6	7.2	6.9	18.5	..	..	..	..	8.8	3.6	8.6
Nigeria[b]	..	..	..	..	..	..	..	..	..	..	..	..
Rwanda	14.0	11.3	11.0	14.8	15.1	10.4	14.1	17.3	15.1	12.0	14.2	13.4
São Tomé and Príncipe	..	..	..	..	..	..	..	..	..	..	..	..
Senegal	2.7	1.6	15.0	14.6	21.0	18.7	19.1	16.1	..	4.2	6.3	16.0
Seychelles	32.4	21.7	17.2	12.4	2.1	8.2	−3.9	1.6	9.2	27.3	21.5	10.0
Sierra Leone	2.9	−1.0	9.1	4.8	10.0	9.0	10.3	5.3	7.8	7.7	0.8	5.7
Somalia	20.1	..	..	..	..	..	..	..	..	19.2	..	..
South Africa	33.9	19.1	15.7	15.0	14.5	14.4	14.1	14.9	15.4	24.4	16.6	15.2
Sudan	4.5	1.2	12.2	16.0	17.0	13.9	17.8	17.4	12.2	3.7	4.0	13.0
Swaziland	..	19.7	24.1	18.3	22.1	17.0	20.6	6.9	2.4	..	16.2	17.1
Tanzania	..	10.1	20.0	19.4	17.3	15.2	16.6	13.3	21.2	..	8.7	16.9
Togo	27.2	21.0	11.3	11.4	8.7	..	..	..	..	16.8	10.8	7.0
Uganda	1.9	5.6	17.6	20.4	20.7	16.9	16.2	21.9	17.5	5.5	14.4	17.6
Zambia	7.8	19.6	10.8	13.1	17.7	23.9	23.1	19.2	19.0	3.2	7.1	13.0
Zimbabwe	12.0	15.6	..	..	..	..	..	..	..	14.6	15.7	..
NORTH AFRICA	**25.9**	**27.6**	**25.2**	**25.3**	**27.4**	**32.5**	**32.2**	**32.5**	**..**	**23.6**	**28.3**	**28.1**
Algeria	41.0	24.3	..	..	..	..	..	..	..	29.4	28.6	..
Egypt, Arab Rep.	21.0	31.1	18.5	21.1	21.8	23.0	23.6	23.6	16.7	21.8	24.7	20.3
Libya	..	..	42.2	34.4	46.0	69.8	66.5	67.1	..	..	..	49.7
Morocco	18.6	25.1	30.7	31.0	30.9	32.2	32.3	32.9	31.2	20.5	21.6	30.6
Tunisia	25.3	23.4	21.8	21.7	20.2	21.7	21.0	21.3	22.8	23.7	22.2	21.9
ALL AFRICA	**24.5**	**20.8**	**19.7**	**20.0**	**20.9**	**23.0**	**22.7**	**22.8**	**17.6**	**20.8**	**18.4**	**20.0**

a. Provisional.

b. For 1994–2000 Nigeria's values were distorted because the official exchange rate used by the government for oil exports and oil value added was significantly overvalued.

Table 2.15 General government final consumption expenditure

	Share of GDP (%)											
										Annual average		
	1980	1990	2003	2004	2005	2006	2007	2008	2009[a]	1980–89	1990–99	2000–09
SUB-SAHARAN AFRICA	**15.1**	**17.5**	**16.4**	**16.6**	**16.7**	**16.4**	**16.0**	**16.3**	**17.6**	**16.5**	**16.8**	**16.3**
Excluding South Africa	..	15.6	13.8	14.1	14.2	13.4	13.1	..	..	15.6	14.4	13.5
Excl. S. Africa & Nigeria	16.1	15.6	13.8	14.1	14.2	13.4	13.1	13.2	13.9	15.6	14.4	13.5
Angola	..	34.5	..	..	..	..	..	..	..	31.5	40.7	..
Benin	8.6	11.0	13.3	13.6	15.0	..	..	..	..	12.7	10.5	12.9
Botswana	21.3	24.1	22.3	21.1	22.4	19.0	19.4	19.8	24.2	24.3	26.7	21.4
Burkina Faso	9.2	21.1	22.2	21.6	22.3	22.0	..	..	..	15.6	22.5	22.3
Burundi	9.2	10.8	22.7	26.1	26.5	28.8	..	..	..	9.3	17.0	22.9
Cameroon	9.7	12.8	10.0	10.2	10.0	9.6	9.2	..	..	10.0	10.6	9.9
Cape Verde	..	14.7	14.7	20.6	20.4	22.1	22.4	20.7	20.8	13.1	17.0	18.6
Central African Republic	15.1	14.9	11.0	10.5	13.3	11.1	2.7	6.6	4.5	15.6	13.9	9.8
Chad	..	10.0	7.6	4.9	5.1	4.9	10.3	12.4	15.6	11.3	8.1	8.4
Comoros	30.9	24.5	14.7	14.3	13.5	14.2	14.3	15.3	15.3	28.6	20.3	14.7
Congo, Dem. Rep.	8.4	11.5	6.3	8.2	8.3	7.8	10.4	11.0	7.9	9.0	9.9	7.9
Congo, Rep.	17.6	13.8	17.4	15.0	13.0	13.9	17.1	12.0	12.2	17.7	18.1	14.5
Côte d'Ivoire	16.9	16.8	8.2	8.3	8.3	8.3	8.7	8.6	8.6	16.5	11.9	8.1
Djibouti	..	31.5	29.5	29.7	27.1	28.0	25.1	..	..	..	31.8	28.0
Equatorial Guinea	..	39.7	3.8	2.9	2.7	2.6	2.3	2.6	3.4	27.4	25.1	3.3
Eritrea	..	..	50.3	52.9	37.2	35.9	31.4	..	..	..	39.7	45.4
Ethiopia	..	13.2	13.4	13.1	12.3	12.1	10.4	9.7	8.2	11.2	9.8	12.6
Gabon	13.2	13.4	10.1	9.3	8.3	8.4	8.9	8.2	11.6	18.3	13.2	9.7
Gambia, The	31.2	13.7	11.0	16.9	18.4	18.1	16.0	15.6	15.9	29.1	13.8	15.3
Ghana	11.2	9.3	11.5	12.2	15.3	11.3	11.6	11.2	9.6	9.0	11.7	11.2
Guinea	..	11.0	8.2	6.9	7.0	8.1	6.8	9.3	0.0	11.6	8.2	7.6
Guinea-Bissau	27.6	10.3	..	..	..	..	..	..	..	18.9	8.4	13.1
Kenya	19.8	18.6	18.1	17.9	17.4	17.5	17.9	16.7	16.3	18.3	15.8	17.0
Lesotho	21.8	25.8	37.4	37.4	39.2	40.4	38.7	44.0	50.4	23.3	33.6	40.2
Liberia	19.1	..	8.5	10.4	11.1	11.5	14.6	19.3	..	22.0	..	12.9
Madagascar	12.1	8.0	9.2	6.9	9.0	8.7	12.3	11.2	11.5	9.8	7.9	9.5
Malawi	19.3	15.1	12.4	12.5	14.3	14.6	14.1	17.3	20.9	17.5	16.6	15.0
Mali	11.6	13.8	8.4	10.0	9.9	9.9	10.3	..	..	12.3	12.7	9.4
Mauritania	45.3	25.9	30.1	21.9	22.7	17.5	21.6	18.8	20.6	30.6	14.5	22.5
Mauritius	14.0	13.6	14.2	14.3	14.8	14.2	13.1	13.2	14.6	12.6	14.0	14.0
Mozambique	12.2	13.5	10.2	10.8	10.4	10.7	11.8	12.1	13.4	13.8	9.7	10.7
Namibia	17.4	30.6	22.2	20.4	19.3	19.5	20.7	20.5	24.2	27.9	31.0	21.5
Niger	10.4	15.0	11.3	12.5	11.5	..	..	..	..	11.9	14.6	12.2
Nigeria	..	..	..	..	..	..	..	..	..	..	..	..
Rwanda	12.5	10.1	13.8	18.4	18.2	18.1	16.5	14.7	14.6	13.0	11.5	15.0
São Tomé and Príncipe	..	..	..	..	..	..	..	..	..	..	..	..
Senegal	24.8	18.4	13.3	13.7	9.6	9.7	10.0	9.7	8.7	19.3	15.0	11.3
Seychelles	28.7	27.7	25.5	28.3	21.3	19.8	16.0	13.3	12.2	33.1	29.0	20.8
Sierra Leone	8.4	7.8	15.6	13.3	13.8	13.8	11.8	12.5	13.8	7.7	10.6	14.3
Somalia	15.6	..	..	..	..	..	..	..	..	17.6	..	..
South Africa	14.3	19.7	19.2	19.4	19.5	19.7	19.0	19.1	21.0	17.4	19.4	19.2
Sudan	16.0	5.8	10.8	11.8	18.2	17.3	15.5	15.8	13.9	11.1	6.1	13.0
Swaziland	27.0	14.3	15.3	16.0	15.6	15.3	14.6	23.6	27.0	21.5	17.2	18.1
Tanzania	..	17.8	15.4	16.9	17.6	17.5	19.3	20.0	19.8	..	14.8	16.3
Togo	22.4	14.2	9.8	9.7	11.5	11.3	9.3	..	..	16.9	12.8	10.0
Uganda	..	7.5	15.7	13.9	14.5	14.1	12.9	11.2	11.4	9.9	11.1	14.1
Zambia	25.5	19.0	14.4	18.1	9.7	10.2	10.4	9.0	13.1	23.0	17.7	11.6
Zimbabwe	18.5	19.4	17.9	21.0	15.7	6.2	3.4	2.1	13.8	20.1	17.6	14.0
NORTH AFRICA	**15.9**	**15.1**	**14.3**	**14.1**	**13.6**	**13.0**	**12.6**	**12.3**	**13.3**	**16.6**	**15.2**	**13.8**
Algeria	15.2	16.1	14.8	13.8	11.5	11.2	11.3	12.9	13.9	17.2	16.6	13.3
Egypt, Arab Rep.	15.7	11.3	12.7	12.8	12.7	12.3	11.3	10.9	11.4	16.2	10.9	11.9
Libya	..	24.4	13.6	13.1	11.8	10.7	11.6	9.3	..	..	24.3	14.4
Morocco	18.3	15.5	18.1	18.7	19.4	18.5	18.2	17.1	18.0	16.6	17.0	18.3
Tunisia	14.5	16.4	15.7	15.4	15.4	14.7	14.1	14.4	13.1	16.5	16.0	15.0
ALL AFRICA	**15.5**	**16.4**	**15.5**	**15.5**	**15.3**	**14.9**	**14.4**	**14.4**	**15.7**	**16.5**	**16.1**	**15.1**

a. Provisional.

Table 2.16 Household final consumption expenditure

	Share of GDP (%)											
										Annual average		
	1980	1990	2003	2004	2005	2006	2007	2008	2009[a]	1980–89	1990–99	2000–09
SUB-SAHARAN AFRICA	**58.9**	**65.3**	**67.7**	**67.7**	**68.0**	**68.3**	**67.8**	**68.1**	**66.9**	**63.3**	**68.0**	**68.0**
Excluding South Africa	..	72.5	73.0	72.1	72.6	73.3	72.8	..	..	72.5	74.1	73.2
Excl. S. Africa & Nigeria	71.6	72.5	73.0	72.1	72.6	73.3	72.8	74.7	74.0	72.4	74.1	73.4
Angola	..	35.8	..	..	..	..	..	..	..	44.5	42.6	..
Benin	97.7	86.8	80.7	80.9	78.1	..	..	..	..	89.7	85.7	81.3
Botswana	52.0	33.2	36.7	38.4	34.5	40.7	42.8	47.9	62.8	40.4	34.5	42.1
Burkina Faso	98.0	73.5	73.3	76.6	72.8	75.2	..	..	..	86.0	68.5	75.2
Burundi	91.4	94.5	85.9	84.9	96.6	91.1	..	..	..	87.5	88.3	89.4
Cameroon	68.6	66.6	72.2	71.4	72.0	71.5	72.2	..	..	65.8	70.9	71.4
Cape Verde	..	93.4	101.1	80.9	75.2	72.9	71.8	70.0	67.2	89.1	88.6	84.0
Central African Republic	93.7	85.7	87.4	89.5	86.6	87.5	95.9	94.4	92.9	85.5	82.4	88.2
Chad	..	97.6	74.4	70.6	59.8	58.7	69.2	60.2	78.5	96.8	92.5	77.9
Comoros	79.2	78.7	88.7	94.2	98.8	100.6	101.2	104.8	105.8	75.9	84.6	96.4
Congo, Dem. Rep.	81.5	79.1	88.7	87.8	85.8	92.8	80.9	80.4	74.4	80.0	81.3	86.0
Congo, Rep.	46.8	62.4	51.8	32.8	35.0	42.8	33.3	39.6	42.2	50.3	53.1	37.3
Côte d'Ivoire	62.8	71.9	70.8	71.7	74.5	72.0	76.8	73.6	72.2	63.9	70.3	72.5
Djibouti	..	78.9	65.2	66.0	64.2	59.9	57.5	..	..	..	73.8	66.3
Equatorial Guinea	..	80.3	16.1	18.2	13.6	11.3	10.8	24.5	24.3	..	61.2	17.1
Eritrea	..	..	90.6	88.6	90.0	81.3	86.2	..	..	..	90.0	83.8
Ethiopia	..	77.2	78.8	78.2	85.1	86.4	85.5	89.9	87.7	78.4	80.5	81.6
Gabon	26.1	49.7	41.7	36.2	33.3	35.6	35.9	32.9	41.1	37.4	43.2	37.1
Gambia, The	63.0	75.6	78.0	74.2	77.6	70.7	77.4	78.4	77.8	64.4	78.8	76.0
Ghana	83.9	85.2	81.5	80.5	81.0	82.6	84.6	86.8	81.7	86.2	80.8	82.9
Guinea	..	66.9	70.3	74.6	74.8	78.0	83.6	80.5	75.2	71.8	73.5	77.3
Guinea-Bissau	73.3	86.9	..	..	..	..	..	..	..	82.0	90.1	100.1
Kenya	62.1	62.8	71.3	71.3	73.2	74.5	74.0	77.2	75.9	63.3	69.6	74.4
Lesotho	130.2	123.3	88.6	88.3	88.7	83.2	88.4	81.3	78.8	146.2	104.0	86.1
Liberia	66.1	..	94.7	90.3	86.4	123.1	228.0	202.3	..	75.8	..	125.4
Madagascar	89.3	86.4	81.9	84.5	86.2	82.0	77.1	78.8	79.7	87.2	87.9	81.3
Malawi	69.9	71.5	84.4	87.5	91.1	84.2	67.0	73.8	61.9	69.8	80.0	79.5
Mali	87.4	79.8	78.3	81.4	79.1	75.3	76.8	..	..	88.1	79.7	78.4
Mauritania	58.2	69.2	74.9	81.2	92.3	63.9	70.4	75.6	72.1	66.3	83.0	76.6
Mauritius	75.6	63.4	60.9	63.7	68.7	70.5	70.3	74.3	74.6	67.1	61.9	66.4
Mozambique	96.7	92.3	86.3	81.4	83.2	80.5	81.9	86.3	84.4	92.3	93.2	83.3
Namibia	44.2	51.2	67.5	62.8	60.9	60.0	56.9	58.1	61.9	61.3	56.3	61.5
Niger	75.1	83.8	83.7	83.6	75.1	..	..	..	..	80.8	82.7	81.9
Nigeria	..	..	..	..	..	..	..	..	..	..	..	..
Rwanda	83.3	83.7	85.8	80.3	79.8	80.1	80.0	78.3	81.1	82.0	94.0	82.6
São Tomé and Príncipe	..	..	..	..	..	..	..	..	..	..	..	..
Senegal	73.1	79.2	77.9	78.4	76.3	79.6	81.4	86.7	83.3	76.4	79.6	79.8
Seychelles	44.2	52.0	52.9	57.0	75.6	72.1	85.7	80.7	71.9	42.7	49.3	65.9
Sierra Leone	90.7	83.5	88.1	87.2	82.2	78.6	82.0	85.8	84.0	83.2	86.6	87.4
Somalia	97.3	..	..	..	..	..	..	..	..	100.6	..	..
South Africa	47.8	57.1	61.8	62.9	63.1	63.1	62.7	61.9	60.4	54.2	61.2	62.3
Sudan	81.9	86.1	73.5	69.5	62.8	64.1	57.8	57.4	66.7	84.8	84.3	68.7
Swaziland	71.8	80.4	66.6	70.5	73.2	73.2	72.7	76.6	72.8	74.7	80.8	72.6
Tanzania	..	80.9	68.6	67.9	68.4	71.4	68.1	69.7	62.3	..	82.3	70.0
Togo	54.5	71.1	84.8	85.8	87.0	..	..	..	..	70.8	80.5	88.3
Uganda	..	91.9	77.1	76.0	73.7	77.8	78.3	73.5	76.1	87.2	84.6	76.4
Zambia	55.2	64.4	72.6	62.0	68.5	58.3	59.0	65.9	61.3	62.9	73.3	70.3
Zimbabwe	67.7	63.1	79.8	81.8	92.0	103.6	98.2	120.5	113.1	63.4	65.2	89.9
NORTH AFRICA	**61.3**	**64.1**	**58.5**	**58.1**	**56.5**	**53.5**	**54.5**	**54.0**	**62.9**	**63.1**	**65.6**	**58.3**
Algeria	41.7	56.8	40.4	38.5	33.6	32.2	31.2	30.4	40.6	51.3	53.3	37.5
Egypt, Arab Rep.	69.2	72.6	73.0	71.7	71.6	70.6	72.4	72.3	76.2	68.3	75.0	73.3
Libya	..	48.4	39.5	44.2	40.2	22.5	24.8	22.9	..	..	58.1	39.0
Morocco	66.8	64.6	57.3	57.1	57.5	57.5	58.4	58.1	57.0	66.7	65.3	58.0
Tunisia	61.5	63.6	63.1	63.4	63.3	63.7	63.8	63.2	63.4	60.8	61.7	62.8
ALL AFRICA	**60.0**	**64.7**	**63.5**	**63.4**	**62.8**	**61.5**	**61.7**	**61.4**	**65.2**	**63.2**	**66.9**	**63.5**

a. Provisional.

Table

2.17 Final consumption expenditure plus discrepancy

	Share of GDP (%)											
										Annual average		
	1980	1990	2003	2004	2005	2006	2007	2008	2009[a]	1980–89	1990–99	2000–09
SUB-SAHARAN AFRICA	**74.7**	**82.9**	**84.0**	**84.1**	**84.3**	**84.1**	**83.3**	**83.9**	**84.5**	**79.9**	**84.6**	**84.0**
Excluding South Africa	..	88.3	86.6	85.8	85.8	85.4	84.8	86.7	87.5	88.1	88.3	86.3
Excl. S. Africa & Nigeria	88.3	88.3	86.6	85.8	85.8	85.4	84.8	86.7	87.5	88.2	88.3	86.3
Angola	..	70.3	80.8	74.9	62.1	50.9	55.0	58.9	79.2	76.0	78.0	68.1
Benin	106.3	97.8	94.0	94.5	93.1	93.1	93.9	92.9	89.3	102.4	96.2	93.5
Botswana	73.3	57.4	59.0	59.5	56.9	59.6	62.2	67.7	87.0	64.7	61.2	63.5
Burkina Faso	107.2	94.6	95.5	98.2	95.2	97.2	..	..	..	101.6	91.0	97.4
Burundi	100.6	105.4	108.7	111.0	123.1	119.9	..	..	..	96.9	105.2	112.3
Cameroon	78.3	79.3	82.2	81.5	81.9	81.1	81.5	..	..	75.8	81.5	81.2
Cape Verde	..	108.1	115.8	101.5	95.6	95.0	94.2	90.8	88.0	102.2	105.6	102.6
Central African Republic	108.9	100.6	98.4	100.0	99.9	98.6	98.5	101.0	97.3	101.1	96.3	98.0
Chad	..	107.7	82.0	75.5	64.9	63.6	79.5	72.6	94.1	108.1	100.5	86.2
Comoros	110.1	103.2	103.4	108.5	112.3	114.8	115.4	120.1	121.1	104.5	104.9	111.1
Congo, Dem. Rep.	89.9	90.7	95.0	96.0	94.1	100.6	91.2	91.4	82.3	89.1	91.2	93.9
Congo, Rep.	64.3	76.2	69.1	47.8	48.0	56.7	50.4	51.6	54.5	68.1	71.2	51.7
Côte d'Ivoire	79.6	88.7	79.0	80.0	82.8	80.4	85.4	82.1	80.8	80.4	82.2	80.6
Djibouti	..	110.4	94.7	95.7	91.4	87.9	82.6	..	..	..	106.4	94.3
Equatorial Guinea	..	120.1	19.9	21.1	16.3	13.9	13.1	27.2	27.8	..	86.3	20.5
Eritrea	..	..	140.9	141.5	127.2	117.2	117.7	..	..	..	129.7	129.2
Ethiopia	..	90.4	92.3	91.2	97.4	98.5	95.8	99.6	95.9	89.5	90.3	94.3
Gabon	39.4	63.1	51.8	45.4	41.7	44.0	44.7	41.1	52.7	55.7	56.4	46.8
Gambia, The	94.2	89.3	88.9	91.1	96.0	88.8	93.4	93.9	93.7	93.5	92.6	91.2
Ghana	95.1	94.5	93.0	92.7	96.3	93.9	96.2	98.0	91.3	95.2	92.5	94.1
Guinea	..	77.8	78.5	81.6	81.7	86.1	90.3	89.7	83.1	83.4	81.7	84.9
Guinea-Bissau	101.0	97.2	..	..	..	..	..	..	..	100.9	98.5	113.2
Kenya	81.9	81.5	89.5	89.2	90.5	91.9	92.0	93.9	92.2	81.7	85.4	91.3
Lesotho	152.0	149.1	125.9	125.7	127.9	123.6	127.1	125.3	129.1	169.5	137.6	126.4
Liberia	85.2	..	103.2	100.7	97.6	134.6	242.5	221.5	..	97.8	..	138.4
Madagascar	101.4	94.5	91.1	91.5	95.1	90.7	89.4	90.1	91.1	97.1	95.8	90.8
Malawi	89.2	86.6	96.8	100.0	105.5	98.8	81.1	91.1	82.8	87.3	96.6	94.6
Mali	98.9	93.6	86.7	91.4	89.0	85.2	87.0	..	..	100.4	92.4	87.8
Mauritania	103.5	95.1	105.0	103.1	115.0	81.4	92.0	94.4	92.6	96.9	97.6	99.1
Mauritius	89.6	77.0	75.1	78.0	83.5	84.7	83.4	87.5	89.2	79.7	75.9	80.4
Mozambique	108.9	105.8	96.5	92.3	93.5	91.2	93.7	98.4	97.8	106.2	102.9	94.0
Namibia	61.6	81.8	89.7	83.2	80.2	79.4	77.6	78.6	86.1	89.2	87.3	82.9
Niger	85.4	98.8	95.0	96.1	86.6	..	..	..	..	92.7	97.3	94.1
Nigeria	..	..	..	..	..	..	..	..	..	..	..	..
Rwanda	95.8	93.8	99.6	98.6	98.0	98.2	96.5	93.0	95.8	95.0	105.5	97.6
São Tomé and Príncipe	..	..	..	..	..	..	..	..	..	..	..	..
Senegal	97.9	97.6	91.2	92.1	85.9	89.3	91.4	96.4	92.0	95.7	94.6	91.1
Seychelles	72.9	79.7	78.5	85.3	96.9	91.9	101.7	94.0	84.1	75.9	78.3	86.7
Sierra Leone	99.1	91.3	103.7	100.4	95.9	92.4	93.9	98.3	97.7	90.9	97.2	101.6
Somalia	112.9	112.5	..	..	..	..	..	..	..	106.3	112.5	..
South Africa	62.1	76.8	81.0	82.2	82.5	82.8	81.7	81.1	81.4	71.5	80.6	81.5
Sudan	97.9	91.8	84.3	81.3	81.0	81.4	73.3	73.2	80.6	95.8	90.4	81.6
Swaziland	98.8	94.7	81.9	86.5	88.8	88.5	87.3	100.2	99.8	96.3	98.0	90.6
Tanzania	..	98.7	83.9	84.8	86.0	89.0	87.4	89.7	82.1	..	97.1	86.3
Togo	76.8	85.3	94.7	95.5	98.5	..	..	..	..	87.7	93.3	98.2
Uganda	100.4	99.4	92.8	89.9	88.3	91.9	91.2	84.7	87.5	97.7	95.7	90.5
Zambia	80.7	83.4	87.0	80.1	78.2	68.5	69.5	74.9	74.4	86.0	91.0	81.9
Zimbabwe	86.2	82.5	97.7	102.8	107.6	109.8	101.6	122.6	126.9	83.5	82.9	103.9
NORTH AFRICA	**77.2**	**79.2**	**72.8**	**72.3**	**70.1**	**66.5**	**67.2**	**66.3**	**76.2**	**79.7**	**80.8**	**72.1**
Algeria	56.9	72.9	55.1	52.3	45.1	43.4	42.5	43.3	54.5	68.5	69.9	50.9
Egypt, Arab Rep.	84.8	83.9	85.7	84.4	84.3	82.9	83.7	83.2	87.6	84.5	85.8	85.2
Libya	..	72.8	53.2	57.3	51.9	33.2	36.4	32.2	..	..	82.4	53.4
Morocco	85.1	80.1	75.5	75.8	76.8	76.0	76.6	75.3	74.9	83.3	82.2	76.3
Tunisia	76.0	80.0	78.8	78.8	78.6	78.5	78.0	77.6	76.5	77.3	77.7	77.8
ALL AFRICA	**75.8**	**81.2**	**79.0**	**78.8**	**77.9**	**76.2**	**76.0**	**75.7**	**80.9**	**79.8**	**82.9**	**78.6**

a. Provisional.

Table 2.18 Final consumption expenditure plus discrepancy per capita

	Current prices ($)											
										Annual average		
	1980	1990	2003	2004	2005	2006	2007	2008	2009[a]	1980–89	1990–99	2000–09
SUB-SAHARAN AFRICA	**450**	**490**	**487**	**584**	**646**	**709**	**792**	**867**	**864**	**449**	**469**	**612**
Excluding South Africa	362	355	323	364	404	466	543	663	654	335	306	424
Excl. S. Africa & Nigeria	375	365	330	372	412	475	554	676	666	345	314	432
Angola	..	677	721	918	1,144	1,346	1,855	2,753	3,232	581	469	1,343
Benin	420	376	455	503	507	543	621	717	666	332	343	503
Botswana	790	1,609	2,661	3,294	3,174	3,599	4,068	4,774	5,273	830	1,844	3,306
Burkina Faso	301	333	317	378	376	394	..	..	..	260	238	311
Burundi	224	210	93	103	133	145	..	..	..	215	170	114
Cameroon	581	723	658	738	763	799	903	..	..	663	631	672
Cape Verde	..	1,034	1,997	1,996	2,001	2,171	2,550	2,788	2,696	809	1,201	2,057
Central African Republic	382	511	283	315	329	349	396	463	441	360	352	332
Chad	..	307	240	344	343	376	525	556	574	221	232	361
Comoros	406	593	583	669	724	754	854	989	984	394	508	684
Congo, Dem. Rep.	476	229	97	110	113	141	146	165	132	296	155	117
Congo, Rep.	605	872	741	665	855	1,258	1,184	1,683	1,417	681	620	915
Côte d'Ivoire	962	760	588	657	704	710	841	934	894	681	630	677
Djibouti	..	892	758	806	805	825	839	..	..	..	834	793
Equatorial Guinea	..	418	1,019	1,869	2,204	2,129	2,569	7,637	4,274	..	410	2,371
Eritrea	..	..	263	308	333	324	338	..	..	..	240	281
Ethiopia	..	226	111	126	160	195	234	320	330	200	160	180
Gabon	2,472	4,057	2,383	2,429	2,636	3,010	3,640	4,121	3,954	2,570	2,723	2,785
Gambia, The	368	316	227	247	290	287	376	465	403	290	324	310
Ghana	383	372	338	384	471	855	1,036	1,197	1,002	350	358	605
Guinea	..	338	305	331	260	258	395	345	339	323	382	315
Guinea-Bissau	134	232	..	..	..	..	..	..	..	171	208	175
Kenya	366	299	392	411	474	563	662	727	680	299	313	501
Lesotho	506	503	609	767	843	870	987	974	986	458	581	740
Liberia	425	..	135	144	155	237	491	492	..	437	..	254
Madagascar	477	258	299	233	272	276	353	444	399	320	245	301
Malawi	178	172	182	198	213	219	194	250	256	150	179	200
Mali	246	262	335	386	399	413	501	..	..	205	244	340
Mauritania	481	488	477	549	716	718	832	1,054	852	450	560	648
Mauritius	1,054	1,933	3,446	4,030	4,219	4,401	4,973	6,422	6,009	1,103	2,486	4,210
Mozambique	316	193	228	259	295	303	344	434	418	275	187	290
Namibia	1,319	1,357	2,288	2,788	2,898	3,095	3,271	3,309	3,675	1,435	1,691	2,820
Niger	362	310	213	232	225	..	..	..	..	274	216	194
Nigeria	..	..	..	..	..	..	..	..	..	..	..	..
Rwanda	214	339	212	234	281	332	382	449	500	270	283	299
São Tomé and Príncipe	..	..	..	..	..	..	..	..	..	..	..	..
Senegal	608	741	586	674	663	723	871	1,040	941	550	580	683
Seychelles	1,667	4,196	6,688	7,234	10,330	10,510	12,276	10,010	7,305	2,170	5,142	8,277
Sierra Leone	335	145	217	224	233	249	288	346	333	248	188	249
Somalia	106	156	..	..	..	..	..	..	..	138	156	..
South Africa	1,818	2,444	2,955	3,860	4,319	4,526	4,845	4,593	4,711	2,094	2,782	3,635
Sudan	364	421	404	465	573	750	843	1,028	1,043	496	325	610
Swaziland	889	1,222	1,328	1,770	1,994	2,078	2,238	2,436	2,527	753	1,469	1,770
Tanzania	..	165	265	287	312	318	356	437	401	..	197	315
Togo	314	354	292	337	347	..	..	..	..	271	308	290
Uganda	99	241	219	274	277	308	354	387	429	231	220	292
Zambia	543	347	339	379	477	609	644	854	737	418	340	498
Zimbabwe	791	693	442	467	482	458	409	418	570	704	543	466
NORTH AFRICA	**853**	**1,104**	**1,179**	**1,270**	**1,362**	**1,465**	**1,724**	**2,060**	**2,240**	**957**	**1,132**	**1,497**
Algeria	1,281	1,789	1,176	1,374	1,405	1,525	1,703	2,152	2,197	1,697	1,217	1,463
Egypt, Arab Rep.	438	626	957	879	980	1,133	1,365	1,662	1,988	529	809	1,242
Libya	..	4,823	2,250	3,298	3,859	3,099	4,236	4,764	..	..	5,111	3,590
Morocco	819	834	1,261	1,432	1,499	1,618	1,846	2,117	2,140	641	986	1,497
Tunisia	1,041	1,206	2,001	2,231	2,271	2,398	2,716	3,070	2,902	961	1,467	2,242
ALL AFRICA	**522**	**601**	**600**	**692**	**757**	**824**	**936**	**1,055**	**1,082**	**541**	**586**	**756**

a. Provisional.

Table 2.19 Gross fixed capital formation

	Share of GDP (%)											
										Annual average		
	1980	1990	2003	2004	2005	2006	2007	2008	2009[a]	1980–89	1990–99	2000–09
SUB-SAHARAN AFRICA	**22.6**	**18.2**	**17.1**	**17.4**	**18.2**	**18.9**	**20.3**	**21.7**	**22.3**	**20.1**	**17.1**	**18.5**
Excluding South Africa	..	17.4	18.5	18.6	19.4	19.3	20.4	21.0	22.0	16.6	17.8	19.3
Excl. S. Africa & Nigeria	18.8	17.4	18.5	18.6	19.4	19.3	20.4	21.0	22.0	17.1	17.8	19.3
Angola	..	11.1	12.7	9.1	8.1	11.3	14.0	16.0	14.8	14.2	23.2	12.7
Benin	..	13.4	18.1	17.5	18.9	18.2	21.4	20.7	25.0	14.8	15.7	19.6
Botswana	34.5	32.4	26.0	24.8	24.5	21.6	23.9	23.3	28.2	29.0	27.2	24.6
Burkina Faso	14.1	17.7	17.5	19.3	19.4	20.8	..	..	..	17.4	21.2	18.2
Burundi	13.9	15.2	10.6	13.0	10.5	16.4	..	..	..	16.1	9.0	9.9
Cameroon	20.0	17.3	18.1	18.3	17.7	16.7	17.1	..	..	21.1	14.5	18.0
Cape Verde	..	22.9	18.7	37.4	37.3	40.6	43.8	48.4	53.8	26.9	29.6	33.9
Central African Republic	6.9	11.4	6.1	6.2	8.9	9.2	8.9	11.6	10.6	10.2	11.2	8.8
Chad	..	4.8	48.6	22.7	16.7	13.2	17.0	23.9	32.7	4.4	11.0	29.2
Comoros	28.5	11.9	10.3	9.4	9.3	9.6	11.2	14.3	12.4	24.3	14.6	10.8
Congo, Dem. Rep.	8.8	12.8	12.2	12.8	14.2	13.0	19.5	23.9	29.8	11.4	8.0	14.3
Congo, Rep.	35.8	17.2	25.5	21.9	21.9	24.4	26.0	21.8	24.3	32.5	24.9	23.5
Côte d'Ivoire	24.4	8.5	9.7	9.8	9.7	9.3	8.7	10.1	11.2	15.8	11.4	10.1
Djibouti	..	14.1	14.4	21.5	19.0	29.6	37.5	..	..	..	11.1	18.6
Equatorial Guinea	..	17.4	41.6	40.5	37.6	31.4	33.3	28.2	36.6	..	59.5	41.5
Eritrea	..	..	28.1	22.3	18.5	12.6	10.6	..	..	..	26.1	22.8
Ethiopia	..	12.9	21.8	25.5	23.0	24.2	23.5	19.8	22.4	15.7	16.5	22.6
Gabon	26.7	21.4	24.0	24.4	21.3	25.9	25.9	24.4	28.4	33.8	25.4	24.6
Gambia, The	..	22.3	19.2	24.8	..	..	..	..	..	18.9	20.1	20.0
Ghana	6.1	14.4	22.9	28.4	29.0	21.6	20.1	21.5	19.6	7.9	19.7	23.2
Guinea	..	22.9	19.8	19.7	18.6	16.6	13.9	15.6	21.6	16.4	20.0	17.4
Guinea-Bissau	28.2	29.9	..	..	..	..	..	..	..	32.0	25.9	12.0
Kenya	18.3	20.6	15.8	16.3	18.7	19.1	19.4	19.7	20.1	18.8	17.6	18.1
Lesotho	35.6	57.0	34.0	27.2	25.7	24.8	25.8	28.8	31.5	40.3	64.4	31.2
Liberia	..	..	9.4	13.2	16.4	..	..	..	..	..	..	9.7
Madagascar	14.4	14.8	17.9	23.4	22.2	25.3	32.4	40.3	32.6	10.8	12.4	24.2
Malawi	22.2	20.1	14.1	16.2	20.2	22.7	24.0	23.3	21.8	15.8	15.2	18.7
Mali	15.5	23.0	24.2	21.0	22.6	22.9	22.4	..	..	17.2	22.5	23.4
Mauritania	..	20.0	25.9	46.4	44.8	29.5	22.4	27.8	25.2	26.6	13.6	28.4
Mauritius	23.2	30.6	22.7	21.6	21.4	24.3	25.1	24.6	26.2	21.2	26.9	23.3
Mozambique	7.6	22.1	22.3	18.6	18.7	17.7	16.1	15.7	21.0	12.2	20.7	21.1
Namibia	27.2	21.2	19.1	18.6	18.6	21.6	23.7	25.7	24.7	18.6	21.0	20.9
Niger	25.5	11.4	14.0	15.8	18.5	..	..	..	..	14.2	9.0	14.2
Nigeria	..	..	..	..	..	..	..	..	..	..	..	..
Rwanda	12.2	14.6	17.9	15.0	15.8	16.0	18.0	22.8	21.8	14.4	14.5	18.2
São Tomé and Príncipe	..	..	..	..	..	..	..	..	..	..	..	..
Senegal	14.6	18.0	21.2	22.7	29.7	28.2	30.9	30.2	27.9	17.4	19.9	26.1
Seychelles	36.5	23.0	10.4	12.7	24.7	26.1	29.5	25.4	24.2	25.6	29.2	24.5
Sierra Leone	14.9	9.6	13.9	10.5	17.0	15.2	13.2	14.7	15.1	11.4	7.2	12.3
Somalia	43.1	14.9	..	..	..	..	..	..	..	26.9	14.9	..
South Africa	25.9	19.1	15.5	16.0	16.8	18.3	20.2	22.5	22.6	23.1	16.3	17.7
Sudan	10.8	10.4	14.1	17.2	24.0	25.1	26.5	22.7	21.8	12.4	10.6	18.8
Swaziland	35.0	14.5	19.1	16.2	15.4	14.1	14.0	15.3	16.9	25.4	16.7	17.1
Tanzania	..	25.8	20.0	21.2	22.5	23.8	25.0	26.3	29.3	..	21.5	22.0
Togo	28.2	25.3	20.9	21.2	22.3	..	..	..	..	19.0	15.6	20.4
Uganda	..	12.7	20.7	20.0	22.2	21.0	21.9	22.7	23.5	9.3	15.9	21.0
Zambia	18.2	13.5	24.1	23.1	22.5	22.6	24.1	22.6	22.1	12.4	12.4	21.5
Zimbabwe	14.1	18.2	13.8	5.1	2.1	2.3	5.4	3.8	2.5	16.0	19.0	6.9
NORTH AFRICA	**26.8**	**24.5**	**19.0**	**19.7**	**20.4**	**21.7**	**24.2**	**25.7**	**25.1**	**27.9**	**21.3**	**21.6**
Algeria	33.8	27.0	24.0	24.1	22.3	22.9	26.0	26.3	33.0	31.9	26.2	24.6
Egypt, Arab Rep.	24.6	26.9	16.3	16.4	17.9	18.7	20.9	22.3	19.0	27.8	20.4	18.6
Libya	..	13.9	9.8	13.9	15.8	20.7	25.0	27.9	..	..	12.7	16.9
Morocco	22.2	24.0	25.1	26.3	27.5	28.1	31.2	33.0	30.7	23.1	22.2	27.8
Tunisia	28.3	24.4	23.4	22.6	22.2	23.5	23.2	25.0	25.9	27.5	25.3	24.3
ALL AFRICA	**24.5**	**21.1**	**17.9**	**18.4**	**19.2**	**20.1**	**22.1**	**23.6**	**23.5**	**23.5**	**19.0**	**19.9**

a. Provisional.

Table 2.20 Gross general government fixed capital formation

	Share of GDP (%)											
										Annual average		
	1980	1990	2003	2004	2005	2006	2007	2008	2009[a]	1980–89	1990–99	2000–09
SUB-SAHARAN AFRICA	**6.6**	**5.6**	**5.2**	**5.4**	**5.4**	**5.8**	**6.5**	**7.6**	**8.7**	**6.1**	**4.8**	**5.8**
Excluding South Africa	..	7.2	6.0	6.5	6.3	6.6	6.8	7.3	8.3	6.6	6.5	6.5
Excl. S. Africa & Nigeria	..	7.2	6.0	6.5	6.3	6.6	6.8	7.3	8.3	6.3	6.5	6.5
Angola	..	..	7.6	4.9	5.0	8.9	11.7	14.1	12.4	..	7.8	8.4
Benin	..	7.4	6.1	5.4	6.7	4.6	7.5	5.8	9.6	9.1	7.5	6.8
Botswana	0.0	8.6	10.6	8.5	7.3	6.1	7.8	12.5	15.1	9.7	11.7	10.0
Burkina Faso	..	9.7	6.3	7.2	7.4	8.0	..	..	..	10.4	10.5	7.0
Burundi	12.8	12.5	8.3	10.7	8.8	..	..	..	..	13.8	9.3	6.9
Cameroon	4.4	5.5	2.3	2.6	2.5	2.4	2.4	..	..	6.9	2.9	2.3
Cape Verde	..	10.3	9.8	7.7	9.0	9.3	10.9	10.4	11.0	19.3	20.3	10.4
Central African Republic	3.7	4.7	2.2	2.0	4.0	3.7	2.7	4.5	3.7	5.5	6.2	3.6
Chad	..	..	12.5	7.8	7.8	8.1	7.3	7.9	10.9	3.8	7.4	9.2
Comoros	23.2	5.2	5.4	4.4	4.5	5.0	6.1	9.3	4.7	18.7	7.0	5.3
Congo, Dem. Rep.	5.1	4.0	2.7	2.8	3.7	3.1	8.8	12.6	23.8	4.4	1.7	5.9
Congo, Rep.	..	5.6	6.7	6.5	6.2	9.5	10.4	8.9	10.7	11.1	6.4	8.5
Côte d'Ivoire	11.4	3.6	2.7	2.8	2.7	3.1	2.6	3.0	3.0	7.1	5.6	2.8
Djibouti	..	9.1	6.7	7.7	9.3	7.5	12.2	..	..	..	6.1	6.6
Equatorial Guinea	..	10.5	9.9	13.1	10.3	15.1	16.9	16.8	20.6	..	6.9	12.4
Eritrea	..	..	20.4	17.0	16.8	11.5	9.4	..	..	..	17.6	17.5
Ethiopia	..	4.0	12.8	15.7	14.7	16.7	16.8	14.0	16.5	4.9	6.6	14.7
Gabon	5.3	3.9	3.7	4.2	4.2	4.8	4.5	4.6	5.2	6.7	6.5	4.3
Gambia, The	..	7.4	5.7	10.9	9.0	7.9	3.7	..	..	10.4	7.8	7.6
Ghana	..	7.5	8.9	12.4	12.0	8.8	8.5	9.4	8.0	6.3	11.1	9.8
Guinea	..	9.7	3.9	3.7	2.8	2.6	2.3	3.5	4.6	7.5	6.1	3.8
Guinea-Bissau	..	27.4	..	..	..	..	..	6.5	9.6	33.3	20.2	9.8
Kenya	0.0	9.7	4.2	4.3	3.8	4.9	3.9	4.4	5.6	0.8	7.0	4.4
Lesotho	9.9	26.2	9.6	8.1	8.1	7.6	10.4	11.0	14.2	17.2	18.7	10.1
Liberia	..	..	0.0	0.0	0.0	..	..	..	..	..	..	0.0
Madagascar	..	7.9	7.8	10.0	8.7	10.5	7.0	7.1	3.1	6.9	6.9	7.3
Malawi	17.5	7.7	..	..	..	..	..	..	..	9.5	9.2	10.2
Mali	..	10.5	6.9	7.5	7.7	8.6	8.4	..	..	10.2	10.1	7.7
Mauritania	..	6.2	12.0	9.1	8.1	..	..	..	..	7.6	5.0	9.1
Mauritius	8.4	11.4	8.9	6.6	6.3	7.7	5.5	4.2	6.7	7.4	9.2	6.6
Mozambique	7.6	12.0	10.5	10.7	8.6	11.8	11.7	11.6	13.1	9.5	12.1	11.3
Namibia	15.7	8.2	6.4	6.3	6.4	6.8	2.9	3.4	5.3	10.7	8.2	5.6
Niger	20.4	7.4	8.3	5.1	6.3	..	..	..	..	11.2	5.6	7.0
Nigeria	..	..	..	..	..	..	..	..	..	..	..	..
Rwanda	12.2	5.9	5.1	8.9	8.7	7.5	8.7	11.0	11.1	12.1	7.2	7.9
São Tomé and Príncipe	..	..	..	..	..	..	..	..	..	..	..	..
Senegal	4.7	4.1	6.2	6.7	10.0	9.7	11.2	10.0	10.1	3.7	4.5	7.9
Seychelles	..	8.2	1.7	3.1	4.6	8.1	4.5	3.3	3.3	12.0	9.9	7.2
Sierra Leone	5.3	3.9	4.8	4.5	5.7	5.1	3.5	6.2	7.7	4.0	3.8	5.1
Somalia	..	..	..	..	..	..	..	..	..	..	..	..
South Africa	6.4	3.9	4.3	4.3	4.3	5.0	6.1	7.9	9.2	5.7	2.8	5.0
Sudan	6.9	..	2.9	5.0	5.8	6.7	9.5	6.5	5.5	4.3	0.7	5.0
Swaziland	11.9	4.5	13.0	10.7	9.8	8.7	8.0	9.8	10.6	8.0	5.4	9.9
Tanzania	..	10.5	5.1	7.1	8.1	7.5	7.5	8.0	8.8	..	6.0	6.3
Togo	20.2	7.3	3.7	5.3	2.8	3.6	2.0	..	..	11.2	3.7	3.0
Uganda	..	6.2	5.1	4.9	5.0	4.6	4.9	4.4	6.1	4.4	5.6	5.3
Zambia	..	6.2	11.4	8.7	7.0	4.1	4.1	5.2	4.3	..	6.8	7.8
Zimbabwe	1.8	3.4	2.1	5.1	2.1	2.3	1.4	0.3	0.8	2.9	3.0	1.9
NORTH AFRICA	**..**	**10.8**	**8.1**	**8.9**	**9.5**	**9.5**	**10.9**	**11.3**	**5.5**	**13.0**	**10.6**	**8.9**
Algeria	11.0	8.2	10.8	10.5	10.8	12.0	16.5	16.1	0.0	13.8	7.2	10.3
Egypt, Arab Rep.	..	14.7	8.3	8.7	9.3	8.0	7.8	7.9	8.0	16.9	14.5	8.6
Libya	..	..	7.9	12.3	14.1	16.7	19.8	22.0	..	..	..	14.9
Morocco	..	4.8	3.8	3.8	3.7	3.6	3.6	4.6	5.9	7.1	4.2	4.3
Tunisia	15.0	8.7	..	..	9.8	..	..	..	..	14.1	11.5	11.1
ALL AFRICA	**..**	**7.8**	**6.4**	**6.9**	**7.2**	**7.4**	**8.4**	**9.2**	**7.4**	**8.9**	**7.2**	**7.2**

a. Provisional.

Table 2.21 Private sector fixed capital formation

	Share of GDP (%)											
										Annual average		
	1980	1990	2003	2004	2005	2006	2007	2008	2009[a]	1980–89	1990–99	2000–09
SUB-SAHARAN AFRICA	**16.4**	**12.9**	**11.8**	**11.8**	**12.5**	**13.5**	**13.7**	**14.2**	**13.4**	**14.4**	**12.4**	**12.6**
Excluding South Africa	..	10.7	12.4	11.9	12.5	13.6	13.3	13.7	13.3	9.8	11.5	12.6
Excl. S. Africa & Nigeria	..	10.7	12.4	11.9	12.5	13.6	13.3	13.7	13.3	9.8	11.5	12.6
Angola	..	1.7	5.1	4.2	3.0	2.4	2.3	1.9	2.4	9.2	16.5	4.3
Benin	..	6.0	12.0	12.1	12.2	13.6	13.9	14.9	15.4	4.5	8.3	12.8
Botswana	34.5	23.8	15.4	16.3	17.3	15.5	16.1	21.3	8.9	19.4	15.5	15.3
Burkina Faso	..	8.0	11.1	..	..	..	..	..	..	8.8	10.8	10.4
Burundi	1.1	2.7	2.3	2.3	1.7	..	..	..	..	2.3	–0.3	1.9
Cameroon	15.6	11.9	15.8	15.7	15.2	14.3	14.7	12.5	12.4	14.2	11.7	15.0
Cape Verde	..	12.6	8.9	29.7	28.4	31.3	32.9	38.0	42.7	7.6	9.3	23.5
Central African Republic	3.2	6.7	3.9	4.1	4.9	5.6	6.2	7.1	6.9	4.7	5.0	5.3
Chad	..	..	36.1	14.9	8.9	5.1	9.7	16.0	21.8	0.6	4.3	20.0
Comoros	5.3	6.7	4.9	5.0	4.8	4.7	5.0	5.0	7.7	5.5	7.7	5.4
Congo, Dem. Rep.	3.7	8.9	9.5	10.0	10.5	9.9	10.7	11.3	6.1	7.1	6.3	8.4
Congo, Rep.	..	11.6	18.8	15.4	15.7	14.9	15.6	12.9	13.5	11.4	18.5	15.1
Côte d'Ivoire	13.0	4.9	7.0	7.1	7.0	6.3	6.1	7.1	8.3	8.7	6.2	7.3
Djibouti	..	5.1	7.7	13.8	9.7	22.0	25.2	..	..	..	5.8	11.9
Equatorial Guinea	..	6.9	31.7	27.4	27.4	16.2	16.4	11.4	16.1	..	52.6	29.1
Eritrea	..	..	7.7	5.3	1.8	1.1	1.2	..	..	..	8.6	5.3
Ethiopia	..	8.9	9.0	9.7	8.3	7.6	6.7	5.9	5.9	12.8	9.9	7.9
Gabon	21.4	17.6	20.2	20.2	17.1	21.1	21.5	19.8	23.2	27.2	18.9	20.4
Gambia, The	..	14.9	13.5	13.9	..	..	..	..	..	8.6	12.3	11.9
Ghana	..	6.9	14.0	16.0	17.0	12.8	11.6	12.1	11.6	3.8	8.6	13.4
Guinea	..	8.8	15.9	16.1	15.8	14.0	11.5	12.1	17.0	8.9	11.7	13.6
Guinea-Bissau	..	8.4	..	..	..	..	..	..	..	10.0	7.7	1.1
Kenya	8.2	10.9	7.8	7.5	6.7	25.4	15.5	15.3	14.5	10.7	9.8	11.5
Lesotho	25.7	30.8	24.4	19.2	17.5	17.3	15.5	17.8	17.3	23.1	46.8	21.1
Liberia	..	..	4.8	4.2	4.3	..	..	..	..	..	..	3.5
Madagascar	..	6.9	10.1	13.4	13.5	14.7	25.4	33.2	29.4	3.6	5.5	16.9
Malawi	4.7	12.4	7.4	7.1	13.0	15.0	9.2	13.9	14.9	6.3	6.0	9.6
Mali	..	12.4	17.3	13.5	15.0	14.3	14.0	..	..	9.9	12.4	15.7
Mauritania	..	13.7	13.9	37.3	36.7	..	..	..	..	19.0	13.9	22.9
Mauritius	14.9	19.2	13.9	15.0	15.1	16.6	19.6	20.4	19.5	13.8	17.7	16.7
Mozambique	0.0	10.1	11.8	8.0	10.1	5.8	4.4	4.1	7.9	2.7	8.6	9.8
Namibia	11.4	13.0	20.1	15.7	16.2	18.4	16.1	14.7	15.6	7.8	12.8	15.4
Niger	5.1	4.0	5.7	10.7	12.2	..	..	..	..	3.0	3.4	7.2
Nigeria	..	..	..	..	..	..	..	..	..	..	..	..
Rwanda	..	8.7	12.8	6.2	7.0	8.5	9.3	11.8	10.6	7.8	7.2	10.3
São Tomé and Príncipe	..	..	..	..	..	..	..	..	..	..	..	..
Senegal	9.9	13.9	15.0	16.0	19.7	18.5	19.7	20.2	17.8	13.7	15.4	18.2
Seychelles	..	14.8	8.7	9.7	20.1	18.1	25.0	22.2	20.9	10.1	19.3	17.2
Sierra Leone	9.5	5.7	9.0	5.9	11.3	10.1	9.7	8.6	7.4	7.3	3.3	7.2
Somalia	..	..	..	..	..	..	..	..	..	..	..	..
South Africa	19.5	15.3	11.2	11.7	12.5	13.4	14.1	14.6	13.4	17.4	13.5	12.7
Sudan	3.8	..	11.2	12.2	18.2	18.4	17.0	16.2	16.3	8.9	9.9	13.8
Swaziland	23.1	10.1	6.0	5.5	5.6	6.7	6.0	5.6	3.0	17.3	11.3	7.0
Tanzania	..	15.3	14.9	14.2	14.4	16.3	17.5	18.3	20.5	..	15.6	15.7
Togo	8.0	18.0	17.2	15.9	19.5	..	..	..	..	7.8	11.8	17.3
Uganda	..	6.5	15.6	15.1	17.3	16.4	16.9	18.3	17.5	5.4	10.3	15.8
Zambia	..	7.2	12.7	14.3	15.5	18.5	20.0	17.4	17.8	4.9	5.7	13.7
Zimbabwe	12.3	14.8	11.7	0.0	0.0	0.0	4.0	3.5	1.7	13.1	16.0	5.0
NORTH AFRICA	**..**	**15.4**	**10.5**	**10.5**	**10.9**	**12.1**	**13.5**	**14.5**	**19.9**	**12.8**	**12.0**	**12.8**
Algeria	22.8	18.8	13.2	13.6	11.5	11.0	9.5	10.2	33.0	18.1	19.0	14.4
Egypt, Arab Rep.	..	12.3	8.1	7.7	8.6	10.7	13.1	14.4	10.9	9.3	5.9	10.0
Libya	..	..	1.9	1.6	1.7	4.0	5.2	5.9	..	..	..	3.2
Morocco	16.7	19.2	21.3	22.4	23.8	24.5	27.6	28.4	24.8	16.1	18.0	23.5
Tunisia	13.3	15.6	..	..	12.3	..	..	..	23.2	13.5	13.8	16.4
ALL AFRICA	**..**	**14.0**	**11.3**	**11.3**	**11.8**	**12.9**	**13.6**	**14.3**	**16.1**	**13.3**	**12.2**	**12.7**

a. Provisional.

Table 2.22 External trade balance (exports minus imports)

	Share of GDP (%)											
										Annual average		
	1980	1990	2003	2004	2005	2006	2007	2008	2009[a]	1980–89	1990–99	2000–09
SUB-SAHARAN AFRICA	**1.2**	**0.8**	**–1.5**	**–1.3**	**–1.3**	**–1.9**	**–2.4**	**–3.8**	**–3.7**	**–0.4**	**–1.5**	**–1.5**
Excluding South Africa	–4.6	–2.5	–4.3	–2.0	–1.9	–1.6	–2.0	–4.4	–5.9	–4.7	–4.6	–2.9
Excl. S. Africa & Nigeria	–8.6	–6.3	–5.7	–5.3	–5.8	–5.3	–5.9	–8.4	–9.4	–6.1	–6.6	–6.1
Angola	..	18.0	6.6	16.0	29.8	37.8	31.1	25.1	6.0	9.1	2.2	19.2
Benin	–21.5	–12.0	–12.8	–12.7	–12.6	–11.3	–15.3	–13.6	–14.3	–17.5	–12.5	–13.2
Botswana	–13.4	5.3	11.0	7.3	16.8	16.4	12.0	–0.1	–11.0	5.3	9.8	8.4
Burkina Faso	–22.3	–13.5	–12.9	–13.5	–15.6	–15.3	..	..	..	–19.6	–13.5	–14.2
Burundi	–14.5	–19.9	–19.3	–24.3	–33.9	–36.2	..	..	..	–13.5	–14.4	–22.3
Cameroon	0.8	2.9	0.3	–0.4	–1.0	2.1	0.8	–3.0	–4.3	0.4	3.7	–0.4
Cape Verde	..	–31.0	–34.5	–38.9	–32.9	–35.6	–38.0	–39.2	–41.8	–29.0	–35.2	–36.5
Central African Republic	–15.9	–12.9	–4.5	–6.2	–8.8	–7.9	–7.4	–12.6	–7.9	–12.1	–7.7	–6.9
Chad	–11.9	–14.4	–34.1	0.2	17.2	22.0	2.5	2.6	–28.0	–13.5	–13.6	–17.1
Comoros	–43.2	–22.9	–13.7	–17.9	–21.6	–24.4	–26.6	–34.4	–33.5	–33.3	–23.0	–21.8
Congo, Dem. Rep.	0.1	0.3	–7.2	–8.8	–8.2	–13.7	–10.8	–15.2	–12.1	–0.8	1.2	–8.2
Congo, Rep.	–0.1	7.9	4.8	29.7	29.7	18.5	23.2	26.3	21.0	–0.5	2.9	24.2
Côte d'Ivoire	–6.2	4.6	10.9	9.2	7.5	10.3	5.9	7.7	8.0	3.2	6.5	9.2
Djibouti	..	–24.6	–9.2	–17.2	–10.3	–17.4	–20.1	..	..	..	–17.5	–12.9
Equatorial Guinea	..	–37.4	20.4	35.1	43.8	53.7	51.6	46.1	32.5	–28.6	–45.8	35.3
Eritrea	..	..	–69.0	–63.8	–45.7	–29.7	–28.2	–18.1	–15.8	..	–55.8	–44.9
Ethiopia	..	–3.3	–14.1	–16.7	–20.4	–22.7	–19.3	–19.4	–18.3	–5.3	–6.8	–16.9
Gabon	33.1	15.2	24.3	30.2	37.0	30.1	29.4	34.6	18.9	9.7	17.7	28.6
Gambia, The	–20.9	–11.7	–9.2	–21.1	–22.8	–17.2	–16.3	–18.6	–19.7	–13.2	–12.6	–14.8
Ghana	–0.7	–9.0	–15.9	–21.1	–25.3	–15.5	–16.3	–19.5	–10.8	–3.1	–12.4	–17.5
Guinea	..	–2.4	–0.1	–2.3	–1.3	–3.3	–4.6	–5.3	–4.7	0.3	–3.0	–3.0
Guinea-Bissau	–29.2	–27.1	..	..	..	..	..	..	..	–32.9	–24.5	–25.2
Kenya	–6.4	–5.6	–6.0	–6.3	–7.5	–9.9	–11.0	–14.2	–13.1	–4.9	–3.7	–9.3
Lesotho	–89.1	–105.1	–58.3	–52.2	–53.8	–49.6	–52.8	–54.0	–60.5	–110.0	–101.9	–57.5
Liberia	–0.1	..	–12.6	–13.9	–14.0	–54.6	–162.5	–141.5	..	2.9	–39.6	–46.7
Madagascar	–16.4	–11.4	–9.0	–14.8	–17.3	–16.0	–21.7	–30.3	–23.7	–7.7	–8.2	–15.0
Malawi	–14.0	–9.6	–13.9	–18.2	–28.1	–24.5	–8.1	–17.4	–7.7	–6.7	–14.3	–15.2
Mali	–14.4	–16.6	–10.9	–12.4	–11.7	–8.1	–9.4	..	..	–17.6	–14.9	–11.2
Mauritania	–29.8	–15.1	–30.9	–49.4	–59.8	–11.0	–14.3	–22.2	–17.8	–24.4	–11.2	–27.5
Mauritius	–10.2	–7.2	1.3	–2.4	–6.0	–11.3	–10.3	–14.7	–10.6	–3.3	–4.1	–4.6
Mozambique	–16.5	–27.9	–18.7	–10.9	–12.2	–8.9	–9.8	11.1	–18.7	–18.4	–23.6	–15.0
Namibia	7.8	–15.5	–9.1	–2.3	0.1	–1.7	–1.3	–6.7	–13.3	–7.6	–10.0	–4.6
Niger	–13.5	–6.9	–9.2	–10.0	–9.2		..	..	..	–8.0	–6.2	–8.8
Nigeria[b]	10.2	14.6	2.3	12.9	15.5	15.1	15.1	12.3	8.7	1.1	4.1	11.4
Rwanda	–11.9	–8.5	–17.6	–13.6	–13.8	–14.2	–14.6	–15.8	–17.5	–10.3	–19.9	–15.8
São Tomé and Príncipe	..	..	..	..	..	..	..	..	..	..	..	..
Senegal	–14.5	–6.8	–12.1	–12.9	–15.6	–17.5	–22.3	–26.6	–19.9	–12.1	–7.1	–15.6
Seychelles	–11.2	–4.3	11.2	2.0	–21.6	–18.0	–31.2	–19.4	–8.3	–2.3	–8.6	–11.1
Sierra Leone	–15.4	–1.3	–17.6	–10.9	–12.9	–7.6	–7.0	–13.0	–12.8	–3.1	–4.5	–14.0
Somalia	–55.3	–28.0	..	..	..	..	..	..	..	–35.1	–28.0	..
South Africa	8.0	5.5	2.3	–0.3	–0.5	–2.4	–2.9	–3.0	–0.9	5.1	2.8	0.3
Sudan	–12.6	–3.0	–4.2	–3.8	–9.9	–10.9	–3.8	0.8	–5.8	–8.3	–6.7	–5.4
Swaziland	–39.4	–9.9	–1.0	–2.7	–4.2	–2.6	–1.3	–15.5	–16.7	–23.5	–15.2	–7.7
Tanzania	..	–24.8	–4.2	–6.4	–8.9	–13.1	–12.8	–16.4	–11.9	..	–19.0	–8.7
Togo	–5.3	–11.9	–13.6	–13.5	–16.9	–19.5	–20.5	..	..	–7.2	–9.6	–17.7
Uganda	–6.6	–12.1	–13.8	–10.1	–10.7	–13.1	–13.3	–7.7	–11.2	–6.2	–11.7	–11.8
Zambia	–4.0	–0.7	–12.4	–4.4	–2.1	8.4	6.4	2.5	3.4	–2.1	–5.6	–4.3
Zimbabwe	–3.2	0.1	–5.7	–7.3	–9.2	–11.4	–9.1	–28.3	–29.1	–0.8	–2.3	–9.9
NORTH AFRICA	**–7.2**	**–5.9**	**4.6**	**5.6**	**8.2**	**10.1**	**6.5**	**5.5**	**–4.5**	**–8.9**	**–3.1**	**4.2**
Algeria	4.0	–1.5	14.4	14.4	23.4	27.1	23.3	23.4	4.3	–2.5	1.6	17.4
Egypt, Arab Rep.	–12.4	–12.7	–2.6	–1.4	–2.3	–1.6	–4.6	–5.6	–6.8	–13.2	–6.7	–4.1
Libya	..	8.6	25.7	31.1	38.1	45.8	38.2	39.9	..	..	3.6	29.1
Morocco	–9.4	–5.4	–2.8	–5.0	–5.6	–5.5	–9.1	–13.4	–10.9	–7.4	–4.9	–6.2
Tunisia	–5.4	–7.0	–3.9	–2.9	–0.4	–2.3	–2.4	–4.2	–3.4	–6.1	–4.3	–3.2
ALL AFRICA	**–2.2**	**–2.0**	**1.1**	**1.6**	**2.7**	**3.1**	**1.4**	**0.2**	**–4.0**	**–3.8**	**–2.2**	**0.9**

a. Provisional.
b. For 1994–2000 Nigeria's values were distorted because the official exchange rate used by the government for oil exports and oil value added was significantly overvalued.

Table 2.23 Exports of goods and services, nominal

	Current prices ($ millions)											
										Annual average		
	1980	1990	2003	2004	2005	2006	2007	2008	2009[a]	1980–89	1990–99	2000–09
SUB-SAHARAN AFRICA	**82,540**	**79,795**	**145,376**	**185,542**	**234,188**	**278,709**	**323,596**	**396,735**	**298,039**	**65,089**	**87,615**	**220,178**
Excluding South Africa	54,029	52,368	98,474	127,656	166,562	200,430	234,106	299,097	220,322	38,654	55,868	157,694
Excl. S. Africa & Nigeria	33,788	40,438	69,589	89,049	114,319	137,465	166,118	212,813	158,411	31,094	43,640	111,379
Angola	..	3,992	9,716	13,780	24,286	33,343	44,707	64,243	39,432	2,613	4,265	25,294
Benin	222	264	487	539	577	538	900	1,019	922	214	327	606
Botswana	563	2,087	3,668	4,444	5,256	5,292	5,877	5,660	3,971	999	2,378	4,268
Burkina Faso	173	340	376	549	542	665	..	..	..	189	286	417
Burundi	81	89	50	64	91	99	..	..	..	111	89	63
Cameroon	1,880	2,251	2,757	3,061	3,393	4,131	4,563	7,718	5,896	2,240	2,198	3,813
Cape Verde	..	43	253	138	171	229	285	345	366	41	79	229
Central African Republic	201	220	154	168	170	207	254	215	290	181	185	197
Chad	175	234	674	2,252	3,234	3,852	3,845	4,413	2,879	153	254	2,189
Comoros	11	36	57	55	55	57	68	74	79	22	40	55
Congo, Dem. Rep.	2,372	2,759	1,483	1,994	2,450	2,621	2,711	2,701	1,017	2,016	1,595	1,799
Congo, Rep.	1,024	1,502	2,825	3,744	5,123	6,507	6,402	8,642	6,884	1,092	1,393	4,734
Côte d'Ivoire	3,561	3,421	6,297	7,517	8,354	9,144	9,465	10,890	9,722	3,142	4,129	7,576
Djibouti	..	244	248	246	288	307	484	..	..	..	210	276
Equatorial Guinea	..	42	2,859	4,724	7,183	8,332	10,299	14,498	7,713	32	160	6,074
Eritrea	..	..	56	64	68	84	86	61	84	..	132	77
Ethiopia	..	672	1,137	1,495	1,855	2,101	2,442	2,950	3,011	608	715	1,794
Gabon	2,770	2,740	3,350	4,465	5,610	5,912	7,203	9,675	5,773	1,964	2,728	5,091
Gambia, The	103	190	158	184	185	203	214	244	223	108	195	192
Ghana	376	993	3,101	3,487	3,907	5,136	6,041	7,140	7,982	554	1,684	4,425
Guinea	..	829	865	862	994	1,108	1,267	1,259	1,671	660	798	1,036
Guinea-Bissau	14	24	..	..	..	..	..	..	..	15	32	62
Kenya	2,144	2,207	3,590	4,283	5,342	5,945	7,062	8,291	7,413	1,805	2,594	5,092
Lesotho	91	98	520	721	703	759	880	936	809	67	187	629
Liberia	613	..	133	171	201	175	208	262	..	519	43	168
Madagascar	539	512	1,264	1,424	1,422	1,640	2,227	2,498	2,447	414	673	1,613
Malawi	307	447	647	655	663	705	936	1,203	1,420	295	465	771
Mali	263	415	1,153	1,237	1,359	1,884	1,871	..	..	255	514	1,262
Mauritania	261	465	356	473	667	1,366	1,548	1,952	1,504	387	465	913
Mauritius	579	1,724	3,180	3,450	3,761	4,009	4,422	4,926	4,161	807	2,257	3,677
Mozambique	383	201	1,348	1,759	2,087	2,722	2,839	3,192	2,454	215	373	1,920
Namibia	1,712	1,220	2,141	2,630	2,937	3,180	4,468	4,787	4,319	1,139	1,543	2,907
Niger	617	372	438	491	512	..	..	..	..	420	325	403
Nigeria	18,859	12,366	28,891	38,609	52,238	62,959	68,061	86,396	62,054	7,725	12,563	46,350
Rwanda	168	145	139	232	295	344	410	680	610	173	107	315
São Tomé and Príncipe	..	..	..	..	..	..	..	..	..	..	..	..
Senegal	837	1,453	1,830	2,126	2,344	2,401	2,875	3,477	3,082	989	1,347	2,237
Seychelles	100	230	671	684	717	860	993	1,091	912	123	298	750
Sierra Leone	252	146	230	247	292	355	346	319	305	187	155	250
Somalia	200	90	..	..	..	..	..	..	..	119	90	..
South Africa	28,555	27,149	46,900	57,890	67,647	78,318	89,549	98,005	77,883	26,088	31,523	62,550
Sudan	806	499	2,613	3,822	4,992	6,015	9,287	12,974	8,230	841	579	5,353
Swaziland	405	658	1,872	2,056	2,250	2,259	2,311	1,795	1,794	394	886	1,779
Tanzania	..	538	2,164	2,520	2,945	3,233	4,093	4,689	4,963	..	949	2,963
Togo	580	545	595	691	850	938	1,048	..	..	464	441	681
Uganda	242	312	722	1,077	1,278	1,519	1,991	3,506	3,753	371	500	1,587
Zambia	1,608	1,180	1,256	2,079	2,482	4,120	4,802	5,267	4,560	1,060	1,099	2,749
Zimbabwe	1,561	2,009	1,856	2,001	1,931	1,957	2,000	1,802	2,040	1,530	2,467	2,053
NORTH AFRICA	**37,505**	**46,844**	**84,346**	**107,367**	**138,842**	**167,469**	**197,126**	**253,603**	**200,244**	**34,399**	**48,912**	**135,256**
Algeria	14,541	14,546	26,028	34,067	48,761	56,953	63,297	79,123	56,798	12,221	12,420	42,760
Egypt, Arab Rep.	6,992	8,647	18,074	22,258	27,214	32,191	39,469	53,800	47,185	6,654	12,435	28,952
Libya	..	11,468	15,011	21,117	29,230	40,275	48,510	62,780	..	..	8,527	27,469
Morocco	3,273	6,830	14,282	16,726	19,234	22,449	26,892	33,312	26,121	3,790	8,363	19,266
Tunisia	3,518	5,353	10,950	13,199	14,402	15,600	18,958	24,588	20,568	3,312	7,168	14,598
ALL AFRICA	**121,315**	**126,751**	**229,724**	**292,911**	**373,037**	**446,193**	**520,752**	**650,506**	**496,886**	**100,090**	**136,561**	**355,318**

a. Provisional.

Table 2.24 Imports of goods and services, nominal

	Current prices ($ millions)											
										Annual average		
	1980	1990	2003	2004	2005	2006	2007	2008	2009[a]	1980–89	1990–99	2000–09
SUB-SAHARAN AFRICA	**75,861**	**74,537**	**149,688**	**181,775**	**220,807**	**259,550**	**306,358**	**384,534**	**317,933**	**66,471**	**90,422**	**215,193**
Excluding South Africa	53,970	53,674	106,770	123,252	152,038	174,847	208,464	279,044	238,718	44,946	62,531	151,820
Excl. S. Africa & Nigeria	40,777	45,400	79,350	95,931	117,132	134,048	165,502	217,932	191,987	37,295	51,235	118,742
Angola	..	2,147	8,801	10,621	15,144	16,287	26,304	43,121	34,901	1,895	4,032	17,472
Benin	524	486	944	1,055	1,119	1,075	1,750	1,928	1,875	447	579	1,181
Botswana	705	1,888	2,780	3,707	3,534	3,451	4,386	5,679	5,273	842	1,916	3,542
Burkina Faso	603	758	928	1,240	1,390	1,547	..	..	..	567	640	1,016
Burundi	214	314	165	225	360	432	..	..	..	254	234	229
Cameroon	1,829	1,931	2,712	3,128	3,562	3,763	4,395	8,435	6,856	2,219	1,816	3,931
Cape Verde	..	148	529	497	500	624	791	945	1,013	118	237	600
Central African Republic	327	411	205	246	289	324	381	464	449	292	282	300
Chad	298	485	1,608	2,241	2,324	2,509	3,670	4,195	4,794	305	469	2,493
Comoros	64	93	101	120	138	156	192	256	258	67	93	143
Congo, Dem. Rep.	2,354	2,731	1,892	2,573	3,036	3,789	3,785	4,468	2,298	2,107	1,537	2,518
Congo, Rep.	1,026	1,282	2,659	2,363	3,318	5,073	4,464	5,541	4,876	1,093	1,309	3,282
Côte d'Ivoire	4,190	2,927	4,796	6,093	7,132	7,356	8,302	9,085	7,866	2,906	3,406	6,147
Djibouti	..	355	305	361	361	441	654	..	..	..	295	365
Equatorial Guinea	..	92	2,256	2,882	3,583	3,179	3,809	5,953	4,328	61	270	2,978
Eritrea	..	..	588	663	603	465	474	361	379	..	482	498
Ethiopia	..	1,069	2,341	3,169	4,359	5,537	6,143	7,976	8,229	1,093	1,330	4,373
Gabon	1,354	1,837	1,882	2,299	2,400	3,037	3,805	4,652	3,685	1,586	1,823	2,667
Gambia, The	153	227	192	269	290	290	320	397	368	137	242	273
Ghana	407	1,522	4,316	5,356	6,617	8,304	10,057	12,690	10,820	709	2,509	6,833
Guinea	..	892	868	947	1,031	1,202	1,460	1,460	1,865	658	905	1,140
Guinea-Bissau	46	90	..	..	..	..	..	..	..	67	91	114
Kenya	2,608	2,691	4,478	5,290	6,740	8,171	10,059	12,563	11,253	2,154	3,071	7,085
Lesotho	475	666	1,072	1,350	1,411	1,462	1,713	1,796	1,764	496	926	1,287
Liberia	614	..	184	235	275	509	1,403	1,454	..	491	180	504
Madagascar	1,202	864	1,756	2,072	2,296	2,525	3,823	5,357	4,484	668	942	2,624
Malawi	480	629	984	1,134	1,438	1,468	1,215	1,911	1,783	384	716	1,213
Mali	520	817	1,630	1,841	1,979	2,360	2,542	..	..	536	882	1,742
Mauritania	473	619	753	1,239	1,778	1,662	1,955	2,747	2,043	576	607	1,422
Mauritius	695	1,915	3,107	3,601	4,138	4,744	5,193	6,295	5,074	853	2,400	4,063
Mozambique	965	888	2,222	2,381	2,891	3,351	3,626	4,586	4,287	773	1,001	2,853
Namibia	1,542	1,584	2,589	2,780	2,927	3,317	4,583	5,387	5,548	1,284	1,844	3,218
Niger	957	545	688	795	825		..	..	..	583	448	629
Nigeria	12,324	8,203	27,360	27,282	34,849	40,726	43,039	61,006	46,999	7,362	11,214	33,073
Rwanda	307	364	464	517	651	787	955	1,423	1,524	354	405	762
São Tomé and Príncipe	..	..	..	..	..	..	..	..	..	..	..	..
Senegal	1,344	1,840	2,662	3,166	3,700	4,037	5,407	6,976	5,637	1,408	1,719	3,725
Seychelles	117	246	593	671	908	1,034	1,313	1,271	975	123	344	850
Sierra Leone	421	154	404	367	452	463	462	575	554	225	191	414
Somalia	534	346	..	..	..	..	..	..	..	403	346	..
South Africa	22,073	21,016	42,967	58,544	68,809	84,706	97,946	106,345	80,328	21,441	27,961	63,596
Sudan	1,763	877	3,367	4,650	7,701	9,995	11,041	12,537	11,391	1,744	1,289	6,856
Swaziland	619	768	1,889	2,117	2,357	2,329	2,350	2,234	2,295	515	1,109	1,948
Tanzania	..	1,595	2,660	3,343	4,205	5,116	6,250	8,090	7,511	..	1,986	4,358
Togo	640	738	833	969	1,206	1,371	1,561	..	..	542	586	1,007
Uganda	324	834	1,597	1,932	2,237	2,820	3,577	4,618	5,557	619	1,039	2,664
Zambia	1,764	1,203	1,796	2,319	2,631	3,221	4,068	4,909	4,118	1,148	1,283	2,757
Zimbabwe	1,771	2,002	2,180	2,413	2,446	2,551	2,455	3,005	3,678	1,598	2,644	2,558
NORTH AFRICA	**38,163**	**53,024**	**72,890**	**89,433**	**103,625**	**115,892**	**151,699**	**199,201**	**193,682**	**40,285**	**53,422**	**111,461**
Algeria	12,847	15,472	16,239	21,808	24,838	25,211	31,633	39,171	50,772	13,875	11,636	24,778
Egypt, Arab Rep.	9,822	14,109	20,219	23,330	29,246	33,931	45,443	62,909	60,048	10,787	16,572	33,962
Libya	..	8,996	8,823	10,723	12,452	14,383	21,074	25,589	..	..	7,464	12,328
Morocco	5,033	8,227	15,691	19,547	22,569	26,044	33,750	45,214	36,088	4,955	9,907	23,634
Tunisia	3,987	6,220	11,918	14,026	14,521	16,322	19,799	26,317	21,894	3,834	7,842	15,503
ALL AFRICA	**115,055**	**127,845**	**222,549**	**271,175**	**324,379**	**375,349**	**458,104**	**583,978**	**509,907**	**107,382**	**143,939**	**326,492**

a. Provisional.

Table 2.25 Exports of goods and services as a share of GDP

	Share of GDP (%)											
										Annual average		
	1980	1990	2003	2004	2005	2006	2007	2008	2009[a]	1980–89	1990–99	2000–09
SUB-SAHARAN AFRICA	**31.9**	**26.4**	**31.0**	**31.2**	**32.6**	**33.3**	**33.8**	**36.0**	**29.8**	**26.9**	**27.2**	**32.4**
Excluding South Africa	29.1	28.0	33.2	34.6	36.4	35.8	35.8	36.3	31.7	25.4	29.9	34.4
Excl. S. Africa & Nigeria	29.0	24.6	31.1	32.6	34.1	34.2	34.5	35.1	30.7	26.4	27.3	32.6
Angola	..	38.9	69.6	69.7	79.3	73.8	75.4	76.3	52.2	34.8	63.4	73.6
Benin	15.8	14.3	13.7	13.3	13.5	11.4	16.2	15.2	13.8	16.6	16.4	14.1
Botswana	53.1	55.1	45.4	44.2	51.2	47.0	47.5	41.8	33.6	62.0	51.5	45.5
Burkina Faso	9.0	11.0	8.8	10.7	10.0	11.5	..	..	..	9.5	11.1	9.7
Burundi	8.8	7.9	8.4	9.6	11.4	10.7	..	..	..	10.4	9.0	8.7
Cameroon	27.9	20.2	20.2	19.4	20.5	23.0	22.1	32.5	26.6	25.7	20.9	22.9
Cape Verde	..	12.7	31.7	14.9	17.1	20.7	21.4	22.5	23.6	15.5	16.9	24.1
Central African Republic	25.2	14.8	13.5	13.2	12.6	14.0	14.8	10.8	14.5	20.5	16.2	14.5
Chad	16.9	13.5	24.6	51.0	61.0	63.2	54.8	52.8	42.1	14.3	16.1	39.4
Comoros	8.7	14.3	17.5	15.1	14.1	14.2	14.7	13.9	14.7	14.7	17.3	15.2
Congo, Dem. Rep.	16.5	29.5	26.1	30.4	34.5	30.7	27.2	23.3	9.6	21.4	23.1	24.4
Congo, Rep.	60.0	53.7	80.8	80.5	84.2	84.2	76.7	73.3	71.9	52.0	60.2	79.1
Côte d'Ivoire	35.0	31.7	45.8	48.6	51.1	52.7	47.8	46.5	41.7	37.1	36.8	46.6
Djibouti	..	53.8	39.9	37.0	40.6	39.9	57.1	..	..	..	43.2	40.7
Equatorial Guinea	..	32.2	96.8	90.1	87.4	86.8	81.9	78.3	74.1	35.9	52.9	89.5
Eritrea	..	..	7.3	6.8	5.8	6.5	6.3	3.7	4.5	..	22.0	8.1
Ethiopia	..	5.6	13.3	14.9	15.1	13.9	12.7	11.4	10.6	6.6	8.1	12.9
Gabon	64.7	46.0	55.3	62.2	64.7	61.9	62.2	66.6	52.2	53.3	54.0	60.7
Gambia, The	42.7	59.9	43.1	46.0	40.0	39.8	32.9	29.6	30.4	47.8	52.6	38.8
Ghana	8.5	16.9	40.7	39.3	36.4	25.2	24.5	25.0	30.5	11.2	25.2	35.8
Guinea	..	31.1	25.1	23.5	33.8	39.3	30.1	33.3	40.7	30.2	23.8	30.3
Guinea-Bissau	12.7	9.9	..	..	..	..	..	..	..	9.9	13.3	30.1
Kenya	29.5	25.7	24.1	26.6	28.5	26.4	26.0	27.6	25.2	25.7	27.6	25.4
Lesotho	21.0	18.1	54.9	59.8	53.4	53.6	55.8	58.7	51.2	16.9	25.0	52.9
Liberia	64.3	..	32.4	37.3	37.9	28.6	28.3	31.1	..	55.3	11.4	28.9
Madagascar	13.3	16.6	23.1	32.6	28.2	29.7	30.3	26.5	28.5	13.6	20.1	27.5
Malawi	24.8	23.8	26.7	25.0	24.0	22.6	27.1	29.5	30.0	23.7	25.1	25.9
Mali	14.7	17.1	26.4	25.4	25.6	32.1	26.2	..	..	15.8	20.8	28.5
Mauritania	36.8	45.6	27.7	30.6	35.9	50.6	54.5	54.4	49.7	47.9	36.7	41.7
Mauritius	51.0	65.0	56.7	54.0	59.9	61.6	58.8	52.9	48.4	54.4	61.5	58.4
Mozambique	10.9	8.2	28.9	30.9	31.7	38.4	35.4	32.3	25.1	6.8	12.8	29.0
Namibia	78.9	51.9	43.4	39.8	40.5	39.9	50.7	53.4	46.6	61.2	49.7	44.2
Niger	24.6	15.0	16.0	16.1	15.0	..	..	..	..	21.0	16.2	16.2
Nigeria	29.4	43.4	42.7	44.0	46.5	42.9	41.0	41.7	35.9	21.4	42.0	42.3
Rwanda	14.4	5.6	7.6	11.1	11.4	11.1	11.0	14.5	11.7	10.4	6.0	10.4
São Tomé and Príncipe	..	..	..	..	..	..	..	..	..	..	..	..
Senegal	23.9	25.4	26.6	26.4	26.9	25.6	25.4	26.4	24.0	27.4	26.4	26.7
Seychelles	68.0	62.5	95.1	97.8	81.1	88.8	96.7	117.8	119.3	62.1	59.9	94.0
Sierra Leone	22.9	22.4	23.2	22.5	23.6	24.9	20.8	16.3	15.7	19.5	19.8	19.9
Somalia	33.2	9.8	..	..	..	..	..	..	..	15.5	9.8	..
South Africa	35.4	24.2	27.9	26.4	27.4	30.0	31.3	35.5	27.3	28.8	23.5	29.7
Sudan	10.6	4.0	14.7	17.6	18.2	16.5	20.0	22.4	15.1	7.4	5.4	16.6
Swaziland	74.6	59.0	104.2	90.1	89.1	84.6	78.3	63.2	59.8	70.2	61.1	83.5
Tanzania	..	12.6	18.6	19.7	20.8	22.6	24.3	22.6	23.2	..	15.9	20.0
Togo	51.1	33.5	33.8	33.5	40.3	42.3	41.9	..	..	46.1	30.2	36.0
Uganda	19.4	7.2	11.4	12.7	14.2	15.3	16.7	24.3	23.4	11.6	9.8	15.1
Zambia	41.4	35.9	28.7	38.3	34.7	38.6	42.1	36.6	35.6	34.4	32.8	33.8
Zimbabwe	23.4	22.9	32.8	35.3	34.6	37.6	39.8	42.4	36.3	21.4	33.3	36.5
NORTH AFRICA	**30.2**	**26.4**	**33.6**	**37.2**	**40.8**	**41.8**	**41.5**	**43.4**	**32.1**	**24.1**	**26.0**	**35.6**
Algeria	34.3	23.4	38.3	40.1	47.6	48.6	46.6	46.3	40.4	23.8	25.8	42.0
Egypt, Arab Rep.	30.5	20.0	21.8	28.2	30.3	29.9	30.3	33.0	25.0	22.2	21.8	25.1
Libya	..	39.7	62.4	63.3	66.4	71.3	67.6	67.4	..	..	28.7	56.9
Morocco	17.4	26.5	28.7	29.4	32.3	34.2	35.7	37.5	28.6	22.2	25.9	31.4
Tunisia	40.2	43.6	43.8	46.9	49.7	50.4	53.2	60.2	52.0	36.9	42.5	49.4
ALL AFRICA	**31.2**	**26.4**	**32.1**	**33.7**	**36.1**	**36.9**	**37.1**	**39.2**	**30.7**	**25.8**	**26.7**	**33.8**

a. Provisional.

Table 2.26 Imports of goods and services as a share of GDP

	Share of GDP (%)											
										Annual average		
	1980	1990	2003	2004	2005	2006	2007	2008	2009[a]	1980–89	1990–99	2000–09
SUB-SAHARAN AFRICA	**30.8**	**25.6**	**32.5**	**32.5**	**33.9**	**35.3**	**36.2**	**39.8**	**33.5**	**27.3**	**28.8**	**33.9**
Excluding South Africa	33.6	30.5	37.4	36.6	38.3	37.4	37.7	40.7	37.6	30.1	34.6	37.3
Excl. S. Africa & Nigeria	37.5	30.8	36.8	37.8	39.9	39.5	40.5	43.4	40.1	32.5	33.8	38.7
Angola	..	20.9	63.1	53.7	49.4	36.1	44.4	51.2	46.2	25.6	61.3	54.4
Benin	37.3	26.3	26.5	26.1	26.1	22.7	31.6	28.8	28.2	34.1	28.9	27.3
Botswana	66.4	49.8	34.4	36.9	34.5	30.7	35.4	41.9	44.6	56.7	41.7	37.0
Burkina Faso	31.3	24.5	21.7	24.3	25.6	26.8	..	..	..	29.2	24.6	24.0
Burundi	23.3	27.8	27.7	33.9	45.3	47.0	..	..	..	23.8	23.4	31.0
Cameroon	27.1	17.3	19.9	19.8	21.5	21.0	21.2	35.5	30.9	25.3	17.2	23.3
Cape Verde	..	43.7	66.3	53.8	50.1	56.3	59.4	61.7	65.4	44.6	52.1	60.6
Central African Republic	41.1	27.6	18.0	19.4	21.4	21.9	22.3	23.4	22.4	32.5	24.0	21.4
Chad	28.9	27.9	58.7	50.8	43.8	41.1	52.3	50.2	70.1	27.7	29.7	56.5
Comoros	51.9	37.1	31.2	33.0	35.8	38.6	41.3	48.3	48.2	47.9	40.2	37.0
Congo, Dem. Rep.	16.4	29.2	33.3	39.2	42.7	44.4	37.9	38.6	21.7	22.2	21.9	32.6
Congo, Rep.	60.1	45.8	76.0	50.8	54.5	65.6	53.5	47.0	50.9	52.6	57.3	54.9
Côte d'Ivoire	41.2	27.1	34.9	39.4	43.6	42.4	41.9	38.8	33.8	33.9	30.3	37.5
Djibouti	..	78.4	49.1	54.2	50.9	57.3	77.1	..	..	..	60.7	53.6
Equatorial Guinea	..	69.6	76.4	55.0	43.6	33.1	30.3	32.1	41.6	64.5	98.6	54.2
Eritrea	..	..	76.3	70.7	51.5	36.3	34.5	21.8	20.3	..	77.8	53.0
Ethiopia	..	8.8	27.4	31.6	35.5	36.6	32.0	30.8	28.8	11.9	14.9	29.7
Gabon	31.6	30.9	31.1	32.0	27.7	31.8	32.9	32.0	33.3	43.6	36.3	32.1
Gambia, The	63.6	71.6	52.3	67.1	62.8	57.0	49.2	48.3	50.1	61.0	65.3	53.6
Ghana	9.2	25.9	56.6	60.4	61.7	40.7	40.8	44.5	41.3	14.3	37.6	53.3
Guinea	..	33.4	25.2	25.8	35.1	42.6	34.7	38.6	45.4	29.9	26.9	33.3
Guinea-Bissau	41.8	37.0	..	..	..	..	..	..	..	42.8	37.7	55.3
Kenya	35.9	31.3	30.0	32.9	36.0	36.3	37.0	41.8	38.3	30.6	31.3	34.7
Lesotho	110.1	123.2	113.2	112.0	107.3	103.2	108.6	112.7	111.7	126.9	126.9	110.4
Liberia	64.4	..	44.9	51.2	51.9	83.2	190.9	172.6	..	52.4	51.0	75.6
Madagascar	29.7	28.0	32.1	47.5	45.6	45.8	52.1	56.8	52.2	21.3	28.3	42.5
Malawi	38.8	33.4	40.6	43.2	52.2	47.1	35.1	46.9	37.7	30.4	39.4	41.1
Mali	29.1	33.7	37.4	37.8	37.3	40.2	35.6	..	..	33.4	35.7	39.6
Mauritania	66.7	60.7	58.6	80.0	95.7	61.6	68.9	76.6	67.6	72.2	47.9	69.2
Mauritius	61.2	72.2	55.1	56.4	65.9	72.9	69.0	67.6	59.1	57.6	65.6	63.0
Mozambique	27.4	36.1	47.6	41.8	43.9	47.2	45.2	46.5	43.8	25.1	36.4	44.0
Namibia	71.1	67.4	52.5	42.1	40.3	41.6	52.0	60.1	59.9	68.7	59.7	48.9
Niger	38.1	22.0	25.2	26.0	24.2	..	..	..	..	29.0	22.4	25.0
Nigeria	19.2	28.8	40.4	31.1	31.0	27.7	25.9	29.5	27.2	20.3	37.8	31.0
Rwanda	26.4	14.1	25.1	24.8	25.2	25.3	25.5	30.3	29.2	20.7	26.0	26.3
São Tomé and Príncipe	..	..	..	..	..	..	..	..	..	..	..	..
Senegal	38.4	32.2	38.7	39.4	42.5	43.0	47.7	53.0	44.0	39.6	33.5	42.2
Seychelles	79.1	66.7	84.0	95.8	102.7	106.9	127.9	137.2	127.6	64.4	68.4	105.2
Sierra Leone	38.2	23.8	40.8	33.5	36.5	32.5	27.8	29.4	28.5	22.5	24.2	33.8
Somalia	88.5	37.7	..	..	..	..	..	..	..	50.6	37.7	..
South Africa	27.3	18.8	25.5	26.7	27.9	32.5	34.2	38.5	28.1	23.8	20.7	29.3
Sudan	23.1	7.1	18.9	21.4	28.1	27.5	23.7	21.6	20.8	15.7	12.1	22.0
Swaziland	114.0	68.9	105.2	92.8	93.4	87.2	79.7	78.7	76.5	93.7	76.3	91.2
Tanzania	..	37.5	22.8	26.1	29.7	35.7	37.1	39.1	35.2	..	34.9	28.7
Togo	56.4	45.3	47.4	47.0	57.2	61.8	62.5	..	..	53.3	39.8	53.7
Uganda	26.0	19.4	25.2	22.8	24.9	28.4	30.1	32.0	34.6	17.8	21.5	26.9
Zambia	45.4	36.6	41.1	42.8	36.8	30.2	35.6	34.1	32.2	36.5	38.4	38.0
Zimbabwe	26.5	22.8	38.5	42.6	43.8	49.0	48.9	70.8	65.4	22.2	35.6	46.4
NORTH AFRICA	**37.3**	**32.3**	**29.0**	**31.6**	**32.6**	**31.7**	**35.0**	**37.9**	**36.6**	**33.0**	**29.1**	**31.4**
Algeria	30.3	24.9	23.9	25.7	24.3	21.5	23.3	22.9	36.1	26.3	24.2	24.6
Egypt, Arab Rep.	42.9	32.7	24.4	29.6	32.6	31.6	34.8	38.6	31.9	35.4	28.5	29.1
Libya	..	31.1	36.7	32.1	28.3	25.5	29.4	27.5	..	..	25.1	27.8
Morocco	26.7	31.9	31.5	34.3	37.9	39.7	44.9	50.9	39.5	29.6	30.9	37.6
Tunisia	45.6	50.6	47.7	49.9	50.1	52.7	55.6	64.4	55.3	43.0	46.8	52.6
ALL AFRICA	**33.4**	**28.4**	**31.0**	**32.1**	**33.4**	**33.8**	**35.7**	**39.0**	**34.7**	**29.6**	**28.9**	**32.9**

a. Provisional.

Table 2.27 Balance of payments and current account

	Exports of goods and services		Imports of goods and services		Total trade (exports and imports)	
	Current prices ($ millions)	Share of GDP (%)	Current prices ($ millions)	Share of GDP (%)	Current prices ($ millions)	Share of GDP (%)
	2009[a]	2009[a]	2009[a]	2009[a]	2009[a]	2009[a]
SUB-SAHARAN AFRICA	**298,039**	**29.8**	**317,933**	**33.5**	**615,972**	**63.3**
Excluding South Africa	220,322	31.7	238,718	37.6	459,041	69.3
Excl. S. Africa & Nigeria	158,411	30.7	191,987	40.1	350,398	70.8
Angola	39,432	52.2	34,901	46.2	74,333	98.5
Benin	922	13.8	1,875	28.2	2,797	42.0
Botswana	3,971	33.6	5,273	44.6	9,245	78.2
Burkina Faso	..	..	..	..	..	..
Burundi	..	..	..	..	..	..
Cameroon	5,896	26.6	6,856	30.9	12,752	57.5
Cape Verde	366	23.6	1,013	65.4	1,379	89.0
Central African Republic	290	14.5	449	22.4	739	36.9
Chad	2,879	42.1	4,794	70.1	7,673	112.2
Comoros	79	14.7	258	48.2	336	62.8
Congo, Dem. Rep.	1,017	9.6	2,298	21.7	3,315	31.3
Congo, Rep.	6,884	71.9	4,876	50.9	11,760	122.8
Côte d'Ivoire	9,722	41.7	7,866	33.8	17,589	75.5
Djibouti	..	..	..	..	..	..
Equatorial Guinea	7,713	74.1	4,328	41.6	12,040	115.6
Eritrea	84	4.5	379	20.3	464	24.7
Ethiopia	3,011	10.6	8,229	28.8	11,240	39.4
Gabon	5,773	52.2	3,685	33.3	9,458	85.5
Gambia, The	223	30.4	368	50.1	591	80.6
Ghana	7,982	30.5	10,820	41.3	18,802	71.8
Guinea	1,671	40.7	1,865	45.4	3,535	86.2
Guinea-Bissau	..	..	..	..	..	..
Kenya	7,413	25.2	11,253	38.3	18,666	63.5
Lesotho	809	51.2	1,764	111.7	2,572	163.0
Liberia	..	..	..	..	..	..
Madagascar	2,447	28.5	4,484	52.2	6,930	80.7
Malawi	1,420	30.0	1,783	37.7	3,203	67.8
Mali	..	..	..	..	..	..
Mauritania	1,504	49.7	2,043	67.6	3,547	117.3
Mauritius	4,161	48.4	5,074	59.1	9,235	107.5
Mozambique	2,454	25.1	4,287	43.8	6,741	68.9
Namibia	4,319	46.6	5,548	59.9	9,868	106.5
Niger	..	..	..	..	..	..
Nigeria	62,054	35.9	46,999	27.2	109,052	63.0
Rwanda	610	11.7	1,524	29.2	2,135	40.9
São Tomé and Príncipe	..	..	..	..	..	..
Senegal	3,082	24.0	5,637	44.0	8,720	68.0
Seychelles	912	119.3	975	127.6	1,887	246.9
Sierra Leone	305	15.7	554	28.5	859	44.2
Somalia	..	..	..	..	..	..
South Africa	77,883	27.3	80,328	28.1	158,210	55.4
Sudan	8,230	15.1	11,391	20.8	19,622	35.9
Swaziland	1,794	59.8	2,295	76.5	4,089	136.3
Tanzania	4,963	23.2	7,511	35.2	12,475	58.4
Togo	..	..	..	..	..	..
Uganda	3,753	23.4	5,557	34.6	9,309	58.0
Zambia	4,560	35.6	4,118	32.2	8,678	67.8
Zimbabwe	2,040	36.3	3,678	65.4	5,718	101.7
NORTH AFRICA	**200,244**	**32.1**	**193,682**	**36.6**	**393,926**	**68.7**
Algeria	56,798	40.4	50,772	36.1	107,570	76.5
Egypt, Arab Rep.	47,185	25.0	60,048	31.9	107,233	56.9
Libya	..	..	..	..	..	..
Morocco	26,121	28.6	36,088	39.5	62,209	68.1
Tunisia	20,568	52.0	21,894	55.3	42,463	107.3
ALL AFRICA	**496,886**	**30.7**	**509,907**	**34.7**	**1,006,794**	**65.4**

a. Provisional.

Net income		Net current transfers		Current account balance		Total reserves including gold	
Current prices ($ millions) 2009[a]	Share of GDP (%) 2009[a]	Current prices ($ millions) 2009[a]	Share of GDP (%) 2009[a]	Current prices ($ millions) 2009[a]	Share of GDP (%) 2009[a]	Current prices ($ millions) 2009[a]	Share of GDP (%) 2009[a]
..	**..**	**..**	**..**	**–12,976**	**–1.6**	**160,688**	**16.8**
..	..	..	..	–1,649	–0.3	121,086	18.1
..	..	..	..	–23,308	–6.3	75,576	15.2
–6,823	–9.0	–370	–0.5	–7,572	–10.0	13,664	18.1
..	..	..	..	..	..	1,230	18.5
–452	–3.8	878	7.4	–526	–4.4	8,704	73.6
..	..	..	..	..	..	1,296	15.9
–17	–1.3	257	19.4	–164	–12.3	323	24.4
–303	–1.4	393	1.8	–1,137	–5.1	3,676	16.6
–54	–3.5	349	22.5	–154	–9.9	366	23.6
..	..	..	..	..	..	211	10.5
..	..	..	..	..	..	617	9.0
..	..	..	..	..	..	..	..
..	..	..	..	..	..	1,615	15.3
..	..	..	..	..	..	3,806	39.7
–890	–3.8	–115	–0.5	1,670	7.2	3,267	14.0
22	2.1	86	8.2	–71	–6.8	242	23.1
..	..	..	..	..	..	3,252	31.2
..	..	..	..	..	..	..	..
–37	–0.1	3,459	12.1	–2,191	–7.7	1,781	6.2
..	..	..	..	..	..	1,993	18.0
–8	–1.1	135	18.4	63	8.6	224	30.6
–296	–1.1	2,078	7.9	–1,198	–4.6	..	..
–168	–4.1	34	0.8	–403	–9.8	..	..
..	..	..	..	..	..	169	20.1
–58	–0.2	2,297	7.8	–1,661	–5.7	3,850	13.1
424	26.8	547	34.7	–32	–2.0	..	..
–128	–14.6	1,101	125.6	–277	–31.6	372	42.5
..	..	..	..	..	..	1,135	13.2
..	..	..	..	..	..	163	3.5
..	..	..	..	..	..	1,604	17.8
..	..	..	..	..	..	238	7.9
27	0.3	224	2.6	–675	–7.9	2,316	27.0
–95	–1.0	764	7.8	–1,171	–12.0	2,181	22.3
–70	–0.8	1,261	13.6	120	1.3	2,051	22.1
..	..	..	..	..	..	656	12.2
–10,020	–5.8	17,977	10.4	21,659	12.5	45,510	26.3
–37	–0.7	604	11.6	–379	–7.3	743	14.2
0	–0.1	5	2.4	–79	–41.3	..	..
..	..	..	..	..	..	2,123	16.6
–111	–14.5	58	7.5	–284	–37.2	191	24.9
–36	–1.8	148	7.6	–193	–9.9	405	20.9
..	..	..	..	..	..	..	..
–6,389	–2.2	–2,684	–0.9	–11,327	–4.0	39,603	13.9
–2,402	–4.4	1,480	2.7	–3,908	–7.1	1,094	2.0
–123	–4.1	192	6.4	–414	–13.8	959	32.0
–175	–0.8	683	3.2	–1,816	–8.5	3,470	16.2
..	..	..	..	..	..	703	24.6
–329	–2.0	1,133	7.1	–451	–2.8	2,994	18.7
–1,363	–10.6	516	4.0	–406	–3.2	1,892	14.8
..	..	..	..	..	..	..	..
..	**..**	**..**	**..**	**–174**	**0.0**	**328,625**	**62.9**
..	..	..	..	..	..	155,112	110.3
–2,076	–1.1	7,960	4.2	–3,349	–1.8	34,897	18.5
578	0.9	–1,572	–2.5	9,381	15.0	103,754	166.4
–1,495	–1.6	7,451	8.2	–4,971	–5.4	23,568	25.8
–2,011	–5.1	1,951	4.9	–1,234	–3.1	11,294	28.5
..	**..**	**..**	**..**	**–13,150**	**–1.1**	**489,313**	**33.1**

Table 2.28 Exchange rates and purchasing power parity

	Official exchange rate (local currency units to $)			Purchasing power parity (PPP) conversion factor (local currency units to international $)			Ratio of PPP conversion factor to market exchange rate		
	2007	2008	2009	2007	2008	2009	2007	2008	2009
SUB-SAHARAN AFRICA									
Excluding South Africa									
Excl. S. Africa & Nigeria									
Angola	49.7	59.7	55.7	76.7	75.0	79.3	0.6	0.8	0.7
Benin	222.0	232.7	233.3	479.3	447.8	472.2	0.5	0.5	0.5
Botswana	3.0	3.4	3.2	6.1	6.8	7.2	0.5	0.5	0.5
Burkina Faso	194.3	201.2	205.5	479.3	447.8	472.2	0.4	0.4	0.4
Burundi	363.1	444.6	500.6	1,081.9	1,185.7	1,230.2	0.3	0.4	0.4
Cameroon	249.3	254.2	243.3	479.3	447.8	472.2	0.5	0.6	0.5
Cape Verde	65.7	64.9	66.8	80.6	75.3	79.4	0.8	0.9	0.8
Central African Republic	264.4	274.7	282.8	479.3	447.8	472.2	0.6	0.6	0.6
Chad	232.9	255.2	221.6	479.3	447.8	472.2	0.5	0.6	0.5
Comoros	227.2	234.6	243.2	359.5	335.9	354.1	0.6	0.7	0.7
Congo, Dem. Rep.	274.8	321.0	414.3	516.7	559.3	809.8	0.5	0.6	0.5
Congo, Rep.	300.1	367.3	289.8	479.3	447.8	472.2	0.6	0.8	0.6
Côte d'Ivoire	288.9	305.7	306.9	479.3	447.8	472.2	0.6	0.7	0.6
Djibouti	86.1	92.3	93.0	177.7	177.7	177.7	0.5	0.5	0.5
Equatorial Guinea	304.3	368.3	242.6	479.3	447.8	472.2	0.6	0.8	0.5
Eritrea	6.9	9.0	9.8	15.4	15.4	15.4	0.4	0.6	0.6
Ethiopia	2.8	3.5	4.3	9.0	9.6	11.8	0.3	0.4	0.4
Gabon	272.6	306.0	245.7	479.3	447.8	472.2	0.6	0.7	0.5
Gambia, The	7.7	8.0	8.1	24.9	22.2	26.6	0.3	0.4	0.3
Ghana	0.7	0.9	1.0	0.9	1.1	1.4	0.8	0.8	0.7
Guinea	1,775.0	1,981.9	2,066.8	4,122.8	5,500.0	..	0.4	0.4	0.4
Guinea-Bissau	211.2	228.5	229.0	479.3	447.8	472.2	0.4	0.5	0.5
Kenya	31.4	34.4	36.3	67.3	69.2	77.4	0.5	0.5	0.5
Lesotho	4.0	4.4	4.5	7.0	8.3	8.5	0.6	0.5	0.5
Liberia	33.2	35.9	38.2	61.3	63.2	68.3	0.5	0.6	0.6
Madagascar	743.2	794.4	852.8	1,873.9	1,708.4	1,956.2	0.4	0.5	0.4
Malawi	48.1	51.3	55.0	140.0	140.5	141.2	0.3	0.4	0.4
Mali	250.5	266.6	275.4	479.3	447.8	472.2	0.5	0.6	0.6
Mauritania	122.3	134.5	125.0	258.6	238.2	262.4	0.5	0.6	0.5
Mauritius	15.9	16.7	16.8	31.3	28.5	32.0	0.5	0.6	0.5
Mozambique	12.0	12.7	13.0	25.8	24.3	27.5	0.5	0.5	0.5
Namibia	4.8	5.3	5.6	7.0	8.3	8.5	0.7	0.6	0.7
Niger	220.0	231.8	241.0	479.3	447.8	472.2	0.5	0.5	0.5
Nigeria	70.7	76.7	75.6	125.8	118.5	148.9	0.6	0.6	0.5
Rwanda	215.1	237.3	261.0	547.0	546.8	568.3	0.4	0.4	0.5
São Tomé and Príncipe	7,514.7	9,049.2	10,364.2	13,536.8	14,695.2	16,208.5	0.6	0.6	0.6
Senegal	259.5	268.9	265.2	479.3	447.8	472.2	0.5	0.6	0.6
Seychelles	3.8	4.7	6.0	6.7	9.5	13.6	0.6	0.5	0.4
Sierra Leone	1,221.5	1,329.2	1,399.7	2,985.2	2,981.5	3,385.7	0.4	0.4	0.4
Somalia	..	..	..	..	..	..	..	..	..
South Africa	4.2	4.5	4.7	7.0	8.3	8.5	0.6	0.5	0.6
Sudan	1.2	1.4	1.3	2.0	2.1	2.3	0.6	0.7	0.6
Swaziland	3.7	4.0	4.2	7.0	8.3	8.5	0.5	0.5	0.5
Tanzania	425.0	458.0	487.3	1,245.0	1,196.3	1,320.3	0.3	0.4	0.4
Togo	229.0	238.6	239.5	479.3	447.8	472.2	0.5	0.5	0.5
Uganda	638.1	664.8	767.5	1,723.5	1,720.4	2,030.3	0.4	0.4	0.4
Zambia	2,866.3	3,126.6	3,492.7	4,002.5	3,745.7	5,046.1	0.7	0.8	0.7
Zimbabwe	..	..	..	9,675.8	6,715,424,238.8	..	..	..	..
NORTH AFRICA									
Algeria	35.6	39.9	35.8	69.3	64.6	72.6	0.5	0.6	0.5
Egypt, Arab Rep.	1.8	2.0	2.2	5.6	5.4	5.5	0.3	0.4	0.4
Libya	0.9	1.1	0.7	1.3	1.2	1.3	0.7	0.9	0.6
Morocco	4.8	5.0	5.0	8.2	7.8	8.1	0.6	0.6	0.6
Tunisia	0.6	0.6	0.6	1.3	1.2	1.4	0.5	0.5	0.5
ALL AFRICA									

Real effective exchange rate (index: 2000 = 100)			Gross domestic product					
			PPP $ billions			Per capita PPP $		
2007	2008	2009	2007	2008	2009	2007	2008	2009
101.5	**104.5**	**105.7**	**1,630.7**	**1,759.6**	**1,812.9**	**2,036.1**	**2,144.0**	**2,155.8**
102.0	105.0	106.6	1,155.6	1,256.7	1,315.6	1,535.4	1,628.1	1,661.8
101.5	104.5	105.7	856.1	932.4	969.7	1,415.3	1,502.2	1,522.6
..	..	..	91.4	105.8	107.5	5,206.4	5,873.0	5,812.0
..	..	..	12.0	12.9	13.5	1,426.9	1,484.8	1,507.9
..	..	..	25.5	26.8	26.1	13,459.8	13,971.3	13,384.5
..	..	..	16.7	17.9	18.7	1,133.6	1,175.4	1,186.9
96.7	99.3	109.4	2.9	3.1	3.3	372.4	386.1	392.1
102.5	105.6	108.0	39.8	41.8	43.0	2,131.2	2,190.6	2,204.9
..	..	..	1.6	1.8	1.8	3,320.3	3,561.3	3,643.6
105.3	113.4	115.8	3.1	3.2	3.3	729.0	747.0	757.4
..	..	..	14.4	14.7	14.6	1,357.0	1,344.4	1,300.1
..	..	..	0.7	0.8	0.8	1,170.3	1,179.1	1,182.9
106.7	106.3	597.2	18.7	20.3	21.1	299.6	316.4	319.1
..	..	..	13.3	14.4	15.6	3,752.4	3,976.3	4,238.0
101.0	105.8	105.7	32.8	34.3	35.9	1,631.7	1,665.5	1,701.2
..	..	..	1.7	1.9	2.0	2,097.3	2,227.5	2,319.5
106.4	115.5	118.1	19.8	22.5	21.5	30,836.7	34,166.0	31,779.1
..	..	..	3.1	2.8	2.9	639.2	571.8	580.5
..	..	..	62.3	70.5	77.4	792.3	874.0	934.4
101.0	104.5	105.3	20.3	21.3	21.3	14,309.1	14,689.5	14,419.2
108.3	114.8	104.4	2.1	2.3	2.4	1,304.7	1,376.5	1,414.6
104.6	99.5	91.8	31.6	35.0	37.0	1,382.6	1,500.5	1,552.4
..	..	..	9.8	10.5	10.5	1,016.9	1,066.2	1,047.8
..	..	..	1.6	1.7	1.7	1,018.6	1,053.7	1,071.2
..	..	..	58.3	60.5	62.6	1,543.1	1,559.6	1,572.6
96.5	87.7	93.2	2.8	3.0	3.0	1,374.2	1,454.2	1,467.6
..	..	..	1.4	1.5	1.6	373.7	391.1	396.0
..	..	..	18.5	20.3	19.7	995.1	1,060.5	1,004.0
95.0	97.8	107.5	10.1	11.2	12.1	696.8	752.1	794.3
..	..	..	13.7	14.7	15.4	1,101.7	1,153.3	1,185.5
..	..	..	6.0	6.4	6.3	1,911.7	1,977.2	1,928.7
..	..	..	14.8	15.9	16.4	11,733.3	12,518.9	12,838.4
..	..	..	17.3	18.9	20.3	791.7	843.8	885.2
..	..	..	13.0	13.9	13.9	6,245.8	6,527.5	6,410.1
..	..	..	9.2	10.3	10.5	654.1	703.8	689.8
104.9	116.5	109.4	295.3	319.9	340.9	1,999.4	2,115.7	2,203.3
..	..	..	9.5	10.8	11.4	1,006.3	1,112.2	1,136.0
..	..	..	0.3	0.3	0.3	1,656.1	1,762.0	1,820.0
..	..	..	20.9	22.1	22.8	1,757.7	1,807.6	1,816.6
..	..	..	1.8	1.8	1.7	21,463.1	21,255.3	19,587.0
96.2	102.8	104.5	4.1	4.4	4.6	750.1	788.6	808.0
..	..	..	..	..	..	..	..	..
90.4	80.4	87.8	482.7	511.4	506.9	10,002.5	10,480.9	10,277.8
..	..	..	81.1	88.6	93.4	2,006.2	2,141.8	2,209.7
..	..	..	5.5	5.8	5.9	4,813.6	4,966.0	4,998.4
..	..	..	49.3	54.1	57.9	1,194.1	1,273.6	1,323.6
98.9	104.3	104.8	5.2	5.4	5.6	830.2	842.4	850.3
101.5	103.6	103.1	33.2	36.8	39.8	1,082.7	1,164.0	1,217.2
120.5	138.8	119.5	15.9	17.2	18.5	1,293.9	1,365.2	1,430.2
..	..	..	..	..	..	..	..	..
98.5	**100.1**	**102.1**	**974.0**	**1,046.3**	**1,094.3**	**6,029.5**	**6,374.8**	**6,563.2**
98.5	103.7	102.1	264.5	276.8	285.2	7,812.4	8,052.2	8,172.5
..	..	..	407.1	445.8	470.8	5,085.5	5,468.4	5,672.6
..	..	..	96.9	102.8	105.9	15,713.7	16,335.9	16,502.0
99.7	100.1	102.4	127.8	137.9	146.1	4,094.6	4,364.5	4,566.5
96.1	82.2	94.2	77.5	82.9	86.3	7,584.0	8,028.9	8,272.5
101.0	**104.0**	**105.0**	**2,602.1**	**2,803.0**	**2,904.5**	**2,703.7**	**2,846.2**	**2,882.3**

Table

2.29 Agriculture value added

	Share of GDP (%)											
										Annual average		
	1980	1990	2003	2004	2005	2006	2007	2008	2009[a]	1980–89	1990–99	2000–09
SUB-SAHARAN AFRICA	**18.5**	**18.9**	**18.6**	**17.1**	**16.5**	**15.9**	**15.5**	**12.7**	**13.1**	**18.4**	**18.3**	**16.2**
Excluding South Africa	31.6	31.3	29.6	27.3	26.6	25.6	24.7	22.4	23.5	31.1	30.7	26.6
Excl. S. Africa & Nigeria	31.6	31.3	26.7	25.7	25.2	24.1	22.8	22.4	23.5	31.1	30.7	25.2
Angola	..	17.9	8.3	8.6	7.7	8.9	8.0	6.6	10.2	15.2	11.3	8.0
Benin	35.4	36.1	32.1	32.1	32.2	..	..	..	..	33.8	36.1	33.7
Botswana	14.7	4.9	2.5	2.0	1.8	1.8	2.1	1.9	3.1	8.7	4.2	2.2
Burkina Faso	29.4	28.8	35.6	32.9	34.1	33.3	..	..	..	29.8	33.8	33.8
Burundi	62.2	55.9	40.1	40.1	34.8	..	..	..	..	58.1	50.8	39.2
Cameroon	31.3	24.6	21.7	20.5	19.5	19.9	19.5	..	..	25.7	24.3	20.9
Cape Verde	..	14.4	6.8	9.7	9.2	9.4	9.2	9.1	9.2	16.6	12.9	9.0
Central African Republic	40.0	47.6	59.7	55.3	54.4	55.0	53.9	52.9	55.5	44.3	48.4	54.9
Chad	45.1	29.3	33.6	23.5	12.3	11.7	12.5	13.6	..	36.9	36.7	25.6
Comoros	34.0	41.4	50.5	50.9	51.0	45.2	45.3	45.8	46.3	36.3	40.2	48.4
Congo, Dem. Rep.	26.8	31.0	51.0	47.3	45.5	45.7	42.5	40.2	42.9	30.4	47.0	47.6
Congo, Rep.	11.7	12.9	6.3	5.5	4.5	4.0	4.4	3.7	4.5	10.0	10.5	5.0
Côte d'Ivoire	25.9	32.5	25.6	23.2	22.8	22.9	23.9	25.0	24.4	27.1	27.2	24.2
Djibouti	..	3.1	3.6	3.6	3.5	3.5	3.9	..	..	3.3	3.4	3.6
Equatorial Guinea	..	61.5	5.5	4.1	2.6	2.8	2.7	2.0	3.5	65.8	41.5	4.6
Eritrea	..	..	14.7	13.9	22.6	24.6	24.3	14.4	14.4	..	22.9	17.8
Ethiopia	..	54.3	41.9	44.2	46.7	47.9	46.2	43.8	50.7	56.5	58.4	40.2
Gabon	6.8	7.3	6.1	5.6	4.9	4.9	4.8	4.1	5.1	7.7	7.7	5.4
Gambia, The	30.8	29.0	31.1	33.7	32.1	30.3	28.7	28.5	27.5	34.0	28.7	31.1
Ghana	60.1	45.1	40.2	41.5	40.9	30.4	29.0	31.0	31.7	52.5	42.6	36.3
Guinea	..	23.8	22.3	25.1	24.2	23.8	25.3	24.9	17.2	24.0	20.1	22.8
Guinea-Bissau	44.3	60.8	..	..	..	..	..	..	..	48.6	56.3	55.0
Kenya	32.6	29.5	29.0	28.0	27.2	26.7	20.1	21.0	22.6	32.4	30.8	26.8
Lesotho	24.6	24.9	10.2	10.1	8.6	9.8	8.2	7.8	8.4	24.7	19.3	9.9
Liberia	35.9	54.4	71.6	68.2	65.8	56.9	55.0	61.3	..	35.8	67.2	66.6
Madagascar	30.1	28.6	29.2	28.8	28.3	27.5	25.7	24.8	29.1	34.3	28.6	28.2
Malawi	43.7	45.0	35.7	34.6	32.6	31.2	30.3	30.1	30.5	44.2	37.3	34.0
Mali	48.3	45.5	38.8	36.4	36.6	36.9	36.5	..	..	44.4	46.7	37.4
Mauritania	30.4	29.6	27.5	25.6	23.7	14.6	18.8	18.9	20.6	30.4	33.9	23.0
Mauritius	13.1	12.9	6.3	6.4	6.0	5.6	4.9	4.4	4.3	14.9	10.2	5.8
Mozambique	37.1	37.1	28.0	27.4	27.0	27.9	27.7	30.5	31.5	39.7	34.7	27.4
Namibia	11.2	11.7	10.9	9.7	11.3	10.5	9.4	9.3	9.4	11.2	11.3	10.4
Niger	43.1	35.3	39.6	..	..	..	..	..	..	38.6	39.4	39.3
Nigeria	..	..	42.7	34.2	32.8	32.0	32.7	..	..	..	..	37.2
Rwanda	45.8	32.5	37.0	38.6	38.4	38.4	35.6	32.5	34.2	40.2	40.6	36.5
São Tomé and Príncipe	..	..	21.1	22.6	16.8	..	..	..	..	..	..	20.0
Senegal	20.1	19.9	17.6	15.9	16.7	14.8	13.4	15.5	16.6	22.0	19.7	16.4
Seychelles	6.8	4.8	3.0	3.0	2.5	2.4	2.1	2.1	2.0	6.1	3.9	2.6
Sierra Leone	33.0	46.9	46.7	44.9	51.6	51.1	49.9	50.2	51.4	40.0	47.9	49.9
Somalia	68.4	65.5	..	..	..	..	..	..	..	66.5	65.5	..
South Africa	6.2	4.6	3.4	3.1	2.7	2.9	3.4	3.2	3.0	5.5	4.1	3.3
Sudan	32.9	40.6	38.8	35.2	32.0	30.1	28.1	26.2	29.7	35.4	42.1	34.7
Swaziland	22.7	10.4	9.6	8.9	8.5	7.5	7.3	7.3	7.3	19.5	12.1	9.1
Tanzania	..	46.0	32.5	33.3	31.8	30.4	30.0	29.7	28.8	..	44.5	31.5
Togo	27.5	33.8	40.8	41.2	43.7	..	..	..	..	31.8	37.4	39.3
Uganda	72.0	56.6	26.1	22.9	26.7	25.6	23.6	22.7	24.7	57.6	47.9	25.6
Zambia	15.1	20.6	22.6	23.0	23.3	22.4	21.8	18.9	21.6	15.9	21.1	22.0
Zimbabwe	15.7	16.5	16.8	20.1	19.2	21.3	22.8	20.2	17.9	16.2	17.0	18.8
NORTH AFRICA	**15.5**	**16.9**	**13.3**	**12.5**	**11.4**	**11.3**	**10.8**	**10.3**	**13.1**	**16.2**	**15.5**	**12.4**
Algeria	8.5	11.4	10.5	10.2	8.2	8.0	8.0	6.9	11.7	9.9	11.2	9.3
Egypt, Arab Rep.	18.3	19.4	16.3	15.2	14.9	14.1	14.1	13.2	13.7	19.8	17.2	15.1
Libya	..	..	4.3	3.0	2.3	2.0	2.1	1.9	..	..	..	3.0
Morocco	18.5	18.3	17.3	16.3	14.7	16.9	13.7	14.6	16.4	16.4	17.8	15.8
Tunisia	14.1	15.7	12.1	12.7	11.2	10.8	10.2	9.8	7.8	13.8	14.0	10.9
ALL AFRICA	**17.2**	**18.0**	**16.4**	**15.1**	**14.4**	**13.9**	**13.5**	**11.6**	**13.1**	**17.4**	**17.1**	**14.6**

a. Provisional.

Table

2.30 Industry value added

	Share of GDP (%)											
										Annual average		
	1980	1990	2003	2004	2005	2006	2007	2008	2009[a]	1980–89	1990–99	2000–09
SUB-SAHARAN AFRICA	**36.9**	**32.1**	**29.9**	**30.9**	**31.7**	**32.0**	**31.9**	**31.7**	**29.6**	**34.2**	**29.6**	**30.6**
Excluding South Africa	24.6	25.1	28.7	30.7	32.1	32.6	32.4	31.0	28.0	24.7	24.9	29.7
Excl. S. Africa & Nigeria	24.6	25.1	26.9	28.2	29.5	30.4	30.4	31.0	28.0	24.7	24.9	28.6
Angola	..	40.8	67.4	66.1	72.6	69.7	67.9	67.5	59.0	39.4	56.9	67.5
Benin	12.3	13.2	13.7	13.3	13.4	..	..	..	..	14.0	13.7	13.7
Botswana	50.7	61.0	49.5	51.0	50.6	54.3	53.1	52.9	39.6	57.5	54.8	51.5
Burkina Faso	20.5	21.0	21.6	23.2	22.7	22.4	..	..	..	21.0	21.1	22.1
Burundi	12.6	19.0	18.9	18.9	20.0	..	..	..	..	15.1	18.7	19.0
Cameroon	25.6	29.5	30.7	30.7	30.4	31.4	30.6	..	..	31.8	30.3	31.8
Cape Verde	..	21.4	19.7	15.2	16.8	17.4	17.8	18.8	20.1	19.0	19.7	17.5
Central African Republic	20.1	19.7	15.7	14.0	14.1	14.2	14.2	14.2	14.6	16.2	20.2	14.8
Chad	8.9	17.7	24.4	47.1	60.4	60.6	54.3	48.8	..	13.5	13.7	37.3
Comoros	13.2	8.3	12.7	12.2	11.0	11.8	11.9	12.0	12.1	12.5	11.4	11.8
Congo, Dem. Rep.	35.0	29.0	21.5	24.5	26.9	27.7	28.4	28.0	24.0	30.1	20.6	24.3
Congo, Rep.	46.6	40.6	61.2	65.9	71.9	75.5	73.1	77.3	71.1	45.1	45.4	69.7
Côte d'Ivoire	19.7	23.2	21.6	23.1	25.9	25.9	25.3	26.1	25.2	20.8	22.2	24.5
Djibouti	..	22.0	16.2	16.6	16.6	16.4	16.9	..	..	20.6	16.6	16.2
Equatorial Guinea	..	10.6	89.2	92.1	94.4	94.4	94.6	95.7	91.9	8.9	38.5	91.5
Eritrea	..	..	24.5	25.6	20.5	18.2	19.2	22.3	22.2	..	18.4	22.0
Ethiopia	..	11.1	14.1	14.1	13.0	12.7	13.3	13.0	10.7	11.6	10.2	13.0
Gabon	60.4	43.0	52.0	55.3	61.4	61.2	60.3	64.3	53.8	53.7	48.2	56.7
Gambia, The	14.9	13.1	14.0	13.2	13.3	14.3	14.8	15.1	15.5	13.7	13.7	14.1
Ghana	12.3	16.9	27.8	27.1	27.5	20.8	20.7	20.4	18.9	13.8	24.5	24.8
Guinea	..	33.3	31.5	33.7	38.9	43.4	43.4	46.7	53.0	33.6	30.0	39.1
Guinea-Bissau	19.7	18.6	..	..	..	..	..	..	..	15.7	12.5	13.0
Kenya	20.8	19.0	17.6	18.2	19.1	18.5	14.9	15.1	15.3	19.4	17.8	17.0
Lesotho	26.5	34.4	33.9	33.9	35.1	36.7	39.0	37.9	34.1	27.7	42.3	35.0
Liberia	28.1	16.8	10.6	13.4	15.7	17.1	18.9	16.8	..	27.8	11.0	13.5
Madagascar	16.1	12.8	15.4	15.9	15.8	16.1	16.3	16.2	16.0	13.8	12.1	15.5
Malawi	22.5	28.9	19.4	17.4	17.0	17.0	16.3	16.1	16.1	22.7	22.7	17.2
Mali	13.2	15.9	23.6	23.9	24.2	24.0	24.2	..	..	14.8	17.0	24.3
Mauritania	26.0	28.8	23.6	28.1	29.3	56.3	38.3	40.6	34.7	27.0	26.6	33.4
Mauritius	26.2	32.8	30.3	29.1	27.6	27.6	28.0	29.2	29.1	28.9	32.1	29.4
Mozambique	34.4	18.4	26.1	27.4	25.3	26.4	25.9	23.7	23.6	24.8	17.1	25.2
Namibia	55.8	38.0	28.3	29.4	29.2	34.6	35.6	37.8	32.7	44.2	30.6	31.9
Niger	22.9	16.2	17.1	..	..	..	..	..	..	19.8	17.4	17.2
Nigeria	..	..	36.8	42.1	43.5	41.9	40.7	..	..	..	..	39.2
Rwanda	21.5	24.6	12.3	13.9	14.1	13.8	13.9	14.9	14.5	21.0	19.5	13.9
São Tomé and Príncipe	..	..	17.8	21.0	20.5	..	..	..	..	..	..	18.7
Senegal	20.1	22.2	24.3	24.9	23.8	23.0	23.6	21.7	21.7	20.7	23.5	23.6
Seychelles	15.6	16.3	27.4	28.2	21.9	20.5	20.2	20.2	19.7	16.5	21.5	24.5
Sierra Leone	21.9	19.2	24.7	24.2	23.6	23.2	24.3	23.5	22.1	15.9	32.4	24.4
Somalia	8.0	..	..	..	..	..	..	..	..	8.0	..	..
South Africa	48.4	40.1	31.7	31.3	31.2	31.2	31.2	32.5	31.1	43.8	35.0	31.7
Sudan	14.1	15.3	22.0	25.8	28.3	29.2	31.2	34.0	26.0	15.2	13.5	25.8
Swaziland	30.2	43.2	47.9	46.7	45.6	48.5	49.4	49.4	49.4	32.3	43.5	47.6
Tanzania	..	17.7	22.5	22.3	22.7	22.9	23.3	23.1	24.3	..	16.4	22.1
Togo	24.8	22.5	22.2	22.8	24.0	..	..	..	..	22.0	21.0	20.4
Uganda	4.5	11.1	24.2	22.1	25.0	24.2	26.6	27.4	25.8	9.4	14.9	24.5
Zambia	42.1	51.3	26.5	27.8	31.6	35.3	38.5	41.4	34.1	45.5	39.2	31.2
Zimbabwe	29.0	33.1	21.6	27.1	29.6	33.9	34.9	32.4	29.0	30.2	30.6	27.7
NORTH AFRICA	**40.3**	**34.3**	**43.0**	**43.0**	**44.8**	**46.3**	**45.0**	**46.6**	**39.3**	**36.3**	**35.9**	**42.4**
Algeria	57.7	48.2	54.8	56.4	61.3	62.3	61.3	62.1	54.5	52.1	49.7	57.8
Egypt, Arab Rep.	36.8	28.7	35.2	36.5	35.9	38.4	36.3	37.5	37.3	30.6	31.8	35.8
Libya	..	..	75.1	68.6	75.5	78.5	76.4	78.2	..	..	..	74.1
Morocco	31.0	33.4	27.9	28.5	28.2	27.2	27.3	30.3	28.5	33.2	32.0	28.2
Tunisia	31.1	29.8	28.3	28.2	28.9	29.2	29.1	32.1	30.0	31.5	28.8	29.3
ALL AFRICA	**38.4**	**33.0**	**35.4**	**36.0**	**37.2**	**38.1**	**37.5**	**38.7**	**33.8**	**35.1**	**32.2**	**35.7**

a. Provisional.

Table 2.31 Services plus discrepancy value added

	Share of GDP (%)											
										Annual average		
	1980	1990	2003	2004	2005	2006	2007	2008	2009[a]	1980–89	1990–99	2000–09
SUB-SAHARAN AFRICA	**44.6**	**49.2**	**51.4**	**52.0**	**51.8**	**52.1**	**52.8**	**55.6**	**57.3**	**47.5**	**52.1**	**53.2**
Excluding South Africa	43.8	43.9	41.8	42.0	41.3	41.8	43.0	46.6	48.5	44.3	44.4	43.7
Excl. S. Africa & Nigeria	43.8	43.9	46.5	46.2	45.2	45.5	47.0	46.6	48.5	44.3	44.4	46.2
Angola	..	41.2	24.3	25.3	19.8	21.4	24.1	25.9	30.8	45.4	31.8	24.5
Benin	52.3	50.7	54.2	54.6	54.4	..	..	..	..	52.2	50.2	52.6
Botswana	34.6	34.1	48.0	47.0	47.6	43.9	44.8	45.2	57.3	33.8	40.9	46.3
Burkina Faso	50.1	50.2	42.8	44.0	43.2	44.4	..	..	..	49.2	45.1	44.1
Burundi	25.1	25.2	41.0	41.0	45.1	..	..	..	..	26.8	30.5	41.7
Cameroon	43.1	46.0	47.6	48.9	50.1	48.8	49.9	..	..	42.5	45.4	47.3
Cape Verde	..	64.3	73.4	75.1	74.0	73.2	73.0	72.1	70.7	64.4	67.4	73.6
Central African Republic	39.9	32.7	24.6	30.7	31.4	30.7	31.9	32.9	29.9	39.5	31.4	30.4
Chad	46.0	53.0	42.0	29.4	27.3	27.8	33.2	37.5	..	49.6	49.6	37.1
Comoros	52.8	50.3	36.7	36.9	38.0	..	..	..	..	51.2	48.4	38.0
Congo, Dem. Rep.	38.2	40.0	27.5	28.3	27.5	26.6	29.1	31.8	33.0	39.6	32.4	28.1
Congo, Rep.	41.7	46.5	32.6	28.6	23.6	20.5	22.6	19.0	24.4	44.9	44.1	25.3
Côte d'Ivoire	54.4	44.3	52.8	53.7	51.3	51.2	50.9	48.9	50.4	52.0	50.6	51.3
Djibouti	..	74.9	80.2	79.8	79.9	80.1	79.3	..	..	76.1	80.0	80.2
Equatorial Guinea	..	27.8	5.3	3.8	3.0	2.9	2.8	2.3	4.7	25.2	20.0	3.8
Eritrea	..	..	60.8	60.5	56.9	57.2	56.5	63.3	63.4	..	58.7	60.1
Ethiopia	..	34.5	44.0	41.8	40.3	39.4	40.5	43.2	38.6	31.9	31.4	40.8
Gabon	32.8	49.7	41.9	39.1	33.8	33.9	34.9	31.7	41.2	38.6	44.0	37.8
Gambia, The	54.3	57.9	54.9	53.1	54.6	55.5	56.5	56.4	57.1	52.3	57.6	54.8
Ghana	27.6	38.1	32.0	31.4	31.6	48.8	50.2	48.6	49.5	33.6	32.9	38.9
Guinea	..	42.9	46.3	41.3	36.9	32.8	31.3	28.4	29.8	42.3	49.9	38.1
Guinea-Bissau	36.1	20.6	..	..	..	..	..	..	..	35.7	31.1	32.0
Kenya	46.6	51.4	53.4	53.7	53.7	54.8	65.0	63.9	62.1	48.2	51.5	56.2
Lesotho	48.9	40.7	55.9	56.0	56.3	53.5	52.8	54.3	57.5	47.6	38.4	55.1
Liberia	36.0	28.8	17.7	18.4	18.4	26.0	26.1	21.9	..	36.4	21.8	19.8
Madagascar	53.9	58.6	55.4	55.3	55.9	56.4	58.1	59.0	54.9	51.9	59.3	56.3
Malawi	33.7	26.1	44.9	47.9	50.3	51.9	53.4	53.8	53.4	33.1	40.1	48.8
Mali	38.5	38.6	37.6	39.8	39.3	39.1	..	..	..	40.8	36.4	38.1
Mauritania	43.6	41.6	48.9	46.3	47.0	29.1	42.9	40.6	44.8	42.6	39.4	43.6
Mauritius	60.7	54.4	63.4	64.4	66.4	66.9	67.1	66.4	66.6	56.2	57.7	64.8
Mozambique	28.5	44.5	45.9	45.2	47.7	45.7	46.4	45.9	44.9	35.6	48.2	47.4
Namibia	33.0	50.2	60.7	60.8	59.5	54.9	55.0	52.8	58.0	44.6	58.1	57.7
Niger	34.0	48.6	43.2	..	..	..	..	..	..	41.6	43.2	43.5
Nigeria	..	..	20.5	23.7	23.7	26.1	26.6	..	..	..	..	23.6
Rwanda	32.6	42.8	50.7	47.6	47.5	47.8	50.4	52.6	51.3	38.8	39.9	49.6
São Tomé and Príncipe	..	..	61.2	56.4	62.7	..	..	..	..	..	..	61.3
Senegal	59.9	57.9	58.2	59.2	59.5	62.2	63.0	62.8	61.7	57.3	56.8	60.0
Seychelles	77.5	78.9	69.6	68.8	75.6	77.1	77.7	77.7	78.3	77.4	74.6	72.8
Sierra Leone	45.0	33.9	28.6	30.9	24.8	25.7	25.9	26.3	26.6	44.2	19.7	25.7
Somalia	23.6	..	..	..	..	..	..	..	..	25.1	..	..
South Africa	45.4	55.3	64.9	65.6	66.2	66.0	65.5	64.3	65.8	50.8	60.9	65.1
Sudan	53.0	44.2	39.3	38.9	39.7	40.8	40.7	39.7	44.3	49.5	44.5	39.6
Swaziland	47.1	46.5	42.5	44.4	45.8	43.9	43.3	43.3	43.3	48.2	44.4	43.3
Tanzania	..	36.4	45.0	44.3	45.5	46.7	46.7	47.2	46.9	..	39.1	46.4
Togo	47.7	43.7	37.1	36.0	32.4	..	..	..	..	46.2	41.7	40.3
Uganda	23.5	32.4	49.7	55.0	48.3	50.2	49.8	49.9	49.5	33.0	37.2	49.8
Zambia	42.8	28.1	50.9	49.1	45.1	42.3	39.8	39.7	44.3	38.6	39.7	46.8
Zimbabwe	55.3	50.4	61.6	52.7	51.2	44.8	42.3	47.5	53.0	53.6	52.4	53.5
NORTH AFRICA	**44.2**	**48.8**	**43.7**	**44.5**	**43.8**	**42.4**	**44.2**	**43.1**	**47.7**	**47.5**	**48.6**	**45.2**
Algeria	33.8	40.5	34.7	33.5	30.5	29.7	30.7	31.0	33.7	38.0	39.1	32.9
Egypt, Arab Rep.	45.0	52.0	48.4	48.3	49.2	47.5	49.6	49.2	49.0	49.7	51.0	49.1
Libya	..	..	20.6	28.4	22.2	19.5	21.5	19.9	..	..	..	23.0
Morocco	50.5	48.3	54.8	55.2	57.1	56.0	59.0	55.0	55.1	50.4	50.2	56.0
Tunisia	54.8	54.5	59.7	59.1	59.9	60.1	60.7	58.1	62.3	54.8	57.3	59.9
ALL AFRICA	**44.4**	**49.1**	**48.2**	**48.8**	**48.4**	**48.0**	**49.1**	**49.8**	**53.1**	**47.5**	**50.7**	**49.8**

a. Provisional.

Table 2.32 Central government finances, expense, and revenue

	Finances Share of GDP (%)								
	Revenue, excluding grants			Expense			Cash surplus or deficit		
	1990	2000	2009	1990	2000	2009	1990	2000	2009
SUB-SAHARAN AFRICA	..	..	..	..	..	..	..	..	..
Excluding South Africa	..	..	..	..	..	..	..	..	..
Excl. S. Africa & Nigeria	..	..	..	..	..	..	..	..	..
Angola	..	..	..	..	..	..	..	..	..
Benin[a]	..	..	17.6	..	..	15.0	..	..	–4.5
Botswana[a]	50.8	..	..	26.7	..	..	19.1	..	..
Burkina Faso	..	..	14.0	..	..	13.0	..	..	–4.8
Burundi[a]	..	..	..	..	..	..	..	..	..
Cameroon[a]	14.3	..	..	14.6	..	..	–5.6	..	..
Cape Verde	..	..	28.7	..	..	28.2	..	..	–3.8
Central African Republic	..	..	..	..	..	..	..	..	..
Chad	..	..	..	..	..	..	..	..	..
Comoros	..	..	..	..	..	..	..	..	..
Congo, Dem. Rep.[a]	10.1	3.7	..	16.7	8.6	..	–6.5	–4.0	..
Congo, Rep.	..	28.6	..	..	19.9	..	..	1.9	..
Côte d'Ivoire[a]	..	..	18.7	..	..	17.6	..	..	0.9
Djibouti	..	..	..	..	..	..	..	..	..
Equatorial Guinea	..	..	..	..	..	..	..	..	..
Eritrea	..	..	..	..	..	..	..	..	..
Ethiopia[a]	12.4	..	..	16.2	..	..	–6.6	..	..
Gabon	..	..	..	..	..	..	..	..	..
Gambia, The[a]	19.4	..	..	17.2	..	..	2.1	..	..
Ghana[a]	12.5	..	15.3	..	..	17.9	..	..	–5.6
Guinea[a]	..	..	..	..	..	..	..	..	..
Guinea-Bissau	..	..	..	..	..	..	..	..	..
Kenya	..	19.7	20.5	..	16.8	21.7	..	2.0	–5.5
Lesotho	44.9	50.7	..	33.6	..	..	–0.6	..	..
Liberia	..	..	..	..	..	..	..	..	..
Madagascar	..	11.7	..	..	10.6	..	..	–2.0	..
Malawi	..	..	..	..	..	..	..	..	..
Mali	..	13.4	17.1	..	11.6	14.6	..	–3.4	–2.1
Mauritania	..	..	..	..	..	..	..	..	..
Mauritius	..	..	23.5	..	..	21.6	..	..	0.6
Mozambique	..	..	..	..	..	..	..	..	..
Namibia	31.3	30.1	..	..	28.5	..	..	–1.6	..
Niger	..	..	..	..	..	..	..	..	..
Nigeria	..	..	..	..	..	..	..	..	..
Rwanda[a]	10.8	..	..	12.7	..	..	–5.4	..	..
São Tomé and Príncipe	..	..	..	..	..	..	..	..	..
Senegal	..	16.9	..	..	12.8	..	..	–0.9	..
Seychelles	..	38.7	36.6	..	43.1	32.7	..	–13.9	4.3
Sierra Leone[a]	5.6	11.4	11.6	..	28.7	22.5	..	–9.3	–3.1
Somalia	..	..	..	..	..	..	..	..	..
South Africa	..	26.3	28.2	..	27.9	33.0	..	–2.0	–4.9
Sudan[a]	..	..	..	..	..	..	..	..	..
Swaziland[a]	..	26.2	..	..	22.6	..	..	–0.8	..
Tanzania	..	..	..	..	..	..	..	..	..
Togo[a]	..	..	18.8	..	..	17.4	..	..	–0.6
Uganda[a]	..	10.8	12.4	..	15.5	13.7	..	–1.9	–0.9
Zambia[a]	20.4	..	..	..	..	..	..	..	..
Zimbabwe[a]	24.1	..	..	24.5	..	..	–2.6	..	..
NORTH AFRICA									
Algeria[a]	..	..	36.6	..	..	25.0	..	..	–4.4
Egypt, Arab Rep.[a]	23.0	..	27.0	24.0	..	30.2	–2.0	..	–6.6
Libya	..	..	..	..	..	..	..	..	..
Morocco	..	..	33.1	..	..	27.9	..	..	1.0
Tunisia[a]	30.7	29.2	31.4	30.4	27.6	29.9	–3.2	–2.7	–1.7
ALL AFRICA									

(continued)

Central government finances, expense, and revenue (continued)

	Finances								
	Share of GDP (%)								
	Net incurrence of liabilities						Total debt		
	Domestic			Foreign					
	1990	2000	2009	1990	2000	2009	1990	2000	2009
SUB-SAHARAN AFRICA	..	..	..	..	..	..	..	..	..
Excluding South Africa	..	..	..	..	..	..	5.8	4.6	1.5
Excl. S. Africa & Nigeria	..	..	..	..	..	..	4.7	4.8	2.0
Angola	..	..	..	..	..	..	3.2	18.7	4.6
Benin[a]	..	..	2.2	..	..	2.1	2.0	3.3	0.6
Botswana[a]	–0.8	..	..	0.0	..	..	2.8	1.2	0.4
Burkina Faso	..	..	4.5	..	..	2.9	1.1	1.8	0.5
Burundi[a]	..	..	..	..	..	..	3.7	3.1	1.5
Cameroon[a]	..	..	..	5.2	..	..	4.6	5.5	1.8
Cape Verde	..	..	4.2	..	..	5.1	1.7	3.0	2.1
Central African Republic	..	..	..	..	..	..	2.0	1.5	1.6
Chad	..	..	..	..	..	..	0.7	1.8	1.1
Comoros	..	..	..	..	..	..	0.4	1.6	2.2
Congo, Dem. Rep.[a]	6.5	..	..	..	..	..	3.7	0.6	6.6
Congo, Rep.	..	..	..	..	..	..	18.6	1.4	1.7
Côte d'Ivoire[a]	..	..	..	..	..	..	11.7	9.8	4.7
Djibouti	..	..	..	..	..	..	2.4	2.4	2.8
Equatorial Guinea	..	..	..	..	..	..	..	..	..
Eritrea	..	..	..	..	..	..	..	0.5	1.2
Ethiopia[a]	5.1	..	..	2.0	..	..	2.0	1.7	0.4
Gabon	..	..	..	..	..	..	3.0	6.9	4.2
Gambia, The[a]	..	..	..	..	..	..	11.9	5.1	3.5
Ghana[a]	..	..	2.8	..	..	2.6	6.2	7.8	0.9
Guinea[a]	..	..	..	..	..	..	6.3	5.0	3.1
Guinea-Bissau	..	..	..	..	..	..	3.5	2.4	1.2
Kenya	..	..	3.0	..	..	..	9.2	4.7	1.3
Lesotho	–7.9	..	..	9.1	..	..	4.3	8.2	2.4
Liberia	..	..	..	..	..	..	0.8	0.1	7.3
Madagascar	..	1.3	..	..	1.7	..	7.2	3.0	0.5
Malawi	..	..	..	..	..	..	7.1	3.6	0.8
Mali	..	–1.0	–4.4	..	3.0	2.6	2.8	3.8	0.9
Mauritania	..	..	..	..	..	..	14.3	7.7	2.6
Mauritius	..	..	3.1	..	..	1.3	5.7	9.9	1.5
Mozambique	..	..	..	..	..	..	3.2	2.3	0.4
Namibia	..	1.0	..	..	0.7	..	..	..	..
Niger	..	..	..	..	..	..	4.0	1.4	0.8
Nigeria	..	..	..	..	..	..	11.7	4.0	0.3
Rwanda[a]	3.3	..	..	..	..	..	0.8	2.1	0.5
São Tomé and Príncipe	..	..	..	..	..	..	..	..	1.8
Senegal	..	0.3	..	..	0.5	..	5.7	4.8	1.6
Seychelles	..	0.7	–6.0	..	13.1	–2.7	5.8	3.4	8.2
Sierra Leone[a]	..	..	..	..	..	..	3.3	7.3	0.4
Somalia	..	..	..	..	..	..	1.2	..	..
South Africa	..	1.6	7.0	..	0.3	1.0	..	2.9	2.7
Sudan[a]	..	..	..	..	..	..	0.4	2.0	0.9
Swaziland[a]	..	..	..	..	..	..	4.0	2.1	1.5
Tanzania	..	..	..	..	..	..	4.2	1.6	0.8
Togo[a]	..	..	2.7	..	..	–0.5	5.3	2.2	1.9
Uganda[a]	..	0.6	1.5	..	2.0	1.8	3.4	1.2	0.4
Zambia[a]	6.8	..	..	1.0	..	..	6.1	5.7	1.3
Zimbabwe[a]	..	..	..	..	..	..	5.4	6.4	1.8
NORTH AFRICA									
Algeria[a]	..	..	5.9	..	..	0.0	14.2	8.2	0.7
Egypt, Arab Rep.[a]	..	..	9.9	..	..	–0.2	7.1	1.8	1.6
Libya	..	..	..	..	..	..	..	..	..
Morocco	..	..	0.1	..	..	1.7	6.9	7.3	3.7
Tunisia[a]	3.6	0.6	0.3	1.8	–0.2	0.0	11.6	9.8	5.3
ALL AFRICA									

Expense														
Share of expense (%)														
Goods and services			Compensation of employees			Interest payments			Subsidies and other transfers			Other expenses		
1990	2000	2009	1990	2000	2009	1990	2000	2009	1990	2000	2009	1990	2000	2009
..	..	..	..	..	..	..	..	..	..	..	..	..	..	..
..	..	..	..	..	..	..	..	..	..	..	..	..	..	..
..	..	..	..	..	..	..	..	..	..	..	..	..	..	..
..	..	..	..	..	..	..	..	..	..	..	..	..	..	..
..	..	17.7	..	..	47.2	..	..	3.3	..	..	29.7	..	..	2.1
35.2	..	..	29.1	..	..	2.8	..	..	31.8	..	..	1.1	..	..
..	..	19.1	..	..	45.8	..	..	3.4	..	..	11.1	..	..	20.7
..	..	..	..	..	..	..	..	..	..	..	..	..	..	..
16.7	..	..	55.6	..	..	7.8	..	..	13.3	..	..	..	..	..
..	..	16.3	..	..	43.3	..	..	5.3	..	..	30.1	..	..	4.9
..	..	..	..	..	..	..	..	..	..	..	..	..	..	..
..	..	..	..	..	..	..	..	..	..	..	..	..	..	..
..	..	..	..	..	..	..	..	..	..	..	..	..	..	..
56.3	59.4	..	25.4	27.4	..	7.4	..	..	..	13.2	..	..	..	..
..	25.6	..	..	27.8	..	..	35.2	..	..	10.9	..	..	0.5	..
..	..	29.5	..	..	38.4	..	..	8.7	..	..	16.3	..	..	7.1
..	..	..	..	..	..	..	..	..	..	..	..	..	..	..
..	..	..	..	..	..	..	..	..	..	..	..	..	..	..
..	..	..	..	..	..	..	..	..	..	..	..	..	..	..
43.1	..	..	48.1	..	..	5.6	..	..	11.2	..	..	0.2	..	..
..	..	..	..	..	..	..	..	..	..	..	..	..	..	..
28.3	..	..	28.7	..	..	21.4	..	..	12.2	..	..	9.4	..	..
..	..	16.5	..	..	39.9	..	..	15.6	..	..	27.9	..	..	..
..	..	..	..	..	..	..	..	..	..	..	..	..	..	..
..	..	..	..	..	..	..	..	..	..	..	..	..	..	..
..	21.3	20.2	..	55.2	37.3	..	17.8	10.3	..	3.4	31.3	..	2.2	0.9
30.8	..	..	38.6	..	..	18.7	..	..	8.9	..	..	2.9	..	..
..	..	..	..	..	..	..	..	..	..	..	..	..	..	..
..	17.7	..	..	40.7	..	..	13.4	..	..	9.7	..	..	18.6	..
..	..	..	..	..	..	..	..	..	..	..	..	..	..	..
..	37.6	30.6	..	36.5	34.4	..	8.0	2.5	..	0.4	15.0	..	17.5	17.5
..	..	..	..	..	..	..	..	..	..	..	..	..	..	..
..	..	11.7	..	..	30.7		..	13.6	..	..	31.0	..	..	10.0
..	..	..	..	..	..	..	..	..	..	..	..	..	..	..
..	20.8	..	..	51.2	..	..	6.6	..	..	10.4	..	..	11.0	..
..	..	..	..	..	..	..	..	..	..	..	..	..	..	..
..	..	..	..	..	..	..	..	..	..	..	..	..	..	..
35.3	..	..	43.5	..	..	7.9	..	..	15.5	..	..	..	..	..
..	..	..	..	..	..	..	..	..	..	..	..	..	..	..
..	26.0	..	..	41.4	..	..	10.7	..	..	18.7	..	..	..	..
..	24.6	37.2	..	36.3	26.8	..	17.3	20.1	..	21.6	15.8	..	..	0.1
..	14.9	24.3	..	23.4	27.6	..	21.9	7.1	..	5.5	22.6	..	34.3	18.3
..	..	..	..	..	..	..	..	..	..	..	..	..	..	..
..	11.3	12.9	..	15.6	13.4	..	18.1	7.2	..	52.9	62.9	..	2.2	4.4
..	..	..	..	..	..	..	..	..	..	..	..	..	..	..
..	26.1	..	..	44.6	..	..	2.3	..	..	27.0	..	..	..	..
..	..	..	..	..	..	..	..	..	..	..	..	..	..	..
..	..	24.1	..	..	40.3	..	..	5.5	..	..	17.6	..	..	12.5
..	55.1	31.2	..	12.3	14.2	..	5.2	8.6	..	27.4	44.7	..	..	1.4
..	..	..	..	..	..	..	..	..	..	..	..	..	..	..
21.7	..	..	40.9	..	..	17.8	..	..	..	..	..	..	..	..
..	..	11.3	..	..	33.7	..	..	1.4	..	..	45.4	..	..	8.3
22.4	..	8.0	26.6	..	24.6	16.3	..	14.0	..	..	44.7	..	..	8.7
..	..	..	..	..	..	..	..	..	..	..	..	..	..	..
..	..	8.9	..	..	47.8	..	..	3.7	..	..	26.6	..	..	12.9
7.0	8.6	6.6	31.4	39.8	35.8	10.9	12.1	7.4	44.9	..	37.7	5.8	..	12.5

(continued)

Table 2.32 Central government finances, expense, and revenue (continued)

	Revenue: Share of revenue (%) — Interest payments			Taxes on income, profits, and capital gains			Taxes on goods and services			Taxes on international trade			Other taxes			Social contributions			Grants and other revenue		
	1990	2000	2009	1990	2000	2009	1990	2000	2009	1990	2000	2009	1990	2000	2009	1990	2000	2009	1990	2000	2009
SUB-SAHARAN AFRICA	..	..	..	..	..	..	..	..	..	..	..	..	..	..	..	..	..	..	..	..	..
Excluding South Africa	..	..	..	..	..	..	..	..	..	..	..	..	..	..	..	..	..	..	..	..	..
Excl. S. Africa & Nigeria	..	..	..	..	..	..	..	..	..	..	..	..	..	..	..	..	..	..	..	..	..
Angola	..	..	..	..	..	..	..	..	..	..	..	..	..	..	..	..	..	..	..	..	..
Benin	..	..	18.4	..	..	17.0	..	..	38.8	..	..	18.4	..	..	5.9	..	..	2.4	..	..	17.5
Botswana	12.9	..	..	37.6	..	..	1.8	..	..	12.9	..	..	0.1	..	..	..	..	..	47.6	..	..
Burkina Faso	..	..	11.6	..	..	13.8	..	..	36.7	..	..	11.6	..	..	2.0	..	..	..	..	..	35.9
Burundi	..	..	..	..	..	..	..	..	..	..	..	..	..	..	..	..	..	..	..	..	..
Cameroon	15.5	..	..	18.9	..	..	22.2	..	..	15.5	..	..	4.6	..	..	1.8	..	..	27.5	..	..
Cape Verde	..	..	12.0	..	..	18.2	..	..	27.6	..	..	12.0	..	..	0.1	..	..	10.1	..	..	32.0
Central African Republic	..	..	..	..	..	..	..	..	..	..	..	..	..	..	..	..	..	..	..	..	..
Chad	..	..	..	..	..	..	..	..	..	..	..	..	..	..	..	..	..	..	..	..	..
Comoros	..	..	..	..	..	..	..	..	..	..	..	..	..	..	..	..	..	..	..	..	..
Congo, Dem. Rep.	37.8	16.4	..	21.9	8.4	..	15.1	15.8	..	37.8	16.4	..	1.1	25.7	..	1.0	..	..	23.1	33.7	..
Congo, Rep.	..	5.0	..	..	..	..	..	15.5	..	..	5.0	..	..	0.0	..	..	3.1	..	..	76.4	..
Côte d'Ivoire	..	..	32.5	..	..	15.3	..	..	20.3	..	..	32.5	..	..	7.9	..	..	6.4	..	..	17.6
Djibouti	..	..	..	..	..	..	..	..	..	..	..	..	..	..	..	..	..	..	..	..	..
Equatorial Guinea	..	..	..	..	..	..	..	..	..	..	..	..	..	..	..	..	..	..	..	..	..
Eritrea	..	..	..	..	..	..	..	..	..	..	..	..	..	..	..	..	..	..	..	..	..
Ethiopia	14.3	..	..	28.2	..	..	24.3	..	..	14.3	..	..	2.2	..	..	1.9	..	..	29.1	..	..
Gabon	..	..	..	..	..	..	..	..	..	..	..	..	..	..	..	..	..	..	..	..	..
Gambia, The	32.4	..	..	9.7	..	..	28.3	..	..	32.4	..	..	0.4	..	..	0.2	..	..	28.9	..	..
Ghana	34.7	..	15.9	20.6	..	22.6	26.8	..	29.3	34.7	..	15.9	..	..	..	..	..	..	10.4	..	32.1
Guinea	..	..	..	..	..	..	..	..	..	..	..	..	..	..	..	..	..	..	..	..	..
Guinea-Bissau	..	..	..	..	..	..	..	..	..	..	..	..	..	..	..	..	..	..	..	..	..
Kenya	..	15.0	10.1	..	28.5	40.0	..	41.4	40.6	..	15.0	10.1	..	0.5	1.0	..	0.0	..	..	14.7	8.2
Lesotho	43.6	41.4	..	8.7	17.2	..	16.0	12.5	..	43.6	41.4	..	0.1	..	..	..	..	..	31.6	28.9	..
Liberia	..	..	..	..	..	..	..	..	..	..	..	..	..	..	..	..	..	..	..	..	..
Madagascar	..	39.6	..	..	11.6	..	..	21.5	..	..	39.6	..	..	1.2	..	..	..	..	..	26.0	..
Malawi	..	..	..	..	..	..	..	..	..	..	..	..	..	..	..	..	..	..	..	..	..
Mali	..	11.3	9.9	..	12.5	19.5	..	41.6	29.2	..	11.3	9.9	..	5.0	10.0	..	..	..	..	29.5	31.4
Mauritania	..	..	..	..	..	..	..	..	..	..	..	..	..	..	..	..	..	..	..	..	..
Mauritius	..	..	2.2	..	..	22.8	..	..	46.3	..	..	2.2	..	..	7.1	..	..	4.1	..	..	17.4
Mozambique	..	..	..	..	..	..	..	..	..	..	..	..	..	..	..	..	..	..	..	..	..
Namibia	25.3	35.1	..	32.6	31.8	..	23.9	22.7	..	25.3	35.1	..	0.9	1.4	..	..	0.5	..	17.2	8.5	..
Niger	..	..	..	..	..	..	..	..	..	..	..	..	..	..	..	..	..	..	..	..	..
Nigeria	..	..	..	..	..	..	..	..	..	..	..	..	..	..	..	..	..	..	..	..	..
Rwanda	20.5	..	..	14.0	..	..	27.1	..	..	20.5	..	..	3.1	..	..	5.4	..	..	30.0	..	..
São Tomé and Principe	..	..	..	..	..	..	..	..	..	..	..	..	..	..	..	..	..	..	..	..	..
Senegal	..	29.5	..	..	21.3	..	..	33.7	..	..	29.5	..	..	3.3	..	..	..	..	..	12.2	..
Seychelles	..	41.0	10.8	..	17.3	19.2	..	5.1	39.7	..	41.0	10.8	..	1.6	..	..	13.8	9.0	..	21.3	21.3
Sierra Leone	38.1	29.4	14.4	29.7	15.4	16.9	22.1	7.6	24.6	38.1	29.4	14.4	0.2	..	..	..	..	..	9.9	47.7	44.1
Somalia	..	..	..	..	..	..	..	..	..	..	..	..	..	..	..	..	..	..	..	..	..
South Africa	..	3.0	2.7	..	51.7	52.6	..	33.1	31.8	..	3.0	2.7	..	2.8	2.4	..	2.1	2.2	..	7.4	8.2
Sudan	..	..	..	..	..	..	..	..	..	..	..	..	..	..	..	..	..	..	..	..	..
Swaziland	..	49.9	..	..	24.1	..	..	13.2	..	..	49.9	..	..	4.1	..	..	..	..	..	8.7	..
Tanzania	..	..	..	..	..	..	..	..	..	..	..	..	..	..	..	..	..	..	..	..	..
Togo	..	..	18.3	..	..	16.7	..	..	34.3	..	..	18.3	..	..	2.8	..	..	..	..	..	28.0
Uganda	..	21.8	9.6	..	9.9	22.0	..	29.4	46.8	..	21.8	9.6	..	0.1	..	..	..	..	..	38.7	21.6
Zambia	17.2	..	..	39.5	..	..	37.4	..	..	17.2	..	..	0.2	..	..	0.0	..	..	5.8	..	..
Zimbabwe	17.1	..	..	43.7	..	..	25.6	..	..	17.1	..	..	1.1	..	..	3.3	..	..	9.2	..	..
NORTH AFRICA																					
Algeria	..	..	4.5	..	..	59.7	..	..	28.0	..	..	4.5	..	..	1.5	..	..	..	..	..	6.3
Egypt, Arab Rep.	12.9	..	4.9	18.1	..	27.8	12.8	..	21.7	12.9	..	4.9	10.2	..	2.2	14.5	..	..	31.5	..	43.4
Libya	..	..	..	..	..	..	..	..	..	..	..	..	..	..	..	..	..	..	..	..	..
Morocco	..	..	6.0	..	..	28.4	..	..	31.4	..	..	6.0	..	..	5.4	..	..	12.1	..	..	16.7
Tunisia	27.5	10.7	5.8	12.3	20.4	27.4	19.1	37.1	31.3	27.5	10.7	5.8	4.8	4.4	4.4	13.0	17.0	19.1	23.4	10.5	11.9
ALL AFRICA																					

a. Data were reported on a cash basis and have been adjusted to the accrual framework.

Table 2.33 Structure of demand

	Share of GDP (%)																	
	Household final consumption expenditure			General government final consumption expenditure			Gross fixed capital formation			Exports of goods and services			Imports of goods and services			Gross national savings		
	1990	2000	2009[a]	1990	2000	2009[a]	1990	2000	2009[a]	1990	2000	2009[a]	1990	2000	2009[a]	1990	2000	2009[a]
SUB-SAHARAN AFRICA	**65.3**	**68.5**	**66.9**	**17.5**	**15.7**	**17.6**	**18.2**	**16.3**	**22.3**	**26.4**	**32.4**	**29.8**	**25.6**	**30.8**	**33.5**	**15.8**	**15.5**	**15.4**
Excluding South Africa	72.5	73.5	..	15.6	13.4	..	17.4	17.4	22.0	28.0	35.7	31.7	30.5	35.1	37.6	12.8	15.2	..
Excl. S. Africa & Nigeria	72.5	73.5	74.0	15.6	13.4	13.9	17.4	17.4	22.0	24.6	31.7	30.7	30.8	35.8	40.1	12.8	15.2	..
Angola	35.8	..	..	34.5	..	..	11.1	15.1	14.8	38.9	89.6	52.2	20.9	62.8	46.2	9.0	23.8	9.7
Benin	86.8	82.4	..	11.0	11.6	..	13.4	18.9	25.0	14.3	15.2	13.8	26.3	28.1	28.2	5.3	10.4	..
Botswana	33.2	30.8	62.8	24.1	25.4	24.2	32.4	25.8	28.2	55.1	53.3	33.6	49.8	41.2	44.6	41.6	41.4	16.4
Burkina Faso	73.5	78.5	..	21.1	20.8	..	17.7	18.7	..	11.0	9.1	..	24.5	25.2	..	15.9	5.1	..
Burundi	94.5	88.5	..	10.8	17.5	..	15.2	6.1	..	7.9	7.8	..	27.8	19.9	..	8.7	4.4	..
Cameroon	66.6	70.2	..	12.8	9.5	..	17.3	16.0	..	20.2	23.3	26.6	17.3	19.7	30.9	16.2	15.3	..
Cape Verde	93.4	92.9	67.2	14.7	21.3	20.8	22.9	19.7	53.8	12.7	27.5	23.6	43.7	61.4	65.4	17.8	9.0	31.3
Central African Republic	85.7	80.8	92.9	14.9	14.0	4.5	11.4	9.5	10.6	14.8	19.8	14.5	27.6	24.1	22.4	6.2	..	..
Chad	97.6	86.8	78.5	10.0	7.7	15.6	4.8	20.9	32.7	13.5	16.9	42.1	27.9	34.7	70.1	2.3	..	..
Comoros	78.7	94.0	105.8	24.5	11.7	15.3	11.9	10.1	12.4	14.3	16.7	14.7	37.1	32.5	48.2	14.4	..	..
Congo, Dem. Rep.	79.1	88.0	74.4	11.5	7.5	7.9	12.8	3.5	29.8	29.5	22.4	9.6	29.2	21.4	21.7	..	..	..
Congo, Rep.	62.4	29.1	42.2	13.8	11.6	12.2	17.2	20.9	24.3	53.7	80.3	71.9	45.8	43.6	50.9	6.9	30.6	..
Côte d'Ivoire	71.9	74.9	72.2	16.8	7.2	8.6	8.5	11.2	11.2	31.7	40.4	41.7	27.1	33.3	33.8	–5.1	8.0	14.8
Djibouti	78.9	76.8	..	31.5	29.7	..	14.1	8.8	..	53.8	35.1	..	78.4	50.4	..	..	5.4	..
Equatorial Guinea	80.3	20.9	24.3	39.7	4.6	3.4	17.4	61.3	36.6	32.2	98.6	74.1	69.6	85.4	41.6	2.1	..	..
Eritrea	..	79.1	..	..	63.8	..	..	23.8	..	..	15.1	4.5	..	81.8	20.3	..	4.4	..
Ethiopia	77.2	73.8	87.7	13.2	17.9	8.2	12.9	20.3	22.4	5.6	12.0	10.6	8.8	24.0	28.8	12.8	15.9	16.1
Gabon	49.7	32.2	41.1	13.4	9.6	11.6	21.4	21.9	28.4	46.0	69.0	52.2	30.9	32.7	33.3	24.3	41.7	..
Gambia, The	75.6	77.8	77.8	13.7	13.7	15.9	22.3	17.4	..	59.9	48.0	30.4	71.6	56.8	50.1	21.9	..	18.8
Ghana	85.2	84.3	81.7	9.3	10.2	9.6	14.4	23.1	19.6	16.9	48.8	30.5	25.9	67.2	41.3	10.5	15.3	15.5
Guinea	66.9	77.7	75.2	11.0	6.8	8.0	22.9	18.9	21.6	31.1	23.6	40.7	33.4	27.9	45.4	19.2	15.4	7.7
Guinea-Bissau	86.9	94.6	..	10.3	14.0	..	29.9	11.3	..	9.9	31.8	..	37.0	51.6	..	14.5	..	..
Kenya	62.8	77.7	75.9	18.6	15.1	16.3	20.6	16.7	20.1	25.7	21.6	25.2	31.3	31.7	38.3	18.5	13.5	15.4
Lesotho	123.3	83.3	78.8	25.8	41.7	50.4	57.0	42.5	31.5	18.1	34.2	51.2	123.2	103.4	111.7	70.5	24.1	28.1
Liberia	..	..	..	..	..	..	..	..	..	..	21.5	..	..	26.0	..	..	..	..
Madagascar	86.4	83.2	79.7	8.0	9.0	11.5	14.8	15.0	32.6	16.6	30.7	28.5	28.0	38.0	52.2	9.1	8.8	..
Malawi	71.5	81.6	61.9	15.1	14.6	20.9	20.1	12.3	21.8	23.8	25.6	30.0	33.4	35.3	37.7	16.4	9.5	..
Mali	79.8	79.4	..	13.8	8.6	..	23.0	24.6	..	17.1	26.8	..	33.7	39.4	..	15.0	15.9	..
Mauritania	69.2	82.8	72.1	25.9	25.8	20.6	20.0	19.4	25.2	45.6	46.2	49.7	60.7	74.2	67.6	18.8	..	..
Mauritius	63.4	60.3	74.0	13.6	14.1	14.6	30.6	22.9	26.2	65.0	61.4	48.4	72.2	61.9	59.1	25.8	26.3	16.7
Mozambique	92.3	80.6	84.4	13.5	9.0	13.4	22.1	31.0	21.0	8.2	10.5	25.1	36.1	37.0	43.8	6.6	10.4	9.1
Namibia	51.2	63.1	61.9	30.6	23.5	24.2	21.2	16.6	24.7	51.9	40.9	46.6	67.4	44.5	59.9	34.8	25.4	26.5
Niger	83.8	83.4	..	15.0	13.0	..	11.4	11.2	..	15.0	17.8	..	22.0	25.7	..	–0.6	5.3	..
Nigeria	..	..	..	..	..	..	..	..	..	43.4	54.0	35.9	28.8	32.0	27.2	..	..	..
Rwanda	83.7	87.7	81.1	10.1	11.0	14.6	14.6	18.3	21.8	5.6	8.7	11.7	14.1	25.7	29.2	11.3	12.9	15.1
São Tomé and Príncipe	..	..	..	..	..	..	..	..	..	..	..	..	..	..	..	..	..	..
Senegal	79.2	76.0	83.3	18.4	12.8	8.7	18.0	22.4	27.9	25.4	27.9	24.0	32.2	37.2	44.0	1.6	13.8	..
Seychelles	52.0	53.9	71.9	27.7	24.2	12.2	23.0	25.2	24.2	62.5	78.2	119.3	66.7	81.4	127.6	21.7	18.5	9.2
Sierra Leone	83.5	100.0	84.0	7.8	14.3	13.8	9.6	6.9	15.1	22.4	18.1	15.7	23.8	39.3	28.5	–1.0	–3.7	7.8
Somalia	..	..	..	..	..	..	14.9	..	..	9.8	..	..	37.7	..	..	..	..	..
South Africa	57.1	63.0	60.4	19.7	18.1	21.0	19.1	15.1	22.6	24.2	27.9	27.3	18.8	24.9	28.1	19.1	15.8	15.4
Sudan	86.1	76.5	66.7	5.8	7.6	13.9	10.4	12.1	21.8	4.0	15.3	15.1	7.1	17.7	20.8	1.2	9.3	12.2
Swaziland	80.4	78.0	72.8	14.3	18.7	27.0	14.5	17.4	16.9	59.0	76.1	59.8	68.9	90.1	76.5	19.7	12.4	2.4
Tanzania	80.9	78.3	62.3	17.8	11.7	19.8	25.8	16.4	29.3	12.6	13.4	23.2	37.5	20.1	35.2	10.1	12.7	21.2
Togo	71.1	92.0	..	14.2	10.2	..	25.3	17.8	..	33.5	30.7	..	45.3	50.7	..	21.0	0.8	..
Uganda	91.9	77.5	76.1	7.5	14.5	11.4	12.7	19.2	23.5	7.2	10.7	23.4	19.4	22.1	34.6	5.6	14.4	17.5
Zambia	64.4	87.4	61.3	19.0	9.5	13.1	13.5	16.0	22.1	35.9	27.1	35.6	36.6	41.5	32.2	19.6	–1.4	19.0
Zimbabwe	63.1	59.9	113.1	19.4	24.3	13.8	18.2	11.8	2.5	22.9	38.6	36.3	22.8	36.4	65.4	15.6	..	..
NORTH AFRICA	**64.1**	**61.1**	**62.9**	**15.1**	**14.4**	**13.3**	**24.5**	**20.2**	**25.1**	**26.4**	**28.3**	**32.1**	**32.3**	**25.3**	**36.6**	**27.6**	**..**	**..**
Algeria	56.8	41.6	40.6	16.1	13.6	13.9	27.0	20.7	33.0	23.4	41.2	40.4	24.9	21.4	36.1	24.3	..	..
Egypt, Arab Rep.	72.6	75.9	76.2	11.3	11.2	11.4	26.9	18.9	19.0	20.0	16.2	25.0	32.7	22.8	31.9	31.1	18.0	16.7
Libya	48.4	45.7	..	24.4	20.8	..	13.9	13.1	..	39.7	35.6	..	31.1	15.5	..	..	..	..
Morocco	64.6	61.4	57.0	15.5	18.4	18.0	24.0	26.0	30.7	26.5	28.0	28.6	31.9	33.4	39.5	25.1	24.3	31.2
Tunisia	63.6	60.7	63.4	16.4	15.6	13.1	24.4	26.0	25.9	43.6	44.5	52.0	50.6	48.2	55.3	23.4	23.2	22.8
ALL AFRICA	**64.7**	**65.1**	**65.2**	**16.4**	**15.1**	**15.7**	**21.1**	**18.1**	**23.5**	**26.4**	**30.7**	**30.7**	**28.4**	**28.5**	**34.7**	**20.8**	**17.2**	**17.6**

a. Provisional.

Table 3.1 Millennium Development Goal 1: eradicate extreme poverty and hunger

	International poverty line[a]															
	Share of population below PPP $1.25 a day				Poverty gap ratio at PPP $1.25 a day				Share of population below PPP $2 a day				Poverty gap ratio at PPP $2 a day			
	Surveys 1990–99[c]		Surveys 2000–09[c]		Surveys 1990–99[c]		Surveys 2000–09[c]		Surveys 1990–99[c]		Surveys 2000–09[c]		Surveys 1990–99[c]		Surveys 2000–09[c]	
	Year	Percent	Year	Percent	Year	Percent	Year	Percent	Year	Percent	Year	Percent	Year	Percent	Year	Percent
SUB-SAHARAN AFRICA																
Angola	..	..	2000	54.3	..	..	2000	29.9	..	..	2000	70.2	..	..	2000	42.4
Benin	..	..	2003	47.3	..	..	2003	15.7	..	..	2003	75.3	..	..	2003	33.5
Botswana	1994	31.2	..	..	1994	11.0	..	..	1994	49.4	..	..	1994	22.3	..	..
Burkina Faso	1998	70.0	2003	56.5	1998	30.2	2003	20.3	1998	87.6	2003	81.2	1998	49.1	2003	39.3
Burundi	1998	86.4	2006	81.3	1998	47.3	2006	36.4	1998	95.4	2006	93.5	1998	64.1	2006	56.1
Cameroon	1996	51.5	2007	9.6	1996	18.9	2007	1.2	1996	74.5	2007	30.4	1996	36.0	2007	8.2
Cape Verde	..	..	2002	21.0	..	..	2002	6.1	..	..	2002	40.9	..	..	2002	15.2
Central African Republic	1992	83.2	2008	62.8	1992	57.4	2008	31.3	1992	91.0	2008	80.1	1992	68.8	2008	46.8
Chad	..	..	2003	61.9	..	..	2003	25.6	..	..	2003	83.3	..	..	2003	43.9
Comoros	..	..	2004	46.1	..	..	2004	20.8	..	..	2004	65.0	..	..	2004	34.2
Congo, Dem. Rep.	..	..	2006	59.2	..	..	2006	25.3	..	..	2006	79.6	..	..	2006	42.4
Congo, Rep.	..	..	2005	54.1	..	..	2005	22.8	..	..	2005	74.4	..	..	2005	38.8
Côte d'Ivoire	1998	24.1	2008	23.8	1998	6.7	2008	7.5	1998	49.2	2008	46.3	1998	18.2	2008	17.8
Djibouti	1996	4.8	2002	18.8	1996	1.6	2002	5.3	1996	15.1	2002	41.2	1996	4.5	2002	14.6
Equatorial Guinea	..	..	..	..	..	..	..	..	..	..	..	..	..	..	..	..
Eritrea	..	..	..	..	..	..	..	..	..	..	..	..	..	..	..	..
Ethiopia	1995	60.5	2005	39.0	1995	21.2	2005	9.6	1995	84.6	2005	77.6	1995	41.2	2005	28.9
Gabon	..	..	2005	4.8	..	..	2005	0.9	..	..	2005	19.6	..	..	2005	5.0
Gambia, The	1998	66.7	2003	34.3	1998	34.7	2003	12.1	1998	82.0	2003	56.7	1998	50.0	2003	24.9
Ghana	1998	39.1	2006	30.0	1998	14.4	2006	10.5	1998	63.3	2006	53.6	1998	28.5	2006	22.3
Guinea	1994	36.8	2007	43.3	1994	11.5	2007	15.0	1994	63.8	2007	69.6	1994	26.5	2007	31.0
Guinea-Bissau	1993	52.1	2002	48.8	1993	20.6	2002	16.5	1993	75.7	2002	77.9	1993	37.4	2002	34.8
Kenya	1997	19.6	2005	19.7	1997	4.6	2005	6.1	1997	42.7	2005	39.9	1997	14.7	2005	15.1
Lesotho	1994	46.2	2003	43.4	1994	25.6	2003	20.8	1994	59.7	2003	62.3	1994	36.1	2003	33.1
Liberia	..	..	2007	83.7	..	..	2007	40.8	..	..	2007	94.8	..	..	2007	59.5
Madagascar	1999	82.3	2005	67.8	1999	44.3	2005	26.5	1999	93.1	2005	89.6	1999	61.0	2005	46.9
Malawi	1998	83.1	2004	73.9	1998	46.0	2004	32.3	1998	93.5	2004	90.5	1998	62.3	2004	51.8
Mali	1994	86.1	2006	51.4	1994	53.1	2006	18.8	1994	93.9	2006	77.1	1994	67.2	2006	36.5
Mauritania	1996	23.4	2000	21.2	1996	7.1	2000	5.7	1996	48.3	2000	44.1	1996	17.8	2000	15.9
Mauritius	..	..	..	..	..	..	..	..	..	..	..	..	..	..	..	..
Mozambique	1997	81.3	2008	60.0	1997	42.0	2008	25.2	1997	92.9	2008	81.6	1997	59.4	2008	42.9
Namibia	1993	49.1	..	..	1993	24.6	..	..	1993	62.2	..	..	1993	36.5	..	..
Niger	1994	78.2	2007	43.1	1994	38.6	2007	11.9	1994	91.6	2007	75.9	1994	56.5	2007	30.6
Nigeria	1996	68.5	2004	64.4	1996	32.1	2004	29.6	1996	86.4	2004	83.9	1996	49.7	2004	46.9
Rwanda	..	..	2005	76.8	..	..	2005	40.9	..	..	2005	89.6	..	..	2005	57.2
São Tomé and Príncipe	..	..	2001	28.6	..	..	2001	8.2	..	..	2001	57.3	..	..	2001	21.6
Senegal	1995	54.1	2005	33.5	1995	19.5	2005	10.8	1995	79.4	2005	60.4	1995	37.9	2005	24.7
Seychelles	..	..	2007	0.3	..	..	2007	0.1	..	..	2007	1.8	..	..	2007	0.4
Sierra Leone	1990	62.8	2003	53.4	1990	44.8	2003	20.3	1990	75.0	2003	76.1	1990	54.0	2003	37.5
Somalia	..	..	..	..	..	..	..	..	..	..	..	..	..	..	..	..
South Africa	1995	21.4	2006	17.4	1995	5.2	2006	3.3	1995	39.9	2006	35.7	1995	15.0	2006	12.3
Sudan	..	..	..	..	..	..	..	..	..	..	..	..	..	..	..	..
Swaziland	1995	78.6	2001	62.9	1995	47.7	2001	29.4	1995	89.3	2001	81.0	1995	61.7	2001	45.8
Tanzania	1992	72.6	2007	67.9	1992	29.7	2007	28.1	1992	91.3	2007	87.9	1992	50.1	2007	47.5
Togo	..	..	2006	38.7	..	..	2006	11.4	..	..	2006	69.3	..	..	2006	27.9
Uganda	1996	64.4	2009	28.7	1996	24.8	2009	8.3	1996	86.0	2009	55.3	1996	44.5	2009	21.3
Zambia	1998	55.4	2004	64.3	1998	26.9	2004	32.8	1998	74.8	2004	81.5	1998	41.7	2004	48.3
Zimbabwe	..	..	..	..	..	..	..	..	..	..	..	..	..	..	..	..
NORTH AFRICA																
Algeria	1995	6.8	..	..	1995	1.4	..	..	1995	23.6	..	..	1995	6.5	..	..
Egypt, Arab Rep.	1996	2.5	2005	<2	1996	0.3	2005	0.4	1996	26.3	2005	18.5	1996	5.0	2005	3.5
Libya	..	..	..	..	..	..	..	..	..	..	..	..	..	..	..	..
Morocco	1999	6.8	2007	2.5	1999	1.2	2007	0.5	1999	24.4	2007	14.0	1999	6.5	2007	3.2
Tunisia	1995	6.5	2000	2.6	1995	1.3	2000	0.5	1995	20.4	2000	12.8	1995	5.8	2000	3.0

Share of population below national poverty line[a] (poverty headcount ratio)				Share of urban population below national poverty line[a] (poverty headcount ratio)				Share of rural population below national poverty line[a] (poverty headcount ratio)			
Surveys 1990–99[c]		Surveys 2000–09[c]		Surveys 1990–99[c]		Surveys 2000–09[c]		Surveys 1990–99[c]		Surveys 2000–09[c]	
Year	Percent	Year	Percent	Year	Percent	Year	Percent	Year	Percent	Year	Percent
..	..	..	..	..	..	2000[e]	62.3	..	..	..	..
..	..	2003[e]	39.0	..	..	2003[e]	29.0	..	..	2003[e]	46.0
1993	47.0	2003	30.6	1993	29.0	2003	19.4	1993	55.0	2003	44.8
..	..	2003[e]	46.4	..	..	2003[e]	19.2	..	..	2003[e]	52.4
..	..	2006[e]	66.9	..	..	2006[e]	34.0	..	..	2006[e]	68.9
..	..	2007[e]	39.9	..	..	2007[e]	12.2	..	..	2007[e]	55.0
..	..	2007[e]	26.6	..	..	2007[e]	13.2	..	..	2007[e]	44.3
..	..	2008[e]	62.0	..	..	2008[e]	49.6	..	..	2008[e]	69.4
..	..	2003[e]	55.0	..	..	2003[e]	24.6	..	..	2003[e]	58.6
..	..	2004[e]	44.8	..	..	2004[e]	34.5	..	..	2004[e]	48.7
..	..	2005	71.3	..	..	2005	61.5	..	..	2005	75.7
..	..	2005	50.1	..	..	..	..	..	..	2005	57.7
1998	36.4[f]	2008	42.7[f]	1998	28.6[f]	2008	29.4[f]	1998	41.5[f]	2008	54.2[f]
..	..	..	..	..	..	..	..	..	..	..	..
..	..	..	..	..	..	..	..	..	..	..	..
1993	69.0	..	..	1993	62.0	..	..	..	..	..	..
1999	44.2	2004	38.9	1999	36.9	2004	35.1	1999	45.4	2004	39.3
..	..	2005	32.7	..	..	2005	29.8	..	..	2005	44.6
..	..	2003[e]	58.0[f]	..	..	2003[e]	39.6[f]	..	..	2003[e]	67.8[f]
1998	39.5	2006	28.5	1998	19.4	2006	10.8	1998	49.6	2006	39.2
..	..	2007[e]	53.0	..	..	2007[e]	30.5	..	..	2007[e]	63.0
..	..	2002[e]	64.7	..	..	2002[e]	51.6	..	..	2002[e]	69.1
..	..	2005[e]	45.9	..	..	2005[e]	33.7	..	..	2005[e]	49.1
1994	66.6[f]	2003	56.6[f]	1994	36.7[f]	2003	41.5[f]	1994	68.9[f]	2003	60.5[f]
..	..	2007	63.8[f]	..	..	2007	55.1[f]	..	..	2007	67.7[f]
1999	71.3	2005	68.7	1999	52.1	2005	52.0	1999	76.7	2005	73.5
1998	65.3	2004	52.4	1998	54.9	2004	25.4	1998	66.5	2004	55.9
..	..	2006[e]	47.4	..	..	2006[e]	25.5	..	..	2006[e]	57.6
..	..	2000[e]	46.3	..	..	2000[e]	25.4	..	..	2000[e]	61.2
..	..	..	..	..	..	..	..	..	..	..	..
1996	60.1	2008	54.7	1996	62.0	2008	49.6	1996	71.3	2008	56.9
..	..	2003[e]	38.0	..	..	2003[e]	17.0	..	..	2003[e]	49.0
..	..	2007[e]	59.5	..	..	2007[e]	36.7	..	..	2007[e]	63.9
..	..	2004[e]	51.7	..	..	2004[e]	43.1	..	..	2004[e]	63.8
..	..	2006[e]	58.5	..	..	2006[e]	23.2	..	..	2006[e]	64.2
..	..	2001	53.8	..	..	2001	45.0	..	..	2001	64.9
..	..	2005[e]	50.8[f]	..	..	2005[e]	35.1[f]	..	..	2005[e]	61.9[f]
..	..	..	..	..	..	..	..	..	..	..	..
..	..	2003[e]	66.4	..	..	2003[e]	47.0	..	..	2003[e]	78.5
..	..	..	..	..	..	..	..	..	..	..	..
1995	31.0	2005	23.0	..	..	..	..	..	..	..	..
..	..	..	..	..	..	..	..	..	..	..	..
..	..	2001[e]	69.2	..	..	2001[e]	49.0	..	..	2001[e]	75.0
..	..	2007[e]	33.4	..	..	..	..	..	..	2007[e]	37.4
..	..	2006	61.7	..	..	2006	36.8	..	..	2006	74.3
1997	44.4	2009	24.5	1997	16.7	2009	9.1	1997	48.7	2009	27.2
1998	66.8	2006	59.3	1998	39.5	2006	26.7	1998	83.0	2006	76.8
..	..	2003[e]	72.0	..	..	..	..	..	..	..	..
1995	22.6	..	..	1995	14.7	..	..	1995	30.3	..	..
1996	19.4	2008	22.0	..	..	2008	10.6	..	..	2008	30.0
..	..	..	..	..	..	..	..	..	..	..	..
..	..	2007	9.0	..	..	2007	4.8	..	..	2007	14.5
1995	6.2	2005	3.8	..	..	..	..	..	..	..	..

(continued)

Table 3.1 Millennium Development Goal 1: eradicate extreme poverty and hunger (continued)

	Share of poorest quintile in national consumption or income[b]				Prevalence of child malnutrition, underweight (% of children under age 5)				Population below minimum dietary energy consumption	
	Surveys 1990–99[c]		Surveys 2000–09[c]		Surveys 1990–99[c]		Surveys 2000–09[c]		Share (%)	Total (millions)
	Year	Percent	Year	Percent	Year	Percent	Year	Percent	2005–07[d]	2005–07[d]
SUB-SAHARAN AFRICA										
Angola	..	..	2000	2	1996	37	2001	27.5	41	7.1
Benin	..	..	2003	6.9	1996	26.8	2006	20.2	12	1.0
Botswana	1994	3.1	..	..	1996	15.1	2000	10.7	25	0.5
Burkina Faso	1998	5.9	2003	7.0	1999	33.7	2009	26.0	9	1.2
Burundi	1998	5.1	2006	9.0	..	..	2000	38.9	62	4.7
Cameroon	1996	5.7	2001	5.6	1998	17.8	2006	16.6	21	3.9
Cape Verde	..	..	2001	4.5	1994	11.8	..	..	10	0.0
Central African Republic	1993	2.0	2003	5.2	1995	23.3	2000	21.8	40	1.7
Chad	..	..	2003	6.3	1997	34.3	2004	33.9	37	3.8
Comoros	..	..	2004	2.6	1996	22.3	2000	25.0	46	0.4
Congo, Dem. Rep.	..	..	2006	5.5	1995	30.7	2007	28.2	69	41.9
Congo, Rep.	..	..	2005	5.0	..	..	2005	11.8	15	0.5
Côte d'Ivoire	1998	5.8	2008	5.6	1999	18.2	2006	16.7	14	2.8
Djibouti	1996	6.4	2002	6.0	1996	16.0	2006	29.6	28	0.2
Equatorial Guinea	..	..	..	..	1997	13.8	2004	10.6	..	..
Eritrea	..	..	..	..	1996	38.3	2002	34.5	64	3.0
Ethiopia	1995	7.2	2005	9.3	..	..	2005	34.6	41	31.6
Gabon	..	..	2005	6.1	..	..	2001	8.8	<5	..
Gambia, The	1998	4.0	2003	4.8	1996	23.2	2006	15.8	19	0.3
Ghana	1998	5.6	2006	5.2	1999	20.3	2008	14.3	5	1.2
Guinea	1994	6.4	2007	6.4	1999	21.2	2008	20.8	17	1.6
Guinea-Bissau	1993	5.2	2002	7.2	..	..	2006	17.4	22	0.3
Kenya	1997	6.0	2005	4.7	1998	17.6	2009	16.4	31	11.2
Lesotho	1995	1.5	2003	3.0	1992	13.8	2005	16.6	14	0.3
Liberia	..	..	2007	6.4	..	..	2007	20.4	33	1.2
Madagascar	1999	5.9	2005	6.2	1997	35.5	2004	36.8	25	4.5
Malawi	1998	4.8	2004	7.0	1998	26.3	2006	15.5	28	3.9
Mali	1994	4.6	2006	6.5	1996	38.2	2006	27.9	12	1.5
Mauritania	1996	6.3	2000	6.2	1996	20.3	2008	16.7	7	0.2
Mauritius	..	..	..	..	1995	13.0	..	..	5	0.1
Mozambique	1997	5.7	2008	5.2	1997	28.1	2003	21.2	38	8.1
Namibia	1993	1.5	..	..	1992	21.5	2007	17.5	19	0.4
Niger	1994	6.0	2007	8.3	1998	45.0	2006	39.9	20	2.7
Nigeria	1996	5.0	2004	5.1	1999	27.3	2008	26.7	6	9.2
Rwanda	..	..	2006	4.2	1996	24.2	2005	18.0	34	3.1
São Tomé and Príncipe	..	..	2001	5.2	..	..	2009	13.1	<5	0.0
Senegal	1995	6.5	2005	6.2	1996	19.6	2005	14.5	17	2.0
Seychelles	..	..	2007	10.8	..	..	..	..	7	0.0
Sierra Leone	1990	1.1	2003	6.1	1990	25.4	2008	21.3	35	1.8
Somalia	..	..	..	..	..	..	2006	32.8	..	..
South Africa	1995	3.6	2000	3.1	1999	10.1	..	..	<5	..
Sudan	..	..	..	..	1993	31.8	2006	31.7	22	8.8
Swaziland	1995	2.7	2001	4.5	..	..	2007	6.1	18	0.2
Tanzania	1992	7.4	2007	6.8	1999	25.3	2005	16.7	34	13.7
Togo	..	..	2006	5.4	1998	23.2	2006	22.3	30	1.8
Uganda	1999	5.9	2009	5.8	1995	21.5	2006	16.4	21	6.1
Zambia	1998	3.3	2004	3.6	1999	19.6	2007	14.9	43	5.2
Zimbabwe	1995	4.6	..	..	1999	11.5	2006	14.0	30	3.7
NORTH AFRICA										
Algeria	1995	6.9	..	..	1995	11.3	2005	3.7	<5	1.4
Egypt, Arab Rep.	1996	9.5	2005	9.0	1998	10.2	2008	6.8	<5	..
Libya	..	..	..	..	1995	4.2	2007	5.6	<5	..
Morocco	1999	6.4	2007	6.5	1997	7.7	2004	9.9	<5	1.6
Tunisia	1995	5.6	2000	5.9	1997	3.3	2006	3.3	<5	..

a. Based on nominal per capita consumption average and distributions estimated from household surveys.
b. Expenditure shares by percentiles of population, ranked by per capita expenditure.
c. Survey year refers to the year in which the underlying household survey data were collected; in cases for which the data collection period bridged two calendar years, the year in which most of the data were collected is reported as the reference year. Data are for the most recent year available during the period specified.
d. Data for a three-year period are used for the estimation of the prevalence of undernourishment.
e. Poverty estimates based on survey data from earlier years are available but not comparable with the most recent year reported here.
f. World Bank estimates.

Table 3.2 Millennium Development Goal 2: achieve universal primary education

	Net primary enrollment ratio (% of relevant age group)			Primary completion rate (% of relevant age group)			Share of cohort reaching grade 5 (% of grade 1 students)			Youth literacy rate (% ages 15–24)		
	1990	2000	2009	1990	2000	2009	1990	2000	2007–08[a]	1991	2000	2009
SUB-SAHARAN AFRICA												
Angola	..	..	..	..	..	..	..	..	..	..	..	73.1
Benin	41.2	..	94.7	19.5	39.3	62.0	27.3	84.2	..	..	..	54.3
Botswana	86.9	82.5	..	89.8	91.0	..	75.7	89.0	..	..	..	95.2
Burkina Faso	..	36.0	63.3	19.3	25.1	43.0	55.6	69.1	75.1	..	..	..
Burundi	..	43.2	98.9	40.9	24.6	52.4	57.2	58.8	72.6	53.6	73.3	76.6
Cameroon	71.1	..	91.6	54.2	49.9	73.4	66.6	..	77.7	..	83.1	..
Cape Verde	92.7	98.9	82.6	53.6	103.2	86.6	53.0	89.1	..	88.2	..	98.2
Central African Republic	57.9	..	66.7	30.4	..	38.0	42.7	..	53.6	..	58.5	64.7
Chad	..	53.5	..	16.3	22.4	33.5	35.6	54.9	..	..	37.6	46.3
Comoros	..	72.9	..	..	..	..	..	..	..	..	80.2	85.3
Congo, Dem. Rep.	..	..	..	..	..	55.9	..	..	..	..	..	67.7
Congo, Rep.	..	..	..	58.8	..	74.1	70.6	..	..	..	..	..
Côte d'Ivoire	..	54.7	57.2	40.1	41.8	46.5	60.8	88.0	66.1	..	60.7	66.6
Djibouti	29.3	26.9	44.4	32.0	28.0	35.4	73.9	..	64.3	..	..	..
Equatorial Guinea	..	68.8	53.5	..	..	46.5	..	..	60.9	..	94.9	97.9
Eritrea	..	37.9	35.7	..	36.4	47.8	..	60.5	73.1	..	..	88.7
Ethiopia	..	40.5	82.7	..	23.0	55.2	..	64.6	45.9	..	..	..
Gabon	..	..	..	..	..	..	..	..	..	..	..	97.6
Gambia, The	51.4	72.1	..	..	74.1	..	..	73.0	..	..	52.6	65.5
Ghana	..	62.9	75.9	..	69.5	82.7	..	66.2	79.0	..	70.7	80.1
Guinea	24.9	46.6	72.9	18.8	32.1	61.7	50.6	..	68.6	..	..	61.1
Guinea-Bissau	..	52.1	..	..	30.7	..	..	..	..	..	59.5	70.9
Kenya	..	64.9	82.6	..	..	..	..	..	..	..	80.3	92.7
Lesotho	70.7	77.5	73.1	58.4	60.1	70.3	66.3	67.2	..	..	90.9	92.0
Liberia	..	75.2	..	..	..	..	..	..	..	..	..	75.6
Madagascar	70.3	67.6	..	37.0	37.6	78.8	34.0	36.1	49.4	..	70.2	..
Malawi	..	..	90.8	28.1	65.4	59.2	32.3	..	50.7	..	..	86.5
Mali	..	..	72.9	..	30.8	59.4	..	..	86.9	..	..	..
Mauritania	..	62.6	76.3	29.1	..	..	63.8	..	..	..	61.3	67.7
Mauritius	97.2	92.9	94.0	113.7	102.8	89.4	..	98.4	97.2	91.2	94.5	96.5
Mozambique	44.0	56.0	90.6	26.4	16.1	56.6	33.8	52.5	53.7	..	..	70.9
Namibia	79.1	88.0	89.1	..	91.6	87.1	..	90.9	91.5	..	..	93.0
Niger	22.8	26.7	54.0	15.8	17.9	40.3	57.0	74.0	61.3	..	..	..
Nigeria	..	63.0	..	..	..	..	..	..	..	..	..	71.8
Rwanda	..	..	..	49.2	22.3		51.5	41.7	48.5	..	77.6	77.2
São Tomé and Príncipe	96.0	..	97.5	77.9	..	83.2	..	..	..	..	..	95.3
Senegal	45.1	57.5	73.1	41.9	39.1	56.9	72.8	72.3	69.8	..	..	65.0
Seychelles	..	..	94.4	..	107.2	105.1	..	91.0	94.9	..	..	..
Sierra Leone	..	..	..	..	..	..	..	..	..	..	..	57.6
Somalia	..	..	..	..	..	..	..	..	..	..	..	..
South Africa	..	89.8	84.7	..	86.6	93.2	..	..	..	..	..	..
Sudan	..	39.2	..	..	35.8	57.2	..	..	86.0	..	77.2	85.9
Swaziland	74.3	71.1	..	62.7	60.3	..	60.0	74.0	..	..	88.4	93.4
Tanzania	51.4	52.9	96.4	..	..	102.3	..	81.4	80.9	..	..	77.4
Togo	62.3	80.2	93.5	35.0	63.2	61.4	44.5	74.7	..	..	74.4	..
Uganda	..	..	92.2	..	..	72.5	..	56.7	57.7	..	..	..
Zambia	..	68.5	90.7	..	61.4	87.1	..	..	71.0	66.4	..	74.6
Zimbabwe	..	83.9	..	93.6	..	..	68.7	..	..	..	..	98.9
NORTH AFRICA												
Algeria	87.5	91.6	93.8	80.8	82.6	90.5	83.8	97.1	94.5	..	..	..
Egypt, Arab Rep.	..	86.0	..	..	87.7	..	..	99.0	..	..	..	..
Libya	..	..	..	..	..	..	..	..	..	..	..	99.9
Morocco	56.2	75.8	89.7	51.4	56.7	80.4	68.9	80.1	84.2	..	..	79.5
Tunisia	92.6	95.8	..	80.3	88.5	..	80.0	93.1	..	..	..	..

a. Data are for the most recent year available during the period specified.

Table 3.3 Millennium Development Goal 3: promote gender equity and empower women

	Ratio of girls to boys in primary and secondary school (%)			Ratio of literate young women to men (% ages 15–24)			Women in national parliament (% of total seats)			Share of women employed in the nonagricultural sector (%)		
	1991	2000	2009	1990	2000	2009	1990	2000	2009	1990	2000	2000–09[a]
SUB-SAHARAN AFRICA												
Angola	..	..	..	..	..	81.1	15.0	16.0	37.3	..	..	..
Benin	..	64.2	..	..	..	66.9	3.0	6.0	10.8	..	..	24.3
Botswana	108.0	101.6	..	107.4	..	103.2	5.0	..	11.1	33.5	42.9	43.4
Burkina Faso	..	70.1	85.6	52.9	..	..	..	8.0	15.3	12.5	..	..
Burundi	79.0	..	92.7	..	91.6	99.2	..	6.0	30.5	14.3	..	..
Cameroon	82.3	..	85.6	..	88.2	..	14.0	6.0	13.9	..	..	22.2
Cape Verde	94.0	..	103.4	..	..	101.7	12.0	11.0	18.1	..	38.9	38.9
Central African Republic	59.1	..	68.7	..	66.6	79.4	4.0	7.0	10.5	..	..	46.8
Chad	40.9	55.8	63.6	..	41.7	72.8	..	2.0	5.2	3.8	..	..
Comoros	..	84.1	..	..	92.4	98.7	0.0	..	3.0	..	..	..
Congo, Dem. Rep.	..	..	76.8	..	..	84.7	5.0	..	8.4	25.9	..	..
Congo, Rep.	88.5	85.7	..	..	..	..	14.0	12.0	7.3	26.1	..	..
Côte d'Ivoire	..	69.3	..	..	73.6	84.6	6.0	..	8.9	..	..	..
Djibouti	72.2	71.0	82.0	..	..	..	0.0	0.0	13.8	..	..	26.7
Equatorial Guinea	..	81.1	..	..	100.2	100.5	13.0	5.0	10.0	10.5	..	..
Eritrea	..	77.4	77.3	..	..	93.6	..	15.0	22.0	..	..	..
Ethiopia	..	65.1	87.9	..	..	..	..	2.0	21.9	..	..	47.3
Gabon	..	95.9	..	..	..	98.0	13.0	8.0	16.7	..	..	..
Gambia, The	..	81.6	..	..	64.3	84.5	8.0	2.0	9.4	20.9	..	..
Ghana	78.0	89.7	95.4	..	86.2	97.3	..	9.0	8.3	..	31.7	31.7
Guinea	44.0	61.5	77.2	..	..	79.1	..	9.0	..	..	..	..
Guinea-Bissau	..	65.5	..	..	61.4	81.3	20.0	..	10.0	10.8	..	..
Kenya	..	97.6	95.4	..	101.1	101.8	1.0	4.0	9.8	21.4	..	..
Lesotho	123.8	107.2	107.1	..	114.9	114.4	..	4.0	25.0	..	..	..
Liberia	..	71.9	..	..	..	114.9	..	..	12.5	..	..	11.4
Madagascar	95.6	..	96.9	..	93.9	..	7.0	8.0	..	..	..	37.7
Malawi	80.9	92.6	100.0	..	..	99.0	10.0	8.0	20.8	10.5	..	..
Mali	57.6	69.5	78.4	..	..	..	..	12.0	10.2	..	..	34.6
Mauritania	68.9	95.3	..	..	81.9	90.8	..	4.0	22.1	..	35.8	35.8
Mauritius	100.4	98.6	101.3	..	101.7	102.1	7.0	8.0	17.1	37.4	38.6	37.1
Mozambique	72.7	74.9	88.3	..	..	81.6	16.0	..	34.8	11.4	..	..
Namibia	110.8	103.2	..	105.5	..	104.2	7.0	22.0	26.9	..	42.8	41.4
Niger	53.0	65.0	75.3	..	..	..	5.0	1.0	12.4	..	..	36.1
Nigeria	76.5	80.2	..	76.8	..	83.6	..	..	7.0	..	18.6	21.1
Rwanda	94.8	96.0	100.3	100.0	97.9	100.5	17.0	17.0	56.3	..	33.0	33.0
São Tomé and Príncipe	..	..	103.1	95.9	..	101.0	12.0	9.0	7.3	..	..	..
Senegal	67.4	81.9	..	..	..	75.7	13.0	12.0	22.0	..	..	10.6
Seychelles	..	103.7	103.5	..	..	..	16.0	24.0	23.5	..	..	..
Sierra Leone	61.8	..	..	..	..	71.1	..	9.0	13.2	..	..	23.2
Somalia	..	..	..	..	..	..	4.0	..	6.1	21.7	..	..
South Africa	103.5	100.3	99.4	..	..	..	3.0	30.0	44.5	..	41.1	44.0
Sudan	..	..	89.4	..	84.4	92.8	..	..	18.1	22.2	..	..
Swaziland	..	95.5	..	..	103.2	103.2	4.0	3.0	13.6	..	..	..
Tanzania	97.1	97.5	96.1	..	..	97.3	..	16.0	30.4	..	..	30.5
Togo	58.1	69.1	..	..	76.0	..	5.0	..	11.1	41.0	..	..
Uganda	77.9	92.8	98.7	81.7	..	..	12.0	18.0	30.7	..	..	39.0
Zambia	..	91.4	95.8	..	..	82.3	7.0	10.0	15.2	16.6	22.0	22.0
Zimbabwe	96.4	94.4	..	..	..	101.1	11.0	14.0	15.2	15.4	20.4	21.9
NORTH AFRICA												
Algeria	81.6	..	..	..	..	..	2.0	3.0	7.7	..	..	13.1
Egypt, Arab Rep.	80.5	92.5	..	..	..	..	4.0	2.0	1.8	20.5	19.0	19.0
Libya	..	..	..	..	..	99.9	..	..	7.7	..	..	15.8
Morocco	68.8	82.4	..	..	..	83.2	0.0	1.0	10.5	..	..	20.8
Tunisia	84.6	99.5	..	..	..	..	4.0	12.0	22.8	..	24.3	25.0

a. Data are for the most recent year available during the period specified.

Table 3.4 Millennium Development Goal 4: reduce child mortality

	Under-five mortality rate (per 1,000)				Infant mortality rate (per 1,000 live births)				Child immunization rate, measles (% of children ages 12–23 months)			
	1990	2000	2008	2009	1990	2000	2008	2009	1990	2000	2008	2009
SUB-SAHARAN AFRICA												
Angola	258	212	166	161	153	126	101	98	38	41	79	77
Benin	184	144	121	118	111	89	76	75	79	70	66	72
Botswana	60	99	59	57	46	66	44	43	87	91	94	94
Burkina Faso	201	188	169	166	110	102	92	91	79	51	75	75
Burundi	189	178	168	166	114	107	102	101	74	76	84	91
Cameroon	148	156	155	154	91	96	95	95	56	49	80	74
Cape Verde	63	41	29	28	49	33	24	23	79	86	96	96
Central African Republic	175	184	172	171	115	119	113	112	82	36	62	62
Chad	201	205	209	209	120	122	124	124	32	28	23	23
Comoros	128	114	105	104	90	81	76	75	87	70	76	79
Congo, Dem. Rep.	199	199	199	199	126	126	126	126	38	46	67	76
Congo, Rep.	104	116	127	128	67	74	80	81	75	34	79	76
Côte d'Ivoire	152	142	121	119	105	97	85	83	56	71	63	67
Djibouti	123	106	95	94	95	84	76	75	85	50	73	73
Equatorial Guinea	198	168	148	145	120	102	90	88	88	51	51	51
Eritrea	150	89	58	55	92	58	41	39	..	86	95	95
Ethiopia	210	148	109	104	124	91	69	67	38	52	74	75
Gabon	93	83	71	69	68	61	53	52	76	55	55	55
Gambia, The	153	131	106	103	104	93	80	78	86	92	91	96
Ghana	120	106	72	69	76	68	49	47	61	90	86	93
Guinea	231	185	146	142	137	111	90	88	35	42	51	51
Guinea-Bissau	240	218	195	193	142	129	117	115	53	71	76	76
Kenya	99	105	86	84	64	66	56	55	78	78	76	74
Lesotho	93	124	91	84	74	86	66	61	80	74	85	85
Liberia	247	198	119	112	165	134	85	80	..	63	64	64
Madagascar	167	100	61	58	102	65	43	41	47	55	70	64
Malawi	218	164	115	110	129	99	71	69	81	73	88	92
Mali	250	217	194	191	139	120	103	101	43	55	71	71
Mauritania	129	122	118	117	81	77	75	74	38	62	65	59
Mauritius	24	19	17	17	21	17	15	15	76	84	98	99
Mozambique	232	183	147	142	155	123	99	96	59	71	77	77
Namibia	73	76	50	48	40	50	35	34	..	69	73	76
Niger	305	227	167	160	144	107	79	76	25	37	66	73
Nigeria	212	190	143	138	126	114	89	86	54	33	41	41
Rwanda	171	180	117	111	103	108	74	70	83	74	92	92
São Tomé and Príncipe	95	86	79	78	62	56	52	52	71	69	93	90
Senegal	151	120	95	93	73	61	52	51	51	48	77	79
Seychelles	15	14	13	12	13	12	11	11	86	97	99	97
Sierra Leone	285	250	198	192	166	150	126	123	..	37	66	71
Somalia	180	180	180	180	109	109	109	109	30	35	24	24
South Africa	62	77	65	62	48	54	45	43	79	72	62	62
Sudan	124	115	109	108	78	73	70	69	57	58	79	82
Swaziland	92	105	77	73	67	71	53	52	85	92	95	95
Tanzania	162	139	111	108	99	86	70	68	80	78	88	91
Togo	150	124	100	98	89	78	66	64	73	58	77	84
Uganda	184	154	130	128	111	94	81	79	52	57	68	68
Zambia	179	166	145	141	108	99	88	86	90	85	85	85
Zimbabwe	81	116	93	90	54	69	58	56	87	75	70	76
NORTH AFRICA												
Algeria	61	46	34	32	51	40	30	29	83	80	88	88
Egypt, Arab Rep.	90	47	23	21	66	38	20	18	86	98	92	95
Libya	36	25	19	19	32	23	17	17	89	93	98	98
Morocco	89	55	39	38	69	46	35	33	79	93	96	98
Tunisia	50	27	21	21	40	23	18	18	93	95	98	98

Table 3.5 Millennium Development Goal 5: improve maternal health

	Maternal mortality ratio (per 100,000 live births)				Births attended by skilled health staff (% of total)			
	Modeled estimate		National estimate		Surveys 1990–99[a]		Surveys 2000–09[a]	
	1990	2008	1990–99[a]	2000–09[a]	Year	Percent	Year	Percent
SUB-SAHARAN AFRICA								
Angola	1,000	610	..	..	1996	22.5	2007	47.3
Benin	790	410	..	397	1996	59.8	2006	74.0
Botswana	83	190	498	198	1996	87	2007	94.6
Burkina Faso	770	560	326	307	1999	31	2006	53.5
Burundi	1,200	970	484	615	..	..	2005	33.6
Cameroon	680	600	..	669	1998	55	2006	63.0
Cape Verde	230	94	..	16	1998	88.5	2005	77.5
Central African Republic	880	850	..	543	1995	45.9	2009	43.7
Chad	1,300	1,200	1,100	1,099	1997	15	2004	14.4
Comoros	530	340	830	380	1996	51.6	2000	61.8
Congo, Dem. Rep.	900	670	..	549	..	..	2007	74.0
Congo, Rep.	460	580	..	781	..	..	2005	83.4
Côte d'Ivoire	690	470	..	543	1999	47.1	2006	56.8
Djibouti	370	300	600	546	..	..	2006	92.9
Equatorial Guinea	1,000	280	74	..	1994	5	2000	64.6
Eritrea	930	280	..	..	1995	20.6	2002	28.3
Ethiopia	990	470	998	673	..	..	2005	5.7
Gabon	260	260	..	519	..	..	2000	85.5
Gambia, The	750	400	..	730	1990	44.1	2006	56.8
Ghana	630	350	..	451	1998	44.3	2008	57.1
Guinea	1,200	680	..	980	1999	34.8	2007	46.1
Guinea-Bissau	1,200	1,000	530	405	1995	25	2006	38.8
Kenya	380	530	910	488	1998	44.3	2009	43.8
Lesotho	370	530	..	762	1993	49.6	2009	61.5
Liberia	1,100	990	..	994	..	..	2007	46.3
Madagascar	710	440	..	498	1997	47.3	2009	43.9
Malawi	910	510	..	807	1992	54.8	2006	53.6
Mali	1,200	830	..	464	1996	40	2006	49.0
Mauritania	780	550	..	686	1991	40	2007	60.9
Mauritius	72	36	..	22	1999	98.5	2005	99.2
Mozambique	1,000	550	..	408	1997	44.2	2008	55.3
Namibia	180	180	..	449	1992	68.2	2007	81.4
Niger	1,400	820	..	648	1998	17.6	2006	32.9
Nigeria	1,100	840	590	545	1999	41.6	2008	38.9
Rwanda	1,100	540	..	750	1992	25.8	2008	52.1
São Tomé and Príncipe	..	..	..	148	..	..	2009	81.7
Senegal	750	410	..	401	1999	48.3	2005	51.9
Seychelles	..	..	560	57	..	..	..	..
Sierra Leone	1,300	970	..	857	..	..	2008	42.4
Somalia	1,100	1,200	..	1,044	1999	32.2	2006	33.0
South Africa	230	410	1,000	166	1998	84.4	2003	91.2
Sudan	830	750	150	1,107	1999	56.9	2006	49.2
Swaziland	260	420	..	589	1994	56	2007	69.0
Tanzania	880	790	229	578	1999	43.8	2005	43.4
Togo	650	350	..	..	1998	50.5	2006	62.0
Uganda	670	430	478	435	1995	37.8	2006	41.9
Zambia	390	470	..	591	1999	47.1	2007	46.5
Zimbabwe	390	790	..	555	1999	72.5	2009	60.2
NORTH AFRICA								
Algeria	250	120	..	..	1992	77	2006	95.2
Egypt, Arab Rep.	220	82	117	55	1998	55.2	2008	78.9
Libya	100	64	..	..	1999	99	..	..
Morocco	270	110	77	132	1995	39.6	2004	62.6
Tunisia	130	60	332	..	1995	80.5	2006	94.6

a. Data are for the most recent year available during the period specified.

Table 3.6 Millennium Development Goal 6: combat HIV/AIDS, malaria, and other diseases

	Prevalence of HIV (% ages 15–49)		Contraceptive use, any method (% of married women ages 15–49)				Children sleeping under insecticide-treated nets (% of children under age 5)	
			Surveys 1990–99[a]		Surveys 2000–09[a]		Surveys 2000–09[a]	
	1990	2009	Year	Percent	Year	Percent	Year	Percent
SUB-SAHARAN AFRICA								
Angola	0.5	2.0	1996	8.1	2001	6.2	2007	18
Benin	0.2	1.2	1996	16.4	2006	17.0	2006	20
Botswana	3.5	24.8	..	..	2007	52.8	..	..
Burkina Faso	3.9	1.2	1999	11.9	2006	17.4	2006	10
Burundi	3.9	3.3	..	..	2005	9.1	2005	8
Cameroon	0.6	5.3	1998	19.3	2006	29.2	2006	13
Cape Verde	..	..	1998	52.9	2005	61.3	..	..
Central African Republic	3.1	4.7	1995	14.8	2006	19.0	2006	15
Chad	1.1	3.4	1997	4.2	2004	2.8	2000	1
Comoros	<0.1	0.1	1996	21.0	2000	25.7	2000	9
Congo, Dem. Rep.	..	..	1991	7.7	2007	20.6	2007	6
Congo, Rep.	5.2	3.4	..	..	2005	44.3	2005	6
Côte d'Ivoire	2.4	3.4	1999	15.0	2006	12.9	2006	3
Djibouti	0.9	2.5	..	..	2008	22.5	2009	20
Equatorial Guinea	0.1	5.0	..	..	..	..	2000	1
Eritrea	0.3	0.8	1995	8.0	2002	8.0	2002	4
Ethiopia	..	..	1990	4.3	2005	14.7	2007	33
Gabon	0.9	5.2	..	..	2000	32.7	..	..
Gambia, The	0.1	2.0	1990	11.8	2001	17.5	2006	49
Ghana	0.3	1.8	1999	22.0	2008	23.5	2008	28
Guinea	1.1	1.3	1999	6.2	2005	9.1	2008	5
Guinea-Bissau	0.3	2.5	..	..	2006	10.3	2006	39
Kenya	3.9	6.3	1998	39.0	2009	45.5	2009	46
Lesotho	0.8	23.6	1992	23.2	2009	47.0	..	..
Liberia	0.3	1.5	..	..	2007	11.4	2009	26
Madagascar	0.2	0.2	1997	19.3	2009	39.9	2009	46
Malawi	7.2	11.0	1996	21.9	2006	41.0	2006	25
Mali	0.4	1.0	1996	6.7	2006	8.2	2006	27
Mauritania	0.2	0.7	1991	3.3	2007	9.3	2004	2
Mauritius	<0.1	1.0	1999	26.0	2002	75.9	..	..
Mozambique	1.2	11.5	1997	5.6	2008	16.2	2008	23
Namibia	1.6	13.1	1992	28.9	2007	55.1	2006	11
Niger	0.1	0.8	1998	8.2	2006	11.2	2009	43
Nigeria	1.3	3.6	1999	15.3	2008	14.6	2008	6
Rwanda	5.2	2.9	1996	13.7	2008	36.4	2008	56
São Tomé and Príncipe	..	..	..	..	2009	38.4	2009	56
Senegal	0.2	0.9	1999	10.5	2005	11.8	2009	29
Seychelles	..	..	..	..	..	..	..	..
Sierra Leone	<0.1	1.6	..	..	2008	8.2	2008	26
Somalia	0.1	0.7	1999	7.9	2006	14.6	2006	11
South Africa	0.7	17.8	1998	56.3	2003	59.9	..	..
Sudan	0.1	1.1	1993	9.9	2006	7.6	2006	28
Swaziland	2.3	25.9	..	..	2007	50.6	2007	1
Tanzania	4.8	5.6	1999	25.4	2005	26.4	2008	26
Togo	0.6	3.2	1999	23.5	2006	16.8	2006	38
Uganda	10.2	6.5	1995	14.8	2006	23.7	2006	10
Zambia	12.7	13.5	1999	22.0	2007	40.8	2008	41
Zimbabwe	10.1	14.3	1999	53.5	2009	64.9	2009	17
NORTH AFRICA								
Algeria	<0.1	0.1	1995	52.0	2006	61.4	..	..
Egypt, Arab Rep.	<0.1	<0.1	1998	51.7	2008	60.3	..	..
Libya	..	..	1995	45.2	..	..	..	..
Morocco	<0.1	0.1	1997	58.8	2004	63.0	..	..
Tunisia	<0.1	<0.1	1995	60.0	2006	60.2	..	..

(continued)

Table 3.6 Millennium Development Goal 6: combat HIV/AIDS, malaria, and other diseases (continued)

	Incidence of tuberculosis (per 100,000 people)			Tuberculosis treatment success rate (% of registered cases)			
				Surveys 1990–99[a]		Surveys 2000–08[a]	
	1990	1999	2009	Year	Percent	Year	Percent
SUB-SAHARAN AFRICA							
Angola	205	245	298	1998	68.0	2008	70.0
Benin	77	84	93	1999	77.0	2008	89.0
Botswana	307	588	694	1999	71.0	2008	65.0
Burkina Faso	95	182	215	1999	61.0	2008	76.0
Burundi	154	295	348	1998	74.0	2008	90.0
Cameroon	81	154	182	1999	75.0	2007	76.0
Cape Verde	175	162	148	..	..	2008	74.0
Central African Republic	145	277	327	1995	37.0	2008	71.0
Chad	125	240	283	1998	64.0	2006	54.0
Comoros	85	59	39	1999	93.0	2008	90.0
Congo, Dem. Rep.	165	315	372	1999	69.0	2008	87.0
Congo, Rep.	169	324	382	1999	61.0	2008	76.0
Côte d'Ivoire	177	338	399	1999	63.0	2008	76.0
Djibouti	619	619	620	1999	72.0	2008	84.0
Equatorial Guinea	86	97	117	1997	82.0	2008	56.0
Eritrea	72	84	99	1999	44.0	2008	76.0
Ethiopia	159	304	359	1999	74.0	2008	84.0
Gabon	153	210	501	1998	50.0	2008	53.0
Gambia, The	185	221	269	1997	70.0	2008	84.0
Ghana	223	212	201	1999	51.0	2008	86.0
Guinea	119	190	318	1999	74.0	2008	78.0
Guinea-Bissau	158	188	229	1999	35.0	2008	70.0
Kenya	112	382	305	1999	79.0	2008	85.0
Lesotho	184	519	634	1999	69.0	2008	73.0
Liberia	199	237	288	1999	74.0	2008	79.0
Madagascar	177	213	261	1997	64.0	2008	81.0
Malawi	258	417	304	1999	71.0	2008	87.0
Mali	275	297	324	1999	69.0	2008	82.0
Mauritania	228	272	330	..	..	2008	68.0
Mauritius	28	25	22	1999	87.0	2008	87.0
Mozambique	181	347	409	1999	71.0	2008	84.0
Namibia	322	616	727	1999	51.0	2008	82.0
Niger	125	149	181	1999	60.0	2008	81.0
Nigeria	131	250	295	1999	75.0	2008	78.0
Rwanda	167	319	376	1999	67.0	2008	87.0
São Tomé and Príncipe	135	116	98	1999	81.0	2008	94.0
Senegal	195	232	282	1999	58.0	2008	84.0
Seychelles	43	37	31	1999	91.0	2008	100.0
Sierra Leone	207	355	644	1999	75.0	2008	86.0
Somalia	285	285	285	1999	88.0	2008	81.0
South Africa	301	479	971	1999	57.0	2008	76.0
Sudan	119	119	119	1999	80.0	2008	81.0
Swaziland	267	691	1257	..	..	2008	68.0
Tanzania	226	232	183	1999	78.0	2008	88.0
Togo	308	367	446	1999	76.0	2008	79.0
Uganda	163	324	293	1999	61.0	2008	70.0
Zambia	297	603	433	1999	69.0	2008	88.0
Zimbabwe	329	628	742	1999	73.0	2008	74.0
NORTH AFRICA							
Algeria	38	47	59	1999	87.0	2008	90.0
Egypt, Arab Rep.	34	27	19	1999	85.0	2008	89.0
Libya	40	40	40	1999	67.0	2008	69.0
Morocco	147	123	92	1999	88.0	2008	85.0
Tunisia	29	26	24	1999	91.0	2008	86.0

a. Data are for the most recent year available during the period specified.

Table 3.7 Millennium Development Goal 7: ensure environmental sustainability

	Forest area (% of total land area)			Terrestrial protected areas (% of total land area)			GDP per unit of energy use (2005 PPP $ per kg of oil equivalent)		
	1990	2000	2010	1990	2000	2009	1990	2000	2008
SUB-SAHARAN AFRICA									
Angola	48.9	47.9	46.9	12.4	12.4	12.4	5.8	4.9	8.8
Benin	52.1	45.8	41.2	23.8	23.8	23.8	3.2	4.3	3.9
Botswana	24.2	22.1	20.0	30.3	30.9	30.9	7.6	9.1	11.6
Burkina Faso	25.0	22.8	20.6	13.3	13.5	13.9	..	..	..
Burundi	11.3	7.7	6.7	3.8	4.8	4.8	..	..	..
Cameroon	51.4	46.8	42.1	7.0	8.7	9.2	5.1	4.6	5.4
Cape Verde	14.3	20.4	21.1	2.5	2.5	2.5	..	..	..
Central African Republic	37.2	36.8	36.3	14.4	14.7	14.7	..	..	..
Chad	10.4	9.8	9.2	9.4	9.4	9.4	..	..	..
Comoros	6.4	4.3	1.6	0.0	0.0	0.0	..	..	..
Congo, Dem. Rep.	70.7	69.4	68.0	10.0	10.0	10.0	1.9	0.8	0.8
Congo, Rep.	66.5	66.1	65.6	5.4	7.8	9.4	10.7	11.5	9.6
Côte d'Ivoire	32.1	32.5	32.7	22.6	22.6	22.6	5.5	4.5	3.1
Djibouti	0.2	0.2	0.3	0.0	0.0	0.0	..	..	..
Equatorial Guinea	66.3	62.1	58.0	7.3	19.2	19.2	..	..	..
Eritrea	..	15.6	15.2	4.9	4.9	5.0	..	3.5	3.8
Ethiopia	15.2	13.7	12.3	17.7	17.7	18.4	1.8	1.9	2.0
Gabon	85.4	85.4	85.4	4.2	5.2	14.9	11.8	11.2	9.4
Gambia, The	44.2	46.1	48.0	1.5	1.5	1.5	..	..	..
Ghana	32.7	26.8	21.7	13.9	14.0	14.0	2.5	2.6	3.4
Guinea	29.6	28.1	26.6	6.8	6.8	6.8	..	..	..
Guinea-Bissau	78.8	75.4	71.9	7.6	16.1	16.1	..	..	..
Kenya	6.5	6.3	6.1	11.5	11.6	11.6	3.0	2.9	3.1
Lesotho	1.3	1.4	1.4	0.5	0.5	0.5	..	..	..
Liberia	51.2	48.1	44.9	18.1	18.1	18.1	..	..	..
Madagascar	23.5	22.6	21.6	2.1	2.9	2.9	..	..	..
Malawi	41.4	37.9	34.4	15.0	15.0	15.0	..	..	..
Mali	11.5	10.9	10.2	2.3	2.3	2.4	..	..	..
Mauritania	0.4	0.3	0.2	0.5	0.5	0.5	..	..	..
Mauritius	19.1	19.1	17.2	1.7	4.5	4.5	..	..	..
Mozambique	55.2	52.4	49.6	14.8	14.8	15.8	0.9	1.3	1.9
Namibia	10.6	9.8	8.9	14.4	14.5	14.5	..	8.4	7.3
Niger	1.5	1.0	1.0	6.8	6.8	6.8	..	..	..
Nigeria	18.9	14.4	9.9	11.6	12.8	12.8	2.0	2.0	2.6
Rwanda	12.9	13.9	17.6	9.9	9.9	10.0	..	..	..
São Tomé and Príncipe	28.1	28.1	28.1	..	..	..	..	..	..
Senegal	48.6	46.2	44.0	24.1	24.1	24.1	6.3	6.0	7.1
Seychelles	88.5	88.5	89.1	42.0	42.0	42.0	..	..	..
Sierra Leone	43.5	40.8	38.1	5.0	5.0	5.0	..	..	..
Somalia	13.2	12.0	10.8	0.6	0.6	0.6	..	..	..
South Africa	7.6	7.6	4.7	6.5	6.9	6.9	3.1	3.0	3.5
Sudan	32.1	29.7	29.4	4.7	4.9	4.9	2.5	3.4	5.3
Swaziland	27.4	30.1	32.7	3.0	3.0	3.0	..	..	..
Tanzania	46.8	42.3	37.7	26.5	26.9	27.7	2.2	2.1	2.6
Togo	12.6	8.9	5.3	11.3	11.3	11.3	2.7	2.0	1.9
Uganda	24.1	19.6	15.2	7.3	7.9	9.7	..	..	..
Zambia	71.0	68.8	66.5	36.0	36.0	36.0	1.8	1.7	2.1
Zimbabwe	57.3	48.8	40.4	18.0	18.0	28.0	..	..	..
NORTH AFRICA									
Algeria	0.7	0.7	0.6	6.3	6.3	6.3	7.1	6.9	6.8
Egypt, Arab Rep.	0.0	0.1	0.1	1.9	4.3	5.9	5.8	6.2	5.8
Libya	0.1	0.1	0.1	0.1	0.1	0.1	..	4.0	5.2
Morocco	11.3	11.2	11.5	1.2	1.5	1.5	9.7	8.3	8.4
Tunisia	4.1	5.4	6.5	1.3	1.3	1.3	6.6	7.1	8.3

(continued)

Millennium Development Goal 7: ensure environmental sustainability (continued)

	Carbon dioxide emissions per capita (metric tons)			Population with sustainable access to an improved water source (%)			Population with sustainable access to improved sanitation (%)		
	1990	2000	2007	1990	2000	2008	1990	2000	2008
SUB-SAHARAN AFRICA									
Angola	0.4	0.7	1.4	36.0	41.0	50.0	25.0	40.0	57.0
Benin	0.1	0.2	0.5	56.0	66.0	75.0	5.0	9.0	12.0
Botswana	1.6	2.5	2.6	93.0	94.0	95.0	36.0	50.0	60.0
Burkina Faso	0.1	0.1	0.1	41.0	60.0	76.0	6.0	8.0	11.0
Burundi	0.1	0.0	0.0	70.0	72.0	72.0	44.0	45.0	46.0
Cameroon	0.1	0.2	0.3	50.0	64.0	74.0	47.0	47.0	47.0
Cape Verde	0.2	0.4	0.6	..	83.0	84.0	..	45.0	54.0
Central African Republic	0.1	0.1	0.1	58.0	63.0	67.0	11.0	22.0	34.0
Chad	0.0	0.0	0.0	38.0	45.0	50.0	6.0	7.0	9.0
Comoros	0.2	0.2	0.2	87.0	92.0	95.0	17.0	28.0	36.0
Congo, Dem. Rep.	0.1	0.0	0.0	45.0	44.0	46.0	9.0	16.0	23.0
Congo, Rep.	0.5	0.3	0.4	..	70.0	71.0	..	30.0	30.0
Côte d'Ivoire	0.5	0.4	0.3	76.0	78.0	80.0	20.0	22.0	23.0
Djibouti	0.7	0.6	0.6	77.0	84.0	92.0	66.0	63.0	56.0
Equatorial Guinea	0.3	0.9	7.5	..	43.0	..	..	51.0	..
Eritrea	..	0.2	0.1	43.0	54.0	61.0	9.0	11.0	14.0
Ethiopia	0.1	0.1	0.1	17.0	28.0	38.0	4.0	8.0	12.0
Gabon	6.6	1.0	1.4	..	85.0	87.0	..	36.0	33.0
Gambia, The	0.2	0.2	0.2	74.0	84.0	92.0	..	63.0	67.0
Ghana	0.3	0.3	0.4	54.0	71.0	82.0	7.0	9.0	13.0
Guinea	0.2	0.2	0.1	52.0	62.0	71.0	9.0	15.0	19.0
Guinea-Bissau	0.2	0.2	0.2	..	55.0	61.0	..	18.0	21.0
Kenya	0.2	0.3	0.3	43.0	52.0	59.0	26.0	29.0	31.0
Lesotho	..	..	..	61.0	74.0	85.0	32.0	29.0	29.0
Liberia	0.2	0.2	0.2	58.0	65.0	68.0	11.0	14.0	17.0
Madagascar	0.1	0.2	0.1	31.0	37.0	41.0	8.0	10.0	11.0
Malawi	0.1	0.1	0.1	40.0	63.0	80.0	42.0	50.0	56.0
Mali	0.0	0.1	0.0	29.0	44.0	56.0	26.0	32.0	36.0
Mauritania	1.3	0.5	0.6	30.0	40.0	49.0	16.0	21.0	26.0
Mauritius	1.4	2.3	3.1	99.0	99.0	99.0	91.0	91.0	91.0
Mozambique	0.1	0.1	0.1	36.0	42.0	47.0	11.0	14.0	17.0
Namibia	0.0	1.0	1.5	64.0	81.0	92.0	25.0	29.0	33.0
Niger	0.1	0.1	0.1	35.0	42.0	48.0	5.0	7.0	9.0
Nigeria	0.5	0.6	0.6	47.0	53.0	58.0	37.0	34.0	32.0
Rwanda	0.1	0.1	0.1	68.0	67.0	65.0	23.0	40.0	54.0
São Tomé and Príncipe	0.6	0.6	0.8	..	79.0	89.0	..	21.0	26.0
Senegal	0.4	0.4	0.5	61.0	65.0	69.0	38.0	45.0	51.0
Seychelles	1.6	7.0	7.3	..	..	..	..	..	..
Sierra Leone	0.1	0.1	0.2	..	55.0	49.0	..	11.0	13.0
Somalia	0.0	0.1	0.1	..	23.0	30.0	..	22.0	23.0
South Africa	9.5	8.4	9.0	83.0	86.0	91.0	69.0	73.0	77.0
Sudan	0.2	0.2	0.3	65.0	61.0	57.0	34.0	34.0	34.0
Swaziland	0.5	1.1	0.9	..	55.0	69.0	..	49.0	55.0
Tanzania	0.1	0.1	0.1	55.0	54.0	54.0	24.0	24.0	24.0
Togo	0.2	0.3	0.2	49.0	55.0	60.0	13.0	12.0	12.0
Uganda	0.0	0.1	0.1	43.0	57.0	67.0	39.0	44.0	48.0
Zambia	0.3	0.2	0.2	49.0	54.0	60.0	46.0	47.0	49.0
Zimbabwe	1.5	1.1	0.8	78.0	80.0	82.0	43.0	44.0	44.0
NORTH AFRICA									
Algeria	3.1	3.8	4.1	94.0	89.0	83.0	88.0	92.0	95.0
Egypt, Arab Rep.	1.3	2.0	2.3	90.0	96.0	99.0	72.0	86.0	94.0
Libya	9.2	9.3	9.3	54.0	54.0	..	97.0	97.0	97.0
Morocco	0.9	1.2	1.5	74.0	78.0	81.0	53.0	64.0	69.0
Tunisia	1.6	2.1	2.3	81.0	90.0	94.0	74.0	81.0	85.0

Table 3.8 Millennium Development Goal 8: develop a global partnership for development

	Debt sustainability					
	Heavily Indebted Poor Countries (HIPC) Debt Initiative		Debt service relief committed ($ millions)[a]	Public and publicly guaranteed debt service (% of exports, excluding worker remittances)		
	Decision point[a]	Completion point[a]		1990	2000	2009
SUB-SAHARAN AFRICA						
Angola	..	..	..	7.1	20.4	8.4
Benin	Jul. 2000	Mar. 2003	460	8.4	10.7	..
Botswana	..	..	..	4.3	2.0	1.0
Burkina Faso	Jul. 2000	Apr. 2002	930	7.7	15.1	..
Burundi	Aug. 2005	Jan. 2009	1,366	40.7	25.1	10.1
Cameroon	Oct. 2000	Apr. 2006	4,917	12.5	14.0	2.5
Cape Verde	..	..	..	8.9	10.5	5.1
Central African Republic	Sep. 2007	Jun. 2009	804	7.5	..	..
Chad	May 2001	..	260	2.3	..	..
Comoros	Jun. 2010	..	136	2.5	..	..
Congo, Dem. Rep.	Jul. 2003	Jul. 2010	15,222	..	..	..
Congo, Rep.	Mar. 2006	Jan. 2010	1,738	30.9	0.5	..
Côte d'Ivoire	Mar. 2009	..	3,415	14.7	14.9	6.6
Djibouti	..	..	..	..	4.8	5.7
Equatorial Guinea	..	..	..	..	..	..
Eritrea	..	..	..	..	2.8	..
Ethiopia	Nov. 2001	Apr. 2004	3,275	33.2	12.2	3.0
Gabon	..	..	..	3.8	8.8	..
Gambia, The	Dec. 2000	Dec. 2007	112	17.3	..	8.7
Ghana	Feb. 2002	Jul. 2004	3,500	19.9	12.0	2.5
Guinea	Dec. 2000	..	800	17.7	17.6	10.1
Guinea-Bissau	Dec. 2000	..	790	22.0	..	..
Kenya	..	..	..	22.7	15.7	4.5
Lesotho	..	..	..	4.1	10.3	2.5
Liberia	Mar. 2008	Jun. 2010	4,600	..	..	11.2
Madagascar	Dec. 2000	Oct. 2004	1,900	31.9	8.4	..
Malawi	Dec. 2000	Aug. 2006	1,628	22.4	10.8	..
Mali	Sep. 2000	Mar. 2003	895	9.7	10.2	..
Mauritania	Feb. 2000	Jun. 2002	1,100	24.8	..	..
Mauritius	..	..	..	4.5	16.4	1.9
Mozambique	Apr. 2000	Sep. 2001	4,300	17.2	7.0	1.4
Namibia	..	..	..	..	..	..
Niger	Dec. 2000	Apr. 2004	1,190	3.2	6.0	..
Nigeria	..	..	..	22.3	8.2	0.7
Rwanda	Dec. 2000	Apr. 2005	1,316	9.1	15.3	4.7
São Tomé and Príncipe	Dec. 2000	Mar. 2007	263	28.6	20.3	16.2
Senegal	Jun. 2000	Apr. 2004	850	13.7	13.2	..
Seychelles	..	..	..	7.6	3.3	6.2
Sierra Leone	Mar. 2002	Dec. 2006	994	7.8	29.6	2.1
Somalia	..	..	..	..	..	..
South Africa	..	..	..	..	5.5	2.4
Sudan	..	..	..	4.5	10.1	5.6
Swaziland	..	..	..	5.3	2.1	2.1
Tanzania	Apr. 2000	Nov. 2001	3,000	25.1	10.3	1.0
Togo	Nov. 2008	..	360	8.6	3.2	..
Uganda	Feb. 2000	May 2000	1,950	47.1	6.5	1.7
Zambia	Dec. 2000	Apr. 2005	3,900	12.6	17.2	1.6
Zimbabwe	..	..	..	18.2	..	..
NORTH AFRICA						
Algeria	..	..	..	63.3	..	..
Egypt, Arab Rep.	..	..	..	23.2	8.5	6.2
Libya	..	..	..	..	..	..
Morocco	..	..	..	23.1	23.0	6.4
Tunisia	..	..	..	23.0	20.0	9.0

(continued)

Table 3.8 Millennium Development Goal 8: develop a global partnership for development (continued)

	Youth unemployment rate (ages 15–24)						Information and communication								
	Total (share of total labor force)		Male (share of male labor force)		Female (share of female labor force)		Fixed-line and mobile telephone subscribers (per 100 people)			Personal computers (per 100 people)			Internet users (per 100 people)		
	Year	Percent	Year	Percent	Year	Percent	1990	2000	2009	1990	2000	2005–09[b]	1995	2000	2009
SUB-SAHARAN AFRICA															
Angola	..	..	..	..	..	..	0.7	0.6	45.5	..	0.1	0.7	..	0.1	3.3
Benin	2002	0.82	2002	1.07	2002	0.61	0.3	1.6	57.8	..	0.2	0.7	..	0.2	2.2
Botswana	2000	13.6	2000	13.23	2000	14.01	2.0	20.8	103.5	..	3.5	6.3	0.1	2.9	6.2
Burkina Faso	..	..	..	..	..	..	0.2	0.7	22.0	0.0	0.1	0.6	..	0.1	1.1
Burundi	..	..	..	..	..	..	0.1	0.6	10.5	..	0.1	0.9	0.0	0.1	0.8
Cameroon	..	..	..	..	..	..	0.3	1.3	39.6	..	0.3	1.1	..	0.3	3.8
Cape Verde	..	..	..	..	..	..	2.3	16.9	91.8	..	5.7	14.0	..	1.8	29.7
Central African Republic	..	..	..	..	..	..	0.2	0.4	4.1	..	0.2	0.3	..	0.1	0.5
Chad	..	..	..	..	..	..	0.1	0.2	24.1	..	0.1	0.2	..	0.0	1.7
Comoros	..	..	..	..	..	..	0.8	1.3	19.0	0.0	0.6	0.9	..	0.3	3.7
Congo, Dem. Rep.	..	..	..	..	..	..	0.1	0.1	15.5	..	..	0.0	..	0.0	0.6
Congo, Rep.	..	..	..	..	..	..	0.7	3.0	59.6	..	0.4	0.6	..	0.0	6.7
Côte d'Ivoire	..	..	..	..	..	..	0.6	4.3	64.7	..	0.5	1.7	0.0	0.2	4.6
Djibouti	..	..	..	..	..	..	1.0	1.4	16.9	0.2	0.9	4.3	0.0	0.2	3.0
Equatorial Guinea	..	..	..	..	..	..	0.3	2.1	67.3	..	0.4	1.5	..	0.1	2.1
Eritrea	..	..	..	..	..	..	..	0.8	3.7	..	0.2	1.0	0.0	0.1	4.9
Ethiopia	2006	24.89	2006	19.51	2006	29.42	0.3	0.4	6.0	..	0.1	0.7	0.0	0.0	0.5
Gabon	..	..	..	..	..	..	2.2	12.9	94.9	..	1.0	3.4	..	1.2	6.7
Gambia, The	..	..	..	..	..	..	0.7	3.0	86.9	..	1.2	3.5	0.0	0.9	7.6
Ghana	2000	16.55	2000	16.42	2000	16.68	0.3	1.8	64.5	0.0	0.3	1.1	0.0	0.2	5.4
Guinea	..	..	..	..	..	..	0.2	0.8	55.9	..	0.4	0.5	0.0	0.1	0.9
Guinea-Bissau	..	..	..	..	..	..	0.6	0.9	35.1	..	..	0.2	..	0.2	2.3
Kenya	..	..	..	..	..	..	0.8	1.3	50.3	0.0	0.5	1.4	0.0	0.3	10.0
Lesotho	..	..	..	..	..	..	0.8	2.3	33.9	..	..	0.3	..	0.2	3.7
Liberia	2007	4.73	2007	5.73	2007	3.73	0.4	0.3	21.3	..	..	..	..	0.0	0.5
Madagascar	2005	2.27	2005	1.74	2005	2.77	0.3	0.8	31.5	..	0.2	0.6	..	0.2	1.6
Malawi	..	..	..	..	..	..	0.3	0.8	16.9	..	0.1	0.2	..	0.1	4.7
Mali	..	..	..	..	..	..	0.1	0.5	29.4	..	0.1	0.8	..	0.1	1.9
Mauritania	..	..	..	..	..	..	0.3	1.3	68.6	..	1.0	4.5	..	0.2	2.3
Mauritius	2009	21.36	2009	18.08	2009	26.25	5.5	38.8	114.9	0.4	10.1	17.6	..	7.3	22.7
Mozambique	..	..	..	..	..	..	0.4	0.8	26.4	..	0.3	1.4	..	0.1	2.7
Namibia	2004	41.7	2004	36.68	2004	47.05	3.7	10.5	62.6	..	4.1	23.9	0.0	1.6	5.9
Niger	2001	3.16	2001	3.95	2001	1.67	0.1	0.2	17.4	..	0.1	0.1	..	0.0	0.8
Nigeria	..	..	..	..	..	..	0.3	0.5	48.2	..	0.6	0.9	..	0.1	28.4
Rwanda	..	..	..	..	..	..	0.2	0.7	24.6	..	..	0.3	..	0.1	4.5
São Tomé and Príncipe	..	..	..	..	..	..	1.9	3.3	44.1	..	..	3.9	..	4.6	16.4
Senegal	2006	14.8	2006	11.92	2006	20.11	0.6	4.6	57.3	0.2	1.6	2.2	0.0	0.4	7.4
Seychelles	2002	20.33	..	..	..	..	12.4	57.4	130.0	..	13.6	21.2	..	7.4	38.7
Sierra Leone	2004	5.15	2004	7.27	2004	3.5	0.3	0.7	20.9	..	..	..	0.0	0.1	0.3
Somalia	..	..	..	..	..	..	0.2	1.4	8.1	..	..	0.9	0.0	0.2	1.2
South Africa	2009	48.15	2009	44.59	2009	52.51	9.4	30.2	102.9	0.7	6.6	8.4	0.7	5.5	9.0
Sudan	..	..	..	..	..	..	0.2	1.2	37.2	..	0.3	10.7	0.0	0.0	9.9
Swaziland	..	..	..	..	..	..	1.6	6.0	59.1	..	1.1	3.7	0.0	0.9	7.6
Tanzania	2006	8.84	2006	7.39	2006	10.11	0.3	0.8	40.3	..	0.3	0.9	..	0.1	1.6
Togo	..	..	..	..	..	..	0.3	1.8	35.8	..	1.9	3.1	0.0	1.9	5.4
Uganda	..	..	..	..	..	..	0.2	0.8	29.4	..	0.3	1.7	0.0	0.2	9.8
Zambia	2000	21.36	2000	23.11	2000	19.48	0.8	1.7	34.8	..	0.7	1.1	0.0	0.2	6.3
Zimbabwe	2002	24.88	2002	28.18	2002	21.4	1.2	4.1	27.0	0.0	1.6	7.6	0.0	0.4	11.4
NORTH AFRICA															
Algeria	2006	24.3	2004	42.85	2004	46.27	3.2	6.1	101.2	0.1	0.7	1.1	0.0	0.5	13.5
Egypt, Arab Rep.	2007	24.8	2007	17.16	2007	47.89	2.8	9.8	79.1	..	1.1	3.9	0.0	0.6	20.0
Libya	..	..	..	..	..	..	5.0	12.1	95.1	..	..	2.2	..	0.2	5.5
Morocco	2009	21.88	2009	22.77	2009	19.37	1.6	13.1	90.1	..	1.2	5.7	0.0	0.7	32.2
Tunisia	2005	30.68	2005	31.35	2005	29.32	3.7	11.2	105.8	0.3	2.2	9.7	0.0	2.7	33.6

Note: 0.0 indicates less than 1 but more than 0.

a. As of 2010.

b. Data are for the most recent year available during the period specified.

Table 4.1 Doing Business indicators

	Overall ranking		Starting a business: Number of procedures		Starting a business: Time required for each procedure (days)		Starting a business: Cost (% of GNI per capita)		Starting a business: Minimum capital (% of GNI per capita)		Registering property: Number of procedures		Registering property: Time required (days)		Registering property: Cost (% of property value)	
	2009	2010	2009	2010	2009	2010	2009	2010	2009	2010	2009	2010	2009	2010	2009	2010
SUB-SAHARAN AFRICA			**9**	**9**	**47**	**45**	**106.8**	**97.0**	**149.0**	**151.9**	**7**	**7**	**72**	**67**	**10.0**	**9.6**
Angola	164	163	8	8	68	68	151.1	163.0	29.0	28.7	7	7	184	184	11.4	11.5
Benin	172	170	7	7	31	31	155.5	152.6	290.8	285.3	4	4	120	120	11.8	11.8
Botswana	50	52	10	10	61	61	2.1	2.2	0.0	0.0	5	5	16	16	5.0	5.0
Burkina Faso	154	151	4	4	14	14	50.3	49.8	428.2	416.2	4	4	59	59	13.2	13.1
Burundi	181	181	11	11	32	32	151.6	129.3	0.0	0.0	5	5	94	94	6.3	5.8
Cameroon	173	168	10	6	35	19	115.0	51.2	182.9	191.8	5	5	93	93	19.2	19.3
Cape Verde	142	132	9	8	24	11	17.0	18.5	38.9	42.4	6	6	73	73	7.6	3.9
Central African Republic	182	182	8	8	22	22	244.9	228.4	507.1	468.6	5	5	75	75	18.6	18.5
Chad	183	183	13	13	75	75	246.4	226.9	369.3	386.7	6	6	44	44	18.7	18.2
Comoros	159	159	11	11	24	24	182.1	176.5	261.8	245.5	5	5	24	24	20.8	20.8
Congo, Dem. Rep.	179	175	14	10	127	84	847.6	735.1	0.0	0.0	6	6	54	54	9.8	7.0
Congo, Rep.	177	177	10	10	160	160	86.5	111.4	96.5	129.8	6	6	55	55	10.3	10.7
Côte d'Ivoire	168	169	10	10	40	40	133.3	133.0	204.9	202.9	6	6	62	62	13.9	13.9
Djibouti	157	158	11	11	37	37	195.1	169.9	500.5	434.1	7	7	40	40	13.2	13.0
Equatorial Guinea	161	164	20	20	136	136	100.4	104.3	12.4	21.3	6	6	23	23	6.2	6.3
Eritrea	180	180	13	13	84	84	76.5	69.2	297.0	268.4	11	11	78	78	9.1	9.1
Ethiopia	103	104	5	5	9	9	18.9	14.1	492.4	367.7	10	10	41	41	2.2	2.1
Gabon	158	156	9	9	58	58	17.8	21.9	26.5	32.7	7	7	39	39	10.5	10.5
Gambia, The	141	146	8	8	27	27	215.1	199.6	0.0	0.0	5	5	66	66	7.6	7.6
Ghana	77	67	7	7	12	12	24.8	20.3	13.4	11.0	5	5	34	34	1.1	1.0
Guinea	178	179	13	13	41	41	139.2	146.6	495.4	519.1	6	6	104	104	13.9	14.0
Guinea-Bissau	175	176	16	17	216	216	181.5	183.3	415.8	415.1	9	9	211	211	6.1	6.1
Kenya	94	98	12	11	34	33	36.5	38.3	0.0	0.0	8	8	64	64	4.2	4.2
Lesotho	137	138	7	7	40	40	27.0	26.0	11.9	12.0	6	6	101	101	8.0	8.0
Liberia	152	155	5	5	20	20	52.9	54.6	0.0	0.0	10	10	50	50	13.2	13.2
Madagascar	138	140	2	2	7	7	6.2	12.9	207.4	248.1	7	7	74	74	9.4	9.8
Malawi	132	133	10	10	39	39	108.0	108.4	0.0	0.0	6	6	88	49	3.2	3.2
Mali	155	153	6	6	8	8	86.9	79.7	334.6	306.8	5	5	29	29	20.0	11.9
Mauritania	167	165	9	9	19	19	34.7	33.6	450.4	412.1	4	4	49	49	5.2	5.2
Mauritius	20	20	5	5	6	6	4.1	3.8	0.0	0.0	4	4	26	26	10.7	10.6
Mozambique	130	126	10	9	26	13	19.3	13.9	0.0	0.0	8	8	42	42	11.3	9.9
Namibia	68	69	10	10	66	66	20.4	18.5	0.0	0.0	9	9	23	23	9.6	9.6
Niger	171	173	9	9	17	17	118.7	118.6	613.7	613.0	4	4	35	35	11.0	11.0
Nigeria	134	137	8	8	31	31	76.7	78.9	0.0	0.0	13	13	82	82	20.9	20.9
Rwanda	70	58	2	2	3	3	10.1	8.8	0.0	0.0	4	4	60	55	0.5	0.4
São Tomé and Príncipe	176	178	10	10	144	144	81.7	77.3	0.0	385.7	7	7	62	62	10.9	10.9
Senegal	151	152	4	4	8	8	63.7	63.1	206.9	205.1	6	6	124	122	20.6	20.6
Seychelles	92	95	10	10	39	39	19.2	17.5	0.0	0.0	4	4	33	33	7.0	7.0
Sierra Leone	143	143	6	6	12	12	118.8	110.7	0.0	0.0	7	7	236	86	12.4	12.2
Somalia	..	..	..	..	..	..	..	..	..	..	..	..	..	..	..	..
South Africa	32	34	6	6	22	22	5.9	6.0	0.0	0.0	6	6	24	24	8.7	8.8
Sudan	153	154	10	10	36	36	36.0	33.6	0.0	0.0	6	6	9	9	3.0	3.0
Swaziland	126	118	12	12	60	56	33.9	33.0	0.5	0.5	9	9	44	44	7.1	7.1
Tanzania	125	128	12	12	29	29	36.8	30.9	0.0	0.0	9	9	73	73	4.4	4.4
Togo	162	160	7	7	75	75	205.0	178.1	514.0	486.9	5	5	295	295	13.1	13.0
Uganda	129	122	18	18	25	25	84.4	94.4	0.0	0.0	13	13	77	77	3.5	3.2
Zambia	84	76	6	6	18	18	28.4	27.9	1.3	0.0	6	5	39	40	6.6	6.6
Zimbabwe	156	157	9	9	97	90	353.8	182.8	0.0	0.0	5	5	31	31	10.1	8.5
NORTH AFRICA	**42**	**42**	**9**	**9**	**13.5**	**13.5**	**12.5**	**10.0**	**10.7**	**11.4**	**8**	**8**	**51**	**51**	**4.8**	**4.7**
Algeria	136	136	14	14	24	24	12.1	12.9	31.0	34.4	11	11	47	47	7.1	7.1
Egypt, Arab Rep.	99	94	6	6	7	7	16.1	6.3	0.0	0.0	7	7	72	72	0.9	0.8
Libya	..	..	..	..	..	..	..	..	..	..	..	..	..	..	..	..
Morocco	114	114	6	6	12	12	16.1	15.8	11.8	11.2	8	8	47	47	4.9	4.9
Tunisia	58	55	10	10	11	11	5.7	5.0	0.0	0.0	4	4	39	39	6.1	6.1

(continued)

Table 4.1 Doing Business indicators (continued)

	Enforcing contracts						Dealing with construction permits						Protecting investors (0 least protection to 10 most protection)			
	Number of procedures		Time required (days)		Cost (% of debt)		Number of procedures		Time required (days)		Cost (% of GNI per capita)		Disclosure index		Director liability index	
	2009	2010	2009	2010	2009	2010	2009	2010	2009	2010	2009	2010	2009	2010	2009	2010
SUB-SAHARAN AFRICA	**39**	**39**	**658**	**652**	**49.0**	**49.7**	**18**	**18**	**245**	**238**	**1,993.4**	**1,775.2**	**5**	**5**	**3**	**3**
Angola	46	46	1,011	1,011	44.4	44.4	12	12	328	328	597.7	694.3	5	5	6	6
Benin	42	42	825	825	64.7	64.7	15	15	410	320	254.4	249.6	6	6	1	1
Botswana	29	29	687	625	28.1	28.1	24	24	167	167	246.2	264.5	7	7	8	8
Burkina Faso	37	37	446	446	83.0	81.7	15	15	132	122	721.2	576.1	6	6	1	1
Burundi	44	44	832	832	38.6	38.6	25	25	212	212	8,262.0	7,047.6	4	4	1	1
Cameroon	43	43	800	800	46.6	46.6	14	14	227	213	1,178.4	1,235.8	6	6	1	1
Cape Verde	37	37	425	425	21.8	21.8	18	18	120	120	523.3	570.7	1	1	5	5
Central African Republic	43	43	660	660	82.0	82.0	21	21	239	239	275.2	259.5	6	6	1	1
Chad	41	41	743	743	45.7	45.7	14	14	164	164	6,383.4	6,684.4	6	6	1	1
Comoros	43	43	506	506	89.4	89.4	18	18	164	164	72.6	68.1	6	6	1	1
Congo, Dem. Rep.	43	43	625	625	151.8	151.8	14	14	248	128	4,505.8	2,692.2	3	3	3	3
Congo, Rep.	44	44	560	560	53.2	53.2	17	17	169	169	179.3	241.1	6	6	1	1
Côte d'Ivoire	33	33	770	770	41.7	41.7	22	21	629	592	230.9	227.6	6	6	1	1
Djibouti	40	40	1,225	1,225	34.0	34.0	16	16	179	179	2,145.6	1,862.8	5	5	2	2
Equatorial Guinea	40	40	553	553	18.5	18.5	18	18	201	201	128.4	220.7	6	6	1	1
Eritrea	39	39	405	405	22.6	22.6	..	..	..	..	..	..	4	4	5	5
Ethiopia	37	37	620	620	15.2	15.2	12	12	128	128	562.0	419.6	4	4	4	4
Gabon	38	38	1,070	1,070	34.3	34.3	16	16	210	210	34.5	42.9	6	6	1	1
Gambia, The	32	32	434	434	37.9	37.9	17	17	146	146	336.4	314.9	2	2	1	1
Ghana	36	36	487	487	23.0	23.0	18	18	220	220	1,099.0	1,017.7	7	7	5	5
Guinea	50	50	276	276	45.0	45.0	32	32	255	255	249.6	419.0	6	6	1	1
Guinea-Bissau	41	40	1,140	1,140	25.0	25.0	15	15	167	167	2,020.0	1,075.0	6	6	1	1
Kenya	40	40	465	465	47.2	47.2	11	11	120	120	161.7	167.8	3	3	2	2
Lesotho	41	41	785	785	19.5	19.5	15	15	601	601	1,278.8	1,290.7	2	2	1	1
Liberia	41	41	1,280	1,280	35.0	35.0	24	24	77	77	28,295.9	29,574.4	4	4	1	1
Madagascar	38	38	871	871	42.4	42.4	16	16	178	178	630.7	654.9	5	5	6	6
Malawi	42	42	432	312	142.4	94.1	21	21	213	268	1,311.3	1,316.7	4	4	7	7
Mali	36	36	626	620	52.0	52.0	14	15	185	168	818.5	505.0	6	6	1	1
Mauritania	46	46	370	370	23.2	23.2	25	25	201	201	506.3	463.2	5	5	3	3
Mauritius	36	36	720	645	17.4	17.4	18	18	107	107	35.5	32.3	6	6	8	8
Mozambique	30	30	730	730	142.5	142.5	17	17	381	381	632.0	530.3	5	5	4	4
Namibia	33	33	270	270	35.8	35.8	12	12	139	139	124.7	113.0	5	5	5	5
Niger	39	39	545	545	59.6	59.6	17	17	265	265	2,355.0	2,352.3	6	6	1	1
Nigeria	40	40	457	457	32.0	32.0	18	18	350	350	573.4	597.5	5	5	7	7
Rwanda	24	24	260	230	78.7	78.7	14	14	210	195	456.1	353.6	7	7	9	9
São Tomé and Príncipe	43	43	1,185	1,185	50.5	50.5	13	13	255	255	631.4	565.1	3	3	1	1
Senegal	44	44	780	780	26.5	26.5	16	16	220	210	463.1	459.0	6	6	1	1
Seychelles	37	37	720	720	14.3	15.4	20	20	144	144	30.3	38.0	4	4	8	8
Sierra Leone	40	40	515	515	149.5	149.5	25	25	283	252	368.5	343.3	6	6	7	7
Somalia	..	..	..	..	..	..	..	..	..	..	..	..	..	..	..	..
South Africa	30	30	600	600	33.2	33.2	17	17	174	174	24.5	23.1	8	8	8	8
Sudan	53	53	810	810	19.8	19.8	19	19	271	271	206.4	192.2	0	0	6	6
Swaziland	40	40	972	972	56.1	56.1	14	14	116	116	147.1	143.0	0	2	1	5
Tanzania	38	38	462	462	14.3	14.3	22	22	328	328	3,281.3	2,756.3	3	3	4	4
Togo	41	41	588	588	47.5	47.5	15	15	277	277	1,285.3	1,241.9	6	6	1	1
Uganda	38	38	510	490	44.9	44.9	18	18	171	171	1,510.5	1,287.8	2	2	5	5
Zambia	35	35	471	471	38.7	38.7	17	17	254	254	2,793.8	2,454.2	3	3	6	6
Zimbabwe	38	38	410	410	32.0	113.1	17	17	1012	1012	13,770.3	8,020.6	8	8	1	1
NORTH AFRICA	**42**	**42**	**705**	**705**	**23.8**	**23.8**	**22**	**22**	**176**	**180**	**408.3**	**362.0**	**6**	**7**	**4**	**4**
Algeria	46	46	630	630	21.9	21.9	22	22	240	240	39.6	44.0	6	6	6	6
Egypt, Arab Rep.	41	41	1,010	1,010	26.2	26.2	25	25	218	218	331.6	293.7	8	8	3	3
Libya	..	..	..	..	..	..	..	..	..	..	..	..	..	..	..	..
Morocco	40	40	615	615	25.2	25.2	19	19	163	163	263.7	251.5	6	7	2	2
Tunisia	39	39	565	565	21.8	21.8	20	20	84	97	998.3	858.7	5	5	5	5

a. Average of the disclosure, director liability, and shareholder suits indexes.
b. Average of the rigidity of hours, difficulty of hiring, and difficulty of firing indexes.

Protecting investors (0 least protection to 10 most protection)				Employing workers											
Shareholder suits index		Investor protection index[a]		Rigidity of hours index (0 least rigid to 100 most rigid)		Difficulty of hiring index (0 least difficult to 100 most difficult)		Difficulty of firing index (0 least difficult to 100 most difficult)		Firing cost (weeks of wages)		Rigidity of employment index[b] (0 least rigid to 100 most rigid)			
2009	2010	2009	2010	2009	2010	2009	2010	2009	2010	2009	2010	2009	2010		
5	**5**	**4.3**	**4.4**	**30**	**30**	**38**	**38**	**40**	**40**	**68**	**67**	**36**	**36**		
6	6	5.7	5.7	60	60	67	67	70	70	58	58	66	66		
3	3	3.3	3.3	40	40	39	39	40	40	36	36	40	40		
3	3	6.0	6.0	0	0	0	0	40	40	90	90	13	13		
4	4	3.7	3.7	20	20	33	33	10	10	34	34	21	21		
5	5	3.3	3.3	53	53	0	0	30	30	26	26	28	28		
6	6	4.3	4.3	20	20	28	28	70	70	33	33	39	39		
6	6	4.0	4.0	33	33	33	33	70	70	93	93	46	46		
5	5	4.0	4.0	40	40	61	61	50	50	22	22	50	50		
3	3	3.3	3.3	20	20	39	39	40	40	36	36	33	33		
5	5	4.0	4.0	40	40	39	39	40	40	100	100	40	40		
4	4	3.3	3.3	47	47	50	72	70	70	31	31	63	63		
3	3	3.3	3.3	40	40	78	78	70	70	33	33	63	63		
3	3	3.3	3.3	47	47	33	33	20	20	49	49	33	33		
0	0	2.3	2.3	40	40	67	67	30	30	56	56	46	46		
4	4	3.7	3.7	60	60	67	67	70	70	133	133	66	66		
5	5	4.7	4.7	40	40	0	0	20	20	69	69	20	20		
5	5	4.3	4.3	20	20	33	33	30	30	40	40	28	28		
3	3	3.3	3.3	60	60	17	17	80	80	43	43	52	52		
5	5	2.7	2.7	40	40	0	0	40	40	26	26	27	27		
6	6	6.0	6.0	20	20	11	11	50	50	178	178	27	27		
1	1	2.7	2.7	20	20	33	33	20	20	26	26	24	24		
5	5	4.0	4.0	27	27	67	67	70	70	87	87	54	54		
10	10	5.0	5.0	0	0	22	22	30	30	47	47	17	17		
8	8	3.7	3.7	20	20	22	22	0	0	44	44	14	14		
6	6	3.7	3.7	20	20	22	22	40	40	84	84	27	27		
6	6	5.7	5.7	40	40	89	89	40	40	30	30	56	56		
5	5	5.3	5.3	0	0	44	44	20	20	84	84	21	21		
4	4	3.7	3.7	20	20	33	33	40	40	31	31	31	31		
3	3	3.7	3.7	20	20	56	56	40	40	31	31	39	39		
9	9	7.7	7.7	13	33	0	0	40	20	35	4	18	18		
9	9	6.0	6.0	33	33	67	67	20	20	134	134	40	40		
6	6	5.3	5.3	20	20	0	0	20	20	24	24	13	13		
3	3	3.3	3.3	53	53	100	100	50	50	35	35	68	68		
5	5	5.7	5.7	0	0	0	0	20	20	50	50	7	7		
3	3	6.3	6.3	40	0	44	11	30	10	26	26	7	7		
6	6	3.3	3.3	67	67	50	50	60	60	91	91	59	50		
2	2	3.0	3.0	53	53	72	72	50	50	38	38	59	59		
5	5	5.7	5.7	13	13	44	44	50	50	39	39	36	36		
6	6	6.3	6.3	40	40	33	33	50	50	189	189	41	41		
..	..	..	..	..	..	..	..	..	..	..	..	..	..		
8	8	8.0	8.0	20	20	56	56	30	30	24	24	35	35		
4	4	3.3	3.3	20	20	39	39	50	50	118	118	36	36		
5	6	2.0	4.3	0	0	11	11	20	20	53	53	10	10		
8	8	5.0	5.0	13	13	100	100	50	50	18	18	54	54		
4	4	3.7	3.7	40	40	61	83	40	40	36	36	54	54		
5	5	4.0	4.0	0	0	0	0	0	0	13	13	0	0		
7	7	5.3	5.3	33	33	22	11	20	20	178	178	21	21		
4	4	4.3	4.3	40	40	0	0	60	60	446	446	33	33		
4	**4**	**4.7**	**4.8**	**28**	**28**	**43**	**40**	**58**	**58**	**63**	**63**	**42**	**42**		
4	4	5.3	5.3	40	40	44	44	40	40	17	17	41	41		
5	5	5.3	5.3	20	20	0	0	60	60	132	132	27	27		
..	..	..	..	..	..	..	..	..	..	..	..	..	..		
1	1	3.0	3.3	40	40	100	89	50	50	85	85	60	60		
6	6	5.3	5.3	13	13	28	28	80	80	17	17	40	40		

Table 4.2 Investment climate

	Private sector fixed capital formation (% of GDP) 2009[a]	Net foreign direct investment ($ millions) 2009[a]	Domestic credit to private sector (% of GDP) 2009[a]	Enterprise Surveys: Firms that believe the court system is fair, impartial, and uncorrupt (%) 2009–10[b]	Enterprise Surveys: Viewed by firms as a major constraint (% of firms): Corruption 2009–10[b]	Crime, theft, and discord 2009–10[b]	Tax rates 2009–10[b]	Finance 2009–10[b]	Electricity 2009–10[b]	Labor regulations 2009–10[b]	Labor skills 2009–10[b]	Transportation 2009–10[b]	Customs and trade regulations 2009–10[b]
SUB-SAHARAN AFRICA	**13.4**	**..**	**64.4**										
Angola	2.4	2,198.5	21.2	23.7	75.6	28.1	26.4	38.5	35.7	26.1	25.9	25.3	35.8
Benin	15.4	..	22.2	9.6	67.8	52.7	67.6	70.3	51.9	16.1	28.2	46.7	51.8
Botswana	8.9	251.3	25.5	79.5	27.4	22.6	16.9	25.5	34.8	14.0	32.2	20.1	15.8
Burkina Faso	..	..	17.5	38.7	70.5	42.2	75.7	75.0	53.9	26.0	37.5	40.3	42.6
Burundi	..	0.3	21.7	..	..	..	..	..	..	..	..	..	..
Cameroon	12.4	–50.0	11.3	32.6	61.3	41.5	45.9	55.1	58.6	21.5	37.8	27.7	26.3
Cape Verde	42.7	120.0	64.0	59.5	29.8	62.3	51.8	36.7	53.1	5.7	49.2	24.0	27.2
Central African Republic	6.9	..	7.0	..	..	..	..	..	..	..	..	..	..
Chad	21.8	..	5.2	31.0	67.2	45.8	59.7	46.5	74.6	28.4	53.1	45.5	57.4
Comoros	7.7	..	16.0	..	..	..	..	..	..	..	..	..	..
Congo, Dem. Rep.	6.1	..	7.5	17.2	72.7	63.3	39.5	73.3	51.7	20.0	65.0	38.8	54.0
Congo, Rep.	13.5	..	4.8	32.3	65.0	44.1	40.9	44.8	71.1	24.5	51.5	48.4	45.9
Côte d'Ivoire	8.3	380.9	17.1	35.3	75.0	53.8	30.5	66.6	39.8	6.1	26.7	38.2	19.4
Djibouti	..	96.9	29.3	..	..	..	..	..	..	..	..	..	..
Equatorial Guinea	16.1	..	7.7	..	..	..	..	..	..	..	..	..	..
Eritrea	..	..	16.6	100.0	0.0	0.0	1.1	0.9	0.2	0.2	1.2	2.2	2.0
Ethiopia	5.9	221.5	..	..	..	..	..	..	..	..	..	..	..
Gabon	23.2	..	10.1	41.3	41.4	34.1	30.9	30.4	58.0	16.4	42.7	48.8	35.1
Gambia, The	..	39.4	18.9	..	..	..	..	..	..	..	..	..	..
Ghana	11.6	1,677.8	..	..	..	..	..	..	..	..	..	..	..
Guinea	17.0	140.9	..	..	..	..	..	..	..	..	..	..	..
Guinea-Bissau	..	..	5.6	..	..	..	..	..	..	..	..	..	..
Kenya	14.5	94.5	31.5	..	..	..	..	..	..	..	..	..	..
Lesotho	17.3	62.9	13.5	33.2	46.7	33.5	47.1	28.6	44.3	11.3	16.5	19.8	21.7
Liberia	..	217.8	16.1	44.3	31.2	26.8	19.0	35.0	59.1	2.6	5.1	39.3	15.6
Madagascar	29.4	..	11.5	28.8	42.7	48.1	40.8	39.4	54.6	2.2	17.0	26.6	18.7
Malawi	14.9	..	14.2	74.3	12.8	22.8	15.6	51.0	37.6	2.7	21.8	24.6	11.0
Mali	..	..	17.4	42.7	24.8	17.3	26.3	48.2	33.5	6.4	12.2	21.4	16.9
Mauritania	..	..	..	..	..	..	..	..	..	..	..	..	..
Mauritius	19.5	218.9	85.1	63.6	50.7	41.5	25.1	46.3	42.9	8.8	45.7	45.8	17.7
Mozambique	7.9	878.4	25.1	..	..	..	..	..	..	..	..	..	..
Namibia	15.6	528.1	46.8	..	..	..	..	..	..	..	..	..	..
Niger	..	..	12.2	49.6	83.7	44.2	60.4	62.0	63.2	5.3	37.1	50.0	31.6
Nigeria	..	5,647.2	37.6	..	..	..	..	..	..	..	..	..	..
Rwanda	10.6	118.7	..	..	..	..	..	..	..	..	..	..	..
São Tomé and Príncipe	..	7.2	34.6	..	..	..	..	..	..	..	..	..	..
Senegal	17.8	..	24.7	..	..	..	..	..	..	..	..	..	..
Seychelles	20.9	242.9	25.1	..	..	..	..	..	..	..	..	..	..
Sierra Leone	7.4	74.3	9.3	29.7	36.9	14.2	42.5	34.6	53.4	11.4	16.0	29.9	26.9
Somalia	..	..	..	..	..	..	..	..	..	..	..	..	..
South Africa	13.4	4,042.4	147.1	..	..	..	..	..	..	..	..	..	..
Sudan	16.3	2,682.2	12.3	..	..	..	..	..	..	..	..	..	..
Swaziland	3.0	58.7	25.0	..	..	..	..	..	..	..	..	..	..
Tanzania	20.5	414.5	15.3	..	..	..	..	..	..	..	..	..	..
Togo	..	..	21.9	14.1	70.2	22.6	43.5	58.6	50.9	3.1	17.2	32.1	27.5
Uganda	17.5	603.7	13.1	..	..	..	..	..	..	..	..	..	..
Zambia	17.8	699.2	12.0	..	..	..	..	..	..	..	..	..	..
Zimbabwe	1.7	..	..	..	..	..	..	..	..	..	..	..	..
NORTH AFRICA	**19.9**	**9,702.9**	**35.2**										
Algeria	33.0	..	16.2	..	..	..	..	..	..	..	..	..	..
Egypt, Arab Rep.	10.9	6,140.4	36.2	..	..	..	..	..	..	..	..	..	..
Libya	..	546.0	10.9	..	..	..	..	..	..	..	..	..	..
Morocco	24.8	1,491.3	64.4	..	..	..	..	..	..	..	..	..	..
Tunisia	23.2	1,525.2	68.4	..	..	..	..	..	..	..	..	..	..

a. Provisional.
b. Data are for the most recent year available during the period specified.

Number of tax payments 2010	Time to prepare, file, and pay taxes (hours) 2010	Total tax rate (% of profit) 2010	Highest marginal tax rate, corporate (%) 2009–10[b]	Time dealing with officials (% of management time) 2009–10[b]	Average time to clear customs (days): Direct exports 2009–10[b]	Average time to clear customs (days): Imports 2009–10[b]	Interest rate spread (lending rate minus deposit rate) 2009	Listed domestic companies 2009	Market capitalization of listed companies (% of GDP) 2009[a]	Turnover ratio for traded stocks (%) 2009[a]
Enterprise Surveys: Regulation and tax administration										
37	**310**	**67**					**..**	**..**	**..**	**..**
31	282	53.2	35.0	12.2	6.7	11.4	8.1	..	..	..
55	270	66.0	..	20.7	9.6	33.0	..	..	..	..
19	152	19.5	25.0	10.2	6.2	3.7	6.3	20	33.8	2.7
46	270	44.9	..	22.2	7.4	16.4	..	..	..	..
32	211	153.4	..	..	..	..	..	..	..	..
44	654	49.1	..	7.0	15.1	24.0	..	..	..	..
43	186	37.1	..	3.9	..	20.5	8.1	..	..	..
54	504	203.8	..	..	..	..	..	..	..	..
54	732	65.4	..	20.8	11.9	27.5	..	..	..	..
20	100	217.9	..	..	..	..	8.6	..	..	..
32	336	339.7	38.0	29.4	18.0	45.4	49.5	..	..	..
61	606	65.5	..	6.0	..	31.4	..	..	..	..
64	270	44.4	25.0	1.6	16.6	31.2	..	38	26.4	2.0
35	90	38.7	..	..	..	..	..	..	..	..
46	492	59.5	..	..	..	..	..	..	..	..
18	216	84.5	..	0.5	9.6	20.1	..	..	..	..
19	198	31.1	..	..	..	..	..	..	..	..
26	488	43.5	..	2.8	3.8	10.3	..	..	..	..
50	376	292.3	..	..	..	..	11.5	..	..	..
33	224	32.7	25.0	..	..	..	..	35	9.6	2.0
56	416	54.6	..	..	..	..	..	..	..	..
46	208	45.9	..	..	..	..	..	..	..	..
41	393	49.7	..	..	..	..	8.8	55	36.6	4.6
21	324	19.6	..	5.6	5.4	4.4	8.2	..	..	..
32	158	43.7	..	7.5	..	6.7	10.1	..	..	..
23	201	37.7	..	17.1	14.2	19.3	33.5	..	..	..
19	157	25.1	..	3.5	9.9	11.2	21.8	15	29.3	..
59	270	52.2	..	2.0	12.9	16.5	..	..	..	..
38	696	68.4	..	..	..	..	..	..	..	..
7	161	24.1	15.0	9.4	10.3	9.8	10.8	88	55.2	8.1
37	230	34.3	32.0	..	..	..	6.2	..	..	..
37	375	9.6	35.0	..	..		4.9	7	9.1	3.0
41	270	46.5	..	22.9	2.6	9.3	..	..	..	..
35	938	32.2	30.0	..	..	..	5.1	214	19.3	11.0
26	148	31.3	..	..	..	..	..	..	..	..
42	424	33.3	..	..	..	..	19.7	..	..	..
59	666	46.0	..	..	..	..	..	..	..	..
16	76	44.1	..	..	..	..	5.6	..	..	..
29	357	235.6	..	7.4	..	12.2	..	..	..	..
..	..	..	..	..	..	..	..	..	..	..
9	200	30.5	34.6	..	..	..	3.2	363	247.0	57.3
42	180	36.1	35.0	..	..	..	..	..	..	..
33	104	36.8	30.0	..	..	..	6.0	5	..	..
48	172	45.2	30.0	..	..	..	7.1	15	..	..
53	270	50.8	..	2.7	6.7	9.0	..	..	..	..
32	161	35.7	45.0	..	..	..	11.2	8	..	..
37	132	16.1	35.0	..	..	..	15.0	19	..	..
49	242	40.3	30.9	..	..	..	..	94	..	..
25	**347**	**54.8**					**5.5**	**..**	**..**	**..**
34	451	72.0	..	..	..	..	6.3	..	..	..
29	433	42.6	20.0	..	..	..	5.5	305	47.7	60.1
..	..	..	40.0	..	..	..	3.5	..	..	..
28	358	41.7	..	..	..	..	..	78	68.8	45.7
8	144	62.8	30.0	..	..	..	..	49	23.1	16.2

Table 4.3 Financial sector infrastructure

	Macroeconomy							
	Foreign currency sovereign ratings		Gross national savings (% of GDP)		Money and quasi money (M2) (% of GDP)		Real interest rate (%)	
	Long-term 2010–11[b]	Short-term 2010–11[b]	2008	2009[c]	2008	2009[c]	2008	2009[c]
SUB-SAHARAN AFRICA			**15.5**	**15.4**	**41.0**	**47.7**	**..**	**..**
Angola	B+	B	23.6	9.7	18.0	31.1	−8.2	22.8
Benin	..	..	10.6	..	32.9	36.4	..	..
Botswana	..	..	34.8	16.4	39.0	46.8	−0.4	20.6
Burkina Faso	..	..	..	..	22.5	24.8	..	..
Burundi	..	..	..	..	34.2	36.7	−6.9	0.4
Cameroon	..	..	..	..	19.3	21.5	..	..
Cape Verde	..	..	26.7	31.3	85.2	84.2	8.9	6.9
Central African Republic	..	..	..	..	14.4	15.5	..	..
Chad	..	..	..	..	11.8	14.7	..	..
Comoros	..	..	..	..	27.1	28.6	4.7	5.7
Congo, Dem. Rep.	..	..	..	..	12.6	14.3	19.9	27.0
Congo, Rep.	..	..	..	..	16.0	22.2	..	..
Côte d'Ivoire	..	..	12.3	14.8	27.8	29.6	..	..
Djibouti	..	..	..	..	74.5	83.0	1.9	..
Equatorial Guinea	..	..	..	..	6.2	12.3	..	..
Eritrea	..	..	..	..	109.8	112.3	..	..
Ethiopia	..	..	17.1	16.1	30.9	0.0	−17.2	..
Gabon	..	..	..	..	16.8	22.1	..	..
Gambia, The	..	..	10.4	18.8	49.5	55.0	19.6	24.1
Ghana	B+	B	8.8	15.5	23.6	0.0	..	..
Guinea	..	..	1.4	7.7	0.0	0.0	..	..
Guinea-Bissau	..	..	..	..	20.8	23.3	..	..
Kenya	..	..	14.2	15.4	40.3	42.7	1.9	7.6
Lesotho	BB-	B	33.5	28.1	34.0	38.6	2.4	9.2
Liberia	..	..	−2.1	..	27.8	35.4	3.6	6.3
Madagascar	..	..	..	..	20.5	22.0	32.8	33.8
Malawi	..	..	..	..	19.7	23.5	15.0	15.6
Mali	..	..	..	..	25.8	25.2	..	..
Mauritania	..	..	..	..	0.0	0.0	..	..
Mauritius	..	..	16.7	16.7	97.0	104.0	13.6	17.5
Mozambique	..	..	3.8	9.1	30.8	35.7	9.4	12.0
Namibia	BBB-	F3	31.6	26.5	36.5	38.5	−0.5	4.4
Niger	..	..	..	..	15.7	17.1	..	..
Nigeria	BB-	B	..	..	30.1	37.1	4.1	19.1
Rwanda	B	B	17.3	15.1	0.0	0.0	3.3	..
São Tomé and Príncipe	..	..	..	..	35.5	35.5	7.6	14.6
Senegal	..	..	16.1	..	33.5	35.1	..	..
Seychelles	B	B	1.6	9.2	60.4	59.3	−13.0	−10.3
Sierra Leone	..	..	5.3	7.8	20.6	23.3	12.0	..
Somalia	..	..	..	..	0.0	0.0	..	..
South Africa	BBB+	F2	14.9	15.4	78.4	80.2	5.4	4.1
Sudan	..	..	17.4	12.2	17.5	20.3	..	..
Swaziland	..	..	6.9	2.4	24.2	27.6	4.3	5.6
Tanzania	..	..	13.3	21.2	27.6	28.8	4.4	7.1
Togo	..	..	..	..	37.8	42.6	..	..
Uganda	..	..	21.9	17.5	20.8	20.6	13.1	3.8
Zambia	B+	B	19.2	19.0	21.5	20.6	6.8	8.3
Zimbabwe	..	..	..	..	0.0	0.0	..	..
NORTH AFRICA			**32.5**	**..**	**67.0**	**75.7**	**..**	**..**
Algeria	..	..	..	..	54.8	64.1	−5.8	19.2
Egypt, Arab Rep.	BB	B	23.6	16.7	84.2	79.8	0.1	1.0
Libya	B	B	67.1	..	28.3	53.7	−15.5	57.8
Morocco	BBB-	F3	32.9	31.2	102.5	104.7	..	..
Tunisia	BBB-	F3	21.3	22.8	60.0	64.2	..	..

a. Data are consolidated for regional security markets where they exist.
b. Data are for the most recent year available during the period specified.
c. Provisional.

Intermediation						Capital markets[a]					
Domestic credit to private sector (% of GDP)		Interest rate spread (lending rate minus deposit rate)		Ratio of bank nonperforming loans to total gross loans (%)		Listed domestic companies		Market capitalization of listed companies (% of GDP)		Turnover ratio for traded stocks (%)	
2008	2009[c]	2008	2009[c]	2008	2009[c]	2008	2009[c]	2008	2009[c]	2008	2009[c]
56.0	**64.4**	**8.6**	**..**	**..**	**..**	**..**	**..**	**..**	**..**	**..**	**..**
12.6	21.2	6.0	8.1	..	..	..	..	..	..	..	..
20.9	22.2	..	..	..	..	..	..	..	..	..	..
21.0	25.5	7.9	6.3	..	..	19	20	26.3	33.8	3.1	2.7
18.4	17.5	..	..	..	..	..	..	..	..	..	..
20.9	21.7	..	..	..	..	..	..	..	..	..	..
10.2	11.3	..	..	..	..	..	..	..	..	..	..
61.1	64.0	6.2	8.1	..	..	..	..	..	..	..	..
7.0	7.0	..	..	..	..	..	..	..	..	..	..
3.7	5.2	..	..	..	..	..	..	..	..	..	..
11.5	16.0	8.0	8.6	..	..	..	..	..	..	..	..
7.1	7.5	35.4	49.5	..	..	..	..	..	..	..	..
3.2	4.8	..	..	..	..	..	..	..	..	..	..
16.3	17.1	..	..	..	..	38	38	30.2	26.4	4.1	2.0
24.7	29.3	9.4	..	..	..	..	..	..	..	..	..
4.4	7.7	..	..	..	..	..	..	..	..	..	..
18.4	16.6	..	..	..	..	..	..	..	..	..	..
17.8	..	3.3	..	..	..	..	..	..	..	..	..
8.5	10.1	..	..	8.5	9.8	..	..	..	..	..	..
17.3	18.9	14.1	11.5	..	..	..	..	..	..	..	..
15.9	..	..	..	7.7	16.2	35	35	11.9	9.6	5.2	2.0
..	..	..	..	..	..	..	..	..	..	..	..
4.9	5.6	..	..	..	..	..	..	..	..	..	..
30.3	31.5	8.7	8.8	9.0	7.9	53	55	36.4	36.6	11.8	4.6
11.1	13.5	8.5	8.2	4.0	4.0	..	..	..	..	..	..
12.5	16.1	10.4	10.1	..	..	..	..	..	..	..	..
11.2	11.5	33.5	33.5	..	..	..	..	..	..	..	..
11.9	14.2	21.8	21.8	..	..	15	15	43.5	29.3	..	..
17.2	17.4	..	..	..	..	..	..	..	..	..	..
..	..	..	..	..	..	..	..	..	..	..	..
87.8	85.1	11.4	10.8	..	..	41	88	37.0	55.2	8.9	8.1
18.3	25.1	7.3	6.2	1.9	1.8	..	..	..	..	..	..
44.9	46.8	5.4	4.9	3.1	2.7	7	7	6.9	9.1	2.8	3.0
10.0	12.2	..	..	..	..	..	..	..	..	..	..
33.9	37.6	3.5	5.1	6.3	6.6	213	214	24.0	19.3	29.3	11.0
..	..	9.8	..	12.6	13.1	..	..	..	..	..	..
29.9	34.6	19.7	19.7	..	..	..	..	..	..	..	..
24.3	24.7	..	..	19.1	18.7	..	..	..	..	..	..
32.3	25.1	7.8	5.6	..	..	..	..	..	..	..	..
7.1	9.3	14.8	..	17.9	16.5	..	..	..	..	..	..
..	..	..	..	..	..	..	..	..	..	..	..
145.1	147.1	3.5	3.2	3.9	5.9	425	363	177.7	247.0	60.6	57.3
10.5	12.3	..	..	..	..	..	..	..	..	..	..
23.6	25.0	6.7	6.0	7.6	8.1	7	5	..	..	..	..
16.1	15.3	6.7	7.1	..	..	14	15	6.2	..	..	..
18.7	21.9	..	..	..	..	..	..	..	..	..	..
13.9	13.1	9.8	11.2	2.2	4.2	6	8	..	..	..	..
15.2	12.0	12.5	15.0	..	..	19	19	..	..	..	..
..	..	..	..	..	..	81	94	..	..	..	..
32.6	**35.2**	**5.7**	**5.5**	**14.8**	**13.2**	**..**	**..**	**..**	**..**	**..**	**..**
13.2	16.2	6.3	6.3	..	..	..	..	..	..	..	..
42.8	36.2	5.7	5.5	14.8	13.4	373	305	52.7	47.7	61.9	60.1
6.8	10.9	3.5	3.5	..	..	..	..	..	..	..	..
63.2	64.4	..	..	6.0	5.5	77	78	74.0	68.8	31.1	45.7
65.8	68.4	..	..	15.5	13.2	49	49	15.6	23.1	25.5	16.2

Table 5.1 International trade and tariff barriers

	Trade											
								Annual average (% of GDP)		Annual growth (%)		
	Total (% of GDP) 2009[a]	Merchandise (% of GDP) 2009[a]	Services (% of GDP) 2009[a]	Exports of goods and services ($ millions) 2009[a]	Imports of goods and services ($ millions) 2009[a]	Exports of goods and services (% of GDP) 2009[a]	Imports of goods and services (% of GDP) 2009[a]	Exports of goods and services 2000–09	Imports of goods and services 2000–09	Exports of goods and services 2009[a]	Imports of goods and services 2009[a]	Terms of trade index (2000 = 100) 2009[a]
SUB-SAHARAN AFRICA	**63.3**	**53.6**	**13.4**	**298,039**	**317,933**	**29.8**	**33.5**	**32.4**	**33.9**	**..**	**..**	**..**
Angola	98.5	75.6	26.2	39,432	34,901	52.2	46.2	73.6	54.4	..	..	..
Benin	42.0	45.7	..	922	1,875	13.8	28.2	14.1	27.3	..	..	..
Botswana	78.2	69.2	15.9	3,971	5,273	33.6	44.6	45.5	37.0	–28.0	–9.3	82.7
Burkina Faso	..	36.0	..	..	..	..	..	9.7	24.0	..	..	..
Burundi	..	35.2	17.1	..	..	..	..	8.7	31.0	..	..	..
Cameroon	57.5	32.7	15.2	5,896	6,856	26.6	30.9	22.9	23.3	–4.8	–5.2	106.9
Cape Verde	89.0	48.1	52.3	366	1,013	23.6	65.4	24.1	60.6	11.9	13.0	58.7
Central African Republic	36.9	20.9	..	290	449	14.5	22.4	14.5	21.4	..	..	..
Chad	112.2	69.5	..	2,879	4,794	42.1	70.1	39.4	56.5	..	..	..
Comoros	62.8	30.4	..	79	258	14.7	48.2	15.2	37.0	..	..	..
Congo, Dem. Rep.	31.3	63.4	..	1,017	2,298	9.6	21.7	24.4	32.6	5.4	–11.9	85.9
Congo, Rep.	122.8	88.7	..	6,884	4,876	71.9	50.9	79.1	54.9	..	..	..
Côte d'Ivoire	75.5	64.2	14.8	9,722	7,866	41.7	33.8	46.6	37.5	9.3	11.0	96.1
Djibouti	..	46.2	42.9	..	..	..	..	40.7	53.6	..	..	..
Equatorial Guinea	115.6	137.3	..	7,713	4,328	74.1	41.6	89.5	54.2	..	..	..
Eritrea	24.7	29.6	..	84	379	4.5	20.3	8.1	53.0	..	..	..
Ethiopia	39.4	33.5	14.4	3,011	8,229	10.6	28.8	12.9	29.7	6.9	16.4	115.3
Gabon	85.5	66.0	..	5,773	3,685	52.2	33.3	60.7	32.1	–4.9	–2.8	124.4
Gambia, The	80.6	43.5	25.5	223	368	30.4	50.1	38.8	53.6	2.5	3.8	71.3
Ghana	71.8	52.1	18.0	7,982	10,820	30.5	41.3	35.8	53.3	..	–14.1	..
Guinea	86.2	58.7	9.8	1,671	1,865	40.7	45.4	30.3	33.3	3.0	16.8	98.8
Guinea-Bissau	..	41.2	..	..	..	..	..	30.1	55.3	..	..	..
Kenya	63.5	49.8	16.1	7,413	11,253	25.2	38.3	25.4	34.7	–7.0	–0.2	114.5
Lesotho	163.0	171.0	12.5	809	1,764	51.2	111.7	52.9	110.4	–17.2	–1.1	157.3
Liberia	..	80.1	162.0	..	..	..	..	28.9	75.6	..	..	..
Madagascar	80.7	51.1	..	2,447	4,484	28.5	52.2	27.5	42.5	9.3	–10.5	88.3
Malawi	67.8	55.4	..	1,420	1,783	30.0	37.7	25.9	41.1	..	..	..
Mali	..	52.7	..	..	..	..	..	28.5	39.6	..	..	..
Mauritania	117.3	92.6	..	1,504	2,043	49.7	67.6	41.7	69.2	..	..	..
Mauritius	107.5	66.0	44.8	4,161	5,074	48.4	59.1	58.4	63.0	–4.8	–4.6	81.0
Mozambique	68.9	60.4	17.1	2,454	4,287	25.1	43.8	29.0	44.0	2.4	14.0	49.3
Namibia	106.5	93.6	12.2	4,319	5,548	46.6	59.9	44.2	48.9	–14.0	5.3	138.2
Niger	..	44.6	..	..	..	..	..	16.2	25.0	..	..	..
Nigeria	63.0	52.9	11.4	62,054	46,999	35.9	27.2	42.3	31.0	..	..	..
Rwanda	40.9	27.2	16.5	610	1,524	11.7	29.2	10.4	26.3	..	..	..
São Tomé and Príncipe	..	64.4	15.4	..	..	..	..	..	..	..	..	..
Senegal	68.0	53.8	..	3,082	5,637	24.0	44.0	26.7	42.2	–8.8	–17.1	91.9
Seychelles	246.9	162.6	93.2	912	975	119.3	127.6	94.0	105.2	10.8	1.7	100.0
Sierra Leone	44.2	38.7	8.7	305	554	15.7	28.5	19.9	33.8	..	..	..
Somalia	..	..	..	..	..	..	..	..	..	..	..	..
South Africa	55.4	47.6	9.4	77,883	80,328	27.3	28.1	29.7	29.3	–19.5	–17.4	126.3
Sudan	35.9	32.1	5.6	8,230	11,391	15.1	20.8	16.6	22.0	..	..	..
Swaziland	136.3	103.3	25.4	1,794	2,295	59.8	76.5	83.5	91.2	–6.1	–3.5	100.0
Tanzania	58.4	44.2	16.7	4,963	7,511	23.2	35.2	20.0	28.7	15.5	14.1	119.3
Togo	..	80.6	..	..	..	..	..	36.0	53.7	..	..	..
Uganda	58.0	42.3	14.9	3,753	5,557	23.4	34.6	15.1	26.9	16.2	25.2	67.2
Zambia	67.8	63.3	7.4	4,560	4,118	35.6	32.2	33.8	38.0	..	..	..
Zimbabwe	101.7	91.9	..	2,040	3,678	36.3	65.4	36.5	46.4	5.2	36.0	102.7
NORTH AFRICA	**68.7**	**53.3**	**18.0**	**200,244**	**193,682**	**32.1**	**36.6**	**35.6**	**31.4**	**–10.3**	**–7.5**	**..**
Algeria	76.5	60.1	..	56,798	50,772	40.4	36.1	42.0	24.6	–3.0	16.7	103.3
Egypt, Arab Rep.	56.9	36.1	18.8	47,185	60,048	25.0	31.9	25.1	29.1	–14.5	–17.9	89.6
Libya	..	73.4	8.7	..	..	..	..	56.9	27.8	..	..	..
Morocco	68.1	51.2	21.1	26,121	36,088	28.6	39.5	31.4	37.6	–13.1	–6.0	99.5
Tunisia	107.3	84.8	21.4	20,568	21,894	52.0	55.3	49.4	52.6	–1.6	6.7	106.0

Structure of merchandise exports (% of total)					Structure of merchandise imports (% of total)				
Food	Agricultural raw materials	Fuel	Ores and metals	Manufactures	Food	Agricultural raw materials	Fuel	Ores and metals	Manufactures
2009	2009	2009	2009	2009	2009	2009	2009	2009	2009
13.7	**3.0**	**36.9**	**15.3**	**30.8**	**11.2**	**1.0**	**16.8**	**1.7**	**66.2**
..	..	..	..	..	..	..	..	..	..
..	..	..	..	..	..	..	..	..	..
5.2	0.2	0.3	16.1	78.0	13.1	0.9	13.3	2.1	69.5
26.8	60.5	0.0	0.6	12.1	15.7	0.7	23.6	0.7	59.0
67.5	4.8	1.9	4.8	20.6	12.5	1.4	2.4	0.6	80.9
..	..	..	..	..	..	..	..	..	..
72.6	0.0	..	0.7	26.7	29.4	1.3	11.6	1.2	56.5
..	..	..	..	..	..	..	..	..	..
..	..	..	..	..	..	..	..	..	..
..	..	..	..	..	..	..	..	..	..
..	..	..	..	..	..	..	..	..	..
..	..	..	..	..	..	..	..	..	..
48.2	5.7	30.0	0.4	15.2	23.2	0.8	25.0	1.2	48.6
0.4	0.0	6.5	0.3	90.7	29.3	0.6	6.5	0.8	62.4
..	..	..	..	..	..	..	..	..	..
..	..	..	..	..	..	..	..	..	..
77.5	11.9	0.0	0.8	8.7	10.9	0.5	15.9	1.2	71.5
..	..	..	..	..	..	..	..	..	..
53.0	1.0	0.0	6.9	39.1	34.3	1.3	15.6	0.6	48.1
..	..	..	..	..	..	..	..	..	..
..	..	..	..	..	..	..	..	..	..
..	..	..	..	..	..	..	..	..	..
44.0	13.2	4.2	2.0	36.6	15.4	1.4	21.5	1.6	60.0
..	..	..	..	..	..	..	..	..	..
..	..	..	..	..	..	..	..	..	..
28.8	5.2	4.9	3.0	57.2	10.7	0.6	10.4	0.4	77.7
86.6	3.8	0.1	0.8	8.6	13.1	1.0	10.4	1.0	74.2
..	..	..	..	..	..	..	..	..	..
..	..	..	..	..	..	..	..	..	..
32.4	0.9	0.0	0.7	64.6	21.7	2.4	15.6	1.1	59.2
23.3	3.1	17.5	3.9	11.7	15.4	1.2	15.4	0.5	55.0
..	..	..	..	..	..	..	..	..	..
..	..	..	..	..	..	..	..	..	..
4.5	1.1	90.4	0.2	3.6	11.8	1.0	1.0	1.8	83.6
42.3	1.7	0.1	31.9	19.4	12.4	1.5	7.8	1.8	76.1
92.4	0.7	0.0	0.0	3.0	35.9	0.9	15.4	1.1	46.6
29.5	1.1	24.0	3.4	41.3	24.2	1.5	23.2	0.9	50.1
..	..	..	..	..	..	..	..	..	..
..	..	..	..	..	..	..	..	..	..
..	..	..	..	..	..	..	..	..	..
10.2	1.9	11.1	29.3	47.5	6.5	0.9	21.5	1.3	64.3
5.6	1.4	92.1	0.3	0.4	14.9	1.1	4.0	0.9	77.8
..	..	..	..	..	..	..	..	..	..
35.5	9.8	1.0	24.6	24.6	8.9	0.9	22.6	1.0	66.5
..	..	..	..	..	..	..	..	..	..
..	..	..	..	..	..	..	..	..	..
7.5	1.4	0.9	81.1	8.4	6.5	0.7	13.9	13.3	65.1
19.4	23.1	0.9	22.3	34.3	22.4	0.4	12.9	5.2	57.6
6.3	**0.4**	**63.6**	**2.4**	**27.2**	**..**	**..**	**..**	**..**	**..**
0.3	0.0	97.7	0.5	1.6	16.3	1.5	1.1	1.4	79.8
..	..	..	..	..	..	..	..	..	..
..	..	..	..	..	..	..	..	..	..
22.1	1.6	2.0	8.8	65.5	11.2	2.1	20.5	2.5	63.0
9.2	0.5	13.6	1.3	75.4	8.6	2.0	11.5	3.1	74.8

(continued)

Table 5.1 International trade and tariff barriers (continued)

	Export indexes (0 low to 1 high)		Competitiveness indicator (%)		Tariff barriers, all products (%)								
	Diversification 2009	Concentration 2009	Sectoral effect 2005–09	Global effect 2005–09	Binding coverage 2010	Simple mean bound rate 2010	Simple mean tariff 2010	Dispersion around the mean 2010	Weighted mean tariff 2010	Share of lines with international peaks 2010	Share of lines with domestic peaks 2010	Share of lines that are bound 2009	Share of lines with specific rates 2010
SUB-SAHARAN AFRICA	**0.61**	**0.42**			**..**	**..**	**..**	**0.9**	**..**	**..**	**..**	**51.9**	**..**
Angola	0.82	0.95	–0.2	16.0	..	..	..	0.9	..	..	..	100.0	..
Benin	0.75	0.35	–1.3	–13.9	39.5	28.7	13.3	0.6	15.4	50.2	0.0	39.3	0.0
Botswana	0.86	0.45	–15.8	–6.4	96.1	19.0	8.8	1.5	5.2	20.2	8.5	96.6	0.0
Burkina Faso	0.72	0.34	–8.2	5.7	39.4	42.5	12.4	..	8.8	44.5	0.0	39.2	0.0
Burundi	0.80	0.59	6.5	–11.5	22.3	67.8	9.8	..	5.5	29.8	1.1	21.8	0.0
Cameroon	0.79	0.48	–0.1	–2.7	..	..	..	0.6	..	..	..	13.3	..
Cape Verde	0.70	0.44	–0.7	11.5	100.0	15.8	14.7	1.3	11.6	44.3	11.9	100.0	0.0
Central African Republic	0.34	0.12	–3.2	–2.1	..	..	..	..	..	..	..	62.5	..
Chad	0.70	0.40	0.9	–3.0	..	..	..	0.6	..	..	..	13.5	..
Comoros	0.75	0.51	–0.2	–3.0	..	..	..	..	..	..	..	..	..
Congo, Dem. Rep.	0.82	0.35	–2.8	20.3	..	..	..	0.5	..	..	..	100.0	..
Congo, Rep.	0.78	0.70	0.0	0.6	..	..	..	..	..	..	..	16.1	..
Côte d'Ivoire	0.71	0.36	7.1	–3.1	33.8	11.2	13.1	0.6	7.3	47.9	0.0	33.1	0.0
Djibouti	0.65	0.33	1.4	12.3	..	..	..	0.4	..	..	..	100.0	..
Equatorial Guinea	0.74	0.73	–0.9	5.6	..	..	..	..	..	..	..	..	..
Eritrea	0.63	0.22	–2.5	2.0	..	..	..	..	..	..	..	..	..
Ethiopia	0.80	0.34	7.4	4.3	..	..	..	0.7	..	..	..	..	..
Gabon	0.85	0.72	–0.1	–4.3	..	..	..	0.6	..	..	..	100.0	..
Gambia, The	0.63	0.26	0.4	19.1	..	..	..	0.2	..	..	..	13.7	..
Ghana	0.81	0.44	8.2	–0.8	..	..	..	0.5	..	..	..	14.3	..
Guinea	0.79	0.49	1.6	–6.4	..	..	..	0.6	..	..	..	38.9	..
Guinea-Bissau	0.80	0.93	–2.6	–3.4	97.6	48.6	13.3	0.6	9.9	51.8	0.0	97.8	0.0
Kenya	0.70	0.22	1.9	1.1	15.2	95.3	12.1	1.0	9.2	36.6	0.8	14.6	0.0
Lesotho	0.86	0.50	–3.0	–4.3	100.0	78.9	9.5	1.5	10.5	21.6	5.7	100.0	0.0
Liberia	0.77	0.60	11.4	–16.5	..	..	..	..	..	..	..	..	..
Madagascar	0.73	0.22	–0.8	0.3	..	..	..	..	..	..	..	29.7	..
Malawi	0.81	0.62	9.2	–0.4	..	..	..	..	..	..	..	31.2	..
Mali	0.87	0.75	–8.9	–5.2	40.5	28.9	12.8	0.6	8.4	47.9	0.0	40.6	0.0
Mauritania	0.82	0.50	12.4	4.5	..	..	..	..	..	..	..	39.3	..
Mauritius	0.70	0.25	0.9	–2.9	..	..	..	3.8	..	..	..	17.8	..
Mozambique	0.73	0.32	–3.4	4.0	..	..	..	0.8	..	..	..	13.6	..
Namibia	0.87	0.31	–2.4	4.0	96.1	19.4	6.3	1.5	1.8	16.7	7.1	96.6	0.0
Niger	0.79	0.51	7.6	6.6	96.6	44.9	13.0	0.6	9.1	48.9	0.0	96.8	0.0
Nigeria	0.85	0.83	0.8	–0.4	19.5	119.4	10.9	0.7	10.6	34.9	0.0	19.2	0.0
Rwanda	0.82	0.40	1.7	21.0	100.0	89.3	9.9	..	6.0	31.4	1.0	100.0	0.0
São Tomé and Príncipe	0.56	0.70	11.5	0.2	..	..	..	..	..	..	..	..	..
Senegal	0.69	0.23	2.0	–9.8	100.0	30.0	13.4	0.6	8.9	50.5	0.0	100.0	0.0
Seychelles	0.84	0.52	6.1	–14.2	..	..	..	..	..	..	..	..	..
Sierra Leone	0.62	0.27	–5.9	9.7	..	..	..	..	..	..	..	100.0	..
Somalia	0.78	0.47	–0.2	5.0	..	..	..	..	..	..	..	..	..
South Africa	0.58	0.14	2.7	–0.5	96.1	19.4	7.6	1.6	4.4	17.9	7.5	96.6	0.0
Sudan	0.74	0.76	0.2	3.6	..	..	..	0.9	..	..	..	..	..
Swaziland	0.71	0.24	1.8	–5.9	96.1	19.4	10.9	1.5	10.2	26.2	12.0	96.6	0.0
Tanzania	0.77	0.29	6.1	–3.6	13.8	120.0	12.9	0.9	8.2	39.9	1.0	13.4	0.0
Togo	0.71	0.25	1.6	–4.5	14.3	80.0	12.8	0.6	14.2	47.3	0.0	14.0	0.0
Uganda	0.73	0.23	4.4	6.5	16.1	73.5	12.1	1.0	8.2	37.5	1.1	15.8	0.0
Zambia	0.86	0.65	5.7	–2.4	..	..	..	0.8	..	..	..	16.7	..
Zimbabwe	0.75	0.19	2.7	–16.9	..	..	..	..	..	..	..	21.0	..
NORTH AFRICA	**..**	**..**			**..**	**..**	**..**	**..**	**..**	**..**	**..**	**..**	**..**
Algeria	0.80	0.56	1.9	–1.5	..	..	..	0.7	..	..	..	..	..
Egypt, Arab Rep.	0.59	0.17	1.2	8.6	..	..	..	4.7	..	..	..	99.3	..
Libya	0.82	0.76	–0.3	2.8	..	..	..	..	..	..	..	..	..
Morocco	0.69	0.15	2.4	–2.2	..	..	..	1.4	..	..	..	100.0	..
Tunisia	0.55	0.16	–0.4	5.7	..	..	..	..	..	..	..	57.6	..

a. Provisional.
b. Data are for the most recent year available during the period specified.

Tariff barriers, primary products (%)			Tariff barriers, manufactured products (%)			Average cost to ship 20 ft container from port to final destination ($)		Average time to clear customs (days)	
Simple mean tariff 2010	Dispersion around the mean 2009	Weighted mean tariff 2010	Simple mean tariff 2010	Dispersion around the mean 2009	Weighted mean tariff 2010	Export 2010	Import 2010	Direct exports 2009–10[b]	Imports 2009–10[b]
..	**0.8**	**..**	**..**	**0.9**	**..**	**1,938**	**2,458**		
..	0.7	..	..	0.9	..	1,850	2,840	6.7	11.4
15.5	0.5	12.4	12.9	0.6	11.7	1,251	1,400	9.6	33.0
6.1	1.4	0.5	9.0	1.5	8.0	3,010	3,390	6.2	3.7
11.4	0.5	8.1	12.5	..	11.7	2,412	4,030	7.4	16.4
15.4	..	9.4	9.1	..	11.5	2,747	4,285	..	..
..	0.5	..	..	0.6	..	1,379	1,978	15.1	24.0
16.2	1.1	12.2	14.3	1.3	9.8	1,200	1,000	..	20.5
..	..	..	..	..	..	5,491	5,554	..	..
..	0.5	..	..	0.6	..	5,902	8,150	11.9	27.5
..	..	..	..	..	..	1,073	1,057	..	..
..	0.5	..	..	0.5	..	3,505	3,735	18.0	45.4
..	..	..	..	..	..	3,818	7,709	..	31.4
15.1	0.5	5.4	12.8	0.6	11.7	1,969	2,577	16.6	31.2
..	0.7	..	..	0.4	..	836	911	..	..
..	..	..	..	..	..	1,411	1,411	..	..
..	..	..	..	..	..	1,431	1,581	9.6	20.1
..	0.5	..	..	..	..	1,890	2,993	..	..
..	0.5	..	..	..	..	1,945	1,955	3.8	10.3
..	0.3	..	..	..	..	831	975	..	..
..	0.3	..	..	..	..	1,013	1,203	..	..
..	0.5	..	..	..	..	855	1,391	..	..
14.6	0.5	10.0	12.9	..	11.7	1,545	2,349	..	..
16.0	0.7	12.6	11.7	..	11.5	2,055	2,190	..	..
9.2	1.4	1.6	9.5	..	8.0	1,680	1,610	5.4	4.4
..	..	..	..	..	..	1,232	1,212	..	6.7
..	..	..	..	..	..	1,197	1,555	14.2	19.3
..	..	..	..	..	..	1,713	2,570	9.9	11.2
12.8	..	7.9	12.8	..	11.7	2,202	3,067	12.9	16.5
..	..	..	..	..	..	1,520	1,523	..	..
..	..	..	..	..	..	737	689	10.3	9.8
..	..	..	..	..	..	1,100	1,475	..	..
4.1	..	2.1	6.7	..	8.0	1,686	1,813	..	..
14.0	..	10.7	12.8	..	11.7	3,545	3,545	2.6	9.3
11.8	..	9.1	10.7	..	11.3	1,263	1,440	..	..
11.5	..	6.4	9.7	..	11.5	3,275	4,990	..	..
..	..	..	..	..	..	690	577	..	..
14.1	..	7.7	13.2	..	11.7	1,098	1,940	..	..
..	..	..	..	..	..	876	876	..	..
..	..	..	..	..	..	1,573	1,639	..	12.2
..	..	..	..	..	..	..	..	..	..
5.4	1.5	1.9	7.8	1.6	8.0	1,531	1,807	..	..
..	0.5	..	..	0.9	..	2,050	2,900	..	..
9.7	1.4	1.3	11.1	1.5	8.0	1,754	1,849	..	..
17.5	0.7	8.7	12.4	0.9	11.5	1,262	1,475	..	..
14.4	0.5	12.4	12.6	0.6	11.7	940	963	6.7	9.0
15.7	0.7	8.8	11.6	1.0	11.5	2,780	2,940	..	..
..	0.5	..	..	0.8	..	2,664	3,315	..	..
..	..	..	..	..	..	3,280	5,101	..	..
..	**..**	**..**	**..**	**..**	**..**	**834**	**996**	**..**	**..**
..	0.5	..	..	0.7	..	1,248	1,428	..	..
..	4.8	..	..	4.7	..	613	698	..	..
..	..	..	..	..	..	..	..	..	..
..	1.2	..	..	1.4	..	700	1,000	..	..
..	..	..	..	..	..	773	858	..	..

Table 5.2 Top three exports and share in total exports, 2009

	First		Second	
	Product	Share of total exports (%)	Product	Share of total exports (%)
SUB-SAHARAN AFRICA				
Angola	Petroleum oils and oils from bituminous minerals, crude	96.3		
Benin	Cashew nuts, in shells	29.5	Cotton, not carded or combed	28.7
Botswana	Diamonds, nonindustrial, unworked or simply sawn or cleaved	27.9	Nickel mattes	19.9
Burkina Faso	Cotton, not carded or combed	52.1	Gold, semi-manufactured, including platinum plated, nonmonetary	19.6
Burundi	Coffee, not roasted, not decaffeinated	76.1	Black tea (fermented) and other partly fermented tea	9.3
Cameroon	Petroleum oils and oils from bituminous minerals, crude	39.6	Cocoa beans, whole or broken, raw or roasted	18.7
Cape Verde	Tunas, yellowfin	16.4	Fish, whole or in pieces	13.5
Central African Republic	Logs, tropical hardwoods, not elsewhere specified	25.8	Diamonds, not mounted or set, unsorted	25.4
Chad	Petroleum oils and oils from bituminous minerals, crude	90.9	Petroleum oils and oils from bituminous minerals, noncrude	5.6
Comoros	Cloves (whole fruit, cloves and stems)	32.1	Vessels and other floating structures for breaking up	26.8
Congo	Petroleum oils and oils from bituminous minerals, crude	87.8		
Congo, Dem. Rep.	Cobalt ores and concentrates	20.7	Petroleum oils and oils from bituminous minerals, crude	16.6
Cote d'Ivoire	Cocoa beans, whole or broken, raw or roasted	36.3	Petroleum oils and oils from bituminous minerals, crude	14.6
Djibouti	Live bovine animals other than purebred breeding animals	27.4	Sheep, live	17.8
Equatorial Guinea	Petroleum oils and oils from bituminous minerals, crude	72.7	Liquefied natural gas	22.2
Eritrea	Prefabricated buildings	19.3	Sheep, live	14.2
Ethiopia	Coffee, not roasted, not decaffeinated	31.0	Sesamum seeds	24.9
Gabon	Petroleum oils and oils from bituminous minerals, crude	69.9	Manganese ores and concentrates	9.8
Gambia, The	Cashew nuts, in shells	44.5	Petroleum oils and oils from bituminous minerals, crude	14.3
Ghana	Cocoa beans, whole or broken, raw or roasted	49.7	Manganese ores and concentrates	8.5
Guinea	Aluminum ores and concentrates	62.9	Aluminum oxide not elsewhere specified	11.2
Guinea-Bissau	Cashew nuts, in shells	92.2		
Kenya	Black tea (fermented) and other partly fermented tea	14.3	Cut flowers and flower buds, fresh	13.8
Lesotho	Diamonds, nonindustrial, unworked or simply sawn or cleaved	33.3	Men's and boys' trousers and shorts, of cotton, not knitted	13.8
Liberia	Cargo vessels and other vessels for transport of goods or persons	42.1	Tankers	19.3
Madagascar	Shrimps and prawns	9.3	Women's and girls' trousers, overalls, breeches, and shorts, of cotton	6.7
Malawi	Tobacco, partly or wholly stemmed	63.0	Dried leguminous vegetables, shelled, not elsewhere specified	8.8
Mali	Cotton, not carded or combed	39.3	Mineral or chemical fertilizers containing nitrogen, phosphorus, potassium	12.5
Mauritania	Iron ores and concentrates, nonagglomerated	45.4	Octopus, other than live, fresh, and chilled	14.4
Mauritius	T-shirts, singlets, and other vests, knitted of cotton	13.4	Cane sugar, raw	12.2
Mozambique	Aluminum, unwrought, not alloyed	38.1	Electrical energy	10.5
Namibia	Natural uranium and its compounds	16.4	Unwrought zinc, containing by weight 99.99 percent or more of zinc	14.5
Niger	Natural uranium and its compounds	70.5	Light oils and preparations	23.8
Nigeria	Petroleum oils and oils from bituminous minerals, crude	86.3	Liquefied natural gas	7.5
Rwanda	Coffee, not roasted, not decaffeinated	29.0	Niobium, tantalum, and vanadium ores and concentrates	20.6
São Tomé & Príncipe	Cocoa beans, whole or broken, raw or roasted	47.1	Wristwatches, other than automatic winding	12.3
Senegal	Phosphoric acid and polyphosphoric acids	25.5	Fish, fresh and chilled, not elsewhere specified	6.8
Seychelles	Tunas, skipjack, and bonito	59.2	Tunas, bigeye (Thunnus obesus)	7.3
Sierra Leone	Diamonds, nonindustrial, unworked or simply sawn or cleaved	21.5	Titanium ores and concentrates	11.8
Somalia	Goats, live	28.3	Sheep, live	24.3
South Africa	Platinum, unwrought or in powder form	9.3	Gold, unwrought, nonmonetary	6.4
Sudan	Petroleum oils and oils from bituminous minerals, crude	91.3		
Swaziland	Cane sugar, raw	15.7	Mixtures of odoriferous substances for the food or drink industries	13.4
Tanzania	Coffee, not roasted, not decaffeinated	9.6	Tobacco, partly or wholly stemmed	9.2
Togo	Cocoa beans, whole or broken, raw or roasted	47.1	Ground	8.3
Uganda	Coffee, not roasted, not decaffeinated	35.4	Fish fillets and other fish meat, fresh or chilled	8.8
Zambia	Refined copper, cathodes and sections of cathodes	49.8	Copper, unrefined, and copper anodes for electrolytic refining	16.5
Zimbabwe	Tobacco, partly or wholly stemmed	22.9	Ferro-chromium containing by weight more than 4% carbon	9.1
NORTH AFRICA				
Algeria	Petroleum oils and oils from bituminous minerals, crude	46.8	Natural gas, in gaseous state	21.0
Egypt, Arab Rep.	Liquefied natural gas	15.8	Petroleum oils and oils from bituminous minerals, crude	15.3
Libya	Petroleum oils and oils from bituminous minerals, crude	79.3	Natural gas, in gaseous state	9.1
Morocco	Phosphoric acid and polyphosphoric acids	6.6	Ignition and other wiring sets of a kind used in vehicles, aircraft or ships	4.8
Tunisia	Petroleum oils and oils from bituminous minerals, crude	9.4	Ignition and other wiring sets of a kind used in vehicles, aircraft or ships	6.1
AFRICA[a]	**Petroleum oils and oils from bituminous minerals, crude**	**44.8 [18.5]**	**Liquefied natural gas**	**3.9 [20.0]**

Note: Includes only products that account for more than 4 percent of total exports.
a. Values in brackets are Africa's share of total world exports.

Third		
Product	Share of total exports (%)	Number of exports accounting for 75 percent of total exports
		1
Copper waste and scrap	6.0	6
Diamonds, nonindustrial, not mounted or set, not elsewhere specified	8.6	16
Sesamum seeds	9.1	3
		1
Bananas, including plantains, fresh	8.4	5
Men's and boys' trousers and shorts, of cotton, not knitted	10.4	9
Logs, tropical wood specified in Subhe	16.7	4
		1
Essential oils, not elsewhere specified	18.6	3
		1
Copper ores and concentrates	14.1	6
Cocoa paste, not defatted	8.0	7
Goats, live	13.2	5
		2
Men's and boys' shirts, of cotton	6.9	19
Cut flowers and flower buds, fresh	10.9	7
Logs, tropical hardwoods, not elsewhere specified	7.0	2
Titanium ores and concentrates	12.3	4
Cocoa butter, fat and oil	5.6	7
Coffee, not roasted, not decaffeinated	4.0	3
		1
Coffee, not roasted, not decaffeinated	5.9	54
Pullovers, cardigans, and similar articles, knitted of cotton	11.0	6
Petroleum oils and oils from bituminous minerals, crude	13.3	4
Vanilla	5.6	31
Black tea (fermented) and other partly fermented tea	6.3	3
Sesamum seeds	8.1	8
Petroleum oils and oils from bituminous minerals, crude	13.2	4
Tunas, skipjack, and bonito	11.2	36
Light oils and preparations	9.0	8
Uranium ores and concentrates	13.3	7
		2
		1
Tin ores and concentrates	11.2	5
Aircraft, unladen weight of 2,000–15,000 kilograms	9.7	4
Fish, frozen, not elsewhere specified	6.0	19
Skipjack and stripbellied bonito	5.4	4
Cocoa beans, whole or broken, raw or roasted	8.5	22
Live bovine animals	21.6	4
Iron ores and concentrates, nonagglomerated	5.6	103
		1
Food preparations not elsewhere specified	10.6	25
Precious metal ores and concentrates, other than silver	8.3	31
Gold, unwrought, nonmonetary	7.7	5
Tobacco, partly or wholly stemmed	7.5	15
Copper ores and concentrates	7.8	4
Cane sugar, raw	8.3	19
Liquefied natural gas	10.8	3
Light oils and preparations	5.3	65
Petroleum oils and oils from bituminous minerals, noncrude	4.8	1
		76
Men's and boys' trousers and shorts, of cotton, not knitted	5.5	94
Natural gas, in gaseous state	**3.7 [9.9]**	**40**

Table 5.3 Regional integration, trade blocs

	Year established	Year of entry into force of most recent agreement	Type of most recent agreement[a]	Merchandise exports within bloc ($ millions) 1990	1995	2000	2005	2007	2008	2009
Economic and Monetary Community of Central African States (CEMAC)	1994	1999	CU	139	120	96	201	305	355	300
Economic Community of the Great Lakes Countries (CEPGL)	1976		NNA	7	8	10	20	29	73	64
Common Market for Eastern and Southern Africa (COMESA)	1994	1994	FTA	1,146	1,367	1,443	2,695	4,021	6,676	6,114
East African Community (EAC)	1996	2000	CU	335	628	689	1075	1,385	1,797	1,572
Economic Community of Central African States (ECCAS)	1983	2004[b]	NNA	160	157	182	255	385	449	378
Economic Community of West African States (ECOWAS)	1975	1993	PTA	1,532	1,875	2,715	5,497	6,717	9,355	7,312
Indian Ocean Commission (IOC)	1984	2005[b]	NNA	63	113	106	162	214	217	183
Southern African Development Community (SADC)	1992	2000	FTA	1,655	3,615	4,427	7,799	12,051	16,011	11,697
West African Economic and Monetary Union (UEMOA)	1994	2000	CU	621	560	741	1,390	1,735	2,281	1,927

	Year established	Year of entry into force of most recent agreement	Type of most recent agreement[a]	Merchandise exports within bloc (% of total bloc exports) 1990	1995	2000	2005	2007	2008	2009
Economic and Monetary Community of Central African States (CEMAC)	1994	1999	CU	2.3	2.1	1.0	0.9	1.1	0.8	1.2
Economic Community of the Great Lakes Countries (CEPGL)	1976		NNA	0.5	0.5	0.8	1.2	1.4	1.9	2.2
Common Market for Eastern and Southern Africa (COMESA)	1994	1994	FTA	4.7	6.1	4.6	4.6	4.5	5.3	7.2
East African Community (EAC)	1996	2000	CU	17.7	19.5	22.6	18.0	17.8	19.2	18.9
Economic Community of Central African States (ECCAS)	1983	2004[b]	NNA	1.4	1.5	1.0	0.6	0.6	0.4	0.6
Economic Community of West African States (ECOWAS)	1975	1993	PTA	8.0	9.0	7.6	9.3	7.8	8.5	9.9
Indian Ocean Commission (IOC)	1984	2005[b]	NNA	3.9	5.9	4.4	4.9	5.8	5.7	5.8
Southern African Development Community (SADC)	1992	2000	FTA	6.6	10.2	9.5	9.3	10.2	10.3	11.0
West African Economic and Monetary Union (UEMOA)	1994	2000	CU	13.0	10.3	13.1	13.4	14.9	15.9	13.2

	Year established	Year of entry into force of most recent agreement	Type of most recent agreement[a]	Merchandise exports by bloc (% of world exports)						
				1990	1995	2000	2005	2007	2008	2009
Economic and Monetary Community of Central African States (CEMAC)	1994	1999	CU	0.2	0.1	0.1	0.2	0.2	0.2	0.2
Economic Community of the Great Lakes Countries (CEPGL)	1976		NNA	0.0	0.0	0.0	0.0	0.0	0.0	0.0
Common Market for Eastern and Southern Africa (COMESA)	1994	1994	FTA	0.7	0.4	0.5	0.6	0.6	0.8	0.7
East African Community (EAC)	1996	2000	CU	0.1	0.1	0.0	0.1	0.1	0.1	0.1
Economic Community of Central African States (ECCAS)	1983	2004[b]	NNA	0.3	0.2	0.3	0.4	0.5	0.7	0.5
Economic Community of West African States (ECOWAS)	1975	1993	PTA	0.6	0.4	0.6	0.6	0.6	0.7	0.6
Indian Ocean Commission (IOC)	1984	2005[b]	NNA	0.0	0.0	0.0	0.0	0.0	0.0	0.0
Southern African Development Community (SADC)	1992	2000	FTA	0.7	0.7	0.7	0.8	0.9	1.0	0.9
West African Economic and Monetary Union (WAEMU/UEMOA)	1994	2000	CU	0.1	0.1	0.1	0.1	0.1	0.1	0.1

Note: **Economic and Monetary Community of Central Africa (CEMAC; formerly Central African Customs and Economic Union [UDEAC]),** Cameroon, the Central African Republic, Chad, the Republic of Congo, Equatorial Guinea, and Gabon; **Economic Community of the Great Lakes Countries (CEPGL),** Burundi, the Democratic Republic of the Congo, and Rwanda; **Common Market for Eastern and Southern Africa (COMESA),** Burundi, Comoros, the Democratic Republic of Congo, Djibouti, the Arab Republic of Egypt, Eritrea, Ethiopia, Kenya, Libya, Madagascar, Malawi, Mauritius, Rwanda, Seychelles, Sudan, Swaziland, Uganda, Zambia, and Zimbabwe; **East African Community (EAC),** Burundi, Kenya, Rwanda, Tanzania, and Uganda; **Economic Community of Central African States (ECCAS),** Angola, Burundi, Cameroon, the Central African Republic, Chad, the Democratic Republic of Congo, the Republic of Congo, Equatorial Guinea, Gabon, and São Tomé and Principe; **Economic Community of West African States (ECOWAS),** Benin, Burkina Faso, Cape Verde, Côte d'Ivoire, the Gambia, Ghana, Guinea, Guinea-Bissau, Liberia, Mali, Niger, Nigeria, Senegal, Sierra Leone, and Togo; **Indian Ocean Commission (IOC),** Comoros, Madagascar, Mauritius, Réunion, and Seychelles; **Southern African Development Community (SADC; formerly Southern African Development Coordination Conference),** Angola, Botswana, the Democratic Republic of the Congo, Lesotho, Madagascar, Malawi, Mauritius, Mozambique, Namibia, Seychelles, South Africa, Swaziland, Tanzania, Zambia, and Zimbabwe; **West African Economic and Monetary Union (UEMOA),** Benin, Burkina Faso, Côte d'Ivoire, Guinea-Bissau, Mali, Niger, Senegal, and Togo.

a. CU is customs union; FTA is free trade agreement; NNA is not notified agreement, which refers to preferential trade agreements established among member countries that are not notified to the World Trade Organization (these agreements may be functionally equivalent to any of the other agreements); and PTA is preferential trade agreement.

b. From the official website of the trade bloc.

Table 6.1 Water and sanitation

	Access, supply side	Access, demand side						Quality of supply	Financing		
	Internal fresh water resources per capita (cubic meters)	Population with sustainable access to an improved water source			Population with sustainable access to improved sanitation			Average duration of insufficient water supply	Committed nominal investment in water projects with private participation ($ millions)	ODA gross disbursements for water supply and sanitation sector ($ millions)	
		(% of total population)	(% of urban population)	(% of rural population)	(% of total population)	(% of urban population)	(% of rural population)				
	2007	2008	2008	2008	2008	2008	2008	2009–10[a]	2000–09[a]	2008	2009
SUB-SAHARAN AFRICA	**4,850**	**60**	**83**	**47**	**31**	**44**	**24**	**..**		**1,668.2**	**1,789.9**
Angola	8,431	50	60	38	57	86	18	9.9	..	22.3	13.9
Benin	1,227	75	84	69	12	24	4	19.0	..	63.5	55.0
Botswana	1,268	95	99	90	60	74	39	3.2	..	2.2	0.0
Burkina Faso	849	76	95	72	11	33	6	4.6	..	60.5	70.7
Burundi	1,284	72	83	71	46	49	46	..	..	15.7	19.2
Cameroon	14,630	74	92	51	47	56	35	23.5	0.0	18.5	8.7
Cape Verde	610	84	85	82	54	65	38	9.8	..	6.4	20.4
Central African Republic	33,119	67	92	51	34	43	28	..	..	1.9	6.7
Chad	1,412	50	67	44	9	23	4	2.7	..	26.0	28.9
Comoros	1,910	95	91	97	36	50	30	..	..	1.3	1.4
Congo, Dem. Rep.	14,395	46	80	28	23	23	23	13.6	..	62.0	73.7
Congo, Rep.	62,516	71	95	34	30	31	29	45.3	0.0	1.8	0.4
Côte d'Ivoire	3,819	80	93	68	23	36	11	27.7	0.0	7.9	30.6
Djibouti	360	92	98	52	56	63	10	..	..	3.2	7.1
Equatorial Guinea	40,485	..	..	..	..	..	..	..	..	0.0	0.0
Eritrea	586	61	74	57	14	52	4	..	..	8.2	7.4
Ethiopia	1,551	38	98	26	12	29	8	..	..	107.1	142.6
Gabon	115,340	87	95	41	33	33	30	1.1	..	18.6	3.2
Gambia, The	1,857	92	96	86	67	68	65	..	..	9.1	5.0
Ghana	1,325	82	90	74	13	18	7	..	0.0	124.4	56.3
Guinea	23,505	71	89	61	19	34	11	..	..	14.7	11.2
Guinea-Bissau	10,383	61	83	51	21	49	9	..	..	3.0	2.6
Kenya	548	59	83	52	31	27	32	..	..	101.3	98.2
Lesotho	2,574	85	97	81	29	40	25	6.1	..	18.8	23.1
Liberia	55,138	68	79	51	17	25	4	2.9	..	7.1	13.1
Madagascar	18,114	41	71	29	11	15	10	8.0	..	17.4	12.8
Malawi	1,118	80	95	77	56	51	57	4.7	..	13.9	16.0
Mali	4,835	56	81	44	36	45	32	12.1	..	47.1	78.0
Mauritania	127	49	52	47	26	50	9	..	..	21.9	23.6
Mauritius	2,182	99	100	99	91	93	90	6.0	0.0	9.5	10.8
Mozambique	4,586	47	77	29	17	38	4	..	..	81.6	95.5
Namibia	2,949	92	99	88	33	60	17	..	0.0	11.8	12.0
Niger	248	48	96	39	9	34	4	..	3.4	38.1	43.7
Nigeria	1,496	58	75	42	32	36	28	..	..	108.7	105.5
Rwanda	1,005	65	77	62	54	50	55	..	..	37.7	28.2
São Tomé and Príncipe	13,829	89	89	88	26	30	19	..	..	0.9	1.0
Senegal	2,169	69	92	52	51	69	38	..	0.0	76.2	58.3
Seychelles	..	..	100	..	..	97	..	..	..	0.2	0.6
Sierra Leone	29,518	49	86	26	13	24	6	0.0	..	13.3	10.0
Somalia	687	30	67	9	23	52	6	..	..	1.9	5.1
South Africa	928	91	99	78	77	84	65	..	0.0	52.7	60.9
Sudan	742	57	64	52	34	55	18	..	120.7	21.8	55.2
Swaziland	2,293	69	92	61	55	61	53	..	..	1.1	0.3
Tanzania	2,035	54	80	45	24	32	21	..	8.5	148.9	173.2
Togo	1,825	60	87	41	12	24	3	..	..	3.0	5.8
Uganda	1,273	67	91	64	48	38	49	..	0.0	64.2	86.4
Zambia	6,513	60	87	46	49	59	43	..	0.0	39.5	50.5
Zimbabwe	985	82	99	72	44	56	37	..	..	12.1	7.6
NORTH AFRICA	**290**	**92**	**95**	**87**	**89**	**94**	**83**	**..**		**464.0**	**542.1**
Algeria	332	83	85	79	95	98	88	..	468.0	4.7	9.0
Egypt, Arab Rep.	23	99	100	98	94	97	92	..	..	56.7	106.0
Libya	97	..	..	..	97	97	96	..	..	0.0	0.0
Morocco	929	81	98	60	69	83	52	..	..	301.0	319.4
Tunisia	410	94	99	84	85	96	64	..	..	98.6	100.4

a. Data are for the most recent year available during the period specified.

Table 6.2 Transportation

	Access, supply side			Access, demand side: Vehicle fleet (per 1,000 people)	
	Road network (km) 2000–08[a]	Rail lines (km) 2009	Road density Ratio to total land (road km/100 sq km of land area) 2000–08[a]	Commercial vehicles 2000–08[a]	Passenger vehicles 2000–08[a]
SUB-SAHARAN AFRICA		..			
Angola	51,429	..	4.0	40.0	8.0
Benin	19,000	..	17.0	21.0	17.0
Botswana	25,798	888	4.0	113.0	56.0
Burkina Faso	92,495	622	34.0	11.0	7.0
Burundi	12,322	..	44.0	6.0	2.0
Cameroon	51,346	977	11.0	..	11.0
Cape Verde	1,350	..	33.0	94.0	67.0
Central African Republic	24,307	..	4.0	0.3	0.3
Chad	40,000	..	3.0	6.0	..
Comoros	880	..	39.0	33.0	31.0
Congo, Dem. Rep.	153,497	3,641	7.0	5.0	..
Congo, Rep.	17,000	..	5.0	26.0	15.0
Côte d'Ivoire	81,996	639	25.0	20.0	16.0
Djibouti	3,065	..	14.0	..	..
Equatorial Guinea	2,880	..	10.0	..	..
Eritrea	4,010	..	3.0	11.0	6.0
Ethiopia	44,359	..	4.0	3.0	1.0
Gabon	9,170	810	3.0	..	..
Gambia, The	3,742	..	33.0	7.0	5.0
Ghana	57,614	..	24.0	33.0	21.0
Guinea	44,348	..	18.0	..	..
Guinea-Bissau	3,455	..	12.0	33.0	27.0
Kenya	63,265	..	11.0	21.0	15.0
Lesotho	5,940	..	20.0	..	..
Liberia	10,600	..	10.0	3.0	2.0
Madagascar	49,827	..	8.0	27.0	8.0
Malawi	15,451	..	13.0	9.0	4.0
Mali	18,912	..	2.0	9.0	7.0
Mauritania	11,066	728	1.0	..	..
Mauritius	2,028	..	99.0	159.0	123.0
Mozambique	30,331	3,116	4.0	13.0	9.0
Namibia	66,467	..	0.0	109.0	52.0
Niger	18,948	..	1.0	5.0	4.0
Nigeria	193,200	..	21.0	31.0	31.0
Rwanda	14,008	..	53.0	4.0	2.0
São Tomé and Príncipe	320	..	33.0	2.0	2.0
Senegal	14,805	..	8.0	23.0	17.0
Seychelles	508	..	110.0	173.0	103.0
Sierra Leone	11,300	..	..	5.0	3.0
Somalia	22,100	..	3.0	..	..
South Africa	362,099	22,051	30.0	159.0	108.0
Sudan	11,900	4,508	1.0	28.0	20.0
Swaziland	3,594	300	21.0	89.0	46.0
Tanzania	87,524	..	9.0	73.0	4.0
Togo	11,652	..	21.0	2.0	2.0
Uganda	70,746	..	29.0	7.0	3.0
Zambia	66,781	..	12.0	18.0	11.0
Zimbabwe	97,267	..	25.0	106.0	91.0
NORTH AFRICA		14,019			
Algeria	111,261	4,723	5.0	112.0	72.0
Egypt, Arab Rep.	104,918	5,195	10.0	43.0	31.0
Libya	83,200	..	5.0	291.0	225.0
Morocco	58,256	2,110	13.0	71.0	53.0
Tunisia	19,371	1,991	12.0	114.0	76.0

(continued)

Table 6.2 Transportation (continued)

	Quality	Pricing		Financing		
	Ratio of paved to total roads (%)	Price of diesel fuel ($ per liter)	Price of gasoline ($ per liter)	Committed nominal investment in transport projects with private participation ($ millions)	ODA gross disbursements for transportation and storage ($ millions)	
	2000–08[a]	2010	2010	2000–08[a]	2008	2009
SUB-SAHARAN AFRICA		1.15	1.25		2,460.5	3,039.4
Angola	10.4	0.43	0.65	53.0	1.8	5.7
Benin	9.5	1.21	1.04	..	99.4	92.3
Botswana	32.6	0.97	0.93	..	0.1	12.9
Burkina Faso	4.2	1.28	1.44	..	38.2	52.5
Burundi	10.4	1.42	1.43	..	34.3	46.0
Cameroon	8.4	1.10	1.20	0.0	92.1	90.2
Cape Verde	69.0	1.33	1.84	..	76.1	55.7
Central African Republic	..	1.69	1.71	..	5.1	15.3
Chad	0.8	1.31	1.32	..	58.2	45.3
Comoros	76.5	..	..	0.5	0.6	2.2
Congo, Dem. Rep.	1.8	1.27	1.28	..	159.4	138.3
Congo, Rep.	7.1	0.84	1.27	735.0	28.2	20.4
Côte d'Ivoire	7.9	1.30	1.68	0.0	6.7	16.0
Djibouti	45.0	1.07	1.63	396.0	3.6	93.8
Equatorial Guinea	..	..	..	..	..	..
Eritrea	21.8	1.07	2.54	..	1.8	2.9
Ethiopia	13.7	0.78	0.91	..	313.8	251.8
Gabon	10.2	..	..	3.9	7.0	75.9
Gambia, The	19.3	..	..	..	6.4	9.7
Ghana	14.9	0.83	0.82	0.0	119.3	116.6
Guinea	9.8	0.95	0.95	159.0	35.5	28.6
Guinea-Bissau	27.9	..	..	..	16.8	15.1
Kenya	14.1	1.27	1.33	404.0	97.5	115.3
Lesotho	18.3	1.07	0.97	..	16.1	6.5
Liberia	6.2	0.96	0.98	..	31.2	49.8
Madagascar	11.6	1.26	1.52	17.5	117.8	42.8
Malawi	45.0	1.54	1.71	..	33.0	22.3
Mali	19.0	1.25	1.42	55.4	81.0	44.6
Mauritania	26.9	0.99	1.16	..	41.6	22.9
Mauritius	98.0	1.23	1.55	..	1.5	0.7
Mozambique	20.8	0.86	1.11	0.0	100.5	100.0
Namibia	12.8	1.09	1.06	..	25.8	53.7
Niger	20.7	1.16	1.07	..	60.7	38.8
Nigeria	15.0	0.77	0.44	382.0	44.4	108.7
Rwanda	19.0	1.62	1.63	..	50.7	26.8
São Tomé and Príncipe	68.1	..	..	..	3.7	1.6
Senegal	29.3	1.34	1.57	264.0	82.9	89.1
Seychelles	96.5	..	..	..	..	..
Sierra Leone	8.0	0.94	0.94	..	22.6	34.2
Somalia	11.8	..	..	..	0.1	1.7
South Africa	17.3	1.14	1.19	3,483.0	0.4	520.5
Sudan	36.3	0.43	0.62	30.0	29.3	78.3
Swaziland	30.0	1.10	1.07	..	0.0	0.4
Tanzania	7.4	1.19	1.22	134.0	162.8	146.4
Togo	21.0	1.17	1.18	..	0.0	0.6
Uganda	23.0	1.11	1.42	404.0	178.5	103.1
Zambia	22.0	1.52	1.66	15.6	77.1	34.6
Zimbabwe	19.0	1.15	1.29	..	0.0	0.0
NORTH AFRICA		0.32	0.48		531.4	890.6
Algeria	73.5	0.19	0.32	108.0	90.4	76.0
Egypt, Arab Rep.	86.9	0.32	0.48	640.0	110.2	145.5
Libya	57.2	0.13	0.17	..	..	..
Morocco	67.8	0.88	1.23	200.0	179.2	344.2
Tunisia	75.2	0.82	0.94	840.0	144.7	320.3

a. Data are for the most recent year available during the period specified.

Table 6.3 Information and communication technology

	Access, supply side: Telephone subscribers (per 100 people)			Access, demand side				Quality: Telephone faults	
	Total 2009	Mainline telephone 2009	Mobile telephone 2009	Unmet demand (% of mainline telephones) 2008	Households with own telephone (% of households) 2008	Average delay for firm in obtaining a mainline phone connection (days) 2009–10[a]	Internet users (per 100 people) 2009	Total (per 100 mainlines) 2009	Cleared by next working day (%) 2009
SUB-SAHARAN AFRICA	**38.8**	**1.5**	**37.3**	**..**	**..**		**8.8**	**..**	**..**
Angola	45.5	1.6	43.8	..	..	9.3	3.3	..	..
Benin	57.8	1.4	56.3	..	..	89.4	2.2	6.6	40.7
Botswana	103.5	7.4	96.1	..	..	17.1	6.2	..	..
Burkina Faso	22.0	1.1	20.9	..	..	19.5	1.1	..	..
Burundi	10.5	0.4	10.1	0.1	..	..	0.8	..	..
Cameroon	39.6	1.7	37.9	..	..	19.2	3.8	..	..
Cape Verde	91.8	14.3	77.5	0.4	..	8.2	29.7	3.0	93.0
Central African Republic	4.1	0.3	3.8	..	..	..	0.5	..	..
Chad	24.1	0.1	24.0	..	..	13.3	1.7	..	..
Comoros	19.0	3.9	15.2	28.3	..	..	3.7	..	..
Congo, Dem. Rep.	15.5	0.1	15.4	..	..	20.1	0.6	..	..
Congo, Rep.	59.6	0.7	58.9	..	..	25.5	6.7	..	..
Côte d'Ivoire	64.7	1.3	63.3	..	..	5.8	4.6	..	..
Djibouti	16.9	2.0	14.9	..	7.2	..	3.0	..	31.0
Equatorial Guinea	67.3	1.5	65.8	..	..	..	2.1	..	..
Eritrea	3.7	1.0	2.8	49.5	..	..	4.9	50.2	24.0
Ethiopia	6.0	1.1	4.9	2.1	..	..	0.5	4.9	66.0
Gabon	94.9	1.8	93.1	..	..	8.6	6.7	..	..
Gambia, The	86.9	2.9	84.0	..	..	..	7.6	..	..
Ghana	64.5	1.1	63.4	0.2	..	..	5.4	1.1	60.0
Guinea	55.9	0.2	55.7	..	..	..	0.9	..	..
Guinea-Bissau	35.1	0.3	34.8	..	..	..	2.3	..	..
Kenya	50.3	1.7	48.7	0.4	..	..	10.0	26.1	47.0
Lesotho	33.9	1.9	32.0	..	..	53.7	3.7	..	..
Liberia	21.3	0.1	21.3	..	..	..	0.5	..	..
Madagascar	31.5	0.9	30.6	0.1	2.4	29.9	1.6	9.5	92.4
Malawi	16.9	1.2	15.7	..	..	45.9	4.7	..	..
Mali	29.4	0.6	28.8	..	..	13.8	1.9	..	..
Mauritania	68.6	2.3	66.3	..	..	..	2.3	..	..
Mauritius	114.9	29.7	85.2	..	73.6	38.6	22.7	..	..
Mozambique	26.4	0.4	26.1	..	..	..	2.7	..	..
Namibia	62.6	6.5	56.1	..	..	..	5.9	..	..
Niger	17.4	0.4	17.0	..	1.4	13.9	0.8	..	..
Nigeria	48.2	0.9	47.2	..	1.8	..	28.4	..	..
Rwanda	24.6	0.3	24.3	..	1.1	..	4.5	0.0	98.0
São Tomé and Príncipe	44.1	4.8	39.3	..	..	..	16.4	..	..
Senegal	57.3	2.2	55.1	..	..	..	7.4	..	92.0
Seychelles	130.0	25.1	104.9	9.8	..	..	38.7	5.0	95.0
Sierra Leone	20.9	0.6	20.4	..	0.8	21.4	0.3	..	..
Somalia	8.1	1.1	7.0	..	..	..	1.2	..	..
South Africa	102.9	8.8	94.2	..	18.1	..	9.0	..	..
Sudan	37.2	0.9	36.3	0.0	..	..	9.9	5.0	95.0
Swaziland	59.1	3.7	55.4	0.2	..	..	7.6	0.6	63.0
Tanzania	40.3	0.4	39.9	..	0.7	..	1.6	..	..
Togo	35.8	2.7	33.1	..	..	51.0	5.4	..	..
Uganda	29.4	0.7	28.7	..	..	..	9.8	..	..
Zambia	34.8	0.7	34.1	..	..	..	6.3	..	..
Zimbabwe	27.0	3.1	23.9	..	..	..	11.4	41.0	..
NORTH AFRICA	**88.1**	**11.3**	**76.9**	**..**	**..**		**21.3**	**..**	**..**
Algeria	101.2	7.4	93.8	..	..	..	13.5	..	..
Egypt, Arab Rep.	79.1	12.4	66.7	0.3	..	..	20.0	0.1	98.3
Libya	95.1	17.2	77.9	..	..	..	5.5	..	..
Morocco	90.1	11.0	79.1	..	26.0	..	32.2	..	..
Tunisia	105.8	12.3	93.5	0.9	..	..	33.6	24.8	78.7

(continued)

Table 6.3 Information and communication technology (continued)

	Pricing									
		Cost of 3-minute call during peak hours ($)		Cost of 3-minute call during off-peak hours ($)		Connection charge ($)				
								Mobile cellular		
	Fixed broadband internet subscription ($ per month)	Fixed telephone local	Cellular local	Fixed telephone local	Cellular local	Residential telephone	Business telephone	Prepaid	Postpaid	Fixed broadband internet
	2009	2009	2009	2009	2009	2009	2009	2009	2009	2009
SUB-SAHARAN AFRICA	**56.9**	**0.19**	**0.64**	**0.13**	**0.65**	**35.7**	**52.4**	**..**	**2.1**	**72.0**
Angola	154.3	0.29	0.65	0.23	0.65	56.7	56.7	..	..	90.8
Benin	112.5	0.13	0.55	0.13	0.55	204.4	372.1	5.3	5.3	31.8
Botswana	56.9	0.19	0.75	0.14	0.75	35.4	51.9	1.4	1.4	94.7
Burkina Faso	87.2	0.24	0.95	0.14	0.95	53.0	53.0	..	6.4	..
Burundi	..	..	..	..	..	..	..	..	..	..
Cameroon	84.7	0.32	0.95	0.16	0.95	42.4	105.9	..	5.3	105.9
Cape Verde	33.3	0.07	0.91	0.05	0.91	25.8	26.4	..	..	29.0
Central African Republic	1,270.7	0.13	0.76	0.13	0.76	75.0	75.0	..	2.1	..
Chad	12.5	0.37	1.14	0.37	1.14	112.5	112.5	1.7	1.7	309.2
Comoros	409.4	0.14	0.64	0.14	0.64	114.4	114.4	..	..	169.4
Congo, Dem. Rep.	..	..	..	..	..	..	..	..	..	..
Congo, Rep.	..	..	..	..	..	..	..	..	..	..
Côte d'Ivoire	42.4	0.38	0.63	0.00	0.63	21.2	21.2	..	..	53.0
Djibouti	56.3	0.09	0.54	0.09	0.54	56.3	56.3	28.1	28.1	28.1
Equatorial Guinea	254.1	..	..	..	..	..	..	..	..	264.7
Eritrea	..	0.02	0.35	0.02	0.35	71.5	71.5	100.2	100.2	..
Ethiopia	517.6	0.02	0.21	0.02	0.21	20.6	20.6	14.4	14.4	..
Gabon	..	..	..	..	..	..	..	..	..	..
Gambia, The	..	..	..	..	..	..	..	..	..	..
Ghana	45.5	0.11	0.31	0.04	..	28.4	28.4	0.7	0.7	63.9
Guinea	..	..	..	..	..	..	..	..	..	..
Guinea-Bissau	..	..	0.57	..	0.57	..	..	1.1	1.1	..
Kenya	38.8	0.11	0.31	0.11	0.31	29.7	..	..	1.3	..
Lesotho	43.7	0.20	0.70	0.15	0.70	39.7	..	..	5.9	53.1
Liberia	..	..	..	..	..	..	..	..	..	..
Madagascar	100.2	0.30	0.65	0.09	0.65	30.2	30.2	..	0.5	0.0
Malawi	490.6	..	0.59	..	0.59	..	..	..	2.8	613.3
Mali	53.0	0.11	0.70	0.11	0.70	81.9	81.9	..	2.1	103.8
Mauritania	57.2	0.23	0.63	0.23	0.63	19.1	19.1	..	1.9	26.6
Mauritius	15.1	0.07	0.13	0.06	0.13	36.0	72.0	3.1	3.1	72.0
Mozambique	80.6	0.18	0.72	0.14	0.72	17.8	17.8	..	0.7	..
Namibia	41.2	0.16	0.89	0.08	0.89	34.6	34.6	..	2.2	..
Niger	254.1	0.16	0.79	0.16	0.79	31.8	..	..	3.2	103.8
Nigeria	105.8	0.20	0.60	0.18	0.60	..	..	..	..	..
Rwanda	88.0	0.20	0.45	0.20	0.45	52.8	..	..	1.8	176.0
São Tomé and Príncipe	202.5	0.10	0.47	0.10	0.47	25.9	25.9	..	8.6	81.0
Senegal	38.1	0.35	0.54	0.35	0.54	21.2	..	..	4.2	40.2
Seychelles	42.8	0.07	0.92	0.05	0.92	48.1	48.1	3.7	3.7	45.9
Sierra Leone	29.3	..	..	..	..	..	..	..	..	..
Somalia	..	..	..	..	..	..	..	..	..	..
South Africa	23.5	0.15	0.89	0.07	0.89	55.2	55.2	..	17.6	64.2
Sudan	26.1	0.00	0.18	0.00	0.18	..	..	..	2.2	43.4
Swaziland	749.2	0.07	0.78	0.04	0.78	25.1	42.0	..	1.8	..
Tanzania	22.7	0.27	0.59	0.27	..	15.2	15.2	0.4	0.4	18.9
Togo	1,049.6	0.19	0.73	0.10	0.73	75.0	75.0	..	2.1	174.9
Uganda	41.9	0.18	0.50	0.11	..	59.1	59.1	..	1.5	145.3
Zambia	47.4	0.78	0.70	0.46	0.70	9.9	29.7	..	..	..
Zimbabwe	..	..	..	..	..	..	..	..	..	..
NORTH AFRICA	**15.1**	**0.05**	**0.41**	**0.04**	**0.41**	**14.8**	**90.2**	**3.7**	**5.3**	**..**
Algeria	15.1	0.08	0.33	0.06	0.33	..	..	..	6.9	..
Egypt, Arab Rep.	8.1	0.03	0.11	0.03	0.11	6.7	90.2	3.2	3.2	0.0
Libya	39.9	..	..	..	..	..	..	..	..	119.6
Morocco	16.0	0.25	1.34	0.25	1.34	74.5	148.9	14.9	14.9	..
Tunisia	11.1	0.02	0.49	0.02	0.49	14.8	37.0	3.7	3.7	..

a. Data are for the most recent year available during the period specified.

Financing					Annual revenue ($ millions)		
Annual investment ($ millions)			Committed nominal investment in telecommunication projects with private participation ($ millions)	ODA gross disbursements for communication ($ millions)			
Fixed telephone service	Mobile communication	Telecommunications			Fixed telephone service	Mobile communication	Telecommunications
2009[a]	2009	2009	2009	2009	2009	2009	2009
143.1	**6,107.9**	**4,070.7**	**11,333.0**	**256.3**	**2,304.4**	**12,497.8**	**15,077.3**
..	..	..	354.0	0.6	..	..	..
0.8	335.9	336.7	127.0	0.7	22.9	315.5	338.4
..	..	..	86.0	0.1	..	279.5	402.8
..	..	118.0	193.0	4.3	..	..	..
..	..	..	–	1.8	..	..	..
..	..	..	278.0	2.1	..	..	..
..	..	..	23.0	0.8	..	..	..
..	..	..	6.0	0.1	..	..	..
..	..	..	68.0	..	..	..	..
..	..	3.9	..	..	..	7.6	27.9
..	203.8	203.8	151.0	4.3	..	726.5	..
..	..	..	110.0	0.1	..	..	..
..	271.5	298.6	318.0	0.9	292.7	1,173.8	1,466.5
7.1	1.2	8.6	..	10.4	22.3	16.2	60.2
..	..	..	..	(0.0)	..	..	..
..	..	..	–	..	25.0	28.8	54.5
..	..	..	..	4.6	270.8	196.4	480.8
..	..	..	91.0	..	..	..	..
..	..	..	–	0.4	..	..	..
..	592.9	640.5	847.0	9.3	..	1,067.3	1,174.0
..	..	..	87.0	0.1	..	..	..
..	..	..	28.0	0.2	..	..	..
40.4	454.6	514.2	278.0	17.3	646.4	1,088.1	1,837.6
..	..	..	11.0	..	..	..	..
..	..	..	24.0	0.3	..	..	..
7.6	..	..	83.0	0.3	32.9	248.4	325.9
..	..	..	73.0	2.0	..	..	..
..	..	63.5	429.0	0.8	50.0	463.4	513.4
..	..	..	43.0	0.0	..	..	..
..	..	..	35.0	6.5	67.7	114.2	..
..	..	..	52.0	19.0	..	..	..
..	..	..	–	(0.7)	..	..	..
..	..	..	87.0	0.5	..	..	..
..	..	644.7	3,057.0	22.8	280.7	5,990.1	6,270.8
..	..	174.3	183.0	2.4	..	..	152.8
..	..	..	..	0.1	..	..	..
38.2	227.2	265.4	256.0	2.4	593.0	692.5	1,285.5
..	..	..	..	..	..	..	..
..	..	..	23.0	0.9	..	..	..
..	..	..	–	0.1	..	..	..
..	..	..	2,387.0	6.2	..	..	..
..	..	..	357.0	0.1	..	..	..
..	20.7	..	25.0	..	..	89.5	..
..	..	..	522.0	2.2	..	..	..
..	..	..	44.0	..	..	..	..
..	..	298.5	283.0	8.2	..	..	686.2
..	..	..	114.0	1.2	..	..	..
49.0	4,000.0	500.0	200.0	0.3	..	..	..
258.7	**1,327.8**	**4,085.3**	**2,716.0**	**29.3**	**3,194.4**	**11,710.3**	**17,337.8**
..	..	..	398.0	0.7	798.4	3,057.2	5,011.9
177.9	1,166.2	3,135.4	1,791.0	2.8	1,039.5	4,717.0	6,513.4
..	..	..	..	..	..	..	..
..	..	684.1	240.0	1.5	1,127.6	2,806.6	4,136.9
80.8	161.6	265.8	287.0	19.2	229.0	1,129.4	1,675.6

Table 6.4 Energy

	Access, demand side								
	Energy production						Electric power consumption (kWh per capita)	GDP per unit of energy use (2005 PPP $ per kg of oil equivalent)	Solid fuels use (% of population)
	Total (billion kWh)	Source[a] (% of total)							
		Hydroelectric	Coal	Natural gas	Nuclear	Oil			
	2008	2008	2008	2008	2008	2008	2008	2008	2006
SUB-SAHARAN AFRICA	**423.9**	**17.2**	**58.0**	**4.4**	**3.1**	**3.8**	**530.9**	**3.2**	**81.6**
Angola	4.0	96.3	0.0	0.0	0.0	3.7	189.3	8.8	47.7
Benin	0.1	0.7	0.0	0.0	0.0	99.3	76.3	3.9	94.3
Botswana	0.6	0.0	100.0	0.0	0.0	0.0	1,503.3	11.6	40.0
Burkina Faso	..	..	..	..	..	..	..	..	95.0
Burundi	..	..	..	..	..	..	..	..	95.0
Cameroon	5.6	76.2	0.0	7.7	0.0	15.9	262.6	5.4	80.6
Cape Verde	..	..	..	..	..	..	..	..	36.2
Central African Republic	..	..	..	..	..	..	..	..	95.0
Chad	..	..	..	..	..	..	..	..	93.0
Comoros	..	..	..	..	..	..	..	..	76.0
Congo, Dem. Rep.	7.5	99.4	0.0	0.4	0.0	0.2	95.1	0.8	95.0
Congo, Rep.	0.5	81.3	0.0	18.7	0.0	0.0	150.2	9.6	83.9
Côte d'Ivoire	5.8	32.7	0.0	65.1	0.0	0.2	186.3	3.1	79.0
Djibouti	..	..	..	..	..	..	..	..	16.0
Equatorial Guinea	..	..	..	..	..	..	..	..	..
Eritrea	0.3	0.0	0.0	0.0	0.0	99.3	..	3.8	62.7
Ethiopia	3.8	87.3	0.0	0.0	0.0	12.4	42.4	2.0	95.0
Gabon	2.0	43.8	0.0	24.7	0.0	31.2	1,158.0	9.4	27.0
Gambia, The	..	..	..	..	..	..	..	..	94.7
Ghana	8.4	74.1	0.0	0.0	0.0	25.9	267.7	3.4	85.9
Guinea	..	..	..	..	..	..	..	..	95.0
Guinea-Bissau	..	..	..	..	..	..	..	..	95.0
Kenya	7.1	40.4	0.0	0.0	0.0	38.4	155.3	3.1	75.0
Lesotho	..	..	..	..	..	..	..	..	71.0
Liberia	..	..	..	..	..	..	..	..	95.0
Madagascar	..	..	..	..	..	..	..	..	95.0
Malawi	..	..	..	..	..	..	..	..	95.0
Mali	..	..	..	..	..	..	..	..	95.0
Mauritania	..	..	..	..	..	..	..	..	60.0
Mauritius	..	..	..	..	..	..	..	..	5.0
Mozambique	15.1	99.9	0.0	0.1	0.0	0.0	461.4	1.9	95.0
Namibia	2.1	67.5	31.1	0.0	0.0	1.4	1,797.3	7.3	57.0
Niger	..	..	..	..	..	..	..	..	95.0
Nigeria	21.1	27.1	0.0	58.2	0.0	14.7	126.5	2.6	78.8
Rwanda	..	..	..	..	..	..	..	..	95.0
São Tomé and Principe	..	..	..	..	..	..	..	..	..
Senegal	2.4	9.5	0.0	1.7	0.0	85.8	158.2	7.1	51.0
Seychelles	..	..	..	..	..	..	..	..	5.0
Sierra Leone	..	..	..	..	..	..	..	..	95.0
Somalia	..	..	..	..	..	..	..	..	95.0
South Africa	255.5	0.5	94.2	0.0	5.1	0.1	4,759.5	3.5	17.3
Sudan	4.5	32.4	0.0	0.0	0.0	67.6	96.4	5.3	89.9
Swaziland	..	..	..	..	..	..	..	..	58.0
Tanzania	4.4	60.1	2.7	36.2	0.0	0.9	83.9	2.6	94.0
Togo	0.1	74.0	0.0	0.0	0.0	24.4	98.8	1.9	95.0
Uganda	..	..	..	..	..	..	..	..	95.0
Zambia	9.7	99.7	0.0	0.0	0.0	0.3	602.4	2.1	85.7
Zimbabwe	8.0	53.4	46.3	0.0	0.0	0.3	1,022.2	..	71.2
NORTH AFRICA	**236.1**	**6.7**	**5.0**	**66.5**	**0.0**	**21.3**	**1,281.7**	**6.4**	**5.4**
Algeria	40.2	0.7	0.0	97.3	0.0	2.0	957.1	6.8	5.0
Egypt, Arab Rep.	131.0	11.2	0.0	68.4	0.0	19.7	1,425.4	5.8	5.0
Libya	28.7	0.0	0.0	41.0	0.0	59.0	3,909.3	5.2	5.0
Morocco	20.8	4.5	56.2	13.8	0.0	24.2	735.6	8.4	6.8
Tunisia	15.3	0.2	0.0	88.7	0.0	10.8	1,298.0	8.3	5.0

a. Shares may not sum to 100 percent because other sources of generated electricity (such as geothermal, solar, and wind) are not shown.
b. Data are for the most recent year available during the period specified.

Quality						Financing	
Firms identifying electricity as major or very severe obstacle to business operation and growth (%) 2009–10[b]	Average delay for firm in obtaining electrical connection (days) 2009–10[b]	Electric power transmission and distribution losses (% of output) 2008	Electrical power outages in a typical month (average) 2009–10[b]	Firms that share or own their own generator (%) 2009–10[b]	Firms using electricity from generator (%) 2009–10[b]	Committed nominal investment in energy projects with private participation ($ millions) 2009	ODA gross disbursements for energy ($ millions) 2009
		10.5				**..**	**1,478.9**
35.7	7.7	14.5	5.4	79.0	17.3	..	4.7
51.9	86.8	92.6	13.9	50.5	10.1	..	16.3
34.8	39.2	52.0	4.5	34.5	0.6	..	0.3
53.9	23.1	..	10.8	28.3	2.5	..	26.1
..	..	..	..	..	..	..	1.9
58.6	17.6	9.7	10.6	34.8	4.5	0.0	57.3
53.1	30.5	..	4.9	48.8	10.9	..	1.9
..	..	..	..	..	..	..	3.4
74.6	10.6	..	22.6	75.5	52.0	..	0.8
..	..	..	..	..	..	..	..
51.7	48.0	11.0	21.8	49.3	4.2	..	132.8
71.1	8.5	76.8	25.3	81.8	43.2	..	0.1
39.8	20.9	23.5	3.8	6.5	1.0	0.0	15.4
..	..	..	..	..	..	..	22.5
..	..	..	..	..	..	..	0.0
0.2	..	..	3.0	36.8	1.0	..	3.1
..	..	9.5	..	..	..	4.0	179.0
58.0	34.5	17.8	7.2	22.9	1.8	..	0.1
..	..	..	..	..	..	..	1.8
..	..	22.1	..	..	..	..	43.9
..	..	..	..	..	..	..	0.8
..	..	..	..	..	..	..	3.4
..	..	14.7	..	..	..	11.0	142.9
44.3	13.9	..	6.8	30.9	0.0	..	0.4
59.1	..	..	5.4	66.5	63.1	..	13.1
54.6	92.1	..	13.6	29.3	5.2	..	5.8
37.6	59.2	..	1.0	25.3	2.1	..	2.3
33.5	32.9	..	5.3	20.1	0.5	..	20.5
..	..	..	..	..	..	..	11.2
42.9	18.7	..	3.2	24.5	0.8	..	5.8
..	..	9.0	..	..	..	..	57.6
..	..	17.6	..	..	..	..	4.5
63.2	37.1	..	20.1	34.5	5.2	..	0.6
..	..	9.4	..	..	..	..	72.7
..	..	..	..	..	..	..	41.9
..	..	..	..	..	..	..	..
..	..	19.5	..	..	..	..	16.5
..	..	..	..	..	..	..	..
53.4	14.8	..	15.9	81.8	36.6	..	30.1
..	..	..	..	..	..	..	..
..	..	8.8	..	..	..	..	4.8
..	..	11.9	..	..	..	..	2.0
..	..	..	..	..	..	..	..
..	..	19.3	..	..	..	..	121.4
50.9	53.9	122.8	11.1	63.6	9.3	..	121.8
..	..	..	..	..	..	27.0	163.0
..	..	23.3	..	..	..	..	8.1
..	..	6.5	..	..	..	..	1.3
		12.5				**..**	**1,106.6**
..	..	18.1	..	..	..	..	2.2
..	..	10.6	..	..	..	..	460.3
..	..	14.0	..	..	..	..	2.5
..	..	11.0	..	..	..	..	454.7
..	..	12.4	..	..	..	..	166.7

Table 7.1 Education

	Literacy rate (%)						Primary education						
	Youth (ages 15–24)			Adult (ages 15 and older)			Gross enrollment ratio (% of relevant age group)			Net enrollment ratio (% of relevant age group)			Student-teacher ratio
	Total 2009	Male 2009	Female 2009	Total 2009	Male 2009	Female 2009	Total 2009	Male 2009	Female 2009	Total 2009	Male 2009	Female 2009	2009
SUB-SAHARAN AFRICA	**75.2**	**79.5**	**70.9**	**65.5**	**74.8**	**56.3**	..	..	..	..	..	..	..
Angola	73.1	80.8	65.5	70.0	82.9	57.6	..	..	..	..	..	..	..
Benin	54.3	64.9	43.4	41.7	54.2	29.1	121.9	129.2	114.2	94.7	..	..	..
Botswana	95.2	93.7	96.7	84.1	83.8	84.4	..	..	..	..	..	..	..
Burkina Faso	..	..	..	..	..	..	78.3	82.9	73.5	63.3	67.1	59.4	48.9
Burundi	76.6	76.9	76.3	66.6	72.6	60.9	146.6	149.1	144.2	98.9	98.2	99.6	51.4
Cameroon	..	..	..	..	..	..	113.8	122.0	105.5	91.6	97.5	85.6	46.3
Cape Verde	98.2	97.3	99.0	84.8	90.1	80.2	98.1	101.8	94.4	82.6	83.6	81.5	23.9
Central African Republic	64.7	72.2	57.3	55.2	69.1	42.1	88.6	103.8	73.6	66.7	76.9	56.6	94.6
Chad	46.3	53.5	39.0	33.6	44.5	23.1	89.7	105.2	74.2	..	..	..	60.9
Comoros	85.3	85.8	84.7	74.2	79.7	68.7	..	..	..	..	..	..	..
Congo, Dem. Rep.	67.7	73.3	62.1	67.0	79.5	54.9	90.3	97.5	83.0	..	..	..	37.3
Congo, Rep.	..	..	..	..	..	..	119.5	123.5	115.5	..	..	..	64.4
Côte d'Ivoire	66.6	72.1	61.0	55.3	64.7	45.3	73.6	81.2	66.0	57.2	62.5	52.0	42.1
Djibouti	..	..	..	..	..	..	54.5	57.6	51.3	44.4	46.8	42.1	..
Equatorial Guinea	97.9	97.7	98.2	93.3	97.0	89.8	81.9	83.6	80.1	53.5	54.0	53.0	24.2
Eritrea	88.7	91.6	85.8	66.6	77.9	56.0	48.3	52.8	43.8	35.7	38.1	33.2	38.5
Ethiopia	..	..	..	..	..	..	102.5	107.1	97.8	82.7	85.2	80.1	57.9
Gabon	97.6	98.6	96.6	87.7	91.4	84.1	..	..	..	..	..	..	..
Gambia, The	65.5	71.0	60.0	46.5	57.6	35.8	..	..	..	..	..	..	..
Ghana	80.1	81.2	78.9	66.6	72.8	60.4	105.2	105.7	104.6	75.9	75.5	76.2	33.1
Guinea	61.1	68.1	53.8	39.5	50.8	28.1	89.8	96.7	82.8	72.9	77.9	67.8	..
Guinea-Bissau	70.9	78.2	63.6	52.2	66.9	38.0	..	..	..	..	..	..	..
Kenya	92.7	91.9	93.6	87.0	90.5	83.5	112.7	113.9	111.4	82.6	82.2	83.0	46.8
Lesotho	92.0	85.7	98.1	89.7	82.9	95.3	104.4	104.6	104.2	73.1	71.2	75.0	..
Liberia	75.6	70.4	80.9	59.1	63.7	54.5	..	..	..	..	..	..	..
Madagascar	..	..	..	..	..	..	160.4	162.3	158.5	..	..	..	47.9
Malawi	86.5	86.9	86.0	73.7	80.6	67.0	119.3	117.6	121.1	90.8	88.5	93.2	..
Mali	..	..	..	..	..	..	94.7	102.9	86.3	72.9	79.3	66.4	50.1
Mauritania	67.7	70.9	64.3	57.5	64.5	50.3	104.4	100.6	108.4	76.3	73.9	78.8	39.1
Mauritius	96.5	95.5	97.6	87.9	90.6	85.3	100.0	100.0	100.1	94.0	93.4	94.6	21.6
Mozambique	70.9	78.1	63.7	55.1	70.1	41.5	114.4	120.7	108.1	90.6	93.2	87.9	61.3
Namibia	93.0	91.1	94.9	88.5	88.9	88.1	112.1	113.0	111.2	89.1	87.1	91.1	30.1
Niger	..	..	..	..	..	..	62.4	69.2	55.2	54.0	60.0	47.6	38.8
Nigeria	71.8	78.1	65.3	60.8	72.0	49.8	..	..	..	..	..	..	..
Rwanda	77.2	77.0	77.4	70.7	75.0	66.8	150.7	149.8	151.4	..	..	..	68.3
São Tomé and Príncipe	95.3	94.9	95.8	88.8	93.7	84.0	131.2	130.7	131.8	97.5	95.5	99.5	26.2
Senegal	65.0	74.2	56.2	49.7	61.8	38.7	83.7	82.1	85.4	73.1	71.7	74.4	34.7
Seychelles	..	..	..	..	..	..	106.2	105.0	107.4	94.4	93.4	95.4	13.8
Sierra Leone	57.6	67.6	48.1	40.9	52.7	30.1	..	..	..	..	..	..	..
Somalia	..	..	..	..	..	..	..	..	..	..	..	..	..
South Africa	..	..	..	..	..	..	101.2	103.2	99.1	84.7	84.7	84.6	..
Sudan	85.9	89.1	82.7	70.2	79.6	60.8	74.0	77.8	70.0	..	..	..	38.4
Swaziland	93.4	91.9	94.9	86.9	87.8	86.2	..	..	..	..	..	..	..
Tanzania	77.4	78.5	76.4	72.9	79.0	66.9	104.9	104.9	104.9	96.4	95.8	97.0	53.7
Togo	..	..	..	..	..	..	115.2	118.8	111.5	93.5	98.1	89.0	41.3
Uganda	..	..	..	..	..	..	121.6	120.8	122.4	92.2	90.9	93.6	49.3
Zambia	74.6	81.8	67.3	70.9	80.6	61.3	112.9	113.5	112.4	90.7	89.6	91.8	..
Zimbabwe	98.9	98.4	99.5	91.9	94.7	89.4	..	..	..	..	..	..	..
NORTH AFRICA	..	..	..	..	..	..	..	..	..	..	..	..	..
Algeria	..	..	..	..	..	..	107.7	111.0	104.2	93.8	94.8	92.9	23.0
Egypt, Arab Rep.	..	..	..	..	..	..	..	..	..	..	..	..	..
Libya	99.9	99.9	99.8	88.9	95.2	82.0	..	..	..	..	..	..	..
Morocco	79.5	86.7	72.1	56.1	68.9	43.9	107.4	111.9	102.7	89.7	91.2	88.1	26.6
Tunisia	..	..	..	..	..	..	..	..	..	..	..	..	..

Secondary education							Tertiary education			Public spending on education (%)	
Gross enrollment ratio (% of relevant age group)			Net enrollment ratio (% of relevant age group)			Student-teacher ratio	Gross enrollment ratio (% of relevant age group)			Share of government expenditure	Share of GDP
Total 2009	Male 2009	Female 2009	Total 2009	Male 2009	Female 2009	2009	Total 2009	Male 2009	Female 2009	2009	2009
..	..	..	..	..	..	..	..	..	..	..	..
..	..	..	..	..	..	..	..	..	..	..	..
..	..	..	..	..	..	..	..	..	..	..	..
..	..	..	..	..	..	..	..	..	..	22.0	8.9
19.8	22.6	16.8	15.4	17.7	13.1	25.6	3.4	4.6	2.2	..	..
21.2	24.6	17.8	..	..	..	26.5	2.7	..	..	23.4	8.3
41.5	45.2	37.7	..	..	..	..	9.0	10.1	8.0	19.2	3.7
81.5	74.7	88.2	63.3	..	..	18.2	14.9	13.1	16.7	15.9	5.9
13.6	17.5	9.8	10.4	13.2	7.7	80.1	2.5	3.5	1.5	..	1.3
24.1	34.1	14.0	..	..	..	32.3	2.0	3.4	0.6	12.6	3.2
..	..	..	..	..	..	..	5.2	..	..	..	..
36.7	47.0	26.2	..	..	..	16.0	6.0	..	..	..	..
..	..	..	..	..	..	..	6.4	10.6	2.2	..	..
..	..	..	..	..	..	..	..	..	..	..	..
30.5	35.1	25.8	..	..	..	..	3.5	4.1	2.8	..	..
..	..	..	..	..	..	..	..	..	..	..	..
31.8	37.1	26.4	27.4	31.6	23.1	42.7	2.0	3.0	1.0	..	..
34.4	38.8	30.0	..	..	..	47.9	..	..	..	..	..
..	..	..	..	..	..	..	..	..	..	..	..
..	..	..	..	..	..	..	..	..	..	..	..
57.2	60.5	53.6	46.1	48.0	44.1	18.3	8.6	10.6	6.6	..	..
37.0	46.3	27.4	..	..	..	..	..	..	..	..	..
..	..	..	..	..	..	..	..	..	..	..	..
59.5	62.4	56.5	49.6	51.1	48.1	29.7	4.1	4.8	3.3	..	..
45.0	37.8	52.3	28.8	21.9	35.7	..	..	..	..	..	..
..	..	..	..	..	..	..	..	..	..	..	..
31.5	32.5	30.6	..	..	..	23.5	3.6	3.8	3.4	..	3.0
29.5	31.5	27.6	25.0	25.7	24.4	..	..	..	..	..	..
38.3	46.4	30.1	30.1	36.6	23.5	..	6.0	8.5	3.5	22.3	4.4
..	..	..	..	..	..	..	3.8	5.3	2.2	..	..
87.2	86.1	88.3	..	..	..	16.0	..	..	..	11.4	3.2
23.4	26.2	20.6	14.7	15.6	13.7	37.9	..	..	..	..	..
..	..	..	..	..	..	..	..	..	..	..	..
11.7	14.5	8.8	..	..	..	27.6	1.4	2.2	0.7	19.3	4.6
..	..	..	..	..	..	..	..	..	..	..	..
26.7	27.5	26.0	..	..	..	..	4.8	5.5	4.1	..	..
50.1	47.3	52.8	..	..	..	..	4.1	4.2	3.9	..	..
..	..	..	..	..	..	..	8.0	10.2	5.9	..	5.8
105.0	102.6	107.5	97.3	95.4	99.2	12.6	..	..	..	..	..
..	..	..	..	..	..	..	..	..	..	18.1	4.3
..	..	..	..	..	..	..	..	..	..	..	..
93.9	91.6	96.1	..	..	..	..	..	..	..	16.9	5.4
38.0	40.3	35.5	..	..	..	22.2	..	..	..	..	..
..	..	..	..	..	..	..	..	..	..	..	..
27.4	30.7	24.1	..	..	..	..	..	..	..	..	..
..	..	..	..	..	..	..	..	..	..	17.6	4.6
27.4	29.8	24.9	..	..	..	18.1	4.1	4.5	3.6	15.0	3.2
48.7	52.8	44.5	46.2	50.5	41.8	..	..	..	..	..	..
..	..	..	..	..	..	..	3.2	3.9	2.5	..	..
..	..	..	..	..	..	..	..	..	..	..	..
..	..	..	..	..	..	..	30.6	25.2	36.3	..	..
..	..	..	..	..	..	..	..	..	..	..	..
..	..	..	..	..	..	..	..	..	..	..	..
..	..	..	..	..	..	..	12.9	13.7	12.0	..	..
..	..	..	..	..	..	..	..	..	..	..	..

Table 7.2 Health

	Mortality						Diseases			
	Life expectancy at birth (years)								Malaria	
	Total 2009	Male 2009	Female 2009	Under-five mortality rate (per 1,000) 2009	Infant mortality rate (per 1,000 live births) 2009	Maternal mortality ratio, modeled estimate (per 100,000 live births) 2008	Prevalence of HIV (% ages 15–49) 2009	Incidence of tuberculosis (per 100,000 people) 2009	Clinical cases reported 2009[c]	Reported deaths 2009
SUB-SAHARAN AFRICA	**52.5**	**51.5**	**53.6**	**130**	**81**	**646**	**5.4**	**344**	**71,675,530**	**113,326**
Angola	47.6	45.6	49.6	161	98	610	2.0	298	2,221,076	10,530
Benin	61.8	60.7	63.0	118	75	410	1.2	93	1,256,708	1,375
Botswana	55.0	55.1	54.8	57	43	190	24.8	694	14,878	6
Burkina Faso	53.3	52.0	54.7	166	91	560	1.2	215	4,399,837	7,982
Burundi	50.9	49.4	52.4	166	101	970	3.3	348	1,757,387	714
Cameroon	51.4	50.8	51.9	154	95	600	5.3	182	1,883,199	4,943
Cape Verde	71.3	68.7	74.1	28	23	94	..	148	65	2
Central African Republic	47.3	45.9	48.8	171	112	850	4.7	327	175,210	667
Chad	48.9	47.7	50.2	209	124	1,200	3.4	283	182,415	221
Comoros	65.8	63.6	68.1	104	75	340	0.1	39	49,679	..
Congo, Dem. Rep.	47.8	46.2	49.4	199	126	670	..	372	6,749,112	21,168
Congo, Rep.	53.7	52.8	54.7	128	81	580	3.4	382	92,855	116
Côte d'Ivoire	58.0	56.7	59.3	119	83	470	3.4	399	1,847,367	18,156
Djibouti	55.7	54.4	57.2	94	75	300	2.5	620	7,120	0
Equatorial Guinea	50.6	49.5	51.8	145	88	280	5.0	117	78,983	23
Eritrea	59.9	57.6	62.2	55	39	280	0.8	99	21,298	23
Ethiopia	55.7	54.3	57.1	104	67	470	..	359	3,043,203	1,121
Gabon	60.9	59.6	62.1	69	52	260	5.2	501	112,840	197
Gambia, The	56.2	54.6	58.0	103	78	400	2.0	269	479,409	240
Ghana	56.8	55.9	57.7	69	47	350	1.8	201	1,899,544	3,378
Guinea	58.3	56.4	60.4	142	88	680	1.3	318	812,471	586
Guinea-Bissau	48.2	46.7	49.8	193	115	1,000	2.5	229	143,011	369
Kenya	54.9	54.5	55.3	84	55	530	6.3	305	8,123,689	..
Lesotho	45.4	45.0	45.7	84	61	530	23.6	634	..	..
Liberia	58.7	57.3	60.1	112	80	990	1.5	288	871,560	1,706
Madagascar	60.8	59.2	62.5	58	41	440	0.2	261	215,110	173
Malawi	53.8	52.9	54.7	110	69	510	11.0	304	5,455,423	6,527
Mali	48.8	48.1	49.5	191	101	830	1.0	324	1,633,423	2,331
Mauritania	57.0	55.0	59.0	117	74	550	0.7	330	167,705	91
Mauritius	72.6	69.2	76.2	17	15	36	1.0	22	..	..
Mozambique	48.1	47.4	48.8	142	96	550	11.5	409	4,310,086	3,747
Namibia	61.6	60.8	62.4	48	34	180	13.1	727	81,812	46
Niger	52.0	51.1	52.9	160	76	820	0.8	181	309,675	2,159
Nigeria	48.1	47.6	48.7	138	86	840	3.6	295	4,295,686	7,522
Rwanda	50.6	48.8	52.5	111	70	540	2.9	376	1,247,583	809
São Tomé and Príncipe	65.8	63.9	67.7	78	52	..	..	98	3,893	23
Senegal	55.9	54.4	57.5	93	51	410	0.9	282	222,232	574
Seychelles	73.7	68.5	79.2	12	11	..	..	31	..	..
Sierra Leone	47.9	46.7	49.2	192	123	970	1.6	644	646,808	1,734
Somalia	50.1	48.7	51.5	180	109	1,200	0.7	285	56,153	45
South Africa	51.6	50.3	53.1	62	43	410	17.8	971	6,072	45
Sudan	58.5	57.0	60.1	108	69	750	1.1	119	2,686,822	1,396
Swaziland	46.3	47.1	45.5	73	52	420	25.9	1,257	6,639	13
Tanzania	56.3	55.5	57.1	108	68	790	5.6	183	40	840
Togo	62.9	61.2	64.6	98	64	350	3.2	446	618,842	1,556
Uganda	53.4	52.8	54.1	128	79	430	6.5	293	9,775,318	6,296
Zambia	46.3	45.8	46.9	141	86	470	13.5	433	2,976,395	3,862
Zimbabwe	45.4	45.3	45.6	90	56	790	14.3	742	736,897	14
NORTH AFRICA	**71.5**	**69.7**	**73.4**	**26**	**23**	**92**	**0.1**	**43**	**239**	**3**
Algeria	72.6	71.2	74.1	32	29	120	0.1	59	..	..
Egypt, Arab Rep.	70.3	68.6	72.2	21	18	82	0.1	19	94	2
Libya	74.5	72.0	77.2	19	17	64	..	40	..	..
Morocco	71.6	69.4	73.9	38	33	110	0.1	92	145	1
Tunisia	74.5	72.5	76.5	21	18	60	0.1	24	..	..

Child immunization rate (% of children ages 12–23 months)		Malnutrition (% of children under age 5)		Births attended by skilled health staff (% of total)	Contraceptive use (% of married women ages 15–49)		Children sleeping under insecticide-treated nets (% of under age 5)	Tuberculosis case detection rate, all forms (%)	Tuberculosis treatment success rate (% of registered cases)	Children with fever receiving any antimalarial treatment same or next day (% of under age 5)
Measles	DPT[b]	Stunting	Underweight		Any method	Modern method				
2009	2009	2007–09[a]	2007–09[a]	2007–09[a]	2007–09[a]	2007–09[a]	2007–09[a]	2009	2008	2007–09[a]
68	**70**						**..**	**48.0**	**79.0**	
77	73	..	..	47.3	..	..	17.7	75.0	70.0	29.3
72	83	..	..	..	..	..	..	47.0	89.0	..
94	96	..	..	94.6	52.8	..	..	62.0	65.0	..
75	82	35.1	26.0	..	..	..	..	14.0	76.0	..
91	92	..	..	..	..	..	..	25.0	90.0	..
74	80	..	..	..	..	..	..	70.0	..	..
96	99	..	..	..	..	..	..	44.0	74.0	..
62	54	..	..	43.7	..	..	..	60.0	71.0	..
23	23	..	..	..	..	..	..	26.0	..	..
79	83	..	..	..	..	..	..	46.0	90.0	..
76	77	45.8	28.2	74.0	20.6	5.8	5.8	46.0	87.0	29.8
76	91	..	..	..	..	..	..	69.0	76.0	..
67	81	..	..	..	..	..	..	27.0	76.0	..
73	89	..	..	..	22.5	..	19.9	71.0	84.0	..
51	33	..	..	..	..	..	..	89.0	56.0	..
95	99	..	..	..	..	..	..	58.0	76.0	..
75	79	..	..	..	..	..	33.1	50.0	84.0	9.5
55	45	..	..	..	..	..	..	42.0	53.0	..
96	98	..	..	..	..	..	..	47.0	84.0	..
93	94	28.6	14.3	57.1	23.5	16.6	28.2	31.0	86.0	43.0
51	57	40.0	20.8	46.1	..	..	4.5	26.0	78.0	..
76	68	..	..	..	..	..	..	59.0	70.0	..
74	75	35.2	16.4	43.8	45.5	38.9	46.1	85.0	85.0	23.2
85	83	..	..	61.5	47.0	..	..	93.0	73.0	..
64	64	39.4	20.4	46.3	11.4	10.3	26.4	52.0	79.0	67.2
64	78	49.2	..	43.9	39.9	28.2	45.8	44.0	81.0	19.7
92	93	..	..	..	..	..	..	49.0	87.0	..
71	74	..	..	..	..	..	..	16.0	82.0	..
59	64	24.2	16.7	60.9	9.3	8.0	..	24.0	68.0	20.7
99	99	..	..	..	..	..	..	41.0	87.0	..
77	76	..	..	55.3	16.2	..	22.8	46.0	84.0	36.7
76	83	29.6	17.5	81.4	55.1	53.5	..	76.0	82.0	..
73	70	..	..	..	..	..	42.8	36.0	81.0	..
41	42	41.0	26.7	38.9	14.6	8.1	5.5	19.0	78.0	33.2
92	97	..	..	52.1	36.4	26.1	55.7	19.0	87.0	5.6
90	98	29.3	13.1	81.7	38.4	..	56.2	49.0	94.0	8.4
79	86	..	..	..	..	..	29.2	31.0	84.0	9.1
97	99	..	..	..	..	..	..	57.0	100.0	..
71	75	37.4	21.3	42.4	8.2	6.0	25.8	31.0	86.0	30.1
24	31	..	..	..	..	..	..	42.0	81.0	..
62	69	..	..	..	..	..	..	74.0	76.0	..
82	84	..	..	..	..	..	..	52.0	81.0	..
95	95	29.5	6.1	69.0	50.6	46.8	0.6	67.0	68.0	0.6
91	85	..	..	..	..	..	25.7	77.0	88.0	56.7
84	89	..	..	..	..	..	..	10.0	79.0	..
68	64	..	..	..	..	..	..	44.0	70.0	..
85	81	45.8	14.9	46.5	40.8	26.5	41.1	80.0	88.0	43.3
76	73	..	..	60.2	64.9	..	17.3	46.0	74.0	23.6
94	**97**								**..**	
88	93	..	..	..	..	..	..	100.0	90.0	..
95	97	30.7	6.8	78.9	60.3	57.6	..	63.0	89.0	..
98	98	21.0	5.6	..	..	..	..	82.0	69.0	..
98	99	..	..	..	..	..	..	93.0	85.0	..
98	99	..	..	..	..	..	..	86.0	86.0	..

(continued)

Table 7.2 Health (continued)

	Water and sanitation						Human resources		
	Population with sustainable access to an improved water source			Population with sustainable access to improved sanitation			Health workers (per 1,000 people)		
	(% of total population) 2008	(% of urban population) 2008	(% of rural population) 2008	(% of total population) 2008	(% of urban population) 2008	(% of rural population) 2008	Physicians 2008–09[a]	Nurses and midwives 2008–09[a]	Community workers 2008
SUB-SAHARAN AFRICA	**60**	**83**	**47**	**31**	**44**	**24**			**..**
Angola	50	60	38	57	86	18	..	..	..
Benin	75	84	69	12	24	4	0.1	0.8	..
Botswana	95	99	90	60	74	39	..	..	..
Burkina Faso	76	95	72	11	33	6	0.1	0.7	..
Burundi	72	83	71	46	49	46	..	..	..
Cameroon	74	92	51	47	56	35	..	..	..
Cape Verde	84	85	82	54	65	38	0.6	1.3	..
Central African Republic	67	92	51	34	43	28	..	..	..
Chad	50	67	44	9	23	4	..	..	..
Comoros	95	91	97	36	50	30	..	..	..
Congo, Dem. Rep.	46	80	28	23	23	23	..	..	..
Congo, Rep.	71	95	34	30	31	29	..	..	..
Côte d'Ivoire	80	93	68	23	36	11	0.1	0.5	..
Djibouti	92	98	52	56	63	10	..	0.8	..
Equatorial Guinea	..	..	..	..	..	..	..	..	..
Eritrea	61	74	57	14	52	4	..	..	..
Ethiopia	38	98	26	12	29	8	..	..	..
Gabon	87	95	41	33	33	30	..	..	..
Gambia, The	92	96	86	67	68	65	0.0	0.6	0.1
Ghana	82	90	74	13	18	7	0.1	1.1	0.2
Guinea	71	89	61	19	34	11	..	..	..
Guinea-Bissau	61	83	51	21	49	9	0.0	0.6	..
Kenya	59	83	52	31	27	32	..	..	..
Lesotho	85	97	81	29	40	25	..	..	..
Liberia	68	79	51	17	25	4	0.0	0.3	..
Madagascar	41	71	29	11	15	10	..	..	..
Malawi	80	95	77	56	51	57	0.0	0.3	0.7
Mali	56	81	44	36	45	32	0.0	0.3	..
Mauritania	49	52	47	26	50	9	0.1	0.7	..
Mauritius	99	100	99	91	93	90	..	..	..
Mozambique	47	77	29	17	38	4	..	..	..
Namibia	92	99	88	33	60	17	..	..	..
Niger	48	96	39	9	34	4	0.0	0.1	..
Nigeria	58	75	42	32	36	28	0.4	1.6	0.1
Rwanda	65	77	62	54	50	55	..	..	..
São Tomé and Príncipe	89	89	88	26	30	19	..	..	..
Senegal	69	92	52	51	69	38	0.1	0.4	..
Seychelles	..	100	..	..	97	..	..	..	..
Sierra Leone	49	86	26	13	24	6	0.0	0.2	0.0
Somalia	30	67	9	23	52	6	..	..	..
South Africa	91	99	78	77	84	65	..	..	..
Sudan	57	64	52	34	55	18	0.3	0.8	..
Swaziland	69	92	61	55	61	53	..	..	..
Tanzania	54	80	45	24	32	21	..	..	..
Togo	60	87	41	12	24	3	0.1	0.3	..
Uganda	67	91	64	48	38	49	..	..	..
Zambia	60	87	46	49	59	43	..	..	..
Zimbabwe	82	99	72	44	56	37	..	..	..
NORTH AFRICA	**92**	**95**	**87**	**89**	**94**	**83**			**..**
Algeria	83	85	79	95	98	88	..	..	..
Egypt, Arab Rep.	99	100	98	94	97	92	2.8	3.5	..
Libya	..	..	..	97	97	96	1.9	6.8	..
Morocco	81	98	60	69	83	52	0.6	0.9	..
Tunisia	94	99	84	85	96	64	1.2	3.3	..

a. Data are for the most recent year available during the period specified.
b. Diphtheria, pertussis, and tetanus toxoid.
c. Malaria cases reported before 2000 can be probable and confirmed or only confirmed, depending on the country.

Health expenditure								
Share of GDP (%)			Share of total health expenditure (%)			Out-of-pocket (% of private expenditure on health)	Private prepaid plans (% of private expenditure on health)	Health expenditure per capita ($)
Total 2009	Public 2009	Private 2009	Public 2009	Private 2009	External resources for health 2009	2009	2009	2009
6.6	**2.9**	**3.7**	**44.0**	**56.0**	**..**	**62.9**	**..**	**76.0**
4.6	4.1	0.5	89.0	11.0	2.7	100.0	0.0	203.8
4.2	2.3	1.9	55.2	44.8	22.6	92.7	7.3	31.9
10.3	8.2	2.1	80.0	20.0	18.8	34.0	6.5	611.9
6.4	3.9	2.4	61.7	38.3	21.9	93.0	3.4	38.1
13.1	6.0	7.1	46.0	54.0	45.2	66.1	0.0	19.8
5.6	1.6	4.0	27.9	72.1	8.1	94.9	0.0	61.1
3.9	2.9	1.0	74.0	26.0	7.4	99.7	0.0	146.1
4.3	1.6	2.6	38.7	61.3	40.4	95.0	0.0	19.3
7.0	3.9	3.1	55.2	44.8	6.9	96.7	0.0	41.8
3.4	2.1	1.3	61.6	38.4	15.3	100.0	0.0	27.8
9.5	4.9	4.7	51.0	49.0	35.8	76.2	0.0	15.6
3.0	1.6	1.4	53.8	46.2	7.2	100.0	0.0	70.1
5.1	1.0	4.1	18.8	81.2	10.6	98.8	1.2	55.3
7.0	5.3	1.6	76.9	23.1	30.2	98.6	1.4	84.5
3.9	3.4	0.5	86.9	13.1	3.2	83.5	0.0	709.4
2.2	1.0	1.2	44.6	55.4	65.6	100.0	0.0	10.1
4.3	2.0	2.2	47.6	52.4	39.5	80.1	1.5	14.7
3.5	1.7	1.8	47.9	52.1	1.7	100.0	0.0	266.3
6.0	3.0	3.0	50.1	49.9	26.3	48.5	3.1	25.6
6.9	3.1	3.8	45.0	55.0	16.8	78.6	6.2	45.1
5.7	0.9	4.9	15.2	84.8	15.6	99.4	0.0	18.8
6.1	1.6	4.5	25.5	74.5	42.0	56.0	0.0	18.4
4.3	1.5	2.9	33.8	66.2	36.1	77.4	8.8	33.2
8.2	5.6	2.6	68.2	31.8	30.4	68.9	0.0	70.0
13.2	5.3	8.0	39.7	60.3	47.0	52.2	0.0	29.4
4.1	2.8	1.4	67.1	32.9	28.3	67.8	15.1	18.0
6.2	3.6	2.6	58.0	42.0	99.1	28.5	14.5	19.1
5.6	2.7	2.9	47.9	52.1	25.6	99.5	0.5	38.4
2.5	1.6	0.9	62.6	37.4	25.6	100.0	0.0	21.9
5.7	2.1	3.6	36.9	63.1	1.6	88.7	6.3	383.1
5.7	4.1	1.5	73.2	26.8	72.0	43.6	1.5	24.7
5.9	4.0	2.0	66.6	33.4	11.9	17.8	61.0	258.0
6.1	3.5	2.6	57.6	42.4	32.6	96.2	3.2	20.0
5.8	2.1	3.7	36.3	63.7	4.9	95.6	3.1	69.3
9.0	3.9	5.1	43.2	56.8	53.2	44.4	10.2	48.2
7.1	2.9	4.2	41.0	59.0	38.7	68.5	0.0	90.7
5.7	3.1	2.5	55.6	44.4	14.0	78.5	17.9	58.9
4.0	3.1	0.9	76.8	23.2	1.4	30.9	0.0	365.7
13.1	0.9	12.2	7.2	92.8	20.4	89.5	1.0	43.9
..	..	..	..	..	..	..	..	..
8.5	3.4	5.1	40.1	59.9	1.9	29.6	66.1	485.4
7.3	2.0	5.3	27.4	72.6	3.2	96.2	1.0	94.6
6.3	4.0	2.3	63.3	36.7	12.2	42.3	18.9	155.8
5.1	3.8	1.4	73.6	26.4	56.5	65.1	14.5	25.3
5.9	1.7	4.2	28.2	71.8	17.4	84.2	4.3	28.9
8.2	1.6	6.7	19.0	81.0	20.9	65.4	0.0	42.5
4.8	2.5	2.2	53.0	47.0	50.3	74.5	4.1	47.1
..	..	..	..	..	..	..	..	..
5.3	**3.0**	**2.3**	**56.8**	**43.2**	**..**	**93.4**	**..**	**173.4**
5.8	5.0	0.8	86.2	13.8	0.0	94.7	5.1	267.9
5.0	2.1	2.9	41.7	58.3	1.5	97.7	1.7	113.3
3.9	2.6	1.3	66.1	33.9	1.0	100.0	0.0	416.7
5.5	1.9	3.6	34.4	65.6	0.2	86.3	13.7	155.7
6.2	3.4	2.9	54.0	46.0	1.2	87.0	11.2	240.0

Table 8.1 Rural development

	Rural population (%)						Rural population density (rural population per sq km of arable land)	
	Share of total population			Annual growth				
	1990	2008	2009	1990	2008	2009	1990	2008
SUB-SAHARAN AFRICA	**71.8**	**63.5**	**63.0**	**2.2**	**1.7**	**1.7**	**286.0**	**358.0**
Angola	62.9	43.3	42.4	0.7	0.6	0.5	231.2	229.5
Benin	65.5	58.8	58.4	2.2	2.5	2.4	194.5	199.7
Botswana	58.1	40.4	39.7	–2.1	–0.4	–0.4	187.0	310.6
Burkina Faso	86.2	80.4	80.0	2.4	2.9	2.9	215.8	194.5
Burundi	93.7	89.6	89.3	2.3	2.6	2.5	572.4	803.8
Cameroon	59.3	43.2	42.4	1.5	0.4	0.3	122.1	138.4
Cape Verde	55.9	40.4	39.6	–2.2	–0.4	–0.5	483.0	309.8
Central African Republic	63.2	61.4	61.3	1.9	1.6	1.6	96.4	138.1
Chad	79.2	73.3	72.9	2.9	2.1	2.0	147.7	186.1
Comoros	72.1	71.9	71.9	2.0	2.3	2.3	402.4	578.6
Congo, Dem. Rep.	72.2	66.0	65.4	3.7	1.8	1.8	400.7	633.4
Congo, Rep.	45.7	38.7	38.3	1.9	0.8	0.9	233.4	285.2
Côte d'Ivoire	60.3	51.2	50.6	3.1	1.0	1.0	312.9	376.7
Djibouti	24.3	12.7	12.3	4.1	–1.3	–1.5	13,614.8	10,785.4
Equatorial Guinea	65.3	60.6	60.5	1.9	2.3	2.3	190.5	305.0
Eritrea	84.2	79.3	78.8	1.3	2.4	2.4	..	583.0
Ethiopia	87.4	83.0	82.7	3.1	2.2	2.2	..	492.4
Gabon	30.9	15.0	14.5	–1.0	–1.3	–1.5	97.0	66.7
Gambia, The	61.7	43.6	42.7	2.3	0.8	0.7	303.6	185.5
Ghana	63.6	50.0	49.2	1.7	0.6	0.6	352.6	265.2
Guinea	72.0	65.6	65.1	3.2	1.5	1.6	547.8	268.6
Guinea-Bissau	71.9	70.2	70.1	0.8	2.1	2.1	294.0	368.4
Kenya	81.8	78.4	78.1	3.1	2.3	2.3	384.1	573.4
Lesotho	86.0	74.5	73.8	1.0	–0.1	–0.1	434.7	430.3
Liberia	54.7	39.9	39.2	–3.8	2.8	2.5	338.7	378.0
Madagascar	76.4	70.5	70.1	2.2	2.2	2.2	316.6	456.6
Malawi	88.4	81.2	80.7	3.5	2.2	2.2	371.3	344.4
Mali	76.7	67.8	67.3	1.4	1.5	1.5	323.3	177.7
Mauritania	60.3	59.0	58.8	1.0	2.1	2.0	299.7	474.2
Mauritius	56.1	57.5	57.5	0.2	0.5	0.4	593.0	838.9
Mozambique	78.9	63.2	62.4	0.2	1.1	1.0	309.7	314.2
Namibia	72.3	63.2	62.6	3.4	1.0	1.0	155.2	168.2
Niger	84.6	83.5	83.4	2.8	3.8	3.8	60.6	84.7
Nigeria	64.7	51.6	50.9	1.6	1.0	0.9	213.2	208.2
Rwanda	94.6	81.7	81.4	–0.4	2.4	2.5	768.7	615.3
São Tomé and Príncipe	56.4	39.4	38.6	0.2	–0.5	–0.5	3,274.5	701.9
Senegal	61.0	57.6	57.4	2.4	2.2	2.2	148.7	201.0
Seychelles	50.7	45.7	45.2	0.9	1.2	0.1	3,549.0	3,970.4
Sierra Leone	67.1	62.2	61.9	0.9	2.0	1.9	563.8	192.8
Somalia	70.3	63.5	63.0	0.0	1.5	1.6	453.7	566.6
South Africa	48.0	39.3	38.8	1.0	–0.1	–0.2	125.7	131.8
Sudan	73.4	56.6	55.7	1.2	0.7	0.6	155.4	113.0
Swaziland	77.1	75.1	74.8	3.2	1.0	1.1	370.2	492.5
Tanzania	81.1	74.5	74.0	2.7	2.3	2.3	229.4	329.6
Togo	69.9	58.0	57.3	1.9	1.3	1.2	130.7	152.3
Uganda	88.9	87.0	86.9	3.2	3.1	3.1	315.3	487.6
Zambia	60.6	64.6	64.4	3.1	2.2	2.2	209.1	346.1
Zimbabwe	71.0	62.7	62.2	1.9	–0.7	–0.3	257.0	209.4
NORTH AFRICA	**51.5**	**47.2**	**46.9**	**1.7**	**1.1**	**1.1**	**823.3**	**1,078.3**
Algeria	47.9	34.8	34.1	0.8	–0.3	–0.3	171.0	159.6
Egypt, Arab Rep.	56.5	57.3	57.2	2.5	1.7	1.7	1,429.4	1,684.1
Libya	24.3	22.5	22.3	2.0	1.2	1.2	58.8	80.8
Morocco	51.6	44.0	43.6	0.5	0.4	0.4	147.0	172.6
Tunisia	42.1	33.5	33.1	0.5	–0.2	–0.2	118.0	122.0

a. Data are for the most recent year available during the period specified.

Share of rural population below the national poverty line				Rural population poverty gap at national poverty line (%)				Share of rural population with sustainable access (%)	
Surveys 1990–99[a]		Surveys 2000–09[a]		Surveys 1990–99[a]		Surveys 2000–07[a]		To an improved water source	To improved sanitation facilities
Year	Percent	Year	Percent	Year	Percent	Year	Percent	2008	2008
..	..	..	..	..	..	..	..	**46.8**	**24.1**
..	..	..	..	..	..	..	..	38.0	18.0
1999	33.0	2003	46.0	1999	9.4	2003	14.0	69.0	4.0
1993	55.0	2003	44.8	..	..	2003	18.4	90.0	39.0
1998	50.7	2003	52.4	1998	15.7	2003	17.6	72.0	6.0
1998	83.2	2006	68.9	1998	45.9	2006	24.2	71.0	46.0
1996	59.6	2007	55.0	..	..	2007	17.5	51.0	35.0
..	..	2007	44.3	..	..	2007	14.3	82.0	38.0
1992	74.4	2008	69.4	1992	42.5	2008	35.0	51.0	28.0
1995	48.6	2003	58.6	1995	26.3	2003	23.3	44.0	4.0
1995	69.4	2004	48.7	..	..	2004	17.8	97.0	30.0
..	..	2005	75.7	..	..	2005	34.9	28.0	23.0
..	..	2005	57.7	..	..	2005	20.6	34.0	29.0
1998	41.5	2008	54.2	1998	14.3	2008	20.3	68.0	11.0
..	..	..	..	..	..	..	..	52.0	10.0
..	..	..	..	..	..	..	..	..	..
..	..	..	..	..	..	..	..	57.0	4.0
1999	45.4	2004	39.3	1999	12.2	2004	8.5	26.0	8.0
..	..	2005	44.6	..	..	2005	16.0	41.0	30.0
1998	79.0	2003	67.8	..	..	2003	30.5	86.0	65.0
1998	49.6	2006	39.2	1998	18.2	2006	13.5	74.0	7.0
1994	82.1	2007	63.0	1994	39.1	2007	22.0	61.0	11.0
..	..	2002	69.1	..	..	2002	27.8	51.0	9.0
1997	52.9	2005	49.1	1997	19.3	2005	17.5	52.0	32.0
1994	68.9	2003	60.5	1993	26.5	..	..	81.0	25.0
..	..	2007	67.7	..	..	2007	26.3	51.0	4.0
1999	76.7	2005	73.5	1999	21.4	2005	28.9	29.0	10.0
1998	66.5	2004	55.9	1998	23.9	2004	8.6	77.0	57.0
..	..	2006	57.6	..	..	..	..	44.0	32.0
1996	68.1	2000	61.2	..	..	2000	24.1	47.0	9.0
..	..	..	..	..	..	..	..	99.0	90.0
1996	71.3	2008	56.9	1996	29.9	2008	22.2	29.0	4.0
1993	69.0	2003	49.0	1993	34.0	2003	16.0	88.0	17.0
1993	66.0	2007	63.9	1993	22.5	2007	21.2	39.0	4.0
1996	69.8	2004	63.8	1992	16.1	2004	26.6	42.0	28.0
..	..	2006	64.2	..	..	2006	26.0	62.0	55.0
..	..	2001	64.9	..	..	2001	24.7	88.0	19.0
1994	71.0	2005	61.9	1994	25.3	2005	21.5	52.0	38.0
..	..	..	..	..	..	..	..	..	..
1990	88.3	2003	78.5	1990	73.1	2003	34.6	26.0	6.0
..	..	..	..	..	..	..	..	9.0	6.0
..	..	..	..	..	..	..	..	78.0	65.0
..	..	..	..	..	..	..	..	52.0	18.0
..	..	2001	75.0	..	..	2001	37.0	61.0	53.0
1992	40.8	2007	37.4	1992	12.7	2007	11.0	45.0	21.0
..	..	2006	74.3	..	..	2006	29.3	41.0	3.0
1997	48.7	2009	27.2	1997	15.2	2009	7.6	64.0	49.0
1998	83.0	2006	76.8	1998	44.5	2006	38.8	46.0	43.0
1995	44.0	..	..	..	..	..	..	72.0	37.0
..	..	..	..	..	..	..	..	**87.4**	**83.0**
1995	30.3	..	..	1995	4.5	..	..	79.0	88.0
..	..	2008	30.0	..	..	..	..	98.0	92.0
..	..	..	..	..	..	..	..	..	96.0
1999	24.2	2007	14.5	..	..	..	..	60.0	52.0
..	..	..	..	..	..	..	..	84.0	64.0

Table 8.2 Agriculture

	Agriculture value added (% of GDP)	Gross production index (1999–2001=100)					Cereal (thousands of metric tons)			Trade			
										Agricultural		Food	
		Agriculture total	Crop	Livestock	Food	Cereal	Production	Exports	Imports	Exports ($ millions)	Imports ($ millions)	Exports ($ millions)	Imports ($ millions)
	2009[a]	2009	2009	2009	2009	2009	2009	2008	2008	2008	2008	2008	2008
SUB-SAHARAN AFRICA	**13.1**	**..**	**128.7**	**125.1**	**130**	**..**	**116,492**	**2,199**	**21,901**	**25,448**	**32,546**	**15,199**	**26,522**
Angola	10.2	196.0	250.0	92.0	198.0	174.0	1,030	1	734	12	2,375	10	1,824
Benin	..	112.0	110.0	135.0	116.0	136.0	1,508	5	226	450	791	300	745
Botswana	3.1	113.0	120.0	112.0	113.0	182.0	56	2	177	150	609	115	467
Burkina Faso	..	140.0	144.0	132.0	136.0	158.0	3,627	11	205	273	294	67	228
Burundi	..	109.0	108.0	118.0	110.0	114.0	300	0	29	57	49	2	44
Cameroon	..	114.0	117.0	105.0	120.0	148.0	2,017	0	551	962	624	681	541
Cape Verde	9.2	118.0	107.0	141.0	118.0	43.0	7	1	103	1	194	1	190
Central African Republic	55.5	119.0	110.0	132.0	123.0	148.0	251	0	31	23	33	16	27
Chad	..	118.0	118.0	120.0	125.0	172.0	2,193	0	147	87	143	54	111
Comoros	46.3	112.0	113.0	103.0	112.0	115.0	26	0	47	8	55	8	51
Congo, Dem. Rep.	42.9	97.0	97.0	96.0	98.0	97.0	1,573	5	902	57	959	11	830
Congo, Rep.	4.5	124.0	116.0	157.0	123.0	183.0	23	0	175	67	469	23	413
Côte d'Ivoire	24.4	110.0	109.0	132.0	120.0	113.0	1,471	38	1,090	4,361	1,224	3,382	1,036
Djibouti	..	147.0	101.0	158.0	147.0	90.0	0	0	201	38	432	37	383
Equatorial Guinea	3.5	91.0	90.0	104.0	89.0	..	..	..	30	3	85	3	53
Eritrea	14.4	126.0	154.0	101.0	126.0	237.0	227	1	119	2	66	2	65
Ethiopia	50.7	149.0	153.0	140.0	151.0	170.0	15,502	2	1,424	1,352	1,347	576	1,131
Gabon	5.1	103.0	104.0	100.0	103.0	127.0	47	0	135	81	391	3	322
Gambia, The	27.5	118.0	114.0	132.0	117.0	177.0	311	0	169	16	111	15	89
Ghana	31.7	154.0	156.0	127.0	155.0	156.0	2,607	0	825	1,532	1,311	1,482	1,214
Guinea	17.2	130.0	133.0	167.0	133.0	169.0	2,659	15	324	58	264	28	220
Guinea-Bissau	..	123.0	120.0	128.0	122.0	146.0	215	0	32	96	67	96	52
Kenya	22.6	124.0	107.0	147.0	126.0	94.0	2,804	30	1,100	2,669	1,344	737	1,175
Lesotho	8.4	75.0	72.0	78.0	72.0	37.0	75	0	259	1	138	1	112
Liberia	..	117.0	115.0	127.0	131.0	169.0	293	0	262	97	217	10	196
Madagascar	29.1	113.0	115.0	111.0	114.0	120.0	4,388	3	276	193	401	150	331
Malawi	30.5	136.0	141.0	153.0	129.0	120.0	3,993	31	259	768	266	103	177
Mali	..	157.0	162.0	153.0	183.0	240.0	6,335	4	252	351	416	144	341
Mauritania	20.6	116.0	116.0	115.0	116.0	129.0	213	..	438	24	470	18	424
Mauritius	4.3	105.0	95.0	138.0	106.0	182.0	1	18	282	372	746	326	562
Mozambique	31.5	123.0	130.0	89.0	102.0	94.0	1,785	30	610	330	616	181	526
Namibia	9.4	102.0	140.0	90.0	101.0	134.0	112	3	371	235	367	190	229
Niger	..	185.0	210.0	153.0	186.0	175.0	3,451	30	320	97	335	87	282
Nigeria	..	134.0	134.0	121.0	135.0	142.0	20,983	5	1,364	856	3,400	696	2,991
Rwanda	34.2	135.0	132.0	158.0	134.0	191.0	651	8	56	235	123	19	105
São Tomé and Príncipe	..	111.0	110.0	125.0	111.0	145.0	4	..	14	5	28	5	23
Senegal	16.6	133.0	130.0	144.0	134.0	175.0	1,869	37	1,533	252	1,793	133	1,633
Seychelles	2	39.0	61.0	44.0	38.0	..	..	0	19	4	90	2	77
Sierra Leone	51.4	197.0	204.0	144.0	201.0	406.0	868	0	214	26	211	23	189
Somalia	..	104.0	96.0	105.0	104.0	54.0	215	0	452	58	518	53	385
South Africa	3	120.0	111.0	130.0	122.0	122.0	14,577	1,279	2,302	5,461	4,896	3,741	3,204
Sudan	29.7	118.0	112.0	123.0	119.0	144.0	5,552	170	1,664	457	1,543	319	1,290
Swaziland	7.3	110.0	101.0	140.0	115.0	24.0	61	1	182	256	224	242	184
Tanzania	28.8	135.0	154.0	104.0	134.0	154.0	5,683	136	546	954	643	361	555
Togo	..	113.0	109.0	137.0	132.0	120.0	1,004	19	307	301	326	247	279
Uganda	24.7	112.0	109.0	120.0	112.0	131.0	2,811	73	439	878	629	198	537
Zambia	21.6	144.0	170.0	106.0	135.0	208.0	2,198	238	48	348	284	190	208
Zimbabwe	17.9	70.0	55.0	107.0	82.0	30.0	919	1	652	534	627	111	475
NORTH AFRICA	**13.1**						**42,172**	**400**	**32,879**	**5,382**	**26,427**	**4,668**	**23,107**
Algeria	11.7	163.0	196.0	121.0	163.0	279.0	5,253	1	9,093	76	7,785	61	7,015
Egypt, Arab Rep.	13.7	137.0	136.0	134.0	139.0	125.0	23,697	258	12,324	1,823	8,661	1,499	7,754
Libya	..	109.0	102.0	116.0	109.0	93.0	207	1	2,276	8	2,266	1	2,091
Morocco	16.4	139.0	142.0	128.0	140.0	163.0	10,430	95	6,127	1,919	5,157	1,718	4,140
Tunisia	7.8	115.0	119.0	110.0	115.0	84.0	2,585	45	3,059	1,555	2,557	1,389	2,107

Share of land area (%)		Agricultural irrigated land (% of agricultural land)	Fertilizer consumption (100 grams per hectare of arable land)	Agricultural machinery (tractors per 100 sq km of arable land)	Agricultural employment (% of total employment)	Agriculture value added per worker (2000 $)	Cereal yield (kilograms per hectare)
Permanent cropland	Cereal cropland						
2009	2009	2000–08[b]	2008	2000–08[b]	2000–08[b]	2009	2009
1.0	**3.8**		**11.6**			**318.3**	**1,296.9**
0.2	1.4	..	8.3	..	..	313.1	587.7
2.7	9.6	..	0.0	..	..	..	1,423.5
0.0	0.2	0.0	..	134.8	..	597.1	569.4
0.2	13.2	..	3.9	..	..	..	1,002.0
15.2	8.8	..	2.2	..	..	..	1,319.4
2.5	2.8	..	8.6	..	..	..	1,524.0
0.7	8.2	..	..	11.2	11.2	2,224.8	223.6
0.1	0.4	..	..	..	..	..	948.3
0.0	2.0	..	..	..	..	..	879.9
29.6	12.9	..	..	..	..	452.9	1,063.9
0.3	0.9	..	0.9	..	..	167.9	788.5
0.2	0.1	..	1.1	..	..	..	861.5
13.4	2.4	..	18.9	32.1	32.1	925.6	1,899.7
..	0.0	..	..	46.2	46.2	..	1,111.1
2.7	..	..	..	..	..	1,004.8	..
0.0	4.5	..	0.0	8.3	8.3	66.1	500.0
0.9	9.2	0.5	7.7	..	..	214.7	1,676.8
0.6	0.1	..	14.1	..	..	1,869.3	2,388.8
0.5	29.6	..	2.6	..	..	275.3	1,049.3
12.5	6.9	..	6.4	4.5	4.5	..	1,659.8
2.8	8.1	..	1.5	39.3	39.3	225.4	1,339.2
8.9	5.3	..	..	..	..	..	1,444.5
0.9	4.1	0.1	33.3	25.2	25.2	334.2	1,203.8
0.1	5.9	..	..	..	..	207.0	421.0
2.3	1.9	..	..	..	..	..	1,609.7
1.0	2.9	2.2	4.3	1.9	1.9	192.2	2,581.7
1.3	19.6	..	1.7	..	..	161.7	2,162.8
0.1	3.3	..	9.0	2.7	2.7	..	1,588.2
0.0	0.2	..	..	9.8	9.8	407.5	875.8
2.0	0.0	21.4	210.1	..	..	5,555.9	8,306.9
0.3	2.6	..	0.0	..	..	219.7	876.6
0.0	0.4	..	0.3	..	..	1,638.1	364.7
0.0	7.2	..	0.4	..	..	..	379.8
3.3	15.1	..	13.3	6.6	6.6	..	1,528.0
11.3	14.4	..	8.3	0.5	0.5	..	1,828.7
46.9	1.1	..	..	..	..	..	4,056.2
0.3	8.6	0.7	2.4	2.1	2.1	245.4	1,134.5
6.5	..	..	29.0	..	..	724.9	..
1.9	8.6	..	..	..	..	..	1,402.3
0.0	0.9	..	..	12.0	12.0	..	371.4
0.8	2.7	..	49.7	43.0	43.0	3,640.8	4,414.2
0.1	4.0	1.3	3.6	12.4	12.4	922.3	587.2
0.8	3.1	..	..	87.1	87.1	1,176.0	1,147.5
1.5	5.8	..	5.9	23.3	23.3	283.0	1,109.5
3.1	13.2	..	4.9	0.5	0.5	..	1,398.4
11.4	9.3	..	3.4	..	..	202.9	1,539.4
0.0	1.4	..	50.1	..	..	215.7	2,066.9
0.3	5.3	..	27.9	..	..	141.4	449.6
0.9	**2.4**		**..**			**2,929.4**	**3,111.3**
0.4	1.3	2.1	6.8	139.6	139.6	2,183.7	1,653.9
0.8	3.1	..	723.6	372.1	372.1	3,024.2	7,571.4
0.2	0.2	..	27.3	218.9	218.9	..	568.8
2.1	12.2	4.4	53.8	..	..	3,306.3	1,910.7
14.2	9.2	4.0	32.1	142.6	142.6	3,602.4	1,812.9

a. Provisional.

b. Data are for the most recent year available during the period specified.

Table 8.3 Producer food prices

	Rice, paddy (current $ per metric ton)					Maize (current $ per metric ton)				
	1991	1995	2000	2005	2008	1991	1995	2000	2005	2008
SUB-SAHARAN AFRICA										
Angola	..	..	..	..	..	..	..	..	..	..
Benin	..	..	..	..	..	..	..	..	..	..
Botswana	..	..	..	..	..	..	..	..	..	..
Burkina Faso	351.5	245.6	119.4	392.2	559.8	212.7	148.5	91.3	192.4	253.7
Burundi	220.4	272.3	277.5	609.2	814.9	270.0	208.2	253.0	314.3	325.2
Cameroon	177.2	136.2	144.6	269.1	337.2	283.6	152.3	163.7	113.2	140.6
Cape Verde	..	..	..	..	..	313.9	432.0	247.9	334.6	461.0
Central African Republic	..	..	..	..	..	..	..	..	..	..
Chad	..	..	..	..	..	..	..	..	..	..
Comoros	..	..	..	..	..	..	..	..	..	..
Congo, Dem. Rep.	..	..	..	..	..	..	..	..	..	..
Congo, Rep.	265.9	150.3	178.4	220.1	362.9	212.7	200.3	262.6	359.6	587.8
Côte d'Ivoire	212.7	220.4	154.5	222.2	506.4	159.5	162.9	119.4	233.0	331.7
Djibouti	..	..	..	..	..	..	..	..	..	..
Equatorial Guinea	..	..	..	..	..	..	..	..	..	..
Eritrea	..	..	..	..	..	..	295.1	354.3	347.0	500.2
Ethiopia	..	260.8	201.6	127.7	734.4	294.7	154.3	119.3	144.7	350.0
Gabon	..	..	..	..	..	..	..	..	..	..
Gambia, The	170.4	206.2	136.9	175.0	258.3	211.3	419.0	134.5	311.2	293.3
Ghana	416.9	393.3	306.6	577.8	826.0	188.9	215.1	171.7	366.5	445.6
Guinea	220.2	245.1	405.5	138.2	128.8	191.0	245.1	166.7	152.0	127.0
Guinea-Bissau	..	..	351.1	474.8	893.2	..	76.2	842.7	1,168.0	1,382.3
Kenya	72.7	107.2	299.9	378.8	627.5	104.3	155.6	190.3	201.7	471.0
Lesotho	..	..	..	..	..	..	..	..	..	..
Liberia	..	..	..	..	..	..	..	..	..	..
Madagascar	119.9	170.0	190.6	125.9	314.9	337.8	178.6	143.8	84.5	226.5
Malawi	139.1	117.8	594.4	718.5	1,060.8	96.3	47.1	111.9	184.7	291.5
Mali	223.3	236.4	154.5	269.7	264.5	134.7	166.3	107.7	197.5	172.0
Mauritania	..	..	..	..	..	..	..	..	..	..
Mauritius	..	..	..	..	..	303.5	287.6	171.4	185.9	221.1
Mozambique	181.1	135.8	90.6	163.3	..	132.7	92.4	51.8	154.5	..
Namibia	..	..	..	..	..	166.6	193.3	145.1	276.6	262.6
Niger	260.4	214.4	154.5	201.0	260.2	163.0	138.2	118.0	173.0	226.4
Nigeria	761.3	652.2	279.4	545.1	519.4	334.8	661.3	198.4	477.5	486.9
Rwanda	199.7	873.4	582.1	480.2	659.2	259.0	194.5	211.0	104.2	138.5
São Tomé and Príncipe	..	..	..	..	..	..	..	..	..	..
Senegal	..	..	..	..	..	..	..	..	..	..
Seychelles	..	..	..	..	..	..	..	..	..	..
Sierra Leone	..	..	..	..	..	..	..	..	..	..
Somalia	..	..	..	..	..	..	..	..	..	..
South Africa	..	..	..	..	..	129.3	159.1	78.5	99.3	200.9
Sudan	962.2	205.2	388.9	497.3	125,651.2	1,538.6	328.1	621.9	184.6	42,295.8
Swaziland	..	..	..	..	..	..	..	..	..	..
Tanzania	..	..	..	..	..	..	..	..	..	..
Togo	283.6	232.4	165.7	258.3	375.2	205.6	190.3	120.8	294.4	495.8
Uganda	..	..	..	..	..	..	..	..	..	..
Zambia	..	..	..	..	..	..	..	..	..	..
Zimbabwe	215.4	288.5	255.1	346.4	..	74.6	121.2	123.8	100.5	..
NORTH AFRICA										
Algeria	270.7	544.5	344.8	421.4	581.2	173.2	335.7	212.6	259.8	358.3
Egypt, Arab Rep.	127.5	193.4	167.9	185.0	269.7	140.5	151.5	174.8	179.3	260.3
Libya	..	..	..	..	..	..	..	..	..	..
Morocco	436.5	445.0	276.4	325.2	405.1	242.3	292.7	223.0	225.8	398.7
Tunisia	..	..	..	..	..	..	..	..	..	..

Sorghum (current $ per metric ton)					Millet (current $ per metric ton)				
1991	1995	2000	2005	2008	1991	1995	2000	2005	2008
..	..	..	..	..	..	..	..	..	..
..	..	..	..	..	..	..	..	..	..
..	..	..	..	..	..	..	..	..	..
212.7	134.4	84.3	178.7	225.3	212.7	152.9	84.3	178.7	217.0
330.6	328.3	374.7	324.2	430.5	..	..	..	..	..
177.2	160.3	313.8	217.0	269.4	..	..	..	..	..
..	..	..	..	..	..	..	..	..	..
..	..	..	..	..	..	..	..	..	..
..	..	..	..	..	..	..	..	..	..
..	..	..	..	..	..	..	..	..	..
..	..	..	..	..	..	..	..	..	..
..	..	..	..	..	..	..	..	..	..
342.4	252.2	2,103.1	336.6	325.4	460.8	391.3	245.7	415.4	376.9
..	..	..	..	..	..	..	..	..	..
..	..	..	..	..	..	..	..	..	..
..	212.4	284.7	391.7	571.0	..	337.2	434.3	645.3	939.4
362.3	193.2	142.1	188.7	446.4	294.7	216.0	144.8	170.0	461.5
..	..	..	..	..	..	..	..	..	..
213.6	193.3	129.0	334.3	316.4	218.8	388.9	128.2	310.1	266.6
217.5	212.9	153.1	424.4	514.9	308.6	245.0	205.9	495.3	619.6
187.0	263.8	179.4	120.7	139.4	..	..	..	..	..
..	..	351.1	854.6	1,287.9	..	..	..	..	..
207.7	194.1	204.1	331.8	319.8	256.6	361.3	311.1	485.5	487.7
..	..	..	..	..	..	..	..	..	..
..	..	..	..	..	..	..	..	..	..
..	..	..	..	..	..	..	..	..	..
176.6	72.0	500.6	514.4	661.0	133.2	65.1	518.6	642.7	919.6
145.3	198.3	87.4	233.6	197.2	156.0	194.3	85.1	254.5	192.7
..	..	..	..	..	..	..	..	..	..
..	..	..	..	..	..	..	..	..	..
63.9	47.9	51.8	141.3	..	..	..	..	..	..
147.8	182.0	157.4	263.2	244.4	147.8	209.5	157.4	263.2	244.4
140.2	96.2	77.3	117.4	154.2	150.1	96.2	108.2	135.1	175.8
368.1	847.7	190.3	509.0	370.2	339.6	413.3	184.5	493.7	402.1
234.0	450.1	211.0	138.8	186.0	..	..	..	..	..
..	..	..	..	..	..	..	..	..	..
..	..	..	..	..	..	..	..	..	..
..	..	..	..	..	..	..	..	..	..
..	..	..	..	..	..	..	..	..	..
..	..	..	..	..	..	..	..	..	..
106.8	132.9	74.9	70.9	214.7	..	..	..	..	..
943.0	92.7	165.6	335.2	3,297.7	1,206.4	278.6	655.1	433.6	5,426.7
..	..	..	..	..	..	..	..	..	..
..	..	..	..	..	..	..	..	..	..
237.5	246.4	140.5	364.6	629.7	265.9	238.4	122.2	305.8	407.5
..	..	..	..	..	..	..	..	..	..
..	..	..	..	..	..	..	..	..	..
69.0	75.0	90.1	100.6	..	71.8	60.0	90.1	100.6	..
152.3	207.7	131.5	160.8	221.7	..	..	..	..	..
141.2	166.9	184.0	186.7	264.3	..	..	..	..	..
..	..	..	..	..	..	..	..	..	..
218.2	402.8	218.3	292.5	384.5	..	..	..	..	..
..	..	..	..	..	..	..	..	..	..

Table 8.4 Environment

	Forest area (% of land area)		Renewable internal fresh water resources: Total (billions of cubic meters)	Renewable internal fresh water resources: Per capita (cubic meters)	Annual fresh water withdrawals (billions of cubic meters)	Water productivity (2000 $ per cubic meter of fresh water withdrawal)	Water pollution: Emissions of organic water pollutants (kilograms per day)	Energy: Energy production (kilotons of oil equivalent)		Energy: Energy use (kilotons of oil equivalent)		Energy: Combustible renewables and waste (% of total energy use)	
	1990	2010	2007	2007	2000–05[a]	2000–07[a]	2000–07[a]	1990	2008	1990	2008	1990	2008
SUB-SAHARAN AFRICA	**31.3**	**28.0**	**3,884**	**4,850**	**103.6**			**475,369**	**809,956**	**310,313**	**497,224**	**56.6**	**57.7**
Angola	48.9	46.9	148	8,431	0.6	14.3	..	28,652	105,837	5,883	10,972	73.5	63.5
Benin	52.1	41.2	10	1,227	0.1	18.2	..	1,774	1,833	1,661	3,005	94.2	61.0
Botswana	24.2	20.0	2	1,268	0.2	29.0	3,246	910	1,002	1,261	2,117	33.4	22.3
Burkina Faso	25.0	20.6	13	849	1.0	2.7	..	..	..	..	..	..	..
Burundi	11.3	6.7	10	1,284	0.3	2.5	..	..	..	..	..	..	..
Cameroon	51.4	42.1	273	14,630	1.0	10.5	..	10,976	10,119	4,980	7,102	76.7	71.0
Cape Verde	14.3	21.1	0	610	0.0	27.2	..	..	..	..	..	..	..
Central African Republic	37.2	36.3	141	33,119	0.1	14.4	..	..	..	..	..	..	..
Chad	10.4	9.2	15	1,412	0.4	3.8	..	..	..	..	..	..	..
Comoros	6.4	1.6	1	1,910	..	..	..	..	..	..	..	..	..
Congo, Dem. Rep.	70.7	68.0	900	14,395	0.6	6.9	..	12,019	22,664	11,798	22,250	84.7	93.4
Congo, Rep.	66.5	65.6	222	62,516	0.0	76.0	..	8,746	13,245	797	1,368	59.5	51.3
Côte d'Ivoire	32.1	32.7	77	3,819	1.4	7.4	..	3,382	11,415	4,323	10,278	73.5	74.0
Djibouti	0.2	0.3	0	360	0.0	29.2	..	..	..	..	..	..	..
Equatorial Guinea	66.3	58.0	26	40,485	0.0	72.1	..	..	..	..	..	..	..
Eritrea	..	15.2	3	586	0.6	1.2	2,540	..	546	..	681	..	80.0
Ethiopia	15.2	12.3	122	1,551	5.6	1.6	32,159	14,052	29,581	14,866	31,704	93.9	92.4
Gabon	85.4	85.4	164	115,340	0.1	39.0	..	14,630	13,519	1,181	2,073	62.9	52.5
Gambia, The	44.2	48.0	3	1,857	0.1	5.9	..	..	..	..	..	..	..
Ghana	32.7	21.7	30	1,325	1.0	5.1	16,048	4,392	6,858	5,291	9,459	73.7	66.8
Guinea	29.6	26.6	226	23,505	1.6	1.9	..	..	..	..	..	..	..
Guinea-Bissau	78.8	71.9	16	10,383	0.2	1.2	..	..	..	..	..	..	..
Kenya	6.5	6.1	21	548	2.7	5.0	..	9,013	15,108	10,940	18,021	77.9	76.9
Lesotho	1.3	1.4	5	2,574	0.1	14.9	5,252	..	..	..	..	..	..
Liberia	51.2	44.9	200	55,138	0.2	3.1	..	..	..	..	..	..	..
Madagascar	23.5	21.6	337	18,114	14.7	0.3	92,770	..	..	..	..	..	..
Malawi	41.4	34.4	16	1,118	1.0	1.8	32,672	..	..	..	..	..	..
Mali	11.5	10.2	60	4,835	6.5	0.4	..	..	..	..	..	..	..
Mauritania	0.4	0.2	0	127	1.6	0.7	..	..	..	..	..	..	..
Mauritius	19.1	17.2	3	2,182	0.7	6.9	15,446	..	..	..	..	..	..
Mozambique	55.2	49.6	100	4,586	0.7	5.7	..	5,608	11,460	5,922	9,314	93.9	81.9
Namibia	10.6	8.9	6	2,949	0.3	13.0	..	..	317	..	1,752	..	11.2
Niger	1.5	1.0	4	248	2.4	0.8	..	..	..	..	..	..	..
Nigeria	18.9	9.9	221	1,496	10.3	4.5	..	150,452	226,793	70,582	111,156	80.2	81.2
Rwanda	12.9	17.6	10	1,005	0.2	11.6	..	..	..	..	..	..	..
São Tomé and Príncipe	28.1	28.1	2	13,829	..	..	..	..	..	..	..	..	..
Senegal	48.6	44.0	26	2,169	2.2	2.2	6,621	964	1,230	1,686	2,859	56.8	41.7
Seychelles	88.5	89.1	..	..	0.0	47.1	..	..	..	..	..	..	..
Sierra Leone	43.5	38.1	160	29,518	0.5	1.3	..	..	..	..	..	..	..
Somalia	13.2	10.8	6	687	3.3	..	..	..	..	..	..	..	..
South Africa	7.6	4.7	45	928	12.5	10.6	229,582	114,535	162,951	90,860	134,489	11.5	10.4
Sudan	32.1	29.4	30	742	37.1	0.3	38,567	8,775	34,874	10,629	15,372	81.8	68.0
Swaziland	27.4	32.7	3	2,293	1.0	1.4	..	..	..	..	..	..	..
Tanzania	46.8	37.7	84	2,035	5.2	2.2	30,322	9,064	17,470	9,733	18,957	91.7	88.2
Togo	12.6	5.3	12	1,825	0.2	8.2	..	1,054	2,138	1,263	2,563	82.8	83.1
Uganda	24.1	15.2	39	1,273	0.3	21.5	2,105	..	..	..	..	..	..
Zambia	71.0	66.5	80	6,513	1.7	1.9	..	4,918	6,790	5,399	7,355	74.3	81.0
Zimbabwe	57.3	40.4	12	985	4.2	1.5	..	8,550	8,533	9,297	9,506	50.9	65.3
NORTH AFRICA	**1.3**	**1.4**	**47**	**290**				**234,657**	**361,445**	**77,234**	**150,155**	**2.8**	**2.3**
Algeria	0.7	0.6	11	332	6.1	9.6	..	100,114	162,044	22,192	37,069	0.1	0.1
Egypt, Arab Rep.	0.0	0.1	2	23	68.2	1.5	..	54,869	87,487	31,825	70,710	3.3	2.1
Libya	0.1	0.1	1	97	4.3	7.9	..	73,173	103,743	11,330	18,221	1.1	0.9
Morocco	11.3	11.5	29	929	12.6	2.9	73,989	773	637	6,941	14,977	4.6	3.2
Tunisia	4.1	6.5	4	410	2.8	7.2	..	5,728	7,534	4,946	9,178	12.9	13.6

a. Data are for the most recent year available during the period specified.
b. Hydrofluorocarbons, perfluorocarbons, and sulphur hexafluoride.

Greenhouse gas emissions																	
		Methane						Nitrous oxide						Other greenhouse gases[b]			
Carbon dioxide (thousands of metric tons)		Total (kilotons of carbon dioxide equivalent)		Agricultural (% of total)		Industrial (% of total)		Total (metric tons of carbon dioxide equivalent)		Agricultural (% of total)		Industrial (% of total)		(thousands of metric tons of carbon dioxide equivalent)		ODA gross disbursements for forestry ($ millions)	ODA gross disbursements for general environment protection ($ millions)
1990	2007	1990	2005	1990	2005	1990	2005	1990	2005	1990	2005	1990	2005	1990	2005	2009	2009
464,110	**682,631**	**..**	**..**	**44.0**	**44.0**	**32.1**	**30.2**	**..**	**..**	**64.5**	**66.1**	**0.3**	**0.8**	**..**	**..**	**120.8**	**588.2**
4,426	24,743	49,530	45,409	26.4	27.9	21.6	11.6	41,667	38,881	39.2	38.4	0.0	0.0	0	20	0.9	2.5
715	3,873	4,847	4,080	36.7	47.8	16.1	8.9	3,695	2,902	50.5	61.5	0.0	0.0	0	0	0.0	13.2
2,169	4,994	5,812	4,501	90.5	84.1	7.7	17.9	5,511	3,081	90.9	92.0	..	0.0	0	0	0.1	3.0
586	1,693	..	..	..	..	..	..	..	..	..	..	..	..	..	..	2.8	10.5
304	180	..	..	..	..	..	..	..	..	..	..	..	..	..	..	0.0	1.9
1,737	6,163	13,503	18,518	55.2	42.4	20.2	17.9	10,530	9,127	68.1	75.9	0.0	0.0	932	419	4.3	12.3
88	308	..	..	..	..	..	..	..	..	..	..	..	..	..	..	..	7.9
198	253	..	..	..	..	..	..	..	..	..	..	..	..	..	..	2.9	18.6
147	385	..	..	..	..	..	..	..	..	..	..	..	..	..	..	0.0	6.0
77	121	..	..	..	..	..	..	..	..	..	..	..	..	..	..	0.0	0.7
4,067	2,433	96,593	56,445	25.6	23.1	47.9	49.6	87,098	54,643	37.9	31.3	0.0	0.0	0	0	4.0	15.5
1,187	1,587	6,231	5,584	37.3	31.9	10.4	7.7	4,307	3,566	48.6	51.8	0.0	0.0	0	5	1.2	3.8
5,793	6,379	11,243	10,997	18.3	17.4	18.9	11.2	7,485	7,364	22.7	29.3	0.0	0.0	0	0	..	1.3
399	487	..	..	..	..	..	..	..	..	..	..	..	..	..	..	0.2	0.5
121	4,793	..	..	..	..	..	..	..	..	..	..	..	..	..	..	0.1	0.5
..	579	1,884	2,467	78.7	73.2	11.0	7.5	1,028	1,189	93.0	90.9	0.0	0.0	0	0	0.5	1.0
3,016	6,504	39,325	52,243	81.6	72.5	9.3	10.0	25,545	30,510	91.9	88.8	0.0	0.0	0	10	7.8	13.5
6,082	2,034	8,103	8,218	0.9	1.1	46.5	79.9	305	482	25.6	23.3	0.0	0.0	0	9	0.2	5.4
191	396	..	..	..	..	..	..	..	..	..	..	..	..	..	..	..	0.4
3,928	9,801	7,238	8,990	48.9	39.5	13.7	10.7	5,187	4,899	75.5	70.5	0.0	0.0	596	15	16.3	18.6
1,055	1,389	..	..	..	..	..	..	..	..	..	..	..	..	..	..	0.7	2.1
253	286	..	..	..	..	..	..	..	..	..	..	..	..	..	..	..	2.2
5,818	11,227	17,952	22,130	74.3	65.5	15.7	18.0	9,222	10,542	91.9	88.8	0.0	0.0	0	0	5.7	35.2
..	..	..	..	..	..	..	..	..	..	..	..	..	..	..	..	0.1	1.2
484	674	..	..	..	..	..	..	..	..	..	..	..	..	..	..	1.1	3.0
986	2,250	..	..	..	..	..	..	..	..	..	..	..	..	..	..	0.7	18.8
612	1,055	..	..	..	..	..	..	..	..	..	..	..	..	..	..	2.2	5.9
421	579	..	..	..	..	..	..	..	..	..	..	..	..	..	..	3.1	14.1
2,664	1,949	..	..	..	..	..	..	..	..	..	..	..	..	..	..	3.5	11.8
1,462	3,884	..	..	..	..	..	..	..	..	..	..	..	..	..	..	..	5.2
1,000	2,598	10,863	12,043	66.3	44.2	17.5	16.9	10,881	9,501	82.0	71.4	0.0	0.0	0	282	1.6	17.9
7	3,034	3,435	5,057	95.8	94.9	3.7	4.7	2,580	3,797	93.2	94.0	0.0	0.0	0	0	1.3	11.6
953	909	..	..	..	..	..	..	..	..	..	..	..	..	..	..	0.2	7.4
45,338	95,194	117,467	130,317	18.5	19.8	47.3	45.5	19,153	21,565	82.1	77.3	0.0	0.0	242	669	0.5	9.9
682	715	..	..	..	..	..	..	..	..	..	..	..	..	..	..	1.0	9.2
66	128	..	..	..	..	..	..	..	..	..	..	..	..	..	..	..	0.2
3,180	5,474	5,277	7,129	68.8	68.3	4.5	4.7	2,976	4,083	88.1	88.5	0.0	0.0	0	0	6.9	54.2
114	623	..	..	..	..	..	..	..	..	..	..	..	..	..	..	..	0.1
388	1,312	..	..	..	..	..	..	..	..	..	..	..	..	..	..	..	1.9
18	601	..	..	..	..	..	..	..	..	..	..	..	..	..	..	..	0.1
333,241	433,173	51,179	63,785	37.3	31.4	52.4	54.3	21,300	24,048	63.3	59.8	3.6	7.3	1,491	2,552	0.0	26.6
5,555	11,512	43,370	67,441	87.1	85.2	21.4	21.5	36,669	49,472	92.0	92.6	0.0	0.0	0	0	2.5	15.1
425	1,063	..	..	..	..	..	..	..	..	..	..	..	..	..	..	0.0	1.1
2,371	6,038	25,817	32,024	73.9	63.2	21.3	20.3	21,468	21,647	82.8	78.8	0.0	0.0	0	0	11.0	30.9
773	1,315	2,752	2,889	52.9	39.8	18.4	14.8	2,209	1,738	74.3	67.5	0.0	0.0	0	0	..	1.2
817	3,202	..	..	..	..	..	..	..	..	..	..	..	..	..	..	2.9	16.9
2,444	2,689	26,944	19,294	66.1	59.3	8.1	5.7	35,669	25,068	75.1	71.7	0.0	3.7	0	0	0.5	11.6
15,510	9,629	10,112	9,539	79.1	73.3	22.2	24.8	7,284	6,114	84.2	85.2	5.9	0.0	0	0	0.0	1.0
231,777	**452,017**	**104,128**	**134,629**	**21.6**	**20.6**	**51.5**	**48.2**	**24,023**	**33,358**	**72.0**	**75.3**	**5.6**	**7.9**	**2,668**	**3,950**	**5.7**	**109.9**
78,831	140,005	40,726	54,219	9.1	8.2	61.2	66.3	3,843	4,898	64.3	58.6	4.4	7.2	326	489	0.2	4.6
75,881	184,508	27,839	46,996	38.0	31.7	33.4	31.2	11,818	18,996	71.5	80.0	8.2	11.5	2,059	3,181	0.0	35.6
40,286	57,287	22,473	14,682	4.9	5.7	79.1	77.6	1,176	1,285	67.2	51.9	0.0	0.0	282	280	..	0.1
23,523	46,368	9,132	10,573	58.8	51.7	6.2	2.6	5,180	5,814	85.1	82.6	0.0	0.0	0	0	0.7	40.9
13,256	23,849	3,958	8,160	44.9	25.5	26.2	32.1	2,006	2,366	59.0	66.4	10.6	4.1	0	0	4.4	22.8

Table 8.5 Fossil fuel emissions

	Carbon dioxide emissions						Carbon dioxide emissions from fossil fuel (thousands of metric tons)					
	Total (thousands of metric tons)			Per capita (metric tons)			Total			Solid fuel consumption		
	1990	2005	2007	1990	2005	2007	1990	2005	2007	1990	2005	2007
SUB-SAHARAN AFRICA	**464,110**	**656,877**	**682,631**	**0.9**	**0.9**	**0.9**	**129,769**	**183,320**	**189,853**	**110,850**	**143,104**	**149,751**
Angola	4,426	19,756	24,743	0.4	1.2	1.4	1,208	5,392	6,753	0	0	0
Benin	715	2,565	3,873	0.1	0.3	0.5	195	700	1,057	0	0	0
Botswana	2,169	4,521	4,994	1.6	2.5	2.6	592	1,234	1,363	592	702	796
Burkina Faso	586	1,173	1,693	0.1	0.1	0.1	160	320	462	0	0	0
Burundi	304	165	180	0.1	0.0	0.0	83	45	49	4	2	2
Cameroon	1,737	3,693	6,163	0.1	0.2	0.3	..	..	..	..	..	..
Cape Verde	88	297	308	0.2	0.6	0.6	24	81	84	0	0	0
Central African Republic	198	235	253	0.1	0.1	0.1	54	64	69	0	0	0
Chad	147	399	385	0.0	0.0	0.0	40	109	105	0	0	0
Comoros	77	110	121	0.2	0.2	0.2	21	30	33	0	0	0
Congo, Dem. Rep.	4,067	2,275	2,433	0.1	0.0	0.0	1,110	621	664	209	273	303
Congo, Rep.	1,187	1,605	1,587	0.5	0.5	0.4	324	438	433	0	0	0
Côte d'Ivoire	5,793	8,160	6,379	0.5	0.4	0.3	1,581	2,227	1,741	0	0	0
Djibouti	399	473	487	0.7	0.6	0.6	109	129	133	0	0	0
Equatorial Guinea	121	4,708	4,793	0.3	7.7	7.5	33	1,285	1,308	0	0	0
Eritrea	..	733	579	..	0.2	0.1	..	200	158	..	0	0
Ethiopia	3,016	5,485	6,504	0.1	0.1	0.1	823	1,497	1,775	0	0	0
Gabon	6,082	1,861	2,034	6.6	1.4	1.4	1,660	508	555	0	0	0
Gambia, The	191	322	396	0.2	0.2	0.2	52	88	108	0	0	0
Ghana	3,928	7,467	9,801	0.3	0.3	0.4	1,072	2,038	2,675	2	0	0
Guinea	1,055	1,359	1,389	0.2	0.1	0.1	288	371	379	0	0	0
Guinea-Bissau	253	264	286	0.2	0.2	0.2	69	72	78	0	0	0
Kenya	5,818	10,944	11,227	0.2	0.3	0.3	1,588	2,987	3,064	110	78	80
Lesotho	..	..	..	..	..	..	..	..	..	..	..	..
Liberia	484	737	674	0.2	0.2	0.2	132	201	184	0	0	0
Madagascar	986	2,173	2,250	0.1	0.1	0.1	269	593	614	9	7	7
Malawi	612	1,037	1,055	0.1	0.1	0.1	167	283	288	13	43	44
Mali	421	568	579	0.0	0.0	0.0	115	155	158	0	0	0
Mauritania	2,664	1,656	1,949	1.3	0.6	0.6	727	452	532	4	0	0
Mauritius	1,462	3,408	3,884	1.4	2.7	3.1	399	930	1,060	54	264	415
Mozambique	1,000	1,854	2,598	0.1	0.1	0.1	273	506	709	42	0	7
Namibia	7	2,656	3,034	0.0	1.3	1.5	2	725	828	0	14	56
Niger	953	824	909	0.1	0.1	0.1	260	225	248	98	103	105
Nigeria	45,338	110,371	95,194	0.5	0.8	0.6	12,374	30,123	25,981	35	8	8
Rwanda	682	689	715	0.1	0.1	0.1	186	188	195	0	0	0
São Tomé and Príncipe	66	128	128	0.6	0.8	0.8	18	35	35	0	0	0
Senegal	3,180	5,529	5,474	0.4	0.5	0.5	868	1,509	1,494	0	114	218
Seychelles	114	696	623	1.6	8.4	7.3	31	190	170	0	0	0
Sierra Leone	388	1,260	1,312	0.1	0.2	0.2	106	344	358	0	0	0
Somalia	18	579	601	0.0	0.1	0.1	5	158	164	0	0	0
South Africa	333,241	407,895	433,173	9.5	8.6	9.0	90,950	111,325	118,224	72,352	95,970	100,415
Sudan	5,555	10,992	11,512	0.2	0.3	0.3	1,516	3,000	3,142	0	0	0
Swaziland	425	1,019	1,063	0.5	0.9	0.9	116	278	290	116	104	109
Tanzania	2,371	5,082	6,038	0.1	0.1	0.1	647	1,387	1,648	3	54	62
Togo	773	1,337	1,315	0.2	0.2	0.2	211	365	359	0	0	0
Uganda	817	2,338	3,202	0.0	0.1	0.1	223	638	874	0	0	0
Zambia	2,444	2,363	2,689	0.3	0.2	0.2	667	645	734	227	98	111
Zimbabwe	15,510	10,780	9,629	1.5	0.9	0.8	4,233	2,942	2,628	3,666	2,318	2,073
NORTH AFRICA	**231,777**	**424,566**	**452,017**	**1.9**	**2.7**	**2.8**	**63,258**	**115,875**	**123,367**	**3,567**	**6,292**	**6,878**
Algeria	78,831	138,741	140,005	3.1	4.2	4.1	21,515	37,866	38,211	825	666	859
Egypt, Arab Rep.	75,881	163,220	184,508	1.3	2.1	2.3	20,710	44,547	50,357	917	924	966
Libya	40,286	55,997	57,287	9.2	9.5	9.3	10,995	15,283	15,635	4	0	0
Morocco	23,523	43,825	46,368	0.9	1.4	1.5	6,420	11,961	12,655	1,278	3,844	4,115
Tunisia	13,256	22,783	23,849	1.6	2.3	2.3	3,618	6,218	6,509	72	0	0

Note: 0 refers to a negligible value that rounds to 0.

Carbon dioxide emissions from fossil fuel (thousands of metric tons)

Liquid fuel consumption			Gas fuel consumption			Gas flaring			Cement production		
1990	2005	2007	1990	2005	2007	1990	2005	2007	1990	2005	2007
42,649	**48,703**	**49,016**	**..**	**..**	**..**	**..**	**..**	**..**	**2,906**	**4,815**	**6,229**
489	1,460	2,296	276	341	435	409	3,412	3,832	35	179	190
154	666	846	0	0	0	0	0	0	41	34	211
0	532	568	0	0	0	0	0	0	0	0	0
160	316	458	0	0	0	0	0	0	0	4	4
79	43	47	0	0	0	0	0	0	0	0	0
..	..	..	..	..	..	..	..	..	..	..	..
24	81	84	0	0	0	0	0	0	0	0	0
54	64	69	0	0	0	0	0	0	0	0	0
40	109	105	0	0	0	0	0	0	0	0	0
21	30	33	0	0	0	0	0	0	0	0	0
838	348	362	0	0	0	0	0	0	63	0	0
265	358	347	1	12	11	46	0	0	12	69	75
1,513	1,228	1,025	0	910	629	0	0	0	68	88	88
109	129	133	0	0	0	0	0	0	0	0	0
33	142	163	0	605	876	0	538	269	0	0	0
..	194	152	..	0	0	..	0	0	..	6	6
777	1,284	1,544	0	0	0	0	0	0	46	213	231
583	408	443	138	65	82	924	0	0	16	35	31
52	87	106	0	1	1	0	0	0	0	0	0
978	1,780	2,417	0	0	0	0	0	0	92	258	258
288	322	330	0	0	0	0	0	0	0	49	49
69	72	78	0	0	0	0	0	0	0	0	0
1,273	2,620	2,669	0	0	0	0	0	0	205	289	315
..	..	..	..	..	..	..	..	..	..	..	..
125	181	163	0	0	0	0	0	0	7	20	21
252	566	570	0	0	0	0	0	0	8	20	37
141	217	219	0	0	0	0	0	0	13	23	25
112	155	158	0	0	0	0	0	0	3	0	0
709	411	476	0	0	0	0	0	0	14	41	56
345	666	645	0	0	0	0	0	0	0	0	0
220	392	605	0	38	82	0	0	0	11	76	116
2	711	772	0	0	0	0	0	0	0	0	0
159	115	136	0	0	0	0	0	0	3	7	7
9,823	12,143	7,789	2,041	5,572	5,594	0	12,075	11,707	476	326	884
177	173	181	0	0	0	0	0	0	8	14	14
18	35	35	0	0	0	0	0	0	0	0	0
801	1,031	841	3	7	5	0	0	0	64	357	429
31	190	170	0	0	0	0	0	0	0	0	0
106	321	326	0	0	0	0	0	0	0	23	32
0	158	164	0	0	0	0	0	0	5	0	0
16,596	11,526	13,599	940	2,269	2,353	0	0	0	1,062	1,559	1,857
1,493	2,955	3,115	0	0	0	0	0	0	23	45	27
0	173	181	0	0	0	0	0	0	0	0	0
571	962	1,102	0	185	278	0	0	0	73	186	206
157	256	250	0	0	0	0	0	0	54	109	109
219	552	786	0	0	0	0	0	0	4	86	88
381	488	535	0	0	0	0	0	0	59	59	88
471	542	502	0	0	0	0	0	0	95	82	54
34,171	**58,630**	**63,212**	**17,482**	**39,841**	**39,810**	**..**	**..**	**..**	**4,167**	**8,848**	**10,342**
6,835	17,270	18,794	10,619	16,706	13,942	2,373	1,688	2,454	862	1,536	2,162
14,323	21,152	23,958	3,552	18,057	20,211	0	0	0	1,918	4,414	5,222
6,058	10,425	10,301	2,599	3,010	3,304	1,969	1,357	1,527	367	492	503
4,541	6,385	6,705	30	237	339	0	0	0	571	1,496	1,496
2,414	3,398	3,454	682	1,831	2,014	1	79	82	449	910	959

Table 9.1 Labor force participation

	Labor force ages 15 and older						Participation rate, ages 15 and older					
	Total (thousands)		Male (% of total labor force)		Female (% of total labor force)		Total (% of total population)		Male (% of male population)		Female (% of female population)	
	2000	2009	2000	2009	2000	2009	2000	2009	2000	2009	2000	2009
SUB-SAHARAN AFRICA	**263,550**	**341,616**	**57.0**	**56.4**	**43.0**	**43.6**	**69.9**	**70.7**	**81.1**	**80.8**	**59.1**	**60.9**
Angola	6,237	8,278	53.3	53.1	46.7	46.9	82.5	81.3	90.2	88.4	75.2	74.5
Benin	2,670	3,699	55.1	53.8	44.9	46.2	72.5	72.7	81.4	77.9	63.9	67.4
Botswana	799	996	52.9	52.6	47.1	47.4	74.9	76.6	80.8	80.9	69.2	72.3
Burkina Faso	5,217	7,140	52.3	52.9	47.7	47.1	84.0	84.4	90.9	90.8	77.5	78.2
Burundi	3,138	4,569	47.0	47.4	53.0	52.6	90.2	89.3	90.0	87.5	90.5	91.0
Cameroon	5,995	7,727	60.9	59.9	39.1	40.1	66.2	67.0	81.4	80.7	51.2	53.5
Cape Verde	156	214	60.3	56.8	39.7	43.2	62.6	66.4	83.2	81.3	45.5	53.5
Central African Republic	1,703	2,074	53.7	53.5	46.3	46.5	78.3	79.0	86.8	86.7	70.4	71.6
Chad	3,277	4,283	54.5	54.8	45.5	45.2	72.3	70.4	80.2	78.2	64.6	62.7
Comoros	251	325	54.3	53.5	45.7	46.5	77.0	79.6	83.8	85.4	70.1	73.7
Congo, Dem. Rep.	18,605	24,927	59.7	59.4	40.3	40.6	70.5	70.8	86.1	85.6	55.5	56.5
Congo, Rep.	1,256	1,594	57.0	56.4	43.0	43.6	71.9	72.7	83.0	82.6	61.1	62.9
Côte d'Ivoire	6,728	8,369	64.8	63.1	35.2	36.9	66.5	66.9	82.1	82.1	49.2	50.8
Djibouti	295	387	58.5	55.9	41.5	44.1	68.8	70.1	81.2	78.7	56.6	61.5
Equatorial Guinea	186	262	72.5	69.2	27.5	30.8	62.8	65.5	93.1	92.0	33.8	39.7
Eritrea	1,383	2,154	58.0	55.5	42.0	44.5	68.4	72.6	82.6	83.4	55.2	62.5
Ethiopia	28,989	39,952	54.8	52.1	45.2	47.9	81.7	85.4	90.9	90.3	72.8	80.7
Gabon	537	711	55.4	53.3	44.6	46.7	73.7	75.5	83.0	81.1	64.6	70.0
Gambia, The	581	766	53.8	53.8	46.2	46.2	78.2	77.8	86.0	85.2	70.0	70.6
Ghana	8,554	10,951	51.6	50.9	48.4	49.1	74.6	74.6	76.6	75.2	72.6	73.8
Guinea	3,954	4,850	53.3	53.1	46.7	46.9	84.4	84.2	89.8	89.2	78.9	79.2
Guinea-Bissau	541	661	57.3	57.6	42.7	42.4	71.4	71.5	83.4	83.8	59.8	59.6
Kenya	14,321	18,712	53.4	53.3	46.6	46.7	81.6	82.2	88.2	88.1	75.2	76.4
Lesotho	810	935	48.0	47.6	52.0	52.4	73.9	74.0	80.1	77.7	68.9	70.8
Liberia	1,123	1,611	52.8	52.4	47.2	47.6	71.3	71.1	76.9	75.8	66.0	66.6
Madagascar	7,273	9,681	51.3	50.8	48.7	49.2	86.8	86.4	89.6	88.7	84.0	84.2
Malawi	4,953	6,309	49.9	50.2	50.1	49.8	77.4	76.8	79.1	78.8	75.8	75.0
Mali	2,959	3,770	64.2	62.7	35.8	37.3	51.6	51.9	68.2	67.0	35.9	37.6
Mauritania	1,031	1,394	59.2	58.0	40.8	42.0	68.5	70.0	81.5	81.0	55.6	59.0
Mauritius	528	567	65.9	63.9	34.1	36.1	60.2	57.5	80.4	74.8	40.6	40.8
Mozambique	8,914	11,004	46.9	48.0	53.1	52.0	86.7	85.8	87.4	86.9	86.0	84.8
Namibia	601	783	54.9	53.5	45.1	46.5	55.8	57.1	63.7	62.6	48.5	51.8
Niger	3,551	4,799	68.9	68.4	31.1	31.6	62.6	62.7	88.1	87.5	38.1	38.9
Nigeria	39,249	49,972	65.4	64.9	34.6	35.1	56.0	56.2	74.1	73.4	38.3	39.2
Rwanda	3,710	4,963	46.9	47.2	53.1	52.8	86.0	86.0	86.4	85.1	85.6	86.7
São Tomé and Príncipe	46	58	63.0	61.9	37.0	38.1	57.3	59.8	73.8	76.0	41.5	44.5
Senegal	4,089	5,405	57.9	56.7	42.1	43.3	75.8	76.4	89.2	88.6	62.8	64.8
Seychelles	..	..	..	..	..	..	..	..	..	..	..	..
Sierra Leone	1,664	2,141	47.9	48.6	52.1	51.4	67.8	66.4	67.8	67.5	67.8	65.4
Somalia	2,944	3,538	58.3	59.1	41.7	40.9	71.3	70.3	84.7	84.7	58.4	56.5
South Africa	15,280	18,849	56.5	56.3	43.5	43.7	52.3	55.0	60.9	63.4	44.3	47.0
Sudan	10,494	13,462	72.1	70.5	27.9	29.5	52.0	52.3	75.1	73.9	28.9	30.8
Swaziland	373	457	58.5	56.6	41.5	43.4	62.3	63.6	78.2	74.9	48.4	53.1
Tanzania	16,767	21,382	50.2	50.6	49.8	49.4	88.9	88.4	90.8	90.6	87.0	86.3
Togo	2,183	2,960	58.0	56.5	42.0	43.5	72.9	74.4	86.3	85.7	60.0	63.6
Uganda	10,500	14,134	53.0	53.5	47.0	46.5	85.0	84.5	91.1	90.6	79.0	78.3
Zambia	4,024	4,812	55.1	56.6	44.9	43.4	70.2	69.2	78.6	79.2	62.1	59.5
Zimbabwe	5,110	5,028	53.2	52.5	46.8	47.5	71.0	66.8	78.5	74.3	64.0	60.0
NORTH AFRICA	**48,019**	**60,451**	**74.4**	**74.1**	**25.6**	**25.9**	**51.2**	**51.7**	**76.4**	**77.0**	**26.1**	**26.6**
Algeria	11,101	14,840	71.7	68.4	28.3	31.6	55.2	58.5	79.0	79.6	31.3	37.2
Egypt, Arab Rep.	21,655	27,417	75.6	77.0	24.4	23.0	48.9	48.8	74.1	75.3	23.8	22.4
Libya	1,831	2,368	78.7	77.5	21.3	22.5	50.5	52.8	75.5	78.9	22.7	24.7
Morocco	10,215	11,982	73.6	74.2	26.4	25.8	53.4	52.3	80.7	80.1	27.5	26.2
Tunisia	3,217	3,844	75.3	73.3	24.7	26.7	48.1	48.0	72.3	70.6	23.8	25.6

Participation rate, ages 15–64						Labor force ages 15–24						Participation rate, ages 15–24					
Total (% of total population)		Male (% of male population)		Female (% of female population)		Total (thousands)		Male (% of total labor force)		Female (% of total labor force)		Total (% of total population)		Male (% of male population)		Female (% of female population)	
2000	2009	2000	2009	2000	2009	2000	2009	2000	2009	2000	2009	2000	2009	2000	2009	2000	2009
71.1	**72.1**	**82.0**	**81.8**	**60.5**	**62.5**	**75,323**	**94,875**	**56.4**	**55.7**	**45.2**	**45.8**	**56.8**	**56.2**	**63.3**	**61.6**	**50.2**	**50.7**
83.9	82.6	91.1	89.1	76.9	76.4	2,182	2,851	53.7	53.1	46.3	46.9	78.3	75.3	84.7	80.6	72.1	70.0
73.4	73.5	81.6	78.2	65.2	68.8	773	991	52.8	49.9	47.2	50.1	60.3	56.7	62.9	55.5	57.6	57.9
76.7	78.8	81.7	82.1	71.8	75.5	231	258	52.7	51.8	47.3	48.2	59.5	59.3	62.4	61.2	56.6	57.5
85.3	85.7	91.5	91.4	79.5	80.2	1,872	2,416	53.6	53.5	46.4	46.5	78.6	77.7	83.3	82.0	73.8	73.2
91.0	89.9	90.5	88.1	91.4	91.6	1,080	1,480	48.2	47.5	51.8	52.5	82.2	77.4	80.0	73.8	84.3	80.9
67.3	68.3	82.7	82.0	52.2	54.5	1,653	2,020	62.3	61.7	37.7	38.3	50.9	49.6	63.2	60.9	38.5	38.2
65.5	69.2	85.1	82.8	48.7	57.0	55	63	60.9	59.8	39.1	40.2	58.5	54.8	72.8	65.9	44.8	43.8
78.7	79.3	87.1	87.1	70.6	71.7	469	576	54.6	54.5	45.4	45.5	64.1	64.2	70.6	70.7	57.7	57.9
72.5	70.6	79.9	77.8	65.2	63.5	929	1,204	49.8	49.0	50.2	51.0	57.0	54.4	56.9	53.2	57.1	55.6
77.9	80.6	84.1	85.9	71.6	75.3	..	..	..	..	..	..	..	..	..	..	..	..
71.9	72.1	87.6	87.0	56.7	57.7	6,353	8,643	58.7	58.6	41.3	41.4	65.9	65.0	77.4	76.2	54.4	53.8
72.3	73.1	84.0	83.5	60.9	62.8	351	414	59.3	58.7	40.7	41.3	55.7	54.1	65.7	63.1	45.6	45.0
67.0	67.5	82.4	82.6	49.9	51.5	1,806	2,177	60.8	60.4	39.2	39.6	51.6	51.8	62.3	62.5	40.8	41.1
70.3	71.8	82.3	80.0	58.4	63.6	80	95	56.8	55.1	43.2	44.9	54.4	50.9	61.4	55.6	47.3	46.0
64.5	66.9	95.2	93.8	34.8	40.7	..	..	..	..	..	..	68.5	..	89.0	..	48.2	..
69.7	74.0	83.6	84.6	56.6	63.9	529	617	58.1	56.2	41.9	43.8	61.2	59.4	71.0	67.2	51.4	51.7
83.7	87.0	92.1	90.9	75.5	83.1	9,679	13,294	53.0	51.2	47.0	48.8	79.0	78.5	83.7	80.3	74.2	76.7
75.9	77.5	84.9	82.8	67.2	72.1	150	186	53.4	53.3	46.6	46.7	62.8	59.9	67.7	63.2	58.0	56.5
78.5	78.0	85.9	85.1	71.2	71.1	157	210	50.8	50.7	49.2	49.3	66.6	65.5	68.0	66.4	65.1	64.6
75.5	75.6	77.1	75.8	73.9	75.3	2,132	2,478	50.5	49.5	49.5	50.5	53.9	51.1	53.5	49.6	54.3	52.6
86.3	86.3	90.5	89.9	82.1	82.6	1,250	1,518	53.1	52.7	46.9	47.3	77.3	76.2	80.4	78.9	74.0	73.4
73.2	73.3	85.1	85.6	61.7	61.3	145	178	57.3	57.7	42.7	42.3	59.4	60.2	68.1	69.5	50.6	51.0
82.9	83.5	89.0	88.8	77.0	78.2	5,033	6,069	53.4	53.1	46.6	46.9	73.4	72.4	78.3	76.8	68.6	68.0
75.1	75.2	81.0	78.5	70.4	72.4	273	299	53.2	52.4	46.8	47.6	64.4	62.0	70.1	66.0	58.9	58.2
73.1	72.9	77.9	76.8	68.4	69.1	333	458	50.9	50.4	49.1	49.6	60.1	58.5	61.4	59.0	58.8	58.0
88.1	87.7	90.4	89.4	85.9	86.0	2,167	2,850	50.5	50.1	49.5	49.9	75.1	73.0	75.8	73.2	74.4	72.8
76.8	76.1	78.2	77.9	75.4	74.4	1,262	1,615	46.0	46.2	54.0	53.8	53.9	53.5	49.7	49.3	58.2	57.7
52.9	53.1	69.9	68.3	37.0	38.7	882	1,072	62.0	60.7	38.0	39.3	41.3	39.3	51.1	47.5	31.4	31.0
70.0	71.6	82.5	82.0	57.4	60.9	298	355	58.1	57.2	41.9	42.8	55.8	53.6	63.1	59.7	48.0	47.2
64.5	62.6	84.7	79.8	44.2	45.4	101	83	64.3	57.6	35.7	42.4	49.2	40.8	62.5	46.4	35.6	35.0
86.8	86.1	87.2	86.0	86.5	85.6	2,662	3,255	46.2	46.9	53.8	53.1	73.7	72.5	69.6	68.3	77.5	76.8
57.2	58.6	65.0	63.9	49.9	53.5	115	136	54.2	52.1	45.8	47.9	30.6	28.9	33.2	30.1	28.0	27.7
63.0	63.3	88.6	88.0	38.6	39.4	1,071	1,511	65.8	66.3	34.2	33.7	53.7	55.1	76.3	76.1	34.2	35.7
56.9	57.3	75.4	74.7	38.7	39.9	7,942	9,312	68.9	68.0	31.1	32.0	31.4	30.0	43.0	40.4	19.6	19.4
87.4	87.2	87.3	86.0	87.5	88.4	1,316	1,664	48.5	48.1	51.5	51.9	76.9	75.1	76.3	73.2	77.5	76.9
60.0	62.5	76.6	78.5	44.0	47.1	14	14	68.5	68.1	31.5	31.9	41.4	40.6	56.3	54.6	26.2	26.2
76.8	77.5	90.4	89.7	63.6	65.7	1,396	1,741	60.4	60.1	39.6	39.9	67.9	66.4	82.0	79.7	53.9	53.1
..	..	..	..	..	..	..	..	..	..	..	..	..	..	..	..	..	..
68.9	67.4	68.5	67.9	69.2	66.8	392	480	43.4	42.7	56.6	57.3	45.4	43.6	40.6	38.2	49.9	48.8
72.8	71.8	86.1	86.1	59.8	57.9	..	..	..	..	..	..	77.6	..	88.7	..	66.6	..
54.8	58.6	63.1	66.6	46.9	50.8	2,629	3,099	54.5	54.9	45.5	45.1	28.7	30.8	31.3	33.7	26.2	27.8
52.7	53.2	75.3	74.0	30.0	32.2	2,434	2,794	63.3	62.1	36.7	37.9	35.1	32.7	43.8	40.0	26.1	25.1
63.8	65.3	79.0	75.8	50.4	55.5	121	147	55.3	55.1	44.7	44.9	52.3	50.0	59.1	55.0	45.8	45.0
90.3	90.0	91.5	91.2	89.1	88.8	5,663	7,077	50.0	49.8	50.0	50.2	82.2	81.4	82.2	81.0	82.2	81.8
73.9	75.6	86.9	86.4	61.3	65.0	674	827	57.7	57.1	42.3	42.9	62.1	60.7	71.9	69.5	52.4	51.9
86.4	85.8	91.8	91.2	81.1	80.5	3,878	5,259	53.2	53.0	46.8	47.0	79.8	78.7	84.6	83.1	74.9	74.2
70.5	69.7	78.7	79.3	62.5	60.0	1,210	1,489	56.1	56.0	43.9	44.0	57.1	57.0	64.0	63.7	50.3	50.3
71.6	67.9	79.0	75.4	64.7	61.2	1,579	1,597	54.5	53.7	45.5	46.3	54.6	50.4	59.7	54.6	49.5	46.3
53.7	**54.5**	**79.6**	**80.5**	**27.7**	**28.3**	**11,760**	**12,769**	**69.8**	**72.3**	**30.3**	**28.0**	**40.6**	**39.8**	**55.7**	**56.7**	**25.1**	**22.5**
57.7	61.1	82.2	82.8	32.7	38.8	3,168	3,455	71.6	68.6	28.4	31.4	45.9	47.1	64.5	63.3	26.6	30.1
51.3	51.6	77.1	79.1	25.2	23.9	5,291	6,257	68.6	73.3	31.4	26.7	36.1	36.5	48.8	52.6	23.0	19.8
52.1	55.0	77.6	81.6	23.7	26.1	453	421	74.0	74.8	26.0	25.2	34.9	36.3	50.8	53.2	18.4	18.7
56.3	55.3	84.3	83.7	29.5	28.3	2,848	2,637	69.5	73.8	30.5	26.2	46.7	41.1	65.3	60.7	28.3	21.5
51.0	50.9	76.0	73.8	25.8	27.8	..	..	..	..	..	..	39.9	..	50.3	..	29.0	..

Table 9.2 Labor force composition

	Sector[a]					
	Agriculture		Industry		Services	
	Male (% of male employment) 2000–09[b]	Female (% of female employment) 2000–09[b]	Male (% of male employment) 2000–09[b]	Female (% of female employment) 2000–09[b]	Male (% of male employment) 2000–09[b]	Female (% of female employment) 2000–09[b]
SUB-SAHARAN AFRICA	..	..	..	..	..	..
Angola	..	..	..	..	..	..
Benin	..	..	..	..	..	..
Botswana	35.1	24.3	19.2	10.8	45.5	64.8
Burkina Faso	..	..	..	..	..	..
Burundi	..	..	..	..	..	..
Cameroon	53.1	68.4	14.1	3.9	25.5	22.5
Cape Verde	..	..	..	..	..	..
Central African Republic	..	..	..	..	..	..
Chad	..	..	..	..	..	..
Comoros	..	..	..	..	..	..
Congo, Dem. Rep.	..	..	..	..	..	..
Congo, Rep.	..	..	..	..	..	..
Côte d'Ivoire	..	..	..	..	..	..
Djibouti	..	..	..	..	..	..
Equatorial Guinea	..	..	..	..	..	..
Eritrea	..	..	..	..	..	..
Ethiopia	8.7	10.3	25.4	19.5	75.6	63.9
Gabon	..	..	..	..	..	..
Gambia, The	..	..	..	..	..	..
Ghana	..	..	..	..	..	..
Guinea	..	..	..	..	..	..
Guinea-Bissau	..	..	..	..	..	..
Kenya	..	..	..	..	..	..
Lesotho	..	..	..	..	..	..
Liberia	..	..	..	..	..	..
Madagascar	81.5	82.5	5.1	1.6	13.4	15.9
Malawi	..	..	..	..	..	..
Mali	49.8	29.9	17.8	14.7	32.4	55.3
Mauritania	..	..	..	..	..	..
Mauritius	9.9	7.6	35.5	25.8	53.9	66.1
Mozambique	..	..	..	..	..	..
Namibia	22.7	8.2	24.3	9.1	48.7	63.1
Niger	..	..	..	..	..	..
Nigeria	..	..	..	..	..	..
Rwanda	..	..	..	..	..	..
São Tomé and Príncipe	30.6	22.8	26.3	5.9	42.6	70.7
Senegal	34.1	33	20.2	4.9	32.5	42
Seychelles	..	..	..	..	..	..
Sierra Leone	66	71.1	10.3	2.5	23.4	26.3
Somalia	..	..	..	..	..	..
South Africa	5.4	3.4	31.2	12.5	57.3	79.1
Sudan	..	..	..	..	..	..
Swaziland	..	..	..	..	..	..
Tanzania	71.2	78	7.3	2.8	21.5	19.2
Togo	..	..	..	..	..	..
Uganda	61.8	75.7	10.3	5.3	27.6	19.2
Zambia	65.2	78.6	8.8	2	26	18.4
Zimbabwe	..	..	..	..	..	..
NORTH AFRICA	30.9	49.7	24.8	9	44.1	41.2
Algeria	20.4	22.3	25.6	28.2	53.8	49.4
Egypt, Arab Rep.	28.3	43.3	25.8	6	45.6	50.6
Libya	..	..	..	..	..	..
Morocco	34.8	60.2	23.8	15.1	41.2	24.5
Tunisia	..	..	..	..	..	..

a. Components may not sum to 100 percent because of unclassified data.
b. Data are for the most recent year available during the period specified.

Status[a]								
Wage and salaried workers			Self-employed workers			Contributing family workers		
Total (% of total employed) 2000–09[b]	Male (% of males employed) 2000–09[b]	Female (% of females employed) 2000–09[b]	Total (% of total employed) 2000–09[b]	Male (% of males employed) 2000–09[b]	Female (% of females employed) 2000–09[b]	Total (% of total employed) 2000–09[b]	Male (% of males employed) 2000–09[b]	Female (% of females employed) 2000–09[b]
..	**..**	**..**	**..**	**..**	**..**	**..**	**..**	**..**
..	..	..	..	..	..	..	..	..
..	..	..	..	..	..	..	..	..
73.2	74.4	71.9	12.2	8.1	16.8	2.2	2.2	2.2
..	..	..	..	..	..	..	..	..
..	..	..	..	..	..	..	..	..
19.2	29.3	8.7	59.3	57	61.7	18.2	9.5	27.2
38.9	43.8	33	31.8	32.6	30.9	10.3	6.5	14.8
..	..	..	..	..	..	..	..	..
..	..	..	..	..	..	..	..	..
..	..	..	..	..	..	..	..	..
..	..	..	..	..	..	..	..	..
..	..	..	..	..	..	..	..	..
..	..	..	..	..	..	..	..	..
..	..	..	..	..	..	..	..	..
..	..	..	..	..	..	..	..	..
..	..	..	..	..	..	..	..	..
46.3	49.3	42.7	42.8	41.8	44	10	7.8	12.7
..	..	..	..	..	..	..	..	..
..	..	..	..	..	..	..	..	..
..	..	..	..	..	..	..	..	..
..	..	..	..	..	..	..	..	..
..	..	..	..	..	..	..	..	..
..	..	..	..	..	..	..	..	..
..	..	..	..	..	..	..	..	..
..	..	..	..	..	..	..	..	..
13.4	16	10.8	43.7	51.6	35.4	52.3	32.1	73
..	..	..	..	..	..	..	..	..
13.6	15.2	11.4	71.4	66.4	78.4	15	18.4	10.2
..	..	..	..	..	..	..	..	..
79.2	77.2	83.2	18	21.2	11.6	2.2	0.9	4.7
..	..	..	..	..	..	..	..	..
81.3	82.2	80.3	22.3	20.4	26.6	1	0.9	1.1
..	..	..	..	..	..	..	..	..
..	..	..	..	..	..	..	..	..
..	..	..	..	..	..	..	..	..
..	..	..	..	..	..	..	..	..
..	..	..	..	..	..	..	..	..
..	..	..	..	..	..	..	..	..
7.6	11.3	3.7	..	..	..	18.1	14.8	21.6
..	..	..	..	..	..	..	..	..
82.4	83.5	80.8	17	16	18.3	0.4	0.3	0.6
..	..	..	..	..	..	..	..	..
..	..	..	..	..	..	..	..	..
10.5	15.3	6.1	78.1	75	80.9	11.4	9.7	13
..	..	..	..	..	..	..	..	..
14.5	22.2	7.5	59.4	67.5	52.1	26.1	10.3	40.5
18.7	25.7	9	59.7	49	29.2	19.6	25.4	61.8
37.7	51	23.1	50.4	38.6	63.2	11.9	10.4	13.6
55.9	**58.6**	**46.5**	**26.4**	**30.3**	**12.8**	**17.6**	**11.2**	**40.6**
59.8	61.9	49.8	31.7	30.7	36.6	8.2	7.1	13.6
61.8	63.7	53.7	25.1	27.7	13.7	13.1	8.6	32.6
..	..	..	..	..	..	..	..	..
44.8	48.8	34.1	28.9	34.5	13.9	26.1	16.5	51.8
64.3	..	..	26.8	..	..	8.7	..	..

Table 9.3 Unemployment

	Unemployment (ages 15 and older)			Youth unemployment (ages 15–24)		
	Total (% of total labor force) 2000–09[b]	Male (% of male labor force) 2000–09[b]	Female (% of female labor force) 2000–09[b]	Total (% of total labor force ages 15–24) 2000–09[b]	Male (% of male labor force ages 15–24) 2000–09[b]	Female (% of female labor force ages 15–24) 2000–09[b]
SUB-SAHARAN AFRICA						
Angola	..	..	..	..	..	..
Benin	0.7	0.9	0.4	0.8	1.1	0.6
Botswana	17.6	15.3	19.9	13.6	13.2	14.0
Burkina Faso	..	..	..	..	..	..
Burundi	..	..	..	..	..	..
Cameroon	2.9	2.5	3.3	..	..	..
Cape Verde	..	..	..	..	..	..
Central African Republic	..	..	..	..	..	..
Chad	..	..	..	..	..	..
Comoros	..	..	..	..	..	..
Congo, Dem. Rep.	..	..	..	..	..	..
Congo, Rep.	..	..	..	..	..	..
Côte d'Ivoire	..	..	..	..	..	..
Djibouti	59.5	54.6	68.6	..	..	..
Equatorial Guinea	..	..	..	..	..	..
Eritrea	..	..	..	..	..	..
Ethiopia	20.5	12.1	29.9	24.9	19.5	29.4
Gabon	..	..	..	..	..	..
Gambia, The	..	..	..	..	..	..
Ghana	10.4	10.1	10.7	16.6	16.4	16.7
Guinea	..	..	..	..	..	..
Guinea-Bissau	..	..	..	..	..	..
Kenya	..	..	..	..	..	..
Lesotho	..	..	..	..	..	..
Liberia	5.6	6.8	4.2	4.7	5.7	3.7
Madagascar	2.6	1.7	3.5	2.3	1.7	2.8
Malawi	7.8	5.4	10.0	..	..	..
Mali	8.8	7.2	10.9	..	..	..
Mauritania	33.0	8.8	41.2	..	..	..
Mauritius	7.3	4.4	12.3	21.4	18.1	26.2
Mozambique	..	..	..	..	..	..
Namibia	37.6	32.5	43.0	41.7	36.7	47.0
Niger	1.5	1.7	0.9	3.2	4.0	1.7
Nigeria	..	..	..	..	..	..
Rwanda	..	..	..	..	..	..
São Tomé and Príncipe	16.7	11.0	24.5	..	..	..
Senegal	10.0	7.9	13.6	14.8	11.9	20.1
Seychelles	5.5	6.1	4.9	20.3	..	..
Sierra Leone	3.4	4.5	2.3	5.2	7.3	3.5
Somalia	..	..	..	..	..	..
South Africa	23.8	22.0	25.9	48.2	44.6	52.5
Sudan	..	..	..	..	..	..
Swaziland	..	..	..	..	..	..
Tanzania	4.3	2.8	5.8	8.8	7.4	10.1
Togo	..	..	..	..	..	..
Uganda	3.2	2.5	3.9	..	..	..
Zambia	12.9	14.1	11.3	21.4	23.1	19.5
Zimbabwe	4.2	4.2	4.1	24.9	28.2	21.4
NORTH AFRICA						
Algeria	11.3	11.0	10.1	24.3	42.8	46.3
Egypt, Arab Rep.	9.4	5.2	22.9	24.8	17.2	47.9
Libya	..	..	..	..	..	..
Morocco	10.0	9.8	10.5	21.9	22.8	19.4
Tunisia	14.2	13.1	17.3	30.7	31.4	29.3

a. Components may not sum to 100 percent because of unclassified data.
b. Data are for the most recent year available during the period specified.

Unemployment by education level[a]								
Primary			Secondary			Tertiary		
Total (% of total unemployment) 2000–09[b]	Male (% of male unemployment) 2000–09[b]	Female (% of female unemployment) 2000–09[b]	Total (% of total unemployment) 2000–09[b]	Male (% of male unemployment) 2000–09[b]	Female (% of female unemployment) 2000–09[b]	Total (% of total unemployment) 2000–09[b]	Male (% of male unemployment) 2000–09[b]	Female (% of female unemployment) 2000–09[b]
..	..	..	..	..	..	..	..	..
..	..	..	..	..	..	..	..	..
65.5	64.4	66.3	27.3	23.9	30.2	..	..	..
47.0	44.4	58.3	19.7	16.7	33.3	6.1	5.6	8.3
..	..	..	..	..	..	..	..	..
..	..	..	..	..	..	..	..	..
..	..	..	..	..	..	..	..	..
..	..	..	..	..	..	..	..	..
..	..	..	..	..	..	..	..	..
..	..	..	..	..	..	..	..	..
..	..	..	..	..	..	..	..	..
..	..	..	..	..	..	..	..	..
..	..	..	..	..	..	..	..	..
..	..	..	..	..	..	..	..	..
..	..	..	..	..	..	..	..	..
..	..	..	..	..	..	..	..	..
35.9	50.6	30.8	13.3	19.0	11.3	3.2	5.7	2.3
..	..	..	..	..	..	..	..	..
..	..	..	..	..	..	..	..	..
..	..	..	..	..	..	..	..	..
..	..	..	..	..	..	..	..	..
..	..	..	..	..	..	..	..	..
..	..	..	..	..	..	..	..	..
..	..	..	..	..	..	..	..	..
..	..	..	..	..	..	..	..	..
43.9	42.9	44.4	23.8	25.8	22.7	9.3	14.0	6.6
..	..	..	..	..	..	..	..	..
..	..	..	..	..	..	..	..	..
..	..	..	..	..	..	..	..	..
44.2	49.5	39.7	48.5	41.4	53.2	6.4	8.1	3.5
..	..	..	..	..	..	..	..	..
..	..	..		..	..	..	..	..
..	..	..	..	..	..	..	..	..
..	..	..	..	..	..	..	..	..
60.7	62.8	59.4	24.1	23.0	24.9	5.9	0.5	9.4
..	..	..	..	..	..	..	..	..
40.2	42.2	37.9	6.9	7.5	6.2	2.5	2.8	2.1
..	..	..	..	..	..	..	..	..
..	..	..	..	..	..	..	..	..
..	..	..	..	..	..	..	..	..
36.2	39.8	32.9	56.3	52.7	59.7	4.5	4.0	5.0
..	..	..	..	..	..	..	..	..
..	..	..	..	..	..	..	..	..
..	..	..	..	..	..	..	..	..
..	..	..	..	..	..	..	..	..
..	..	..	..	..	..	..	..	..
..	..	..	..	..	..	..	..	..
..	..	..	..	..	..	..	..	..
59.3	65.2	32.5	23.0	21.4	30.4	11.4	6.6	33.0
..	..	..	..	..	..	..	..	..
..	..	..	..	..	..	..	..	..
51.1	57.7	36.6	22.4	21.7	23.9	21.6	16.2	33.5
41.4	46.0	31.9	37.7	37.3	38.5	13.6	9.0	23.3

Table 9.4 Migration and population

	International migration							Population				
	Migrant stock			Worker remittances, received		Migrant remittance inflows		Population dynamics				
	Share of population (%) 2005	Total 2005	Net migration 2005	Total ($ millions) 2009	Share of GDP (%) 2009	Total ($ millions) 2009	Share of GDP (%) 2009	Total (millions) 2009	Male (% of total) 2009	Female (% of total) 2009	Annual growth rate (%) 2009	Fertility rate (births per woman) 2009
SUB-SAHARAN AFRICA	**2.1**	**16,338,433**	**-1,599,939**	**..**	**..**	**20,791.3**	**2.2**	**841.0**	**49.8**	**50.2**	**2.5**	**5.0**
Angola	0.3	56,055	175,000	0.2	0.0	..	..	18.5	49.3	50.7	2.6	5.6
Benin	2.4	187,584	98,831	..	..	251.3	3.8	8.9	50.5	49.5	3.1	5.4
Botswana	4.4	80,148	20,000	61.6	0.5	87.9	0.7	1.9	50.0	50.0	1.5	2.8
Burkina Faso	5.6	772,814	100,000	..	..	99.3	1.2	15.8	49.9	50.1	3.4	5.8
Burundi	1.1	81,566	191,600	28.2	2.1	28.2	2.1	8.3	49.0	51.0	2.8	4.5
Cameroon	1.2	211,880	–12,121	129.2	0.6	147.6	0.7	19.5	50.0	50.0	2.2	4.5
Cape Verde	2.3	11,183	–12,500	145.8	9.4	146.2	9.4	0.5	47.8	52.2	1.4	2.7
Central African Republic	1.8	75,623	–45,000	..	..	..	..	4.4	49.1	50.9	1.9	4.7
Chad	3.6	358,446	218,966	..	..	..	..	11.2	49.7	50.3	2.6	6.1
Comoros	2.3	13,661	–10,000	..	..	..	..	0.7	50.2	49.8	2.4	3.9
Congo, Dem. Rep.	0.8	480,105	–236,676	..	..	..	..	66.0	49.6	50.4	2.7	5.9
Congo, Rep.	3.8	128,838	3,527	..	..	14.8	0.2	3.7	49.9	50.1	1.9	4.3
Côte d'Ivoire	12.3	2,371,277	–338,732	..	..	185.5	0.8	21.1	50.9	49.1	2.3	4.5
Djibouti	13.7	110,333	0	6.0	0.6	32.5	3.1	0.9	50.0	50.0	1.7	3.8
Equatorial Guinea	1	5,800	15,000	..	..	..	..	0.7	49.6	50.4	2.6	5.3
Eritrea	0.3	14,612	229,376	..	..	..	..	5.1	49.2	50.8	2.9	4.5
Ethiopia	0.7	554,021	–340,460	261.6	0.9	261.6	0.9	82.8	49.7	50.3	2.6	5.2
Gabon	17.9	244,550	9,566	..	..	..	..	1.5	50.0	50.0	1.8	3.2
Gambia, The	15.2	231,739	31,127	72.2	9.8	79.8	10.9	1.7	49.6	50.4	2.7	5.0
Ghana	7.6	1,669,267	11,690	114.5	0.4	114.5	0.4	23.8	50.7	49.3	2.1	3.9
Guinea	4.4	401,217	–425,000	50.5	1.2	63.7	1.6	10.1	50.5	49.5	2.4	5.3
Guinea-Bissau	1.3	19,219	1,181	..	..	49.5	5.9	1.6	49.5	50.5	2.2	5.7
Kenya	2.2	790,071	25,144	631.5	2.1	1,686.2	5.7	39.8	50.0	50.0	2.6	4.9
Lesotho	0.3	6,247	–36,000	28.5	1.8	414.1	26.2	2.1	47.2	52.8	0.8	3.3
Liberia	2.9	96,793	62,452	7.0	0.8	25.1	2.9	4.0	49.7	50.3	4.2	5.8
Madagascar	0.2	39,699	–5,000	..	..	..	..	19.6	49.8	50.2	2.7	4.6
Malawi	2	278,806	–30,000	..	..	..	..	15.3	49.7	50.3	2.8	5.5
Mali	1.4	165,448	–134,204	..	..	431.0	4.8	13.0	49.4	50.6	2.4	6.5
Mauritania	2.2	66,053	30,000	..	..	..	..	3.3	50.7	49.3	2.3	4.4
Mauritius	3.3	40,824	0	..	..	211.2	2.5	1.3	49.6	50.4	0.5	1.5
Mozambique	1.9	406,075	–20,000	31.5	0.3	111.1	1.1	22.9	48.6	51.4	2.3	5.0
Namibia	6.6	131,630	–1,000	5.3	0.1	13.6	0.1	2.2	49.3	50.7	1.9	3.3
Niger	1.4	182,960	–28,497	..	..	93.7	1.7	15.3	50.1	49.9	3.9	7.1
Nigeria	0.7	972,126	–170,000	18230.2	10.5	9,584.8	5.5	154.7	50.1	49.9	2.3	5.6
Rwanda	4.8	435,749	5,931	88.1	1.7	92.6	1.8	10.0	48.4	51.6	2.8	5.3
São Tomé and Príncipe	3.5	5,387	–7,000	2.0	1.0	2.0	1.0	0.2	49.5	50.5	1.6	3.7
Senegal	2	220,208	–100,000	..	..	1,364.7	10.6	12.5	49.6	50.4	2.6	4.7
Seychelles	10.2	8,441	..	11.6	1.5	12.5	1.6	0.1	..	..	1.2	2.3
Sierra Leone	3	152,101	336,000	32.7	1.7	46.7	2.4	5.7	48.7	51.3	2.4	5.2
Somalia	0.3	21,271	–200,000	..	..	..	..	9.1	49.6	50.4	2.3	6.4
South Africa	2.6	1,248,732	700,001	..	..	902.3	0.3	49.3	49.3	50.7	1.1	2.5
Sudan	1.7	639,686	–531,781	..	..	2,992.7	5.5	42.3	50.4	49.6	2.2	4.1
Swaziland	3.4	38,574	–46,077	2.0	0.1	93.5	3.1	1.2	48.9	51.1	1.5	3.5
Tanzania	2	797,701	–345,000	11.9	0.1	23.3	0.1	43.7	49.9	50.1	2.9	5.5
Togo	3.1	182,823	–3,570	..	..	337.1	11.8	6.6	49.5	50.5	2.4	4.2
Uganda	2.3	652,408	–5,000	749.7	4.7	749.7	4.7	32.7	50.1	49.9	3.3	6.3
Zambia	2.4	287,337	–81,713	41.3	0.3	41.3	0.3	12.9	49.9	50.1	2.5	5.7
Zimbabwe	3.1	391,345	–700,000	..	..	..	..	12.5	48.3	51.7	0.5	3.4
NORTH AFRICA	**0.8**	**1,192,628**	**-1,048,004**	**15145.3**	**4.0**	**17,458.3**	**3.3**	**166.7**	**50.2**	**49.8**	**1.6**	**2.6**
Algeria	0.7	242,446	–140,000	..	..	2,058.7	1.5	34.9	50.5	49.5	1.5	2.3
Egypt, Arab Rep.	0.3	246,745	–291,405	7149.6	3.8	7,149.6	3.8	83.0	50.3	49.7	1.8	2.8
Libya	10.4	617,536	14,000	0.0	0.0	16.0	0.0	6.4	51.7	48.3	2.0	2.6
Morocco	0.2	51,020	–550,000	6269.1	6.9	6,269.5	6.9	32.0	49.1	50.9	1.2	2.3
Tunisia	0.3	34,881	–80,599	1726.6	4.4	1,964.5	5.0	10.4	50.3	49.7	1.0	2.1

Population													
Age composition (% of total)									Dependency ratio (% of working-age population)	Geographic distribution (%)			
Ages 0–14			Ages 15–64			Ages 65 and older				Share of total population		Annual growth	
Total 2009	Male 2009	Female 2009	Total 2009	Male 2009	Female 2009	Total 2009	Male 2009	Female 2009	2009	Rural population 2009	Urban population 2009	Rural population 2009	Urban population 2009
42.6	**43.1**	**42.0**	**54.3**	**54.1**	**54.5**	**3.1**	**2.8**	**3.4**	**84.8**	**63.0**	**37.0**	**1.7**	**3.8**
45.0	45.4	44.5	52.6	52.4	52.8	2.5	2.2	2.7	90.2	42.4	57.6	0.5	4.2
43.1	43.4	42.7	53.7	54.0	53.4	3.2	2.6	3.9	86.2	58.4	41.6	2.4	4.1
33.3	33.6	33.0	62.9	63.3	62.5	3.8	3.1	4.5	58.9	39.7	60.3	−0.4	2.7
46.3	47.2	45.4	51.7	51.2	52.2	2.0	1.6	2.4	93.5	80.0	20.0	2.9	5.5
38.4	39.2	37.6	58.8	58.6	59.1	2.8	2.2	3.3	70.0	89.3	10.7	2.5	5.6
40.9	41.2	40.6	55.5	55.5	55.5	3.6	3.2	3.9	80.1	42.4	57.6	0.3	3.7
36.2	38.0	34.5	59.6	59.0	60.2	4.2	3.0	5.3	67.8	39.6	60.4	−0.5	2.6
40.6	41.2	40.1	55.5	55.3	55.6	3.9	3.5	4.3	80.2	61.3	38.7	1.6	2.3
45.7	46.2	45.3	51.4	51.3	51.6	2.8	2.6	3.1	94.4	72.9	27.1	2.0	4.4
38.1	38.6	37.7	58.8	58.7	58.9	3.1	2.7	3.4	70.1	71.9	28.1	2.3	2.6
46.7	47.2	46.2	50.7	50.5	50.8	2.6	2.3	3.0	97.3	65.4	34.6	1.8	4.5
40.5	40.8	40.1	55.7	55.7	55.8	3.8	3.5	4.2	79.5	38.3	61.7	0.9	2.5
40.6	40.1	41.3	55.5	56.0	55.0	3.9	4.0	3.7	80.2	50.6	49.4	1.0	3.7
36.1	36.4	35.7	60.7	60.7	60.7	3.2	2.9	3.6	64.8	12.3	87.7	−1.5	2.2
41.0	41.5	40.5	56.1	55.9	56.4	2.9	2.6	3.2	78.2	60.5	39.5	2.3	3.0
41.5	42.6	40.5	56.0	55.5	56.5	2.5	1.9	3.0	78.5	78.8	21.2	2.4	5.0
43.5	44.0	43.1	53.3	53.1	53.5	3.2	2.9	3.4	87.6	82.7	17.3	2.2	4.3
36.1	36.5	35.8	59.5	59.5	59.6	4.3	4.0	4.7	68.0	14.5	85.5	−1.5	2.4
42.3	42.9	41.7	54.9	54.5	55.3	2.8	2.6	3.0	82.2	42.7	57.3	0.7	4.2
38.4	38.8	38.0	58.0	57.8	58.1	3.6	3.4	3.8	72.5	49.2	50.8	0.6	3.5
42.8	43.2	42.4	54.0	54.0	53.9	3.3	2.8	3.7	85.3	65.1	34.9	1.6	3.8
42.6	43.2	42.1	53.9	53.7	54.1	3.5	3.2	3.8	85.5	70.1	29.9	2.1	2.5
42.8	43.1	42.5	54.6	54.5	54.6	2.6	2.4	2.8	83.3	78.1	21.9	2.3	4.0
38.8	41.4	36.6	56.4	54.4	58.2	4.7	4.2	5.2	77.3	73.8	26.2	−0.1	3.6
42.7	43.3	42.1	54.2	53.9	54.5	3.1	2.8	3.4	84.6	39.2	60.8	2.5	5.3
42.9	43.2	42.6	54.0	53.9	54.2	3.0	2.9	3.2	85.0	70.1	29.9	2.2	3.8
46.2	46.9	45.5	50.7	50.2	51.2	3.1	2.9	3.3	97.2	80.7	19.3	2.2	5.4
44.2	45.2	43.2	53.5	52.7	54.4	2.3	2.2	2.4	86.8	67.3	32.7	1.5	4.1
39.5	40.1	38.9	57.9	57.8	57.9	2.7	2.1	3.2	72.9	58.8	41.2	2.0	2.8
22.6	23.2	22.1	70.1	70.9	69.3	7.3	5.9	8.6	42.7	57.5	42.5	0.4	0.6
44.0	45.4	42.7	52.8	51.8	53.7	3.3	2.9	3.7	89.6	62.4	37.6	1.0	4.4
36.9	37.6	36.2	59.5	59.3	60.7	3.6	3.1	4.1	68.0	62.6	37.4	1.0	3.5
49.9	50.9	48.9	48.1	47.3	48.9	2.0	1.8	2.2	108.0	83.4	16.6	3.8	4.4
42.5	43.0	42.0	54.3	54.1	54.6	3.1	2.9	3.4	84.0	50.9	49.1	0.9	3.8
42.3	43.3	41.3	55.2	54.7	55.8	2.5	2.1	2.9	81.0	81.4	18.6	2.5	4.3
40.7	41.5	39.8	55.4	55.0	55.7	4.0	3.5	4.4	80.6	38.6	61.4	−0.5	2.9
43.6	44.3	42.8	54.0	53.4	54.7	2.4	2.3	2.5	85.0	57.4	42.6	2.2	3.2
..	..	..	..	..	..	..	..	..	..	45.2	54.8	0.1	2.0
43.4	44.4	42.5	54.8	53.8	55.7	1.8	1.8	1.8	82.6	61.9	38.1	1.9	3.3
44.9	45.4	44.4	52.4	52.1	52.7	2.7	2.5	3.0	90.9	63.0	37.0	1.6	3.5
30.5	31.1	29.9	65.0	65.3	64.7	4.5	3.5	5.4	53.8	38.8	61.2	−0.2	1.9
39.1	39.6	38.7	57.3	57.1	57.4	3.6	3.3	3.9	74.6	55.7	44.3	0.6	4.2
39.3	40.4	38.3	57.3	56.7	57.9	3.3	2.9	3.8	74.5	74.8	25.2	1.1	2.6
44.7	45.2	44.2	52.2	52.0	52.4	3.1	2.8	3.4	91.6	74.0	26.0	2.3	4.6
39.9	40.3	39.5	56.6	56.5	56.6	3.5	3.1	3.9	76.7	57.3	42.7	1.2	4.1
48.9	49.1	48.6	48.6	48.6	48.6	2.5	2.3	2.8	105.8	86.9	13.1	3.1	4.5
46.2	46.6	45.9	50.7	50.6	50.8	3.0	2.8	3.3	97.1	64.4	35.6	2.2	2.9
39.9	41.4	38.5	56.0	54.9	57.0	4.1	3.7	4.5	78.5	62.2	37.8	−0.3	1.8
29.9	**30.4**	**29.3**	**65.3**	**65.2**	**65.4**	**4.8**	**4.4**	**5.3**	**53.4**	**46.9**	**53.1**	**1.1**	**2.0**
27.3	27.7	27.0	68.1	68.2	67.9	4.6	4.1	5.1	46.9	34.1	65.9	−0.3	2.5
32.3	32.9	31.8	63.1	63.0	63.3	4.6	4.1	5.0	58.4	57.2	42.8	1.7	1.9
30.1	29.8	30.5	65.6	66.1	65.1	4.2	4.1	4.4	52.4	22.3	77.7	1.2	2.2
28.4	29.4	27.4	66.3	65.7	66.8	5.4	4.9	5.8	50.9	43.6	56.4	0.4	1.8
23.2	23.8	22.6	70.0	69.9	70.2	6.7	6.2	7.2	42.8	33.1	66.9	−0.2	1.6

Table 10.1 HIV/AIDS

	Estimated number of people living with HIV/AIDS (thousands)			Estimated HIV prevalence rate (%) Adults (ages 15–49) Point estimate			Low estimate			High estimate		
	1990	2000	2009	1990	2000	2009	1990	2000	2009	1990	2000	2009
SUB-SAHARAN AFRICA												
Angola	28	140	200	0.5	1.9	2.0	0.2	1.4	1.6	1.4	2.4	2.4
Benin	6	49	60	0.2	1.4	1.2	<0.1	1.2	1.0	3.7	1.7	1.3
Botswana	23	260	320	3.5	26.0	24.8	2.9	25.1	23.8	4.2	27.1	25.8
Burkina Faso	160	150	110	3.9	2.3	1.2	2.6	1.9	1.0	4.8	2.7	1.5
Burundi	93	170	180	3.9	5.2	3.3	3.7	5.1	2.9	4.0	5.4	3.5
Cameroon	33	460	610	0.6	5.5	5.3	0.3	5.0	4.9	2.4	6.0	5.8
Cape Verde	..	..	..	..	..	..	..	..	..	..	..	..
Central African Republic	44	190	130	3.1	9.4	4.7	2.0	8.4	4.2	6.2	11.4	5.2
Chad	31	130	210	1.1	3.0	3.4	0.5	2.0	2.8	2.0	4.0	5.1
Comoros	<1.0	<0.1	<0.5	<0.1	<0.1	0.1	<0.1	<0.1	0.1	<0.1	<0.1	0.1
Congo, Dem. Rep.	..	..	..	..	..	..	1.2	1.1	1.2	1.6	1.5	1.6
Congo, Rep.	63	68	77	5.2	3.9	3.4	3.6	3.5	3.1	6.4	4.5	3.8
Côte d'Ivoire	140	640	450	2.4	6.9	3.4	1.3	6.2	3.1	7.2	7.6	3.9
Djibouti	3	12	14	0.9	2.9	2.5	<0.1	2.0	..	3.5	4.1	3.2
Equatorial Guinea	<0.5	4	20	0.1	1.5	5.0	<0.1	1.0	3.5	0.2	2.5	6.6
Eritrea	5	25	25	0.3	1.2	0.8	0.1	0.9	0.6	0.9	1.6	1.0
Ethiopia	..	..	..	..	..	..	..	..	..	..	..	..
Gabon	4	34	46	0.9	5.2	5.2	0.6	4.1	4.2	1.5	6.6	6.2
Gambia, The	<1.0	4	18	0.1	0.5	2.0	0.1	0.3	1.3	1.7	1.1	2.9
Ghana	22	250	260	0.3	2.3	1.8	0.2	2.0	1.6	1.5	2.8	2.0
Guinea	34	78	79	1.1	1.7	1.3	0.5	1.1	1.1	7.6	2.7	1.6
Guinea-Bissau	1	13	22	0.3	1.8	2.5	0.1	1.5	2.0	0.4	2.2	3.0
Kenya	400	1,500	1,500	3.9	9.0	6.3	3.0	8.6	5.8	6.6	9.6	6.5
Lesotho	6	240	290	0.8	24.5	23.6	0.6	23.0	22.3	1.2	26.1	25.2
Liberia	3	52	37	0.3	3.3	1.5	0.1	2.2	1.3	0.6	4.5	1.8
Madagascar	12	17	24	0.2	0.2	0.2	0.2	0.2	0.2	0.2	0.2	0.3
Malawi	310	850	920	7.2	14.2	11.0	3.3	13.0	10.0	10.8	15.5	12.1
Mali	15	91	76	0.4	1.7	1.0	0.1	1.3	0.8	2.0	2.0	1.3
Mauritania	2	8	14	0.2	0.6	0.7	0.1	0.5	0.6	0.2	0.7	0.9
Mauritius	<0.5	3	9	<0.1	0.3	1.0	<0.1	0.2	0.7	0.2	0.4	1.3
Mozambique	76	750	1,400	1.2	8.6	11.5	0.9	7.8	10.6	1.5	9.4	12.2
Namibia	11	150	180	1.6	15.3	13.1	0.9	12.9	11.1	2.3	18.1	15.5
Niger	4	51	61	0.1	1.0	0.8	0.1	1.0	0.8	0.1	1.0	0.9
Nigeria	590	2,600	3,300	1.3	3.9	3.6	0.2	3.3	3.3	2.1	4.3	4.0
Rwanda	160	170	170	5.2	3.8	2.9	4.3	3.5	2.5	8.4	4.6	3.3
São Tomé and Príncipe	..	..	..	..	..	..	..	..	..	..	..	..
Senegal	6	30	59	0.2	0.6	0.9	0.1	0.5	0.7	0.2	0.7	1.0
Seychelles	..	..	..	..	..	..	..	..	..	..	..	..
Sierra Leone	<0.5	21	49	<0.1	0.9	1.6	<0.1	0.4	1.4	<0.1	1.6	2.1
Somalia	2	9	34	0.1	0.2	0.7	<0.1	<0.1	0.5	0.3	0.3	1.0
South Africa	140	4,200	5,600	0.7	16.1	17.8	0.6	15.7	17.2	0.9	16.6	18.3
Sudan	12	61	..	0.1	0.3	1.1	<0.1	0.1	0.9	0.4	0.5	1.4
Swaziland	9	120	180	2.3	22.3	25.9	1.8	21.0	24.9	2.7	23.6	27.0
Tanzania	600	1,400	1,400	4.8	7.3	5.6	4.3	6.9	5.3	5.3	8.0	6.1
Togo	11	99	120	0.6	3.6	3.2	0.1	2.8	2.5	1.2	4.3	3.8
Uganda	870	980	1,200	10.2	7.3	6.5	8.6	6.7	5.9	11.5	7.7	6.9
Zambia	500	810	980	12.7	14.4	13.5	3.4	13.8	12.8	26.4	15.2	14.1
Zimbabwe	510	1,700	1,200	10.1	24.8	14.3	8.7	23.8	13.4	11.7	26.1	15.4
NORTH AFRICA												
Algeria	..	6	18	<0.1	<0.1	0.1	<0.1	<0.1	0.1	<0.1	<0.1	0.1
Egypt, Arab Rep.	<0.5	3	11	<0.1	<0.1	<0.1	<0.1	<0.1	<0.1	<0.1	<0.1	<0.1
Libya	..	..	..	..	..	..	..	..	..	..	..	..
Morocco	3	13	3	<0.1	0.1	0.1	<0.1	0.1	0.1	<0.1	0.1	0.2
Tunisia	<0.2	<1.0	2	<0.1	<0.1	<0.1	<0.1	<0.1	<0.1	<0.1	<0.1	0.1

Estimated HIV prevalence rate (%)					
	Young men (ages 15–24)			Young women (ages 15–24)	
Point estimate	Low estimate	High estimate	Point estimate	Low estimate	High estimate
2009	2009	2009	2009	2009	2009
0.6	0.4	0.9	1.6	1.1	2.2
0.3	0.2	0.4	0.7	0.5	1.1
5.2	3.7	7.3	11.8	9.0	15.9
0.5	0.3	0.6	0.8	0.6	1.2
1.0	0.8	1.2	2.1	1.6	2.7
1.6	1.2	2.1	3.9	3.1	5.4
..	..	..	..	..	..
1.0	0.6	1.4	2.2	1.4	3.1
1.0	0.7	2.0	2.5	1.7	5.2
0.1	0.1	0.1	<0.1	<0.1	<0.1
..	0.4	0.6	..	0.9	1.5
1.2	0.9	1.6	2.6	2.1	3.6
0.7	0.5	1.1	1.5	1.1	2.3
0.8	..	..	1.9	..	..
1.9	1.0	3.2	5.0	2.7	7.9
0.2	0.1	0.3	0.4	0.2	0.7
..	..	..	..	..	..
1.4	0.8	2.0	3.5	2.1	5.2
0.9	0.5	1.6	2.4	1.4	4.0
0.5	0.4	0.7	1.3	0.9	1.8
0.4	0.3	0.6	0.9	0.6	1.3
0.8	0.5	1.1	2.0	1.5	2.9
1.8	1.3	2.4	4.1	3.0	5.4
5.4	4.1	7.4	14.2	11.2	19.2
0.3	0.1	0.5	0.7	0.2	1.2
0.1	0.1	0.4	0.1	<0.1	0.1
3.1	2.3	4.2	6.8	5.3	9.2
0.2	0.1	0.4	0.5	0.2	0.9
0.4	0.2	1.4	0.3	0.1	0.5
0.3	0.2	0.4	0.2	0.1	0.3
3.1	2.4	4.4	8.6	7.0	12.1
2.3	1.3	3.6	5.8	3.7	8.6
0.2	0.2	0.3	0.5	0.4	0.6
1.2	0.9	1.6	2.9	2.3	3.9
1.3	0.9	1.6	1.9	1.3	2.3
..	..	..	..	..	..
0.3	0.2	0.4	0.7	0.5	1.0
..	..	..	..	..	..
0.6	0.3	1.0	1.5	0.9	2.5
0.4	..	..	0.6	..	..
4.5	4.1	5.0	13.6	12.3	15.0
0.5	..	..	1.3	..	..
6.5	4.8	8.8	15.6	12.6	21.3
1.7	1.3	2.3	3.9	3.1	5.3
0.9	0.6	1.2	2.2	1.5	3.1
2.3	1.8	2.8	4.8	4.0	6.4
4.2	3.2	5.5	8.9	7.3	12.0
3.3	2.5	4.4	6.9	5.3	9.3
0.1	<0.1	0.2	<0.1	<0.1	0.1
<0.1	<0.1	<0.1	<0.1	<0.1	<0.1
..	..	..	..	..	..
0.1	<0.1	0.3	0.1	<0.1	0.1
<0.1	<0.1	0.1	<0.1	<0.1	<0.1

(continued)

Table 10.1 HIV/AIDS (continued)

	Deaths of adults and children due to HIV/AIDS (thousands)									AIDS orphans (ages 0–17, thousands)								
	Point estimate			Low estimate			High estimate			Point estimate			Low estimate			High estimate		
	1990	2000	2009	1990	2000	2009	1990	2000	2009	1990	2000	2009	1990	2000	2009	1990	2000	2009
SUB-SAHARAN AFRICA																		
Angola	<1.0	9.2	11.0	<0.5	5.6	7.7	3.2	13.0	16.0	2.1	54.0	140.0	<1.0	23.0	95.0	9.9	95.0	200.0
Benin	<0.2	3.0	2.7	<0.1	1.7	1.8	18.0	5.4	3.7	<0.5	11.0	30.0	<0.1	3.7	18.0	470.0	110.0	53.0
Botswana	<1.0	13.0	5.8	<0.5	11.0	2.3	<1.0	16.0	14.0	1.0	45.0	93.0	<1.0	36.0	71.0	1.7	59.0	120.0
Burkina Faso	6.7	15.0	7.1	4.1	11.0	4.8	11.0	19.0	9.7	13.0	130.0	140.0	5.2	96.0	100.0	71.0	180.0	170.0
Burundi	3.9	14.0	15.0	3.1	11.0	12.0	4.7	16.0	17.0	10.0	120.0	200.0	7.7	98.0	170.0	14.0	150.0	230.0
Cameroon	<1.0	27.0	37.0	<0.5	22.0	29.0	9.3	33.0	46.0	1.3	100.0	330.0	<1.0	67.0	270.0	36.0	210.0	420.0
Cape Verde	..	..	..	..	..	..	..	..	..	..	..	..	..	..	..	..	..	..
Central African Republic	1.0	14.0	11.0	<1.0	11.0	8.8	5.8	20.0	13.0	2.0	69.0	140.0	1.2	43.0	110.0	49.0	100.0	180.0
Chad	1.4	7.9	11.0	<1.0	4.7	8.1	2.9	12.0	15.0	5.1	43.0	120.0	2.1	22.0	79.0	11.0	79.0	170.0
Comoros	<0.1	<0.1	<0.1	<0.1	<0.1	<0.1	<0.1	<0.1	<0.1	..	..	<0.1	..	..	<0.1	..	..	<0.1
Congo, Dem. Rep.	..	..	..	12.0	23.0	26.0	26.0	34.0	40.0	..	..	..	46.0	270.0	350.0	210.0	430.0	510.0
Congo, Rep.	3.0	5.7	5.1	<1.0	4.8	4.1	6.2	7.1	6.4	6.9	48.0	51.0	<0.2	31.0	41.0	31.0	72.0	66.0
Côte d'Ivoire	3.9	48.0	36.0	2.1	34.0	29.0	12.0	65.0	44.0	7.3	230.0	440.0	4.0	140.0	330.0	16.0	410.0	550.0
Djibouti	<0.1	<1.0	1.0	<0.1	<0.5	<1.0	<1.0	1.3	1.4	..	..	..	..	..	..	..	..	..
Equatorial Guinea	<0.1	<0.2	<1.0	<0.1	<0.2	<1.0	<0.1	<0.5	1.4	<0.1	<0.5	4.1	<0.1	<0.2	2.5	<0.1	<1.0	6.4
Eritrea	<0.2	1.6	1.7	<0.1	<1.0	1.0	<1.0	2.5	2.5	<0.5	7.0	19.0	<0.1	3.2	12.0	2.6	16.0	28.0
Ethiopia	..	..	..	..	..	..	..	..	..	..	..	..	..	..	..	..	..	..
Gabon	<0.2	1.8	2.4	<0.1	1.4	1.6	<0.5	2.5	3.4	<0.2	6.0	18.0	<0.1	4.1	12.0	<0.5	9.2	25.0
Gambia, The	<0.1	<0.2	<1.0	<0.1	<0.1	<0.5	<1.0	<1.0	1.2	<0.1	<1.0	2.8	<0.1	<0.5	1.4	6.6	6.5	6.5
Ghana	<1.0	15.0	18.0	<0.5	11.0	14.0	6.9	20.0	22.0	1.3	47.0	160.0	<1.0	33.0	120.0	58.0	110.0	210.0
Guinea	1.1	6.1	4.7	<0.5	2.5	3.1	15.0	14.0	6.9	2.5	36.0	59.0	1.1	9.9	34.0	110.0	97.0	120.0
Guinea-Bissau	<0.1	<1.0	1.2	<0.1	<0.5	<1.0	<0.1	<1.0	1.6	<0.2	2.2	9.7	<0.1	1.3	7.7	<0.5	3.1	12.0
Kenya	10.0	120.0	80.0	6.7	98.0	61.0	22.0	140.0	99.0	17.0	710.0	1,200.0	10.0	550.0	980.0	40.0	960.0	1,400.0
Lesotho	..	12.0	14.0	<0.1	10.0	10.0	<0.2	15.0	18.0	<0.1	38.0	130.0	<0.1	29.0	110.0	<0.2	51.0	160.0
Liberia	<0.1	3.5	3.6	<0.1	2.0	2.8	<0.2	5.7	4.6	<0.1	15.0	52.0	<0.1	7.3	34.0	<0.5	25.0	76.0
Madagascar	<1.0	1.3	1.7	<1.0	1.0	1.4	1.4	1.5	2.0	6.6	9.4	11.0	4.0	7.3	9.3	12.0	12.0	14.0
Malawi	11.0	64.0	51.0	4.1	53.0	38.0	22.0	77.0	67.0	25.0	380.0	650.0	7.1	280.0	540.0	68.0	500.0	780.0
Mali	<0.5	6.9	4.4	<0.1	3.8	3.0	4.3	11.0	6.1	<0.5	29.0	59.0	<0.1	11.0	36.0	15.0	82.0	93.0
Mauritania	<0.1	<0.5	<1.0	<0.1	<0.5	<1.0	<0.2	<1.0	1.0	<0.5	1.3	3.6	<0.1	<1.0	2.7	<0.5	1.9	4.8
Mauritius	<0.1	<0.1	<0.5	<0.1	<0.1	<0.5	<0.2	<0.2	<1.0	<0.1	<0.2	1.0	<0.1	<0.1	<0.5	<0.5	<0.5	<1.0
Mozambique	2.2	36.0	74.0	1.5	28.0	57.0	3.3	45.0	92.0	6.6	180.0	670.0	2.1	84.0	..	5.6	150.0	..
Namibia	<0.5	6.7	6.7	<0.2	5.1	2.5	<1.0	8.8	11.0	<1.0	23.0	70.0	<0.5	17.0	50.0	1.4	33.0	96.0
Niger	<0.2	2.9	4.3	<0.1	2.3	3.3	<0.2	3.5	5.6	<0.5	13.0	57.0	<0.5	11.0	44.0	<0.5	16.0	73.0
Nigeria	10.0	200.0	220.0	<0.5	110.0	170.0	21.0	250.0	260.0	12.0	1,100.0	2,500.0	<0.5	300.0	1,800.0	94.0	1,700.0	3,100.0
Rwanda	8.4	15.0	4.1	5.6	12.0	<1.0	13.0	21.0	97.0	32.0	160.0	130.0	19.0	130.0	98.0	92.0	240.0	180.0
São Tomé and Principe	..	–	..	..	..	..	..	..	..	..	..	..	..	..	..	..	..	..
Senegal	<0.5	1.6	2.6	<0.2	1.3	1.9	<0.5	2.0	3.5	<1.0	7.3	19.0	<0.5	5.4	15.0	1.4	9.4	25.0
Seychelles	..	–	..	..	..	..	..	..	..	..	..	..	..	..	..	..	..	..
Sierra Leone	<0.1	<1.0	2.8	<0.1	<0.5	2.1	<0.1	1.9	3.7	<0.1	1.5	15.0	<0.1	<1.0	9.2	<0.1	5.1	26.0
Somalia	<0.2	<0.5	..	<0.1	<0.1	..	<1.0	<1.0	..	..	..	..	..	..	..	..	..	..
South Africa	2.9	170.0	310.0	2.0	140.0	260.0	4.3	210.0	390.0	4.4	430.0	1,900.0	2.3	340.0	1,600.0	7.4	550.0	2,400.0
Sudan	<1.0	3.0	..	<0.1	<0.5	..	3.5	6.5	..	..	..	..	..	..	..	..	..	..
Swaziland	<0.5	5.7	7.0	<0.2	4.7	4.6	<0.5	7.1	10.0	<1.0	23.0	69.0	<0.5	18.0	55.0	<1.0	29.0	86.0
Tanzania	21.0	110.0	86.0	16.0	90.0	69.0	27.0	130.0	110.0	53.0	750.0	1,300.0	37.0	610.0	1,100.0	75.0	940.0	1,500.0
Togo	<0.5	5.6	7.7	<0.1	3.8	5.3	2.0	7.4	10.0	<0.5	19.0	66.0	<0.1	8.5	47.0	23.0	39.0	89.0
Uganda	37.0	89.0	64.0	22.0	76.0	49.0	83.0	100.0	80.0	280.0	1,000.0	1,200.0	180.0	800.0	1,000.0	770.0	1,400.0	1,400.0
Zambia	23.0	66.0	45.0	<1.0	55.0	30.0	46.0	76.0	60.0	74.0	540.0	690.0	<0.1	340.0	570.0	210.0	740.0	810.0
Zimbabwe	14.0	130.0	83.0	9.7	110.0	70.0	19.0	150.0	97.0	29.0	670.0	1,000.0	18.0	550.0	910.0	53.0	840.0	1,200.0
NORTH AFRICA																		
Algeria	<0.1	<0.2	<1.0	<0.1	<0.1	<1.0	<0.1	<0.5	1.1	..	..	..	..	..	..	..	..	..
Egypt, Arab Rep.	<0.1	<0.2	<0.5	<0.1	<0.1	<0.5	<1.0	<0.5	<1.0	..	..	..	..	..	..	..	..	..
Libya	..	..	..	..	..	..	..	..	..	..	..	..	..	..	..	..	..	..
Morocco	<0.2	<1.0	1.2	<0.1	<0.5	<1.0	0.5	<1.0	1.6	..	..	..	..	..	..	..	..	..
Tunisia	<0.1	<0.1	<0.1	<0.1	<0.1	<0.1	<0.1	<0.1	<0.2	..	..	..	..	..	..	..	..	..

HIV-positive pregnant women receiving antiretrovirals to reduce the risk of mother-to-child transmission				ODA gross disbursements ($ millions)			
	Share of total (WHO/UNAIDS methodology, %)						
Total	Point estimate	Low estimate	High estimate	For social mitigation of HIV/AIDS		For STD control, including HIV/AIDS	
2009	2009	2009	2009	2007	2009	2007	2009
				76.7	**91.9**	**2,777.2**	**3,776.4**
3,053	19	12	36	1.8	0.5	22.8	13.9
1,703	46	29	92	0.0	0.0	9.6	17.1
12,406	>95	74	>95	2.3	1.5	43.1	211.8
2,084	32	19	60	1.0	0.3	22.7	37.6
1,837	12	9	22	0.7	1.1	12.0	30.7
9,092	27	18	50	0.0	0.2	31.8	28.5
61	..	..	..	..	..	1.0	0.5
2,157	34	23	67	0.0	0.0	2.4	4.5
989	6	3	12	0.0	0.0	4.6	9.5
1	..	10	33	..	..	0.3	0.1
2,232	..	4	11	1.2	0.3	41.2	40.1
441	12	8	23	..	0.0	4.2	5.7
11,064	54	36	95	0.2	0.3	46.1	64.8
63	10	6	21	..	0.0	5.4	0.7
365	26	16	50	..	..	0.4	0.9
464	34	21	71	0.0	0.0	11.3	15.8
6,721	..	13	40	1.4	3.7	246.5	206.7
577	30	20	60	0.0	..	3.2	3.9
885	..	43	95	0.0	..	3.1	6.2
3,643	27	18	53	0.6	0.1	43.2	58.8
783	17	11	34	0.0	0.0	6.6	6.9
383	24	16	49	0.0	..	2.4	5.9
58,591	73	50	95	4.7	5.2	223.7	377.1
8,846	64	48	95	2.7	5.3	19.2	29.6
377	16	10	33	..	0.0	7.7	5.1
17	..	1	5	0.0	0.0	12.1	9.7
33,156	58	40	95	3.8	3.1	149.4	150.1
1,710	..	26	82	0.0	0.1	26.2	25.6
68	..	12	37	0.0	..	2.7	0.8
41	..	33	95	..	..	1.3	0.9
68,248	70	51	95	6.2	8.4	153.9	192.9
6,744	88	61	95	0.0	0.1	83.9	119.7
1,737	..	25	74	0.0	0.0	6.9	13.2
44,723	22	15	42	1.0	0.0	222.1	356.2
7,030	65	43	95	1.6	0.5	101.4	135.1
11	..	..	..	..	0.0	0.6	0.1
917	..	16	45	..	0.1	17.1	19.0
12	..	..	..	..	..	0.0	0.0
637	19	12	36	0.0	0.2	6.9	13.2
..	..	0	0	0.0	..	7.9	1.3
188,200	88	66	95	9.9	11.4	284.2	560.1
245	2	1	3	0.2	0.1	14.4	12.0
8,182	88	68	95	0.2	0.6	20.1	27.2
58,833	70	48	95	6.1	7.1	206.5	257.1
1,451	26	15	67	0.0	0.0	11.6	17.2
46,948	53	37	95	5.4	7.2	241.3	259.0
47,175	69	50	95	1.6	3.4	145.2	223.8
28,208	56	41	95	2.4	7.2	97.5	71.2
				0.0	**0.0**	**15.8**	**14.7**
65	..	14	59	..	..	1.7	1.2
11	..	3	10	..	0.0	1.4	4.2
..	..	..	..	..	..	1.5	0.0
90	..	13	49	..	..	5.8	5.7
3	..	6	25	0.0	..	5.1	3.0

Table 11.1 Malaria

	Population (millions)		Clinical cases of malaria reported[a]		Reported deaths due to malaria		Under-five mortality rate (per 1,000)		Children sleeping under insecticide-treated nets (% of children under age 5)	Children with fever receiving any antimalarial treatment (% of children under age 5 with fever)	Pregnant women receiving two doses of intermittent preventive treatment (%)	ODA disbursements for malaria control ($ millions)	
	2008	2009	2008	2009	2008	2009	2008	2009	2000–09[b]	2000–09[b]	2000–09[b]	2008	2009
SUB-SAHARAN AFRICA	**820.7**	**841.0**	**62,920,801**	**71,675,530**	**104,331**	**113,326**	**133**	**130**				**682.8**	**1,158.8**
Angola	18.0	18.5	2,151,072	2,221,076	9,465	10,530	166	161	17.7	29.3	2.5	30.4	29.4
Benin	8.7	8.9	1,147,005	1,256,708	918	1,375	121	118	20.1	54.0	3.0	14.1	15.9
Botswana	1.9	1.9	17,886	14,878	12	6	59	57	..	..	..	0.0	..
Burkina Faso	15.2	15.8	3,688,338	4,399,837	7,834	7,982	169	166	9.6	48.0	1.3	3.6	20.7
Burundi	8.1	8.3	1,424,026	1,757,387	1,511	714	168	166	8.3	30.0	..	22.5	7.8
Cameroon	19.1	19.5	1,650,749	1,883,199	7,673	4,943	155	154	13.1	57.8	5.8	6.1	9.6
Cape Verde	0.5	0.5	35	65	2	2	29	28	..	..	..	..	..
Central African Republic	4.3	4.4	152,260	175,210	456	667	172	171	15.1	57.0	8.7	2.7	0.0
Chad	10.9	11.2	462,573	182,415	1,018	221	209	209	0.6	53.0	..	0.8	0.3
Comoros	0.6	0.7	46,426	49,679	47	..	105	104	9.3	62.7	..	0.3	0.2
Congo, Dem. Rep.	64.3	66.0	3,938,597	6,749,112	17,940	21,168	199	199	5.8	29.8	5.1	36.4	89.0
Congo, Rep.	3.6	3.7	117,291	92,855	143	116	127	128	6.1	48.0	..	0.1	0.2
Côte d'Ivoire	20.6	21.1	1,343,654	1,847,367	1,249	18,156	121	119	3.0	36.0	8.3	1.9	16.2
Djibouti	0.8	0.9	3,528	7,120	..	0	95	94	19.9	9.5	..	1.5	0.2
Equatorial Guinea	0.7	0.7	62,312	78,983	4	23	148	145	0.7	48.6	..	6.3	3.4
Eritrea	4.9	5.1	10,572	21,298	19	23	58	55	4.2	3.6	..	5.9	0.7
Ethiopia	80.7	82.8	2,532,645	3,043,203	1,169	1,121	109	104	33.1	9.5	..	34.9	140.3
Gabon	1.4	1.5	77,278	112,840	156	197	71	69	..	..	..	1.3	3.9
Gambia, The	1.7	1.7	508,846	479,409	403	240	106	103	49.0	62.6	32.5	5.7	6.0
Ghana	23.4	23.8	3,050,513	1,899,544	3,889	3,378	72	69	28.2	43.0	43.7	19.2	43.3
Guinea	9.8	10.1	657,003	812,471	441	586	146	142	4.5	43.5	2.9	1.2	0.0
Guinea-Bissau	1.6	1.6	128,758	143,011	487	369	195	193	39.0	45.7	7.4	1.5	1.6
Kenya	38.8	39.8	839,904	8,123,689	..	..	86	84	46.1	23.2	15.0	39.8	73.5
Lesotho	2.0	2.1	..	..	..	..	91	84	..	..	..	..	0.0
Liberia	3.8	4.0	606,952	871,560	345	1,706	119	112	26.4	67.2	45.1	13.8	13.0
Madagascar	19.1	19.6	116,538	215,110	276	173	61	58	45.8	19.7	6.4	22.7	26.7
Malawi	14.8	15.3	4,580,226	5,455,423	6,748	6,527	115	110	24.7	24.9	44.5	30.7	20.4
Mali	12.7	13.0	1,045,424	1,633,423	1,227	2,331	194	191	27.1	31.7	4.0	9.6	14.7
Mauritania	3.2	3.3	199,791	167,705	..	91	118	117	2.1	20.7	..	1.4	–
Mauritius	1.3	1.3	..	..	..	..	17	17	..	..	..	..	..
Mozambique	22.4	22.9	4,831,491	4,310,086	4,424	3,747	147	142	22.8	36.7	43.1	31.5	26.6
Namibia	2.1	2.2	128,531	81,812	171	46	50	48	10.5	9.8	10.0	0.4	3.8
Niger	14.7	15.3	596,858	309,675	2,461	2,159	167	160	42.8	33.0	0.3	14.7	19.6
Nigeria	151.2	154.7	2,834,174	4,295,686	8,677	7,522	143	138	5.5	33.2	4.9	36.5	267.4
Rwanda	9.7	10.0	772,197	1,247,583	566	809	117	111	55.7	5.6	17.2	37.3	62.6
São Tomé and Príncipe	0.2	0.2	1,647	3,893	16	23	79	78	56.2	8.4	59.8	2.4	(0.0)
Senegal	12.2	12.5	443,828	222,232	741	574	95	93	29.2	9.1	52.2	26.8	27.1
Seychelles	0.1	0.1	..	..	..	..	13	12	..	..	..	..	..
Sierra Leone	5.6	5.7	851,478	646,808	871	1,734	198	192	25.8	30.1	10.3	7.1	5.8
Somalia	8.9	9.1	56,408	56,153	49	45	180	180	11.4	7.9	0.9	3.9	1.2
South Africa	48.8	49.3	7,796	6,072	43	45	65	62	..	..	..	..	0.0
Sudan	41.3	42.3	3,145,944	2,686,822	1,388	1,396	109	108	27.6	54.2	..	44.1	13.3
Swaziland	1.2	1.2	5,881	6,639	10	13	77	73	0.6	0.6	0.5	0.3	2.6
Tanzania	42.5	43.7	3,812,350	40	12,434	840	111	108	25.7	56.7	30.2	89.8	99.1
Togo	6.5	6.6	602,908	618,842	2,663	1,556	100	98	38.4	47.7	18.1	5.0	0.3
Uganda	31.7	32.7	10,184,961	9,775,318	2,372	6,296	130	128	9.7	61.3	16.2	25.2	54.4
Zambia	12.6	12.9	3,080,301	2,976,395	3,781	3,862	145	141	41.1	43.3	60.3	25.4	24.8
Zimbabwe	12.5	12.5	1,003,846	736,897	232	14	93	90	17.3	23.6	6.3	0.1	1.8
NORTH AFRICA	**164.1**	**166.7**	**12,186**	**239**	**3**	**3**	**28**	**26**	**..**	**..**	**..**	**..**	**..**
Algeria	34.4	34.9	11,964	..	..	..	34	32	..	..	..	..	..
Egypt, Arab Rep.	81.5	83.0	80	94	2	2	23	21	..	..	..	..	..
Libya	6.3	6.4	..	..	..	..	19	19	..	..	..	..	..
Morocco	31.6	32.0	142	145	1	1	39	38	..	..	..	..	..
Tunisia	10.3	10.4	..	..	..	..	21	21	..	..	..	..	..

a. Malaria cases reported before 2000 can be probable and confirmed or only confirmed, depending on the country.
b. Data are for the most recent year available during the period specified.

Table 12.1 Aid and debt relief

	Net official development assistance ($ millions)									
	From all donors		From DAC donors		From non-DAC donors		From multilateral donors		From other donors	
	2008	2009	2008	2009	2008	2009	2008	2009	2008	2009
SUB-SAHARAN AFRICA	**40,484.5**	**44,704.2**	**21,336.6**	**22,660.0**	**322.7**	**201.5**	**14,295.0**	**16,248.1**	**41.1**	**32.1**
Angola	368.8	239.5	209.9	131.5	8.3	9.7	150.6	98.4	0.0	0.0
Benin	641.4	682.9	305.0	325.7	4.3	3.4	332.0	353.8	0.1	0.1
Botswana	720.3	279.6	682.7	223.4	–1.5	–0.4	39.0	56.6	0.0	0.1
Burkina Faso	1,001.0	1,083.9	475.3	452.9	7.2	1.7	518.6	629.3	0.1	0.2
Burundi	508.5	548.8	255.1	260.9	0.2	0.2	253.2	287.8	0.1	0.1
Cameroon	548.8	649.4	298.4	267.7	9.9	1.0	240.5	380.7	0.3	0.3
Cape Verde	221.8	195.9	162.7	161.9	0.4	–0.4	58.6	34.5	..	0.0
Central African Republic	256.4	236.9	128.5	98.6	0.2	0.5	127.7	137.7	..	..
Chad	418.7	561.2	277.5	355.5	0.4	–0.1	140.9	205.8	0.1	0.2
Comoros	37.3	50.6	20.8	28.1	1.2	0.9	15.2	21.6	..	..
Congo, Dem. Rep.	1,768.5	2,353.6	985.5	1,099.3	5.4	2.7	777.6	1,251.6	0.3	0.0
Congo, Rep.	485.1	283.0	382.6	226.1	0.2	0.4	102.3	56.4	0.0	0.1
Côte d'Ivoire	623.3	2,366.3	200.2	1,722.6	2.5	2.3	420.5	641.4	0.8	0.4
Djibouti	120.9	162.2	66.1	97.7	9.6	10.8	45.1	53.7	..	..
Equatorial Guinea	32.1	31.6	18.5	25.1	0.1	0.0	13.5	6.5	0.0	..
Eritrea	143.6	144.8	52.5	43.4	6.8	14.8	84.3	86.6	6.7	13.3
Ethiopia	3,327.8	3,820.0	1,843.4	1,816.6	31.0	19.6	1,453.4	1,983.9	20.2	8.0
Gabon	62.1	77.6	37.6	52.5	0.7	0.0	23.8	25.0	0.0	..
Gambia, The	93.8	128.0	27.9	21.9	4.4	1.1	61.6	105.1	0.1	0.1
Ghana	1,305.0	1,582.6	725.7	820.3	3.7	6.2	575.6	756.1	0.2	0.6
Guinea	327.6	214.7	209.9	171.0	0.5	–3.9	117.1	47.5	0.1	0.2
Guinea-Bissau	131.6	145.5	52.9	50.6	0.4	1.0	78.3	93.9	0.0	..
Kenya	1,362.7	1,778.0	953.2	1,224.0	1.9	5.4	407.5	548.6	0.8	0.7
Lesotho	143.8	123.0	66.0	70.7	–0.3	4.7	78.1	47.7	0.4	0.7
Liberia	1,249.5	505.0	819.2	340.8	27.0	1.0	403.3	163.3	0.4	0.1
Madagascar	842.9	445.5	274.5	241.6	3.9	1.5	564.6	202.4	0.3	0.3
Malawi	923.7	772.4	432.0	435.2	9.3	3.8	482.4	333.4	0.1	0.1
Mali	964.1	985.1	531.4	574.7	0.1	1.6	432.7	408.9	0.4	0.4
Mauritania	319.7	286.7	139.1	122.2	24.2	20.7	156.4	143.8	0.2	..
Mauritius	109.7	155.6	16.1	63.6	–1.9	–1.9	95.5	93.8	0.0	0.0
Mozambique	1,996.1	2,013.3	1,341.3	1,287.7	3.0	1.7	651.9	723.9	0.0	..
Namibia	210.2	326.2	150.0	246.5	2.4	1.3	57.8	78.4	0.1	0.0
Niger	606.7	470.0	269.1	255.3	1.7	2.0	336.0	212.7	0.1	0.1
Nigeria	1,290.2	1,659.1	637.2	687.5	2.0	2.2	651.0	969.4	0.9	1.2
Rwanda	933.2	934.4	451.6	519.8	1.7	2.8	479.9	411.0	0.2	0.0
São Tomé and Príncipe	47.3	30.7	26.4	19.7	0.1	0.0	20.8	11.0	..	..
Senegal	1,064.2	1,017.6	554.4	514.4	38.2	4.6	471.6	498.7	0.4	0.3
Seychelles	12.5	23.2	5.0	11.8	0.2	0.1	7.3	11.4	0.1	0.1
Sierra Leone	366.8	437.3	174.9	196.3	–0.9	0.4	192.9	240.5	0.1	0.1
Somalia	758.3	661.7	565.6	499.5	8.0	9.6	184.7	152.5	0.2	0.1
South Africa	1,124.9	1,075.0	881.7	861.3	1.6	2.6	241.6	211.1	1.3	1.5
Sudan	2,383.6	2,288.9	1,820.9	1,911.0	103.8	60.7	459.0	317.2	5.8	2.4
Swaziland	69.9	58.0	17.8	18.5	–0.7	–0.7	52.8	40.1	0.0	0.0
Tanzania	2,330.7	2,934.2	1,372.9	1,408.8	–2.3	–1.4	960.1	1,526.8	0.1	0.1
Togo	329.6	499.0	176.0	361.8	–0.6	1.0	154.2	136.2	0.1	0.1
Uganda	1,641.3	1,785.9	1,005.7	1,013.3	4.0	3.8	631.5	768.8	0.3	0.2
Zambia	1,116.2	1,268.7	703.9	700.6	0.4	2.1	412.0	566.0	0.0	0.0
Zimbabwe	612.4	736.8	532.4	620.4	0.1	0.4	80.0	115.9	0.0	0.1
NORTH AFRICA	**3,375.9**	**2,870.5**	**2,129.1**	**1,866.5**	**151.8**	**31.0**	**837.1**	**771.4**	**1.3**	**0.7**
Algeria	319.4	319.2	244.7	200.1	–26.7	11.8	101.4	107.3	0.1	0.0
Egypt, Arab Rep.	1,344.3	925.1	967.3	580.0	107.0	122.3	270.0	222.8	0.9	0.4
Libya	60.2	39.2	52.2	32.2	1.9	0.9	6.1	6.0	0.1	0.0
Morocco	1,062.6	911.6	614.4	704.7	78.4	–98.2	369.8	305.1	0.2	0.2
Tunisia	331.6	473.9	250.6	349.5	–8.8	–5.8	89.8	130.2	0.0	0.1

(continued)

Table 12.1 Aid and debt relief (continued)

	Net private official development assistance ($ millions)						Net official development assistance					
	From all donors		From DAC donors		From non-DAC donors		Share of GDP (%)		Per capita ($)		Share of gross capital formation (%)	
	2008	2009	2008	2009	2008	2009	2008	2009	2008	2009	2008	2009
SUB-SAHARAN AFRICA	**5,263.1**	**6,626.6**	**5,237.8**	**6,614.5**	**25.3**	**12.1**	**4.0**	**4.7**	**49.3**	**53.2**	**20.7**	**24.4**
Angola	3,049.8	2,461.3	3,049.8	2,461.3	..	..	0.4	0.3	20.5	12.9	2.7	2.1
Benin	3.8	–34.7	3.8	–34.7	..	..	9.6	10.3	74.0	76.4	46.4	41.1
Botswana	–92.1	2.0	–92.1	2.0	..	..	5.3	2.4	374.9	143.4	16.4	9.8
Burkina Faso	16.5	2.1	16.5	2.1	..	..	12.4	13.3	65.7	68.8	..	..
Burundi	–37.8	–26.9	–37.8	–26.9	..	..	43.5	41.4	63.0	66.1	..	..
Cameroon	93.3	45.7	93.3	45.7	..	..	2.3	2.9	28.8	33.3	..	..
Cape Verde	44.5	49.0	44.5	49.0	..	..	14.5	12.6	444.7	387.5	29.9	23.5
Central African Republic	–22.3	5.9	–22.5	5.9	0.2	..	12.9	11.8	59.1	53.6	111.2	111.2
Chad	43.5	20.2	43.5	20.2	..	..	5.0	8.2	38.4	50.1	20.2	24.2
Comoros	1.4	0.3	1.4	0.3	..	..	7.0	9.5	57.9	76.8	49.2	76.3
Congo, Dem. Rep.	–1.9	–27.4	–1.9	–27.4	..	..	15.3	22.3	27.5	35.6	64.0	74.6
Congo, Rep.	123.8	166.5	123.8	166.5	..	..	4.1	3.0	134.2	76.8	18.6	12.0
Côte d'Ivoire	36.6	–1,886.0	36.6	–1,886.0	..	..	2.7	10.2	30.3	112.3	26.2	90.4
Djibouti	32.6	50.4	32.6	50.4	..	..	12.3	15.5	142.3	187.7	..	..
Equatorial Guinea	–1,016.0	448.2	–1,016.0	448.2	..	..	0.2	0.3	48.7	46.7	0.6	0.7
Eritrea	–5.8	4.5	–5.8	4.5	..	..	8.7	7.7	29.1	28.5	..	..
Ethiopia	–137.8	240.3	–142.9	239.4	5.0	0.9	12.8	13.4	41.2	46.1	64.7	59.7
Gabon	–241.6	–294.4	–241.6	–294.4	..	..	0.4	0.7	42.8	52.6	1.8	2.5
Gambia, The	1.3	10.9	1.3	10.9	..	..	11.4	17.5	56.5	75.1	46.2	67.3
Ghana	209.4	253.8	209.1	253.8	0.3	0.0	4.6	6.0	55.9	66.4	21.3	30.9
Guinea	–59.0	0.6	–59.0	0.6	..	..	8.7	5.2	33.3	21.3	55.7	24.2
Guinea-Bissau	–15.1	–9.1	–15.1	–9.1	..	..	15.5	17.4	83.5	90.3	..	..
Kenya	–25.7	444.1	–25.7	444.1	..	..	4.5	6.1	35.2	44.7	22.3	29.0
Lesotho	–4.5	–2.8	–4.5	–2.8	..	..	9.0	7.8	70.2	59.5	31.4	24.8
Liberia	559.9	1,132.7	559.9	1,132.7	..	..	148.3	57.6	329.4	127.7	741.5	..
Madagascar	205.9	270.4	205.9	270.4	..	..	8.9	5.2	44.1	22.7	22.2	15.9
Malawi	–4.7	31.4	–4.7	31.4	..	..	22.7	16.3	62.2	50.6	86.3	65.6
Mali	–25.3	–26.5	–25.3	–26.7	..	0.2	11.1	11.0	75.9	75.7	..	..
Mauritania	–8.7	23.8	–8.7	23.8	..	..	8.9	9.5	99.4	87.1	32.1	37.7
Mauritius	818.6	1,526.6	803.0	1,526.6	15.6	..	1.2	1.8	86.4	122.0	4.3	8.5
Mozambique	–52.5	58.2	–52.5	58.2	..	..	20.2	20.6	89.2	87.9	128.9	98.2
Namibia	317.3	289.8	317.3	289.8	..	..	2.3	3.5	98.7	150.2	8.3	13.0
Niger	–30.2	16.7	–30.2	16.7	..	0.1	11.3	8.7	41.3	30.7	..	..
Nigeria	1,713.2	1,209.8	1,713.2	1,209.8	..	..	0.6	1.0	8.5	10.7	..	..
Rwanda	10.3	81.1	10.3	81.1	0.0	..	19.9	17.9	96.0	93.5	87.2	82.3
São Tomé and Príncipe	–4.9	3.1	–4.9	3.1	..	..	27.3	16.1	295.5	188.7	..	..
Senegal	163.3	274.1	162.6	273.9	0.7	0.2	8.1	7.9	87.2	81.2	26.7	28.4
Seychelles	33.6	48.3	33.6	48.3	..	0.0	1.4	3.0	144.0	263.7	5.3	12.5
Sierra Leone	1.8	11.6	1.8	11.6	..	..	18.8	22.5	66.0	76.8	127.5	148.8
Somalia	3.7	6.1	3.7	6.1	..	..	..	..	84.9	72.4	..	..
South Africa	5,504.6	–377.1	5,504.3	–377.3	0.3	0.2	0.4	0.4	23.1	21.8	1.9	1.9
Sudan	–13.5	16.3	–16.8	5.7	3.3	10.6	4.1	4.2	57.6	54.1	15.8	16.6
Swaziland	1.9	–3.8	1.9	–3.8	..	..	2.5	1.9	59.8	48.9	16.1	11.4
Tanzania	122.2	189.8	122.2	189.8	..	..	11.3	13.7	54.9	67.1	42.1	46.1
Togo	31.6	–86.5	31.6	–86.5	..	..	11.4	17.5	51.0	75.4	..	..
Uganda	111.7	64.0	111.7	64.0	..	..	11.4	11.1	51.8	54.6	49.5	46.8
Zambia	380.2	–30.1	380.2	–30.1	..	..	7.8	9.9	88.4	98.1	34.4	44.7
Zimbabwe	16.0	–96.5	16.0	–96.5	..	..	14.4	13.1	49.1	58.8	252.5	581.9
NORTH AFRICA	**20,880.4**	**9,244.6**	**20,693.6**	**9,167.0**	**186.8**	**77.6**	**0.6**	**0.5**	**20.6**	**17.2**	**2.1**	**1.8**
Algeria	295.8	2,728.9	294.5	2,727.0	1.3	1.9	0.2	0.2	9.3	9.1	0.6	0.6
Egypt, Arab Rep.	15,267.8	4,392.2	15,252.5	4,357.5	15.3	34.7	0.8	0.5	16.5	11.1	3.7	2.5
Libya	1,914.2	1,073.7	1,910.0	1,035.6	4.2	38.1	0.1	0.1	9.6	6.1	0.2	..
Morocco	1,588.6	811.7	1,583.8	809.9	4.8	1.8	1.2	1.0	33.6	28.5	3.1	2.8
Tunisia	1,396.7	58.5	1,235.4	57.3	161.3	1.2	0.8	1.2	32.1	45.4	3.0	4.5

a. As of 2010.

Net official development assistance				Food aid shipments (thousands of tons)				Heavily Indebted Poor Countries (HIPC) Debt Initiative				
Share of imports of goods and services (%)		Share of central government expenditures (%)		Cereal		Noncereal				In nominal terms		
								Decision point[a]	Completion point[a]	Debt service relief committed ($ millions)[a]	Assistance delivered under MDRI ($ millions)[a]	Total HIPC and MDRI assistance ($ millions)[a]
2007	2008	2007	2008	2008	2009	2008	2009					
8.8	**12.0**	**..**	**..**	**3,284.1**	**2,631.6**	**3,460.2**	**3,066.9**					
0.6	0.5	..	..	24.3	9.4	0.0	0.0	..	..	..	..	..
26.1	..	64.3	68.2	12.5	5.2	9.7	16.7	Jul. 2000	Mar. 2003	460	1,130	1,590
10.7	4.7	..	..	0.0	0.0	0.0	0.0	..	..	..	..	..
34.0	..	98.5	102.5	34.6	34.4	39.3	21.8	Jul. 2000	Apr. 2002	930	1,207	2,137
83.4	102.0	..	..	57.8	50.9	24.3	47.7	Aug. 2005	Jan. 2009	1,366	93	1,459
6.5	9.4	..	..	8.5	4.7	12.7	8.7	Oct. 2000	Apr. 2006	4,917	1,285	6,202
17.5	17.6	54.0	44.9	27.5	4.6	11.4	17.5	..	..	..	..	..
..	..	..	..	7.5	20.4	13.1	17.4	Sep. 2007	Jun. 2009	804	280	1,084
..	..	..	..	50.5	56.2	69.9	100.2	May 2001	..	260	..	260
..	..	..	..	0.2	0.0	0.0	7.5	Jun. 2010	..	136	..	136
..	..	..	..	90.6	78.2	86.3	141.4	Jul. 2003	Jul. 2010	15,222	1,035	16,257
..	..	..	..	4.4	7.3	2.7	3.7	Mar. 2006	Jan. 2010	1,738	203	1,941
5.7	23.9	14.9	57.6	17.3	21.9	12.0	21.4	Mar. 2009	..	3,415	..	3,415
16.9	27.3	..	..	8.8	7.1	7.6	21.0	..	..	..	..	..
..	..	..	..	0.0	0.0	0.0	0.0	..	..	..	..	..
..	..	..	..	32.0	14.8	17.2	0.0	..	..	..	..	..
34.5	42.0	..	..	679.7	571.2	979.1	904.1	Nov. 2001	Apr. 2004	3,275	3,277	6,552
..	..	..	..	0.0	0.0	0.0	0.0	..	..	..	..	..
23.5	35.3	..	..	11.4	7.2	2.5	10.4	Dec. 2000	Dec. 2007	112	370	482
10.1	14.1	22.3	33.8	47.8	36.3	38.9	29.1	Feb. 2002	Jul. 2004	3,500	3,862	7,362
7.5	13.6	..	..	22.3	14.7	30.0	11.3	Dec. 2000	..	800	..	800
44.0	..	..	..	5.7	8.8	6.1	2.1	Dec. 2000	..	790	..	790
10.7	15.4	20.9	27.9	307.8	220.0	213.8	216.7	..	..	..	..	..
8.0	6.7	17.3	..	18.7	32.0	15.2	6.2	..	..	..	..	..
54.1	27.3	43884.0	..	53.8	33.9	35.0	22.3	Mar. 2008	Jun. 2010	4,600	265	4,865
..	..	76.2	..	41.5	43.1	28.5	20.7	Dec. 2000	Oct. 2004	1,900	2,385	4,285
..	..	..	..	179.4	82.0	57.2	70.7	Dec. 2000	Aug. 2006	1,628	1,570	3,198
23.1	..	82.1	74.9	35.2	43.6	19.1	23.0	Sep. 2000	Mar. 2003	895	1,977	2,872
..	..	..	..	38.2	39.6	50.0	25.2	Feb. 2000	Jun. 2002	1,100	875	1,975
1.6	2.8	..	8.4	0.0	0.0	0.0	0.0	..	..	..	..	..
30.9	44.1	..	..	133.7	80.1	135.4	157.4	Apr. 2000	Sep. 2001	4,300	2,029	6,329
4.3	5.9	..	..	5.8	9.3	4.2	0.3	..	..	..	..	..
30.2	..	..	..	74.1	74.8	55.8	40.2	Dec. 2000	Apr. 2004	1,190	1,057	2,247
1.6	2.8	8.6	..	0.0	0.0	0.0	0.0	..	..	..	..	..
63.8	61.0	..	..	31.6	16.9	16.1	22.4	Dec. 2000	Apr. 2005	1,316	510	1,826
40.9	29.3	..	..	1.0	1.5	6.8	6.0	Dec. 2000	Mar. 2007	263	65	328
14.6	..	..	..	10.6	20.4	24.9	11.3	Jun. 2000	Apr. 2004	850	2,460	3,310
0.9	2.0	4.5	9.3	0.0	0.0	3.5	0.0	..	..	..	..	..
53.2	64.8	92.3	101.9	27.2	25.9	25.9	15.1	Mar. 2002	Dec. 2006	994	661	1,655
..	..	..	..	180.1	92.9	317.9	281.8	..	..	..	..	..
0.9	1.2	1.3	1.1	0.0	0.0	0.0	0.0	..	..	..	..	..
17.1	16.8	..	..	498.7	405.6	520.9	427.8	..	..	..	..	..
2.8	2.1	..	..	12.8	13.4	16.2	2.4	..	..	..	..	..
25.9	37.2	..	..	77.4	65.6	75.3	24.7	Apr. 2000	Nov. 2001	3,000	3,806	6,806
18.7	..	75.3	100.6	0.6	1.8	5.0	25.0	Nov. 2008	..	360	..	360
28.9	32.0	75.1	86.9	208.0	223.7	158.2	96.0	Feb. 2000	May 2000	1,950	3,483	5,433
16.2	23.1	..	..	89.1	32.7	24.5	11.8	Dec. 2000	Apr. 2005	3,900	2,742	6,642
..	..	..	..	115.6	119.6	287.6	178.1	..	..	..	..	..
1.5	**1.6**	**7.0**	**..**	**43.2**	**19.0**	**25.6**	**12.2**					
..	..	0.8	0.9	16.5	17.1	21.4	11.5	..	..	..	..	..
1.9	1.6	2.7	1.6	26.7	1.9	4.3	0.7	..	..	..	..	..
0.2	0.1	..	..	..	..	..	..	..	..	..	..	..
2.2	2.3	3.9	3.6	0.0	0.0	0.0	0.0	..	..	..	..	..
1.1	2.0	2.7	4.0	0.0	0.0	0.0	0.0	..	..	..	..	..

Table 12.2 Status of Paris Declaration indicators

	PDI-1		PDI-2			PDI-3		PDI-4		PDI-5			
	Operational national development strategies[a]		Reliable public financial management[b]		Reliable country procurement systems[c]	Government budget estimates comprehensive and realistic (%)		Technical assistance aligned and coordinated with country programs (%)		Aid for government sectors uses country public financial management systems (%)		Aid for government sectors uses of country procurement systems (%)	
	2005	2007	2005	2007	2007	2005	2007	2005	2007	2005	2007	2005	2007
SUB-SAHARAN AFRICA													
Angola[d]	..	..	..	..	..	..	..	..	..	..	..	..	..
Benin	C	C	4.0	3.5	..	46.7	28.5	56.3	53.9	51.8	47.5	64.1	63.3
Botswana[d]	..	..	..	..	..	..	..	..	..	..	..	..	..
Burkina Faso	C	B	4.0	4.0	..	67.5	92.2	3.4	56.4	44.5	43.2	60.4	53.8
Burundi	D	C	2.5	3.0	..	39.3	53.9	42.6	41.0	24.5	32.7	19.4	34.6
Cameroon	C	C	3.5	3.5	B	..	85.7	..	29.9	..	53.1	..	63.1
Cape Verde	C	C	3.5	4.0	..	85.1	90.2	92.7	39.3	64.1	22.5	53.5	22.1
Central African Republic	D	D	2.0	2.0	..	..	36.4	..	36.5	..	23.8	..	10.2
Chad	C	C	3.0	9.0	..	..	87.9	..	64.4	..	1.0	..	10.6
Comoros[d]	..	..	..	..	..	..	..	..	..	..	..	..	..
Congo, Dem. Rep.	D	D	2.5	2.5	..	81.0	58.3	10.7	38.1	12.9	0.0	30.8	0.8
Congo, Rep.	..	..	..	..	..	..	..	..	..	..	..	..	..
Côte d'Ivoire	D	E	2.5	2.0	..	..	64.4	..	30.9	..	0.0	..	9.3
Djibouti[d]	..	..	..	..	..	..	..	..	..	..	..	..	..
Equatorial Guinea[d]	..	..	..	..	..	..	..	..	..	..	..	..	..
Eritrea[d]	..	..	..	..	..	..	..	..	..	..	..	..	..
Ethiopia	C	B	3.5	4.0	..	74.4	61.7	27.3	66.8	45.2	46.7	42.8	41.4
Gabon	..	..	9.0	9.0	..	..	22.4	..	70.4	..	4.7	..	32.3
Gambia, The[d]	..	..	..	..	..	..	..	..	..	..	..	..	..
Ghana	C	B	3.5	4.0	C	96.1	94.5	40.4	73.8	62.1	50.8	51.9	56.1
Guinea[d]	..	..	..	..	..	..	..	..	..	..	..	..	..
Guinea-Bissau[d]	..	..	..	..	..	..	..	..	..	..	..	..	..
Kenya	D	C	3.5	3.5	..	90.9	64.2	60.2	63.8	47.3	53.6	44.7	36.8
Lesotho[d]	..	..	..	..	..	..	..	..	..	..	..	..	..
Liberia	D	D	9.0	9.0	..	..	0.0	..	35.3	..	32.0	..	0.0
Madagascar	C	C	3.0	3.5	..	..	87.0	..	70.9	..	21.5	..	25.9
Malawi	C	C	3.0	3.0	C	53.6	63.7	46.6	52.3	54.7	49.9	35.0	35.4
Mali	C	C	4.0	3.5	..	60.0	72.6	15.1	75.4	29.5	34.4	44.6	34.8
Mauritania	B	C	2.0	2.5	..	65.4	57.4	19.5	53.4	4.4	8.3	19.7	22.2
Mauritius[d]	..	..	..	..	..	..	..	..	..	..	..	..	..
Mozambique	C	C	3.5	3.5	..	83.3	82.5	38.1	26.9	35.8	43.5	38.0	53.8
Namibia[d]	..	..	..	..	..	..	..	..	..	..	..	..	..
Niger	C	C	3.5	3.5	B	99.5	90.7	15.3	50.2	27.1	25.5	48.7	36.5
Nigeria	..	C	3.0	3.0	..	..	6.3	..	70.6	..	0.0	..	0.0
Rwanda	B	B	3.5	4.0	B	49.0	51.0	57.8	83.6	39.2	42.0	46.0	42.9
São Tomé and Príncipe[d]	..	..	..	..	..	..	..	..	..	..	..	..	..
Senegal	C	C	3.5	3.5	B	88.9	87.7	18.1	54.1	22.7	19.0	28.9	41.3
Seychelles[d]	..	..	..	..	..	..	..	..	..	..	..	..	..
Sierra Leone	D	C	3.5	3.5	B	..	53.6	..	22.5	..	20.1	..	38.3
Somalia[d]	..	..	..	..	..	..	..	..	..	..	..	..	..
South Africa	..	..	..	..	..	70.8	..	95.1	..	38.1	..	43.7	..
Sudan	D	D	2.5	2.0	..	..	84.6	..	53.2	..	3.1	..	0.4
Swaziland[d]	..	..	..	..	..	..	..	..	..	..	..	..	..
Tanzania	B	B	4.5	4.0	B	89.5	83.6	49.5	60.5	65.9	71.5	61.2	68.5
Togo	..	..	2.0	2.0	..	..	68.9	..	28.9	..	4.4	..	15.5
Uganda	B	B	4.0	4.0	B	79.1	98.4	41.6	58.1	60.2	57.0	54.2	36.9
Zambia	C	B	3.0	3.5	C	51.9	73.5	32.4	34.5	34.1	59.4	43.5	71.0
Zimbabwe[d]	..	..	..	..	..	..	..	..	..	..	..	..	..
NORTH AFRICA													
Algeria[d]	..	..	..	..	..	..	..	..	..	..	..	..	..
Egypt, Arab Rep.	..	..	9.0	9.0	..	58.2	57.4	76.3	86.2	28.2	12.0	24.9	22.7
Libya	..	..	..	..	..	..	..	..	..	..	..	..	..
Morocco	..	..	9.0	9.0	..	..	79.8	..	82.2	..	78.9	..	81.1
Tunisia[d]	..	..	..	..	..	..	..	..	..	..	..	..	..

Note: See *Technical notes* for further details. PDI is Paris Declaration Indicator. Status will be updated in the fourth quarter of 2011.

a. Ratings range from A to E, where A means the development strategy substantially achieves good practices; B means it is largely developed toward achieving good practices; C means it reflects action taken toward achieving good practices; D means it incorporates some elements of good practice; and E means it reflects little action toward achieving good practices.

b. Ratings range from 1 (low) to 6 (high).

c. Ratings range from A (high) to D (low). Indicator was not collected in 2005.

d. Did not take part in the Survey on Monitoring the Paris Declaration.

PDI-6 Project implementation units parallel to country structures (number)		PDI-7 Aid disbursements on schedule and recorded by government (%)		PDI-8 Bilateral aid that is untied (%)		PDI-9 Aid provided in the framework of program-based approaches (%)		PDI-10 Donor missions coordinated (%)		PDI-10 Country analysis coordinated (%)		PDI-11 Existence of a monitorable performance assessment framework[a]		PDI-12 Existence of a mutual accountability review[a]	
2005	2007	2005	2007	2005	2007	2005	2007	2005	2007	2005	2007	2005	2007	2005	2007
..	..	..	..	..	..	..	..	..	..	..	..	..	..	..	..
29.0	58.0	53.0	31.6	79.3	98.8	60.8	49.0	14.5	25.1	37.5	44.0	C	C	B	B
..	..	..	..	..	..	..	..	..	..	..	..	..	..	..	..
131.0	102.0	91.7	91.6	92.4	91.8	45.3	57.2	16.8	12.8	45.2	39.0	C	C	B	B
37.0	29.0	52.5	44.4	59.8	90.6	53.6	35.5	24.3	13.5	55.0	73.8	D	D	B	A
..	38.0	..	50.8	..	98.5	..	39.6	..	25.8	..	49.2	D	D	..	B
10.0	18.0	92.2	96.4	22.3	60.3	36.7	30.9	10.5	43.4	34.1	64.5	D	C	A	B
..	11.0	..	45.2	..	86.7	..	34.3	..	9.8	..	23.2	D	D	..	B
..	17.0	..	0.0	..	81.2	..	1.5	..	18.1	..	35.0	D	D	..	..
..	..	..	..	..	..	..	..	..	..	..	..	..	..	..	..
34.0	146.0	82.9	19.5	88.1	93.9	53.8	20.8	38.4	21.3	35.2	22.9	D	D	B	B
..	..	..	..	..	..	..	..	..	..	..	..	D	D	..	..
..	29.0	..	67.0	..	91.7	..	2.6	..	65.0	..	75.0	D	E	..	B
..	..	..	..	..	..	..	..	..	..	..	..	..	..	..	..
..	..	..	..	..	..	..	..	..	..	..	..	..	..	..	..
..	..	..	..	..	..	..	..	..	..	..	..	..	..	..	..
103.0	56.0	95.9	73.4	38.8	82.2	52.6	65.6	26.7	29.4	49.5	69.5	C	C	A	A
..	5.0	..	16.8	..	99.7	..	0.0	..	4.7	..	36.8	..	..	..	B
..	..	..	..	..	..	..	..	..	..	..	..	..	..	..	..
45.0	16.0	91.6	82.3	89.9	91.8	52.7	68.8	19.7	39.0	39.9	59.8	C	C	A	A
..	..	..	..	..	..	..	..	..	..	..	..	..	..	..	..
..	..	..	..	..	..	..	..	..	..	..	..	..	..	..	..
17.0	21.0	44.0	46.5	78.3	84.5	44.6	30.5	9.2	48.4	32.3	78.0	C	C	B	B
..	..	..	..	..	..	..	..	..	..	..	..	..	..	..	..
..	16.0	..	0.0	..	82.4	..	21.3	..	11.0	..	65.6	D	D	..	B
..	48.0	..	79.5	..	83.9	..	43.5	..	23.8	..	41.6	C	C	..	B
69.0	51.0	57.7	58.1	96.9	90.5	31.8	42.0	23.8	22.3	60.0	60.8	C	C	A	A
65.0	60.0	70.7	68.2	95.0	93.4	48.1	40.6	7.4	15.2	30.0	39.3	D	D	B	B
23.0	27.0	39.4	52.1	72.9	67.0	36.7	35.1	13.8	11.4	58.9	25.4	C	C	B	B
..	..	..	..	..	..	..	..	..	..	..	..	..	..	..	..
40.0	20.0	70.1	73.7	89.0	90.8	46.3	46.4	46.5	16.8	63.2	31.7	C	B	A	A
..	..	..	..	..	..	..	..	..	..	..	..	..	..	..	..
52.0	47.0	73.2	77.5	83.8	84.3	31.2	49.0	20.9	15.4	39.9	31.8	D	D	B	B
..	23.0	..	7.1	..	99.2	..	3.9	..	19.1	..	32.8	..	C	..	B
48.0	41.0	65.6	66.8	81.6	95.1	41.5	38.4	8.5	20.8	36.4	42.0	C	C	B	B
..	..	..	..	..	..	..	..	..	..	..	..	..	..	..	..
23.0	55.0	69.3	60.8	90.8	93.0	57.3	38.9	15.1	16.6	40.5	28.1	C	C	B	B
..	..	..	..	..	..	..	..	..	..	..	..	..	..	..	..
..	2.0	..	29.7	..	91.6	..	26.9	..	27.1	..	56.3	D	D	..	B
..	..	..	..	..	..	..	..	..	..	..	..	..	..	..	..
15.0	..	44.2	..	97.2	97.4	26.5	..	18.8	..	75.0	..	..	..	A	..
..	105.0	..	51.6	..	79.9	..	19.2	..	14.9	..	44.7	D	D	..	B
..	..	..	..	..	..	..	..	..	..	..	..	..	..	..	..
56.0	28.0	70.2	60.8	94.6	98.9	55.5	60.8	17.3	15.8	38.3	64.9	B	B	A	A
..	13.0	..	14.3	..	56.1	..	38.9	..	15.1	..	20.7	..	..	..	B
54.0	55.0	84.0	74.4	81.0	85.4	49.9	65.7	17.2	21.0	40.1	54.0	B	B	B	B
24.0	34.0	50.1	85.1	99.1	99.6	47.1	46.8	14.7	15.9	45.8	46.4	D	C	A	B
..	..	..	..	..	..	..	..	..	..	..	..	..	..	..	..
..	..	..	..	..	..	..	..	..	..	..	..	..	..	..	..
100.0	32.0	29.2	78.9	46.7	75.0	61.2	48.9	18.1	21.6	40.0	56.1	..	..	A	B
..	..	..	..	..	..	..	..	..	..	..	..	..	..	..	..
..	47.0	..	68.3	..	90.1	..	70.3	..	11.7	..	25.0	..	..	..	B
..	..	..	..	..	..	..	..	..	..	..	..	..	..	..	..

Table 12.3 Capable states

	Investment climate			Enforcing contracts		
	Firms that believe the court system is fair, impartial, and uncorrupt (%)	Viewed by firms as major or very severe constraints (% of firms)				
		Corruption	Crime, theft, and disorder	Number of procedures	Time required (days)	Cost (% of claim)
	2009–10[b]	2009–10[b]	2009–10[b]	2010	2010	2010
SUB-SAHARAN AFRICA				**39**	**652**	**49.7**
Angola	23.7	75.6	28.1	46	1,011	44.4
Benin	9.6	67.8	52.7	42	825	64.7
Botswana	79.5	27.4	22.6	29	625	28.1
Burkina Faso	38.7	70.5	42.2	37	446	81.7
Burundi	..	..	..	44	832	38.6
Cameroon	32.6	61.3	41.5	43	800	46.6
Cape Verde	59.5	29.8	62.3	37	425	21.8
Central African Republic	..	..	..	43	660	82.0
Chad	31.0	67.2	45.8	41	743	45.7
Comoros	..	..	..	43	506	89.4
Congo, Dem. Rep.	17.2	72.7	63.3	43	625	151.8
Congo, Rep.	32.3	65.0	44.1	44	560	53.2
Côte d'Ivoire	35.3	75.0	53.8	33	770	41.7
Djibouti	..	..	..	40	1,225	34.0
Equatorial Guinea	..	..	..	40	553	18.5
Eritrea	100.0	0.0	0.0	39	405	22.6
Ethiopia	..	..	..	37	620	15.2
Gabon	41.3	41.4	34.1	38	1,070	34.3
Gambia, The	..	..	..	32	434	37.9
Ghana	..	..	..	36	487	23.0
Guinea	..	..	..	50	276	45.0
Guinea-Bissau	..	..	..	40	1,140	25.0
Kenya	..	..	..	40	465	47.2
Lesotho	33.2	46.7	33.5	41	785	19.5
Liberia	44.3	31.2	26.8	41	1,280	35.0
Madagascar	28.8	42.7	48.1	38	871	42.4
Malawi	74.3	12.8	22.8	42	312	94.1
Mali	42.7	24.8	17.3	36	620	52.0
Mauritania	..	..	..	46	370	23.2
Mauritius	63.6	50.7	41.5	36	645	17.4
Mozambique	..	..	..	30	730	142.5
Namibia	..	..	..	33	270	35.8
Niger	49.6	83.7	44.2	39	545	59.6
Nigeria	..	..	..	40	457	32.0
Rwanda	..	..	..	24	230	78.7
São Tomé and Príncipe	..	..	..	43	1,185	50.5
Senegal	..	..	..	44	780	26.5
Seychelles	..	..	..	37	720	15.4
Sierra Leone	29.7	36.9	14.2	40	515	149.5
Somalia	..	..	..	..	..	..
South Africa	..	..	..	30	600	33.2
Sudan	..	..	..	53	810	19.8
Swaziland	..	..	..	40	972	56.1
Tanzania	..	..	..	38	462	14.3
Togo	14.1	70.2	22.6	41	588	47.5
Uganda	..	..	..	38	490	44.9
Zambia	..	..	..	35	471	38.7
Zimbabwe	..	..	..	38	410	113.1
NORTH AFRICA				**42**	**705**	**23.8**
Algeria	..	..	..	46	630	21.9
Egypt, Arab Rep.	..	..	..	41	1,010	26.2
Libya	..	..	..	..	..	..
Morocco	..	..	..	40	615	25.2
Tunisia	..	..	..	39	565	21.8

a. Average of the disclosure, director liability, and shareholder suits indexes.
b. Data are for the most recent year available during the period specified.

Protecting investors (0 least desirable to 10 most desirable)				Regulation and tax administration			
Disclosure index	Director liability index	Shareholder suits index	Investor protection index[a]	Number of tax payments	Time required to prepare, file, and pay taxes (hours)	Total tax rate (% of profit)	Extractive Industries Transparency Initiative status
2010	2010	2010	2010	2010	2010	2010	2010
5	**3**	**5**	**4.4**	**37**	**310**	**67.4**	
5	6	6	5.7	31	282	53.2	
6	1	3	3.3	55	270	66.0	
7	8	3	6.0	19	152	19.5	
6	1	4	3.7	46	270	44.9	Candidate
4	1	5	3.3	32	211	153.4	
6	1	6	4.3	44	654	49.1	Candidate
1	5	6	4.0	43	186	37.1	
6	1	5	4.0	54	504	203.8	
6	1	3	3.3	54	732	65.4	Candidate
6	1	5	4.0	20	100	217.9	
3	3	4	3.3	32	336	339.7	Candidate
6	1	3	3.3	61	606	65.5	Candidate
6	1	3	3.3	64	270	44.4	Candidate
5	2	0	2.3	35	90	38.7	
6	1	4	3.7	46	492	59.5	Intent to implement
4	5	5	4.7	18	216	84.5	
4	4	5	4.3	19	198	31.1	Intent to implement
6	1	3	3.3	26	488	43.5	Candidate
2	1	5	2.7	50	376	292.3	
7	5	6	6.0	33	224	32.7	Compliant
6	1	1	2.7	56	416	54.6	Candidate
6	1	5	4.0	46	208	45.9	
3	2	10	5.0	41	393	49.7	
2	1	8	3.7	21	324	19.6	
4	1	6	3.7	32	158	43.7	Compliant
5	6	6	5.7	23	201	37.7	Candidate
4	7	5	5.3	19	157	25.1	
6	1	4	3.7	59	270	52.2	Candidate
5	3	3	3.7	38	696	68.4	Candidate
6	8	9	7.7	7	161	24.1	
5	4	9	6.0	37	230	34.3	
5	5	6	5.3	37	375	9.6	
6	1	3	3.3	41	270	46.5	Compliant
5	7	5	5.7	35	938	32.2	Compliant
7	9	3	6.3	26	148	31.3	
3	1	6	3.3	42	424	33.3	Intent to implement
6	1	2	3.0	59	666	46.0	
4	8	5	5.7	16	76	44.1	
6	7	6	6.3	29	357	235.6	Candidate
..	..	..	..	..	..	..	
8	8	8	8.0	9	200	30.5	
0	6	4	3.3	42	180	36.1	
2	5	6	4.3	33	104	36.8	
3	4	8	5.0	48	172	45.2	Candidate
6	1	4	3.7	53	270	50.8	Candidate
2	5	5	4.0	32	161	35.7	
3	6	7	5.3	37	132	16.1	Candidate
8	1	4	4.3	49	242	40.3	
7	**4**	**4**	**4.8**	**25**	**347**	**54.8**	
6	6	4	5.3	34	451	72.0	
8	3	5	5.3	29	433	42.6	
..	..	..	..	..	..	..	
7	2	1	3.3	28	358	41.7	
5	5	6	5.3	8	144	62.8	

Table 12.4 Governance and anticorruption indicators

	Governance indicators[a]											
	Voice and accountability		Political stability and absence of violence		Government effectiveness		Regulatory quality		Rule of law		Control of corruption	
	1996	2009	1996	2009	1996	2009	1996	2009	1996	2009	1996	2009
SUB-SAHARAN AFRICA												
Angola	–1.5	–1.1	–2.3	–0.2	–1.3	–0.9	–1.1	–1.0	–1.6	–1.2	–1.1	–1.3
Benin	0.7	0.3	1.0	0.4	..	–0.5	–0.1	–0.4	–0.3	–0.7	..	–0.6
Botswana	0.8	0.4	0.7	0.9	0.3	0.6	0.9	0.6	0.6	0.6	0.5	0.9
Burkina Faso	–0.3	–0.3	–0.2	–0.1	–0.9	–0.7	–0.2	–0.1	–0.3	–0.3	–0.3	–0.4
Burundi	–1.5	–0.7	–2.0	–1.4	..	–1.1	–1.1	–1.2	–0.9	–1.2	..	–1.1
Cameroon	–1.2	–1.0	–1.3	–0.4	–1.1	–0.8	–0.8	–0.7	–1.5	–1.1	–1.1	–0.9
Cape Verde	0.8	0.8	1.0	0.8	..	0.0	–0.6	0.0	0.5	0.5	..	0.7
Central African Republic	–0.5	–1.0	–0.2	–2.0	..	–1.4	..	–1.1	–0.3	–1.3	..	–0.8
Chad	–0.9	–1.4	–0.9	–1.8	..	–1.5	–1.1	–1.1	–0.9	–1.5	..	–1.4
Comoros	0.0	–0.3	1.0	–1.0	..	–1.8	..	–1.6	..	–1.1	..	–0.8
Congo, Dem. Rep.	–1.6	–1.4	–1.9	–2.1	–1.5	–1.7	–2.3	–1.6	–2.3	–1.7	–2.5	–1.4
Congo, Rep.	–0.5	–1.0	–0.8	–0.4	–0.9	–1.2	–1.2	–1.3	–1.4	–1.2	–0.3	–1.2
Côte d'Ivoire	–0.8	–1.2	0.0	–1.5	0.2	–1.2	0.0	–1.0	–0.7	–1.3	0.5	–1.2
Djibouti	–0.7	–1.1	0.2	0.5	..	–0.9	–0.1	–0.6	–0.2	–0.6	..	–0.3
Equatorial Guinea	–1.7	–1.8	–0.9	0.0	–1.3	–1.7	–1.5	–1.3	–1.2	–1.3	–1.1	–1.6
Eritrea	–1.1	–2.2	0.3	–0.8	..	–1.4	..	–2.3	–0.3	–1.2	..	–0.3
Ethiopia	–0.8	–1.3	–1.0	–1.7	–1.3	–0.4	–1.9	–1.0	–1.0	–0.8	–1.1	–0.7
Gabon	–0.4	–1.1	–0.2	0.1	–1.0	–0.7	0.0	–0.6	–0.9	–0.5	–1.1	–0.9
Gambia, The	–1.3	–1.1	0.1	0.3	–0.2	–0.7	–1.8	–0.3	0.4	–0.4	0.4	–0.6
Ghana	–0.3	0.5	–0.1	0.2	–0.5	0.1	0.1	0.1	–0.3	–0.1	–0.3	0.1
Guinea	–1.1	–1.4	–1.4	–1.9	–0.9	–1.3	0.1	–1.2	–1.4	–1.6	0.4	–1.2
Guinea-Bissau	–0.3	–0.8	–0.6	–0.5	–0.9	–1.1	0.4	–1.2	–1.7	–1.4	–1.0	–1.1
Kenya	–0.8	–0.3	–0.7	–1.3	–0.2	–0.7	–0.4	–0.2	–1.1	–1.1	–1.1	–1.1
Lesotho	–0.2	–0.1	0.6	0.4	..	–0.3	–0.6	–0.6	–0.3	–0.3	..	0.1
Liberia	–1.4	–0.3	–2.6	–1.0	–1.5	–1.2	–2.6	–1.2	–2.3	–1.1	–1.7	–0.6
Madagascar	0.4	–0.6	0.1	–0.7	–0.9	–0.6	–0.8	–0.5	–1.0	–0.7	0.4	–0.2
Malawi	0.0	–0.2	–0.3	–0.1	–0.9	–0.5	–0.2	–0.5	–0.4	–0.2	–0.3	–0.5
Mali	0.7	0.2	0.7	–0.3	–1.5	–0.8	0.1	–0.4	–0.6	–0.4	–0.3	–0.7
Mauritania	–1.0	–1.0	0.6	–1.2	..	–0.9	–1.1	–0.7	–0.9	–0.8	..	–0.7
Mauritius	0.8	0.8	0.8	0.6	0.3	0.7	0.0	0.9	0.9	0.9	0.6	0.7
Mozambique	0.0	–0.1	–0.5	0.5	–0.1	–0.3	–1.0	–0.3	–0.8	–0.6	–0.2	–0.4
Namibia	0.6	0.3	0.5	0.8	0.5	0.2	0.2	0.1	0.3	0.3	0.6	0.2
Niger	–1.0	–0.7	0.0	–1.2	–0.9	–0.8	–1.5	–0.5	–0.9	–0.6	–0.3	–0.7
Nigeria	–1.8	–0.9	–1.6	–2.0	–1.2	–1.2	–1.1	–0.7	–1.6	–1.2	–1.1	–1.1
Rwanda	–1.3	–1.3	–2.0	–0.3	..	–0.2	–1.6	–0.3	–1.4	–0.5	..	0.1
São Tomé and Príncipe	0.5	0.2	1.0	0.2	..	–0.7	..	–0.8	..	–0.7	..	–0.4
Senegal	–0.1	–0.3	–0.6	–0.1	–0.1	–0.4	–0.3	–0.3	–0.3	–0.3	–0.3	–0.5
Seychelles	0.0	0.0	1.0	0.7	..	0.2	..	–0.6	..	0.1	..	0.3
Sierra Leone	–0.9	–0.3	–2.3	–0.4	–1.5	–1.2	–1.2	–0.8	–1.3	–1.0	–1.7	–1.0
Somalia	–1.9	–2.0	–2.3	–3.3	–1.5	–2.3	–2.5	–2.6	–2.1	–2.5	–1.7	–1.7
South Africa	0.9	0.6	–1.3	0.0	0.3	0.5	0.1	0.4	0.0	0.1	0.5	0.1
Sudan	–2.0	–1.6	–2.6	–2.6	–1.3	–1.3	–1.5	–1.2	–1.6	–1.3	–1.1	–1.2
Swaziland	–1.1	–1.2	0.0	0.0	..	–0.7	0.4	–0.5	0.8	–0.6	..	–0.3
Tanzania	–0.6	–0.1	–0.2	0.1	–0.8	–0.4	0.1	–0.4	–0.3	–0.4	–1.1	–0.4
Togo	–1.0	–1.0	–0.5	–0.2	–0.9	–1.4	0.4	–0.8	–1.4	–0.9	–1.0	–1.1
Uganda	–0.5	–0.5	–1.2	–1.1	–0.6	–0.6	0.3	–0.2	–0.5	–0.4	–0.3	–0.9
Zambia	–0.5	–0.3	–0.5	0.5	–0.7	–0.7	0.3	–0.5	–0.5	–0.5	–1.1	–0.5
Zimbabwe	–0.6	–1.6	–0.6	–1.4	–0.3	–1.7	–0.8	–2.3	–0.9	–1.9	–0.3	–1.5
NORTH AFRICA												
Algeria	–1.3	–1.0	–2.7	–1.2	–0.6	–0.6	–1.1	–0.9	–1.4	–0.7	–0.3	–0.5
Egypt, Arab Rep.	–1.0	–1.1	–0.9	–0.6	0.2	–0.3	0.4	–0.1	0.1	0.0	–0.2	–0.4
Libya	–1.8	–1.9	–1.8	0.6	–1.0	–1.1	–2.0	–1.0	–1.4	–0.8	–1.1	–1.1
Morocco	–0.6	–0.8	–0.5	–0.4	0.2	–0.1	0.3	0.0	0.1	–0.2	0.5	–0.2
Tunisia	–0.9	–1.3	0.0	0.2	0.5	0.4	0.7	0.1	–0.2	0.2	–0.2	0.0

a. The rating scale for each criterion ranges from –2.5 (weak performance) to 2.5 (very high performance).

b. 0–20 indicates that budget documents provide scant or no information, 21–40 indicates minimal information, 41–60 indicates some information, 61–80 indicates significant information, and 81–100 indicates extensive information. In 2008 the International Budget Partnership made three changes in the methodology applied to its Open Budget Survey, which is the basis for the open budget index.

c. Data are for the most recent year available during the period specified.

Share of firms (%)								
Expected to pay informal payment to public officials to get things done	Expected to give gifts to obtain an operating license	Expected to give gifts in meetings with tax officials	Expected to give gifts to secure a government contract	Identifying corruption as a major constraint	Mean corruption perceptions index score (0 low to 10 high)		Open budget index overall score[b]	
2009–10[c]	2009–10[c]	2009–10[c]	2009–10[c]	2009–10[c]	2008	2010	2008	2010
48.9	39.1	34.2	58.6	75.6	1.9	1.9	3.0	26.0
54.5	44.6	26.8	59	67.8	3.1	2.8	..	..
7.3	2.9	8.4	1	27.4	5.8	5.8	62.0	51.0
8.5	4.1	6.7	11.8	70.5	3.5	3.1	14.0	5.0
..	..	..	..	..	1.9	1.8	..	..
51.2	39.6	30.8	58.8	61.3	2.3	2.2	5.0	2.0
6	0	1.1	0	29.8	5.1	5.1	..	..
..	..	..	..	..	2.0	2.1	..	..
41.8	52.6	21.2	47.3	67.2	1.6	1.7	7.0	0.4
..	..	..	..	..	2.5	2.1	..	..
65.7	53.8	54.4	75.7	72.7	1.7	2.0	0.0	6.0
81.8	..	37.1	49.9	65	1.9	2.1	..	..
38.5	31.8	13.6	28.5	75	2.0	2.2	..	..
..	..	..	..	..	..	3.2	..	..
..	..	..	..	..	1.7	1.9	0.0	0.0
0	0	0	0	0	2.6	2.6	..	..
..	..	..	..	..	2.6	2.7	..	..
41.8	0	22.8	26.6	41.4	3.1	2.8	..	..
..	..	..	..	..	1.9	3.2	..	..
..	..	..	..	..	3.9	4.1	49.0	54.0
..	..	..	..	..	1.6	2.0	..	..
..	..	..	..	..	1.9	2.1	..	..
..	..	..	..	..	2.1	2.1	57.0	49.0
28.1	3.3	9.2	16.7	46.7	3.2	3.5	..	..
55.4	49.6	54.4	51.6	31.2	2.4	3.3	2.0	40.0
21.8	18.6	6.8	9	42.7	3.4	2.6	..	..
10.8	3.5	11.4	2.8	12.8	2.8	3.4	28.0	47.0
19.4	42.4	20.2	22.8	24.8	3.1	2.7	..	35.0
..	..	..	..	..	2.8	2.3	..	..
5.9	0	0.3	8.8	50.7	5.5	5.4	..	..
..	..	..	..	..	2.6	2.7	..	28.0
..	..	..	..	..	4.5	4.4	47.0	53.0
35.2	32.5	13.7	43.4	83.7	2.8	2.6	26.0	3.0
..	..	..	..	..	2.7	2.4	19.0	18.0
..	..	..	..	..	3.0	4.0	0.0	11.0
..	..	..	..	..	2.7	3.0	0.0	0.0
..	..	..	..	..	3.4	2.9	3.0	3.0
..	..	..	..	..	4.8	4.8	..	..
20.4	8.7	8.6	33.9	36.9	1.9	2.4	..	..
..	..	..	..	..	1.0	1.1	..	..
..	..	..	..	..	4.9	4.5	87.0	92.0
..	..	..	..	..	1.6	1.6	0.0	8.0
..	..	..	..	..	3.6	3.2	..	..
..	..	..	..	..	3.0	2.7	35.0	45.0
16.7	15.7	16.4	5.5	70.2	2.7	2.4	..	..
..	..	..	..	..	2.6	2.5	51.0	55.0
..	..	..	..	..	2.8	3.0	47.0	36.0
..	..	..	..	..	1.8	2.4	..	..
..	..	..	..	..	3.2	2.9	1.0	1.0
..	..	..	..	..	2.8	3.1	43.0	49.0
..	..	..	..	..	2.6	2.2	..	..
..	..	..	..	..	3.5	3.4	27.0	28.0
..	..	..	..	..	4.4	4.3	..	..

Table 12.5 Country Policy and Institutional Assessment ratings

	CPIA overall rating (IDA resource allocation index)[a]		Economic management							
			Average[b]		Macroeconomic management		Fiscal policy		Debt policy	
	2008	2009	2008	2009	2008	2009	2008	2009	2008	2009
SUB-SAHARAN AFRICA	**3.2**	**3.2**	**3.4**	**3.4**	**3.5**	**3.6**	**3.4**	**3.4**	**3.2**	**3.1**
Angola	2.7	2.8	3.0	3.0	3.0	3.0	3.0	3.0	3.0	3.0
Benin	3.6	3.5	4.0	3.7	4.5	4.0	4.0	3.5	3.5	3.5
Botswana[c]	..	..	..	..	..	..	..	..	..	..
Burkina Faso	3.7	3.8	4.3	4.3	4.5	4.5	4.5	4.5	4.0	4.0
Burundi	3.0	3.1	3.3	3.3	3.5	3.5	3.5	3.5	3.0	3.0
Cameroon	3.2	3.2	3.7	3.7	4.0	4.0	4.0	4.0	3.0	3.0
Cape Verde	4.2	4.2	4.5	4.5	4.5	4.5	4.5	4.5	4.5	4.5
Central African Republic	2.5	2.6	2.8	3.0	3.5	3.5	3.0	3.0	2.0	2.5
Chad	2.5	2.5	2.7	2.5	2.5	2.5	2.5	2.5	3.0	2.5
Comoros	2.3	2.5	2.0	2.3	2.5	3.0	1.5	2.0	2.0	2.0
Congo, Dem. Rep.	2.7	2.7	3.2	3.2	3.5	3.5	3.5	3.5	2.5	2.5
Congo, Rep.	2.7	2.8	2.8	3.0	3.5	3.5	2.5	3.0	2.5	2.5
Côte d'Ivoire	2.7	2.8	2.5	2.8	3.0	3.5	2.5	2.5	2.0	2.5
Djibouti	3.1	3.2	3.0	3.0	3.5	3.5	3.0	3.0	2.5	2.5
Equatorial Guinea[c]	..	..	..	..	..	..	..	..	..	..
Eritrea	2.3	2.2	2.2	1.8	2.0	2.0	2.0	2.0	2.5	1.5
Ethiopia	3.4	3.4	3.3	3.7	2.5	3.5	4.0	4.0	3.5	3.5
Gabon[c]	..	..	..	..	..	..	..	..	..	..
Gambia, The	3.2	3.3	3.5	3.5	4.0	4.0	3.5	3.5	3.0	3.0
Ghana	3.9	3.8	3.7	3.7	3.5	3.5	3.5	3.5	4.0	4.0
Guinea	3.0	2.8	3.0	2.3	3.0	2.5	3.5	2.5	2.5	2.0
Guinea-Bissau	2.6	2.6	1.8	2.2	2.0	2.5	2.5	2.5	1.0	1.5
Kenya	3.6	3.7	4.0	4.2	4.0	4.5	4.0	4.0	4.0	4.0
Lesotho	3.5	3.5	4.0	4.0	4.0	4.0	4.0	4.0	4.0	4.0
Liberia[d]	..	2.8	..	3.2	..	3.5	..	3.5	..	2.5
Madagascar	3.7	3.5	3.8	3.7	4.0	4.0	3.5	3.0	4.0	4.0
Malawi	3.4	3.4	3.3	3.2	3.5	3.0	3.5	3.5	3.0	3.0
Mali	3.7	3.7	4.3	4.3	4.5	4.5	4.0	4.0	4.5	4.5
Mauritania	3.3	3.2	3.5	3.2	3.5	3.5	3.0	2.5	4.0	3.5
Mauritius[c]	..	..	..	..	..	..	..	..	..	..
Mozambique	3.7	3.7	4.3	4.5	4.5	4.5	4.0	4.5	4.5	4.5
Namibia[c]	..	..	..	..	..	..	..	..	..	..
Niger	3.3	3.3	3.7	3.8	4.0	4.0	3.5	3.5	3.5	4.0
Nigeria	3.4	3.5	4.3	4.3	4.0	4.0	4.5	4.5	4.5	4.5
Rwanda	3.7	3.8	3.8	3.8	4.0	4.0	4.0	4.0	3.5	3.5
São Tomé and Príncipe	3.0	2.9	2.8	2.8	3.0	3.0	3.0	3.0	2.5	2.5
Senegal	3.6	3.7	3.8	4.0	4.0	4.0	3.5	4.0	4.0	4.0
Seychelles[c]	..	..	..	..	..	..	..	..	..	..
Sierra Leone	3.1	3.2	3.7	3.7	4.0	4.0	3.5	3.5	3.5	3.5
Somalia[d]	..	..	..	..	..	..	..	..	..	..
South Africa[c]	..	..	..	..	..	..	..	..	..	..
Sudan	2.5	2.5	2.7	2.7	3.5	3.5	3.0	3.0	1.5	1.5
Swaziland[c]	..	..	..	..	..	..	..	..	..	..
Tanzania	3.8	3.8	4.3	4.3	4.5	4.5	4.5	4.5	4.0	4.0
Togo	2.7	2.8	2.7	2.8	3.0	3.0	3.0	3.0	2.0	2.5
Uganda	3.9	3.9	4.5	4.5	4.5	4.5	4.5	4.5	4.5	4.5
Zambia	3.5	3.4	3.7	3.5	4.0	4.0	3.5	3.0	3.5	3.5
Zimbabwe	1.4	1.9	1.0	1.7	1.0	2.0	1.0	2.0	1.0	1.0
NORTH AFRICA										
Algeria[c]	..	..	..	..	..	..	..	..	..	..
Egypt, Arab Rep.[c]	..	..	..	..	..	..	..	..	..	..
Libya[c]	..	..	..	..	..	..	..	..	..	..
Morocco[c]	..	..	..	..	..	..	..	..	..	..
Tunisia[c]	..	..	..	..	..	..	..	..	..	..

Structural policies							
Average[b]		Trade		Financial sector		Business regulatory environment	
2008	2009	2008	2009	2008	2009	2008	2009
3.2	3.2	3.7	3.7	3.0	3.0	3.1	3.1
2.8	2.8	4.0	4.0	2.5	2.5	2.0	2.0
3.7	3.7	4.0	4.0	3.5	3.5	3.5	3.5
..	..	..	..	..	..	..	..
3.5	3.5	4.0	4.0	3.0	3.0	3.5	3.5
2.8	3.0	3.5	4.0	2.5	2.5	2.5	2.5
3.2	3.2	3.5	3.5	3.0	3.0	3.0	3.0
3.8	3.8	4.0	4.0	4.0	4.0	3.5	3.5
2.7	2.7	3.5	3.5	2.5	2.5	2.0	2.0
2.8	2.8	3.0	3.0	3.0	3.0	2.5	2.5
2.7	2.7	3.0	3.0	2.5	2.5	2.5	2.5
2.7	2.5	4.0	3.5	2.0	2.0	2.0	2.0
2.8	3.0	3.5	3.5	2.5	3.0	2.5	2.5
3.3	3.3	4.0	4.0	3.0	3.0	3.0	3.0
3.7	3.7	4.0	4.0	3.5	3.5	3.5	3.5
..	..	..	..	..	..	..	..
1.5	1.5	1.5	1.5	1.0	1.0	2.0	2.0
3.2	3.2	3.0	3.0	3.0	3.0	3.5	3.5
..	..	..	..	..	..	..	..
3.3	3.3	3.5	3.5	3.0	3.0	3.5	3.5
4.0	4.0	4.0	4.0	4.0	4.0	4.0	4.0
3.3	3.3	4.0	4.0	3.0	3.0	3.0	3.0
3.2	3.2	4.0	4.0	3.0	3.0	2.5	2.5
3.8	4.0	4.0	4.0	3.5	4.0	4.0	4.0
3.3	3.3	3.5	3.5	3.5	3.5	3.0	3.0
..	2.8	..	3.0	..	2.5	..	3.0
3.5	3.5	4.0	4.0	3.0	3.0	3.5	3.5
3.5	3.5	4.0	4.0	3.0	3.0	3.5	3.5
3.5	3.5	4.0	4.0	3.0	3.0	3.5	3.5
3.3	3.3	4.0	4.0	2.5	2.5	3.5	3.5
..	..	..	..	..	..	..	..
3.7	3.7	4.5	4.5	3.5	3.5	3.0	3.0
..	..	..	..	..	..	..	..
3.3	3.3	4.0	4.0	3.0	3.0	3.0	3.0
3.3	3.5	3.5	3.5	3.5	3.5	3.0	3.5
3.5	3.8	3.5	4.0	3.5	3.5	3.5	4.0
3.2	3.0	4.0	4.0	2.5	2.5	3.0	2.5
3.8	3.8	4.0	4.0	3.5	3.5	4.0	4.0
..	..	..	..	..	..	..	..
3.2	3.2	3.5	3.5	3.0	3.0	3.0	3.0
..	..	..	..	..	..	..	..
..	..	..	..	..	..	..	..
2.7	2.7	2.5	2.5	2.5	2.5	3.0	3.0
..	..	..	..	..	..	..	..
3.8	3.8	4.0	4.0	4.0	4.0	3.5	3.5
3.2	3.2	4.0	4.0	2.5	2.5	3.0	3.0
3.8	3.8	4.0	4.0	3.5	3.5	4.0	4.0
3.7	3.5	4.0	4.0	3.5	3.5	3.5	3.0
1.5	2.2	2.0	3.0	1.0	1.5	1.5	2.0
..	..	..	..	..	..	..	..
..	..	..	..	..	..	..	..
..	..	..	..	..	..	..	..
..	..	..	..	..	..	..	..
..	..	..	..	..	..	..	..

(continued)

Table 12.5 Country Policy and Institutional Assessment ratings (continued)

	Policies for social inclusion and equity											
	Average[b]		Gender equality		Equity of public resource use		Building human resources		Social protection and labor		Policies and institutions for environmental sustainability	
	2008	2009	2008	2009	2008	2009	2008	2009	2008	2009	2008	2009
SUB-SAHARAN AFRICA	3.1	3.1	3.2	3.2	3.2	3.2	3.3	3.3	3.0	3.0	2.9	2.9
Angola	2.7	2.9	3.0	3.5	2.5	2.5	2.5	2.5	2.5	3.0	3.0	3.0
Benin	3.3	3.3	3.5	3.5	3.0	3.0	3.5	3.5	3.0	3.0	3.5	3.5
Botswana[c]	..	..	..	..	..	..	..	..	..	..	..	..
Burkina Faso	3.6	3.6	3.5	3.5	4.0	4.0	3.5	3.5	3.5	3.5	3.5	3.5
Burundi	3.3	3.3	4.0	4.0	3.5	3.5	3.0	3.0	3.0	3.0	3.0	3.0
Cameroon	3.1	3.1	3.0	3.0	3.0	3.0	3.5	3.5	3.0	3.0	3.0	3.0
Cape Verde	4.3	4.3	4.5	4.5	4.5	4.5	4.5	4.5	4.5	4.5	3.5	3.5
Central African Republic	2.2	2.5	2.5	2.5	2.0	2.5	2.0	2.5	2.0	2.0	2.5	3.0
Chad	2.4	2.4	2.5	2.5	2.5	2.5	2.5	2.5	2.5	2.5	2.0	2.0
Comoros	2.5	2.6	3.0	3.0	2.5	2.5	2.5	3.0	2.5	2.5	2.0	2.0
Congo, Dem. Rep.	2.9	2.8	3.0	2.5	3.0	3.0	3.0	3.0	3.0	3.0	2.5	2.5
Congo, Rep.	2.7	2.7	3.0	3.0	2.5	2.5	3.0	3.0	2.5	2.5	2.5	2.5
Côte d'Ivoire	2.3	2.4	2.5	2.5	1.5	2.0	2.5	2.5	2.5	2.5	2.5	2.5
Djibouti	3.0	3.2	2.5	3.0	3.0	3.0	3.5	3.5	3.0	3.0	3.0	3.5
Equatorial Guinea[c]	..	..	..	..	..	..	..	..	..	..	..	..
Eritrea	3.0	2.8	3.5	3.5	3.0	2.5	3.5	3.5	3.0	2.5	2.0	2.0
Ethiopia	3.6	3.6	3.0	3.0	4.5	4.5	4.0	4.0	3.5	3.5	3.0	3.0
Gabon[c]	..	..	..	..	..	..	..	..	..	..	..	..
Gambia, The	3.2	3.3	3.5	3.5	3.0	3.5	3.5	3.5	2.5	2.5	3.5	3.5
Ghana	4.0	3.9	4.0	4.0	4.0	4.0	4.5	4.5	4.0	3.5	3.5	3.5
Guinea	3.0	3.0	3.5	3.5	3.0	3.0	3.0	3.0	3.0	3.0	2.5	2.5
Guinea-Bissau	2.6	2.5	2.5	2.5	3.0	3.0	2.5	2.0	2.5	2.5	2.5	2.5
Kenya	3.2	3.5	3.0	3.0	3.0	3.5	3.5	4.0	3.0	3.5	3.5	3.5
Lesotho	3.3	3.3	4.0	4.0	3.0	3.0	3.5	3.5	3.0	3.0	3.0	3.0
Liberia[d]	..	2.5	..	2.5	..	3.0	..	2.5	..	2.5	..	2.0
Madagascar	3.7	3.6	3.5	3.5	4.0	4.0	3.5	3.5	3.5	3.5	4.0	3.5
Malawi	3.4	3.5	3.5	3.5	3.5	3.5	3.0	3.5	3.5	3.5	3.5	3.5
Mali	3.4	3.4	3.5	3.5	3.5	3.5	3.5	3.5	3.5	3.5	3.0	3.0
Mauritania	3.5	3.4	4.0	4.0	3.5	3.5	3.5	3.5	3.0	3.0	3.5	3.0
Mauritius[c]	..	..	..	..	..	..	..	..	..	..	..	..
Mozambique	3.4	3.3	3.5	3.5	3.5	3.5	4.0	3.5	3.0	3.0	3.0	3.0
Namibia[c]	..	..	..	..	..	..	..	..	..	..	..	..
Niger	3.0	3.1	2.5	2.5	3.5	3.5	3.0	3.5	3.0	3.0	3.0	3.0
Nigeria	3.2	3.2	3.0	3.0	3.5	3.5	3.0	3.0	3.5	3.5	3.0	3.0
Rwanda	3.9	3.9	3.5	3.5	4.5	4.5	4.5	4.5	3.5	3.5	3.5	3.5
São Tomé and Príncipe	2.8	2.8	3.0	3.0	3.0	3.0	3.0	3.0	2.5	2.5	2.5	2.5
Senegal	3.4	3.4	3.5	3.5	3.5	3.5	3.5	3.5	3.0	3.0	3.5	3.5
Seychelles[c]	..	..	..	..	..	..	..	..	..	..	..	..
Sierra Leone	2.9	3.1	3.0	3.0	3.0	3.0	3.5	3.5	3.0	3.5	2.0	2.5
Somalia[d]	..	..	..	..	..	..	..	..	..	..	..	..
South Africa[c]	..	..	..	..	..	..	..	..	..	..	..	..
Sudan	2.3	2.3	2.0	2.0	2.5	2.5	2.5	2.5	2.5	2.5	2.0	2.0
Swaziland[c]	..	..	..	..	..	..	..	..	..	..	..	..
Tanzania	3.7	3.7	3.5	3.5	4.0	4.0	4.0	4.0	3.5	3.5	3.5	3.5
Togo	2.7	2.7	3.0	3.0	2.0	2.0	3.0	3.0	3.0	3.0	2.5	2.5
Uganda	3.8	3.8	3.5	3.5	4.0	4.0	4.0	4.0	3.5	3.5	4.0	4.0
Zambia	3.5	3.5	3.5	3.5	3.5	3.5	4.0	4.0	3.0	3.0	3.5	3.5
Zimbabwe	1.5	1.6	2.5	2.5	1.0	1.5	1.0	1.0	1.0	1.0	2.0	2.0
NORTH AFRICA												
Algeria[c]	..	..	..	..	..	..	..	..	..	..	..	..
Egypt, Arab Rep.[c]	..	..	..	..	..	..	..	..	..	..	..	..
Libya[c]	..	..	..	..	..	..	..	..	..	..	..	..
Morocco[c]	..	..	..	..	..	..	..	..	..	..	..	..
Tunisia[c]	..	..	..	..	..	..	..	..	..	..	..	..

Note: The rating scale for each indicator ranges from 1 (low) to 6 (high). The most recent external review of the CPIA ratings and methodology was in 2004.

a. Calculated as the average of the average ratings of each cluster.

b. All criteria are weighted equally.

c. Not an International Development Association (IDA) member.

d. Not rated in the IDA resource allocation index.

Public sector management and institutions

Average[b]		Property rights and rule-based governance		Quality of budgetary and financial management		Efficiency of revenue mobilization		Quality of public administration		Transparency, accountability, and corruption in public sector	
2008	2009	2008	2009	2008	2009	2008	2009	2008	2009	2008	2009
2.9	**3.0**	**2.8**	**2.8**	**3.0**	**3.0**	**3.4**	**3.4**	**2.9**	**2.9**	**2.7**	**2.7**
2.4	2.4	2.0	2.0	2.5	2.5	2.5	2.5	2.5	2.5	2.5	2.5
3.3	3.3	3.0	3.0	3.5	3.5	3.5	3.5	3.0	3.0	3.5	3.5
..	..	..	..	..	..	..	..	..	..	..	..
3.5	3.7	3.5	3.5	4.0	4.5	3.5	3.5	3.5	3.5	3.0	3.5
2.6	2.6	2.5	2.5	3.0	3.0	3.0	3.0	2.5	2.5	2.0	2.0
2.9	2.9	2.5	2.5	3.0	3.0	3.5	3.5	3.0	3.0	2.5	2.5
4.0	4.0	4.0	4.0	4.0	4.0	3.5	3.5	4.0	4.0	4.5	4.5
2.3	2.4	2.0	2.0	2.0	2.5	2.5	2.5	2.5	2.5	2.5	2.5
2.2	2.2	2.0	2.0	2.0	2.0	2.5	2.5	2.5	2.5	2.0	2.0
2.2	2.4	2.5	2.5	1.5	2.0	2.5	2.5	2.0	2.5	2.5	2.5
2.2	2.2	2.0	2.0	2.5	2.5	2.5	2.5	2.0	2.0	2.0	2.0
2.6	2.6	2.5	2.5	2.5	2.5	3.0	3.0	2.5	2.5	2.5	2.5
2.5	2.6	2.0	2.0	2.0	2.5	4.0	4.0	2.0	2.0	2.5	2.5
2.8	2.8	2.5	2.5	3.0	3.0	3.5	3.5	2.5	2.5	2.5	2.5
..	..	..	..	..	..	..	..	..	..	..	..
2.7	2.7	2.5	2.5	2.5	2.5	3.5	3.5	3.0	3.0	2.0	2.0
3.3	3.2	3.0	3.0	4.0	3.5	4.0	3.5	3.0	3.5	2.5	2.5
..	..	..	..	..	..	..	..	..	..	..	..
2.9	2.9	3.0	3.0	3.0	3.0	3.5	3.5	3.0	3.0	2.0	2.0
3.9	3.8	3.5	3.5	4.0	3.5	4.5	4.5	3.5	3.5	4.0	4.0
2.6	2.6	2.0	2.0	3.0	3.0	3.0	3.0	3.0	3.0	2.0	2.0
2.6	2.6	2.5	2.5	2.5	2.5	3.0	3.0	2.5	2.5	2.5	2.5
3.3	3.3	2.5	2.5	3.5	3.5	4.0	4.0	3.5	3.5	3.0	3.0
3.4	3.4	3.5	3.5	3.0	3.0	4.0	4.0	3.0	3.0	3.5	3.5
..	2.8	..	2.5	..	2.5	..	3.5	..	2.5	..	3.0
3.6	3.3	3.5	3.5	3.5	3.0	4.0	4.0	3.5	3.5	3.5	2.5
3.4	3.4	3.5	3.5	3.0	3.0	4.0	4.0	3.5	3.5	3.0	3.0
3.4	3.4	3.5	3.5	3.5	3.5	3.5	3.5	3.0	3.0	3.5	3.5
3.0	3.0	3.0	3.0	3.0	3.0	3.5	3.5	3.0	3.0	2.5	2.5
..	..	..	..	..	..	..	..	..	..	..	..
3.3	3.4	3.0	3.0	3.5	4.0	4.0	4.0	3.0	3.0	3.0	3.0
..	..	..	..	..	..	..	..	..	..	..	..
3.2	3.1	3.0	3.0	3.5	3.5	3.5	3.5	3.0	3.0	3.0	2.5
2.9	2.9	2.5	2.5	3.0	3.0	3.0	3.0	3.0	3.0	3.0	3.0
3.5	3.5	3.0	3.0	4.0	4.0	3.5	3.5	3.5	3.5	3.5	3.5
3.1	3.1	2.5	2.5	3.0	3.0	3.5	3.5	3.0	3.0	3.5	3.5
3.4	3.4	3.5	3.5	3.0	3.0	4.0	4.0	3.5	3.5	3.0	3.0
..	..	..	..	..	..	..	..	..	..	..	..
2.7	2.9	2.5	2.5	3.5	3.5	2.5	2.5	2.5	3.0	2.5	3.0
..	..	..	..	..	..	..	..	..	..	..	..
..	..	..	..	..	..	..	..	..	..	..	..
2.3	2.2	2.0	2.0	2.0	2.0	3.0	3.0	2.5	2.5	2.0	1.5
..	..	..	..	..	..	..	..	..	..	..	..
3.5	3.5	3.5	3.5	3.5	3.5	4.0	4.0	3.5	3.5	3.0	3.0
2.2	2.4	2.5	2.5	2.0	2.5	2.5	3.0	2.0	2.0	2.0	2.0
3.4	3.3	3.5	3.5	4.0	4.0	3.5	3.5	3.0	3.0	3.0	2.5
3.2	3.2	3.0	3.0	3.5	3.5	3.5	3.5	3.0	3.0	3.0	3.0
1.6	2.0	1.0	1.5	1.5	2.0	3.5	3.5	1.0	1.5	1.0	1.5
..	..	..	..	..	..	..	..	..	..	..	..
..	..	..	..	..	..	..	..	..	..	..	..
..	..	..	..	..	..	..	..	..	..	..	..
..	..	..	..	..	..	..	..	..	..	..	..
..	..	..	..	..	..	..	..	..	..	..	..

Table 12.6 Polity indicators

	Revised combined polity score (–10 strongly autocratic to 10 strongly democratic)			Institutionalized democracy (0 low to 10 high)			Institutionalized autocracy (0 low to 10 high)		
	1995	2000	2009	1995	2000	2009	1995	2000	2009
SUB-SAHARAN AFRICA									
Angola	–2.0	–3.0	–2.0	..	1.0	2.0	..	4.0	4.0
Benin	6.0	6.0	7.0	6.0	6.0	7.0	0.0	0.0	0.0
Botswana	7.0	8.0	8.0	7.0	8.0	8.0	0.0	0.0	0.0
Burkina Faso	–5.0	–3.0	0.0	0.0	0.0	2.0	5.0	3.0	2.0
Burundi	0.0	–1.0	6.0	..	1.0	7.0	..	2.0	1.0
Cameroon	–4.0	–4.0	–4.0	1.0	1.0	1.0	5.0	5.0	5.0
Cape Verde	..	..	..	..	..	..	..	..	..
Central African Republic	5.0	5.0	–1.0	5.0	5.0	1.0	0.0	0.0	2.0
Chad	–4.0	–2.0	–2.0	0.0	1.0	1.0	4.0	3.0	3.0
Comoros	0.0	–1.0	9.0	..	1.0	9.0	..	2.0	0.0
Congo, Dem. Rep.	0.0	0.0	5.0	..	..	6.0	..	..	1.0
Congo, Rep.	5.0	–6.0	–4.0	6.0	0.0	0.0	1.0	6.0	4.0
Côte d'Ivoire	–6.0	4.0	0.0	0.0	5.0	..	6.0	1.0	..
Djibouti	–7.0	2.0	2.0	0.0	3.0	3.0	7.0	1.0	1.0
Equatorial Guinea	–5.0	–5.0	–5.0	0.0	0.0	0.0	5.0	5.0	5.0
Eritrea	–6.0	–6.0	–7.0	0.0	0.0	0.0	6.0	6.0	7.0
Ethiopia	1.0	1.0	1.0	3.0	3.0	3.0	2.0	2.0	2.0
Gabon	–4.0	–4.0	3.0	0.0	0.0	4.0	4.0	4.0	1.0
Gambia, The	–7.0	–5.0	–5.0	0.0	0.0	0.0	7.0	5.0	5.0
Ghana	–1.0	2.0	8.0	1.0	3.0	8.0	2.0	1.0	0.0
Guinea	–1.0	–1.0	–1.0	1.0	1.0	1.0	2.0	2.0	2.0
Guinea-Bissau	5.0	5.0	6.0	5.0	5.0	7.0	0.0	0.0	1.0
Kenya	–5.0	–2.0	7.0	0.0	2.0	7.0	5.0	4.0	0.0
Lesotho	8.0	4.0	8.0	8.0	..	8.0	0.0	..	0.0
Liberia	0.0	0.0	6.0	..	3.0	7.0	..	3.0	1.0
Madagascar	9.0	7.0	0.0	9.0	7.0	3.0	0.0	0.0	3.0
Malawi	6.0	6.0	6.0	6.0	6.0	6.0	0.0	0.0	0.0
Mali	7.0	6.0	7.0	7.0	6.0	7.0	0.0	0.0	0.0
Mauritania	–6.0	–6.0	–2.0	0.0	0.0	0.0	6.0	6.0	2.0
Mauritius	10.0	10.0	10.0	10.0	10.0	10.0	0.0	0.0	0.0
Mozambique	5.0	5.0	5.0	5.0	5.0	5.0	0.0	0.0	0.0
Namibia	6.0	6.0	6.0	6.0	6.0	6.0	0.0	0.0	0.0
Niger	8.0	5.0	–3.0	8.0	6.0	0.0	0.0	1.0	3.0
Nigeria	–6.0	4.0	4.0	0.0	4.0	4.0	6.0	0.0	0.0
Rwanda	–6.0	–4.0	–3.0	0.0	0.0	0.0	6.0	4.0	3.0
São Tomé and Principe	..	..	..	..	..	..	..	..	..
Senegal	–1.0	8.0	7.0	2.0	8.0	7.0	3.0	0.0	0.0
Seychelles	..	..	..	..	..	..	..	..	..
Sierra Leone	–7.0	0.0	7.0	0.0	..	8.0	7.0	..	1.0
Somalia	0.0	0.0	0.0	..	..	..	..	..	..
South Africa	9.0	9.0	9.0	9.0	9.0	9.0	0.0	0.0	0.0
Sudan	–7.0	–7.0	–4.0	0.0	0.0	0.0	7.0	7.0	4.0
Swaziland	–9.0	–9.0	–9.0	0.0	0.0	0.0	9.0	9.0	9.0
Tanzania	–1.0	–1.0	–1.0	2.0	2.0	2.0	3.0	3.0	3.0
Togo	–2.0	–2.0	–4.0	1.0	1.0	1.0	3.0	3.0	5.0
Uganda	–4.0	–4.0	–1.0	0.0	0.0	1.0	4.0	4.0	2.0
Zambia	6.0	1.0	7.0	6.0	3.0	7.0	0.0	2.0	0.0
Zimbabwe	–6.0	–3.0	1.0	0.0	1.0	3.0	6.0	4.0	2.0
NORTH AFRICA									
Algeria	–3.0	–3.0	2.0	1.0	1.0	3.0	4.0	4.0	1.0
Egypt, Arab Rep.	–6.0	–6.0	–3.0	0.0	0.0	1.0	6.0	6.0	4.0
Libya	–7.0	–7.0	–7.0	0.0	0.0	0.0	7.0	7.0	7.0
Morocco	–7.0	–6.0	–6.0	0.0	0.0	0.0	7.0	6.0	6.0
Tunisia	–3.0	–3.0	–4.0	1.0	1.0	1.0	4.0	4.0	5.0

Technical notes

1. Basic indicators

TABLE 1.1. BASIC INDICATORS

Population is total population based on the de facto definition of population, which counts all residents regardless of legal status or citizenship—except for refugees not permanently settled in the country of asylum, who are generally considered part of the population of their country of origin. The values shown are midyear estimates.

Population growth rate for year *t* is the exponential rate of growth of midyear population from year *t*–1 to *t*, expressed as a percentage. Population is based on the de facto definition of population, which counts all residents regardless of legal status or citizenship—except for refugees not permanently settled in the country of asylum, who are generally considered part of the population of the country of origin.

Land area is the land surface area of a country, excluding inland waters, national claims to continental shelf, and exclusive economic zones.

Population density is midyear population divided by land area in square kilometers. Population is based on the de facto definition of population, which counts all residents regardless of legal status or citizenship—except for refugees not permanently settled in the country of asylum, who are generally considered part of the population of their country of origin. Land area is a country's total area, excluding area under inland water bodies, national claims to continental shelf, and exclusive economic zones. In most cases the definition of inland water bodies includes major rivers and lakes.

Gross national income (GNI) per capita, World Bank Atlas method, is GNI, calculated using the *World Bank Atlas* method (see box 1), divided by midyear population. It is similar in concept to GNI per capita in current prices, except that the use of three-year averages of exchange rates smooths out sharp fluctuations from year to year.

Gross domestic product (GDP) per capita is gross domestic product divided by midyear population. GDP is the sum of gross value added by all resident producers in the economy plus any product taxes and minus any subsidies not included in the value of the products. It is calculated without making deductions for depreciation of fabricated assets or for depletion and degradation of natural resources. Growth rates are in real terms and have been calculated by the least-squares method using constant 2000 exchange rates (box 2).

Life expectancy at birth is the number of years a newborn infant would live if prevailing patterns of mortality at the time of its birth were to remain the same throughout its life.

Under-five mortality rate is the probability that a newborn baby will die before reaching age 5, if subject to current age-specific mortality rates. The probability is expressed as a rate per 1,000.

Gini index is the most commonly used measure of inequality. The coefficient ranges from 0, which reflects complete equality, to 100, which indicates complete inequality (one person has all the income or consumption, all others have none). Graphically, the Gini index can be easily represented by the area between the Lorenz curve and the line of equality.

Adult literacy rate is the percentage of adults ages 15 and older who can, with understanding, read and write a short, simple statement on their everyday life.

Net official development assistance per capita is calculated by dividing net disbursements

Box 2 **Growth rates**

Growth rates are calculated as annual averages and represented as percentages. Except where noted, growth rates of values are computed from constant price series. Rates of change from one period to the next are calculated as proportional changes from the earlier period. Least squares growth rates are used wherever there is a sufficiently long time series to permit a reliable calculation. No growth rate is calculated if more than half the observations in a period are missing. The least squares growth rate, *r*, is estimated by fitting a linear regression trend line to the logarithmic annual values of the variable in the relevant period. The regression equation takes the form

$$\ln X_{t = a + bt}$$

which is equivalent to the logarithmic transformation of the compound growth equation,

$$X_t = X_o(1 + r)^2$$

In this equation X is the variable, t is time, and $a = \ln X_o$ and $b = \ln(1 + r)$ are parameters to be estimated. If b^* is the least squares estimate of b, the average annual growth rate, r, is obtained as $[\exp(b^*) - 1]$ multiplied by 100 for expression as a percentage. The calculated growth rate is an average rate that is representative of the available observations over the entire period. It does not necessarily match the actual growth rate between any two periods.

of loans and grants from all official sources on concessional financial terms by midyear population. This indicator shows the importance of aid flows in sustaining per capita income and consumption levels, although exchange rate fluctuations, the actual rise of aid flows, and other factors vary across countries and over time.

Regional aggregates for GNI per capita, GDP per capita, life expectancy at birth, and adult literacy rates are weighted by population.

Source: Data on population and life expectancy are from the United Nations Population Division *World Population Prospects: The 2008 Revision*, census reports and other statistical publications from national statistical offices, Eurostat *Demographic Statistics*, Secretariat of the Pacific Community Statistics and Demography Programme, U.S. Census Bureau International Database, and World Bank estimates based on data from these sources as well as household surveys conducted by national agencies, Macro International, the U.S. Centers for Disease Control and Prevention, and refugees statistics from the United Nations High Commissioner for Refugees. Data on land are from Food and Agriculture Organization electronic files and website. Data on GNI per capita and GDP per capita are from World Bank national accounts data and Organisation for Economic Co-operation and Development (OECD) national accounts data files. Data on under-five mortality are from the Inter-agency Group for Child Mortality Estimation *Level & Trends in Child Mortality: Report 2010.* Data on Gini index for developing countries are from the World Bank Development Research Group and are based on primary household survey data obtained from government statistical agencies and World Bank country departments (http://iresearch.worldbank.org/PovcalNet/jsp/index.jsp) and for high-income economies are from the Luxembourg Income Study database. Data on literacy are from United Nations Educational, Scientific and Cultural Organization Institute for Statistics. Data on aid flows are from the OECD *Geographic Distribution of Aid Flows to Developing Countries*.

2. National and fiscal accounts

Africa Development Indicators uses the 1993 System of National Accounts (1993 SNA) to compile national accounts data. Botswana, Cameroon, Chad, the Democratic Republic of the Congo, Ethiopia, Kenya, Lesotho, Namibia, Senegal, Sierra Leone, and South Africa report data using the 1993 SNA. Although more countries are adopting the 1993 SNA, many still follow the 1968 SNA, and some low-income countries use concepts from the 1953 SNA.

Reporting periods: For most economies the fiscal year is concurrent with the calendar year. However, there are few countries whose ending date reported is for the fiscal year of the central government, though fiscal years for other government levels and reporting years for statistical surveys may differ. Reporting end dates are as follows for the following countries: Botswana (June 30); Egypt (June 30), Ethiopia (July 7), Gambia, The (June 30), Kenya (June 30), Lesotho (March 31), Malawi (March 31),

Most of the data used to compute the indicators in this volume of *Africa Development Indicators* come from the African country national statistical systems, the only primary source of the statistics related to country economic, social, and environmental issues. While international and specialized institutions may review, make comparable, and estimate missing values, the true sources of the data are the national statistical systems, and the data coverage and quality improvement depend on strengthening their capacity.

National statistical systems

In general a national statistical system consists of a central statistical office, a national office or institute of statistics, and its regional agencies, sectors' statistical units in key ministries (finance, education, health, transport, agriculture), and a Central Bank statistical unit. Some large programs may also have specialized statistical units.

Africa's national statistical systems were designed on Europe's model, ruled by the same principles drafted in a statistical law—a law that ensures the independence of the system and the essence of the role it plays within or together with the government (produce and centralize, process, publish and disseminate basic information needed for administrative management). In the past most African countries reviewed and updated their statistical laws to address new aspects of statistical information.

The system is usually coordinated by a national council of statistics, a multisector body at the ministerial level that approves the overall strategies and policies related to the statistical operations in the country as well as the yearly action plan for statistical production. It meets once or twice a year. In most countries, these councils have been weak institutions incapable of playing their central role of coordination and quality control. It seems, however, that in recent years, thanks to PARIS21's new National Strategy for the Development of Statistics process and STATCAP, they have been able to play a stronger role in both developing and coordinating national statistical systems.

The major element of the national statistical system is the central statistical office. In the context of weak systems, these offices tend to concentrate all national production, often substituting the sector departments. However, that does not preclude most of these offices from facing incredible difficulties that hamper their power to produce statistics in a timely and accurate manner. Most African central statistical offices now have websites where the core of their production is displayed (see table).

In more and more countries, statistical training is provided by national schools sometimes linked with central statistical offices, while regional schools of statistics train statisticians at high and intermediate levels. As a result, most central statistical offices are staffed with trained statisticians, but a critical mass of statisticians is yet to be reached to support regular statistical production. In addition, there is a concentration at the central statistical office, while in general, sector departments of statistics lack trained statisticians.

National Strategies for the Development of Statistics

The National Strategy for the Development of Statistics approach developed by PARIS21 and endorsed by the Marrakech Action Plan for Statistics in 2004 gives an efficient tool to organize the development of national statistical systems. If the Poverty Reduction Strategy Paper is the vehicle for coordination and prioritization for national development planning in the region, the National Strategy for the Development of Statistics is the equivalent for statistical systems. Based on the principles of strategic management used in statistical systems in developed countries, the strategy's guidelines were discussed and reviewed by a number of managers of statistical offices in developing countries and have taken into account previous attempts of statistical planning.

A National Strategy for the Development of Statistics provides a guide for strengthening statistical capacity across the entire national statistical system. The strategy envisages where the national statistical systems should be in 5–10 years and sets milestones for getting there. It presents a comprehensive and unified framework for continual assessment of evolving user needs and priorities for statistics and for building the capacity needed to meet these needs in a more coordinated, synergistic, and efficient manner. It also provides a framework for mobilizing, harnessing, and leveraging resources (both national and international) and a basis for effective and results-oriented strategic management of the national statistical system.

The PARIS21 Report (March 2011) on National Strategy for the Development of Statistics status for International Development Association countries shows that 22 countries are currently implementing a strategy and that 15 are designing a strategy or awaiting their adoption by country authorities.

Role of partners

For a long time donors have substituted government at both the demand and financial levels and provided methodological support for the adoption of up to date techniques and measurements. According to the 2010 Partner Report on Support to Statistics, Africa received nearly half of total statistical support, equivalent to $716 million in commitments, of which 9 countries (Burkina Faso, Ethiopia, Kenya, Malawi, Mali, Mozambique, Nigeria, Sudan, and Tanzania) received a little less than half of this amount.

Challenges in supporting national capacity

After years of decline, the capacity of African countries to produce and disseminate good quality, reliable, relevant, and timely statistics has improved due in part to an increase in the demand for data. However, this demand has rarely been used to build a sustainable statistical capacity. Data production from some administrative sources and surveys has improved, but large gaps remain in national accounts, household surveys, and most administrative data. If data dissemination has progressed with the development of national data archives, very few countries have adopted data

(continued)

access policies. The use of data by nationals, the raison d'être of statistical capacity building, is still very limited.

In the past, the policy environment has been friendlier to statistical development, but progress remains precarious:

- The industry of indicators has flourished with Poverty Reduction Strategy/Millennium Development Goals monitoring and evaluation, but availability of good statistics has rarely been cited as a condition for transparency, accountability, and good governance in development policies. Hence, the commitment of governments continues to be fragile.
- Most of the countries have designed National Strategies for the Development of Statistics, but implementation of action programs is still meager. National statistical offices have gained more autonomy despite the resistance to enforcing new laws or taking advantage of new institutional arrangements.
- For more than 20 years, Africa has benefitted from a training center network; however, trained statisticians are not being adequately hired by statistical offices due to budgetary constraints.
- Statistical knowledge and new techniques are available but transferred to African statisticians in ad hoc and uncoordinated manners, resulting in a permanent resort to technical assistance. Some attempts have been made to address this—but in an ad hoc manner and without a systematic capacity-building program approach.
- Finally, despite recent efforts, inadequate financing of statistical operations remains the major constraint to statistical development.

References

PARIS21. 2004. "A Guide to Designing a National Strategy for the Development of Statistics (NSDS)." PARIS21 Secretariat, Paris.

———. 2010. "Partner Report on Support to Statistics (PRESS)." PARIS21 Secretariat, Paris.

———. 2011. *National Strategies for the Development of Statistics Progress Report: NSDS Summary Table for IDA and Lower Middle Income Countries.* Paris: PARIS21 Secretariat.

World Bank. 2004. "Better Data for Better Results: An Action Plan for Improving Development Statistics." Paper presented at the Second International Roundtable on Managing for Development Results, February 4–5, Marrakech, Morocco.

Country	Statistical office website
Angola	
Benin	www.insae-bj.org
Botswana	www.cso.gov.bw/
Burkina Faso	www.insd.bf/fr/
Burundi	www.isteebu.bi/
Cameroon	www.statistics-cameroon.org
Cape Verde	www.ine.cv/
Central African Republic	www.stat-centrafrique.com/
Chad	www.inseed-tchad.org
Comoros	
Congo, Dem. Rep.	www.ins.cd/
Congo, Rep.	www.cnsee.org
Côte d'Ivoire	www.ins.ci/
Equatorial Guinea	www.dgecnstat-ge.org
Eritrea	
Ethiopia	www.csa.gov.et/
Gabon	www.stat-gabon.org
Gambia	www.gambia.gm/Statistics/
Ghana	www.statsghana.gov.gh/
Guinea	www.stat-guinee.org
Guinea-Bissau	www.stat-guinebissau.com/
Kenya	www.knbs.or.ke/
Lesotho	www.bos.gov.ls/
Liberia	www.lisgis.org
Madagascar	www.instat.mg/
Malawi	www.nso.malawi.net/
Mali	http://instat.gov.ml/
Mauritania	www.ons.mr/
Mauritius	www.gov.mu/portal/site/cso
Mozambique	www.ine.gov.mz/
Namibia	www.npc.gov.na/cbs/
Niger	www.stat-niger.org
Nigeria	www.nigerianstat.gov.ng/
Rwanda	www.statistics.gov.rw/
São Tomé and Príncipe	www.ine.st/
Senegal	www.ansd.sn/
Seychelles	www.nsb.gov.sc/
Sierra Leone	www.statistics.sl/
Somalia	
South Africa	www.statssa.gov.za/
South Sudan	http://ssccse.org
Sudan	www.cbs.gov.sd/
Swaziland	www.gov.sz/
Tanzania	www.nbs.go.tz/
Togo	www.stat-togo.org
Uganda	www.ubos.org
Zambia	www.zamstats.gov.zm/
Zimbabwe	www.zimstat.co.zw
Total	**44**

Namibia (March 31), Sierra Leone (June 30), South Africa (March 31), Swaziland (March 31), Uganda (June 30), and Zimbabwe (June 30). The reporting period for national accounts data is either calendar year or fiscal year basis. Most economies report national accounts and balance of payments data using calendar years, but some report on fiscal years. Fiscal year data are assigned to the calendar year that contains the larger share of the fiscal year. If a country's fiscal year ends before June 30, data are shown in that first calendar year of the fiscal year; if the fiscal year ends on or after June 30, data are shown in the second calendar year of the fiscal year. Balance of payments data are reported by calendar year.

Revisions to national accounts data: National accounts data are revised by national statistical offices when methodologies change or data sources improve. This in turn means that Africa Development Indicators national accounts data are also revised when data sources change.

- *Ghana:* The Ghana Statistical Service revised Ghana's national accounts series from 1993 to 2006. New GDP data are about 60 percent higher than previously reported and incorporate improved data sources and methodology.
- *Guinea-Bissau:* National accounts data for 2003–09 are revised. The new data have broader coverage of all sectors of the economy, and the new base year is 2005. GDP in current prices is on average 89 percent higher than previous estimates.
- *Namibia:* The Central Bureau of Statistics has revised national accounts data for 2000–07. An expanded survey has resulted in a substantial upward adjustment to estimates of output, particularly in mining, services, and manufacturing. The constant price series were rebased from 1995 to 2004 prices. GDP in current prices averages 14 percent higher than previous estimates.
- *South Africa:* The base year has been changed from 2000 to 2005. Data are revised from 2000 onward with official government data.

National currencies: As of January 2009, multiple hard currencies such as the rand, pound sterling, euro, and U.S. dollar are in use in Zimbabwe. However, data are reported in U.S. dollars, the most frequently used currency.

Table 2.1. Gross domestic product, nominal

Gross domestic product (GDP), nominal, is the sum of gross value added by all resident producers in the economy plus any product taxes and minus any subsidies not included in the value of the products. It is calculated without making deductions for depreciation of fabricated assets or for depletion and degradation of natural resources. GDP figures are shown at market prices (also known as purchaser values) and converted from domestic currencies using single-year official exchange rates. For the few countries where the official exchange rate does not reflect the rate effectively applied to actual foreign exchange transactions, an alternative conversion factor is used.

The sum of the components of GDP by industrial origin (presented here as value added) will not normally equal total GDP for several reasons. First, components of GDP by expenditure are individually rescaled and summed to provide a partially rebased series for total GDP. Second, total GDP is shown at purchaser value, while value added components are conventionally reported at producer prices. As explained above, purchaser values exclude net indirect taxes, while producer prices include indirect taxes. Third, certain items, such as imputed bank charges, are added in total GDP.

Source: World Bank and Organisation for Economic Co-operation and Development national accounts data.

Table 2.2. Gross domestic product, real

Gross domestic product (GDP), real, is obtained by converting national currency GDP series to U.S. dollars using constant 2000 exchange rates. For countries where the official exchange rate does not effectively reflect the rate applied to actual foreign exchange transactions, an alternative currency conversion factor has been used. Growth rates are in real terms and calculated by the least-squares method using constant 2000 exchange rates (see box 2).

Sub-Saharan Africa in 2011 has an unprecedented opportunity for transformation and sustained growth. Until the global economic crisis, Africa's economy had been growing 5 percent a year for a decade. Growth declined in 2009 but rebounded in 2010, thanks mainly to prudent macroeconomic policies (figure 1). Progress toward the Millennium Development Goals has been fast enough that several countries (Ethiopia, Ghana, and Malawi) are likely to achieve most of the goals. Africa's private sector is increasingly attracting investment, and—if policymakers' response to the global crisis is a guide—the climate for market-oriented, pro-poor reforms is robust.

Figure 1 Growth and poverty reduction in Africa

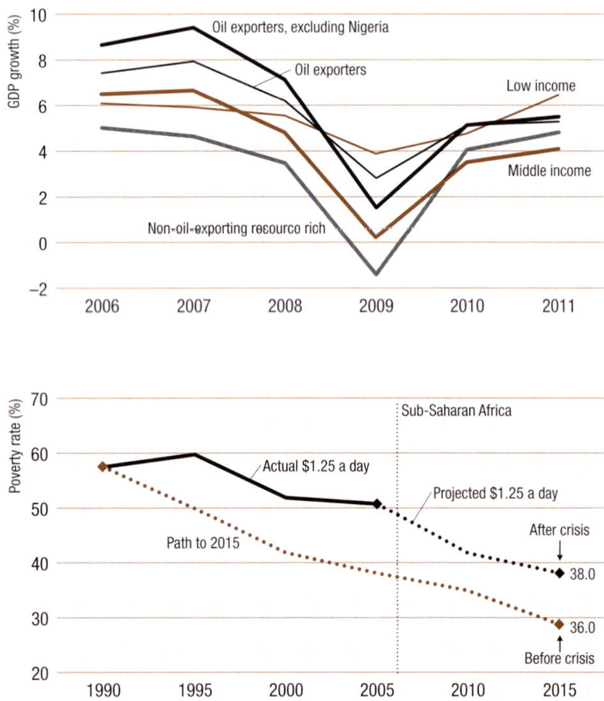

But Africa continues to face long-term development challenges: dependence on a few primary commodities, low human capital, weak governance, low youth employment, low empowerment of women, and climate change, to name a few. If we can address these challenges, Africa could be on the brink of a takeoff, much like China 30 years ago and India 20 years ago.

To that end, the World Bank's strategy for Africa has two pillars and a foundation. The two pillars are:

- *Competitiveness and employment.* The strategy seeks to help diversify African countries' exports and generate productive employment, especially for the 7–10 million young people entering the labor force every year. The strategy will require a mix of proactive government policies that target sectors—which helped Kenya's cut flowers and Mali's mangoes—with more "neutral" policies, including infrastructure and skill-building, that enable different industries to flourish, as shown by the dynamic growth of the information, communications, and technology sector in Africa.
- *Vulnerability and resilience.* Africa's poor are subject to a series of shocks that conspire to keep them poor: macroeconomic shocks; health shocks such as malaria or HIV/AIDS; natural disasters, which are likely to increase with climate change; and conflict and political violence. The strategy seeks to build resilience to these shocks by, for example, improving macroeconomic policies, promoting public health interventions, adapting to the effects of climate change with greater use of irrigation and water management, and strengthening institutions of resource-sharing and consensus-building. The strategy will also support countries in the event of a shock through, for instance, health insurance and safety net programs, such as Rwanda's nearly universal insurance scheme or Ethiopia's public works program.

The foundation of the strategy is *governance and public sector capacity.* Of Africa's $48 billion infrastructure deficit, $17 billion can be filled by efficiency improvements in the management of infrastructure. Teachers in public primary schools in Uganda are absent about 20 percent of the time. Yet governance problems—vested interests—stand in the way of these efficiency gains. The strategy will help address these problems by approaching governance from both the demand and supply sides. We aim to strengthen citizen voice using data, knowledge, and the power of information, communications, and technology so that they can demand good governance from their leaders. On the supply side, we will continue to strengthen the capacity of the public sector, focusing on incentives within the civil service.

The World Bank will implement the strategy using its three instruments—finance, knowledge, and partnerships—but we will reverse the order. The first instrument is partnership—with African governments, the domestic and international private sector, civil society, and development partners. We will tailor our interventions depending on what others are doing. Since Rwanda and Niger receive substantial amounts of money for "vertical health programs" such as HIV/AIDS or malaria, the Bank uses its resources to help these countries improve their health systems. The second instrument is knowledge, which we will use to promote a more evidence-based public debate. Studies on leakage of public funds, teacher absenteeism, and student learning outcomes, by informing the public about the quality of public services, have stimulated a vigorous debate, which has brought about change. The third instrument, finance, will be used as a source of leveraging. How can we turn a $500 million lending envelope to a country into $3 billion in external resources to that country, just as the Bujagali dam in Uganda used $150 million of the Bank's IDA resources to crowd in $650 million additional resources from public and private sources?

The strategy proposes a 10-year vision of a continent whose per capita income is 50 percent higher than today, whose poverty rate has fallen 12 percentage points, whose area includes at least 5 middle-income countries and 15 countries increasing agricultural productivity faster than 5 percent a year, and whose share of

Africa's future and the World Bank's support to it (continued)

world trade has doubled to 8 percent. To track progress towards these goals, the strategy has a three-tier results monitoring framework based on a results chain that links Africa's progress with the World Bank's contribution to those results with the use of World Bank instruments (figure 2).

Figure 2 The Africa strategy's three-tier results monitoring framework

Needless to say, this strategy is not without risks. The global economy could face another serious downturn, political violence could break out in parts of the continent, and we may lack the resources to carry out the plans. But the themes of the strategy, as well as the focus on partnerships—not to mention the palpable optimism on the continent—make us confident that Africa can seize this opportunity and realize its full potential ti sustain growth and reduce poverty.

References

World Bank. 2011. *Africa's Future and the World's Support to It.* Washington, DC: World Bank.

Source: World Bank and Organisation for Economic Co-operation and Development national accounts data.

TABLE 2.3. GROSS DOMESTIC PRODUCT GROWTH

Gross domestic product (GDP) growth is the average annual growth rate of real GDP (table 2.2) at market prices based on constant local currency. Aggregates are based on constant 2000 U.S. dollars.

Source: World Bank and Organisation for Economic Co-operation and Development national accounts data.

TABLE 2.4. GROSS DOMESTIC PRODUCT PER CAPITA, REAL

Gross domestic product (GDP) per capita, real, is calculated by dividing real GDP (table 2.2) by corresponding midyear population.

Source: World Bank and Organisation for Economic Co-operation and Development national accounts data.

TABLE 2.5. GROSS DOMESTIC PRODUCT PER CAPITA GROWTH

Gross domestic product (GDP) per capita growth is the average annual growth rate of real GDP per capita (table 2.4).

Source: World Bank and Organisation for Economic Co-operation and Development national accounts data.

TABLE 2.6. GROSS NATIONAL INCOME, NOMINAL

Gross national income, nominal, is the sum of value added by all resident producers plus any product taxes (less subsidies) not included in the valuation of output plus net receipts of primary income (compensation of employees and property income) from abroad. Data are converted from national currency in current prices to U.S. dollars at official annual exchange rates.

Source: World Bank and Organisation for Economic Co-operation and Development national accounts data.

TABLE 2.7. GROSS NATIONAL INCOME, *WORLD BANK ATLAS* METHOD

Gross national income (GNI), World Bank At*las method,* (formerly GNP) is the sum of value added by all resident producers plus any product taxes (less subsidies) not included in the valuation of output plus net receipts of primary income (compensation of employees and property income) from abroad. GNI, calculated in national currency, is usually converted to U.S. dollars at official exchange rates for comparisons across economies, although an alternative rate is used when the official exchange rate is judged to diverge by an exceptionally large margin from the rate actually applied in international transactions. To smooth fluctuations in prices and exchange rates, the *World Bank Atlas* method (see box 1) of conversion is used.

This method applies a conversion factor that averages the exchange rate for a given year and the two preceding years, adjusted for the difference between the rate of inflation in the country and that in Japan, the United Kingdom, the United States, and the euro area. Growth rates are calculated by the least-squares method (see box 2).

Source: World Bank and Organisation for Economic Co-operation and Development national accounts data.

Table 2.8. Gross national income per capita, *World Bank Atlas* method
Gross national income (GNI) per capita, World Bank Atlas *method,* is GNI, calculated using the *World Bank Atlas* method (see box 1), divided by midyear population.

Source: World Bank and Organisation for Economic Co-operation and Development national accounts data.

Table 2.9. Gross domestic product deflator (local currency series)
Gross domestic product (GDP) deflator (local currency series) is nominal GDP in current local currency divided by real GDP in constant 2000 local currency, expressed as an index with base year 2000. GDP is the sum of gross domestic and foreign value added claimed by residents plus net factor income from abroad (the income residents receive from abroad for factor services including labor and capital) less similar payments made to nonresidents who contribute to the domestic economy, divided by midyear population. It is calculated by the *World Bank Atlas* method using constant 2000 exchange rates (see box 1).

Source: World Bank and Organisation for Economic Co-operation and Development national accounts data.

Table 2.10. Gross domestic product deflator (U.S. dollar series)
Gross domestic product (GDP) deflator (U.S. dollar series) is nominal GDP in current U.S. dollars (table 2.1) divided by real GDP in constant 2000 U.S. dollars (table 2.2), expressed as an index with base year 2000. The series shows the effects of domestic price changes and exchange rate variations.

Source: World Bank and Organisation for Economic Co-operation and Development national accounts data.

Table 2.11. Consumer price index
Consumer price index reflects changes in the cost to the average consumer of acquiring a basket of goods and services that may be fixed or changed at specified intervals, such as yearly. The Laspeyres formula is generally used.

Source: International Monetary Fund International Financial Statistics database and data files.

Table 2.12. Price indexes
Inflation, GDP deflator, is measured by the annual growth rate of the GDP implicit deflator and shows the rate of price change in the economy as a whole.

Consumer price index is a change in the cost to the average consumer of acquiring a basket of goods and services that may be fixed or changed at specified intervals, such as yearly. The Laspeyres formula is generally used.

Exports of goods and services price index is calculated by dividing the national accounts exports of goods and services in current U.S. dollars by exports of goods and services in constant 2000 U.S. dollars.

Imports of goods and services price index is calculated by dividing the national accounts imports of goods and services in current U.S. dollars by imports of goods and services in constant 2000 U.S. dollars.

Source: World Bank and Organisation for Economic Co-operation and Development national accounts data.

Table 2.13. Gross domestic savings
Gross domestic savings is calculated by deducting total consumption (table 2.17) from nominal gross domestic product (table 2.1).

Source: World Bank and Organisation for Economic Co-operation and Development national accounts data.

Table 2.14. Gross national savings
Gross national savings is the sum of gross domestic savings (table 2.13), net factor income from abroad, and net private transfers from

abroad. Net public transfers from abroad are included.

Source: World Bank and Organisation for Economic Co-operation and Development national accounts data.

Table 2.15. General government final consumption expenditure

General government final consumption expenditure is all current expenditure for purchases of goods and services by all levels of government, including capital expenditure on national defense and security. Other government capital expenditure is included in capital formation.

Source: World Bank and Organisation for Economic Co-operation and Development national accounts data.

Table 2.16. Household final consumption expenditure

Household final consumption expenditure (formerly *private consumption*) is the market value of all goods and services, including durable products (such as cars, washing machines, and home computers), purchased by households. It excludes purchases of dwellings but includes imputed rent for owner-occupied dwellings. It also includes payments and fees to governments to obtain permits and licenses.

Here, household consumption expenditure includes the expenditures of nonprofit institutions serving households, even when reported separately by the country.

Source: World Bank and Organisation for Economic Co-operation and Development national accounts data.

Table 2.17. Final consumption expenditure plus discrepancy

Final consumption expenditure plus discrepancy (formerly *total consumption*) is the sum of household final consumption expenditure (table 2.16) and general government final consumption expenditure (table 2.15), shown as a share of gross domestic product. This estimate includes any statistical discrepancy in the use of resources relative to the supply of resources. Private consumption, not separately shown here, is the value of all goods and services purchased or received as income in kind by households and nonprofit institutions. It excludes purchases of dwellings but includes imputed rent for owner-occupied dwellings. In practice, it includes any statistical discrepancy in the use of resources.

Source: World Bank and Organisation for Economic Co-operation and Development national accounts data.

Table 2.18. Final consumption expenditure plus discrepancy per capita

Final consumption expenditure plus discrepancy per capita is final consumption expenditure plus discrepancy in current U.S. dollars (table 2.17) divided by midyear population.

Source: World Bank and Organisation for Economic Co-operation and Development national accounts data.

Table 2.19. Gross fixed capital formation

Gross fixed capital formation consists of gross domestic fixed capital formation plus net changes in the level of inventories. Gross capital formation comprises outlays by the public sector (table 2.20) and the private sector (table 2.21). Examples include improvements in land, dwellings, machinery, and other equipment. Due to statistical discrepancies, for some countries the sum of gross private investment and gross public investment does not total gross domestic investment.

Source: World Bank and Organisation for Economic Co-operation and Development national accounts data.

Table 2.20. Gross general government fixed capital formation

Gross general government fixed capital formation is gross domestic fixed capital formation (see table 2.19) for the public sector.

Source: World Bank and Organisation for Economic Co-operation and Development national accounts data.

Table 2.21. Private sector fixed capital formation

Private sector fixed capital formation is gross domestic fixed capital formation (see table 2.19) for the private sector.

Source: World Bank and Organisation for Economic Co-operation and Development national accounts data.

Table 2.22. External trade balance (exports minus imports)

External trade balance is the difference between free on board exports (table 2.23) and cost, insurance, and freight imports (table 2.24) of goods and services (or the difference between gross domestic savings and gross capital formation). The resource balance is shown as a share of nominal gross domestic product (table 2.1).

Source: World Bank and Organisation for Economic Co-operation and Development national accounts data.

Table 2.23. Exports of goods and services, nominal

Exports of goods and services, nominal, represent the value of all goods and other market services provided to the rest of the world. They include the value of merchandise, freight, insurance, transport, travel, royalties, license fees, and other services, such as communication, construction, financial, information, business, personal, and government services. They exclude labor and property income (formerly called factor services) as well as transfer payments and are expressed in current U.S. dollars.

Source: World Bank and Organisation for Economic Co-operation and Development national accounts data.

Table 2.24. Imports of goods and services, nominal

Imports of goods and services, nominal, represent the value of all goods and other market services received from the rest of the world. They include the value of merchandise, freight, insurance, transport, travel, royalties, license fees, and other services, such as communication, construction, financial, information, business, personal, and government services. They exclude labor and property income (formerly called factor services) as well as transfer payments and are expressed in current U.S. dollars.

Source: World Bank and Organisation for Economic Co-operation and Development national accounts data.

Table 2.25. Exports of goods and services as a share of GDP

Exports of goods and services represent the value of all goods and other market services provided to the rest of the world. They include the value of merchandise, freight, insurance, transport, travel, royalties, license fees, and other services, such as communication, construction, financial, information, business, personal, and government services. They exclude labor and property income (formerly called factor services) as well as transfer payments and are expressed as a proportion of real GDP.

Source: World Bank and Organisation for Economic Co-operation and Development national accounts data.

Table 2.26. Imports of goods and services as a share of GDP

Imports of goods and services represent the value of all goods and other market services received from the rest of the world. They include the value of merchandise, freight, insurance, transport, travel, royalties, license fees, and other services, such as communication, construction, financial, information, business, personal, and government services. They exclude labor and property income (formerly called factor services) as well as transfer payments and are expressed as a proportion of real GDP.

Source: World Bank and Organisation for Economic Co-operation and Development national accounts data.

Table 2.27. Balance of payments and current account

Exports of goods and services represent the value of all goods and other market services provided to the rest of the world. They include the value of merchandise, freight, insurance, transport, travel, royalties, license fees, and other services, such as communication, construction, financial, information, business, personal, and government services. They exclude labor and property income (formerly called factor services) as well as transfer payments and are expressed in current U.S. dollars and as a proportion of real GDP.

Imports of goods and services represent the value of all goods and other market services received from the rest of the world. They include the value of merchandise, freight, insurance, transport, travel, royalties, license fees, and other services, such as communication, construction, financial, information, business, personal, and government services. They exclude labor and property income (formerly called factor services) as well as transfer payments and are expressed in current U.S. dollars and as a proportion of real GDP.

Total trade is the sum of exports and imports of goods and services.

Net income is the receipts and payments of employee compensation paid to nonresident workers and investment income (receipts and payments on direct investment, portfolio investment, other investments, and receipts on reserve assets).

Net current transfers are recorded in the balance of payments whenever an economy provides or receives goods, services, income, or financial items without a quid pro quo.

Current account balance is the sum of net exports of goods, services, net income, and net current transfers. All transfers not considered to be capital are current.

Total reserves including gold are the holdings of monetary gold, special drawing rights, reserves of International Monetary Fund (IMF) members held by the IMF, and holdings of foreign exchange under the control of monetary authorities.

Source: Data on exports and imports of goods and services are from World Bank and Organisation for Economic Co-operation and Development national accounts data. Data on net income, net current transfers, current account balance, and total reserves are from the IMF International Financial Statistics database and data files.

Table 2.28. Exchange rates and purchasing power parity

Official exchange rate is the exchange rate determined by national authorities or the rate determined in the legally sanctioned exchange market.

Purchasing power parity (PPP) conversion factor is the number of units of a country's currency required to buy the same amount of goods and services in the domestic market as a U.S. dollar would buy in the United States.

Ratio of PPP conversion factor to market exchange rate is the national price level, making it possible to compare across countries the costs of the bundle of goods that make up gross domestic product.

Real effective exchange rate is the nominal effective exchange rate (a measure of the value of a currency against a weighted average of several foreign currencies) divided by a price deflator or index of costs.

Gross domestic product (GDP), PPP, is gross domestic product converted to international dollars using purchasing power parity rates. An international dollar has the same purchasing power over GDP as the U.S. dollar has in the United States. GDP is the sum of gross value added by all resident producers in the economy plus any product taxes and minus any subsidies not included in the value of the products.

It is calculated without making deductions for depreciation of fabricated assets or for depletion and degradation of natural resources.

Gross domestic product (GDP) per capita, PPP, is GDP per capita based on purchasing power parity (PPP). PPP GDP is gross domestic product converted to international dollars using purchasing power parity rates. An international dollar has the same purchasing power over GDP as the U.S. dollar has in the United States. GDP at purchaser prices is the sum of gross value added by all resident producers in the economy plus any product taxes and minus any subsidies not included in the value of the products. It is calculated without making deductions for depreciation of fabricated assets or for depletion and degradation of natural resources.

Source: International Monetary Fund International Financial Statistics database. Data on PPP are from the World Bank International Comparison Program database.

Table 2.29. Agriculture value added

Agriculture value added is the gross output of forestry, hunting, and fishing, as well as crop cultivation and livestock production (International Standard Industrial Classification [ISIC] revision 3 divisions 1–5) less the value of their intermediate inputs. It is calculated without making deductions for depreciation of fabricated assets or depletion and degradation of natural resources. For countries that report national accounts data at producer prices (Angola, Benin, Cape Verde, Comoros, the Republic of Congo, Côte d'Ivoire, Gabon, Ghana, Liberia, Niger, Rwanda, São Tomé and Príncipe, Seychelles, Togo, and Tunisia), gross value added at market prices is used as the denominator. For countries that report national accounts data at basic prices (all other countries), gross value added at factor cost is used as the denominator. Value added at basic prices excludes net taxes on products; value added at producer prices includes net taxes on products paid by producers but excludes sales or value added taxes.

Source: World Bank and Organisation for Economic Co-operation and Development national accounts data files.

TABLE 2.30. INDUSTRY VALUE ADDED

Industry value added is the gross output of mining, manufacturing, construction, electricity, water, and gas (International Standard Industrial Classification revision 3 divisions 10– 45) less the value of their intermediate inputs. It is calculated without making deductions for depreciation of fabricated assets or depletion and degradation of natural resources For countries that report national accounts data at producer prices (Angola, Benin, Cape Verde, Comoros, the Republic of Congo, Côte d'Ivoire, Gabon, Ghana, Liberia, Niger, Rwanda, São Tomé and Príncipe, Seychelles, Togo, and Tunisia), gross value added at market prices is used as the denominator. For countries that report national accounts data at basic prices (all other countries), gross value added at factor cost is used as the denominator. Value added at basic prices excludes net taxes on products; value added at producer prices includes net taxes on products paid by producers but excludes sales or value added taxes.

Source: World Bank and Organisation for Economic Co-operation and Development national accounts data files.

TABLE 2.31. SERVICES PLUS DISCREPANCY VALUE ADDED

Services plus discrepancy value added is the gross output of all other branches of economic activity, including wholesale and retail trade (including hotels and restaurants), transport, and government, financial, professional, and personal services, such as education, health care, and real estate (International Standard Industrial Classification revision 3 divisions 50–99), less the value of their intermediate inputs. Also included are imputed bank service charges, import duties, and any statistical discrepancies noted by national compilers or arising from rescaling. It is calculated without making deductions for depreciation of fabricated assets or depletion and degradation of natural resources. For countries that report national accounts data at producer prices (Angola, Benin, Cape Verde, Comoros, the Republic of Congo, Côte d'Ivoire, Gabon, Ghana, Liberia, Niger, Rwanda, São Tomé and Príncipe, Seychelles, Togo, and Tunisia), gross value added at market prices is used as the denominator. For countries that report national accounts data at basic prices (all other countries), gross value added at factor cost is used as the denominator. Value added at basic prices excludes net taxes on products; value added at producer prices includes net taxes on products paid by producers but excludes sales or value added taxes.

Source: World Bank and Organisation for Economic Co-operation and Development national accounts data files.

TABLE 2.32. CENTRAL GOVERNMENT FINANCES, EXPENSE, AND REVENUE

Revenue, excluding grants, is cash receipts from taxes, social contributions, and other revenues, such as fines, fees, rent, and income from property or sales. Grants are also considered as revenue but are excluded here.

Expense is cash payments for operating activities of the government in providing goods and services. It includes compensation of employees (such as wages and salaries), interest and subsidies, grants, social benefits, and other expenses such as rent and dividends.

Cash surplus or deficit is revenue (including grants) minus expense, minus net acquisition of nonfinancial assets. In the 1986 *Government Finance Statistics Manual* nonfinancial assets were included under revenue and expenditure in gross terms. This cash surplus or deficit is closest to the earlier overall budget balance (still missing is lending minus repayments, which are now a financing item under net acquisition of financial assets).

Net incurrence of liabilities is domestic financing (obtained from residents) and foreign financing (obtained from nonresidents), or the means by which a government provides financial resources to cover a budget deficit or allocates financial resources arising from a budget surplus. The net incurrence of liabilities should be offset by the net acquisition of financial assets (a third financing item). The difference between the cash surplus or deficit and the three financing items is the net change in the stock of cash.

Total debt is the entire stock of direct government fixed-term contractual obligations to others outstanding on a particular date. It includes domestic and foreign liabilities such as currency and money deposits, securities other than shares, and loans. It is the gross amount of government liabilities minus the amount of equity and financial derivatives held by the government. Because debt is a stock rather than a flow, it is measured as of a given date, usually the last day of the fiscal year.

Goods and services include all government payments in exchange for goods and services used for the production of market and nonmarket goods and services. Own-account capital formation is excluded.

Compensation of employees consists of all payments in cash and in kind (such as food and housing) to employees in return for services rendered and of government contributions to social insurance schemes such as social security and pensions that provide benefits to employees.

Interest payments (expense) include interest payments on government debt—including long-term bonds, long-term loans, and other debt instruments—to domestic and foreign residents, expressed as a proportion of expense.

Subsidies and other transfers include all unrequited, nonrepayable transfers on current accounts to private and public enterprises; grants to foreign governments, international organizations, and other government units; and social security, social assistance benefits, and employer social benefits in cash and in kind.

Other expenses are spending on dividends, rent, and other miscellaneous expenses, including provision for consumption of fixed capital.

Interest payments (revenue) include interest payments on government debt—including long-term bonds, long-term loans, and other debt instruments—to domestic and foreign residents, expressed as a proportion of revenue.

Taxes on income, profits, and capital gains are levied on the actual or presumptive net income of individuals, on the profits of corporations and enterprises, and on capital gains, whether realized or not, on land, securities, and other assets. Intragovernmental payments are eliminated in consolidation.

Taxes on goods and services include general sales and turnover or value added taxes, selective excises on goods, selective taxes on services, taxes on the use of goods or property, taxes on extraction and production of minerals, and profits of fiscal monopolies.

Taxes on international trade include import duties, export duties, profits of export or import monopolies, exchange profits, and exchange taxes.

Other taxes include employer payroll or labor taxes, taxes on property, and taxes not allocable to other categories, such as penalties for late payment or nonpayment of taxes.

Social contributions include social security contributions by employees, employers, and self-employed individuals, and other contributions whose source cannot be determined. They also include actual or imputed contributions to social insurance schemes operated by governments.

Grants and other revenue include grants from other foreign governments, international organizations, and other government units; interest; dividends; rent; requited, nonrepayable receipts for public purposes (such as fines, administrative fees, and entrepreneurial income from government ownership of property); and voluntary, unrequited, nonrepayable receipts other than grants.

Source: International Monetary Fund, *Government Finance Statistics Yearbook* and data files, and World Bank and Organisation for Economic Co-operation and Development GDP estimates.

TABLE 2.33. STRUCTURE OF DEMAND

Household final consumption expenditure (formerly *private consumption*) is the market value of all goods and services, including durable products (such as cars, washing machines, and home computers), purchased by households.

General government final consumption expenditure (formerly *general government consumption*) is all government current expenditures for purchases of goods and services.

Gross fixed capital formation (formerly *gross domestic investment*) consists of outlays on additions to the fixed assets of the economy plus net changes in the level of inventories.

Exports of goods and services represent the value of all goods and other market services provided to the rest of the world. They include the value of merchandise, freight, insurance, transport, travel, royalties, license fees, and other services, such as communication, construction, financial, information, business, personal, and government services. They exclude labor and property income (formerly called *factor services*) as well as transfer payments and are expressed as a proportion of real GDP.

Imports of goods and services represent the value of all goods and other market services received from the rest of the world. They include the value of merchandise, freight, insurance, transport, travel, royalties, license fees, and other services, such as communication, construction, financial, information, business, personal, and government services. They exclude labor and property income (formerly called factor services) as well as transfer payments and are expressed as a proportion of real GDP.

Gross national savings is the gross national income less total consumption, plus net transfers.

Source: World Bank and Organisation for Economic Co-operation and Development national accounts data files.

3. Millennium Development Goals

TABLE 3.1. MILLENNIUM DEVELOPMENT GOAL 1: ERADICATE EXTREME POVERTY AND HUNGER

Share of population below PPP $1.25 a day is the percentage of the population living on less than $1.25 a day at 2005 international prices. As a result of revisions in purchasing power parity (PPP) exchange rates, poverty rates in this edition cannot be compared with those in editions before 2009.

Poverty gap ratio at PPP $1.25 a day is the mean shortfall from the poverty line (counting the nonpoor as having zero shortfall), expressed as a percentage of the poverty line. This measure reflects the depth of poverty as well as its incidence.

Share of population below PPP $2 a day is the percentage of the population living on less than $2 a day at 2005 international prices. As a result of revisions in PPP exchange rates, poverty rates in this edition cannot be compared with those in editions before 2009.

Poverty gap ratio at PPP $2 a day is the mean shortfall from the poverty line (counting the nonpoor as having zero shortfall), expressed as a percentage of the poverty line. This measure reflects the depth of poverty as well as its incidence.

Share of population below national poverty line (poverty headcount ratio) is the percentage of the population living below the national poverty line. National estimates are based on population-weighted subgroup estimates from household surveys.

Share of poorest quintile in national consumption or income is the share of consumption, or in some cases income, that accrues to the poorest 20 percent of the population.

Prevalence of child malnutrition, underweight, is the percentage of children under age 5 whose weight for age is more than two standard deviations below the median for the international reference population ages 0–59 months. The reference population, adopted by the World Health Organization in 1983, is based on children from the United States, who are assumed to be well nourished.

Population below minimum dietary energy consumption (also referred to as prevalence of undernourishment) is the population whose dietary energy consumption is continuously below a minimum dietary energy requirement for maintaining a healthy life and carrying out a light physical activity with an acceptable minimum bodyweight for attained height.

Source: Data on poverty are from the World Bank Development Research Group. Data are based on primary household survey data obtained from government statistical agencies and World Bank country departments

In developing countries, poverty measures are among the main indicators of economic development and progress in alleviating poverty. But poverty is multidimensional, and no single indicator can adequately capture all its aspects. To do so, poverty measures must be sufficiently informative on social welfare and comparable over time and across space. The World Bank uses consumption poverty as its main index and sets the poverty line at $1.25 (in 2005 purchasing power parity [PPP] terms; Chen and others 2008) per person per day; an alternative poverty line at $2 (2005 PPP) per person per day measures extreme poverty. Consumption poverty alone does not give a full picture of a country's economic condition, let alone the priorities governments should set in their efforts to alleviate poverty. Health, education, wealth inequality, and gender equality are just some of the dimensions of poverty not fully captured. These topics are covered by the Millennium Development Goals—in addition to poverty and hunger—ensuring that they will receive international attention.

A multidimensional index of poverty attempts to capture various dimensions of welfare (Alkire and Foster 2007; Alkire and others 2010). Can a single indicator combining measures of health and education, consumption poverty, and gender inequality be sufficiently informative on social welfare to be policy relevant? The conceptual issues underlying the construction of these indices are not new (see Ravallion 2010, 2011 for a discussion), and measures of consumption poverty face similar challenges, but they differ from multidimensional indices of poverty, especially in the assumptions underlying the aggregation of information.

Constructing consumption poverty measures requires an adequate protocol to aggregate several varieties into one measure. The consumption aggregate rightly captures social welfare if the weights given to each variety consumed reflect societal preferences. When goods making the consumption poverty index are marketable and markets are functioning properly, market prices reflect the weights that the consumption of these items have in the social welfare function. Thus, theoretically, all expenditure levels of marketable items can be aggregated into one index of consumption that *fully* reflects social welfare.

Multidimensional indices of poverty extend this approach by adding the consumption of nonmarketable items. The key assumptions underlying the construction of these indexes thus relate to the weights (or prices) assigned to nonmarketable items entering into the aggregation. For example, how does one compare an individual with a $2 daily consumption level and a 75-year life expectancy with an individual with a $3 daily consumption level but a 60-year life expectancy? In a perfect "market for life expectancy," one could observe how much individuals might pay for a longer life expectancy, and assuming market perfection, willingness to pay would capture the social weight of life expectancy in consumption terms. However, without observable prices, policymakers will need to choose social weights, an exercise highly arbitrary and subject to political capture.

The relevance and credibility of multidimensional indices of poverty therefore depend crucially on the choice of social weights assigned to each dimension of poverty (Alkire and others 2000). On one hand, weights need to be sufficiently flexible to reflect a social welfare function that varies both over time and across space; on the other, the choice of welfare weights is politically charged, so governments might not be able to afford such flexibility without undermining the legitimacy of their choices. Governments need transparency and accountability so that they can produce an index that fully reflects social welfare. Then, if these weights do not correspond to societal preferences, aggregating consumption poverty and life expectancy into a single index will not reduce the dimensionality of the problem at hand. A multidimensional index of poverty constructed from consumption poverty and life expectancy will still need to be complemented by those same indices of consumption poverty (or life expectancy) to provide a full picture of social welfare, a prerequisite for policy decisions. The usefulness of such aggregation effort must then be revisited.

References

Alkire, Sabina, and James Foster. 2007. "Counting and Multidimensional Poverty Measurement." Working Paper 7, Oxford Poverty and Human Development Initiative, University of Oxford.

Alkire, Sabina, and Maria Emma Santos. 2010. *Acute Multidimensional Poverty: A New Index for Developing Countries.* Oxford, UK: University of Oxford, Oxford Poverty & Human Development Initiative, Oxford Department of International Development, Queen Elizabeth House.

Alkire, Sabina, Maria Emma Santos, Suman Seth, and Gatson Yalonetzky. 2010. *Is the Multidimensional Poverty Index Robust to Different Weights?* Oxford, UK: University of Oxford, Oxford Poverty & Human Development Initiative, Queen Elizabeth House.

Chen, Shaohua, and Martin Ravallion. 2008. "The Developing World is Poorer than We Thought, but No Less Successful in the Fight against Poverty." Policy Research Working Paper 4703, World Bank, Washington, DC.

Deaton, A., and S. Zaidi. 2002. "A Guide to Aggregating Consumption Expenditures." Living Standards Measurement Study Working Paper 135, World Bank, Washington, DC.

Hentschel, J., and P. Lanjouw. 1996. "Constructing an Indicator of Consumption for the Analysis of Poverty." Living Standards Measurement Study Working Paper 124, World Bank, Washington, DC.

Ravallion, M. 2010. "Mashup Indices of Development." Policy Research Working Paper 5432, World Bank, Washington, DC.

Ravallion, M. 2011. "On Multidimensional Indices of Poverty." *Journal of Economic Inequality* 9 (2): 235–248.

(http://iresearch.worldbank.org/PovcalNet/jsp/index.jsp). Data on national poverty are from the Global Poverty Working Group and are based on World Bank country poverty assessments and country poverty reduction strategies. Efforts have been made to harmonize these data series with those published on the United Nations Millennium Development Goals website (www.un.org/millenniumgoals), but some differences in timing, sources, and definitions remain. Data on child malnutrition are from World Health Organization Global Database on Child Growth and Malnutrition. Data on population below minimum dietary energy consumption are from the Food and Agriculture Organization (www.fao.org/economic/ess/food-security-statistics/en/).

Table 3.2. Millennium Development Goal 2: achieve universal primary education

Primary education provides children with basic reading, writing, and mathematics skills, along with an elementary understanding of such subjects as history, geography, natural science, social science, art, and music.

Net primary enrollment ratio is the ratio of children of official primary school age, based on the International Standard Classification of Education 1997, who are enrolled in primary school to the population of the corresponding official primary school age.

Primary completion rate is the percentage of students completing the last year of primary school. It is calculated as the total number of students in the last grade of primary school minus the number of repeaters in that grade divided by the total number of children of official graduation age.

Share of cohort reaching grade 5 is the percentage of children enrolled in grade 1 of primary school who eventually reach grade 5. The estimate is based on the reconstructed cohort method.

Youth literacy rate is the percentage of people ages 15–24 who can, with understanding, both read and write a short, simple statement about their everyday life.

Source: Data are from the United Nations Educational, Scientific and Cultural Organization Institute for Statistics. Efforts have been made to harmonize these data series with those published on the United Nations Millennium Development Goals website (www.un.org/millenniumgoals), but some differences in timing, sources, and definitions remain.

Table 3.3. Millennium Development Goal 3: promote gender equality and empower women

Ratio of girls to boys in primary and secondary school is the ratio of female to male gross enrollment rate in primary and secondary school.

Ratio of literate young women to men is the ratio of the female youth literacy rate to the male youth literacy rate.

Women in national parliament are the percentage of parliamentary seats in a single or lower chamber occupied by women.

Share of women employed in the nonagricultural sector is women wage employees in the nonagricultural sector as a share of total nonagricultural employment.

Source: Data on net enrollment and literacy are from the United Nations Educational, Scientific and Cultural Organization Institute for Statistics. Data on women in national parliaments are from the Inter-Parliamentary Union Parline database (www.ipu.org). Data on women's employment are from the International Labour Organization Key Indicators of the Labour Market database.

Table 3.4. Millennium Development Goal 4: reduce child mortality

Under-five mortality rate is the probability that a newborn baby will die before reaching age 5, if subject to current age-specific mortality rates. The probability is expressed as a rate per 1,000.

Infant mortality rate is the number of infants dying before reaching one year of age, per 1,000 live births.

Child immunization rate, measles, is the percentage of children ages 12–23 months who received vaccinations for measles before 12 months or at any time before the survey. A child is considered adequately immunized against measles after receiving one dose of vaccine.

Source: Data on under-five and infant mortality are from the Inter-agency Group for Child Mortality Estimation *Level & Trends in Child Mortality: Report 2010*, based mainly on household surveys, censuses, and vital registration, supplemented by the World Bank Human Development Network and Development Data Group estimates based on vital registration and sample registration. Data on child immunization are from the World Health Organization and the United Nations Children's Fund (www.who.int/immunization_monitoring/routine/en/).

TABLE 3.5. MILLENNIUM DEVELOPMENT GOAL 5: IMPROVE MATERNAL HEALTH

Maternal mortality ratio, modeled estimate, is the number of women who die from pregnancy-related causes during pregnancy and childbirth, per 100,000 live births. Data are estimated by a regression model using information on fertility, birth attendants, and HIV prevalence.

Maternal mortality ratio, national estimate, is the number of women who die during pregnancy and childbirth, per 100,000 live births.

Births attended by skilled health staff are the percentage of deliveries attended by personnel who are trained to give the necessary supervision, care, and advice to women during pregnancy, labor, and the postpartum period; to conduct deliveries on their own; and to care for newborns.

Source: Data on maternal mortality (modeled) are from the World Health Organization, United Nations Children's Fund (UNICEF), United Nations Population Fund, and the World Bank *Trends in Maternal Mortality: 1990–2008*. Data on maternal mortality (national) and births attended by skilled health staff are from UNICEF *State of the World's Children* and Childinfo and from Demographic and Health Surveys by Macro International.

TABLE 3.6. MILLENNIUM DEVELOPMENT GOAL 6: COMBAT HIV/AIDS, MALARIA, AND OTHER DISEASES

Prevalence of HIV is the percentage of people ages 15–49 who are infected with HIV.

Contraceptive use, any method, is the percentage of women ages 15–49, married or in union, who are practicing, or whose sexual partners are practicing, any form of contraception.

Children sleeping under insecticide-treated nets are the percentage of children under age 5 with access to an insecticide-treated net to prevent malaria.

Incidence of tuberculosis is the estimated number of new tuberculosis cases (pulmonary, smear positive, and extrapulmonary), per 100,000 people.

Tuberculosis treatment success rate is the percentage of new, registered smear-positive (infectious) cases that were cured or in which a full course of treatment was completed.

Source: Data on HIV prevalence are from the Joint United Nations Programme on HIV/AIDS and the World Health Organization (WHO) *Report on the Global AIDS Epidemic*. Data on contraceptive use are from household surveys, including Demographic and Health Surveys by Macro International and Multiple Indicator Cluster Surveys by the United Nations Children's Fund (UNICEF). Data on insecticide-treated net use are from UNICEF *State of the World's Children* and Childinfo and from Demographic and Health Surveys by Macro International. Data on tuberculosis are from the WHO *Global Tuberculosis Control Report*.

TABLE 3.7. MILLENNIUM DEVELOPMENT GOAL 7: ENSURE ENVIRONMENT SUSTAINABILITY

Forest area is land under natural or planted stands of trees, whether productive or not.

Terrestrial protected areas are those officially documented by national authorities.

Gross domestic product (GDP) per unit of energy use is the GDP in purchasing power parity (PPP) U.S. dollars per kilogram of oil equivalent of energy use. PPP GDP is gross domestic product converted to 2000 constant international dollars using PPP rates. An international dollar has the same purchasing power over GDP as a U.S. dollar has in the United States.

Carbon dioxide emissions per capita are those stemming from the burning of fossil fuels and the manufacture of cement divided by midyear population. They include carbon dioxide produced during consumption of solid, liquid, and gas fuels and gas flaring.

Population with sustainable access to an improved water source is the percentage of the population with reasonable access to an adequate amount of water from an improved source, such as a household connection, public standpipe, borehole, protected well or spring, or rainwater collection. Unimproved sources include vendors, tanker trucks, and unprotected wells and springs. Reasonable access is defined as the availability of at least 20 liters a person a day from a source within 1 kilometer of the dwelling.

Population with sustainable access to improved sanitation is the percentage of the population with at least adequate access to excreta disposal facilities that can effectively prevent human, animal, and insect contact with excreta. Improved facilities range from simple but protected pit latrines to flush toilets with a sewerage connection. The excreta disposal system is considered adequate if it is private or shared (but not public) and if it hygienically separates human excreta from human contact. To be effective, facilities must be correctly constructed and properly maintained.

Source: Data on forest area are from the Food and Agricultural Organization *Global Forest Resources Assessment*. Data on nationally protected areas are from the United Nations Environment Programme and the World Conservation Monitoring Centre, as compiled by the World Resources Institute, and based on data from national authorities, national legislation, and international agreements. Data on energy use are from electronic files of the International Energy Agency. Data on carbon dioxide emissions are from the Carbon Dioxide Information Analysis Center, Environmental Sciences Division, Oak Ridge National Laboratory. Data on access to water and sanitation are from the World Health Organization and United Nations Children's Fund Joint Monitoring Programme (www.wssinfo.org).

Table 3.8. Millennium Development Goal 8: develop a global partnership for development

Heavily Indebted Poor Countries (HIPC) Debt Initiative decision point is the date at which a HIPC with an established track record of good performance under adjustment programs supported by the International Monetary Fund (IMF) and the World Bank commits to undertake additional reforms and to develop and implement a poverty reduction strategy.

HIPC Debt Initiative completion point is the a country successfully completes the key structural reforms agreed on at the decision point, including developing and implementing its poverty reduction strategy. The country then receives the bulk of debt relief under the HIPC Debt Initiative without further policy conditions.

Debt service relief committed is the amount of debt service relief, calculated at the Enhanced HIPC Initiative decision point, that will allow the country to achieve debt sustainability at the completion point.

Public and publicly guaranteed debt service is the sum of principal repayments and interest actually paid in foreign currency, goods, or services on long-term obligations of public debtors and long-term private obligations guaranteed by a public entity. Exports refer to exports of goods, services, and income. Worker remittances are not included here, though they are included with income receipts in other World Bank publications, such as *Global Development Finance*.

Youth unemployment rate is the percentage of the labor force ages 15–24 without work but available for and seeking employment. Definitions of labor force and unemployment may differ by country.

Fixed-line and mobile telephone subscribers are subscribers to a fixed-line telephone service, which connects a customer's equipment to the public switched telephone network, or to a public mobile telephone service, which uses cellular technology.

Personal computers are self-contained computers designed for use by a single individual.

Internet users are people with access to the Internet.

Source: Data on HIPC countries are from the International Development Association and International Monetary Fund "Heavily Indebted Poor Countries (HIPC) Initiative and Multilateral Debt Relief Initiative—Status of Implementation." Data on external debt are mainly from reports to the World Bank through its Debtor Reporting System from member countries that have received International Bank for Reconstruction and Development loans or International Development Association credits, as well as from

World Bank and IMF files. Data on youth unemployment are from the International Labour Organization Key Indicators of the Labour Market database. Data on telephone subscribers, personal computers, and Internet users are from the International Telecommunication Union *World Telecommunication/ICT Development Report* and database, and from World Bank estimates.

4. Private sector development

TABLE 4.1. DOING BUSINESS INDICATORS

Number of startup procedures to start a business is the number of procedures required to start a business, including interactions to obtain necessary permits and licenses and to complete all inscriptions, verifications, and notifications to start operations.

Time required for each procedure to start a business is the number of calendar days needed to complete each procedure to legally operate a business. If a procedure can be sped up at additional cost, the fastest procedure, independent of cost, is chosen.

Cost to start a business is normalized by presenting it as a percentage of gross national income (GNI) per capita.

Minimum capital is the paid-in minimum capital requirement, which reflects the amount an entrepreneur needs to deposit in a bank or with a notary before registration and up to three months following incorporation. It is reported as a percentage of the country's income per capita.

Number of procedures to register property is the number of procedures required for a business to secure rights to property.

Time required to register property is the number of calendar days needed for a business to secure rights to property.

Cost to register property is the official costs required by law to register a property, including fees, transfer taxes, stamp duties, and any other payment to the property registry, notaries, public agencies, and lawyers. Other taxes, such as capital gains tax or value added tax, are excluded from the cost measure. Both costs borne by the buyer and those borne by the seller are included. If cost estimates differ across sources, the median reported value is used. It is reported as a percentage of property value, which is assumed to be equivalent to 50 times income per capita.

Number of procedures to enforce a contract is the number of independent actions, mandated by law or courts, that demand interaction between the parties of a contract or between them and the judge or court officer.

Time required to enforce a contract is the number of calendar days from the filing of the lawsuit in court until the final determination and, in appropriate cases, payment.

Cost to enforce a contract is court and attorney fees, where the use of attorneys is mandatory or common, or the cost of an administrative debt recovery procedure, expressed as a percentage of the debt value.

Number of procedures to deal with construction permits is the number of procedures required to obtain construction-related permits.

Time required to deal with construction permits is the average wait, in days, to obtain a construction-related permit, from the day the establishment applied for it to the day it was granted.

Cost to deal with construction permits is all the fees associated with completing the procedures to legally build a warehouse, including those associated with obtaining land use approvals and reconstruction design clearances; receiving inspections before, during, and after construction; getting utility connections; and registering the warehouse property. Nonrecurring taxes required for the completion of the warehouse project also are recorded. The building code, information from local experts, and specific regulations and fee schedules are used as sources for costs. If several local partners provide different estimates, the median reported value is used. It is reported as a percentage of the country's income per capita.

Disclosure index measures the degree to which investors are protected through disclosure of ownership and financial information. Higher values indicate more disclosure.

Director liability index measures a plaintiff's ability to hold directors of firms liable for damages to the company. Higher values indicate greater liability.

Shareholder suits index measures shareholders' ability to sue officers and directors for misconduct. Higher values indicate greater power for shareholders to challenge transactions.

Investor protection index measures the degree to which investors are protected through disclosure of ownership and financial information regulations. It is the average of the disclosure, director liability, and shareholder suits indexes. Higher values indicate better protection.

Rigidity of hours index, a measure of employment regulation, is an average of scores in five areas: whether night work is unrestricted, whether weekend work is unrestricted, whether the work week can consist of 5.5 days, whether the workweek can extend to 50 hours or more (including overtime) for two months a year to respond to a seasonal increase in production, and whether paid annual vacation is 21 working days or fewer. For each question the answer no is assigned a score of 1 and the answer yes a 0.

Difficulty of hiring index indicates the applicability and maximum duration of fixed-term contracts and minimum wage for a trainee or first-time employee. It measures whether fixed-term contracts are prohibited for permanent tasks, the maximum cumulative duration of fixed-term contracts, and the ratio of the minimum wage for a trainee or first time employee to the average value added per worker.

Difficulty of firing index indicates the extent of notification and approval requirements for termination of a redundant worker or group of redundant workers, obligation to reassign or retrain, and priority rules for redundancy and reemployment. It has eight components: whether redundancy is disallowed as a basis for terminating workers, whether the employer needs to notify a third party (such as a government agency) to terminate 1 redundant worker, whether the employer needs to notify a third party to terminate a group of 25 redundant workers, whether the employer needs approval from a third party to terminate 1 redundant worker, whether the employer needs approval from a third party to terminate a group of 25 redundant workers, whether the law requires the employer to reassign or retrain a worker before making the worker redundant, whether priority rules apply for redundancies, and whether priority rules apply for reemployment. For the first question the answer yes is assigned a score of 10, and the rest of the questions do not apply. For the fourth question the answer yes is assigned a score of 2 and the answer no a 0. For every other question the answer yes is assigned a score of 1 and the answer no a 0.

Firing cost indicates the notice requirements, severance, payments, and penalties due when terminating a redundant worker, expressed in weeks of salary.

Rigidity of employment index measures the regulation of employment, specifically the hiring and firing of workers and the rigidity of working hours. This index is the average of three subindexes: the rigidity of hours index, the difficulty of hiring index, and the difficulty of firing index.

Source: Data are from the World Bank Doing Business project (http://rru.worldbank.org/DoingBusiness/).

Table 4.2. Investment climate

Private sector fixed capital formation is private sector fixed capital formation (table 2.21) divided by nominal gross domestic product (table 2.1).

Net foreign direct investment is net inflows of investment to acquire a lasting management interest (10 percent or more of voting stock) in an enterprise operating in an economy other than that of the investor. It is the sum of equity capital, reinvestment of earnings, other long-term capital, and short-term capital as shown in the balance of payments. This series shows net inflows (new investment inflows less disinvestment) in the reporting economy from foreign investors.

Domestic credit to private sector is financial resources provided to the private sector, such as through loans, purchases of nonequity securities, and trade credits and other accounts receivable that establish a claim for repayment. For some countries these claims include credit to public enterprises.

Firms that believe the court system is fair, impartial, and uncorrupt are the percentage of firms that believe the court system is fair, impartial, and uncorrupt.

Corruption is the percentage of firms identifying corruption as a major constraint to current operation.

Crime, theft, and disorder are the percentage of firms identifying crime, theft, and disorder as a major constraint to current operation.

Tax rates are the percentage of firms identifying tax rates as a major constraint to current operation.

Finance is the percentage of firms identifying access to finance or cost of finance as a major constraint to current operation.

Electricity is the percentage of firms identifying electricity as a major constraint to current operation.

Labor regulations are the percentage of firms identifying labor regulations as a major constraint to current operation.

Labor skills are the percentage of firms identifying skills of available workers as a major constraint to current operation.

Transportation is the percentage of firms identifying transportation as a major constraint to current operation.

Customs and trade regulations are the percentage of firms identifying customs and trade regulations as a major constraint to current operation.

Number of tax payments is the number of taxes paid by businesses, including by electronic filing. The tax is counted as paid once a year even if payments are more frequent.

Time to prepare, file, and pay taxes is the number of hours it takes to prepare, file, and pay (or withhold) three major types of taxes: the corporate income tax, the value added or sales tax, and labor taxes, including payroll taxes and social security contributions.

Total tax rate is the total amount of taxes payable by the business (except for labor taxes) after accounting for deductions and exemptions as a percentage of profit.

Highest marginal tax rate, corporate, is the highest rate shown on the schedule of tax rates applied to the taxable income of corporations.

Time dealing with officials is the average percentage of senior management's time that is spent in a typical week dealing with requirements imposed by government regulations (for example, taxes, customs, labor regulations, licensing, and registration), including dealings with officials, completing forms, and the like.

Average time to clear customs, direct exports, is the average number of days to clear direct exports through customs.

Average time to clear customs, imports, is the average number of days to clear imports through customs.

Interest rate spread is the interest rate charged by banks on loans to prime customers minus the interest rate paid by commercial or similar banks for demand, time, or savings deposits.

Listed domestic companies are domestically incorporated companies listed on a country's stock exchanges at the end of the year. They exclude investment companies, mutual funds, and other collective investment vehicles.

Market capitalization of listed companies, also known as market value, is the share price of a listed domestic company's stock times the number of shares outstanding.

Turnover ratio for traded stocks is the total value of shares traded during the period divided by the average market capitalization for the period. Average market capitalization is calculated as the average of the end-of-period values for the current period and the previous period.

Source: Data on private sector fixed capital formation are from the World Bank World Development Indicators database. Data on net foreign direct investment are from the International Monetary Fund (IMF) Balance of Payments database, supplemented by data from the United Nations Conference on Trade and Development and official national sources. Data on domestic credit to the private sector are from the International Monetary Fund International Financial Statistics database and data files, World Bank and Organisation for Economic Co-operation and Development gross domestic product (GDP) estimates, and the World Bank World Development Indicators database. Data on investment climate constraints to firms are based on enterprise surveys conducted by the World Bank and its partners (http://rru.worldbank.org/EnterpriseSurveys). Data on regulation and tax administration and highest marginal corporate tax rates are from the World Bank Doing Business project (http://rru.worldbank.org/DoingBusiness). Data on time dealing with officials and average time to clear customs are from World Bank Enterprise Surveys (http://rru.worldbank.org/EnterpriseSurveys/). Data on interest rate spreads are from the IMF International Financial Statistics database and data files and the World Bank World Development Indicators database. Data on listed domestic companies, turnover ratios for traded stocks, and market capitalization are from Standard

& Poor's *Global Stock Markets Factbook* and supplemental Standard & Poor's data.

Table 4.3. Financial sector infrastructure

Foreign currency sovereign ratings are long- and short-term foreign currency ratings that assess a sovereign's capacity and willingness to honor in full and on time its existing and future obligations issued in foreign currencies. Short-term ratings have a time horizon of less than 13 months for most obligations, or up to 3 years for U.S. public finance, in line with industry standards, to reflect the unique risk characteristics of bond, tax, and revenue anticipation notes that are commonly issued with terms up to 3 years. Short-term ratings thus place greater emphasis on the liquidity necessary to meet financial commitments in a timely manner.

Gross national savings is the sum of gross domestic savings (table 2.13) and net factor income and net private transfers from abroad. The estimate here also includes net public transfers from abroad.

Money and quasi money (M2) are the sum of currency outside banks, demand deposits other than those of the central government, and the time, savings, and foreign currency deposits of resident sectors other than the central government. This definition of money supply is frequently called M2 and corresponds to lines 34 and 35 in the International Monetary Fund International Financial Statistics.

Real interest rate is the lending interest rate adjusted for inflation as measured by the gross domestic product deflator.

Domestic credit to private sector is financial resources provided to the private sector, such as through loans, purchases of nonequity securities, and trade credits and other accounts receivable, that establish a claim for repayment. For some countries these claims include credit to public enterprises.

Interest rate spread is the interest rate charged by banks on loans to prime customers minus the interest rate paid by commercial or similar banks for demand, time, or savings deposits.

Ratio of bank nonperforming loans to total gross loans is the value of nonperforming loans divided by the total value of the loan portfolio (including nonperforming loans before the deduction of specific loan-loss provisions). The loan amount recorded as nonperforming should be the gross value of the loan as recorded on the balance sheet, not just the amount overdue.

Listed domestic companies are domestically incorporated companies listed on a country's stock exchanges at the end of the year. They exclude investment companies, mutual funds, and other collective investment vehicles.

Market capitalization of listed companies, also known as market value, is the share price of a listed domestic company's stock times the number of shares outstanding.

Turnover ratio for traded stocks is the total value of shares traded during the period divided by the average market capitalization for the period. Average market capitalization is calculated as the average of the end-of-period values for the current period and the previous period.

Source: Data on foreign currency sovereign ratings are from Fitch Ratings (www.fitchratings.com/). Data on gross national savings are from World Bank national accounts data, and Organisation for Economic Co-operation and Development national accounts data files. Data on money and quasi money and domestic credit to the private sector are from the International Monetary Fund International Financial Statistics and data files and World Bank and OECD estimates of GDP. Data on real interest rates are from the IMF International Financial Statistics database and data files using World Bank data on the GDP deflator and the World Bank World Development Indicators database. Data on interest rate spreads are from the International Monetary Fund, International Financial Statistics and data files. Data on ratios of bank nonperforming loans to total are from the International Monetary Fund *Global Financial Stability Report*. Data on bank branches are from surveys of banking and regulatory institutions by the World Bank Research Department and Financial Sector and Operations Policy Department and the World Development Indicators database. Data on listed domestic companies and turnover ratios for traded stocks are from Standard & Poor's *Emerging Stock Markets Factbook* and supplemental data and the World Bank's World Development Indicators database.

Data on market capitalization of listed companies are from Standard & Poor's *Emerging Stock Markets Factbook* and supplemental data, World Bank and OECD estimates of GDP, and the World Bank World Development Indicators database.

5. Trade and regional integration

TABLE 5.1. INTERNATIONAL TRADE AND TARIFF BARRIERS

Total trade is the sum of exports and imports of goods and services measured as a share of gross domestic product.

Merchandise trade is the sum of imports and exports of merchandise divided by nominal gross domestic product.

Services trade is the sum of imports and exports of wholesale and retail trade (including hotels and restaurants), transport, and government, financial, professional, and personal services such as education, health care, and real estate (International Standard Industrial Classification revision 3 divisions 50–99) less the value of their intermediate inputs. Also included are imputed bank service charges, import duties, and any statistical discrepancies noted by national compilers or arising from rescaling. It is calculated without making deductions for depreciation of fabricated assets or depletion and degradation of natural resources. For countries that report national accounts data at producer prices (Angola, Benin, Cape Verde, Comoros, the Republic of Congo, Côte d'Ivoire, Gabon, Ghana, Liberia, Niger, Rwanda, São Tomé and Príncipe, Seychelles, Togo, and Tunisia), gross value added at market prices is used as the denominator. For countries that report national accounts data at basic prices (all other countries), gross value added at factor cost is used as the denominator. Value added at basic prices excludes net taxes on products; value added at producer prices includes net taxes on products paid by producers but excludes sales or value added taxes.

Exports of goods and services represent the value of all goods and other market services provided to the rest of the world. They include the value of merchandise, freight, insurance, transport, travel, royalties, license fees, and other services, such as communication, construction, financial, information, business, personal, and government services. They exclude labor and property income (formerly called factor services) as well as transfer payments and are expressed in current U.S. dollars and as a proportion of nominal GDP.

Imports of goods and services represent the value of all goods and other market services received from the rest of the world. They include the value of merchandise, freight, insurance, transport, travel, royalties, license fees, and other services, such as communication, construction, financial, information, business, personal, and government services. They exclude labor and property income (formerly called factor services) as well as transfer payments and are expressed in current U.S. dollars and as a proportion of nominal GDP.

Annual growth of exports and *imports* is calculated using real imports and exports.

Terms of trade index measures the relative movement of export and import prices. This series is calculated as the ratio of a country's export unit values or prices to its import unit values or prices and shows changes over a base year (2000) in the level of export unit values as a percentage of import unit values.

Structure of merchandise exports and *imports* components may not sum to 100 percent because of unclassified trade.

Food comprises the commodities in Standard International Trade Classification (SITC) sections 0 (food and live animals), 1 (beverages and tobacco), and 4 (animal and vegetable oils and fats) and SITC division 22 (oil seeds, oil nuts, and oil kernels).

Agricultural raw materials comprise the commodities in SITC section 2 (crude materials except fuels), excluding divisions 22, 27 (crude fertilizers and minerals excluding coal, petroleum, and precious stones), and 28 (metalliferous ores and scrap).

Fuel comprises SITC section 3 (mineral fuels).

Ores and metals comprise the commodities in SITC sections 27, 28, and 68 (nonferrous metals).

Manufactures comprise the commodities in SITC sections 5 (chemicals), 6 (basic manufactures), 7 (machinery and transport equipment), and 8 (miscellaneous manufactured goods), excluding division 68.

Export diversification index measures the extent to which exports are diversified. It is constructed as the inverse of a Herfindahl index, using disaggregated exports at four digits (following the SITC revision 3). The total number of products exported includes only those whose value exceeds $100,000 or 0.3 percent of the country's total exports, whichever is smaller. The maximum number of three-digit products that could be exported is 261. Ranging from 0 to 1, the index reveals the extent of the differences between the structure of trade of the country or country group and the world average. An index value closer to 1 indicates a bigger difference from the world average. A higher value indicates more export diversification. The index is computed by measuring absolute deviation of the country share from world structure.

Export concentration index, also known as the Herfindahl-Hirschmann index, is a measure of the degree of market concentration. The total number of products exported includes only those whose value exceeds $100,000 or 0.3 percent of the country's total exports, whichever is smaller. The maximum number of three-digit products that could be exported is 261. It has been normalized to a scale of 0–1. An index value close to 1 indicates a very concentrated market (maximum concentration). Values closer to 0 reflect a more equal distribution of market shares among exporters or importers. This type of concentration indicator is vulnerable to cyclical fluctuations in relative prices, with commodity price rises making commodity exporters look more concentrated.

Competitiveness indicator has two aspects: *sectoral effect* and *global effect*. To calculate both indicators, growth of exports is decomposed into three components: the growth rate of total international trade over the reference period (2005–09); the sectoral effect, which measures the contribution to a country's export growth of the dynamics of the sectoral markets where the country sells its products, assuming that sectoral market shares are constant; and the competitiveness effect, which measures the contribution of changes in sectoral market shares to a country's export growth.

Tariff barriers are a form of duty based on the value of an import.

Binding coverage is the percentage of product lines with an agreed bound rate.

Simple mean bound rate is the unweighted average of all the lines in the tariff schedule in which bound rates have been set.

Simple mean tariff is the unweighted average of effectively applied rates or most favored nation rates for all products subject to tariffs calculated for all traded goods.

Dispersion around the mean is calculated as the coefficient of variation of the applied tariff rates, including preferential rates that a country applies to its trading partners available at the six-digit product level of the Harmonized System in a country's customs schedule.

Weighted mean tariff is the average of effectively applied rates or most favored nation rates weighted by the product import shares corresponding to each partner country.

Share of lines with international peaks is the share of lines in the tariff schedule with tariff rates that exceed 15 percent.

Share of lines with domestic peaks is the share of lines in the tariff schedule with tariff rates that are more than three times the simple average tariff .

Share of lines that are bound is the share of lines in the country's tariff schedule bound subject to World Trade Organization negotiation agreements.

Share of lines with specific rates is the share of lines in the tariff schedule that are set on a per unit basis or that combine ad valorem and per unit rates.

Primary products are commodities classified in SITC revision 2 sections 0–4 plus division 68.

Manufactured products are commodities classified in SITC revision 2 sections 5–8 excluding division 68.

Average cost to ship 20 ft container from port to destination is the cost of all operations associated with moving a container from onboard a ship to the considered economic center, weighted based on container traffic for each corridor.

Average time to clear customs, direct exports, is the average number of days to clear direct exports through customs.

Average time to clear customs, imports, is the average number of days to clear imports through customs.

Source: Data on trade and services are from World Bank and Organisation for Economic

Co-operation and Development national accounts data. Data on merchandise trade are from the World Trade Organization and World Bank GDP estimates. Data on the competitiveness indicator are from the Organisation for Economic Co-operation and Development *African Economic Outlook 2011: Africa and Its Emerging Partners*. Data on the export concentration index and diversification index data are from the United Nations Conference on Trade and Development Statistical Office data files (http://unctadstat.unctad.org), with Standard International Trade Classification groups from the United Nations Statistics Division (http://unstats.un.org/unsd/cr/registry/regcst.asp?Cl=14). Data on tariffs are calculated by World Bank staff using the World Integrated Trade Solution system (http://wits.worldbank.org) and data from the United Nations Conference on Trade and Development Trade Analysis and Information System database and the World Trade Organization Integrated Data Base and Consolidated Tariff Schedules database. Data on global imports are from the United Nations Statistics Division COMTRADE database. Data on merchandise exports and imports are from World Bank country desks. Data on shipping costs are from the World Bank Sub-Saharan Africa Transport Policy Program. Data on average time to clear customs are from World Bank Enterprise Surveys (http://rru.worldbank.org/EnterpriseSurveys/).

Table 5.2 Top three exports and share in total exports, 2009

Top exports and *share of total exports* are based on exports disaggregated at the four-digit level (following the Standard International Trade Classification revision 3).

Number of exports accounting for 75 percent of total exports is the number of exports in a country that account for 75 percent of the country's exports.

Source: Organisation for Economic Co-operation and Development *African Economic Outlook 2011: Africa and Its Emerging Partners*.

Table 5.3 Regional integration, trade blocs

Type of most recent agreement includes customs union, under which members substantially eliminate all tariff and nontariff barriers among themselves and establish a common external tariff for nonmembers; economic integration agreement, which liberalizes trade in services among members and covers a substantial number of sectors, affects a sufficient volume of trade, includes substantial modes of supply, and is nondiscriminatory (in the sense that similarly situated service suppliers are treated the same); free trade agreement, under which members substantially eliminate all tariff and nontariff barriers but set tariffs on imports from nonmembers; partial scope agreement, which is a preferential trade agreement notified to the World Trade Organization (WTO) that is not a free trade agreement, a customs union, or an economic integration; and not notified agreement, which is a preferential trade arrangement established among member countries that is not notified to the WTO (the agreement may be functionally equivalent to any of the other agreements).

Merchandise exports within bloc are the sum of merchandise exports by members of a trade bloc to other members of the bloc. They are shown both in U.S. dollars and as a percentage of total merchandise exports by the bloc.

Merchandise exports by bloc are the sum of merchandise exports within bloc and to the rest of the world as a share of total merchandise exports by all economies in the world.

Source: Data on merchandise trade flows are published in the International Monetary Fund (IMF) *Direction of Trade Statistics Yearbook* and *Direction of Trade Statistics Quarterly*. The data in the table were calculated using the IMF's Direction of Trade database. The information on trade bloc membership is from the World Bank Policy Research Report *Trade Blocs* (2000), the United Nations Conference on *Trade and Development Trade and Development Report 2007*, the World Trade Organization Regional Trade Agreements Information System, and the World Bank and the Center for International Business at the Tuck School of Business at Dartmouth College's Global Preferential Trade Agreements Database (http://wits.worldabnk.org/gptad/).

6. Infrastructure

TABLE 6.1. WATER AND SANITATION

Internal fresh water resources per capita are the sum of total renewable resources, which include internal flows of rivers and groundwater from rainfall in the country and river flows from other countries.

Population with sustainable access to an improved water source is the percentage of the population with reasonable access to an adequate amount of water from an improved source, such as a household connection, public standpipe, borehole, protected well or spring, or rainwater collection. Unimproved sources include vendors, tanker trucks, and unprotected wells and springs. Reasonable access is defined as the availability of at least 20 liters a person a day from a source within one kilometer of the user's dwelling.

Population with sustainable access to improved sanitation is the percentage of the population with at least adequate access to excreta disposal facilities that can effectively prevent human, animal, and insect contact with excreta. Improved facilities range from simple but protected pit latrines to flush toilets with a sewerage connection. The excreta disposal system is considered adequate if it is private or shared (but not public) and if it hygienically separates human excreta from human contact. To be effective, facilities must be correctly constructed and properly maintained.

Average duration of insufficient water supply is the average duration of water shortages in a typical month in the last fiscal year.

Committed nominal investment in water projects with private participation is annual committed investment in water projects with private investment, including projects for potable water generation and distribution and sewerage collection and treatment projects.

Official development assistance (ODA) gross disbursements for water supply and sanitation sector are disbursements for water supply and sanitation by bilateral, multilateral, and other donors. The release of funds to, or the purchase of goods or services for a recipient; by extension, the amount thus spent. Disbursements record the actual international transfer of financial resources or of goods or services valued at the cost of the donor.

Source: Data on fresh water resources are from the Food and Agriculture Organization AQUASTAT database. Data on access to water and sanitation are from the World Health Organization and United Nations Children's Fund Joint Monitoring Programme (www.wssinfo.org). Data on insufficient water supply are from World Bank Enterprise Surveys (http://rru.worldbank.org/EnterpriseSurveys/). Data on committed nominal investment in potable water projects with private participation are from the World Bank Private Participation in Infrastructure Project Database (http://ppi.worldbank.org). Data on official development assistance disbursements are from the Development Assistance Committee of the Organisation for Economic Co-operation and Development *Geographical Distribution of Financial Flows to Developing Countries*, *Development Co-operation Report*, and International Development Statistics database (www.oecd.org/dac/stats/idsonline).

TABLE 6.2. TRANSPORTATION

Road network is the length of motorways, highways, main or national roads, secondary or regional roads, and other roads.

Rail lines are the length of railway route available for train service, irrespective of the number of parallel tracks.

Road density, ratio to total land, is the total length of national road network per 100 square kilometers of total land area.

Vehicle fleet is the number of motor vehicles, including cars, buses, and freight vehicles but not two-wheelers.

Commercial vehicles are the number of commercial vehicles that use at least 24 liters of diesel fuel per 100 kilometers.

Passenger vehicles are road motor vehicles, other than two-wheelers, intended for the carriage of passengers and designed to seat no more than nine people (including the driver).

Road network in good or fair condition is the length of the national road network, including the interurban classified network without the urban and rural network, that is in good or fair condition, as defined by each country's road agency.

Ratio of paved to total roads is the length of paved roads—which are those surfaced with crushed stone (macadam) and hydrocarbon binder or bituminized agents, with concrete, or with cobblestones—as a percentage of all the country's roads.

Price of diesel fuel and *gasoline* is the price as posted at filling stations in a country's capital city. When several fuel prices for major cities were available, the unweighted average is used. Since super gasoline (95 octane/A95/premium) is not available everywhere, it is sometime replaced by regular gasoline (92 octane/A92), premium plus gasoline (98 octane/A98), or an average of the two.

Committed nominal investment in transport projects with private participation is annual committed investment in transport projects with private investment, including projects for airport runways and terminals, railways (including fixed assets, freight, intercity passenger, and local passenger), toll roads, bridges, and tunnels.

Official development assistance (ODA) gross disbursements for transportation and storage are disbursements for transportation and storage by bilateral, multilateral, and other donors.

Disbursements record the actual international transfer of financial resources or of goods or services valued at the cost of the donor.

Source: Data on length of road network and vehicle fleet are from the International Road Federation *World Road Statistics* and electronic files, except where noted. Data on rail lines and ratio of paved to total roads are from the World Bank Transportation, Water, and Information and Communications Technologies Department, Transport Division. Data on fuel and gasoline prices are from the German Agency for Technical Cooperation. Data on committed nominal investment in transport projects with private participation are from the World Bank Private Participation in Infrastructure Project Database (http://ppi.worldbank.org). Data on official development assistance disbursements are from the Development Assistance Committee of the Organisation for Economic Co-operation and Development *Geographical Distribution of Financial Flows to Developing Countries*, *Development Co-operation Report*, and International Development Statistics database (www.oecd.org/dac/stats/idsonline).

Table 6.3. Information and communication technology

Telephone subscribers are subscribers to a main telephone line service, which connects a customer's equipment to the public switched telephone network or to a cellular telephone service.

Unmet demand is the number of applications for connection to the public switched telephone network that have been held back because of a lack of technical facilities (equipment, lines, and the like) divided by the number of main telephone lines.

Households with own telephone are the percentage of households possessing a telephone.

Average delay for firm in obtaining a mainline phone connection is the average actual delay in days that firms experience when obtaining a telephone connection, measured from the day the establishment applied to the day it received the service or approval.

Internet users are people with access to the Internet.

Telephone faults are the total number of reported faults for the year divided by the total number of mainlines in operation multiplied by 100. The definition of fault can vary. Some countries include faulty customer equipment; others distinguish between reported and actual found faults. There is also sometimes a distinction between residential and business lines. Another consideration is the time period: some countries report this indicator on a monthly basis; in these cases data are converted to yearly estimates.

Telephone faults cleared by next working day are the percentage of faults in the public switched telephone network that have been corrected by the end of the next working day.

Fixed broadband Internet monthly subscription is the monthly subscription charge for fixed (wired) broadband Internet service. Fixed (wired) broadband is considered any dedicated connection to the Internet at downstream speeds equal to, or greater than, 256 kbit/s, using DSL. Where several offers are available, preference should be given to the 256 kbit/s connection. Taxes should be included. If not included, it should be specified in a note including the applicable tax rate.

Cost of 3-minute fixed telephone local phone call during peak hours is the cost of a three-minute local call during peak hours. Local call refers to a call within the same exchange area using the subscriber's own terminal (that is, not from a public telephone).

Cost of 3-minute cellular local call during peak hours is the cost of a three-minute cellular local call during peak hours.

Residential telephone connection charge is the initial, one-time charge involved in applying for basic telephone service. Where charges differ by exchange areas, the charge reported is for the largest urban area.

Business telephone connection charge is the one-time charge involved in applying for business basic telephone service. Where charges differ by exchange area, the charge reported is for the largest urban area.

Mobile cellular prepaid connection charge is the initial, one-time charge for a new subscription. Refundable deposits should not be counted. Although some operators waive the connection charge, this does not include the cost of the Subscriber Identity Module (SIM) card. The price of the SIM card should be included in the connection charge (for a prepaid service the cost of SIM is equivalent to connection charge). It should also be noted if free minutes or free SMS are included in the connection charge. Taxes should be included. If not included, it should be specified in a note including the applicable tax rate.

Mobile cellular postpaid connection charge is the initial, one-time charge for a new postpaid subscription. Refundable deposits should not be counted. Although some operators waive the connection charge, this does not include the cost of the Subscriber Identity Module (SIM) card. The price of the SIM card should be included in the connection charge. It should also be noted if free minutes or free SMS are included in the connection charge. Taxes should be included. If not included, it should be specified in a note including the applicable tax rate.

Fixed broadband Internet connection charge is the initial, one-time charge for a new fixed (wired) broadband Internet connection. The tariffs should represent the cheapest fixed (wired) broadband entry plan. Refundable deposits should not be counted. Taxes should be included. If not included, it should be specified in a note including the applicable tax rate.

Annual investment in fixed telephone service is the annual investment in equipment for fixed telephone service.

Annual investment in mobile communication is the capital investment on equipment for mobile communication networks.

Annual investment in telecommunications is the expenditure associated with acquiring the ownership of telecommunication equipment infrastructure (including supporting land and buildings and intellectual and nontangible property such as computer software). It includes expenditure on initial installations and on additions to existing installations.

Committed nominal investment in telecommunication projects with private participation is annual committed investment in telecommunication projects with private investment, including projects for fixed or mobile local telephony, domestic long-distance telephony, and international long-distance telephony.

Official development assistance (ODA) gross disbursements for communication are disbursements for communication by bilateral, multilateral, and other donors. Disbursements record the actual international transfer of financial resources or of goods or services valued at the cost of the donor.

Revenue from fixed telephone services is revenue received for the connection (installation) of telephone service (including charges for transferring or cancelling a service); revenue from recurring charges for subscription to telephone (and broadband and Internet access if not able to be separated from fixed telephone), including equipment rentals where relevant; and revenue from calls (local, national, and international).

Revenue from mobile networks is revenue from the provision of mobile cellular communications services, including all voice and data (narrowband and broadband) services. It refers to revenue earned by retailers, not by wholesalers.

Total revenue from all telecommunication services is the total (gross) telecommunication revenue earned from all (fixed, mobile, and data, including Internet) operators (both network and virtual) offering services within the country. It excludes revenues from non-telecommunications services as well as repayable subscribers' contributions or deposits. It refers to revenue earned by retailers, and by wholesalers.

Source: Data on telephone subscribers, unmet demand, reported phone faults, cost of local and cellular calls, households with telephone, Internet users and pricing, telephone and Internet connection charges, and annual investment and revenue on telecommunications are from the International Telecommunications Union data files. Data on delays for firms in obtaining a telephone connection are from World Bank Enterprise Surveys (http://rru.worldbank.org/EnterpriseSurveys/). Data on committed nominal investment are from the World Bank Private Participation in Infrastructure Project Database (http://ppi.worldbank.org). Data on official development assistance disbursements are from the Development Assistance Committee of the Organisation for Economic Co-operation and Development Geographical Distribution of Financial Flows to Developing Countries, Development Co-operation Report, and International Development Statistics database (www.oecd.org/dac/stats/idsonline).

TABLE 6.4. ENERGY

Electricity production is measured at the terminals of all alternator sets in a station. In addition to hydropower, coal, oil, gas, and nuclear power generation, it covers generation by geothermal, solar, wind, and tide and wave energy, as well as that from combustible renewable and waste. Production includes the output of electricity plants that are designed to produce electricity only as well as that of combined heat and power plants.

Hydroelectric refers to electricity produced by hydroelectric power plants.

Coal refers to all coal and brown coal, both primary (including hard coal and lignite-brown coal) and derived fuels (including patent fuel, coke oven coke, gas coke, coke oven gas, and blast furnace gas). Peat is also included.

Natural gas refers to natural gas but excludes natural gas liquids.

Nuclear refers to electricity produced by nuclear power plants.

Oil refers to crude oil and petroleum products.

Electric power consumption is the production of power plants and combined heat and power plants, less distribution losses and own use by heat and power plants.

GDP per unit of energy use is nominal GDP in purchasing power parity (PPP) U.S. dollars divided by apparent consumption, which is equal to indigenous production plus imports and stock changes minus exports and fuels supplied to ships and aircraft engaged in international transport.

Solid fuels use is the percentage of the population using solid fuels as opposed to modern fuels. Solid fuels include fuel wood, straw, dung, coal, and charcoal. Modern fuels include electricity, liquefied petroleum gas, natural gas, kerosene, and gasoline. The indicator is based on the main type of fuel used for cooking because cooking occupies the largest share of overall household energy needs. However, many households use more than one type of fuel for cooking and, depending on climatic and geographical conditions, heating with solid fuels can also contribute to indoor air pollution.

Firms identifying electricity as major or very severe obstacle to business operation and growth are the percentage of firms that responded "major" or "very severe" to the following question: "Please tell us if any of the following issues are a problem for the operation and growth of your business. If an issue (infrastructure, regulation, and permits) poses a problem, please judge its severity as an obstacle on a five-point scale that ranges from 0 = no obstacle to 5 = very severe obstacle."

Average delay for firm in obtaining electrical connection is the average actual delay in days that firms experience when obtaining an electrical connection, measured from the day the establishment applied to the day it received the service or approval.

Electric power transmission and distribution losses are technical and nontechnical losses, including electricity losses due to operation of the system and the delivery of electricity as well as those caused by unmetered supply. This comprises all losses due to transport and distribution of electrical energy and heat.

Electrical power outages in a typical month is the average number of electrical power outages in a typical month.

Firms that share or own their own generator are the percentage of firms that responded "Yes" to the following question: "Does your establishment own or share a generator?"

Firms using electricity from generator are the percentage of firms using electricity supplied from a generator or generators that the firm owns or shares.

Committed nominal investment in energy projects with private participation is annual committed investment in energy projects with private investment, including projects for electricity generation, transmission, and distribution as well as natural gas transmission and distribution.

Official development assistance (ODA) gross disbursements for energy are disbursements for energy by bilateral, multilateral, and other donors. Disbursements record the actual international transfer of financial resources or of goods or services valued at the cost of the donor.

Source: Data on electricity production and consumption are from the International Energy Agency (www.iea.org/stats/index.asp), *Energy Statistics of Non-OECD Countries*, *Energy Balances of Non-OECD Countries*, *Energy Statistics of OECD Countries*, and *Energy Balances of OECD Countries*. Data on PPP GDP per unit of energy use are from the International Energy Agency (www.iea.org/stats/index.asp) and World Bank PPP data. Data on solid fuels use are from household survey data, supplemented by World Bank Project Appraisal Documents. Data on firms identifying electricity as a major or very severe obstacle to business operation and growth, delays for firms in obtaining an electrical connection, electrical outages of firms, firms that share or own their own generator, and firms using electricity from generator are from World Bank Enterprise Surveys (http://rru.worldbank.org/EnterpriseSurveys/). Data on transmission and distribution losses are from the International Energy Agency (www.iea.org/stats/index.asp), *Energy Statistics of Non-OECD Countries*, *Energy Balances of Non-OECD Countries*, *Energy Statistics of OECD Countries*, and *Energy Balances of OECD Countries* and the United Nations *Energy Statistics Yearbook*. Data on committed nominal investment are from the World Bank Private Participation in Infrastructure Project Database (http://ppi.worldbank.org). Data on official development assistance disbursements are from the Development Assistance Committee of the Organisation for Economic Co-operation and Development *Geographical Distribution of Financial Flows to Developing Countries*, *Development Co-operation Report*, and International Development Statistics database (www.oecd.org/dac/stats/idsonline).

7. Human development

Table 7.1. Education

Youth literacy rate is the percentage of people ages 15–24 who can, with understanding, both read and write a short, simple statement about their everyday life.

Adult literacy rate is the proportion of adults ages 15 and older who can, with understanding, read and write a short, simple statement on their everyday life.

Primary education provides children with basic reading, writing, and mathematics skills along with an elementary understanding of such subjects as history, geography, natural science, social science, art, and music.

Secondary education completes the provision of basic education that began at the primary level and aims to lay the foundations for lifelong learning and human development by offering more subject- or skill-oriented instruction using more specialized teachers.

Tertiary education, whether or not at an advanced research qualification, normally requires, as a minimum condition of admission, the successful completion of education at the secondary level.

Gross enrollment ratio is the ratio of total enrollment, regardless of age, to the population of the age group that officially corresponds to the level of education shown.

Net enrollment ratio is the ratio of children of official school age, based on the International Standard Classification of Education 1997, who are enrolled in school to the population of the corresponding official school age.

Student-teacher ratio is the number of students enrolled in school divided by the number of teachers, regardless of their teaching assignment.

Public spending on education is current and capital public expenditure on education plus subsidies to private education at the primary, secondary, and tertiary levels by local, regional, and national government, including municipalities. It excludes household contributions.

Source: United Nations Educational, Scientific and Cultural Organization (UNESCO) Institute for Statistics.

Table 7.2. Health

Life expectancy at birth is the number of years a newborn infant would live if prevailing patterns of mortality at the time of its birth were to remain the same throughout its life. Data are World Bank estimates based on data from the United Nations Population Division, the United Nations Statistics Division, and national statistical offices.

Under-five mortality rate is the probability that a newborn baby will die before reaching age 5, if subject to current age-specific mortality rates. The probability is expressed as a rate per 1,000.

Infant mortality rate is the number of infants dying before reaching age 1, per 1,000 live births.

Maternal mortality ratio, modeled estimate, is the number of women who die from pregnancy-related causes during pregnancy and childbirth, per 100,000 live births. The data are estimated by a regression model using information on fertility, birth attendants, and HIV prevalence.

Prevalence of HIV is the percentage of people ages 15–49 who are infected with HIV.

Incidence of tuberculosis is the number of tuberculosis cases (pulmonary, smear positive, and extrapulmonary) in a population at a given point in time, per 100,000 people. This indicator is sometimes referred to as "point prevalence." Estimates include cases of tuberculosis among people with HIV.

Clinical malaria cases reported are the sum of cases confirmed by slide examination or rapid diagnostic test and probable and unconfirmed cases (cases that were not tested but treated as malaria). National malaria control programs often collect data on the number of suspected cases, those tested, and those confirmed. Probable or unconfirmed cases are calculated by subtracting the number tested from the number suspected. Not all cases reported as malaria are true malaria cases; most health facilities lack appropriate diagnostic services. The misdiagnosis may have led to under- or overreporting malaria cases and missing diagnosis of other treatable diseases.

Reported malaria deaths are all deaths in health facilities that are attributed to malaria, whether or not confirmed by microscopy or by rapid diagnostic test.

Child immunization rate is the percentage of children ages 12–23 months who received vaccinations before 12 months or at any time before the survey for four diseases—measles and diphtheria, pertussis (whooping cough), and tetanus (DPT). A child is considered adequately immunized against measles after receiving one dose of vaccine and against DPT after receiving three doses.

Stunting is the percentage of children under age 5 whose height for age is more than two standard deviations below the median for the international reference population ages 0–59 months. For children up to age 2, height is measured by recumbent length. For older children, height is measured by stature while standing. The reference population adopted by the World Health Organization (WHO) in 1983 is based on children from the United States, who are assumed to be well nourished.

Underweight is the percentage of children under age 5 whose weight for age is more than two standard deviations below the median reference standard for their age as established by the WHO, the U.S. Centers for Disease Control and Prevention, and the U.S. National Center for Health Statistics. Data are based on children under age 3, 4, and 5, depending on the country.

Births attended by skilled health staff are the percentage of deliveries attended by personnel trained to give the necessary supervision, care, and advice to women during pregnancy, labor, and the postpartum period; to conduct deliveries on their own; and to care for newborns.

Contraceptive use is the percentage of women ages 15–49, married or in union, who are practicing, or whose sexual partners are practicing, any form of contraception. Modern methods of contraception include female and male sterilization, oral hormonal pills, the intrauterine device, the male condom, injectables, the implant (including Norplant), vaginal barrier methods, the female condom, and emergency contraception.

Children sleeping under insecticide-treated nets are the percentage of the children under age 5 with access to an insecticide-treated net to prevent malaria.

Tuberculosis case detection rate, all forms, is the percentage of newly notified tuberculosis cases (including relapses) to estimated incident cases (case detection, all forms).

Tuberculosis treatment success rate is the percentage of new, registered smear-positive (infectious) cases that were cured or in which a full course of treatment was completed.

Children with fever receiving any antimalarial treatment same or next day are the percentage of children under age 5 in malaria-risk areas with fever being treated with any antimalarial drugs.

Population with sustainable access to an improved water source is the percentage of population with reasonable access to an adequate amount of water from an improved source, such as a household connection, public standpipe, borehole, protected well or spring, or rainwater collection. Unimproved sources include vendors, tanker trucks, and unprotected wells and springs. Reasonable access is defined as the availability of at least 20 liters a person a day from a source within 1 kilometer of the dwelling.

Population with sustainable access to improved sanitation is the percentage of the population with at least adequate access to excreta disposal facilities that can effectively prevent human, animal, and insect contact with excreta. Improved facilities range from simple but protected pit latrines to flush toilets with a sewerage connection. The excreta disposal system is considered adequate if it is private or shared (but not public) and if it hygienically separates human excreta from human contact. To be effective, facilities must be correctly constructed and properly maintained.

Physicians are the number of physicians, including generalists and specialists, per 1,000 people.

Nurses and midwives are the number of professional nurses, auxiliary nurses, enrolled nurses, and other nurses, such as dental nurses and primary care nurses, and professional midwives, auxiliary midwives, and enrolled midwives, per 1,000 people.

Community workers is the number of community workers, which includes various types of community health aides, many with country-specific occupational titles such as community health officers, community health-education workers, family health workers, woman health visitors, and health extension package workers, per 1,000 people.

Total health expenditure is the sum of public and private health expenditure. It covers the provision of health services (preventive and curative), family planning activities, nutrition activities, and emergency aid designated for health but does not include provision of water and sanitation.

Public health expenditure consists of recurrent and capital spending from government (central and local) budgets, external borrowings and grants (including donations from international agencies and nongovernmental organizations), and social (or compulsory) health insurance funds.

Private health expenditure includes direct household (out-of-pocket) spending, private insurance, charitable donations, and direct service payments by private corporations.

External resources for health are funds or services in kind that are provided by entities not part of the country in question. The resources may come from international organizations, other countries through bilateral arrangements, or foreign nongovernmental organizations. These resources are part of total health expenditure.

Out-of-pocket expenditure is any direct outlay by households, including gratuities and in-kind payments, to health practitioners and suppliers of pharmaceuticals, therapeutic appliances, and other goods and services whose primary intent is to contribute to the restoration or enhancement of the health status of individuals or population groups. It is a part of private health expenditure.

Private prepaid plans are expenditure on health by private insurance institutions. Private insurance enrollment may be contractual or voluntary, and conditions and benefits or a basket of benefits are agreed on a voluntary basis between the insurance agent and the beneficiaries. They are thus not controlled by government units for the purpose of providing social benefits to members.

Health expenditure per capita is the sum of public and private health expenditures divided by total population. It covers the provision of health services (preventive and curative), family planning activities, nutrition activities, and emergency aid designated for health but does not include provision of water and sanitation.

Source: Data on life expectancy at birth, under-five mortality, infant mortality, maternal mortality, prevalence of HIV, incidence of tuberculosis, child immunization, malnutrition, births attended by skilled health staff, contraceptive use, children sleeping under insecticide-treated nets, and children receiving antimalarial drugs are from World Bank staff estimates based on various sources, including census reports, the United Nations Population Division *World Population Prospects*, national statistical offices, household surveys conducted by national agencies and Macro International, the World Health Organization (WHO), and the United Nations Children's Fund (UNICEF). Data on clinical malaria cases reported and reported malaria deaths are from the WHO *World Malaria Report 2010*. Data on physicians, nurses, and community health workers are from the WHO Global Atlas of the Health Workforce (http://apps.who.int/globalatlas/). Data on tuberculosis are from the WHO *Global Tuberculosis Control Report*. Data on access to water and sanitation are from the WHO and UNICEF Fund Joint Monitoring Programme (www.wssinfo.org). Data on health expenditure are from the WHO National Health Account database (www.who.int/nha/en), supplemented by country data.

8. Agriculture, rural development, and Environment

Table 8.1. Rural development

Rural population is the difference between the total population and the urban population.

Rural population density is the rural population divided by the arable land area. Arable land includes land defined by the Food and Agriculture Organization (FAO) as land under temporary crops (double-cropped areas are counted once), temporary meadows for mowing or pasture, land under market or kitchen gardens, and land temporarily fallow. Land abandoned as a result of shifting cultivation is excluded.

Share of rural population below the national poverty line is the percentage of the rural population living below the national poverty line.

Rural population poverty gap at national poverty line is the mean shortfall from the poverty line (counting the nonpoor as having zero shortfall), expressed as a percentage of the poverty line. This measure reflects the depth of poverty as well as its incidence.

Share of rural population with sustainable access to an improved water source is the percentage of the rural population with reasonable access to an adequate amount of water from an improved source, such as a household connection, public standpipe, borehole, protected well or spring, or rainwater collection. Unimproved sources include vendors, tanker trucks, and unprotected wells and springs.

Reasonable access is defined as the availability of at least 20 liters a person a day from a source within 1 kilometer of the dwelling.

Share of rural population with sustainable access to improved sanitation facilities is the percentage of the rural population with at least adequate access to excreta disposal facilities that can effectively prevent human, animal, and insect contact with excreta. Improved facilities range from simple but protected pit latrines to flush toilets with a sewerage connection. The excreta disposal system is considered adequate if it is private or shared (but not public) and if it hygienically separates human excreta from human contact. To be effective, facilities must be correctly constructed and properly maintained.

Source: Data on rural population are calculated from urban population shares from the United Nations Population Division *World Urbanization Prospects* and from total population figures from the World Bank. Data on rural population density are from the FAO and World Bank population estimates. Data on rural population below the poverty line and the rural population poverty gap are from the Global Poverty Working Group and are based on World Bank' country poverty assessments and country poverty reduction strategies. Data on access to water and sanitation are from the World Health Organization and United Nations Children's Fund Joint Monitoring Programme (www.wssinfo.org).

Table 8.2. Agriculture

Agriculture value added is the gross output of forestry, hunting, and fishing, crop cultivation, and livestock production (International Standard Industrial Classification [ISIC] revision 3 divisions 1–5) less the value of their intermediate inputs. It is calculated without making deductions for depreciation of fabricated assets or depletion and degradation of natural resources. For countries that report national accounts data at producer prices (Angola, Benin, Cape Verde, Comoros, the Republic of Congo, Côte d'Ivoire, Gabon, Ghana, Liberia, Niger, Rwanda, São Tomé and Príncipe, Seychelles, Togo, and Tunisia), gross value added at market prices is used as the denominator. For countries that report national accounts data at basic prices (all other countries), gross value added at factor cost is used as the denominator. Value added at basic prices includes net taxes on products; value added at producer prices includes net taxes on products paid by producers but excludes sales or value added taxes.

Total agriculture gross production index is total agricultural production relative to the base period 1999–2001.

Crop gross production index is agricultural crop production relative to the base period 1999–2001. It includes all crops except fodder crops.

Livestock gross production index covers meat and milk from all sources, cheese, eggs, honey, raw silk, wool, and hides and skins.

Food gross production index covers food crops that are considered edible and that contain nutrients. Coffee and tea are excluded because, although edible, they have no nutritive value.

Cereal gross production index covers cereals that are considered edible and that contain nutrients.

Cereal production is crops harvested for dry grain only. Cereal crops harvested for hay or harvested green for food, feed, or silage and those used for grazing are excluded.

Cereal includes wheat, rice, maize, barley, oats, rye, millet, sorghum, buckwheat, and mixed grains.

Agricultural exports and *imports* are expressed in current U.S. dollars at free on board prices. The term agriculture in trade refers to both food and agriculture and does not include forestry and fishery products.

Food exports and *imports* are expressed in current U.S. dollars at free on board prices for exports and cost, insurance, and freight prices for imports.

Permanent cropland is land cultivated with crops that occupy the land for long periods and need not be replanted after each harvest, such as cocoa, coffee, and rubber. It includes land under flowering shrubs, fruit trees, nut trees, and vines but excludes land under trees grown for wood or timber.

Cereal cropland refers to harvested area, although some countries report only sown or cultivated area.

Agricultural irrigated land is areas equipped to provide water to the crops, including areas equipped for full and partial control irrigation, spate irrigation areas, and equipped wetland or inland valley bottoms.

Fertilizer consumption is the aggregate of nitrogenous, phosphate, and potash fertilizers.

Agricultural machinery refers to the number of wheel and crawler tractors (excluding garden tractors) in use in agriculture at the end of the calendar year specified or during the first quarter of the following year. Arable land includes land defined by the Food and Agriculture Organization (FAO) as land under temporary crops (double-cropped areas are counted once), temporary meadows for mowing or pasture, land under market or kitchen gardens, and land temporarily fallow. Land abandoned as a result of shifting cultivation is excluded.

Agricultural employment includes people who work for a public or private employer and who receive remuneration in wages, salary, commission, tips, piece rates, or pay in kind. Agriculture corresponds to division 1 (ISIC revision 2) or tabulation categories A and B (ISIC revision 3) and includes hunting, forestry, and fishing.

Agriculture value added per worker is the output of the agricultural sector (ISIC divisions 1–5) less the value of intermediate inputs. Agriculture comprises value added from forestry, hunting, fishing, crop cultivation, and livestock production. Data are in constant 2000 U.S. dollars.

Cereal yield is dry grain only and includes wheat, rice, maize, barley, oats, rye, millet, sorghum, buckwheat, and mixed grains. Cereal crops harvested for hay or harvested green for food, feed, or silage and those used for grazing are excluded.

Source: Data on agriculture value added are from Organisation for Economic Co-operation and Development and World Bank national accounts data files. Data on crop, livestock, food, and cereal production, cereal exports and imports, agricultural exports and imports, permanent cropland, cereal cropland, agricultural machinery, cereal yield, and fertilizer consumption are from FAO

Transformation of Rwanda's coffee sector: an African success story

Punam Chuhan-Pole and Manka S. Angwafo

For many years, Rwanda's coffee sector was stuck in a "low-quality/low-quantity trap." Compulsory production, substantial export taxes, and a monopsony export control agency meant that producers had little incentive to invest in producing high-quality coffee. Highly volatile world coffee prices in the 1980s (and state capture during boom years), coupled with the country's economic deterioration during the 1994 genocide, left coffee producers in an even worse situation.

The post-genocide regime set out to revitalize and transform the coffee sector. Changes were implemented in several waves. The first began in the late 1990s, when the government removed a variety of trade barriers, created incentives for groups and individuals to transfer their efforts from semiwashed to fully washed (higher value) coffee as an end product, and facilitated entrepreneurship in the coffee industry. More substantial reform efforts began in 2000, when the government, working with consultants and donors, studied the potential for adding value to Rwandan coffee by producing higher-quality, washed, and fermented specialty coffee. In 2002, the government issued a national coffee strategy that outlined a plan for capturing a larger share of the specialty-coffee sector. In the intervening years, more than 100 coffee washing stations were built (table 1).

Table 1 Growth in the specialty coffee sector

	2001	2002	2003	2004	2005	2006	2007	2008	2009
Washing stations	—	1	10	25	45	76	112	—	112
Green specialty coffee exported (tons)	—	30	300	800	1,200	3,000	2,300	2,455	3,045
Specialty coffee buyers	—	2	8	16	25	30	30	—	—
Total value of specialty cofee exported ($ thousands)	—	90	720	1,850	3,168	8,000	7,800	8,060	11,600

— is not available.
Source: U.S. Agency for International Development

Rwanda's approach to liberalizing its coffee sector has resulted in the country's coffee farmers having the opportunity to sell higher-quality beans for a higher price. Indeed, the average export price of coffee nearly doubled over 2003–2008, from $1.60 to $3.10 (figure 1). For smallholder farmers and other participants in the coffee value chain (figure 2), producing specialty coffee means not just more income but expanded connections to world markets and positive effects from informal economic cooperation at coffee washing stations. Coffee washing stations had created 4,000 jobs as of 2006, and Rwandan coffee exports generated more than $47 million in revenue in 2008, compared with $35 million in 2007.

Figure 1 Average farmer and export prices, 2003–08

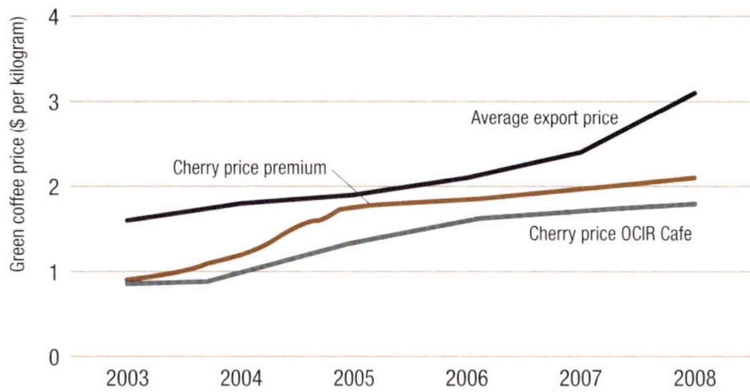

Source: Rwanda Ministry of Agriculture and Animal Husbandry and Ministry of Trade and Industry (2008).

Figure 2 Value chain for washed coffee

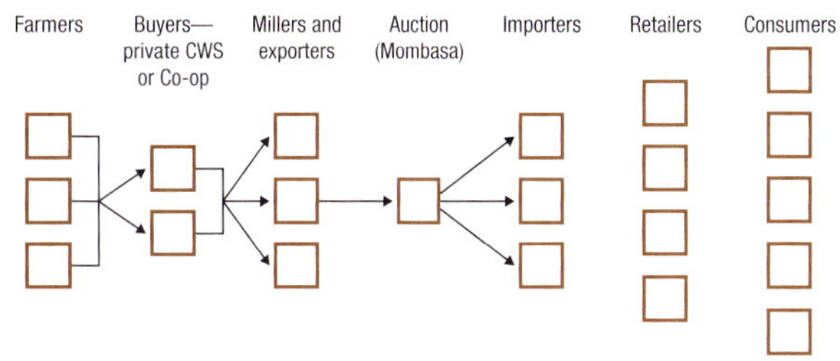

Rwanda's experience shows that reforming policies can unleash private sector activity and pave the way for growth. The willingness of the government to allow liberalization of the coffee sector has paid off. Rwanda could further improve the performance of this sector—for example, by implementing further price incentives for producers to focus on high-quality coffee, improving management of producer cooperatives, and reducing still-high transportation costs related to poor infrastructure and the country's landlocked status.

Source: Adapted from K. Boudreaux. 2010. "A Better Brew for Success in Rwanda: Economic Liberalization in the Coffee Sector." In *Yes Africa Can: Success Stories from a Dynamic Continent,* ed. P. Chuhan-Pole and M. Angwafo. World Bank: Washington, DC.

electronic files and website. Data on agricultural employment are from the International Labour Organization Key Indicators of the Labour Market database.

Table 8.3. Producer food prices

Prices in U.S. dollars are equal to producer prices in local currency times the exchange rate of the selected year. The main source for exchange rates is the International Monetary Fund. Where official and commercial exchange rates differ significantly, the commercial exchange rate may be applied. Producer prices are prices received by farmers for primary agricultural products as defined in the 1993 System of National Accounts.

The producer price is the amount receivable by the producer from the purchaser for a unit of a good or service produced as output minus any value added tax or similar deductible tax invoiced to the purchaser. It excludes any transport charges invoiced separately by the producer. Time series refer to the national average prices of individual commodities comprising all grades, kinds, and varieties received by farmers when they participate in their capacity as sellers of their own products at the farm gate or first point of sale.

Source: Data are from Food and Agriculture Organization electronic files and website.

TABLE 8.4. ENVIRONMENT

Forest area is land under natural or planted stands of trees, whether productive or not.

Renewable internal fresh water resources refer to internal renewable resources (internal river flows and groundwater from rainfall) in the country.

Annual fresh water withdrawals refer to total water withdrawals, not counting evaporation losses from storage basins. Withdrawals also include water from desalination plants in countries where they are a significant source. Withdrawals can exceed 100 percent of total renewable resources where extraction from nonrenewable aquifers or desalination plants is considerable or where there is significant water reuse. Withdrawals for agriculture and industry are total withdrawals for irrigation and livestock production and for direct industrial use (including withdrawals for cooling thermoelectric plants). Withdrawals for domestic uses include drinking water, municipal use or supply, and use for public services, commercial establishments, and homes.

Water productivity is calculated as gross domestic product in constant prices divided by annual total water withdrawal.

Emissions of organic water pollutants are measured in terms of biochemical oxygen demand, which refers to the amount of oxygen that bacteria in water will consume in breaking down waste. This is a standard water-treatment test for the presence of organic pollutants.

Energy production refers to forms of primary energy—petroleum (crude oil, natural gas liquids, and oil from nonconventional sources), natural gas, solid fuels (coal, lignite, and other derived fuels), and combustible renewable and waste—and primary electricity, all converted into oil equivalents.

Energy use refers to use of primary energy before transformation to other end-use fuels, which is equal to indigenous production plus imports and stock changes, minus exports and fuels supplied to ships and aircraft engaged in international transport.

Combustible renewables and waste comprise solid biomass, liquid biomass, biogas, industrial waste, and municipal waste, measured as a percentage of total energy use.

Carbon dioxide emissions are those stemming from the burning of fossil fuels and the manufacture of cement. They include carbon dioxide produced during consumption of solid, liquid, and gas fuels and gas flaring.

Methane emissions, total, are those from human activities such as agriculture and from industrial methane production.

Methane emissions, agricultural, are those from animals, animal waste, rice production, agricultural waste burning (nonenergy, on-site), and savannah burning.

Methane emissions, industrial, are those from the handling, transmission, and combustion of fossil fuels and biofuels.

Nitrous oxide emissions, total, are those from agricultural biomass burning, industrial activities, and livestock management.

Nitrous oxide emissions, agricultural, are those produced through fertilizer use (synthetic and animal manure), animal waste management, agricultural waste burning (nonenergy, on-site), and savannah burning.

Nitrous oxide emissions, industrial, are those produced during the manufacturing of adipic acid and nitric acid.

Other greenhouse gas emissions are by-product emissions of hydrofluorocarbons, perfluorocarbons, and sulfur hexafluoride.

Official development assistance (ODA) gross disbursements for forestry are disbursements for forestry by bilateral, multilateral, and other donors. Disbursements record the actual international transfer of financial resources or of goods or services valued at the cost of the donor.

Official development assistance (ODA) gross disbursements for general environment protection are disbursements for general

Food prices in Africa

Sailesh Tiwari and Hassan Zaman

Although global food prices remain high, the World Bank's nominal food price index has stabilized in recent months after peaking during the food price crisis in February. Still, prices are only 6 percent less than the 2008 peaks and continuing uncertainties are likely to keep them volatile. The primary drivers of the most recent surge in food prices include: severe weather events in key grain exporting countries, such as the Argentina, Australia, Canada, Kazakhstan, and the Russian Federation in the second half of 2010; broad increases in prices of agricultural commodities and the resultant increases in competition for land and other inputs; and the link between higher oil prices and the diversion of key food commodities into the production of biofuels.

In Africa, however, domestic prices of key food commodities have been driven largely by the variability of local supply, as opposed to global trends. The continent's isolated agricultural markets might be a reason for the low pass-through of global prices. One particularly salient consequence is that local shortfalls in production—related either to poor rains and drought or to supply disruptions resulting from conflict—often lead to significant differences in price movements within countries. The price of rice in Benin, for instance, rose 33 percent in Bohicon but fell 4 percent in Cotonou between March and April 2011. A low average increase in food prices can mask significant increases in poverty in specific parts of a country, a primary reason some countries have isolated pockets of food insecurity.

Recent food price trends in Africa underscore this point. Eastern Africa was hit with a drought severely affecting the secondary season harvests, and as a result the prices of maize and sorghum—the region's two main staples—have risen sharply since February. Maize prices in Kenya and Uganda had almost doubled by May, and in Tanzania (Dar es Salaam) they were 59 percent higher than a year ago. By contrast, favorable prospects for maize harvests have led to steady or declining prices across Southern Africa.

Western Africa, where sorghum and millet are the staple crops, still enjoys adequate supplies from the bumper harvests of previous years. The prices of these crops have remained stable in Burkina Faso, Mali, and Niger, and even where there has been some seasonal increase, as in some markets in Chad, the price levels remain lower than where they were last year. However, rising costs of importing fuel and food grains, such as rice and wheat, pose a significant threat to the region's macroeconomic stability. Net importers of food and fuel will likely see external and fiscal balances erode and inflationary pressures build up, as import bills grow and governments shelter domestic consumers from high international prices. Already, Sierra Leone has reduced import duties on rice and petroleum products by 10 percent to avert growing unrest over rising prices of essential commodities.

environment protection by bilateral, multilateral, and other donors. Disbursements record the actual international transfer of financial resources or of goods or services valued at the cost of the donor.

Source: Data on forest area and deforestation are from the Food and Agriculture Organization (FAO) *Global Forest Resources Assessment*. Data on fresh water resources and withdrawals are from the World Resources Institute, supplemented by FAO AQUASTAT data. Data on emissions of organic water pollutants are from the World Bank. Data on energy production and use and combustible renewable and waste are from the International Energy Agency. Data on carbon dioxide emissions are from Carbon Dioxide Information Analysis Center, Environmental Sciences Division, Oak Ridge National Laboratory. Data on methane emissions, nitrous oxide emissions, and other greenhouse gas emissions are from the International Energy Agency. Data on official development assistance disbursements are from the Development Assistance Committee of the Organisation for Economic Co-operation and Development *Geographical Distribution of Financial Flows to Developing Countries*, *Development Co-operation Report*, and International Development Statistics database (www.oecd.org/dac/stats/idsonline).

Table 8.5. Fossil fuel emissions

Carbon dioxide emissions are those stemming from the burning of fossil fuels and the manufacture of cement. They include carbon dioxide produced during consumption of solid, liquid, and gas fuels and gas flaring.

Carbon dioxide emissions per capita are carbon dioxide emissions divided by midyear population.

Fossil fuel is any hydrocarbon deposit that can be burned for heat or power, such as petroleum, coal, and natural gas.

Total carbon dioxide emissions from fossil fuels is the sum of all fossil fuel emissions (solid fuel consumption, liquid fuel consumption, gas fuel consumption, gas flaring, and cement production).

Carbon dioxide emissions from solid fuel consumption refer mainly to emissions from use of coal as an energy source and from secondary fuels derived from hard and soft coal (such as coke-oven coke).

Carbon dioxide emissions from liquid fuel consumption refer to emissions from use of crude petroleum and natural gas liquids as an energy source and from secondary fuels derived from oil (such as jet fuel).

Carbon dioxide emissions from gas fuel consumption refer mainly to emissions from use of natural gas as an energy source and from secondary fuels derived from natural gas (such as blast furnace gas).

Carbon dioxide emissions from gas flaring refer mainly to emissions from gas flaring activities.

Carbon dioxide emissions from cement production refer mainly to emissions during cement production. Cement production is a multistep process, and carbon dioxide is actually released from klinker production during the process.

Source: Data on carbon dioxide emissions and fossil fuels are from Carbon Dioxide Information Analysis Center Environmental Sciences Division, Oak Ridge National Laboratory.

9. Labor, migration, and population

Table 9.1. Labor force participation

Labor force is people ages 15 and older who meet the International Labour Organization (ILO) definition of the economically active population. It includes both the employed and the unemployed. While national practices vary in the treatment of such groups as the armed forces and seasonal or part-time workers, the labor force generally includes the armed forces, the unemployed, and first-time job seekers but excludes homemakers and other unpaid caregivers and workers in the informal sector.

Participation rate is the percentage of the population of the specified age group that is economically active—that is, all people who supply labor for the production of goods and services during a specified period.

Source: ILO Key Indicators of the Labour Market database.

Table 9.2. Labor force composition

Agriculture corresponds to division 1 (International Standard Industrial Classification [ISIC] revision 2) or tabulation categories A and B (ISIC revision 3) and includes hunting, forestry, and fishing.

Industry corresponds to divisions 2–5 (ISIC revision 2) or tabulation categories C–F (ISIC revision 3) and includes mining and quarrying (including oil production), manufacturing, construction, and public utilities (electricity, gas, and water).

Services correspond to divisions 6–9 (ISIC revision 2) or tabulation categories G–P (ISIC revision 3) and include wholesale and retail trade and restaurants and hotels; transport, storage, and communications; financing, insurance, real estate, and business services; and community, social, and personal services.

Wage and salaried workers are workers who hold the type of jobs defined as paid employment jobs, where incumbents hold explicit (written or oral) or implicit employment contracts that give them a basic remuneration that is not directly dependent on the revenue of the unit for which they work.

Self-employed workers are self-employed workers with employees (employers), self-employed workers without employees (own-account workers), and members of producer cooperatives. Although the contributing family workers category is technically part of the self-employed according to the classification used by the International Labour Organization (ILO), and could therefore be combined with the other self-employed categories to derive the total self-employed, they are reported here as a separate category to emphasize the difference between the two statuses, since the socioeconomic implications associated with each status can vary substantially. This practice follows that of the ILO *Key Indicators of the Labour Market*.

Contributing family workers are unpaid workers who hold self-employment jobs as own-account workers in a market-oriented establishment operated by a related person living in the same household.

Source: ILO Key Indicators of the Labour Market database.

Table 9.3. Unemployment

Unemployment is the share of the labor force of the specified subgroup without work but available for and seeking employment.

Primary education provides children with basic reading, writing, and mathematics skills along with an elementary understanding of such subjects as history, geography, natural science, social science, art, and music.

Secondary education completes the provision of basic education that began at the primary level and aims to lay the foundations for lifelong learning and human development by offering more subject- or skill-oriented instruction using more specialized teachers.

Tertiary education, whether or not at an advanced research qualification, normally requires, as a minimum condition of admission, the successful completion of education at the secondary level.

Source: International Labour Organization Key Indicators of the Labour Market database.

TABLE 9.4. MIGRATION AND POPULATION

Migrant stock is the number of people born in a country other than that in which they live. It includes refugees.

Net migration is the annual number of immigrants less the annual number of emigrants, including both citizens and noncitizens. Data are five-year estimates.

Worker remittances, received, comprise current transfers by migrant workers and wages and salaries by nonresident workers.

Migrant remittance flows are the sum of worker remittances, compensation of employees, and migrants' transfers, as recorded in the International Monetary Fund *Balance of Payments.*

Population is total population based on the de facto definition of population, which counts all residents regardless of legal status or citizenship, except for refugees not permanently settled in the country of asylum, who are generally considered part of the population of their country of origin. The values shown are midyear estimates.

Fertility rate is the number of children that would be born to a woman if she were to live to the end of her childbearing years and bear children in accordance with current age-specific fertility rates.

Age composition refers to the percentage of the total population that is in specific age groups.

Dependency ratio is the ratio of dependents —people younger than 15 or older than 64— to the working-age population (ages 15–64).

Rural population is calculated as the difference between the total population and the urban population.

Urban population is the midyear population of areas defined as urban in each country.

Source: Data on migration are from the United Nations Population Division *Trends in Total Migrant Stock: The 2008 Revision*. Data on population are from the United Nations Population Division *World Population Prospects: The 2008 Revision*, census reports and other statistical publications from national statistical offices, Eurostat *Demographic Statistics*, Secretariat of the Pacific Community Statistics and Demography Programme, U.S. Census Bureau International Database, and World Bank estimates based on data from these sources as well as household surveys conducted by national agencies, Macro International, the U.S. Centers for Disease Control and Prevention, and refugees statistics from the United Nations High Commissioner for Refugees. Data on dependency ratio are from World Bank staff estimates based on various sources, including census reports, the United Nations Population Division *World Population Prospects*, national statistical offices, household surveys conducted by national agencies, and Macro International. Data on worker remittances are from the International Monetary Fund *Balance of Payments Statistics Yearbook* and data files. Data from migrant remittance flows are from World Bank staff estimates based on the International Monetary Fund *Balance of Payments Statistics Yearbook 2008.*

10. HIV/AIDS

TABLE 10.1. HIV/AIDS

Estimated number of people living with HIV/AIDS is the number of people in the specified age group living with HIV.

Estimated HIV prevalence rate is the percentage of the population of the specified age subgroup who are infected with HIV. Depending on the reliability of the data available, there may be uncertainty surrounding each estimate. Therefore, plausible bounds are presented for each subgroup rate (low and high estimate).

Deaths of adults and children due to HIV/AIDS are the estimated number of adults and children that have died in a specific year,

Every country in Africa has been affected by migration. Often viewed as a "brain drain," migration can generate substantial benefits for origin countries through remittances, investments, contacts with foreign markets, technology transfer, enhanced skills of returning emigrants, and even increased demand for education (World Bank 2011a). About 30 million Africans (roughly 3 percent of the population) have left their origin country—and sometimes the continent. Some two-thirds of migrants from Sub-Saharan Africa, particularly the poorer, go to other countries in the region; the bulk of migrants remain in their subregions.[1] By contrast, more than 90 percent of North African migrants leave the region, in part because of their proximity to Europe and the Middle East. The top destinations for African migrants are France (9 percent of total emigrants), Côte d'Ivoire (8 percent), South Africa (6 percent), Saudi Arabia (5 percent), and the United States and the United Kingdom (4 percent each). The percentage of a country's population that has emigrated is especially large in countries with small populations or histories of conflict.

Migrant remittance flows to Africa reached nearly $40 billion (2.6 percent of GDP) in 2010 (roughly equally divided between North Africa and Sub-Saharan Africa), almost double the amount in 2005 and more than four times the $9.1 billion received in 1990. Remittances are Africa's largest source of foreign capital after foreign direct investments (figure 1). Including flows through informal channels, the volume of remittances is likely even higher (Ratha 2007; Ratha, Mohapatra, and Plaza 2009). Nigeria accounted for about half the officially recorded remittances to Sub-Saharan Africa in 2010 (World Bank 2011). Other large remittance recipients include Ethiopia, Kenya, Senegal, South Africa, Sudan, and Uganda. But smaller countries are not the largest recipients of remittances as a share of GDP, which include Lesotho, which received 27 percent of GDP in 2009. In Cape Verde, Gambia, Guinea-Bissau, Liberia, Senegal, Sierra Leone, and Togo remittances were 7–10 percent of GDP. Egypt and Morocco, the two largest North African recipients both in dollar-denominated flows and as a share of GDP, account for three-quarters of flows to the region.

Figure 1 Remittances and other resource flows to Africa, 1990–2010

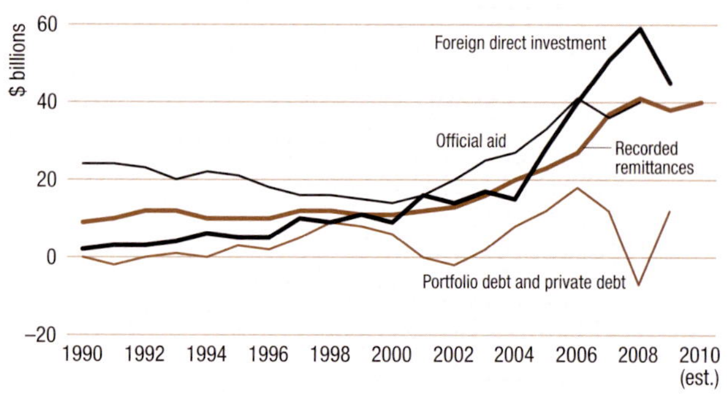

Source: Authors' analysis based on data from the World Bank Global Development Finance 2010 database.

Remittances tend to be more stable than other sources of foreign exchange, are often countercyclical (helping sustain consumption and investment during downturns), and improve sovereign creditworthiness and debt sustainability by increasing the level and stability of foreign exchange receipts (Chami, Hakura, and Montiel 2009; IMF 2010; Avendano, Gaillard, and Nieto-Parra 2009; World Bank 2006). At the micro level, both country and cross-country analyses have shown that remittances reduce poverty (Adams and Page 2003, 2005; Gupta, Pattillo, and Wagh 2009; Anyanwu and Erhijakpor 2010). Studies of Burkina Faso (Wouterse 2010), Ghana (Adams 2006; Quartey and Blankson 2004; Adams, Cuecuecha, and Page 2008), Lesotho (Gustafsson and Makonnen 1993), Morocco (Bourchachen 2000; Sorensen 2004), and Nigeria (Odozia, Awoyemia, and Omonona 2010) conclude that remittances are associated with a reduced share of people in poverty, and in some cased reduced depth and severity of poverty as well. Remittances also spur spending on health, education, housing, and investments.[2]

The Africa Migration Project household surveys show that buying land, building a home, and starting a business were among the highest uses of remittances—15 percent in Senegal, 20 percent in Uganda, 36 percent in Burkina Faso, 55 percent in Kenya, and 57 percent in Nigeria (Plaza, Navarrete, and Ratha 2011). Education was the second highest use of remittances from outside Africa into Nigeria and Uganda, the third highest into Burkina Faso, and the fourth highest into Kenya. In addition, remittances insure against adverse shocks. For example, Ethiopian households that receive international remittances were less likely than other households to sell their productive assets, such as livestock, to cope with food shortages (Mohapatra, Joseph, and Ratha 2009). And remittances enable poorer households in KwaZulu-Natal province, South Africa, to access better medical care (Nagarajan 2009).

However, the cost of sending remittances continues to remain high for Africa, averaging $23 for a $200 transaction, compared with less than $16 for most developing regions. The cost of cross-border remittances within Africa, if permitted at all, tends to be even higher. These high costs reflect the limited reach and expense of formal financial services (relative to average African incomes), the exchange controls on outward transfers in Africa, and the dominance of a few large money transfer companies, which often work exclusively with commercial banks, post offices, and other providers (IFAD 2009; Irving, Mohapatra, and Ratha 2010). Governments in Africa and in migrant-destination countries outside Africa should discourage such exclusive agreements. Post offices, credit cooperatives, rural banks, and microfinance institutions have large networks (particularly among the poor), providing a unique opportunity to expand formal remittance markets among the poor and in rural areas.[3]

Despite these challenges, the rapid adoption of mobile money transfer services is demonstrating enormous potential to broaden the reach of formal remittance markets and expand access to formal financial services. Money transfer services through mobile phone networks have increased significantly in Africa, for example through M-pesa in Kenya (by end 2010, M-Pesa had more than 12 million customers), Zain/Airtel in more than 15 African countries, Orange Money in West Africa, MTN and Ecobank in Benin, Splash in Sierra Leone, and Wizzit in South Africa. Some mobile money transfer service providers offer basic deposit and savings accounts in partnership with African banks, such as the "M-Kesho" low-cost savings account offered by Safaricom, in partnership with Equity Bank. These services are used mostly for domestic money transfers, while their use for cross-border remittances remains limited (other than a few pilots) because of concerns over money laundering, insufficient maturity of branchless banking infrastructure on the receiving end, and lack of customer awareness and trust in new services (Bold 2010).

Large remittance inflows can present a macroeconomic challenge, however, by causing the exchange rate to appreciate, potentially reducing the production of tradable goods. Policymakers in countries that receive very large remittance flows should be alert to their impacts on the exchange rate. In addition to maintaining a flexible exchange rate and considering remittance inflows when crafting targets for reserves policies and money supply growth, African policymakers can implement microeconomic interventions to ease labor market rigidities and reforms to improve competitiveness.

African governments can potentially improve their access to international capital markets by issuing bonds that are securitized by future remittance inflows (Ketkar and Ratha 2009) and by floating bonds aimed at the African diaspora (Okonjo-Iweala and Ratha 2011). Some measures to expedite these instruments include facilitating flows through formal remittance channels, obtaining sovereign ratings, and implementing a securitization law. Multilateral and bilateral donors can play a role in such transactions. Any increase in foreign currency debt, however, should be accompanied by prudential risk management.

Notes

1. In West Africa, for example, more than 70 percent of intra-African emigration is within the subregion (World Bank 2011a).
2. See Adams, Cuecuecha, and Page (2008a) for evidence from Ghana and Elbadawi and Roushdy (2009) for Egypt.
3. A recent survey by the Universal Postal Union found that 81 percent of post offices in Sub-Saharan Africa are outside the three largest cities, where more than 80 percent of Africans live; by contrast, mainstream commercial banks in Africa are concentrated in the largest cities (Clotteau and Anson 2011).

References

Adams, Richard H. 2006. "Remittances and Poverty in Ghana." Policy Research Working Paper 3838, World Bank, Washington, DC.

Adams, Richard H., Alfredo Cuecuecha, and John Page. 2008. "The Impact of Remittances on Poverty and Inequality in Ghana." Policy Research Working Paper 4732, World Bank, Washington, DC.

Adams, Richard H., and John Page. 2003. "International Migration, Remittances and Poverty in Developing Countries." Policy Research Working Paper 3179, World Bank, Washington, DC.

——. 2005. "Do International Migration and Remittances Reduce Poverty in Developing Countries?" *World Development* 33 (10): 1645–69.

Anyanwu, John C., and Andrew E. O. Erhijakpor. 2010. "Do International Remittances Affect Poverty in Africa?" *African Development Review* 22 (1): 51–91

Avendaño, Rolando, Norbert Gaillard, and Sebastián Nieto Parra. 2009. "Are Workers' Remittances Relevant for Credit Rating Agencies?" OECD Development Centre Working Paper 282, Organisation for Economic Cooperation and Development, Paris.

Bold, Chris. 2010. "Borderless, Branchless Banking." Consultative Group to Assist the Poor. http://technology.cgap.org/2010/12/14/borderless-branchless-banking/

Bourchachen, J. 2000. "Apports des transferts des résidents à l'etranger à la réduction de la pauvreté : Cas du Maroc." www.yabiladi.com/clocs/Transfert_sociaux.rme.pdf.

Chami, Ralph, Dalia Hakura, and Peter Montiel. 2009. "Remittances: An Automatic Stabilizer?" IMF Working Paper 09/91, International Monetary Fund, Washington, DC.

Clemens, Michael. 2009 "Skill Flow: A Fundamental Reconsideration of Skilled-Worker Mobility and Development". Working Paper 180, Center of Global Development, Washington, DC.

Elbadawi, Asmaa, and Rania Roushdy. 2009. "Impact of International Migration and Remittances on Child Schooling and Child Work: The Case of Egypt." Paper Prepared for the World Bank's MENA International Migration Program Funded by the European Commission, World Bank, Washington, DC.

Gupta, Sanjeev, Catherine A. Pattillo, and Smita Wagh. 2009. "Impact of Remittances on Poverty and Financial Development in Sub-Saharan Africa." *World Development* 37 (1): 104–15.

Gustafsson, Bjorn, and Negatu Makonnen. 1993. "Poverty and Remittances in Lesotho." *Journal of African Economies* 2 (1): 49–73.

IFAD (International Fund for Agriculture and Development). 2009. *Sending Money Home to Africa.* Rome: International Fund for Agricultural Development.

IMF (International Monetary Fund). 2010. "Staff Guidance Note on the Application of the Joint Bank-Fund Debt Sustainability Framework for Low-Income Countries." Prepared by the staffs of the IMF and the World Bank, January 22.

Irving, Jacqueline, Sanket Mohapatra, and Dilip Ratha. 2010. "Migrant Remittance Flows: Findings from a Global Survey of Central Banks." Working Paper 194, World Bank, Washington, DC.

Ketkar, Suhas, and Dilip Ratha, eds. 2009. *Innovative Financing for Development.* Washington, DC: World Bank.

Lachaud. Jean-Pierre. 1999. "Envoi de fonds, inegalite et pauvrete au Burkina Faso." Documents de travail 40, Groupe d'Economie du Développement de l'Université Montesquieu Bordeaux IV.

Lucas, Robert E.B., and Oded Stark. 1985. "Motivations to Remit: Evidence from Botswana." *Journal of Political Economy* 93 (5): 901–18.

(continued)

Mohapatra, Sanket, George Joseph, and Dilip Ratha. 2009. "Remittances and Natural Disasters: Ex-Post Response and Contribution to Ex-Ante Preparedness." Policy Research Working Paper 4972, World Bank, Washington, DC.

Nagarajan, Subha. 2009. "Migration, Remittances, and Household Health: Evidence from South Africa." Ph.D. dissertation, George Washington University, Washington, DC.

Odozia, John C., Timothy T. Awoyemia, and Bolarin T. Omonona. 2010. "Household Poverty and Inequality: The Implication of Migrants' Remittances in Nigeria." *Journal of Economic Policy Reform* 13 (2): 191–99

Okonjo-Iweala, Ngozi, and Dilip Ratha, 2011. "Homeward Bond." *New York Times*.

Quartey, Peter. 2006. "The Impact of Migrant Remittances on Household Welfare in Ghana." Research Paper 158, AERC, Nairobi.

Quartey, Peter, and Theresa Blankson. 2004. *Do Migrant Remittances Minimize the Impact of Macro-volatility on the Poor in Ghana.* Report prepared for the Global Development Network, University of Ghana, Legon.

Plaza, Sonia, Mario Navarrete, and Dilip Ratha. 2011. "Migration and Remittances Household Surveys in Sub-Saharan Africa: Methodological Aspects and Main Findings." Background paper, World Bank, DEC-PREM, Migration and Remittances Unit, Washington, DC.

Ratha, Dilip, Sanket Mohapatra, Çağlar Özden, Sonia Plaza, and Abebe Shimeles. 2011. *Leveraging Migration for Africa: Remittances, Skills, Investments.* A joint report of the African Development Bank and the World Bank, Washington, DC.

Ratha, Dilip, Sanket Mohapatra, and Sonia Plaza. 2009. "Beyond Aid: New Sources and Innovative Mechanisms for Financing Development in Sub-Saharan Africa." In *Innovative Financing for Development,* ed. Suhas Ketkar and Dilip Ratha, 143–183. Washington DC: World Bank.

Sorensen, Ninna Nyberg. 2004. "Migrant Remittances as a Development Tool: The Case of Morocco." IOM Working Paper 2, International Organization for Migration, Geneva. www.belgium.iom.int/pan-europeandialogue/documents/remittances_morocco.pdf.

Tevera, Daniel, and Abel Chikanda. 2009. "Migrant Remittances and Household Survival in Zimbabwe." Working Paper, Southern African Migration Project, Cape Town.

World Bank. 2006. *Diaspora Networks and the International Migration of Skills: How Countries Can Draw on Their Talent Abroad,* ed. Yevgeny Kuznetsov. World Bank: Washington, DC.

———. 2011. *Leveraging Migration for Africa: Remittances, Skills, Investments.* A joint report of the African Development Bank and the World Bank, Washington, DC.

Wouterse, Fleur. 2010. "Remittances, Poverty, Inequality and Welfare: Evidence from the Central Plateau of Burkina Faso." *Journal of Development Studies* 46 (4): 771–89.

based on the modeling of HIV surveillance data using standard and appropriate tools.

AIDS orphans are the estimated number of children who have lost their mother or both parents to AIDS before age 17 since the epidemic began in 1990. Some of the orphaned children included in this cumulative total are no longer alive; others are no longer under age 17.

HIV-positive pregnant women receiving antiretrovirals to reduce the risk of mother-to-child transmission are the number of pregnant women infected with HIV who received antiretrovirals during the last 12 months to reduce the risk of mother-to-child transmission.

Share of HIV-positive pregnant women receiving antiretrovirals, World Health Organization/ Joint United Nations Programme on HIV/AIDS (WHO/UNAIDS) methodology, is the percentage of pregnant women infected with HIV who received antiretrovirals to reduce the risk of mother-to-child transmission divided by the total number of pregnant women infected with HIV in the last 12 months. The WHO/UNAIDS methodology may differ from country methodologies.

Official development assistance (ODA) disbursements for social mitigation of HIV/AIDS are spending on special programs to address the consequences of HIV/AIDS, such as social, legal, and economic assistance to people living with HIV/AIDS (including food security and employment); spending on support to vulnerable groups and children orphaned as a result of HIV/AIDS; and spending on human rights advocacy for people affected by HIV/AIDS.

Official development assistance (ODA) disbursements for sexually transmitted disease (STD) control, including HIV/AIDS, are spending on all activities related to STDs and HIV/AIDS control, such as information, education, communication, testing, prevention, and treatment.

Source: Data on number of people living with HIV/AIDS, HIV prevalence rate, deaths due to HIV/AIDS, AIDS orphans, and HIVpositive pregnant women receiving antiretrovirals are from UNAIDS and WHO *Report on the Global AIDS Epidemic.* A more detailed explanation of methods and assumptions can be found on the UNAIDS reference group on estimates, modeling, and projections website (www.unaids.org/en/KnowledgeCentre/HIVData/Epidemiology/) and in a series of papers published in *Sexually Transmitted Infections,* "Improved Methods and Tools for HIV/AIDS Estimates and Projections," 2008, 84 (Suppl I); 2006, 82 (Suppl III); and 2004, 80 (Suppl I). Data on official development assistance disbursements are from the Development Assistance Committee of the Organisation for Economic Co-operation and Development *Geographical Distribution of Financial Flows to Developing Countries, Development Co-operation Report,* and International Development Statistics database (www.oecd.org/dac/stats/idsonline).

11. Malaria

TABLE 11.1. MALARIA

Population is total population based on the de facto definition of population, which counts all residents regardless of legal status or citizenship—except for refugees not permanently settled in the country of asylum, who are generally considered part of the population of their country of origin. The values shown are midyear estimates.

Clinical malaria cases reported are the sum of cases confirmed by slide examination or rapid diagnostic test and probable and unconfirmed cases (cases that were not tested but treated as malaria). National malaria control programs often collect data on the number of suspected cases, those tested, and those confirmed. Probable or unconfirmed cases are calculated by subtracting the number tested from the number suspected. Not all cases reported as malaria are true malaria cases; most health facilities lack appropriate diagnostic services. The misdiagnosis may have led to under- or overreporting malaria cases and missing diagnosis of other treatable diseases.

Reported malaria deaths are all deaths in health facilities that are attributed to malaria, whether or not confirmed by microscopy or by rapid diagnostic test.

Under-five mortality rate is the probability that a newborn baby will die before reaching age 5, if subject to current age-specific mortality rates. The probability is expressed as a rate per 1,000.

Children sleeping under insecticide-treated nets is the percentage of children under age 5 with access to an insecticide-treated net to prevent malaria.

Children with fever receiving any antimalarial treatment are the percentage of children under age 5 in malaria-risk areas with fever being treated with any antimalarial drugs.

Pregnant women receiving two doses of intermittent preventive treatment are the number of pregnant women receiving two or more doses of sulfadoxine pyrimethamine during an antenatal care visit. In some country surveys the site of treatment (during the antenatal care visit) is not specified. This approach has been shown to be safe, inexpensive, and effective.

Official development assistance (ODA) disbursements for malaria control are spending on prevention and control of malaria.

Source: Data on population are from the United Nations Population Division *World Population Prospects: The 2008 Revision*, census reports and other statistical publications from national statistical offices, Eurostat *Demographic Statistics*, Secretariat of the Pacific Community Statistics and Demography Programme, U.S. Census Bureau International Database, and World Bank estimates based on data from these sources as well as household surveys conducted by national agencies, Macro International, the U.S. Centers for Disease Control and Prevention, and refugees statistics from the United Nations High Commissioner for Refugees. Data on clinical cases of malaria reported and reported malaria deaths are from the World Health Organization (WHO) *World Malaria Report 2009.* Data on children with fever receiving antimalarial drugs and pregnant women receiving two doses of intermittent preventive treatment are from Demographic Health Surveys, Multiple Indicator Cluster Surveys, and national statistical offices. Data on deaths due to malaria are from the United Nations Statistics Division and based on WHO estimates. Data on under-five mortality are harmonized estimates of the WHO, United Nations Children's Fund, and the World Bank, based mainly on household surveys, censuses, and vital registration, supplemented by World Bank estimates based on household surveys and vital registration. Data on insecticide-treated bednet use are from Demographic and Health Surveys and Multiple Indicator Cluster Surveys. Data on official development assistance disbursements are from the Development Assistance Committee of the Organisation for Economic Co-operation and Development *Geographical Distribution of Financial Flows to Developing Countries*, *Development Co-operation Report*, and International Development Statistics database (www.oecd.org/dac/stats/idsonline).

12. Capable states and partnership

TABLE 12.1. AID AND DEBT RELIEF

Official development assistance is flows to developing countries and multilateral institutions provided by official agencies, including state and local governments, or by their executive agencies, that are administered with the promotion of the economic development and welfare of developing countries as their main objective and that are concessional in character and convey a grant element of at least 25 percent.

Net official development assistance (ODA) from all donors is net ODA from the Organisation for Economic Co-operation and Development's (OECD) Development Assistance Committee (DAC), non-DAC bilateral donors (Organization of Petroleum Exporting Countries [OPEC], the former Council for Mutual Economic Assistance [CMEA] countries, and China), and multilateral donors. OPEC countries are Algeria, Iran, Iraq, Kuwait, Libya, Nigeria, Qatar, Saudi Arabia, the United Arab Emirates, and Venezuela. The former CMEA countries are Bulgaria, Czechoslovakia, the former German Democratic Republic, Hungary, Poland, Romania, and the former Soviet Union.

Net official development assistance (ODA) from DAC donors is net ODA from OECD's DAC donors, which are Australia, Austria, Belgium, Canada, Denmark, Finland, France, Germany, Greece, Ireland, Italy, Japan, Luxembourg, the Netherlands, New Zealand, Norway, Portugal, Spain, Sweden, Switzerland, the United Kingdom, and the United States.

Net official development assistance (ODA) from non-DAC donors is net ODA from OECD's non-DAC donors, which include the Czech Republic, Hungary, Iceland, Israel, the Republic of Korea, Kuwait, Poland, Saudi Arabia, the Slovak Republic, Taiwan (China), Thailand, Turkey, the United Arab Emirates, and other donors.

Net official development assistance (ODA) from multilateral donors is net ODA from multilateral sources, such as the African Development Fund, the European Development Fund for the Commission of the European Communities, the International Development Association, the International Fund for Agricultural Development, Arab- and OPEC-financed multilateral agencies, and UN programs and agencies. Aid flows from the International Monetary Fund (IMF) Trust Fund and Structural Adjustment Facility are also included. UN programs and agencies include the United Nations Technical Assistance Programme, the United Nations Development Programme, the United Nations Office of the High Commissioner for Refugees, the United Nations Children's Fund, and the World Food Programme. Arab- and OPEC-financed multilateral agencies include the Arab Bank for Economic Development in Africa, the Arab Fund for Economic and Social Development, the Islamic Development Bank, the OPEC Fund for International Development, the Arab Authority for Agricultural Investment and Development, the Arab Fund for Technical Assistance to African and Arab Countries, and the Islamic Solidarity Fund.

Net private official development assistance (ODA) is private ODA transactions broken, which comprise direct investment, portfolio investment, and export credits (net). Private transactions are undertaken by firms and individuals resident in the reporting country. Portfolio investment corresponds to bonds and equities. Inflows into emerging countries' stocks markets, are, however, heavily understated.

Accordingly, the coverage of portfolio investment differs in these regards from the coverage of bank claims, which include export credit lending by banks. The bank claims data represent the net change in bank claims after adjusting for exchange rate changes and are therefore a proxy for net flow data but are not themselves a net flow figure. They differ in two further regards from other OECD data. First, they relate to loans by banks resident in countries that report quarterly to the Bank for International Settlements. Second, no adjustment has been made to exclude short-term claims.

Net official development assistance (ODA) as a share of gross domestic product (GDP) is calculated by dividing the nominal total net ODA from all donors by nominal GDP. For a given level of aid flows, devaluation of a recipient's currency may inflate the ratios shown in the table. Thus, trends for a given country and comparisons across countries that have implemented different exchange rate policies should be interpreted carefully.

Net official development assistance (ODA) per capita is calculated by dividing the nominal total net ODA (net disbursements of loans and grants from all official sources on concessional financial terms) by midyear population. These ratios offer some indication of the importance of aid flows in sustaining per capita income and consumption levels, although exchange rate fluctuations, the actual rise of aid flows, and other factors vary across countries and over time.

Net official development assistance (ODA) as a share of gross capital formation is calculated by dividing the nominal total net ODA by gross capital formation. These data highlight the relative importance of the indicated aid flows in maintaining and increasing investment in these economies. The same caveats mentioned above apply to their interpretation. Furthermore, aid flows do not exclusively finance investment (for example, food aid finances consumption), and the share of aid going to investment varies across countries.

Net official development assistance (ODA) as a share of imports of goods and services is calculated by dividing nominal total net ODA by imports of goods and services.

Net official development assistance (ODA) as a share of central government expenditure is calculated by dividing nominal total net ODA by central government expenditure.

Food aid shipments are transfers of food commodities (food aid received) from donor to recipient countries on a total-grant basis or on highly concessional terms. Processed and blended cereals are converted into their grain equivalent by applying the conversion factors included in the Rule of Procedures under the 1999 Food Aid Convention to facilitate comparisons between deliveries of different commodities. Deliveries of food aid refer to quantities of commodities that actually reached the recipient country during a given period. For cereals the period refers to July–June, beginning in the year shown.

Heavily Indebted Poor Countries (HIPC) Debt Initiative decision point is the date at which an HIPC with an established track record of good performance under adjustment programs supported by the International Monetary Fund and the World Bank commits to undertake additional reforms and to develop and implement a poverty reduction strategy.

HIPC Debt Initiative completion point is the date at which the country successfully completes the key structural reforms agreed on at the decision point, including developing and implementing its poverty reduction strategy. The country then receives the bulk of debt relief under the HIPC Initiative without further policy conditions.

Debt service relief committed is the amount of debt service relief, calculated at the decision point, that will allow the country to achieve debt sustainability at the completion point.

The Multilateral Debt Relief Initiative (MDRI) is meant to provide additional support to HIPCs to achieve the Millennium Development Goals while ensuring that the financing capacity of the international financial institutions is preserved. The MDRI provides a framework that commits to achieve two objectives: deepening debt relief to HIPCs while safeguarding the long-term financial capacity of the International Development Association (IDA) and the African Development Fund; and encouraging the best use of additional donor resources for development by allocating them to low-income countries on the basis of policy performance. Debt relief to be provided under the MDRI will be in addition to existing debt relief commitments by IDA and other creditors under the Enhanced HIPC Debt Initiative. The MDRI calls for 100 percent cancellation of IDA, African Development Fund, and IMF debt for countries that reach the HIPC completion point. The costs include principal and interest forgone for all multilateral financial institutions participating in the initiative, except for the IMF, whose costs reflect the stock of debt eligible for MDRI relief, which is the debt outstanding (principal only) as of end-2004 that has not been repaid by the member and is not covered by HIPC assistance.

Source: Data on net official development assistance are from the Development Assistance Committee of the Organisation for Economic Co-operation and Development *Geographical Distribution of Financial Flows to Developing Countries*, *Development Co-operation Report*, and International Development Statistics database (www.oecd.org/dac/stats/idsonline). Data on food aid shipments are based on data compiled by from the Food and Agriculture Organization based on information from the World Food Programme. Data on HIPC countries are from IDA and IMF "Heavily Indebted Poor Countries (HIPC) Initiative and Multilateral Debt Relief Initiative (MDRI)—Status of Implementation." Data on external debt are mainly from reports to the World Bank through its Debtor Reporting System from member countries that have received International Bank for Reconstruction and Development loans or IDA credits, as well as World Bank and IMF files.

Table 12.2. Status of Paris Declaration indicators

The third round of Monitoring the Paris Declaration began in the fourth quarter of 2010 and was completed in March 2011. These data will be updated online in the fourth quarter of 2011.

The Paris Declaration is the outcome of the 2005 Paris High-Level Forum on Aid Effectiveness, where 60 partner countries, 30 donor countries, and 30 development agencies committed to specific actions to further country ownership, harmonization, alignment, managing for development results, and mutual accountability for the use of aid. Participants agreed on 12 indicators. These indicators include good national development strategies, reliable country systems for procurement and public financial management, the development and use of results frameworks, and mutual assessment of progress. Qualitative desk reviews by the Organisation for Economic Co-operation and Development's Development Assistance Committee and the World Bank and a survey questionnaire for governments and donors are used to calculate the indicators.

PDI-1 Operational national development strategies are the extent to which a country has an operational development strategy to guide its aid coordination effort and overall development. The score is based on the World Bank *2005 Comprehensive Development Framework Progress Report*. An operational strategy calls for a coherent long-term strategy derived from it; specific targets serving a holistic, balanced, and well sequenced development strategy; and capacity and resources for its implementation.

PDI-2a Reliable public financial management is the World Bank annual Country Policy and Institutional Assessment rating for the quality of public financial management. Measured on a scale of 1 (worst) to 5 (best), its focus is on how much existing systems adhere to broadly accepted good practices and whether a reform program is in place to promote improved practices.

PDI-2b Reliable country procurement systems measure developing countries' procurement systems. Donors use national procurement procedures when the funds they provide for the implementation of projects and programs are managed according to the national procurement procedures as they were established in the general legislation and implemented by government. The use of national procurement procedures means that donors do not make additional or special requirements for governments on the procurement of works, goods, and services. (Where weaknesses in national procurement systems have been identified, donors may work with partner countries to improve the efficiency, economy, and transparency of their implementation.) The objective of this indicator is to measure and encourage improvements in developing countries' procurement systems.

PDI-3 Government budget estimates comprehensive and realistic are the percentage of aid that is accurately recorded in the national budget, thereby allowing scrutiny by parliaments.

PDI-4 Technical assistance aligned and coordinated with country programs is the percentage of technical cooperation that is free standing and embedded and that respects ownership (partner countries exercise effective leadership over their capacity development programs), alignment (technical cooperation in support of capacity development aligns with countries' development objectives and strategies), and harmonization (when more than one donor is involved in supporting partner-led capacity development, donors coordinate their activities and contributions).

PDI-5a and *5b Aid for government sectors uses country public financial management* and *country procurement systems* is the percentage of donors that use country, rather than donor, systems for managing aid disbursement.

PDI-6 Project implementation units parallel to country structures is the number of parallel project implementation units, which refers to units created outside existing country institutional structures. The survey guidance distinguishes between project implementation units and executing agencies and describes three typical features of parallel project implementation units: they are accountable to external funding agencies rather than to country implementing agencies (ministries, departments, agencies, and the like), most of the professional staff is appointed by the donor, and the personnel salaries often exceed those of civil service personnel. Interpretation of the Paris Declaration survey question on this subject was controversial in a number of countries. It is unclear whether within countries all donors applied the same criteria with the same degree of rigor or that across countries the same standards were used. In several cases the descriptive part of the survey results indicates that some donors applied a legalistic criterion of accountability to the formal executing agency, whereas the national coordinator and other donors would have preferred greater recognition of the substantive reality of accountability to the donor. Some respondents may have confused the definitional question (Is the unit "parallel"?) with the aid management question (Is the parallelism justified in terms of the developmental benefits and costs?).

PDI-7 Aid disbursements on schedule and recorded by government are the percentage of funds that are disbursed within the year they are scheduled and accurately recorded by partner authorities.

PDI-8 Bilateral aid that is untied is the percentage of aid that is untied. Tied aid is aid provided on the condition that the recipient uses it to purchase goods and services from suppliers based in the donor country.

PDI-9 Aid provided in the framework of program-based approaches is the percentage of development cooperation that is based on the principles of coordinated support for a locally owned program of development, such as a national development strategy, a sector program, a thematic program, or a program of a specific organization. Program-based approaches share the following features: leadership by the host country or organization; a single comprehensive program and budget framework; a formalized process for donor coordination and harmonization of donor procedures for reporting, budgeting, financial management, and procurement; and efforts to increase the use of local systems for program design and implementation, financial management, monitoring, and evaluation.

PDI-10a Donor missions coordinated are the percentage of missions undertaken jointly by two or more donors and missions undertaken by one donor on behalf of another (delegated cooperation).

PDI-10b Country analysis coordinated is the percentage of country analytic work that is undertaken by one or more donors jointly or undertaken by one donor on behalf of another donor (including work undertaken by one and used by another when it is cofinanced and formally acknowledged in official documentation and undertaken with substantive involvement from government).

PDI-11 Existence of a monitorable performance assessment framework measures the extent to which the country has realized its commitment to establishing performance frameworks. The indicator relies on the scorings of the 2005 Comprehensive Development Framework Progress Report and considers three criteria: the quality of development information, stakeholder access to development information, and coordinated country-level monitoring and evaluation. The assessments therefore reflect both the extent to which sound data on development outputs, outcomes, and impacts are collected and various aspects of the way information is used, disseminated among stakeholders, and fed back into policy.

PDI-12 Existence of a mutual accountability review indicates whether there is a mechanism for mutual review of progress on aid effectiveness commitments. This is an important innovation of the Paris Declaration because it develops the idea that aid is more effective when both donors and partner governments are accountable to their constituents for the use of resources to achieve development results and when they are accountable to each other. The specific focus is mutual accountability for the implementation of the partnership commitments included in the Paris Declaration and any local agreements on enhancing aid effectiveness.

Source: Organisation for Economic Co-operation and Development *2008 Survey on Monitoring the Paris Declaration: Making Aid More Effective by 2010*.

Table 12.3. Capable states

Firms that believe the court system is fair, impartial, and uncorrupt are the percentage of firms that believe the court system is fair, impartial, and uncorrupt.

Corruption is the percentage of firms identifying corruption as a major constraint to current operation.

Crime, theft, and disorder are the percentage of firms identifying crime, theft, and disorder as a major constraint to current operation.

Number of procedures to enforce a contract is the number of independent actions, mandated by law or courts, that demand interaction between the parties of a contract or between them and the judge or court officer.

Time required to enforce a contract is the number of calendar days from the filing of the lawsuit in court until the final determination and, in appropriate cases, payment.

Cost to enforce a contract is court and attorney fees, where the use of attorneys is mandatory or common, or the cost of an administrative debt recovery procedure, expressed as a percentage of the debt value.

Protecting investors disclosure index measures the degree to which investors are protected through disclosure of ownership and financial information. Higher values indicate more disclosure.

Director liability index measures a plaintiff's ability to hold directors of firms liable for damages to the company. Higher values indicate greater liability.

Shareholder suits index measures shareholders' ability to sue officers and directors for misconduct. Higher values indicate greater power for shareholders to challenge transactions.

Investor protection index measures the degree to which investors are protected through disclosure of ownership and financial information regulations. Higher values indicate better protection.

Number of tax payments is the number of taxes paid by businesses, including electronic filing. The tax is counted as paid once a year even if payments are more frequent.

Time required to prepare, file, and pay taxes is the number of hours it takes to prepare, file, and pay (or withhold) three major types of taxes: the corporate income tax, the value added or sales tax, and labor taxes, including payroll taxes and social security contributions.

Total tax rate is the total amount of taxes payable by the business (except for labor taxes) after accounting for deductions and exemptions as a percentage of gross profit. For further details on the method used for assessing the total tax payable, see the World Bank *Doing Business 2006*.

Extractive Industries Transparency Initiative (EITI) status refers to a country's implementation status for the EITI, a multistakeholder approach to increasing governance and transparency in extractive industries. It includes civil society, the private sector, and government and requires a work plan with a timeline and budget to ensure sustainability, independent audit of payments and disclosure of revenues, publication of results in a publicly accessible manner, and an approach that covers all companies and government agencies. The EITI supports improved governance in resource-rich countries through the verification and full publication of company payments and government revenues from oil, gas, and mining. *Intent to implement* indicates that a country intends to implement the EITI but has not yet met the four initial requirements to join: an unequivocal public statement of its intention to implement the EITI; a commitment to work with civil society and companies on EITI implementation; a senior official appointed to lead EITI implementation; and a widely distributed, fully costed work plan with measurable targets, a timetable for implementation, and an assessment of government, private sector, and civil society capacity constraints. *Candidate* indicates that a country has met the four initial requirements to join the EITI and has begun a range of activities to strengthen revenue transparency, as documented in the country's work plan. Once a country has become an EITI candidate, it has two years to be validated as compliant. *Compliant* indicates that a country has successfully undergone validation, an independent assessment of a country's progress toward the EITI goals by the EITI International Board. Validation is based on the country's work plan, the EITI validation grid and indicator assessment tools, and company forms that detail private companies' extractive industry activities; the board provides guidance for countries' future activity related to EITI compliance. Countries must undergo validation every five years or at the request of the EITI International Board.

Source: Data on investment climate constraints to firms are World Bank Enterprise Surveys (http://rru.worldbank.org/EnterpriseSurveys). Data on enforcing contracts, protecting investors, and regulation and tax administration are from the World Bank Doing Business project (http://rru.worldbank.org/DoingBusiness/). Data on corruption perceptions index are from Transparency International (www.transparency.org/policy_research/surveys_indices/cpi). Data on the EITI are from the EITI website (www.eitransparency.org).

Table 12.4. Governance and anticorruption indicators

Voice and accountability measure the extent to which a country's citizens are able to participate in selecting their government and to enjoy freedom of expression, freedom of association, and a free media.

Political stability and absence of violence measure the perceptions of the likelihood that the government will be destabilized or overthrown by unconstitutional or violent means, including domestic violence or terrorism.

Government effectiveness measures the quality of public services, the quality and degree of independence from political pressures of the civil service, the quality of policy formulation and implementation, and the credibility of the government's commitment to such policies.

Regulatory quality measures the ability of the government to formulate and implement sound policies and regulations that permit and promote private sector development.

Rule of law measures the extent to which agents have confidence in and abide by the rules of society, in particular the quality of contract enforcement, the police, and the courts, as well as the likelihood of crime and violence.

Control of corruption measures the extent to which public power is exercised for private gain, including petty and grand forms of corruption, as well as "capture" of the state by elites and private interests.

Expected to pay informal payment to public officials to get things done is the percentage of firms that expected to make informal payments or give gifts to public officials to "get things done" with regard to customs, taxes, licenses, regulations, services, and the like.

Expected to give gifts to obtain an operating license is the percentage of firms that expected to give gifts or an informal payment to get an operating license.

Expected to give gifts in meetings with tax officials is the percentage of firms that answered yes to the question "Was a gift or informal payment expected or requested during a meeting with tax officials?"

Expected to give gifts to secure a government contract is the percentage of firms that expected to make informal payments or give gifts to public officials to secure a government contract.

Share of firms identifying control of corruption as a major constraint measures the extent to which public power is exercised for private gain, including petty and grand forms of corruption, as well as "capture" of the state by elites and private interests.

Mean corruption perceptions index score is the country's score in Transparency International's annual corruption perceptions index, which ranks more than 150 countries in terms of perceived levels of corruption, as determined by expert assessments and opinion surveys.

Open budget index overall score is the country's score on a subset of 91 questions from the Open Budget Survey. The questions focus on the public availability of eight key budget documents (with a particular emphasis on the executive's budget proposal) and the information they contain. The open budget index is calculated based on detailed questionnaires completed by local experts in 59 participating countries from every continent. In 2008, based on inputs received from researchers and extensive in-house reviews, the International Budget Partnership made three changes in its methodology. The first change concerns the timing of the release of the eight key budget documents assessed by the survey. The second is the inclusion of the enacted budget in calculating country scores for the index. The third is revisions to the answers of a few questions used to assess Brazil and Nigeria.

Source: Data on governance indicators are from the World Bank Institute Worldwide Governance Indicators database, which relies on 33 sources, including surveys of enterprises and citizens and expert polls, gathered from 30 organizations around the world. Data on corruption perceptions index scores are from Transparency International (www.transparency.org). Data on the open budget index are from www.openbudgetindex.org.

TABLE 12.5. COUNTRY POLICY AND INSTITUTIONAL ASSESSMENT RATINGS

The Country Policy and Institutional Assessment (CPIA) assesses the quality of a country's present policy and institutional framework. "Quality" means how conducive that framework is to fostering sustainable, poverty-reducing growth and the effective use of development assistance. The CPIA is conducted annually for all International Bank for Reconstruction and Development and International Development Association borrowers and has evolved into a set of criteria grouped into four clusters with 16 criteria that reflect a balance between ensuring that all key factors that foster pro-poor growth and poverty alleviation are captured, without overly burdening the evaluation process.

- Economic management
  - *Macroeconomic management* assesses the quality of the monetary, exchange rate, and aggregate demand policy framework.
  - *Fiscal policy* assesses the short- and medium-term sustainability of fiscal policy (taking into account monetary and exchange rate policy and the sustainability of the public debt) and its impact on growth.
  - *Debt policy* assesses whether the debt management strategy is conducive to minimize budgetary risks and ensure long-term debt sustainability.
- Structural policies
  - *Trade* assesses how the policy framework fosters trade in goods. It covers two areas: trade regime restrictiveness—which focuses on the height of tariff barriers, the extent to which nontariff barriers are used, the transparency and predictability of the trade regime, and customs and trade facilitation —which includes the extent to which the customs service is free of corruption, relies on risk management, processes duty collections and refunds promptly, and operates transparently.
  - *Financial sector* assesses the structure of the financial sector and the policies and regulations that affect it. It covers three dimensions: financial stability; the sector's efficiency, depth, and resource mobilization strength; and access to financial services.
  - *Business regulatory environment* assesses the extent to which the legal, regulatory, and policy environment helps or hinders private business in investing, creating jobs, and becoming more productive. The emphasis is on direct regulations of business activity and regulation of goods and factor markets. It measures three subcomponents: regulations affecting entry, exit, and competition; regulations of ongoing business operations; and regulations of factor markets (labor and land).
- Policies for social inclusion and equity
  - *Gender equality* assesses the extent to which the country has enacted and put in place institutions and programs to enforce laws and policies that promote equal access for

While the definition of armed conflict (associated with the number of battle-related deaths) is fairly well accepted, fragility remains somewhat ill-defined. Indeed, some people prefer the term "fragile situations" to fragile states. Using the harmonized Country Policy and Institutional Assessment (CPIA) score (less than or equal to 3.2 as a threshold), the World Bank has defined fragile states as low-income countries with a low institutional level. However, *World Development Report 2011* broadened the definition to include conflict indicators, such as annual homicide rates of more than 10 per 100,000 people, annual battle deaths of more than 1,000 people, and the presence of a UN peacekeeping mission. Using the *World Development Report* definition, 20 of Sub-Saharan Africa's 47 countries are either fragile or conflict-affected.

Map 1 The cohort of fragile states was unchanged over 2005–09

Country Policy and Institutional Assessment (International Development Association countries only) scores

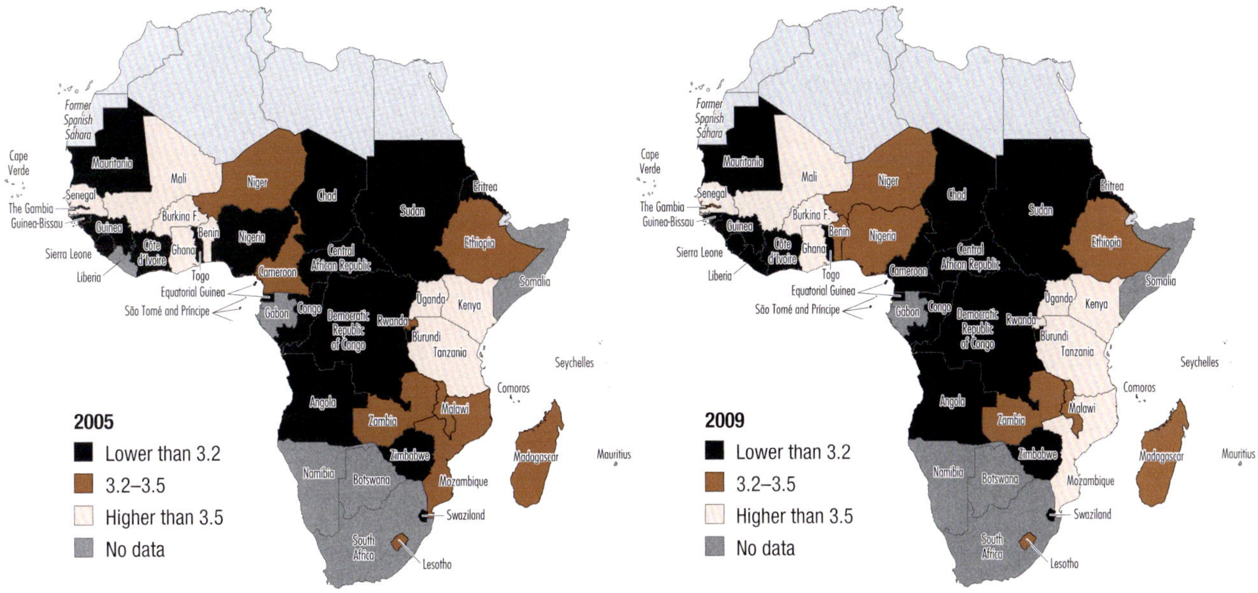

The cohort of fragile states (both core and marginal) remained fairly constant over 2005–09 (map 1), with only one country leaving the core set of fragile states (Nigeria) and two leaving the marginal fragile states (Mozambique and Rwanda). While many countries have stagnant CPIA scores, Angola, Burundi, Central African Republic, Liberia, and Sierra Leone have slightly improved, but they are still on the fragility threshold. Five countries' scores have fallen (Chad, Côte d'Ivoire, Eritrea, Somalia, and Zimbabwe), and the number of violently disputed elections (Côte d'Ivoire, Kenya) and military coups d'état (Mauritania, Guinea, Madagascar, Niger) has risen.

Since the 1990s, Africa has had the most countries in armed conflict, with a peak in 1998–99 when almost half of the countries in fragile or conflict situations in Sub-Saharan Africa were involved in armed conflict. Global trends suggest a gradual decline in the numbers of both armed conflicts and battle-related deaths, both in and outside Africa; the annual average number of conflict-affected states in Sub-Saharan Africa fell from 16 in the 1990s to 6 in 2007 (Human Security Report Project 2008). This positive trend has increased the responsibility of post-conflict recovery interventions and international peacekeeping—some 78,400 UN and AU peacekeeping troops work in Sub-Saharan Africa (map 2).

Despite these trends, armed conflict and violence remain critical challenges to development. The data remain unreliable, but some figures suggest the challenges are massive. Since 1998 the conflict and humanitarian crisis in the Democratic Republic of the Congo has caused the deaths of 5.4 million people (International Rescue Committee 2008), mostly from disease and malnutrition, and the rape of some 1.8 million women (Peterman, Palermo, and Bredenkamp 2011). Some 2 million people were killed during the civil war between northern and southern Sudan and between 180,000–400,000 persons died as a result of armed conflict in Darfur (Degomme and Guha-Sapir 2010). And in 2010 there were around 10.3 million internally displaced persons and 2.5 million refugees across Sub-Saharan Africa. Violence is not simply related to armed conflict; in 2006 the Southern Africa region had the highest intentional homicide rate in the world of 37 per 100,000 people (United Nations Office on Drugs and Crime 2010).

Fragile and conflict-affected states (both core and marginal) are finding it hard to achieve the Millennium Development Goals and are the most vulnerable to external shocks, such as oil and food price increases. Most of the core fragile countries have very high (more than 35 percent) and high (24–35 percent)

(continued)

undernourishment (FAOSTAT 2010). Despite some success—in Ethiopia, Guinea, and Niger—most fragile countries in Africa are far from the maternal mortality and infant mortality targets. While such countries as Cameroon are on target for access to safe water, core fragile countries such as Burundi, the Democratic Republic of the Congo, and Sudan remain way off. Most of those countries are also cereal net importers. Around 6.4 million people in Sudan and 2.4 million in Somalia need external assistance due to conflict and rising food prices (Barungi and others 2011).

Map 2 Conflict, political stability, and violence in Africa

Political stability and absence of violence index, 2009

Refugees and peacekeeping operations, 2011

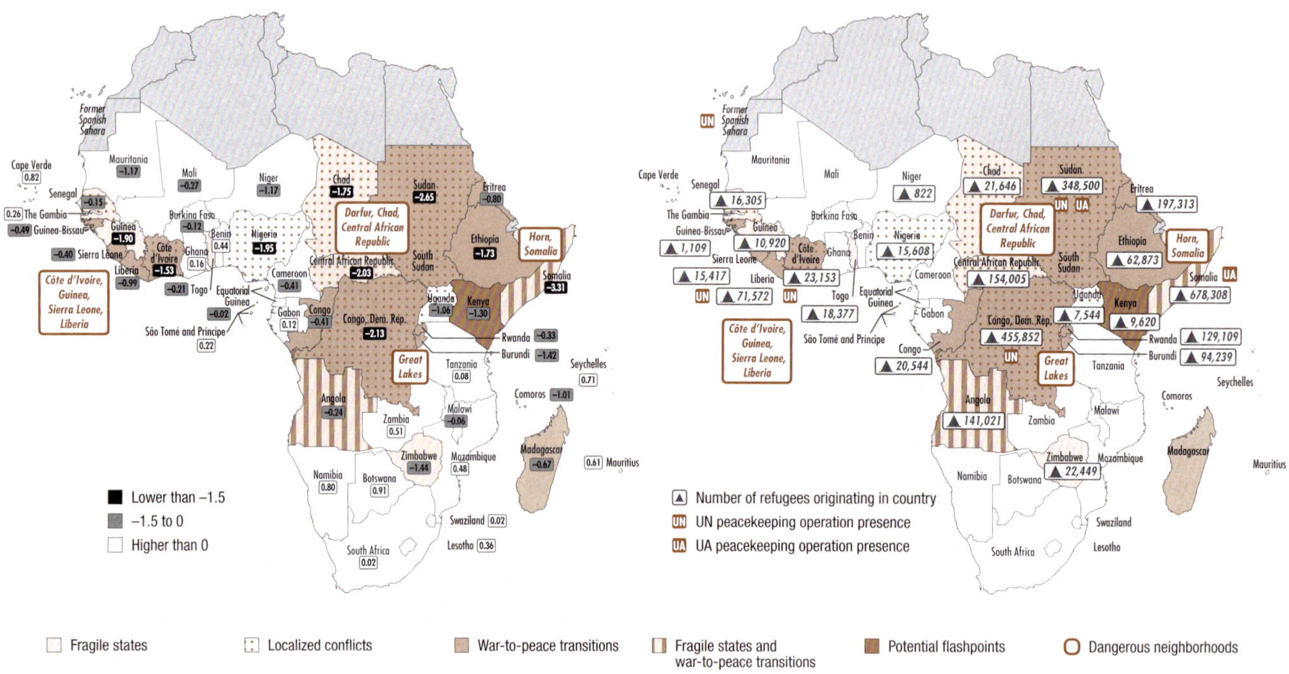

According to the literature, risk factors associated with conflict and violence in Sub-Saharan Africa include low per capita income, horizontal and vertical inequality between groups, ethnic fractionalization, political repression, electoral crisis, legacies of colonialism, superpower rivalry, and competition for natural resources (World Bank 2011; African Development Bank 2008). While the causality between natural resources and conflict is not empirical, the armed conflict in eastern Congo associated with the illicit exploitation of minerals is but one example of the challenges confronting African states. Most African countries are endowed with natural resources, some of which are fragile or conflict-affected, such as Namibia or Botswana. The connections between natural resources and conflict highlight the presence of weak accountability, poor governance, and weak institutions. Other aggravating challenges are high levels of unemployment and underemployment, particularly in urban areas, as well as rising food prices, the poor performance of security and justice institutions, and large-scale corruption.

But all is not about failure in fragile and conflict-affected states. The last years have also produced some post-conflict successes, such as in Mozambique, Sierra Leone, and Rwanda, which has focused on generating rapid economic growth to deal with its history of genocide. Also, Uganda implemented an amnesty program to reintegrate former rebel soldiers into society while sustaining its objectives of increased and sustained inclusive economic growth.

Figure 1 Net official development aid to fragile states in Sub-Saharan Africa, 1960–2005

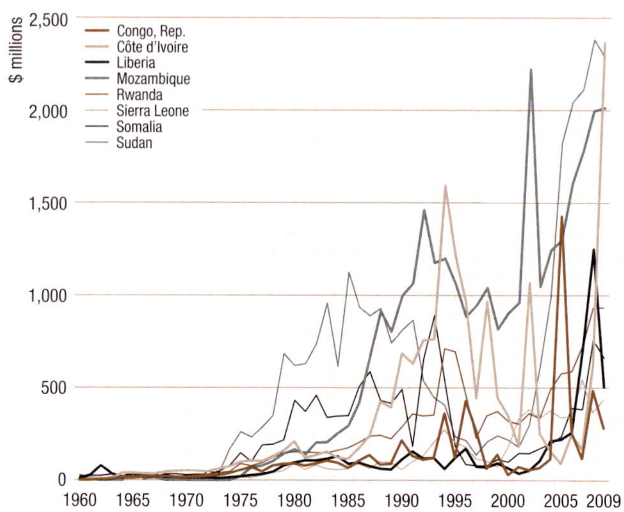

Governance, conflict-affected and fragile states in Africa (continued)

World Development Report 2011 highlights ways external support can support such transitions. While official aid started to peak in the 1990s and average volumes have been increasing, aid has been volatile. Sustained internal and external support is required to help countries move from fragility to peace and prosperity for the long term.

References

African Development Bank. 2008. *Africa Development Report 2008/2009: Conflict Resolution, Peace and Reconstruction in Africa*. Oxford, UK: Oxford University Press.

Barungi, Barbara, Kazuhiro Numasawa, Adeleke Salami, and Adalbert Nshimyumuremyi. 2011. "The Impact of the 2010–11 Surge in Food Prices on African Countries in Fragile Situations." *Africa Economic Brief* 2 (4).

Degomme, Olivier and Debarati Guha-Sapir. 2010. "Patterns of Mortality Rates in Darfur conflict." *The Lancet* 375 (9711): 294–300.

FAOSTAT. 2010. "FAO Hunger MAP in 2010: Prevalence of Undernourishment in Developing Countries." Food and Agriculture Organization, Rome.

Human Security Report Project. 2008. *Human Security Brief 2007.* Vancouver, Canada: Human Security Report Project.

International Rescue Committee. 2008. *Mortality in the DRC: An Ongoing Crisis.* New York: International Rescue Committee.

Peterman, Amber, Tia Palermo, and Caryn Bredenkamp. 2011. "Estimates and Determinants of Sexual Violence against Women in the Democratic Republic of Congo." *American Journal of Public Health* 101 (6): 1060.

United Nations Office on Drugs and Crime. 2010. *Update Report No. 5.* New York: United Nations.

World Bank. 2011. *World Development Report 2011: Conflict, Security, and Development.* Washington, DC: World Bank.

men and women to human capital development and productive and economic resources and that give men and women equal status and protection under the law.

- *Equity of public resource use* assesses the extent to which the pattern of public expenditures and revenue collection affects the poor and is consistent with national poverty reduction priorities. The assessment of the consistency of government spending with the poverty reduction priorities takes into account the extent to which individuals, groups, or localities that are poor, vulnerable, or have unequal access to services and opportunities are identified; a national development strategy with explicit interventions to assist those individuals, groups, and localities has been adopted; and the composition and incidence of public expenditures are tracked systematically and their results fed back into subsequent resource allocation decisions. The assessment of the revenue collection dimension takes into account the incidence of major taxes—for example, whether they are progressive or regressive —and their alignment with poverty reduction priorities. When relevant, expenditure and revenue collection trends at the national and subnational levels should be considered. The expenditure component receives two-thirds of the weight in computing the overall rating.
- *Building human resources* assesses the national policies and public and private sector service delivery that affect access to and quality of health and nutrition services, including: population and reproductive health; education, early childhood development, and training and literacy programs; and prevention and treatment of HIV/AIDS, tuberculosis, and malaria.
- *Social protection and labor* assess government policies in the area of social protection and labor market regulation, which reduce the risk of becoming poor, assist those who are poor to better manage further risks, and ensure a minimal level of welfare for all people. Interventions include social safety net programs, pension and old-age savings programs, protection of basic labor standards, regulations to reduce segmentation and inequity in labor markets, active labor market programs (such as public works or job training), and community driven initiatives. In interpreting the guidelines it is important to take

into account the size of the economy and its level of development.
    - *Policies and institutions for environmental sustainability* assess the extent to which environmental policies foster the protection and sustainable use of natural resources and the management of pollution. Assessment of environmental sustainability requires multidimensional criteria (that is, for air, water, waste, conservation management, coastal zones management, and natural resources management).
- Public sector management and institutions
    - *Property rights and rule-based governance* assess the extent to which private economic activity is facilitated by an effective legal system and rule-based governance structure in which property and contract rights are reliably respected and enforced. Three dimensions are rated separately: legal basis for secure property and contract rights; predictability, transparency, and impartiality of laws and regulations affecting economic activity and their enforcement by the legal and judicial system; and crime and violence as an impediment to economic activity.
    - *Quality of budgetary and financial management* assesses the extent to which there is a comprehensive and credible budget, linked to policy priorities; effective financial management systems to ensure that the budget is implemented as intended in a controlled and predictable way; and timely and accurate accounting and fiscal reporting, including timely and audited public accounts and effective arrangements for follow-up.
    - *Efficiency of revenue mobilization* assesses the overall pattern of revenue mobilization—not only the tax structure as it exists on paper but revenue from all sources as they are actually collected.
    - *Quality of public administration* assesses the extent to which civilian central government staffs (including teachers, health workers, and police) are structured to design and implement government policy and deliver services effectively. Civilian central government staffs include the central executive together with all other ministries and administrative departments, including autonomous agencies. It excludes the armed forces, state-owned enterprises, and subnational governments.
    - *Transparency, accountability, and corruption in public sector* assess the extent to which the executive branch can be held accountable for its use of funds and the results of its actions by the electorate and by the legislature and judiciary and to which public employees within the executive branch are required to account for the use of resources, administrative decisions, and results obtained. Both levels of accountability are enhanced by transparency in decisionmaking, public audit institutions, access to relevant and timely information, and public and media scrutiny.

Source: World Bank Group CPIA database (www.worldbank.org/ida).

TABLE 12.6. POLITY INDICATORS

Revised combined polity score is computed by subtracting the institutionalized autocracy score from the institutionalized democracy score. The resulting unified polity scale ranges from +10 (strongly democratic) to –10 (strongly autocratic).

Institutionalized democracy is conceived as three essential, interdependent elements. One is the presence of institutions and procedures through which citizens can express effective preferences about alternative policies and leaders. Second is the existence of institutionalized constraints on the exercise of power by the executive. Third is the guarantee of civil liberties to all citizens in their daily lives and in acts of political participation. Other aspects of plural democracy—such as the rule of law, systems of checks and balances, freedom of the press, and so on—are means to, or

In the mid-1980s, Sub-Saharan Africa was dominated by fully autocratic regimes—31 of 40 in the database were fully autocratic, with just 3 full-fledged democracies (Botswana, Gambia, and Mauritius) and 6 intermediate regimes, most of which had a heavy weight of autocracy, according to Polity IV scores[1] (figure 1). By end 2009, it had 12 fully democratic regimes (Benin, Comoros, Ghana, Kenya, Lesotho, Mali, Senegal, Sierra Leone, South Africa and Zambia, in addition to the already democratic Botswana and Mauritius) and only 3 fully autocratic regimes (Eritrea, Somalia, and Swaziland), with most countries classified as intermediate—a remarkable shift. Most intermediate regimes now have significant democratic elements (Burkina Faso, Côte d'Ivoire, the Democratic Republic of the Congo, Ethiopia, Mozambique, Nigeria, Rwanda, Uganda, Tanzania, and Zimbabwe).

Figure 1 Polity scores, 1985 and 2009

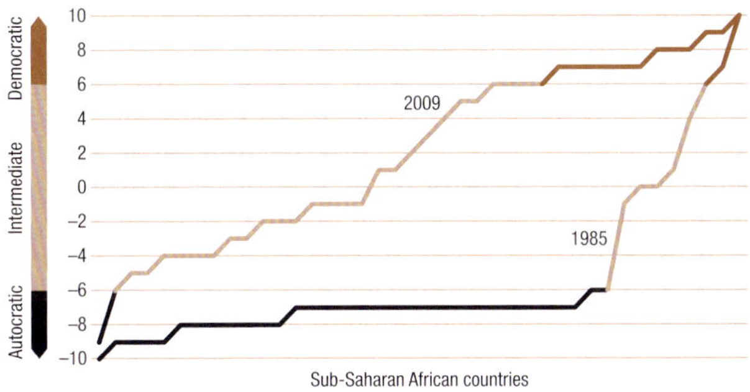

So, why has increasing democratization in the Africa region not resulted in more substantial improvements in public policies for growth, poverty reduction, and human development? Although the democratic wave has been shown to influence public policies, it has disappointed by not addressing critical accountability relations in improving public goods for human development and a competitive business sector. For example, the transition to competitive elections in African countries is associated with the abolition of school fees, which in turn is associated with higher rates of school attendance than in nondemocracies (Harding and Stasavage 2011). Yet the quality of education services is poor, with teachers on the public payroll often absent from their jobs (Glewwe and Kremer 2006) and learning among children falling far short of functional literacy (Uwezo 2010).

Political economy analysis suggests that the disappointments are due largely to widespread clientelistic practices in electoral competition—the provision of private benefits to select citizens in exchange for political support (Robinson and Verdier 2002; Keefer and Khemani 2005). Providing secure jobs to teachers on the public payroll is more important for political survival and extracting rents from political office than it is for managing teachers better and holding them accountable for quality learning outcomes. Clientelism has been traced to underlying conditions of entrenched inequality, social polarization, and lack of information and credible political promises.

Nevertheless, sustained political competition, democratic conditions, and new research in Africa suggest there is substantial scope to undercut clientelism through well designed (and evaluated) interventions that better inform citizens and that enable them to deliberate, communicate, and hold governments more accountable for broad public interest policies. For example, in Benin, a civil society group organized town hall meetings with political candidates in the first round of the 2006 presidential elections, to discuss specific policy proposals informed by empirical evidence. Where the meetings were held, voter turnout was higher and support for clientelist political platforms was lower (Wantchekon 2009) than where they were not. Better data, better evidence, and better communication with citizens could be the key to overcoming political constraints to good development policies in Africa.

Note

1. Polity IV is a database ranking countries on their levels of democracy, based on surveys of political scientists.

References

Glewwe, Paul, and Michael Kremer. 2006. "Schools, Teachers, and Education Outcomes in Developing Countries." *Handbook on the Economics of Education,* ed. Erik Hanushek & F. Welch. Oxford, UK: Elsevier.

Harding, Robin, and David Stasavage. 2011. "What Democracy Does (and Doesn't) Do for Basic Services: School Fees, School Quality, and African Elections." Working Paper, New York University, New York.

Keefer, Philip, and Stuti Khemani. 2005. "Democracy, Public Expenditures, and the Poor." *World Bank Research Observer* 20: 1–27.

Robinson, James A., and Thierry Verdier 2002. "The Political Economy of Clientelism." CEPR Discussion Paper 3205, Center for Economic Policy and Research, Washington, DC.

Uwezo. 2010. *Are Our Children Learning? Annual Learning Assessment.* Nairobi, Kenya. http://uwezo.net/index.php?i=68

Wantchekon, Leonard. 2009. "Can Informed Public Deliberation Overcome Clientelism? Experimental Evidence from Benin." Working Paper, New York University, New York. http://politics.as.nyu.edu/docs/IO/2807/expertinformationjuly.pdf.

specific manifestations of, these general principles. Coded data on civil liberties are not included. This is an additive eleven-point scale (0–10). The operational indicator of democracy is derived from codings of the competitiveness of political participation using weights.

Institutionalized autocracy is a pejorative term for some very diverse kinds of political systems whose common properties are a lack of regularized political competition and concern for political freedoms. The term *autocracy* is used and defined operationally in terms of the presence of a distinctive set of political characteristics. In mature form autocracies sharply restrict or suppress competitive political participation. Their chief executives are chosen in a regularized process of selection within the political elite, and once in office they exercise power with few institutional constraints. Most modern autocracies also exercise a high degree of directiveness over social and economic activity, but this is regarded here as a function of political ideology and choice, not a defining property of autocracy. Social democracies also exercise relatively high degrees of directiveness.

Source: Data are from the Integrated Network for Societal Conflict Research Polity IV Project, Political Regime Characteristics and Transitions, 1800–2009 (www.systemicpeace.org/inscr/inscr.htm).

Technical notes references

Chen, Shaohua, and Martin Ravallion. 2008. "The Developing World Is Poorer Than We Thought, But No Less Successful in the Fight Against Poverty." Policy Research Working Paper 4703. World Bank, Washington, DC.

FAO (Food and Agriculture Organization of the United Nations). 2010. *Global Forest Resources Assessment 2010.* Rome: Food and Agriculture Organization.

IDA (International Development Association) and IMF (International Monetary Fund). 2010. "Heavily Indebted Poor Countries (HIPC) Initiative and Multilateral Debt Relief Initiative (MDRI)—Status of Implementation." International Development Association and International Monetary Fund, Washington, DC.

IEA (International Energy Agency). Various years. *Energy Statistics of OECD Countries.* Paris: International Energy Agency.

ILO (International Labour Organization). Various years. *Key Indicators of the Labor Market.* Geneva: International Labour Organization.

IMF (International Monetary Fund). 2010. *Global Financial Stability.* Washington, DC: International Monetary Fund.

———. Various years. *Balance of Payments Statistics Yearbook.* Parts 1 and 2. Washington, DC: International Monetary Fund.

———. Various years. *Direction of Trade Statistics Quarterly.* Washington, DC: International Monetary Fund.

———. Various years. *Direction of Trade Statistics Yearbook.* Washington, DC: International Monetary Fund.

IRF (International Road Federation). 2010. *World Road Statistics.* Geneva.

OECD (Organisation for Economic Co-operation and Development). 2011. *African Economic Outlook 2011: Africa and its Emerging Partners.* Paris: Organisation for Economic Co-operation and Development.

OECD (Organisation for Economic Co-operation and Development) DAC (Development Assistance Committee). Various years. *Geographical Distribution of Financial Flows to Developing Economies.* Paris: Organisation for Economic Co-operation and Development.

Ravallion, Martin, Shaohua Chen, and Prem Sangraula. 2008. "Dollar a Day Revisited." Policy Research Working Paper 4620. World Bank, Development Research Group, Washington, DC.

Standard & Poor's. 2000. *The S&P Emerging Market Indices: Methodology, Definitions, and Practices.* New York: Standard & Poor's.

———. 2010. *Global Stock Markets Factbook 2010.* New York: Standard & Poor's.

UNAIDS (Joint United Nations Programme on HIV/AIDS) and WHO (World Health Organization). Various years. *Report on the Global AIDS Epidemic.* Geneva: Joint United nations Programme on HIV/AIDS.

UNCTAD (United Nations Conference on Trade and Development). 1995. *Handbook of International Trade and Development.* New York and Geneva: United Nations Conference on Trade and Development.

———. 2007. *Trade and Development Report 2007: Regional Cooperation for Development.* New York and Geneva: United Nations Conference on Trade and Development.

UNESCO (United Nations Educational, Scientific, and Cultural Organization). 1997. *International Standard Classification of Education.* Paris: United Nations Educational, Scientific, and Cultural Organization.

UNICEF (United Nations Children's Fund). Various issues. *The State of the World's Children.* New York: Oxford University Press.

United Nations. 2006. *Standard International Trade Classification Revision 4.* New York: United Nations, Department of Economic and Social Affairs.

United Nations Population Division. 2009a. *Trends in Total Migrant Stock: The 2008 Revision.* New York: United Nations, Department of Economic and Social Affairs.

———. 2009b. *World Population Prospects: The 2008 Revision.* New York: United Nations, Department of Economic and Social Affairs.

———. Various years. *World Population Prospects.* New York: United Nations, Department of Economic and Social Affairs.

———. Various years. *Energy Statistics Yearbook.* New York: United Nations.

———. Various years. *World Urbanization Prospects.* New York: United Nations.

United Nations Statistics Division. n.d. "International Standard Industrial Classification of All Economic Activities, Third Revision." [http://unstats.un.org/unsd/cr/registry/]. New York.

WHO (World Health Organization). 2011. *Global Atlas of the Health Workforce.* Geneva: World Health Organization.

———. Various years. *World Malaria Report.* Geneva: World Health Organization.

WHO (World Health Organization), UNICEF (United Nations Children's Fund), UNFPA (United Nations Population Fund), and World Bank. 2010. *Trends in Maternal Mortality: 1990–2008: Estimates Developed by WHO, UNICEF, UNFPA and the World Bank.* Geneva: World Health Organization.

World Bank. 2000. *Trade Blocs.* New York: Oxford University Press.

———. Various years. *Global Development Finance: External Debt of Developing Countries.* **Washington, DC: World Bank.**

WTO (World Trade Organization). n.d. Regional Trade Agreements Gateway. [www.wto.org/English/tratop_e/region_e/region_e.htm]. Geneva.

Map of Africa

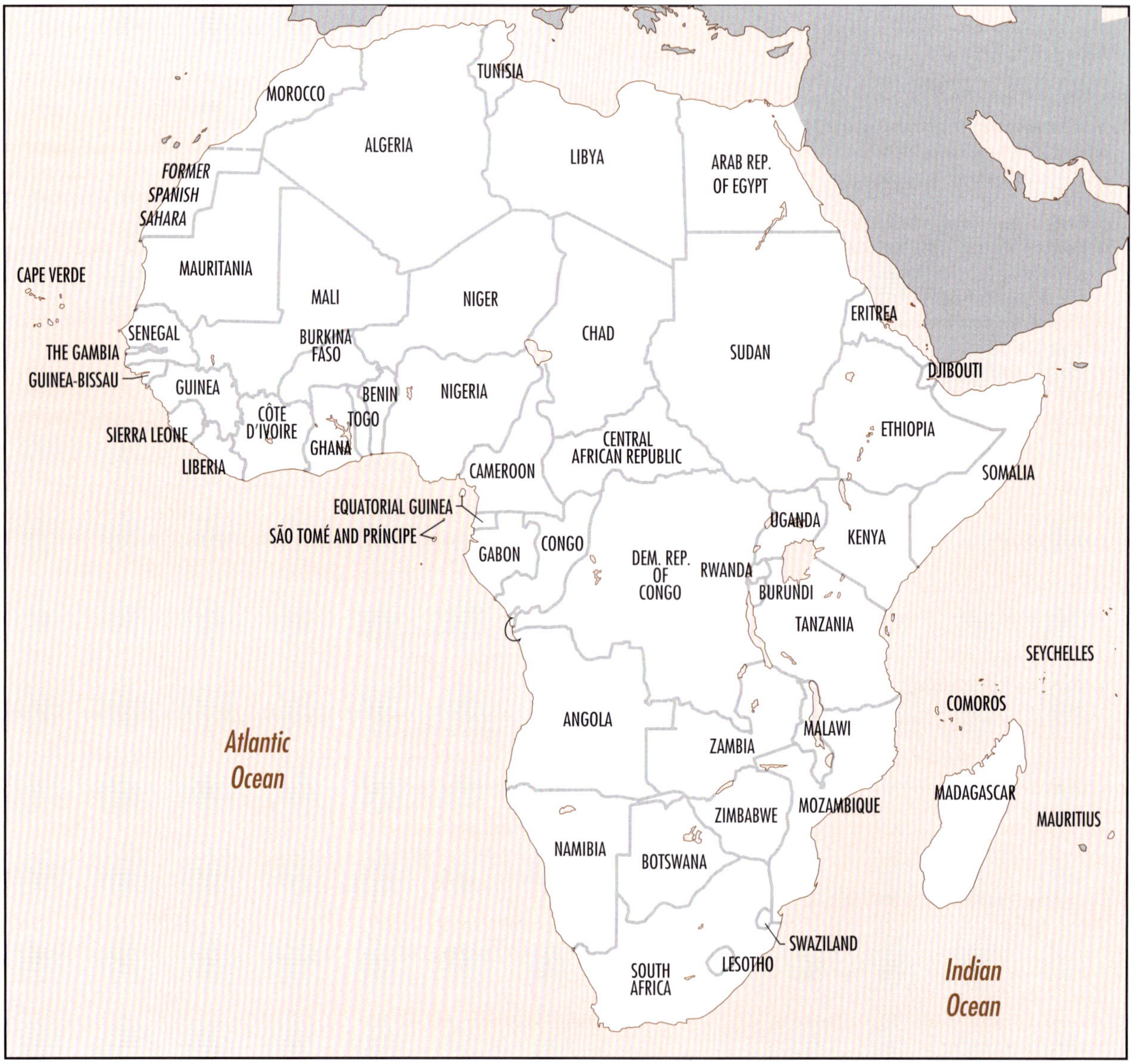

Users Guide

Africa Development Indicators 2011–Multiple User CD-ROM

Introduction

This CD-ROM is part of the Africa Development Indicators suite of products. It was produced jointly by the Office of the Chief Economist and the Operational Quality and Knowledge Services Departments of the Africa Region in collaboration with the Development Data Group of the Development Economics Vice Presidency. It uses the latest version of the World Bank's Data Platform version 3.0.

The CD-ROM contains about 1,700 macroeconomic, sectoral, and social indicators, covering 53 African countries. Time series include data from 1961 to 2009. Doing business and enterprise survey data have data for 2010. It also contains the full contents of the print version of *Africa Development Indicators 2011* and *The Little Data Book on Africa*.

The new Data Platform version 3.0 has sophisticated features: enhanced mapping and charting, a choice of data selection techniques and versatile display options. We invite you to explore it.

A note about the data

Users should note that the data for the Africa Development Indicators suite of products are drawn from the same database. The cutoff date for data is May 2011.

Help

This guide explains how to use the main functions of the CD-ROM. For details about additional features, click *Help* on the menu bar or the *Help* icon; or call one of the hotline numbers listed in the *Help* menu and on the copyright page of this booklet.

Installation

As is usual for Windows® products, you should make sure that other applications are closed while you install the CD-ROM.

To install:

1. Insert the CD-ROM into your CD drive. The installation window should open automatically.
2. If the installation window does not open, click on *Start*, select *Run*. Type D:\RUN.BAT and follow the instructions.
3. DataPlatform requires Microsoft® Internet Explorer 6.0 or higher. If you do not have Internet Explorer, it may be downloaded at no charge from www.microsoft.com. It does not need to be your default browser.

You can delete this program at any time by clicking on the *Remove ADI 2011* icon in the *WB Development Data* program folder.

Issues during installation

This section covers some of the issues that may occur during installation. It also provides all the troubleshooting steps you need to resolve the issue.

My Internet Explorer flickers when I try to launch the application on my desktop

You may experience this problem if you are using Microsoft Vista. This occurs because Internet Explorer 7 and higher versions block the application when there is an IP address in the URL for security reasons. *ADI 2011* is a secure application. Please follow these directions to resolve this issue:

1. Go to *Tools > Internet Options > Security Tab*
2. Select *Local Intranet*
3. Check the *Enabled Protected Mode* checkbox.

I am getting an Internet Explorer security warning message. Is this a security risk?

This is not a security risk. *ADI 2011* is a secure application. You can continue working if this message appears. To permanently disable this message, please follow these directions:

1. Go to *Tools > Internet Options > Security Tab*
2. Select *Local Intranet*
3. Check the *Enabled Protected Mode* checkbox.

I am getting the following message: "MSXML 5.0 from Microsoft Corporation. If you trust this website and the add-on and want to allow it to run, click here."

This message occurs the first time a web page attempts to execute a higher version of a plug-in in Internet Explorer. This is to alert the user the plug-in has been updated with a newer version and prompts this message for user approval. Please right click on the message and run the plug-in. To permanently disable this message, please follow these directions:

1. Go to *Tools > Internet Options > Security Tab*
2. Select *Local Intranet*
3. Check the *Enabled Protected Mode* checkbox.

This change requires Internet Explorer to restart. Please close the existing browser window and re-launch the application by clicking on the *ADI 2011* shortcut desktop icon.

NOTE: When *ADI 2011* launches after installation, the MS-DOS window remains on top of the browser. You should NOT close the window, but you can minimize the MS-DOS window.

Operation

To start the CD-ROM, click on the *ADI 2011* CD-ROM icon on your desktop. An ActiveX security pop-up warning may appear when clicking on a link. ActiveX is a framework for defining reusable controls that perform particular functions in Microsoft Windows. If you receive this security alert, please click *Yes* as the links are not a virus or security risk to your computer.

For detailed instructions, refer to the on-screen *Help* menu or tool tips (on-screen explanations of buttons that are displayed when the cursor rolls over them).

Features and instructions

ADI 2011 has two main screens—a text window featuring the contents of the *Africa Development Indicators 2011* book and other related tables, and a separate window featuring the ADI 2011 time series database.

Home

On the opening text screen you can access each element of the *ADI 2011* CD-ROM. Use the browser controls to link to the *Africa Development Indicators 2011* book, time series database, and other related information.

Database

Select variables

1. Click on each of the *Country, Series,* and *Year* tabs and make your selections on each screen. There are many ways to make a selection—see below, or use the *Help* menu. A *Search* option is also available.
2. Highlight the items you want.
3. Click on the *Select* button to move them into the *Selected* box.
4. Deselect items at any time by highlighting them and clicking on the *Remove* icon.
5. When selection is complete, click on *Next* to move to the next screen.

Making selections

- *Country:* You can select countries and group aggregates from an alphabetical list, group hierarchies, or by *Classification* (region, income group, or lending category). Aggregate data have been calculated only when there were adequate country data.
- *Series:* You can choose from an alphabetical list or by topic, or create your own custom indicators derived from indicators within the *ADI database.*
- *Year:* Select time periods from the list box. On all screens you can click *Notes* to view definition and source information for a highlighted item.

View results

On the *Report* tab, data are presented in a two-dimensional grid. Data for the third dimension are presented on separate screens. You can change the selection displayed by clicking on the third dimension list box. You can also change the scale (to millions, for example) and the number of digits after the decimal. Click on a column header to sort the results. Select *Show Notes* to view source notes and footnotes. To scale series individually click the *Series Level Settings* icon.

Please do not use the browser *Back* and *Forward* buttons on the *View Report* window. This will cause you to lose the report. You will not be able to retrieve data and will have to select the variables again.

Changing the orientation. You can view the result in six different orientations (countries down/periods across, series down/countries across, and so on). To change the orientation, click on *Customize* and drag and drop the dimensions to your desired orientation. *Customize* also has various formatting options for the report.

Saving. You can save the report or you can save the data in another format. You can also save your query selections for later use.

- *Saving the report in Excel.* Select the *Export Report as Excel File* icon on the toolbar. This will save the report in the same format.
- *Saving the report in PDF.* Select the *Export Report as PDF File* icon on the toolbar. This will save the report in the same format. Adobe Reader is required to view files downloaded in PDF format. If you do not have Adobe Reader, it can be downloaded from *www.Adobe.com.*
- *Saving the data or notes in another format.* Select the *Export Data and Notes as CSV File* icon on the toolbar. Saving data as a CSV file will allow you to export all countries, series, and years on to one file. The file will not retain the report format.
- *Saving a query.* Select the *Save Selections as Query* icon on the toolbar. Your query will be saved as "XXXYYY.dp." There is no need to open the file. If you wish to manually edit the query file, select *Notepad.*

Click on *Help* for more details.

Chart

On the *Chart* tab, data are displayed based on the report orientation setting. Click on *Customize* to change the chart type, add a title and to access various formatting options. You can set different chart types for each variable.

Adobe Flash Player 8 or higher is required to view the new features of the charts. It is a free and lightweight installation from www.Adobe.com. If you do not have the application already installed on your desktop, a message will appear asking you to download Adobe Flash Player. Please click "OK" when the message appears. It will take you directly to the Adobe website.

Printing and saving. Right-click on the chart image to print the chart. Click on the appropriate icon to save the chart or save the underlying data.

Map

On the *Map* tab, selected countries are colored according to their data values for the selected indicator and year. The country name and data value will appear as the cursor rolls over the map. The legend scale is based on the report scale and precision settings. To activate the zoom option for a closer look at the map, click directly on the desired location. Click the Reset link to zoom out.

Adobe Flash Player 8 or higher is required to view the new features of the maps. It is a free and lightweight installation from www.Adobe.com. If you do not have the application already installed on your desktop, a message will appear asking you to download Adobe Flash Player. Please click "OK" when the message appears. It will take you directly to the Adobe website.

Changing the map intervals and colors. The default interval range is an equal number of countries. Use the list boxes to set an equal interval range or to change the map color palette. You can also choose to map all countries or only your selected ones.

Printing and saving. Right-click on the map image to print the map. Click on the appropriate icon to save the map or save the underlying data.

License agreement

You must read and agree to the terms of this License Agreement prior to using this CD-ROM product. Use of the software and data contained on the CD-ROM is governed by the terms of this License Agreement. If you do not agree with these terms, you may return the product unused to the World Bank for a full refund of the purchase price.

1. **LICENSE.** In consideration of your payment of the required license fee, the WORLD BANK (the "Bank") hereby grants you a nonexclusive license to use the enclosed data and DataPlatform retrieval program (collectively the "program") subject to the terms and conditions set forth in this license agreement.

2. **OWNERSHIP.** As a licensee you own the physical media on which the program is originally or subsequently recorded. The Bank, however, retains title and ownership of the program recorded on the original CD-ROM and all subsequent copies of the program. This license is not a sale of the program or any copy thereof.

3. **COPY RESTRICTIONS.** The program and accompanying written materials are copyrighted. You may make one copy of the program solely for backup purposes. Unauthorized copying of the program or of the written materials is expressly forbidden and punishable by law.

4. **USE.** You may not modify, adapt, translate, reverse-engineer, decompile, or disassemble the program. You may not modify, adapt, translate, or create derivative works based on any written materials without the prior written consent of the Bank. If you have purchased the single-user version of this product, you may use the Program only on a single laptop/desktop computer used by one person and you may not distribute copies of the Program or accompanying written materials to others.

If you have purchased the multiple-user version of this product, the license is valid for up to 15 authorized users. Should you need to make the program available for additional users through a network, including an intranet, please send a request, indicating the number of users you would like to add, to: World Bank Publications, Marketing and Rights, 1818 H Street NW, Washington DC 20433, fax 202 522 2422, e-mail pubrights@worldbank.org. The Bank will invoice you for an additional fee, depending on the number of users added to the license.

For additional information, please contact World Bank Publications, Marketing and Rights, 1818 H Street NW, Washington DC 20433, fax 202 522 2422, e-mail pubrights@worldbank.org.

5. **TRANSFER RESTRICTIONS.** This program is licensed only to you, the licensee, and may not be transferred to anyone without prior written consent of the Bank.

6. **LIMITED WARRANTY AND LIMITATIONS OF REMEDIES.** The Bank warrants the CD-ROM on which the program is furnished to be free from defects in materials and workmanship under normal use for a period of ninety (90) days from the delivery to you as evidenced by a copy of your receipt. The Bank's entire liability and your exclusive remedy shall be the replacement of any CD-ROMs not meeting the Bank's limited warranty. Defective CD-ROMs should be returned within the warranty period, with a copy of your receipt, to the address specified in section 9 below.

EXCEPT AS PROVIDED ABOVE, THE PRODUCT IS PROVIDED "AS IS" WITHOUT WARRANTY OF ANY KIND, EITHER EXPRESSED OR IMPLIED, INCLUDING, BUT NOT LIMITED TO, THE IMPLIED WARRANTIES OF MERCHANTABILITY AND FITNESS FOR A PARTICULAR PURPOSE. THE BANK DOES NOT WARRANT THAT THE FUNCTIONS CONTAINED IN THE PROGRAM WILL MEET YOUR REQUIREMENTS OR THAT THE OPERATION OF THE PROGRAM WILL BE UNINTERRUPTED OR ERROR-FREE.

IN NO EVENT WILL THE BANK BE LIABLE TO YOU FOR ANY DAMAGES ARISING OUT OF THE USE OR INABILITY TO USE THE PROGRAM.

THE ABOVE WARRANTY GIVES YOU SPECIFIC LEGAL RIGHTS IN THE UNITED STATES, WHICH MAY VARY FROM STATE TO STATE. SOME STATES DO NOT ALLOW THE EXCLUSION OF IMPLIED WARRANTIES OR LIMITATION OF EXCLUSION OF LIABILITY FOR INCIDENTAL OR CONSEQUENTIAL DAMAGES, SO PARTS OF THE ABOVE LIMITATIONS AND EXCLUSIONS MAY NOT APPLY TO YOU.

7. **TERMINATION.** This license is effective from the date you open the sealed package until terminated. You may terminate it by destroying the CD-ROM containing the program and its documentation and any backup copy thereof or by returning this material to the Bank. If any of the terms and conditions of this license are broken, the Bank reserves the right to terminate the license and demand that you return or destroy all copies of the program in your possession without refund to you.

8. **GOVERNING LAW.** This license shall be governed by the laws of the District of Columbia, in the United States of America, without reference to conflicts of law thereof.

9. **GENERAL.** If you have any questions concerning this product, you may contact the Bank by writing to CD-ROM Inquiries, The World Bank, 1818 H Street NW, Washington DC 20433, fax 202 522 1785, e-mail data@worldbank.org. All queries on rights and licenses should be addressed to World Bank Publications, Marketing and Rights, 1818 H Street NW, Washington DC 20433, fax 202 522 2422, e-mail pubrights@worldbank.org.